NORTH POLAR REGION

GLOBAL SATELLITE MOSAIC

The beauty and complexity of Earth's landscape is nowhere more universally revealed than with the Global Satellite Mosaic. The mosaic was compiled for the National Geographic Society by NASA's Jet Propulsion Laboratory from more than 500 satellite images from the National Oceanic and Atmospheric Administration. The cloud-free images show Earth in its natural colors as it appears seen from space. One can easily identify the world's major glaciers, deserts, rain forests, and rain forests. For example, follow the green ribbon of lush vegetation as the Nile into the stark, dry Sahara. The mountain ranges seem to rise off the map thanks to digital elevation databases from the Department of Defense. The deepest areas of the ocean floor are colored dark blue in contrast to the light blue areas highlighting continental shelves, submarine ridges, and underwater mountains.

BIOSPHERE

Thousands of satellite images contributed to show a picture of biological productivity. In the oceans, red, yellow, green indicate waters rich in phytoplankton. On the land, dark green areas show high potential plant productivity; tan areas suffer from productivity limitations due to aridity and temperature.

THE W

SATELL

SOUTH POLAR
REGION

ANTARCTICA

THE NEED FOR SATELLITES

WORLD
TE MAP

**SURFACE
TEMPERATURE**

For information regarding available maps call toll free 1-800-962-1643 or write to National Geographic Maps, PO Box 4357, Evergreen, CO 80437-4357
You can reach us on the Internet at nationalgeographic.com

This registration code provides access to documents

and other sources available at the

Worlds Together, Worlds Apart 3E StudySpace site:

wwnorton.com/studyspace

FMES-LKIC

THIRD EDITION
VOLUME C

Worlds Together, WORLDS APART

ROBERT TIGNOR

JEREMY ADELMAN

STEPHEN ARON

STEPHEN KOTKIN

SUZANNE MARCHAND

GYAN PRAKASH

MICHAEL TSIN

THIRD EDITION
VOLUME C
1750 TO THE PRESENT

Worlds Together, WORLDS APART

W · W · NORTON & COMPANY
NEW YORK · LONDON

W. W. Norton & Company has been independent since its founding in 1923, when William Warder Norton and Mary D. Herter Norton first published lectures delivered at the People's Institute, the adult education division of New York City's Cooper Union. The firm soon expanded its program beyond the Institute, publishing books by celebrated academics from America and abroad. By mid-century, the two major pillars of Norton's publishing program—trade books and college texts—were firmly established. In the 1950s, the Norton family transferred control of the company to its employees, and today—with a staff of four hundred and a comparable number of trade, college, and professional titles published each year—W. W. Norton & Company stands as the largest and oldest publishing house owned wholly by its employees.

Editor: Jon Durbin
Developmental Editor: Alice Vigliani
Copy Editor: Ellen Lohman
Project Editor: Rebecca Homiski
Photo Editor: Stephanie Romeo
Production Manager: Benjamin Reynolds
Managing Editor, College: Marian Johnson
Marketing Manager: Tamara McNeill
Emedia Editor: Steve Hoge
Design Director: Rubina Yeh
Ancillary Editor: Lorraine Klimowich
Editorial Assistant: Jason Spears
Layout Artist: Brad Walrod
Composition: TexTech, Inc.
Cartographer: Carto-Graphics/Alice Thiede

The Library of Congress has cataloged the one-volume edition as follows:

Worlds together, worlds apart : a history of the world from the beginnings of humankind to the present / Robert Tignor ... [et al.]. — 3rd ed.
    p. cm.
  Includes bibliographical references and index.
  ISBN 978-0-393-93492-2 (hardcover)
1. World history.   I. Tignor, Robert L.
  D21.W94 2011
  909—dc22

                                                          2010036837

This edition:
ISBN: 978-0-393-93497-7 (pbk.)

W. W. Norton & Company, Inc., 500 Fifth Avenue, New York, NY 10110
wwnorton.com

W. W. Norton & Company Ltd., Castle House, 75/76 Wells Street, London W1T 3QT

4 5 6 7 8 9

Contents in Brief

Contents

Global Connections & Disconnections Features

Primary Sources

Maps

Preface

The New Edition

Worlds Together, Worlds Apart has set the standard for two editions for those instructors who want to teach a globally integrated world history survey course. Just as the dynamic field of world history evolves, so has Worlds Together, Worlds Apart with each edition. With the Third Edition, Worlds Together, Worlds Apart continues to offer a highly coherent, cutting-edge survey of the field, while becoming more streamlined and accessible for a wider range of students. The Third Edition offers a number of improvements over the first two. First, the chapters are shorter. We cut the narrative by 50,000 words, reducing its length by nearly 20 percent. We shrank the text to highlight even more clearly the distinctive world history stories and themes that each chapter is built around. Readers should be in little doubt now about what truly counted globally in each of the time periods that the chapters cover. The new edition should also be a good page turner for students for while we reduced the length of the book to just over 840 pages, we did not dramatically cut back on the map, illustration, and primary-source programs. By shortening the text, we also wanted to allow instructors to make greater use of outside reading materials, especially primary sources, so vital to understanding the life and thought of people living in different time periods and which are locations. Second, pedagogically, we have re-written the chapter introductions to emphasize the themes even more strongly. We have also added a new pedagogy feature called "Storylines," which is designed to provide the reader with a snapshot of the main chapter themes and show how they relate to each major region of the world. We also went through all the pedagogical features with great care to make sure that the prose and questions were pitched at a good level for a wide range of students. Third, we are pleased to announce the publication of Worlds Together, Worlds Apart: A Companion Reader. Long-time users of the book have been asking for a primary-source reader designed to accompany Worlds Together, Worlds Apart since its First Edition. The new companion reader has been carefully assembled by Ken Pomeranz, Laura Mitchell, and James Given, all of whom teach the world history survey course at the University of California, Irvine, and all of whom have been teaching with Worlds Together, Worlds Apart for many years. The companion reader contains nearly 150 primary sources (both visual and textual) and will greatly enhance an instructor's ability to teach students how to analyze primary sources, while building off the key themes and topics of Worlds Together, Worlds Apart. Finally, Norton StudySpace offers an exciting new feature called World History Tours powered by Google Maps. These digitally based tours trace global developments over time, touching down on locations to launch documents and images for analysis. For example, the Silk Road tour follows the bubonic plague from its eastern origins to Europe, chronicling this movement through journals and images from the Muslim world, Italy, and England.

Since work began on *Worlds Together, Worlds Apart*, world history has gained even more prominence in college classrooms and historical studies. Courses in the history of the world now abound, often replacing the standard surveys of European history and western civilization overviews. Graduate history students receive training in world history, and journals routinely publish studies in this field. A new generation of textbooks was needed to help students and instructors make sense of this vast, complex, and rapidly evolving field.

We believe that *Worlds Together, Worlds Apart* remains the most cutting-edge, engaging, readable, and useful text available for all students of world history. We also believe that this text, one that has advanced the teaching of this field, could have only grown out of the highly collaborative effort of a team of scholars and teachers rather than the more typical single- or two-author efforts. Indeed, the idea to build each chapter around stories of world history significance and the execution of this model grew out of our monthly team meetings and our joint writing efforts during the development stage. As a team-driven text, *Worlds Together, Worlds Apart* also has the advantage of area experts to make sure the material is presented accurately, which is always a challenge for the single- or two-author texts, especially in world history. Finally, our book also reads with a single voice due to the extraordinary efforts of our general editor, and leader, Robert Tignor, who with every edition makes the final major sweep through the text to make sure that the voice, style, and level of detail are consistent throughout. Building on these distinctive strengths, we have worked hard and thoughtfully to make the Third Edition of *Worlds Together, Worlds Apart* the best one so far. While there are many exciting additions to the main text and support package, we have made every effort to remain true to our original vision.

OUR GUIDING PRINCIPLES

Five principles inform this book, guiding its framework and the organization of its individual chapters. The first is that **world history is global history**. There are many fine histories of the individual regions of the world, which we have endeavored to make good use of. But unlike the authors of many other so-called world histories, we have chosen not to deal with the great regions and cultures of the world as separate units, reserving individual chapters to East Asia, South Asia, Southwest Asia, Europe, Africa, and the Americas. Our goal is to place each of these regions in its largest geographical context. Accordingly, we have written chapters that are truly global in that most major regions of the world are discussed in each one. We achieved these globally integrated chapters

by building each around a significant world history story or theme. There are a number of wonderful examples throughout the book, including the peopling of the earth (Chapter 1), the building of the Silk Road (Chapter 6), the rise of universal religions (Chapters 8 and 9), the Black Death (Chapter 11), the effects of New World silver on the economies of the world (Chapter 13), alternative visions to nineteenth-century capitalism (Chapter 15), the rise of nation states and empires (Chapter 16), and so on. It would be misleading, of course, to say that the context is the world, because none of these regions, even the most highly developed commercially, enjoyed commercial or cultural contact with peoples all over the globe before Columbus's voyage to the Americas and the sixteenth century. But the peoples living in the Afro-Eurasian landmass, probably the single most important building block for our study, were deeply influenced by one another, as were the more scattered peoples living in the Americas and in Africa below the Sahara. Products, ideas, and persons traveled widely across the large land units of Eurasia, Africa, and the Americas. Indeed, Afro-Eurasia was not divided or thought of as divided into separate landmasses until recent times. It is in this sense that our world history is global.

The second principle informing this work is **the importance of chronology in framing world history**. Rather than telling the story of world history by analyzing separate geographical areas, we have elected to frame the chapters around significant world history themes and periods that transcended regional and cultural boundaries—moments or periods of meaningful change in the way that human beings organized their lives. Some of these changes were dramatic and affected many people. Environments changed; the earth became drier and warmer; humans learned to domesticate plants and animals; technological innovations in warfare, political organization, and commercial activities occurred; and new religious and cultural beliefs spread far and wide. These changes swept across large landmasses, paying scant heed to preexisting cultural and geographical unity. They affected peoples living in widely dispersed societies. In other cases, changes occurred in only one locality while other places retained their traditions or took alternative routes. Chronology helps us understand the ways in which the world has, and has not, shared a common history.

The third principle is **historical and geographical balance**. Ours is not a history focused on the rise of the West. We seek to pay attention to the global histories of all peoples and not to privilege those developments that led directly into European history as if the rest of the history of the world was but a prelude to the rise of western civilization. We deal with peoples living outside Europe on their own terms and try to see world history from their perspective. Even more significantly, while we describe societies that obviously influenced Europe's historical development, we do so in a context very different from that which western historians have stressed. Rather than simply viewing these cultures in terms of their role in western development, we seek to understand them in their own terms and to illuminate the ways they influenced other parts of the world. From our perspective, it is historically inaccurate to annex Mesopotamia and Egypt to western civilization, because these territories lay well outside Europe and had a large influence on Africa, South Asia, and East Asia as well as on Europe. Indeed, our presentation of Europe in the period leading up to and including the founding of the Roman Empire is different from many of the standard treatments. The Europeans we describe are rather rough, wild-living, warring peoples living on the fringes of the settled parts of the world and looked down on by more politically stable communities. They hardly seem to be made of the stuff that will catapult Europeans to world leadership a millennium later—indeed, they were very different people from those who, as the result of myriad intervening and contingent events, founded the nineteenth- and twentieth-century empires whose ruins are still all around us.

Our fourth principle is **an emphasis on connections and what we call disconnections across societal and cultural boundaries**. World history is not the history of separate regions of the world at different periods of time. It is the history of the connections among peoples living often at great distances from one another, and it is also the history of the resistances of peoples living within and outside societies to connections that threatened to put them in subordinate positions or to rob them of their independence.

A stress on connections inevitably foregrounds those elements within societies that promoted long-distance ties. Merchants are important, as are military men and political potentates seeking to expand their polities. So are scholars and religious leaders, particularly those who believed that they had universalistic messages with which to convert others to their visions. Perhaps most important of all in pre-modern world history, certainly the most understudied, are the nomadic pastoral peoples, who were often the agents for the transmission of products, peoples, and ideas across long and harsh distances. They exploded onto the scene of settled societies at critical junctures, erasing old cultural and geographical barriers and producing new unities, as the Arabs did in the seventh century CE and the Mongols in the thirteenth century. *Worlds Together, Worlds Apart* is not intended to convey the message that the history of the world is a story of increasing integration. What for one ruling group brought benefits in the form of increased workforces, material prosperity, and political stability often meant enslavement, political subordination, and loss of territory for other groups. The historian's task, then, is not only to represent the different experiences of increased connectedness, describing worlds that came together, but also to be attentive to the opposite trends, describing peoples and communities that remained apart.

The fifth and final principle is that **world history is a narrative of big themes and high-level comparisons**. *Worlds*

Together, Worlds Apart is not a book of record. Indeed, in a work that covers the whole of the historical record of humankind from the beginnings of history to the present, the notion that no event or individual worthy of attention would be excluded is the height of folly. We have sought to offer clear themes and interpretations in order to synthesize the vast body of data that often overwhelms histories of the world. Our aspiration is to identify the main historical forces that have moved history, to highlight those monumental innovations that have changed the way humans lived, and to describe the creation and evolution of those bedrock institutions, many of which, of course, endure. In this regard, self-conscious cross-cultural comparisons of developments, institutions, and even founding figures receive attention to make students aware that some common institutions, such as slavery, did not have the same features in every society. Or, in the opposite fashion, the seemingly diverse terms that were used, say, to describe learned and religious men in different parts of the world—monks in Europe, ulama in Islam, Brahmans in India, and scholar-gentries in China—often meant much the same thing in very different settings. We have constructed *Worlds Together, Worlds Apart* around big ideas, stories, and themes rather than filling the book with names and dates that encourage students only to memorize rather than understand world history concepts.

OUR MAJOR THEMES

The primary organizing framework of *Worlds Together, Worlds Apart*—one that runs through the chapters and connects the different parts of the volume—is the theme of **interconnection and divergence**. While describing movements that facilitated global connectedness, this book also shows how different regions developed their own ways of handling or resisting connections and change. Throughout history, different regions and different population groups often stood apart from the rest of the world until touched by traders or explorers or missionaries or soldiers. Some of these regions welcomed global connections. Others sought to change the nature of their connections with the outside world, and yet others resisted efforts to bring them into the larger world. All, however, were somehow affected by their experience of connection. Yet, the history of the world is not simply one of increasing globalization, in which all societies eventually join a common path to the present. Rather, it is a history of the ways in which, as people became linked, their experience of these global connections diverged.

Besides the central theme of interconnection and divergence, other themes also stand out in *Worlds Together, Worlds Apart*. First, the book discusses **how the recurring efforts of people to cross religious, political, and cultural borders brought the world together**. Merchants and educated men and women traded goods and ideas. Whole communities, in addition to select groups, moved to safer or more promising environments. **The transregional crossings of ideas, goods, and peoples produced transformations and conflicts**—a second important theme. Finally, the movement of ideas, peoples, products, and germs over long distances upset the balance of power across the world and within individual societies. Such movements changed the relationship of different population groups with other peoples and areas of the world and led over time to dramatic shifts in the ascendancy of regions. **Changes in power arrangements within and between regions explain which parts of the world and regional groups benefited from integration and which resisted it.** These three themes (exchange and migration, conflict and resistance, and alterations in the balance of power) weave themselves through every chapter of this work. While we highlight major themes throughout, we tell the stories of the people caught in these currents of exchange, conflict, and changing power relations, paying particular attention to the role that gender and the environment play in shaping the evolution of societies.

The history of the world is not a single, sweeping narrative. On the contrary, the last 5,000 years have produced multiple histories, moving along many paths and trajectories. Sometimes these histories merge, intertwining themselves in substantial ways. Sometimes they disentangle themselves and simply stand apart. Much of the time, however, they are simultaneously together and apart. In place of a single narrative, the usual one being the rise of the West, this book maps the many forks in the road that confronted the world's societies at different times and the surprising turns and unintended consequences that marked the choices that peoples and societies made, including the unanticipated and dramatic rise of the West in the nineteenth century. Formulated in this way, world history is the unfolding of many possible histories, and readers of this book should come away with a reinforced sense of the unpredictability of the past, the instability of the present, and the uncertainty of the future.

OVERVIEW OF VOLUME ONE

Volume One of *Worlds Together, Worlds Apart* deals with the period from the beginnings of human history through the Mongol invasions of the thirteenth century and the spread of the Black Death across Afro-Eurasia. It is divided into eleven chapters, each of which marks a distinct historical period. Hence, each chapter has an overarching theme or small set of themes that hold otherwise highly diverse material together.

Chapter 1, "Becoming Human," presents biological and cultural perspectives on the way that early hominoids became truly human. We believe that this chapter is important in establishing the global context of world history. We believe too that our chapter is unique in its focus on how humans became humans, so we discuss how early humans became bipedal and how they developed complex cognitive processes such as language and artistic abilities. Recent research indicates that *Homo sapiens* originated in Africa, probably no more than 200,000 years ago. These early men and women walked out of the African landmass sometime between 120,000 and 50,000 years ago, gradually populating all regions of the world. What is significant in this story is that the different population groups around the world, the so-called races of humankind, have only recently broken off from one another. Also in this chapter, we describe the domestication of plants and animals and the founding of the first village settlements around the globe.

NEW: Discussions of the role that dogs played in human evolution and the latest findings on the origins of humans.

Chapter 2, "Rivers, Cities, and First States, 4000–2000 BCE," covers the period during which five of the great river basins experienced extraordinary breakthroughs in human activity. On the flood plains of the Tigris and Euphrates in Mesopotamia, the Nile in Egypt, the Indus valley in modern-day northern India and Pakistan, and the Yellow and Yangzi rivers in China, men and women mastered annual floods and became expert in seeding and cultivating foodstuffs. In these areas, populations became dense. Riverine cultures had much in common. They had highly developed hierarchical political, social, and cultural systems, priestly and bureaucratic classes, and organized religious and cultural systems. But they also differed greatly, and these differences were passed from generation to generation. The development of these major complex societies certainly is a turning point in world history.

Extensive climatic and technological changes serve as major turning points for **Chapter 3, "Nomads, Territorial States, and Microsocieties, 2000–1200 BCE."** Drought, environmental degradation, and political instability brought the first riverine societies to a crashing end around 2000 BCE. When aridity forced tribal and nomadic peoples living on the fringes of the settled populations to move closer to settled areas, they brought with them an insurmountable military advantage. They had become adept at yoking horses to war chariots, and hence they were in a position to subjugate or intermarry with the peoples in the settled polities in the river basins. Around 2000 BCE these peoples established new territorial kingdoms in Mesopotamia, Egypt, the Indus valley, and China, which gave way a millennium later (1000 BCE) to even larger, militarily and politically more powerful states. In the Americas, the Mediterranean, sub-Saharan Africa, and the

Pacific worlds, microsocieties arose as an alternative form of polity in which peoples lived in much smaller-scale societies that showcased their own unique and compelling features.

NEW: Expanded discussions of how the Egyptian pyramids were built and their role in Egyptian cosmology and fuller integration of material on the environmental catastrophe that shaped the third millennium BCE.

Chapter 4, "First Empires and Common Cultures in Afro-Eurasia, 1200–350 BCE," describes the different ways in which larger-scale societies grew and became unified. In the case of the world's first empires, the neo-Assyrian and Persian, political power was the main unifying element. Both states established different models that future empires would emulate. The Assyrians used brutal force to intimidate and subjugate different groups within their societies and neighboring states. The Persians followed a pattern that relied less on coercion and more on tributary relationships, while reveling in cultural diversity. The Zhou state in China offered yet a third way of political unity, basing its rule on the doctrine of the mandate of heaven, which legitimated its rulers' succession as long as they were able to maintain stability and order. Vedic society in South Asia offers a dramatically different model in which religion and culture were the main unifying forces. Religion moves to the forefront of the narrative in other ways in this chapter. The birth of monotheism occurred in the Zoroastrian and Hebrew faiths and the beginnings of Buddhism. All three religions endure today.

NEW: Revised and expanded discussion of the origins of Judaism.

The last millennium before the common era witnessed some of the most monumental developments in human history. In the six and half centuries discussed in **Chapter 5, "Worlds Turned Inside Out, 1000–350 BCE,"** teachers and thinkers, rather than kings, priests, and warriors, came to the fore. Men like Confucius, the Buddha, Plato, and Aristotle, to name only the best known of this brilliant group, offered new insights into the natural world and provided new guidelines for how to govern justly and live ethically. In this era, small-scale societies, benefiting from more intimate relationships, took the place of the first great empires, now in decline. These highly individualistic cultures developed new strategies for political organization, even including experimenting with a democratic polity. In Africa, the Bantu peoples spread across sub-Saharan Africa, and the Sudanic peoples of Meroe created a society that blended Egyptian and sub-Saharan influences. These were all dynamic hybrid societies building on existing knowledge. Equally dramatic transformations occurred in the Americas, where the Olmec and Chavín peoples were creating hierarchical societies of the like never before seen in their part of the world.

NEW: Increased discussion of the first millennium as an "axial age."

Chapter 6, "Shrinking the Afro-Eurasian World, 350 BCE–250 CE," describes three major forces that simultaneously integrated large segments of the Afro-Eurasian landmass culturally and economically. First, Alexander and his armies changed the political and cultural landscape of North Africa and Southwest and South Asia. Culturally, Alexander spread Hellenism through North Africa and Southwest and central Asia, making it the first cultural system to achieve a transregional scope. Second, it was in the post-Alexander world that these commercial roads were stabilized and intensified. For the first time, a trading network, known as the Silk Road, stretching from Palmyra in the West to central Asia in the East, came into being. Buddhism was the first religion to seize on the Silk Road's more formal existence as its followers moved quickly with the support of the Mauryan Empire to spread their ideas into central Asia. Finally, we witness the growth of a "silk road of the seas" as new technologies and bigger ships allowed for a dramatic expansion in maritime trade from South Asia all the way to Egypt and East Africa.

Chapter 7, "Han Dynasty China and Imperial Rome, 300 BCE–300 CE," compares Han China and the Roman Empire, the two political, economic, and cultural systems that dominated much of the Afro-Eurasian landmass from 200 BCE to 200 CE. Both the Han Dynasty and the Roman Empire ruled effectively in their own way, providing an instructive comparative case study. Both left their imprint on Afro-Eurasia, and rulers for centuries afterward tried to revive these glorious polities and use them as models of greatness. This chapter also discusses the effect of state sponsorship on religion, as Christianity came into existence in the context of the late Roman Empire and Buddhism was introduced to China during the decline of the Han.

Out of the crumbling Roman Empire new polities and a new religion emerged, the major topic of **Chapter 8, "The Rise of Universal Religions, 300–600 CE."** The Byzantine Empire, claiming to be the successor state to the Roman Empire, embraced Christianity as its state religion. The Tang rulers patronized Buddhism to such a degree that Confucian statesmen feared it had become the state religion. Both Buddhism and Christianity enjoyed spectacular success in the politically fragmented post-Han era in China and in the feudal world of western Europe. These dynamic religions represent a decisive transformation in world history. Christianity enjoyed its eventual successes through state sponsorship via the Roman and Byzantine empires and by providing spiritual comfort and hope during the chaotic years of Rome's decline. Buddhism grew through imperial sponsorship and significant changes to its fundamental beliefs, when adherents to the faith deified Buddha and created notions of an afterlife. In Africa a wide range of significant developments and a myriad of cultural practices existed; yet large common cultures also arose. The Bantu peoples spread throughout the southern half of the landmass, spoke closely related languages, and developed similar political institutions based on the prestige of individuals of high achievement. In the Americas the Olmecs established their own form of the city-state, while the Mayans owed their success to a decentralized common culture built around a strong religious belief system and a series of spiritual centers.

NEW: Revised discussions of what enables a religion to become "universal."

In **Chapter 9, "New Empires and Common Cultures, 600–1000 CE,"** in a relatively remote corner of the Arabian Peninsula another world religion, Islam, exploded with world-changing consequences. The rise of Islam provides a contrast to the way in which universalizing religions and political empires interacted. Islam and empire arose in a fashion quite different from Christianity and the Roman Empire. Christianity took over an already existing empire—the Roman—after suffering persecution at its hands for several centuries. In contrast, Islam created an empire almost at the moment of its emergence. By the time the Abbasid Empire came into being in the middle of the eighth century, Islamic armies, political leaders, and clerics exercised power over much of the Afro-Eurasian landmass from southern Spain, across North Africa, all the way to Central Asia. The Tang Empire in China, however, served as a counterweight to Islam's power both politically and intellectually. Confucianism enjoyed a spectacular recovery in this period. With the Tang rulers, Confucianism slowed the spread of Buddhism and further reinforced China's development along different, more secular pathways. Japan and Korea also enter world history at this time, as tributary states to Tang China and as hybrid cultures that mixed Chinese customs and practices with their own. The Christian world split in this period between the western Latin church and the eastern Byzantine church. Both branches of Christianity played a role in unifying societies, especially in western Europe, which lacked strong political rule.

NEW: Reorganized to integrate material on the agricultural revolutions that spread across Afro-Eurasia as a result of the rise of Islam between 600 and 1000 BCE.

In the three centuries from 1000 to 1300 (**Chapter 10, "Becoming 'the World,' 1000–1300 CE"**) Afro-Eurasia experienced an unprecedented rise in prosperity and population that even spread into West and East Africa. Just as importantly, the world in this period divided into regional zones that are recognizable today. And trade grew rapidly.

A view of the major trading cities of this time demonstrates how commerce transformed cultures. Sub-Saharan Africa also underwent intense regional integration via the spread of the Mande-speaking peoples and the Mali Empire.

The Americas witnessed their first empire in the form of the Chimu peoples in the Andes. This chapter ends with the Mongol conquests of the twelfth and thirteenth centuries, which brought massive destruction. The Mongol Empire, however, once in place, promoted long-distance commerce, scholarly exchange, and travel on an unprecedented scale. The Mongols brought Eurasia, North Africa, and many parts of sub-Saharan Africa into a new connectedness. The Mongol story also underscores the important role that nomads played throughout the history of the early world.

NEW: Expanded discussion of the Crusades.

The Black Death brought Afro-Eurasia's prosperity and population growth to a catastrophic end as discussed in **Chapter 11, "Crises and Recovery in Afro-Eurasia, 1300s–1500s."** The dying and destruction of the fourteenth century saw traditional institutions give way and forced peoples to rebuild their cultures. The polities that came into being at this time and the intense religious experimentation that took place effected a sharp break with the past. The bubonic plague wiped out as much as two-thirds of the population in many of the densely settled locations of Afro-Eurasia. Societies were brought to their knees by the Mongols' depredations as well as by biological pathogens. In the face of one of humanity's grimmest periods, peoples and societies demonstrated tremendous resilience as they looked for new ways to rebuild their communities, some turning inward and others seeking inspiration, conquests, and riches elsewhere. Volume One concludes on the eve of the "Columbian Exchange," the moment when "old" worlds discovered "new" ones and a vast series of global interconnections and divergences commenced.

NEW: Expanded discussion of the Renaissance.

OVERVIEW OF VOLUME TWO

The organizational structure for Volume Two reaffirms the commitment to write a decentered, global history of the world. Christopher Columbus is not the starting point, as he is in so many modern world histories. Rather, we begin in the eleventh and twelfth centuries with two major developments in world history: the Mongols and the Black Death. The first, set forth in **Chapter 10, "Becoming 'the World,' 1000–1300 CE,"** describes a world that was divided for the first time into regions that are recognizable today. This world experienced rapid population growth, as is shown by a simple look at the major trading cities from Asia in the East to the Mediterranean in the West. Yet nomadic peoples remain a force as revealed in the Mongol invasions of Afro-Eurasia.

NEW: Expanded discussion of the Crusades.

Chapter 11, "Crises and Recovery in Afro-Eurasia, 1300s–1500s," describes how the Mongol warriors, through their conquests and the integration of the Afro-Eurasian world, spread the bubonic plague, which brought death and depopulation to much of Afro-Eurasia. Both these stories set the stage for the modern world and are clear-cut turning points in world history. The primary agents of world connection described in this chapter were dynasts, soldiers, clerics, merchants, and adventurers who rebuilt the societies that disease and political collapse had destroyed.

NEW: Expanded discussion of the Renaissance.

The Mongols joined the two hemispheres, as we describe in **Chapter 12, "Contact, Commerce, and Colonization, 1450s–1600,"** bringing the peoples and products of the Western Hemisphere into contact and conflict with Eurasia and Africa. It is the collision between the Eastern and Western Hemispheres that sets in motion modern world history and marks a distinct divide or turning point between the premodern and the modern. Here, too, disease and increasing trade linkages were vital. Unprepared for the advanced military technology and the disease pool of European and African peoples, the Amerindian population experienced a population decline even more devastating than that caused by the Black Death.

NEW: Expanded discussion of the Protestant Reformation.

Europeans sailed across the Atlantic Ocean to find a more direct, less encumbered route to Asia and came upon lands, peoples, and products that they had not expected. One item, however, that they had sought in every part of the world and that they found in abundance in the Americas was precious metal. In **Chapter 13, "Worlds Entangled, 1600–1750,"** we discuss how New World silver from Mexico and Peru became the major currency of global commerce, oiling the long-distance trading networks that had been revived after the Black Death. The effect of New World silver on the world economy was so great that it, even more than the Iberian explorations of the New World, brought the hemispheres together and marks the true genesis of modern world history. Sugar also linked the economies and polities of western Europe, Africa, and the Americas and was a powerful force in a triangular trade centered on the Atlantic Ocean. This trade involved the shipment of vast numbers of African captives to the Americas, where they toiled on sugar, tobacco, cotton, and rice slave plantations.

Chapter 14, "Cultures of Splendor and Power, 1500–1780," discusses the Ottoman scientists, Safavid and Mughal artists, and Chinese literati, as well as European thinkers, whose notable achievements were rooted in their own cultures but tempered by awareness of the intellectual activities of others. In this chapter, we look closely at how culture is created as a historical process and describe how the massive increase in wealth during this period, growing out of global trade, led to one of the great periods of cultural flourishing in world history.

NEW: Discussions of the Seven Years' War as the first global war.

Around 1800, transformations reverberated outward from the Atlantic world and altered economic and political relationships in the rest of the world. In **Chapter 15, "Reordering the World, 1750–1850,"** we discuss how political revolutions in the Americas and Europe, new ideas about how to trade and organize labor, and a powerful rhetoric of freedom and universal rights underlay the beginning of "a great divide" between peoples of European descent and those who were not. These forces of laissez-faire capitalism, industrialization, the nation-state, and republicanism not only attracted diverse groups around the world; they also threatened groups that put forth alternative visions. Ideas of freedom, as manifested in trading relations, labor, and political activities, clashed with a traditional world based on inherited rights and statuses and further challenged the way men and women had lived in earlier times. These political, intellectual, and economic reorderings changed the way people around the world saw themselves and thus represent something quite novel in world history.

NEW: Discussions of "industriousness" and how the work habits of westerners were changing in the period before the Industrial Revolution.

These new ways of envisioning the world did not go unchallenged, as **Chapter 16, "Alternative Visions of the Nineteenth Century,"** makes clear. Here, intense resistance to evolving modernity reflected the diversity of peoples and their hopes for the future. Wahabbism in Islam, the strongman movement in Africa, Indian resistance in America and Mexico, socialism and communism in Europe, the Taiping Rebellion in China, and the Indian Mutiny in South Asia catapulted to historical prominence prophets and leaders whose visions often drew on earlier traditions and led these individuals to resist rapid change.

NEW: Streamlined discussions comparing the alternative visions of the nineteenth century.

Chapter 17, "Nations and Empires, 1850–1914," discusses the political, economic, military, and ideological power that thrust Europe and North America to the fore of global events and led to an era of nationalism and modern imperialism, new forces in world history. Yet this period of seeming European supremacy was to prove short-lived.

As **Chapter 18, "An Unsettled World, 1890–1914,"** demonstrates, even before World War I shattered Europe's moral certitude, many groups at home (feminists, Marxists, and unfulfilled nationalists) and abroad (anti-colonial nationalists) had raised a chorus of complaints about European and North American dominance. As in Chapter 14, we look at the processes by which specific cultural movements rose and reflected the concerns of individual societies. Yet here, too, syncretistic movements emerged in many cultures and reflected the sway of global imperialism, which by then had become a dominant force.

NEW: Revised discussions of cultural modernism.

Chapter 19, "Of Masses and Visions of the Modern, 1910–1939," briefly covers World War I and then discusses how, from the end of World War I until World War II, different visions of being modern competed around the world. It is the development of modernism and its effects on multiple cultures that integrate the diverse developments discussed in this chapter. In the decades between the world wars, proponents of liberal democracy struggled to defend their views and often to impose their will on authoritarian rulers and anticolonial nationalists.

NEW: Discussions of the Spanish Civil War as a global phenomenon.

Chapter 20, "The Three-World Order, 1940–1975," presents World War II and describes how new adversaries arose after the war. A three-world order came into being—the First World, led by the United States and extolling capitalism, the nation-state, and democratic government; the Second World, led by the Soviet Union and favoring authoritarian polities and economies; and the Third World, made up of former colonies seeking an independent status for themselves in world affairs. The rise of this three-world order dominates the second half of the twentieth century and constitutes another major theme of world history.

NEW: Expanded discussions of the Holocaust.

In **Chapter 21, "Globalization, 1970–2000,"** we explain that, at the end of the cold war, the modern world, while clearly more unified than before, still had profound cultural differences and political divisions. At the beginning of the twenty-first century, capital, commodities, peoples, and ideas move rapidly over long distances. But cultural tensions and political impasses continue to exist. It is the rise of this form of globalism that represents a vital new element as humankind heads into a new century and millennium.

We close with an **Epilogue,** which tracks developments since the turn of the millennium. These last few years have brought profound changes to the world order, yet we hope readers of *Worlds Together, Worlds Apart* will see more clearly how this most recent history is, in fact, entwined with trends of much longer duration that are the chief focus of this book.

NEW: Fully up-to-date on the global financial collapse, wars in the Middle East, and the Obama presidency.

INNOVATIVE PEDAGOGICAL PROGRAM, MADE BETTER

Worlds Together, Worlds Apart is designed for maximum readability. The crisp, clear, and succinct narrative, built around memorable world history stories and themes, is reinforced through a highly innovative pedagogical program designed to help students think critically and master the core content. All the pedagogical elements have been carefully revised for the Third Edition to ensure that students will find them highly useful. Highlights of this innovative program are described below.

NEW "STORYLINES" FEATURE

New "Storylines" features provide a thematic snapshot of the chapter and appear right after the chapter introduction. Each "Storylines" feature highlights the chapter themes and shows how they apply to each region of the world.

STELLAR MAP PROGRAM WITH NEW GUIDING QUESTIONS

The book's more than 120 beautiful maps are designed to reinforce the main stories and themes in each chapter. Most chapters open with a beautiful two-page map of the world to highlight the main storyline of the chapter. Within the chapter are four to five more maps that focus on the regions covered. Enhanced captions with new guiding questions help students learn how to read historical maps and to understand the relationship between geography and history.

REVISED FOCUS-QUESTION SYSTEM

The focus-question system has been fully revised and now contains more manageable questions in order to help the reader remain alert to key concepts and questions on every page of the text. Focus questions guide students' reading in three ways: (1) a focus question box at the beginning of the chapter previews the chapter's contents, (2) relevant questions reappear at the start of the section where they are discussed, and (3) running heads on right-hand pages keep these questions in view throughout the chapter.

PRIMARY-SOURCE DOCUMENTS WITH NEW QUESTIONS FOR ANALYSIS

The authors have selected three to five primary-source documents for each chapter that reinforce the chapter's main themes and help students learn how to analyze primary sources. Many of them challenge students to see world history through the eyes of others and from different perspectives. The questions for analysis after each document have been carefully revised to draw students into the document, moving from simpler to more complex. Additional primary sources are available in *Worlds Together, Worlds Apart: A Companion Reader* and in the Digital History Reader, which is part of the Norton StudySpace website.

GLOBAL CONNECTIONS & DISCONNECTIONS

Each chapter contains one thematic feature built around key individuals or phenomena that exemplify the main emphasis of the text. Among the many topics are how historians use technology to date bones and objects from early history, the use of ritual funeral objects in the contexts of religion and trade, the role of libraries in early world history, the travels of Marco Polo and Ibn Battuta, coffee drinking and coffeehouses in different parts of the world, cartography and maps as expressions of different worldviews, the growth of universities around the world, and Che Guevera as a radical visionary who tried to export revolution throughout the Third World.

STREAMLINED CHAPTER CHRONOLOGIES

Chapter chronologies appear at the end of each chapter, and they are organized regionally rather than temporally. The chapter chronologies have been streamlined for the Third Edition to make it easier for students to identify the most important events, to track unifying concepts, and to see influences across cultures and societies within a given time period.

REVISED STUDY QUESTIONS

New Study Questions appear at the end of each chapter. Each question has been carefully crafted to ensure that students can identify chapter themes, master core content, and identify the most important comparisons and connections from the reading.

FURTHER READINGS

A section at the back of the book includes an ample list of up-to-date suggestions for further reading, broken down by chapter and annotated so that students can see what each work covers.

RESOURCES FOR INSTRUCTORS

INSTRUCTOR'S MANUAL

Amy Hudnall and Neva Specht
Appalachian State University
Includes chapter outlines, lecture ideas, classroom activities, recommended books, recommended film lists with annotations, and recommended websites.

TEST BANK/COMPUTERIZED TEST BANK

Sara Jorgensen and Andrea Becksvoort
University of Tennessee, Chattanooga
The Test Bank has been revised in accordance with the Norton Assessment Guidelines. Questions are organized around a Concept Map and are ranked by knowledge type, difficulty, and section reference.

All Norton test banks are available with Exam View Test Generator software, allowing instructors to effortlessly create, administer, and manage assessments. The convenient and intuitive testmaking wizard makes it easy to create customized exams with no software learning curve. Other key features include the ability to create paper exams with algorithmically generated variables and to export files directly to Blackboard, WebCT, and Angel.

INSTRUCTOR'S RESOURCE DISC

This helpful classroom presentation tool features:
- Lecture PowerPoint slides that include a suggested classroom-lecture script in the notes field. These are particularly helpful to first-time teachers of the course.
- A separate set of art PowerPoints featuring photographs and maps, retouched for in-class projection.

DOWNLOADABLE INSTRUCTOR'S RESOURCES

wwnorton.com/instructors
Instructional content for use in lecture and distance education, including coursepacks, test banks, PowerPoint lecture slides, images, figures, and more.

COURSEPACKS

Available at no cost to professors or students, Norton coursepacks for online or hybrid courses are available in a variety of formats, including all versions of Blackboard and WebCT. With just a simple download from our instructor's website, an instructor can bring high-quality Norton digital media into a new or existing online course (no extra student passwords required), and it's theirs to keep forever. Content includes chapter-based assignments, test banks and quizzes, interactive learning tools, and selected content from the StudySpace website.

NORTON GRADEBOOK

With the free, easy-to-use Norton Gradebook, instructors can easily access StudySpace student quiz results and avoid email inbox clutter. No course setup required. For more information and an audio tour of the Gradebook, visit wwnorton.com/college/nrl/gradebook.

NORTON ONLINE

Norton Online provides a seamless and flexible online learning environment featuring proven resources that help students succeed. By integrating Norton's market-leading textbooks with interactive tools in an easy-to-use learning-management system, Norton Online provides a high-quality online course that can be used right away or customized to suit an instructor's specific needs.

RESOURCES FOR STUDENTS

STUDYSPACE: YOUR PLACE FOR A BETTER GRADE

StudySpace tells students what they know, shows them what they need to review, and then gives them an organized study plan to master the material.

Students rely on effective and well-designed online resources to help them succeed in their courses—StudySpace is unmatched in providing a one-stop solution that's closely aligned with their textbook. This free and easy-to-navigate website offers students an impressive range of exercises, interactive-learning tools, assessment, and review materials, including:

Quiz+ Quiz+ doesn't just tell students how they did; it shows them how they can do better. With Quiz+, students are presented with a targeted study plan that offers specific page references and links to the ebook and other online learning tools.

NEW: World History Tours powered by Google Maps. These tours trace global developments over time, touching down on locations to launch documents and images for analysis.

NEW: Nearly 100 new documents increase the collection of readings to 350 sources. Each source is accompanied by a media analysis worksheet that offers students a simple guided method to *Observe* a document's primary themes, *Express* an opinion or respond to the author's objective, and *Connect* the document to broader historical relevance.

Engaging Review Materials include chapter summaries and outlines, focus questions, flashcards with audio pronunciations, and diagnostic quizzes.

More Help with Geography: iMaps offer students tools to view maps one layer of information at a time, focusing on specific geographic sections.

Map Review Worksheets provide each map in the textbook as a label-less image; students are given a list of labels to connect to the map. These worksheets can be printed out so that the exercises can be completed off line.

Chrono-Sequencers: These interactive chapter chronologies challenge students to reassemble sequences of events and reinforce their understanding of the flow of history.

Research Topics and Documents: Each chapter clusters primary sources around a topic, complete with an opening question and introduction to help students focus on the connections between the documents.

EBOOK AND CUSTOM VERSIONS

Ebook: Same great book, *one-third* the price!

An affordable and convenient alternative, Norton ebooks retain the content and design of the print book and allow students to highlight and take notes with ease, print chapters as needed, and search the text. Norton ebooks are available online and as downloadable PDFs. They can be purchased directly from our website or with a registration folder that can be sold in the bookstore.

Chapter Select

With Chapter Select instructors can create a custom ebook that contains only the chapters they want to assign. For more information, go to nortonebooks.com: includes pricing and purchasing details as well as instructions about how to create a custom ebook using Chapter Select.

ACKNOWLEDGMENTS

Worlds Together, Worlds Apart would never have happened without the full support of Princeton University. In a highly unusual move, and one for which we are truly grateful, the university helped underwrite this project with financial support from its 250th Anniversary Fund for undergraduate teaching and by allowing release time for the authors from campus commitments.

The history department's support of the effort over many years has been exceptional. Four chairs made funds and departmental support available, including the department's incomparable administrative talents. We would be remiss if we did not single out the department manager, Judith Hanson, who provided us with assistance whenever we needed it. We also thank Eileen Kane, who provided help in tracking down references and illustrations and in integrating changes into the manuscript. We also would like to thank Pamela Long, who made all of the complicated arrangements for ensuring that we were able to discuss matters in a leisurely and attractive setting. Sometimes that meant arranging for long-distance conference calls. She went even further and proofread the entire manuscript, finding many errors that we had all overlooked.

We drew shamelessly on the expertise of the departmental faculty, and although it might be wise simply to include a roster of the Princeton history department, that would do an injustice to those of whom we took most advantage. So here they are: Mariana Candido, Robert Darnton, Sheldon Garon, Anthony Grafton, Molly Greene, David Howell, Harold James, William Jordan, Emmanuel Kreike, Michael Mahoney, Arno Mayer, Kenneth Mills, John Murrin, Susan Naquin,

Willard Peterson, Theodore Rabb, Bhavani Raman, Stanley Stein, and Richard Turits. When necessary, we went outside the history department, getting help from L. Carl Brown, Michael Cook, Norman Itzkowitz, Martin Kern, Thomas Leisten, Heath Lowry, and Peter Schaefer. Two departmental colleagues—Natalie Z. Davis and Elizabeth Lunbeck—were part of the original team but had to withdraw because of other commitments. Their contributions were vital, and we want to express our thanks to them. David Gordon, now at Bowdoin College, used portions of the text while teaching an undergraduate course at the University of Durban in South Africa and shared comments with us. Shamil Jeppie, like David Gordon a graduate of the Princeton history department, now teaching at the University of Cape Town in South Africa, read and commented on various chapters.

Beyond Princeton, we have also benefited from exceptionally gifted and giving colleagues who have assisted this book in many ways. Colleagues at Louisiana State University, the University of Florida, the University of North Carolina, the University of Pennsylvania, and the University of California at Los Angeles, where Suzanne Marchand, Michael Tsin, Holly Pittman, and Stephen Aron, respectively, are now teaching, pitched in whenever we turned to them. Especially helpful have been the contributions of James Gelvin, Naomi Lamoreaux, Gary Nash, and Joyce Appleby at UCLA; Michael Bernstein at Tulane University; and Maribel Dietz, John Henderson, Christine Kooi, David Lindenfeld, Reza Pirbhai, and Victor Stater at Louisiana State University. It goes without saying that none of these individuals bears any responsibility for factual or interpretive errors that the text may contain. Xinru Liu would like to thank her Indian mentor, Romila Thapar, who changed the way we think about Indian history.

The quality and range of reviews on this project were truly exceptional. The final version of the manuscript was greatly influenced by the thoughts and ideas of numerous instructors. We wish to particularly thank our consulting reviewers, who read multiple versions of the manuscript from start to finish.

First Edition Consultants
Hugh Clark, Ursinus College
Jonathan Lee, San Antonio College
Pamela McVay, Ursuline College
Tom Sanders, United States Naval Academy

Second Edition Consultants
Jonathan Lee, San Antonio College
Pamela McVay, Ursuline College
Steve Rapp, Georgia State University
Cliff Rosenberg, City University of New York

First Edition Reviewers
Lauren Benton, New Jersey Institute of Technology
Ida Blom, University of Bergen, Norway

Ricardo Duchesne, University of New Brunswick
Major Bradley T. Gericke, United States Military Academy
John Gillis, Rutgers University
David Kenley, Marshall University
John Kicza, Washington State University
Matthew Levinger, Lewis and Clark College
James Long, Colorado State University
Adam McKeown, Columbia University
Mark McLeod, University of Delaware
John Mears, Southern Methodist University
Michael Murdock, Brigham Young University
David Newberry, University of North Carolina, Chapel Hill
Tom Pearcy, Slippery Rock State University
Oliver B. Pollak, University of Nebraska, Omaha
Ken Pomeranz, University of California, Irvine
Major David L. Ruffley, United States Air Force Academy
William Schell, Murray State University
Major Deborah Schmitt, United States Air Force Academy
Sarah Shields, University of North Carolina, Chapel Hill
Mary Watrous-Schlesinger, Washington State University

Second Edition Reviewers
William Atwell, Hobart and William Smith Colleges
Susan Besse, City University of New York
Tithi Bhattacharya, Purdue University
Mauricio Borrerero, St. John's University
Charlie Briggs, Georgia Southern University
Antoinne Burton, University of Illinois, Urbana-Champaign
Jim Cameron, St. Francis Xavier University
Kathleen Comerford, Georgia Southern University
Duane Corpis, Georgia State University
Denise Davidson, Georgia State University
Ross Doughty, Ursinus College
Alison Fletcher, Kent State University
Phillip Gavitt, Saint Louis University
Brent Geary, Ohio University
Henda Gilli-Elewy, California State Polytechnic University, Pomona
Fritz Gumbach, John Jay College
William Hagen, University of California, Davis
Laura Hilton, Muskingum College
Jeff Johnson, Villanova University
David Kammerling-Smith, Eastern Illinois University
Jonathan Lee, San Antonio College
Dorothea Martin, Appalachian State University
Don McGuire, State University of New York, Buffalo
Pamela McVay, Ursuline College
Joel Migdal, University of Washington
Anthony Parent, Wake Forest University
Sandra Peacock, Georgia Southern University
David Pietz, Washington State University
Jared Poley, Georgia State University

John Quist, Shippensburg State University
Steve Rapp, Georgia State University
Paul Rodell, Georgia Southern University
Ariel Salzman, Queen's University
Bill Schell, Murray State University
Claire Schen, State University of New York, Buffalo
Jonathan Skaff, Shippensburg State University
David Smith, California State Polytechnic University,
    Pomona
Neva Specht, Appalachian State University
Ramya Sreeniva, State University of New York, Buffalo
Charles Stewart, University of Illinois,
    Urbana-Champaign
Rachel Stocking, Southern Illinois University,
    Carbondale
Heather Streets, Washington State University
Tim Teeter, Georgia Southern University
Charlie Wheeler, University of California, Irvine
Owen White, University of Delaware
James Wilson, Wake Forest University

Third Edition Reviewers
Henry Antkiewicz, Eastern Tennessee State University
Anthony Barbieri-Low, University of California,
    Santa Barbara
Andrea Becksvoort, University of Tennessee, Chattanooga
Hayden Bellonoit, United States Naval Academy
John Bloom, Shippensburg University
Kathryn Braund, Auburn University
Catherine Candy, University of New Orleans
Karen Carter, Brigham Young University
Stephen Chappell, James Madison University
Jessey Choo, University of Missouri, Kansas City
Timothy Coates, College of Charleston
Gregory Crider, Wingate University
Denise Davidson, Georgia State University
Jessica Davidson, James Madison University
Sal Diaz, Santa Rosa Junior College
Todd Dozier, Baton Rouge Community College
Richard Eaton, University of Arizona
Lee Farrow, Auburn University, Montgomery
Bei Gao, College of Charleston
Behrooz Ghamari-Tabrizi, University of Illinois,
    Urbana-Champaign
Steven Gish, Auburn University, Montgomery
Jeffrey Hamilton, Baylor University
Barry Hankins, Baylor University
Brian Harding, Mott Community College
Tim Henderson, Auburn University, Montgomery
Marjorie Hilton, University of Redlands
Richard Hines, Washington State University
Lisa Holliday, Appalachian State University
Jonathan Lee, San Antonio College
David Kalivas, University of Massachusetts, Lowell

Christopher Kelley, Miami University, Ohio
Kenneth Koons, Virginia Military Institute
Michael Kulikowski, Pennsylvania State University
Benjamin Lawrence, University of California, Davis
Lu Liu, University of Tennessee, Knoxville
David Longfellow, Baylor University
Harold Marcuse, University of California,
Santa Barbara
Dorothea Martin, Appalachian State University
David Mayes, Sam Houston State University
James Mokhiber, University of New Orleans
Mark Munzinger, Radford College
David Murphree, Virginia Tech University
Joshua Nadel, North Carolina Central University
Wing Chung Nq, University of Texas, San Antonio
Robert Norrell, University of Tennessee, Knoxville
Chandrika Paul, Shippensburg University
Beth Pollard, San Diego State University
Timothy Pytell, California State University,
    San Bernardino
Stephen Rapp, Professional Historian
Alice Roberti, Santa Rosa Junior College
Aviel Roshwald, Georgetown University
James Sanders, Utah State University
Lynn Sargeant, California State University, Fullerton
William Schell, Murray State University
Michael Seth, James Madison University
Barry Stentiford, Grambling State University
Gabrielle Sutherland, Baylor University
Lisa Tran, California State University, Fullerton
Michael Vann, California State University, Sacramento
Peter Von Sivers, University of Utah
Andrew Wackerfuss, Georgetown University
Ted Weeks, Southern Illinois University, Carbondale
Angela White, Indiana University of Pennsylvania
Jennifer Williams, Nichols State University
Andrew Wise, State University of New York, Buffalo
Eloy Zarate, Pasadena City College
William Zogby, Mohawk Valley Community College

We also want to thank Nancy Khalek (Ph.D. Princeton University), who now teaches at Brown University. Nancy was our jack-of-all-trades who helped in any way she could. She attended all the monthly meetings during the development of the early volume. She provided critiques of the manuscript, helped with primary research, worked on the photo program and the Global Connections & Disconnections features, and contributed content to the student website. She was invaluable. For the Third Edition, Nancy has authored a number of the new digital World History Tours powered by Google Maps. We would also like to thank Neva Specht and Amy Hudnall (both from Appalachian State University), who have authored the Instructor's Manual for the last two editions. They have filled the manual with many wonderful classroom exercises and a highly useful annotated suggested films list. Finally, we'd like to thank our two newcomers, Sara Jorgensen and Andrea Becksvoort (both from the University of Tennessee, Chattanooga) for thoroughly revising the test bank.

Our association with the publisher of this volume, W. W. Norton & Company, has been everything we could have asked for. Jon Durbin took us under the wing of the Norton firm. He attended all of our monthly meetings for the first two editions spanning the better part of four years across the creation of both volumes. How he put up with some of our interminable discussions will always be a mystery, but his enthusiasm for the endeavor never flagged, even when we seemed to grow weary. He has brought the same energy and determination to the Third Edition. Sandy Lifland was the ever-watchful and ever-careful development editor for each volume for the First Edition and a good portion of the Second Edition. She let us know when we were making sense and when we needed to explain ourselves more fully. Alice Falk was our talented and insightful co-developmental editor for the Second Edition. Between the efforts of Sandy and Alice, our vision became a reality. For the Third Edition, Alice Vigliani was an unimaginably superb development editor. She took a book that we were all very proud of, and she has helped bring it closest to our original vision. She responded immediately to all queries, kept everyone on an even keel, shrank the text where it was too wordy, and demanded that we add color and vitality where the writing flagged. If the Third Edition showcases the big world history stories better than ever, and it is easier to read and more accessible than the first two (and we believe that this is the case), we owe these improvements to her. Rebecca Homiski did a fabulous job as our project editor on the Second and Third editions, coordinating the responses of up to twelve authors on both volumes combined and locking down all the details on the project. We also want to thank Ellen Lohman for copyediting the manuscript ably and with just the right touch for the Second and Third Editions. Stephanie Romeo led the charge again, finding all the new photos we requested, and Rubina Yeh integrated the new "Storylines" features and the new chapter chronologies into her already gorgeous design. Debra Morton-Hoyt has provided us again with what have to be the most distinctive and appealing world history book covers in the field. Ben Reynolds guided the manuscript through the production process, and Jason Spears capably pulled together all the important loose ends to get the manuscript ready for copyediting, working on the photo captions, glossary, and art manuscript, among other tasks. On the media front, we want to thank Steve Hoge for creating the Norton StudySpace website, which includes the impressive Norton Digital History Reader and the exciting new Norton World History Tours powered by Google Maps. On the print ancillary front, we'd like to thank Lorraine Klimowich and Rachel Comerford for finding an excellent group of authors to create the instructor's manual and test bank. Carla Zimowsk, the information officer for the history department at Princeton University, simplified the multiple transmission of revised chapters among all twelve of the authors, no easy task. She made what is a very complicated set of procedures easy to understand and workable.

Finally, we must recognize that while this project often kept us apart from family members, their support held our personal worlds together.

ROBERT TIGNOR (Ph.D. Yale University) is Professor Emeritus and the Rosengarten Professor of Modern and Contemporary History at Princeton University and the three-time chair of the history department. With Gyan Prakash, he introduced Princeton's first course in world history nearly twenty years ago. Professor Tignor has taught graduate and undergraduate courses in African history and world history and written extensively on the history of twentieth-century Egypt, Nigeria, and Kenya. Besides his many research trips to Africa, Professor Tignor has taught at the University of Ibadan in Nigeria and the University of Nairobi in Kenya.

JEREMY ADELMAN (D.Phil. Oxford University) is currently the Director of the Council for International Teaching and Research at Princeton University and the Walter S. Carpenter III Professor of Spanish Civilization and Culture. He has written and edited five books, including *Republic of Capital: Buenos Aires and the Legal Transformation of the Atlantic World*, which won the best book prize in Atlantic history from the American Historical Association, and most recently *Sovereignty and Revolution in the Iberian Atlantic*. Professor Adelman is the recent recipient of a Guggenheim Memorial Foundation Fellowship and the Frederick Burkhardt Award from the American Council of Learned Societies.

STEPHEN ARON (Ph.D. University of California, Berkeley) is professor of history at the University of California, Los Angeles, and executive director of the Institute for the Study of the American West, Autry National Center. A specialist in frontier and Western American history, Aron is the author of *How the West Was Lost: The Transformation of Kentucky from Daniel Boone to Henry Clay* and *American Confluence: The Missouri Frontier from Borderland to Border State*. He is currently editing the multi-volume *Autry History of the American West* and writing a book with the tentative title *Can We All Just Get Along: An Alternative History of the American West*.

PETER BROWN (Ph.D. Oxford University) is the Rollins Professor of History at Princeton University. He previously taught at London University and the University of California, Berkeley. He has written on the rise of Christianity and the end of the Roman Empire. His works include *Augustine of Hippo*, *The World of Late Antiquity*, *The Cult of the Saints*, *Body and Society*, *The Rise of Western Christendom*, and *Poverty and Leadership in the Later Roman Empire*. He is presently working on issues of wealth and poverty in the late Roman and early medieval Christian worlds.

BENJAMIN ELMAN (Ph.D. University of Pennsylvania) is professor of East Asian studies and history at Princeton University. He is currently serving as the chair of the Princeton East Asian Studies Department. He taught at the University of California, Los Angeles, for over fifteen years. His teaching and research fields include Chinese intellectual and cultural history, 1000–1900; the history of science in China, 1600–1930; the history of education in late imperial China; and Sino-Japanese cultural history, 1600–1850. He is the author of five books: *From Philosophy to Philology: Intellectual and Social Aspects of Change in Late Imperial China*; *Classicism, Politics, and Kinship: The Ch'ang-chou School of New Text Confucianism in Late Imperial China*; *A Cultural History of Civil Examinations in Late Imperial China*; *On Their Own Terms: Science in China, 1550–1900*; and *A Cultural History of Modern Science in China*. He is the creator of Classical Historiography for Chinese History at www.princeton.edu/~classbib/, a bibliography and teaching website published since 1996.

STEPHEN KOTKIN (Ph.D. University of California, Berkeley) is professor of European and Asian history as well as international affairs at Princeton University. He formerly directed Princeton's program in Russian and Eurasian studies (1996–2009). He is the author of *Magnetic Mountain: Stalinism as a Civilization, Uncivil Society: 1989 and the Implosion of the Communist Establishment*, and *Armageddon Averted: The Soviet Collapse, 1970–2000*. He is a coeditor of *Mongolia in the Twentieth Century: Landlocked Cosmopolitan*. Professor Kotkin has twice been a visiting professor in Japan.

XINRU LIU (Ph.D. University of Pennsylvania) is associate professor of early Indian history and world history at the College of New Jersey. She is associated with the Institute of World History and the Chinese Academy of Social Sciences. She is the author of *Ancient India and Ancient China, Trade and Religious Exchanges*, AD 1–600; *Silk and Religion, an Exploration of Material Life and the Thought of People*, AD 600–1200; *Connections across Eurasia, Transportation, Communication, and Cultural Exchange on the Silk Roads*, co-authored with Lynda Norene Shaffer; and *A Social History of Ancient India* (in Chinese). Professor Liu promotes South Asian studies and world history studies in both the United States and the People's Republic of China.

SUZANNE MARCHAND (Ph.D. University of Chicago) is professor of European and intellectual history at Louisiana State University, Baton Rouge. Professor Marchand also spent a number of years teaching at Princeton University. She is the author of *Down from Olympus: Archaeology and Philhellenism in Germany, 1750–1970* and *German Orientalism in the Age of Empire: Religion, Race and Scholarship*.

HOLLY PITTMAN (Ph.D. Columbia University) is professor of art history at the University of Pennsylvania, where she teaches art and archaeology of Mesopotamia and the Iranian Plateau. She also serves as curator in the Near East Section of the University of Pennsylvania Museum of Archaeology and Anthropology. Previously she served as a curator in the Ancient Near Eastern Art Department of the Metropolitan Museum of Art. She has written extensively on the art and culture of the Bronze Age in the Middle East and has participated in excavations in Cyprus, Turkey, Syria, Iraq, and Iran, where she currently works. Her research investigates works of art as media through which patterns of thought, cultural development, and historical interactions of ancient cultures of the Near East are reconstructed.

GYAN PRAKASH (Ph.D. University of Pennsylvania) is professor of modern Indian history at Princeton University and a member of the Subaltern Studies Editorial Collective. He is the author of *Bonded Histories: Genealogies of Labor Servitude in Colonial India, Another Reason: Science and the Imagination of Modern India,* and *Mumbai Fables*. Professor Prakash edited *After Colonialism: Imperial Histories and Postcolonial Displacements* and *Noir Urbanisms*, coedited *The Space of the Modern City* and *Utopia/Dystopia*, and has written a number of articles on colonialism and history writing. He is currently working on a history of the city of Bombay. With Robert Tignor, he introduced the modern world history course at Princeton University.

BRENT SHAW (Ph.D. Cambridge University) is the Andrew Fleming West Professor of Classics at Princeton University, where he is director of the Program in the Ancient World. He was previously at the University of Pennsylvania, where he chaired the Graduate Group in Ancient History. His principal areas of specialization as a Roman historian are Roman family history and demography, sectarian violence and conflict in Late Antiquity, and the regional history of Africa as part of the Roman Empire. He has published *Spartacus and the Slaves Wars*; edited the papers of Sir Moses Finley, *Economy and Society in Ancient Greece*; and published in a variety of books and journals, including the *Journal of Roman Studies*, the *American Historical Review*, the *Journal of Early Christian Studies*, and *Past & Present*.

MICHAEL TSIN (Ph.D. Princeton) is associate professor of history and international studies at the University of North Carolina at Chapel Hill. He previously taught at the University of Illinois at Chicago, Princeton University, Columbia University, and the University of Florida. Professor Tsin's primary interests include the histories of modern China and colonialism. He is the author of *Nation, Governance, and Modernity in China: Canton, 1900–1927.* He is currently writing a social history of the reconfiguration of Chinese identity in the twentieth century.

NORTH
AMERICA

ATLANTIC
OCEAN

SAHARA

Niger R.

PACIFIC
OCEAN

SOUTH

AMERICA

| 0 | 1000 | 2000 Miles |
| 0 | 1000 | 2000 Kilometers |

THE GEOGRAPHY OF THE ANCIENT AND MODERN WORLDS

Today, we believe the world to be divided into continents, and most of us think that it was always so. Geographers usually identify six inhabited continents: Africa, North America, South America, Europe, Asia, and Australia. Inside these continents they locate a vast number of subcontinental units, such as East Asia, South Asia, Southeast Asia, the Middle East, North Africa, and sub-Saharan Africa. Yet this geographical understanding would have been completely alien to premodern men and women, who did not think that they inhabited continents bounded by large bodies of water. Lacking a firm command of the seas,

they saw themselves living on contiguous landmasses, and they thought these territorial bodies were the main geographical units of their lives. Hence, in this volume we have chosen to use a set of geographical terms, the main one being *Afro-Eurasia*, that more accurately reflect the world that the premoderns believed that they inhabited.

The most interconnected and populous landmass of premodern times was Afro-Eurasia. The term *Eurasia* is widely used in general histories, but we think it is in its own ways inadequate. The preferred term from our perspective must be *Afro-Eurasia*, for the interconnected

MAP 15-1   REVOLUTIONS OF NATIONAL INDEPENDENCE IN THE ATLANTIC WORLD, 1776–1829

Influenced by Enlightenment thinkers and the French Revolution, colonies gained independence from European powers (and in the case of Greece, from the Ottoman Empire) in the late eighteenth and early nineteenth centuries. Which European powers granted independence to their colonial possessions in the Americas during this period? What were the first two colonial territories to become independent in the Americas? Given that the second American republic arose from a violent slave revolt, why do you suppose the United States was reluctant to recognize its political independence? According to your reading, why did colonies in Spanish and Portuguese America obtain political independence decades after the United States won its independence?

THE NORTH AMERICAN WAR OF INDEPENDENCE, 1776–1783

By the mid-eighteenth century, Britain's colonies in North America swelled with people and prosperity. Bustling port cities like Charleston, Philadelphia, New York, and Boston saw inflows of African slaves, European migrants, and manufactured goods, while agricultural staples flowed out. A "genteel" class of merchants and landowning planters dominated colonial affairs.

But with settlers arriving from Europe and slaves from Africa, land was a constant source of dispute. Planters struggled with independent farmers (yeomen). Sons and daughters of farmers, often unable to inherit or acquire land near their parents, moved westward, where they came into conflict with Indian peoples. To defend their lands, many Indians allied with Britain's rival, France. After losing the Seven Years' War (see Chapter 13), however, France ceded its Canadian colony to Britain. This left many Indians no choice but to turn to Britain to help them resist the aggressive advances of land-hungry colonists. British officials did make some concessions to Indian interests, most visibly by issuing the Proclamation of 1763, which drew a line at the crest of the Appalachians beyond which Indian lands were to be protected from colonial settlement. Still, Britain did not have the troops to police the line, so while the proclamation antagonized some colonists, it did not really secure Indian lands.

ASSERTING INDEPENDENCE FROM BRITAIN Even as tensions simmered and sometimes boiled over into bloodshed on the western frontier of British North America, the situation of the British in North America still looked very strong in the mid-1760s. At that point, Britain stood supreme in the Atlantic world, with its greatest foes defeated and its empire expanding. Political revolution seemed unimaginable. And yet, a decade later, that is what occurred.

The spark came from King George III, who insisted that colonists help pay for Britain's war with France and for the benefits of being subjects of the British Empire. It seemed only reasonable to King George and his ministers, faced with staggering war debts, that colonists contribute to the crown that protected them. Accordingly, the king's officials imposed taxes on a variety of commodities and tried to end the lucrative smuggling by which colonists had been evading the restrictions that mercantilism was supposed to impose on colonial trade. To the king's surprise and dismay, colonists raised vigorous objections to the new measures and protested having to pay taxes when they lacked political representation in the British Parliament. (See Primary Source: The Other Revolution of 1776.)

In 1775, resistance in the form of petitions and boycotts turned into open warfare between a colonial militia and British troops in Massachusetts. Once blood was spilled, more radical voices came to the fore. Previously, leaders of the resistance to taxation without representation had claimed to revere the British Empire while fearing its corruptions. Now calls for severing the ties to Britain became more prominent. Thomas Paine, a recent immigrant from England, captured the new mood in a pamphlet he published in 1776, arguing that it was "common sense" for people to govern themselves. Later that year, the Continental Congress (in which representatives from thirteen colonies gathered) adapted part of Payne's popular pamphlet for the Declaration of Independence.

Drawing on Enlightenment themes (see Chapter 14), the declaration written by Thomas Jefferson stated the people's "natural rights" to govern themselves. It also drew inspiration from the writings of the British philosopher John Locke, notably the idea that governments should be based on a **social contract** in which the law binds both ruler and people. Locke had even written that the people had the right to rebel against their government if it broke the contract and infringed on their rights.

With the Declaration of Independence, the rebels announced their right to rid themselves of the English king and form their own government. But neither the Declaration of Independence nor Locke's writings explained how these colonists (now calling themselves Americans) should organize a nonmonarchical government—or how thirteen weakly connected colonies (now calling themselves states) might prevail against the world's most powerful empire. Nonetheless,

The Boston Massacre. Paul Revere's idealized view of the Boston Massacre of March 5, 1770. In the years after the Seven Years' War, Bostonians grew increasingly disenchanted with British efforts to enforce imperial regulations. When British troops fired on and killed several members of an angry mob in what came to be called the "Boston Massacre," the resulting frenzy stirred revolutionary sentiments among the populace.

THE OTHER REVOLUTION OF 1776

The year 1776 is mainly known as the year American colonists declared their independence from the British Empire. But it also marked the publication of Adam Smith's An Inquiry into the Nature and Causes of the Wealth of Nations, *the most important book in the history of economic thought. Smith, a Scottish philosopher, felt that constraints on trade (by governments or private monopolies) prevented people from achieving their full potential and thereby impoverished nations. Although he was not opposed to colonies per se, in this selection Smith warns British authorities that mercantilist controls on their colonies are not only unjust but counterproductive. Thus, "free trade" is tied to the fate of Europe's colonies.*

The exclusive trade of the mother countries tends to diminish, or, at least, to keep down below what they would otherwise rise to, both the enjoyments and industry of all those nations in general, and of the American colonies in particular. . . . By rendering the colony produce dearer in all other countries, it lessens its consumption, and thereby cramps the industry of the colonies, and both the enjoyments and the industry of all other countries, which both enjoy less when they pay more for what they enjoy, and produce less when they get less for what they produce.

By rendering the produce of all other countries dearer in the colonies, it cramps, in the same manner, the industry of all other countries, and both the enjoyments and the industry of the colonies. It is a clog which, for the supposed benefit of some particular countries, embarrasses the pleasures, and encumbers the industry of all other countries; but of the colonies more than of any other.

It not only excludes, as much as possible, all other countries from one particular market; but it confines, as much as possible, the colonies to one particular market: and the difference is very great between being excluded from one particular market, when all others are open, and being confined to one particular market, when all others are shut up. The surplus produce of the colonies, however, is the original source of all that increase of enjoyments and industry which Europe derives from the discovery and colonization of America; and the exclusive trade of the mother countries tends to render this source much less abundant than it otherwise would be.

➢ *In terms of the American colonies, who is "the mother country"?*
➢ *According to Smith, how does exclusive trade between the mother country and the colonists diminish the colonies' development?*

Source: Adam Smith, *An Inquiry into the Nature and Causes of the Wealth of Nations,* Book 4, edited by Edwin Cannan (Chicago: University of Chicago Press, 1776/1977), pp. 105–106.

the colonies soon became embroiled in a revolution that would turn the world upside down.

During their War of Independence, Americans designed new political arrangements. First, individual states elected delegates to constitutional conventions, where they drafted written constitutions to govern the workings of each state. Second, by eliminating royal authority, the state constitutions gave extensive powers to legislative bodies, whose members "the people" would elect. But who constituted the people? That is, who had voting rights? Not women. Not slaves. Not Indians. Not even adult white men who owned no property.

Despite the limited extent of voting rights, the notion that all men were created equal overturned former social hierarchies. Thus common men no longer automatically deferred to gentlemen of higher rank. Many women claimed that their contributions to the revolution's cause (by managing farms and shops in their husbands' absence) earned them greater equality in marriage, including property rights. In letters to her husband, John Adams, who was a representative in the Continental Congress and a champion of American independence, Abigail Adams stopped referring to the family farm as "yours" and instead called it "ours." Most revolutionary of all, many slaves sided against the Revolution, for it was the British who offered them freedom—most directly in exchange for military service.

Alas, their hopes for freedom were thwarted when Britain conceded the loss of its rebellious American colonies. That improbable outcome owed to a war in which British armies won most of the major battles but could not finish off the

Abigail Adams. Abigail Adams was the wife of John Adams, a leader in the movement for American independence and later the second president of the United States. Abigail's letters to her husband testified to the ways in which revolutionary enthusiasm for liberty and equality began to reach into women's minds. In the spring of 1776, Abigail wrote to implore that the men in the Continental Congress "remember the ladies, and be more generous and favorable to them than your ancestors. . . . If particular care and attention is not paid to the Ladies we are determined to foment a Rebellion, and will not hold ourselves bound by any Laws in which we have no voice, or Representation."

Continental Army under the command of General George Washington. Washington hung on and held his troops together long enough to convince the French that the American cause was not hopeless and that supporting it might be a way to settle a score against the British. This they did, and with the Treaty of Paris (1783) the United States gained its independence.

BUILDING A REPUBLICAN GOVERNMENT With independence, the former colonists had to build a new government. They generally agreed that theirs was not to be a monarchy. But what it *was* to be remained through the 1780s a source of much debate, involving heated words and sometimes heated action.

Amid the political revolution against monarchy, the prospect of a social revolution of women, slaves, and artisans generated a reaction against what American elites called the "excesses of democracy." Their fears increased after farmers in Massachusetts, led by Daniel Shays, interrupted court proceedings in which the state tried to foreclose on their properties for nonpayment of taxes. The farmers who joined in Shays's rebellion in 1786 also denounced illegitimate taxation—this time, by their state's government. Acting in the interests of the fledgling government, Massachusetts militiamen defeated the rebel army. But to save the young nation from falling into "anarchy," propertied men convened the Constitutional Convention in Philadelphia a year later.

This gathering aimed to forge a document that would create a more powerful national government and a more unified nation. After fierce debate, the convention drafted a charter for a **republican government** in which power and rulership would rest with representatives of the people—not a king. When it went before the states for approval, the Constitution was controversial. Its critics, known as Anti-Federalists, feared the growth of a potentially tyrannical national government and insisted on including a Bill of Rights to protect individual liberties from abusive government intrusions. Ultimately the Constitution won ratification, and the Bill of Rights was soon amended to it.

Ratification of the Constitution and the addition of the Bill of Rights did not end arguments about the scope and power of the national government of the United States, although they did quiet the most heated controversies. In an uneasy truce, political leaders agreed not to let the debate over whether to abolish slavery escalate into a cause for disunion. As the frontier pushed westward, however, the question of which new states would or would not allow slavery sparked debates again. Initially the existence of ample land postponed a confrontation. In 1800, Thomas Jefferson's election as the third president of the United States marked the triumph of a model of sending pioneers out to new lands in order to reduce conflict on old lands. In the same year, however, a Virginia slave named Gabriel Prosser raised an army of slaves to seize the state capital at Richmond and won support from white artisans and laborers for a more inclusive republic. His dream of an egalitarian revolution fell victim to white terror and black betrayal, though: twenty-seven slaves, including Prosser, went to the gallows. With them, for the moment, died the dream of a multiracial republic in which all men were truly created equal.

But the issue of slavery did not go away. Indeed, with ideas of the dignity and rights of free labor gaining popularity in the northern states, the truce by which political leaders tried to keep debates over slavery from escalating into a cause for disunion became even more uneasy.

In a larger Atlantic world context, the American Revolution ushered in a new age based on ideas of freedom. The successful defiance of Europe's most powerful empire and the establishment of a nonmonarchical, republican form of government sent shock waves through the Americas and Europe and even into distant corners of Asia and Africa.

THE FRENCH REVOLUTION, 1789–1799

Partly inspired by the American Revolution, French men and women soon began to call for liberty too—and the result profoundly shook Europe's dynasties and social hierarchies. Its impact, though, reached well beyond Europe, for the French Revolution, even more than the American, inspired rebels and terrified rulers around the globe.

The "Tennis Court Oath." Locked out of the chambers of the Estates-General, the deputies of the Third Estate reconvened at a nearby indoor tennis court in June 1789; there they swore an oath not to disband until the king recognized the sovereignty of a national assembly.

ORIGINS AND OUTBREAK For decades, enlightened thinkers had attacked France's old regime—the court, the aristocracy, and the church—at the risk of imprisonment or exile. But by the mid-eighteenth century, discontent had spread beyond the educated few. In the countryside, peasants grumbled about having to pay taxes and tithes to the church, whereas nobles and clergy paid almost no taxes. Also, despite improved health and nutrition, peasants still suffered occasional deprivation. A combination of these pressures, as well as a fiscal crisis, unleashed the French Revolution of 1789.

Ironically, the king himself opened the door to revolution. Eager to weaken his rival, England, Louis XVI spent huge sums in support of the American rebels—and thereby overloaded the state's debt. It was not the size of the debt but the French king's inability to raise funds that put him in a bind. To restore his credit, Louis needed to raise taxes on the privileged classes, but to do so he was forced to convene the Estates-General, a medieval advisory body that had not met for over a century. Like the American colonists, French nobles argued that taxation gave them the right of representation. When the king reluctantly agreed to summon the Estates-General in 1788, he still thought he would prevail. After all, the delegates of the clergy (the First Estate) and the aristocracy (the Second Estate) could overrule the delegates representing everyone else (the Third Estate), because each estate voted as one body. This meant that it was possible to outvote the Third Estate.

However, when the delegates assembled, the Third Estate refused to be outvoted. It insisted that those who worked and paid taxes *were* the nation, and it demanded that all delegates sit together in one chamber and vote as individuals. The privileged few, critics claimed, were parasites. As arguments raged, peasants began to attack castles in another indication that "the people" were throwing off old inequalities. Soon delegates of the Third Estate declared themselves to be the "National Assembly," the body that should determine France's future.

On July 14, 1789, a Parisian crowd attacked a medieval armory in search of weapons. Not only did this armory—the Bastille—hold gunpowder, but it was also an infamous prison for political prisoners. The crowd stormed the prison and murdered the commanding officer, then cut off his head and paraded it through the streets of Paris. On this day (Bastille Day), the king made the fateful decision not to call out the army, and the capital city belonged to the crowd. As news spread to the countryside, peasants torched manor houses and destroyed municipal archives containing records of the hated feudal dues. Barely three weeks later, the French National Assembly abolished the feudal privileges of the nobility and the clergy. It also declared a new era of liberty, equality, and fraternity.

REVOLUTIONARY TRANSFORMATIONS The "Declaration of the Rights of Man and Citizen" followed a few weeks later. It echoed the Americans' Declaration of Independence, but in more radical terms. It guaranteed all citizens of the French nation inviolable liberties and gave all men equality under the law. It also proclaimed that "the principle of all sovereignty rests essentially in the nation." Thus, the French Revolution connected more closely the concept of a people with a nation. Both the rhetorical and the real war against feudal privileges ushered in the end of dynastic and aristocratic rule in Europe.

Relations in social hierarchies changed too, as women felt that the new principles of citizenship should include women's

Women March on Versailles. On October 5, 1789, a group of market women, many of them fishwives (traditionally regarded as leaders of the poor), marched on the Paris city hall to demand bread. Quickly, their numbers grew, and they redirected their march to Versailles, some twelve miles away and the symbol of the entire political order. In response to the women, the king finally appeared on the balcony and agreed to sign the revolutionary decree and return with the women to Paris.

rights. In 1791, a group of women demanded the right to bear arms to defend the revolution, but they stopped short of claiming equal rights for both sexes. In their view, women would become citizens by being good revolutionary wives and mothers, not because of any natural rights. In the same year, Olympe de Gouges composed the "Declaration of the Rights of Woman and Citizen," proposing rights to divorce, hold property in marriage, be educated, and have public careers. The all-male assembly did not take up these issues, believing that a "fraternity" of free *men* composed the nation. (For a statement claiming similar rights for women in Britain, see Primary Source: Mary Wollstonecraft on the Rights of Women.)

As the revolution gained momentum, more nobles and clergy fled the country. In late 1790, all clergy had to take an oath of loyalty to the new state—an action that enraged Catholics. Meanwhile, the revolutionary ranks began to splinter, as men and women argued over the revolution's proper goals. Soon a new National Convention was elected by universal manhood suffrage, meaning that all adult males could vote—the first such election in Europe. In 1792, the first French Republic was proclaimed. But radicalization continued, and by early 1793 Louis XVI had lost his head to the guillotine, and France was at war with many of its neighbors.

THE TERROR After the king's execution, radicals known as Jacobins, who wanted to extend the revolution beyond France's borders, launched the Reign of Terror to purge the nation of its internal enemies. Jacobin leaders, including the lawyer Maximilien Robespierre, oversaw the execution of as many as 40,000 so-called enemies of the people—mostly peasants and laborers.

To spread revolution to other parts of Europe, the radicals instituted the first national draft. By 1794 France's army numbered some 800,000 soldiers, making it the world's largest. Most French officers now came from the middle classes, some even from the lower class. Foot soldiers identified with the French fatherland and demonstrated their solidarity by singing songs like "The Marseillaise."

The revolutionaries understood that to change society they would have to eliminate all symbols of the old regime. So they changed street names to honor revolutionary heroes, destroyed monuments to the royal family, adopted a new flag, eliminated titles, and insisted that everyone be addressed as "Citizen." They were so exhilarated by the new world they were creating that they changed time itself. Now they reckoned time not from the birth of Christ but from the moment the French Republic was proclaimed. Thus September 22, 1792, became day 1 of year 1 of the new age. The radicals also unsuccessfully attempted to replace the Catholic faith, which they accused of corruption and inequality, with a religion of reason.

By mid-1794, enthusiasm for Robespierre's measures had lost popular support, and Robespierre himself went to the guillotine on 9 Thermidor (July 28, 1794). His execution marked the end of the Terror. Several years later, following more political turmoil, a coup d'état brought to power a thirty-year-old general from the recently annexed Mediterranean island of Corsica.

The general, **Napoleon Bonaparte** (1769–1821), put security and order ahead of social reform. True, his regime retained many of the revolutionary changes, especially those associated with more efficient state government, but retreating from the Jacobins' anti-Catholicism, he allowed religion to be freely practiced again in France. Determined not only to reform France but also to prevail over its enemies, he retreated from republican principles. Napoleon first was a member of a three-man consulate; then he became first consul; finally, he proclaimed himself emperor. But he took the title Emperor of the French, not Emperor of France, and prepared a constitution subject to a vote of approval. He also

Primary Source

MARY WOLLSTONECRAFT ON THE RIGHTS OF WOMEN

As revolutionaries stressed the rights of "man" across the Atlantic world, Mary Wollstonecraft (1759–1797), an English writer, teacher, editor, and proponent of spreading education, resented her male colleagues' celebration of their newfound liberties. In A Vindication of the Rights of Woman *(1792), one of the founding works of modern feminism, she argued that the superiority of men was as arbitrary as the divine right of kings. For this, male progressives denounced her. The author is a "hyena in petticoats," noted one critic. In fact, she was arguing that women had the same rights to be reasonable creatures as men and that education should be available equally to both sexes.*

I love man as my fellow; but his sceptre, real or usurped, extends not to me, unless the reason of an individual demands my homage; and even then the submission is to reason, and not to man. In fact, the conduct of an accountable being must be regulated by the operations of its own reason; or on what foundation rests the throne of God?

It appears to me necessary to dwell on these obvious truths, because females have been insulated, as it were; and while they have been stripped of the virtues that should clothe humanity, they have been decked with artificial graces that enable them to exercise a short-lived tyranny. Love, in their bosoms, taking the place of every nobler passion, their sole ambition is to be fair, to raise emotion instead of inspiring respect; and this ignoble desire, like the servility in absolute monarchies, destroys all strength of character. Liberty is the mother of virtue, and if women be, by their very constitution, slaves, and not allowed to breathe the sharp invigorating air of freedom, they must ever languish like exotics, and be reckoned beautiful flaws in nature. Let it also be remembered, that they are the only flaw.

As to the argument respecting the subjection in which the sex has ever been held, it retorts on man. The many have always been enthralled by the few; and monsters, who scarcely have shown any discernment of human excellence, have tyrannized over thousands of their fellow-creatures. Why have men of superior endowments submitted to such degradation? For, is it not universally acknowledged that kings, viewed collectively, have ever been inferior, in abilities and virtue, to the same number of men taken from the common mass of mankind—yet have they not, and are they not still treated with a degree of reverence that is an insult to reason? China is not the only country where a living man has been made a God. *Men* have submitted to superior strength to enjoy with impunity the pleasure of the moment; *women* have only done the same, and therefore till it is proved that the courtier, who servilely resigns the birthright of a man, is not a moral agent, it cannot be demonstrated that woman is essentially inferior to man because she has always been subjugated.

→ *Wollstonecraft compares men to kings and women to slaves. What are her criticisms of kings, and why does she call them "monsters"?*

→ *In what ways are Wollstonecraft's ideas an outgrowth of Enlightenment thinking?*

→ *Do you find Wollstonecraft's arguments compelling? Explain why or why not.*

SOURCE: Mary Wollstonecraft, *A Vindication of the Rights of Woman*, edited by Miriam Brody (New York: Penguin Books, 1792/1993), pp. 122–23.

centralized government administration and created a system of rational tax collection. Most important, he created a civil legal code—the "Code Napoleon"—that applied throughout all of France (and the French colonies, including the Louisiana Territory). By designing a law code applicable to the nation as a whole, Napoleon created a model that would be widely imitated by emerging nation-states in Europe and the Americas in the century to come.

NAPOLEON'S EMPIRE, 1799–1815

Determined to extend the reach of French influence, Napoleon had his armies trumpet the principles of liberty, equality, and fraternity wherever they went. Many local populations actually embraced the French, regarding them as liberators from the old order. Although Napoleon thought the entire world would take up his cause, this was not always the case, as he learned in Egypt. After defeating Mamluk troops there in 1798, Napoleon soon faced a rebellious local Egyptian population.

In Portugal, Spain, and Russia, French troops also faced fierce popular resistance. Portuguese and Spanish soldiers and peasants formed bands of resisters called guerrillas, and British troops joined them to fight the French in the Peninsular War (1808–1813). In Germany and Italy, as local inhabitants grew tired of hearing that the French occupiers' ways were superior, many looked to their past for inspiration to oppose the French. Now they discovered something they had barely recognized before: *national* traditions and borders.

Battle of the Pyramids. The French army invaded Egypt with grand ambitions and high hopes. Napoleon brought a large cadre of scholars along with his 36,000-man army, intending to win Egyptians to the cause of the French Revolution and to establish a French imperial presence on the banks of the Nile. This idealized portrait of the famous Battle of the Pyramids, fought on July 21, 1798, shows Napoleon and his forces crushing the Mamluk military forces.

In fact, one of the ironies of Napoleon's attempt to bring all of Europe under French rule was that instead of creating a unified continent, it laid the foundations for nationalist strife.

In Europe, Napoleon extended his empire from the Iberian Peninsula to the Austrian and Prussian borders (see Map 15-2). By 1812, when he invaded Russia, however, his forces were too overstretched and undersupplied to survive the harsh winter. Until this point, divisions among his enemies had aided Napoleon's progress. But after his failed attack on Russia, all the major European powers united against him. Forced to retreat, Napoleon and his army were vanquished in Paris. Subsequently Napoleon escaped exile to lead his troops one last time; but at the Battle of Waterloo in Belgium in 1815, armies from Prussia, Austria, Russia, and Britain crushed his troops as they made their last stand.

In 1815, delegates from the victorious states met at the Congress of Vienna. They agreed to respect one another's borders and to cooperate in preventing future revolutions and war. They restored thrones to monarchs deposed by the French under Napoleon, and they returned France itself to the care of a new Bourbon king. Great Britain and Russia—one a constitutional monarchy (ruled by a prime minister and legislative body, with oversight by a king), the other an autocracy (in which the ruler did not share power with anyone)—cooperated to prevent any future attempts to dominate the continent.

The impact of the French Revolution and Napoleon's conquests, however, was far-reaching. In numerous German states, the changes introduced under French revolutionary occupation remained in place. Napoleon's occupation of the Italian peninsula also sparked underground movements for liberty and for Italian unification, much to the chagrin of Austrian and French monarchs. These upheavals even affected Spain and Portugal's links to their colonies in the Americas. The stage was now set for a century-long struggle between those who wanted to restore society as it was before the French Revolution and those who wanted to guarantee a more liberal order based on individual rights, limited government, and free trade.

REVOLUTIONS IN THE CARIBBEAN AND IBERIAN AMERICA

From North America and France, revolutionary enthusiasm spread through the Caribbean and into Spanish and Portuguese America. But unlike the colonists' war of independence that produced the United States, political upheaval in the rest of the Americas began first of all from subordinated people of color (see Map 15-3).

Even before the French Revolution, Andean Indians rebelled against Spanish colonial authority. In a spectacular uprising in the 1780s, they demanded freedom from forced labor and compulsory consumption of Spanish wares. After an army

MAP 15-2   NAPOLEON'S EMPIRE, 1812

Early in the first decade of the nineteenth century, Napoleon controlled almost all of Europe. What major states were under French control? What countries were allied to France? Compare this map with the European part of Map 15-1, and explain how Napoleon redrew the map of Europe. What major country was not under French control? How was Napoleon able to control and build alliances with so many states and kingdoms?

of 40,000 to 60,000 Andean Indians besieged the ancient capital of Cuzco and nearly vanquished Spanish armies, it took Spanish forces many years to eliminate the insurgents.

After this uprising, Iberian American elites who feared their Indian or slave majorities renewed their loyalty to the Spanish or Portuguese crown. They hesitated to imitate the independence-seeking Anglo-American colonists, lest they unleash a social revolution. Ultimately, however, the French Revolution and Napoleonic wars shattered the ties between

Spain and Portugal and their American colonies. Nonetheless, elites limited local power by interpreting "liberty" to apply just to property-owning classes.

REVOLUTION IN SAINT DOMINGUE (HAITI)   It was only in the French colony of Saint Domingue (modern-day Haiti) that slaves carried out a successful revolt. The French Revolution had sent shock waves through this highly prized French colony. There, it led to loss of the colony and

Legend:

■ United Provinces of Central America, 1823–1838

— Republic of Colombia, 1819–1830

■ Mexico, 1867

MAP 15-3   LATIN AMERICAN NATION BUILDING

Creating strong, unified nation-states proved difficult in Latin America. The map highlights this experience in Mexico, the United Provinces of Central America, and the Republic of Colombia. In each case, the governments' territorial and nation-building ambitions failed to some degree. During what period did a majority of the colonies in Latin America gain independence? Which European countries lost the most in Latin America during this period? Why did all these colonies gain their independence during this time?

emancipation for its slaves, along with considerable bloodshed. At the time the island's black slave population numbered 500,000, compared with 40,000 white French settlers and about 30,000 free "people of color" (individuals of mixed black and white ancestry, as well as freed black slaves). Almost two-thirds of the slaves were relatively recent arrivals, brought to the colony to toil on its renowned sugar plantations. The slave population was an angry majority.

After the events of 1789 in France, white settlers in Saint Domingue sought self-government, while slaves borrowed the revolutionary language to denounce their masters. As civil war erupted, Dominican slaves fought French forces that had arrived to restore order. (See Global Connections & Disconnections: Inspirations for Slave Rebellion on Haiti.) Finally, in 1793, the National Convention in France abolished slavery. The argument that revolutionary principles (liberty, fraternity, equality) should apply to the French colonies as well as to the nation won out over claims that abolition would mean economic disaster.

Once liberated, the former slaves took control of the island, but their struggles were not over. First they had to fight British and Spanish forces on the island. Then Napoleon took power in France, restored slavery, and sent an army to suppress forces led by Toussaint L'Ouverture, a former slave. But before long a combination of guerrilla fighters and yellow fever crippled the French army, which

INSPIRATIONS FOR SLAVE REBELLION ON HAITI

As the ideals of the French Revolution spread through Europe and overseas, they had a tumultuous effect on the island of Saint Domingue (renamed Haiti after it acquired independence). By the 1780s Saint Domingue was France's richest colony, whose wealth came from sugar plantations that used a vast, highly coerced slave population. About 40,000 whites ruthlessly exploited 500,000 enslaved Africans. The slaves' lives were short and brutal, lasting on average only fifteen years; hence the wealthy planter class had to replenish their labor supplies from Africa at frequent intervals.

White planters on the island had the reputation of great wealth. But they knew their privileges were vulnerable, so they were eager to amass quick fortunes so that they could sell out and return to France. These men and women were vastly outnumbered by the enslaved, who were seething with resentment, at a time when abolitionist sentiments were gaining ground in Europe and even circulating among slaves in the Americas.

Yet, the planters greeted the onset of the French Revolution in 1789 with enthusiasm. They saw an opportunity to assert their independence from France and to engage in wider trading contacts with North America and the rest of the world. They ignored the fact that the ideals of the French Revolution—especially its slogan of liberty, equality, and fraternity—could inspire the island's free blacks, free mulattoes, and slaves. Indeed, no sooner had the white planters thrown in their lot with the Third Estate in France than a slave rebellion broke out in Saint Domingue. From its beginnings in 1791, it led, after great loss of life to African slaves and French soldiers, to the proclamation of an independent state in Haiti in 1804, ruled by African Americans. Haiti became the Americas' second independent republican government.

The revolution had many sources of inspiration. It was both French and African. According to a later West Indian scholar, a group of black Jacobins, determined to carry the ideals of the French Revolution to their logical end point—the abolition of slavery—made up the revolutionary cadre. Their undisputed leader was Toussaint L'Ouverture, a freed black who had learned about French abolitionist writings. But given that most of the slaves had arrived from Africa very recently, African cultural and political ideals also fueled slave resistance.

At a secret meeting in 1791, the persons who were to lead the initial stage of the revolution gathered to affirm their commitment to one another at a voodoo ritual, presided over by a tall, black priestess "with strange eyes and bristly hair." Voodoo was a mixture of African and New World religious beliefs that existed among slave communities in many parts of the Americas (see Chapter 14). One

Toussaint L'Ouverture. In the 1790s, Toussaint L'Ouverture led the slaves of the French colony of Saint Domingue in the world's largest and most successful slave insurrection. Toussaint embraced the principles of the French Revolution and demanded that universal rights be applied to people of African descent.

description of the ceremony relates that after performing a ritual dance accompanied by an African song, the priestess sacrificed a pig and served its blood to each participant. Then, "at a signal from the priestess, everyone threw themselves on their knees and swore blindly to obey the orders of Boukman, who had been proclaimed supreme chief of the rebellion." Boukman, a voodoo chief himself, initiated the revolution against the planters, though Toussaint L'Ouverture later assumed leadership of the revolt.

Inspired by both voodoo and the French Revolution, the rebellion in Saint Domingue caused the deaths or maiming of hundreds of thousands of African slaves and French soldiers. Thereafter, as white planters yielded to a black political elite, the old sugar economy collapsed. Slave shipments no longer arrived, and sugar was no longer exported.

ultimately surrendered and left. Toussaint L'Ouverture died in a French jail, having been captured while negotiating a settlement. Nonetheless, in 1804 General Jean-Jacques Dessalines declared "Haiti" independent.

The revolt had serious environmental consequences. Not only did sugarcane fields become scorched battlefields, but freed slaves rushed to stake out independent plots on the old plantations and in wooded areas. In both places, the new peasant class energetically cleared the land. The small country soon became deforested, and intensive cultivation caused erosion and soil depletion. Haiti fell into a vicious cycle of environmental degradation and poverty.

Moreover, independence did not bring international recognition from fellow revolutionaries. France's commitment to empire ultimately overrode its commitment to the ideals of republican citizenship. Indeed, Toussaint and the slaves of Saint Domingue had been more loyal to the ideals of liberty than the French themselves were. Even Thomas Jefferson, author of the Declaration of Independence and U.S. president at the time, refused to recognize Haiti. Like other American slave owners, he worried that the example of a successful slave uprising might inspire similar revolts in the United States.

BRAZIL AND CONSTITUTIONAL MONARCHY Brazil was a prized Portuguese colony whose path to independence saw little political turmoil and no social revolution. In 1807, French troops stormed Lisbon, the capital of Portugal, but not before the royals and their associates fled to Rio de Janeiro, then the capital of Brazil. There they made reforms in administration, agriculture, and manufacturing, and they established schools, hospitals, and a library. In fact, the royals' migration prevented the need for colonial claims for autonomy, because with their presence Brazil was now the center of the Portuguese empire. Furthermore, the royal family willingly shared power with the local planter aristocracy, so the economy prospered and slavery expanded.

In 1821, the exiled Portuguese king returned to Lisbon, instructing his son Pedro to preserve the family lineage in Rio de Janeiro. Soon, however, Brazilian elites rejected Portugal altogether. Fearing that colonists might topple the dynasty in Rio de Janeiro and spark regional disputes, in 1822 Pedro declared Brazil an independent empire. Shortly thereafter he established a constitutional monarchy, which would last until the late nineteenth century.

Now Brazilian business elites and bureaucrats cooperated to minimize conflicts, lest a slave revolt erupt. They crushed regional uprisings, like the fledgling Republic of the Equator, and a campaign seeking a decentralized federation of southern provinces free from the Rio de Janeiro rulers. Even the largest urban slave revolt in the Americas, led by African Muslims in the state of Bahia, was quashed in a matter of days. By the 1840s, Brazil had achieved a political stability unmatched in the Americas. Its socially controlled transition from colony to nation was unique in Latin America.

Revolution in Saint Domingue. In 1791, slaves and people of color rose up against white planters. This engraving was based on a German report on the uprising and depicts white fears of slave rebellion as much as the actual events themselves.

As the Brazilian state and its ruling elite expanded the agrarian frontier, here, too, occurred the same kind of terrible environmental degradation that had taken place in Haiti. Landowners oversaw the clearing of ancient hardwood forests so that slaves and squatters could plant coffee trees. The clearing process had begun with sugarcane in the coastal regions, but it accelerated with coffee plantings in the hilly regions of São Paulo. In fact, coffee was a worse threat to Brazil's forests than any other invader in the previous 300 years. Consider that coffee trees thrive on soils that are neither soggy nor overly dry. Therefore planters razed the "virgin" forest, which contained a balanced variety of trees and undergrowth, and Brazil's once-fertile soil suffered rapid depletion by the single-crop industry. Within one generation the clear-cutting led to infertile soils and extensive erosion, which drove planters further into the frontier to destroy even more old forest and plant more coffee groves. The environmental impact was monumental: between 1788 and 1888, when slavery was abolished, Brazil produced about 10 million tons of coffee at the expense of 300 million tons of ancient forest biomass (the accumulated biological material from living organisms).

MEXICO'S INDEPENDENCE When Napoleon occupied Spain, he sparked a crisis in the Spanish empire. Because the ruling Spanish Bourbons fell captive to Napoleon in 1807 and then spent many years under comfortable house

Miguel Hidalgo y Costilla. At the center of this mural by Juan O'Gorman is the revolutionary Mexican priest Miguel Hidalgo y Costilla, who led the first uprising against Spanish rulers. This painting suggests the rebellion was a multiclass and multiethnic movement.

arrest, colonial elites in Buenos Aires (Argentina), Caracas (Venezuela), and Mexico City (Mexico) enjoyed self-rule without an emperor. Once the Bourbons returned to power in 1814 after Napoleon was crushed, creoles (American-born Spaniards) resented it when Spain reinstated peninsulars (colonial officials born in Spain). Inspired by Enlightenment thinkers and chafing at the efforts to restore Iberian authority, the creoles wanted to keep their elite privileges and get rid of the peninsulars.

In Mexico, the royal army prevailed as long as there was any hope that the emperor in Madrid could maintain political authority. But from 1810 to 1813 two rural priests, Father Miguel Hidalgo and Father José María Morelos, galvanized an insurrection of peasants, Indians, and artisans. They sought an end to abuses by the elite, denounced bad government, and called for redistribution of wealth, return of land to the Indians, and respect for the Virgin of Guadalupe (who later became Mexico's patron saint). The rebellion nearly choked off Mexico City, the colony's capital, which horrified peninsulars and creoles alike. In response, they overcame their own disputes to plead with Spanish armies to rescue them from the rebels. Years later, the royal armies eventually crushed the uprising.

Despite the military victory, Spain's hold on its colony weakened. After all, during the years of conflict the colonists had enjoyed some autonomy and had begun electing representatives to local assemblies. Moreover, like the creoles of

South America, those of Mexico were identifying themselves more as Mexicans and less as Spanish Americans. So when the Spanish king appeared unable to govern effectively abroad and even within Spain, the colonists considered home rule. A critical factor was the army, which remained faithful to the crown. However, when anarchy seemed to spread through Spain in 1820, Mexican generals (with support of the creoles) proclaimed Mexican independence in 1821. In many ways, as with Brazil, independence from Spain was a way to curb further turmoil within Mexico. But unlike in Brazil, Mexican secession did not lead to stability.

OTHER SOUTH AMERICAN REVOLUTIONS The loosening of Spain's grip on its colonies was more prolonged and militarized than Britain's separation from its American colonies. Indeed, the struggle for independence from Spain transformed the nature of political leadership in South America. Venezuela's **Simón Bolívar** (1783–1830), the son of a merchant-planter family who was educated on Enlightenment texts, dreamed of a land governed by reason. He revered Napoleonic France as a model state built on military heroism and constitutional proclamations. So did the Argentine leader General José de San Martín (1778–1850). Men like Bolívar, San Martín, and their many generals waged extended wars of independence against Spanish armies and their allies between 1810 and 1824. In some areas, like present-day Uruguay and Venezuela, the wars left entire provinces depopulated.

Simón Bolívar. Bolívar fought Spanish armies from Venezuela to Bolivia, securing the independence of five countries. He wanted to transform the former colonies into modern republics and used many of the icons of revolution from the rest of the Atlantic world—among his favorite models were George Washington and Napoleon Bonaparte. This image portrays Bolívar in a quintessential Napoleonic pose on horseback.

What started in South America as a political revolution against Spanish colonial authority escalated into a social struggle among Indians, mestizos, slaves, and whites. The militarized populace threatened the planters and merchants; rural folk battled against aristocratic creoles; Andean Indians fled the mines and occupied great estates. Provinces fought their neighbors. Popular armies, having defeated Spanish forces by the 1820s, fought civil wars over the new postcolonial order.

New states and collective identities of nationhood now emerged. However, a narrow elite led these political communities, and their guiding principles were contradictory. Simón Bolívar, for instance, urged his followers to become "American," to overcome their local identities. He wanted the liberated countries to form a Latin American confederation, urging Peru and Bolivia to join Venezuela, Ecuador, and Colombia in the "Gran Colombia." But local identities prevailed, giving way to unstable national republics. Bolívar died surrounded by enemies; San Martín died in exile. The real heirs to independence were local military chieftains, who often

forged alliances with landowners. Thus the legacy of the Spanish American revolutions was contradictory: the triumph of wealthy elites under a banner of liberty, yet often at the expense of poorer, ethnic, and mixed populations.

CHANGE AND TRADE IN AFRICA

> → *How did abolition of the slave trade affect African society?*

Africa also was swept up in revolutionary tides, as increased domestic and world trade—including the selling of African slaves—shifted the terms of state building across the continent. Around Lake Victoria, in the highlands of present-day Rwanda and Burundi, and in southern Africa, the early nineteenth century saw new, more powerful kingdoms emerge. Other regimes shattered from internal rivalries. The main catalyst for Africa's political shake-up was the rapid growth and then the demise of the Atlantic slave trade.

ABOLITION OF THE SLAVE TRADE

Even as it enriched and empowered some Africans and many Europeans, the slave trade became a subject of fierce debate in the late eighteenth century. Some European and American revolutionaries argued that slave labor was inherently less productive than free wage labor and ought to be abolished. At the same time, another group favoring abolition of the slave trade insisted that traffic in slaves was immoral. In London they created committees, often led by Quakers, to lobby Parliament for an end to the slave trade. Quakers in Philadelphia did likewise. Pamphlets, reports, and personal narratives denounced the traffic in people. (See Primary Source: Frederick Douglass Asks, "What to the Slave Is the Fourth of July?")

In response to abolitionist efforts, North Atlantic powers moved to prohibit the slave trade. Denmark acted first in 1803, Great Britain followed in 1807, and the United States joined the campaign in 1808. Over time, the British persuaded the French and other European governments to do likewise. To enforce the ban, Britain posted a naval squadron off the coast of West Africa to prevent any slave trade above the equator and compelled Brazil's emperor to end slave imports. After 1850, Atlantic slave-shipping dropped sharply.

But until the 1860s, slavers continued to buy and ship captives illegally. British squadrons that stopped these smugglers took the freed captives to the British base at Sierra Leone and resettled them there. Liberia, too, became a refuge for freed captives and for former slaves returning from the Americas.

Primary Source

FREDERICK DOUGLASS ASKS,
"WHAT TO THE SLAVE IS THE FOURTH OF JULY?"

Frederick Douglass spent the first twenty years of his life as a slave. After running away in 1838, he toured the northern United States delivering speeches that attacked the institution of slavery. The publication of his autobiography in 1845 cemented his standing as a leading abolitionist. In the excerpt below, taken from an address delivered on July 5, 1852, Douglass contrasts the freedom and natural rights extolled in the Declaration of Independence and celebrated on the Fourth of July with the dehumanizing condition—and lack of freedom—of African American slaves.

Fellow-Citizens—pardon me, and allow me to ask, why am I called upon to speak here to-day? What have I, or those I represent, to do with your national independence? Are the great principles of political freedom and of natural justice, embodied in that Declaration of Independence, extended to us? and am I, therefore, called upon to bring our humble offering to the national altar, and to confess the benefits, and express devout gratitude for the blessings, resulting from your independence to us? . . .

But, such is not the state of the case. I say it with a sad sense of the disparity between us. I am not included within the pale of this glorious anniversary! Your high independence only reveals the immeasurable distance between us. The blessings in which you this day rejoice, are not enjoyed in common. The rich inheritance of justice, liberty, prosperity, and independence, bequeathed by your fathers, is shared by you, not by me. The sunlight that brought life and healing to you, has brought stripes and death to me. This Fourth of July is *yours,* not *mine. You* may rejoice, *I* must mourn. . . .

. . . Must I undertake to prove that the slave is a man? That point is conceded already. Nobody doubts it. The slaveholders themselves acknowledge it in the enactment of laws for their government. They acknowledge it when they punish disobedience on the part of the slave. There are seventy-two crimes in the state of Virginia, which, if committed by a black man (no matter how ignorant he be) subject him to the punishment of death; while only two of these same crimes will subject a white man to the like punishment. What is this but the acknowledgment that the slave is a moral, intellectual, and responsible being. The manhood of the slave is conceded. It is admitted in the fact that southern statute books are covered with enactments forbidding, under severe fines and penalties, the teaching of the slave to read or write. When you can point to any such laws, in reference to the beasts of the field, then I may consent to argue the manhood of the slave. When the dogs in your streets, when the fowls of the air, when the cattle on your hills, when the fish of the sea, and the reptiles that crawl, shall be unable to distinguish the slave from a brute, then will I argue with you that the slave is a man!

↷ *What examples does Douglass give of the disparity between slaves and free white Americans?*

↷ *How does Douglass suggest that slaves are human beings?*

↷ *What is the significance of the last sentence of the speech?*

SOURCE: David W. Blight (ed.), *Narrative of the Life of Frederick Douglass: An American Slave, Written by Himself* (Boston: Bedford Books, 1993), pp. 141–45.

NEW TRADE WITH AFRICA

Even as the Atlantic slave trade died down, Europeans promoted commerce with Africa. Now they wanted Africans to export raw materials and to purchase European manufactures. This "legitimate" trade aimed to raise the Africans' standards of living by substituting trade in produce for trade in slaves. West Africans responded by exporting palm kernels and peanuts. The real bonanza was in vegetable oils to lubricate machinery and make candles and in palm oil to produce soap. European merchants argued that by becoming vibrant export societies, Africans would earn the wealth to profitably import European wares.

LEGITIMATE COMMERCE Arising in the age of legitimate commerce, Africa's palm and peanut plantations were less devastating to the environment than their predecessors in the West Indies had been. There, planters had felled

Chasing Slave Dhows. From being the major proponents of the Atlantic slave trade the British became its chief opponents, using their naval forces to suppress those European and African slave traders who attempted to subvert the injunction against slave trading. Here a British vessel chases an East African slaving dhow trying to run slaves from the island of Zanzibar.

forests to establish sugar estates (see Chapter 12). In West Africa, where palm products became crucial exports, the palm tree had always grown wild. Although intensive cultivation caused some deforestation, the results were not as extreme as in the Caribbean.

Legitimate commerce gave rise to a new generation of successful West African merchants. There were many rags-to-riches stories, like that of King Jaja of Opobo (1821–1891). Kidnapped and sold into slavery as a youngster, he started out paddling canoes carrying palm oil to coastal ports. Ultimately becoming the head of a coastal canoe house, as a merchant-prince and chief he founded the port of Opobo and could summon a flotilla of war canoes on command. Another freed slave, a Yoruba, William Lewis, made his way back to Africa and settled in Sierra Leone in 1828. Starting with a few utensils and a small plot of land, he became a successful merchant who sent his son Samuel to England for his education. Samuel eventually became an important political leader in Sierra Leone.

EFFECTS IN AFRICA   Just as the slave trade shaped African political communities, its demise brought sharp adjustments. For some, it was a welcome end to the constant drainage of people. For others, it was a disaster because it cut off income necessary to buy European arms and luxury goods. Many West African regimes, like the Yoruba kingdom, collapsed once chieftains could no longer use the slave trade to finance their retinues and armies.

The rise of free labor in the Atlantic world and the dwindling foreign slave trade had another effect: they strengthened slavery in Africa itself. In some areas by the mid-nineteenth century, slaves accounted for more than half the population. No longer did they comfortably serve in domestic employment; instead, they toiled on palm oil plantations or, in East Africa, on clove plantations. They also served in the military forces, bore palm oil and ivory to markets as porters, or paddled cargo-carrying canoes along rivers leading to the coast. In 1850, northern Nigeria's ruling class had more slaves than independent Brazil, and almost as many as the United States. No longer the world's supplier of slaves, Africa itself had become the world's largest slaveholding region.

ECONOMIC REORDERING

> → *How did the industrial revolution reorder society?*

Behind the political and social upheavals, profound changes were occurring in the world economy. Until the middle of the eighteenth century, global trade touched only the edges of societies, most of which produced for their own subsistence. Surpluses of special goods, from porcelains to silks, entered trade arteries but did not change the cultures that produced them. An exception was the Americas, where especially in the slave societies of the Caribbean, Brazil, and the southern United States, plantations produced goods for export. Yet, this commercial specialization anticipated developments to come, in which communities would be transformed to produce for other societies and less and less for themselves. This gradual, halting, but ineluctable process would gather speed in the eighteenth century and bring the world together in ways that were unimaginable during the age of older European empires.

AN INDUSTRIOUS REVOLUTION

Many of these developments took place first in northwestern Europe and British North America. Here, as elsewhere in the world, households had always produced mainly for themselves and made available for marketplaces only meager surpluses of goods and services. But dramatic changes occurred when family members, including wives and children, decided to work harder and longer in order to produce more for the market and purchase more in the market. For the first time, farmers were able to produce enough food to feed large and growing nonagrarian populations. In these locations, peasant farming gave way to specialized production for the market. In what scholars recently have come to call an **industrious revolution,** households in the countryside and the cities devoted less time to leisure activities; by working more and using income earned through hard work, they were able to live at higher standards than they had before.

This industrious revolution began in the second half of the seventeenth century, gained speed in the eighteenth century, and laid the foundations for the industrial revolution of the late eighteenth and early nineteenth centuries. The willingness on the part of families to work more and an eagerness to eat more diverse foods, to wear better clothes, and to consume products that had once been available as luxuries only to the wealthy classes led in turn to a large expansion in trade—both regionally and globally. By the eighteenth century, separate trading spheres described in earlier chapters were merging increasingly into integrated circuits. As we have observed, sugar and silver were the pioneering products. But by the eighteenth century, other staples joined the long-distance trading business; these staples, moreover, were linked to each other. Tea, for instance, was truly a beverage of world trade. Its leaves came from China, the sugar to cut its bitterness from the Caribbean, the slaves to harvest the sweetener from Africa, and the ceramics from which to drink a proper cup from the English Midlands.

The significance of growing cross-cultural trade and specialization, and the shift away from a few precious cargoes to basic staples, can be seen in the story of a single commodity: soap. By the 1840s, the American entrepreneur William Colgate was importing palm oil from West Africa, coconut oil from Malabar and Ceylon, and poppy seed oil from South Asia, all to make aromatic bars of soap. A London barber called Andrew Pears added glycerine to his product to give it a clean transparent look, and his grandson-in-law, Thomas Barratt, launched an aggressive marketing campaign—in 1886 buying a painting from the *Illustrated London News* called "Bubbles" to enhance the image of his family's soap. Colgate and his Atlantic rivals in the toiletry trade like Pears advertised their products as necessities for the prim and proper home. Pears promised African and Indian buyers that his product would actually whiten their skin.

Global trading trickled its way down from elites to ordinary folk. Even ordinary people could purchase imported goods with their earnings. Thus, the poor began to enjoy— some would say the addictions of—coffee, tea, and sugar, and eventually even felt the need to use soap. European artisans and farmers purchased tools, furnishings, and home decorations. Slaves and colonial laborers also used their meager earn

New Farming Technologies. Although new technologies only gradually transformed agriculture, the spread of more intensive cultivation led to increased yields.

ings to buy imported cotton cloth made in Europe from the raw cotton they themselves had picked several seasons earlier.

The expansion of global trade had important social and political consequences. In many dynastic societies, merchants had long stood high in the social hierarchy, but few extended their business beyond provincial confines. As new goods flowed from ever more distant corners of the globe, immense fortunes grew. To support their enterprise, traders needed new services, in insurance, bookkeeping, and the recording of legal documents. Trade helped nurture the emergence of new classes of professionals—accountants and lawyers. The new cities of the commercial revolution hubs like Bristol, Bombay, and Buenos Aires provided the homes and flourishing neighborhoods for a class of men and women known as the **bourgeoisie**.

As Europe moved to the center of a new economic order, one class in particular moved to the top: the trader-financiers. Like the merchandiser, the financier did not have to emerge from the high and mighty of Eurasia's dynasties. Consider Mayer Amschel Rothschild (1744–1812): born the son of a money changer in the Jewish ghetto of Frankfurt, Rothschild progressed from coin dealing to money changing, then from trading textiles to lending funds to kings and governments. By the time of his death he owned the world's biggest banking operation and his five sons were running powerful branches in London, Paris, Vienna, Naples, and Frankfurt.

By extending credit, families like the Rothschilds also enabled traders to ship goods across long distances without having to worry about immediate payment. All these financial changes implied world integration through the flow of goods as well as the flow of money. In the 1820s, sizeable funds amassed in London flowed to Egypt, Mexico, and New York to support trade, public investment, and, of course, speculation.

THE INDUSTRIAL REVOLUTION

Trade and finance repositioned western Europe's relationship with the rest of the world. So did the emergence of manufacturing—a big leap, as in agriculture, in the output, in this case of industrial commodities. The heart of this process was a gradual accumulation and diffusion of technical knowledge. Lots of little inventions, their applications, and their diffusion across the Atlantic world gradually built up a stock of technical knowledge and practice. Historians have traditionally called these changes the **industrial revolution,** a term first used by the British economic historian Arnold Toynbee in the late nineteenth century. Although the term suggests radical and rapid economic change, the reality was much more gradual and less dramatic than originally believed. Yet, the term still has great validity, for the major economic changes that occurred in Britain, northwestern Europe, and North America catapulted these countries ahead of the rest of the world in industrial and agricultural output and standards of living.

Nowhere was this industrial revolution more evident than in Britain. Britain had a few advantages, like large supplies of coal and iron—key materials used in manufactured products. It also had a political and social environment that allowed merchants and industrialists to invest heavily while also expanding their internal and international markets. Among their investments was the application of steam power to textile production—which enabled Britain's manufacturers to produce cheaper goods in larger quantities. Finally, Britain had access to New World lands as sources of financial investment, raw materials, and markets for manufactured goods. These factors' convergence in Britain promoted self-sustaining economic growth.

An example of the new alliance of the inventor and the investor that fueled the industrial revolution was the advent of the steam engine. Such engines burned coal to boil water, and the resulting steam drove mechanized devices. There were several tinkerers working on the device. But the most famous was James Watt (1736–1819) of Scotland, who managed to separate steam condensers from piston cylinders so that pistons could stay hot and run constantly, and who also joined forces with the industrialist Matthew Boulton, who marketed the steam engine and set up a laboratory where Watt could refine his device. The steam engine catalyzed a revolution in transportation. Steam-powered engines also improved sugar refining, pottery making, and other industrial processes, generating more products at lower cost than when workers had made them by hand.

Technical changes made possible the consolidation of textile manufacturing within a single factory. With new machinery, a single textile operator handled many looms and spindles at once and produced bolts of cloth with stunning efficiency. Gone were the hand tools, the family traditions, and the loosely organized and dispersed systems of households putting out cloth for local merchants to carry to markets. The material was also stronger, finer, and more uniform. All the while, the price of cotton cloth almost halved between 1780 and 1850. As England became the world's largest cloth producer, it imported cotton from Brazil, Egypt, India, and the United States.

Most raw cotton for the British cloth industry had come from colonial India until 1793, when the American inventor Eli Whitney (1765–1825) patented a "cotton gin" that separated cotton seeds from fiber. After that, cotton farming spread so quickly in the southern United States that by the 1850s it was producing more than 80 percent of the world's cotton supply. In turn, every black slave in the Americas and many Indians in British India were consumers of cheap, British-produced cotton shirts.

It is important to note that the industrial revolution did not imply the creation of large-scale industries. The large factory was rare in manufacturing. Indeed, the largest employers at the time were the slave plantations of the Americas that produced the staples for industrial consumption. Small-scale production remained the norm, mass production the exception. Lyonese silks relied on the Jacquard loom, refined between 1800 and 1820, which allowed weavers to reassert their traditional control over the production of fashionable fabrics while increasing productivity. The new looms cut labor costs by eliminating some tasks, but they required skilled, precision handling. Here, as in many places, innovations in-

A Cotton Textile Mill in the 1830s. The region of Lancashire became one of the major industrial hubs for textile production in the world. By the 1830s, mills had made the shift from artisanal work to highly mechanical mass production. Among the great breakthroughs was the discovery that cloth could be printed with designs, such as paisley or calico (as in this image), and marketed to middle-class consumers.

→ *How did the industrial revolution reorder society?*

MAP 15-4 INDUSTRIAL EUROPE AROUND 1850

By 1850 much of western Europe was industrial and urban, with major cities linked to one another through a network of railroads. According to this map, what natural resources contributed to the growth of the industrial revolution? What effects did it have on urban population densities? Explain how the presence of an extensive railroad system helped to accelerate industrialization. According to your reading, why were the effects of the industrial revolution more rapidly apparent in Great Britain and in north-central Europe?

creased the efficiency and quality of production and saved labor, but they did not lead to large-scale production. The silks of Lyon, cutlery of Solingen, calicoes of Alsace, and cottons of Pawtucket, Rhode Island, were all products of small firms in heavily industrialized belts.

Wherever the industrial revolution took hold, it allowed societies to outdistance rivals in manufacturing and elevated them to a new place in the emerging global economic order (see Map 15-4). But why did this revolution cluster mainly in the Atlantic world? This is an important question, because the unequal distribution of global wealth, the gap between the haves and have-nots, really took off in this era of revolutions. In much of Asia and Africa, technical change altered modes of production and business practices, but it was not followed by a continuous cascade of changes. The great mystery was China, the home of astronomical water clocks and gunpowder. Why did China not become the epicenter of the industrial revolution?

There are two reasons. China did not foster experimental science of the kind that allowed Watt to stumble onto the possibility of steam, or Procter and Gamble to invent floating soap. Experimentation, testing, and the links between thinkers and investors were a distinctly Atlantic phenomenon. The Qing, like the Mughal and Ottoman dynasties, swept the great minds into the bureaucracy and reinforced the old agrarian system based on peasant exploitation and tribute. Second, Chinese rulers did not support overseas expansion and trade that helped create the commercial revolution in the Atlantic world. The agrarian dynasties of China and India neither showered favors on local merchants nor effectively shut out interlopers. This made them vulnerable to cheap manufactured imports from European traders backed by their governments extolling the virtues of free trade.

The effects were profound. Historically, Europe had a trade imbalance with partners to the east—furs from Russia, and spices and silks from Asia. It made up for this with silver from the Americas. But the new economic order meant that by the nineteenth century, western Europe not only had manufactures like soap to export to Asia, it also had capital. One of Europe's biggest debtors was none other than the sultan of the Ottoman Empire, whose tax system could not keep up with spending necessary to keep the realm together. More and more, Asian, African, and American governments found themselves borrowing from Europe's financiers just as their people were buying industrial products from Europe and selling their primary products to European consumers and producers.

WORKING AND LIVING

The industrious revolution brought more demanding work routines—not only in the manufacturing economies of western Europe and North America but also on the farms and plantations of Asia and Africa. Although the European side of the story is better known, cultivators toiled harder and for longer hours throughout the rest of the world.

URBAN LIFE AND WORK ROUTINES Increasingly, Europe's workers made their livings in cities. London, Europe's largest city in 1700, saw its population nearly double over the next century to almost 1 million. By the 1820s, population growth was even greater in the industrial hubs of Leeds, Glasgow, Birmingham, Liverpool, and Manchester. By contrast, in the Low Countries (Belgium and the Netherlands) and France, where small-scale, rural-based manufacturing flourished, the shift to cities was less extreme.

For most urban dwellers, cities were not healthy places. Water that powered the mills, along with chemicals used in dyeing, went directly back into waterways that provided drinking water. Overcrowded tenements shared just a few out-

A Model Textile Mill. In the nineteenth century, the English industrialist and reformer Robert Owen tried to create humane factories. Worried about the terrible conditions in most textile mills, Owen created clean and orderly working environments in his mills and had the work rules posted on the walls. Like most of his contemporaries, Owen employed children, as can be seen in this image.

houses. Most European cities as late as 1850 had no running water, no garbage pickup, no underground sewer system. The result was widespread disease. (In fact, no European city at this time had as clean a water supply as the largest towns of the ancient Roman Empire once had.)

As families found jobs in factories, their wages bolstered family revenues. Children, wives, and husbands increasingly worked outside the home for cash, though some still made handicrafts inside the home as well. Urban employers experimented with paying according to the tasks performed or the number of goods produced per day. To earn subsistence wages, men, women, and children frequently stayed on the job for twelve or more hours at a time.

Changes in work affected the understanding of time. Whereas most farmers' workloads had followed seasonal rhythms, after 1800 industrial settings imposed a rigid concept of work discipline. To keep the machinery operating, factory and mill owners installed huge clocks and used bells or horns to signify the workday's beginning and end. Employers also measured output per hour and compared workers' performance. Josiah Wedgwood, a maker of teacups and other porcelain, installed a Boulton & Watt steam engine in his manufacturing plant and made his workers use it efficiently. He rang a bell at 5:45 in the morning so employees could start work as day broke. At 8:30 the bell rang for breakfast, 9:00 to call them back, and 12:00 for a half-hour lunch; it last tolled when darkness put an end to the workday. Sometimes, though, factory clocks were turned back in the morning and forward at night, falsely extending the exhausted laborers' workday.

Despite higher production, industrialization imposed numbing work routines and paltry wages. Worse, however, was having no work at all. As families abandoned their farmland and depended on wages, being idle meant having no income. Periodic downturns in the economy put wage workers at risk, and many responded by organizing protests. In 1834, the British Parliament centralized the administration of all poor relief and deprived able-bodied workers of any relief unless they joined a workhouse, where working conditions resembled those of a prison.

SOCIAL PROTEST AND EMIGRATION While entrepreneurs accumulated private wealth, the effects of the industrial revolution on working-class families raised widespread concern. In the 1810s in England, groups of jobless craftsmen, called Luddites, smashed the machines that had left them unemployed. In 1849, the English novelist Charlotte Brontê published a novel, *Shirley,* depicting the misfortunes caused by the power loom. Charles Dickens described a mythic Coketown to evoke pity for the working class in his 1854 classic, *Hard Times.* Both Elizabeth Gaskell, in England, and Émile Zola, in France, described the hardships of women whose malnourished children were pressed into the workforce too early. Gaskell and Zola also highlighted the hunger, loneliness, and illness that prostitutes and widows

endured. These social advocates sought protective legislation for workers, including curbing child labor, limiting the workday, and, in some countries, legalizing prostitution for the sake of monitoring the prostitutes' health.

Some people, however, could not wait for legislative reform. Thus, the period saw unprecedented emigration, as unemployed workers or peasants abandoned their homes to seek their fortunes in America, Canada, and Australia. During the Irish Potato Famine of 1845–1849, at least one million Irish citizens left their country (and a further million or so died) when fungi attacked their subsistence crop. Desperate to escape starvation, they booked cheap passage to North America on ships so notorious for disease and malnutrition that they earned the name "Coffin Ships." Those who did survive faced discrimination in their new land, for many Americans feared the immigrants would drive down wages or create social unrest.

PERSISTENCE AND CHANGE IN AFRO-EURASIA

→ *How did the Atlantic revolutions affect Afro-Eurasian societies?*

Western Europe's military might, its technological achievements, and its economic strength represented a threat to the remaining Afro-Eurasian empires. Across the continent, western European merchants and industrialists sought closer economic and (in some cases) political ties. They did so in the name of gaining "free" access to Asian markets and products. In response, Russian and Ottoman rulers modernized their military organizations and hoped to achieve similar economic strides while distancing themselves from the democratic principles of the French Revolution. The remote Chinese empire was largely unaffected by the upheavals in Europe and America—until the first Opium War of the early 1840s forced the Chinese to acknowledge their military weaknesses. Thus, changes in the Atlantic world unleashed new pressures around the globe, though with varying degrees of intensity.

REVAMPING THE RUSSIAN MONARCHY

Some eastern European dynasties responded to the pressures by strengthening their traditional rulers, through modest reforms and the suppression of domestic opposition. This was how Russian rulers reacted. Tsar Alexander I (r. 1801–1825) was fortunate that Napoleon committed several blunders and

Decembrists in St. Petersburg. Russians energetically participated in the coalition that defeated Napoleon, but the ideas of the French Revolution greatly appealed to the educated upper classes, including aristocrats of the officer corps. In December 1825, at the death of Tsar Alexander I, some regimental officers staged an uprising of about 3,000 men, demanding a constitution and the end of serfdom. But Nicholas I, the new tsar, called in loyal troops and brutally dispersed the "Decembrists," executing or exiling their leaders.

lost his formidable army in the Russian snows. Yet the French Revolution and its massive, patriotic armies struck at the heart of Russian political institutions, which rested upon a huge peasant population laboring as serfs.

The tsars could no longer easily justify their absolutism by claiming that enlightened despotism was the most advanced form of government, since a new model, rooted in popular sovereignty and the concept of the nation, had arisen. One response was to highlight the heroic resistance of the Russian people that had led to victory over the French. Tsar Alexander glorified patriots who had either fought in the war or grown up hearing about it, but he was not interested in allowing any new political order.

In December 1825, when Alexander died unexpectedly and childless, there was a question over succession. Some Russian officers launched a patriotic revolt, hoping to convince Alexander's brother Constantine to take the throne (and to guarantee a constitution) in place of a more conservative brother, Nicholas. The Decembrists, as they were called, came primarily from elite families and were familiar with western European life and institutions. A few Decembrists called for a constitutional monarchy to replace Russia's despotism; others favored a tsar-less republic and the abolition of serfdom. But the officers' conspiracy failed to win over conservatives or the peasantry, who still believed in the tsar's divine right to rule. Constantine supported Nicholas's claim to power, so Nicholas (r. 1825–1855) became tsar and brutally suppressed the insurrectionists. For the time being, the influence of the French Revolution was quashed.

Still, Alexander's successors faced a world in which powerful European states had constitutions and national armies of citizens, not subjects. In trying to maintain absolute rule, Russian tsars portrayed the monarch's family as the ideal historical embodiment of the nation with direct ties to the peo-

ple. Nicholas himself prevented rebellion by expanding the secret police, enforcing censorship, conducting impressive military exercises, and maintaining serfdom. After suppressing a revolt in the empire's Polish provinces, he sought a closer alliance with conservative monarchies in Austria and Prussia. And in the 1830s he introduced a conservative ideology that stressed religious faith, hierarchy, and obedience. Even some officials and members of society who supported the monarchy wondered whether this would be enough to enable Russia to remain a competitive great power.

REFORMING EGYPT AND THE OTTOMAN EMPIRE

Unlike in Russia, where Napoleon's army had reached Moscow, the Ottoman capital in Istanbul never faced a threat by French troops. Still, Napoleon's invasion of Egypt shook the Ottoman Empire and led European merchants to press Ottoman rulers for more commercial concessions. Even before this trauma, imperial authorities faced the challenge posed by increased trade with Europe—and the greater presence of European merchants and missionaries. In addition, many non-Muslim religious communities in the sultan's empire wanted the European powers to advance their interests. In the wake of Napoleon, who had promised to remake Egyptian society, reformist energies swept from Egypt to the center of the Ottoman domain. (See Primary Source: An Egyptian Intellectual's Reaction to the French Occupation of Egypt.)

REFORMS IN EGYPT In Egypt, far-reaching changes came with **Muhammad Ali**, a skillful modernizing ruler. After the French withdrawal in 1801, Muhammad Ali (r. 1805–1848) won a chaotic struggle for supreme power in Egypt and

AN EGYPTIAN INTELLECTUAL'S REACTION TO THE FRENCH OCCUPATION OF EGYPT

In the 1798 invasion of Egypt, Napoleon Bonaparte attempted to win rank-and-file Egyptian support against the country's Mamluks, who were the most powerful group in Egypt at the time though the country was still under the authority of the Ottoman sultan. Bonaparte portrayed himself as a liberator and invoked the ideals of the French Revolution, as he had done with great success all over Europe. His Egyptian campaign did not succeed, however, and local opposition was bitter. The chronicler Abd al-Rahman al-Jabarti has left one of the most perceptive accounts of these years.

On Monday news arrived that the French had reached Damanhur and Rosetta [in the Nile Delta]. . . . They printed a large proclamation in Arabic, calling on the people to obey them. . . . In this proclamation were inducements, warnings, all manner of wiliness and stipulations. Some copies were sent from the provinces to Cairo and its text is:

In the name of God, the Merciful, the Compassionate. There is no God but God. He has no son nor has He an associate in His Dominion.

On behalf of the French Republic which is based upon the foundation of liberty and equality, General Bonaparte, Commander-in-Chief of the French armies makes known to all the Egyptian people that for a long time the Sanjaqs [its Mamluk rulers] who lorded it over Egypt have treated the French community basely and contemptuously and have persecuted its merchants with all manner of extortion and violence. Therefore the hour of punishment has now come.

Unfortunately, this group of Mamluks . . . have acted corruptly for ages in the fairest land that is to be found upon the face of the globe. However, the Lord of the Universe, the Almighty, has decreed the end of their power.

O ye Egyptians . . . I have not come to you except for the purpose of restoring your rights from the hands of the oppressors and that I more than the Mamluks serve God. . . .

And tell them also that all people are equal in the eyes of God and the only circumstances which distinguish one from the other are reason, virtue, and knowledge. . . . Formerly, in the lands of Egypt there were great cities, and wide canals and extensive commerce and nothing ruined all this but the avarice and the tyranny of the Mamluks.

[Jabarti then challenged the arguments in the French proclamation and portrayed the French as godless invaders, inspired by false ideals.] They follow this rule: great and small, high and low, male and female are all equal. Sometimes they break this rule according to their whims and inclinations or reasoning. Their women do not veil themselves and have no modesty. . . . Whenever a Frenchman has to perform an act of nature he does so where he happens to be, even in full view of people, and he goes away as he is, without washing his private parts after defecation. . . .

His saying "[all people] are equal in the eyes of God" the Almighty is a lie and stupidity. How can this be when God has made some superior to others as is testified by the dwellers in the Heavens and on Earth? . . .

So those people are opposed to both Christians and Muslims, and do not hold fast to any religion. You see that they are materialists, who deny all God's attributes. . . . May God hurry misfortune and punishment upon them, may He strike their tongues with dumbness, may He scatter their hosts, and disperse them.

↬ *When the proclamation speaks of "the fairest land that is to be found upon the face of the globe," what land is it referring to?*

↬ *Why do you think Napoleon's appeals to the ideals of the French Revolution failed with Egyptians?*

↬ *Why does al-Jabarti claim that the invaders are godless even though the proclamation clearly suggests otherwise?*

SOURCE: Abd al-Rahman al-Jabarti, *Napoleon in Egypt: al-Jabarti's Chronicle of the French Occupation, 1798,* translated by Shmuel Moreh (Princeton, NJ: Markus Wiener Publishing, 1993), pp. 24–29.

Muhammad Ali. The Middle Eastern ruler who most successfully assimilated the educational, technological, and economic advances of nineteenth-century Europe was Muhammad Ali, ruler of Egypt from 1805 until 1848.

aligned himself with influential Egyptian families. Yet he looked to revolutionary France for a model of modern state-building. As with Napoleon (and with Simón Bolívar in Latin America), the key to his hold on power was the army. With the help of French advisors, the modernized Egyptian army became the most powerful fighting force in the Middle East.

Muhammad Ali also made reforms in education and agriculture. He established a school of engineering and opened the first modern medical school in Cairo under the supervision of a French military doctor. And his efforts in the countryside made Egypt one of the world's leading cotton exporters. A summer crop, cotton required steady watering when the Nile's irrigation waters were in short supply. So Muhammad Ali's Public Works Department, advised by European engineers, deepened the irrigation canals and constructed a series of dams across the Nile. These efforts transformed Egypt, making it the most powerful state in the eastern Mediterranean and alarming the Ottoman state (which still controlled Egypt) and the great powers in Europe.

Muhammad Ali's modernizing reforms, however, disrupted the habits of the peasantry. After all, incorporation into the industrial world economy involved harder work (as English wage workers had discovered), often with little addi-

tional pay. Because irrigation improvements permitted year-round cultivation, Egyptian peasants now had to plant and harvest three crops instead of one or two. Moreover, the state controlled the prices of cultivated products, so peasants saw little profit from their extra efforts. Young men also faced conscription into the state's enlarged army, while whole families had to toil, unpaid, on public works projects. In addition, a state-sponsored program of industrialization aimed to put Egypt on a par with Europe: before long, textile and munitions factories employed 200,000 workers. But Egypt had few skilled laborers or cheap sources of energy, so by the time of Muhammad Ali's death in 1849 few of the factories survived.

External forces also limited Muhammad Ali's ambitious plans. At first, his new army enjoyed spectacular success. At the bidding of the Ottoman sultan, the Egyptian military fought well against Greek nationalists (who ultimately won independence in 1829) and carried out conquests in Sudan. But Muhammad Ali overplayed his hand when he sent forces into Syria in the 1830s and later when he threatened Anatolia, the heart of the Ottoman state. Fearing that an Egyptian ruler might attempt to overthrow the Ottoman sultan and threaten the balance of power in the eastern Mediterranean region, the European powers compelled Egypt to withdraw from Anatolia and reduce its army. In the name of free trade, European merchants pressed for free access to Egyptian markets, just as they did in Latin America and Africa.

OTTOMAN REFORMS Under political and economic pressures like those facing Muhammad Ali in Egypt, Ottoman rulers also made reforms. Indeed, military defeats and humiliating treaties with Europe were painful reminders of the sultans' vulnerability. Stunned by Napoleon's defeat of the Mamluks in Egypt and disenchanted with privileged janissaries who resisted reform efforts, in 1805 Sultan Selim III tried to create a new source of military strength: the New Order infantry, trained by western European officers. But before he could bring this force up to fighting strength, the janissaries stormed the palace and killed New Order officers. They overturned the New Order army and deposed Selim in 1807. Over the next few decades, janissary military men and clerical scholars (*ulama*) cobbled together an alliance that continuously thwarted reformers.

Why did reform falter in the Ottoman state before it could be implemented? After all, in France and Spain, the old regimes were also inefficient and burdened with debts and military losses. But reform was possible only if the forces of restraint—especially in the military—were weak and the reformers strong. In the Ottoman Empire, the janissary class had grown powerful, providing the main resistance to change. Ottoman authority depended on clerical support, and the Muslim clergy also resisted change. Blocked at the top, Ottoman rulers were hesitant to appeal for popular support in a struggle against anti-reformers. Such an appeal, in the new age of popular sovereignty and national feeling, would be dangerous for an unelected dynasty in a multiethnic and multireligious realm.

Mahmud II (r. 1808–1839), who acknowledged Europe's rising power, broke the political deadlock. He shrewdly manipulated his conservative opponents. Convincing some clerics that the janissaries neglected traditions of discipline and piety, and promising that a new corps would pray fervently, the sultan won the *ulama*'s support and in 1826 established a European-style army corps. When the janissaries plotted their inevitable mutiny, Mahmud rallied clerics, students, and subjects. The schemers retreated to their barracks, only to be shelled by the sultan's artillery and then destroyed in flames. Thousands of other janissaries were rounded up and executed.

The sultan could now pursue reform within an autocratic framework. Like Muhammad Ali in Egypt, Mahmud brought in European officers to advise his forces. Here, too, military reform spilled over into nonmilitary areas. The Ottoman modernizers created a medical college, then a school of military sciences. To understand Europe better and to create a first-rate diplomatic corps, the Ottomans schooled their officials in European languages and had European classics translated into Turkish. As Mahmud's successors extended reforms into civilian life, this era—known as the Tanzimat, or Reorganization period—saw legislation that guaranteed equality for all Ottoman subjects, regardless of religion.

The reforms, however, stopped well short of revolutionary change. For one thing, reform relied too much on the personal whim of rulers. Also, the bureaucratic and religious infrastructure remained committed to old ways. Moreover, any effort to reform the rural sector met resistance by the landed interests. Finally, the merchant classes profited from business with a debt-ridden sultan. By preventing the empire's fiscal collapse through financial support to the state, bankers lessened the pressure for reform and removed the spark that had fired the revolutions in Europe. Together, these factors impeded reform in the Ottoman Empire.

Yet, by failing to make greater reforms, the empire lost economic and military ground to its European neighbors. For centuries, European traders had needed Islam's goods and services more than the other way around. By the nineteenth century, however, the ties of trade and financial dependency bound the Ottomans to Europe on terms that the Europeans controlled.

COLONIAL REORDERING IN INDIA

Europe's most important colonial possession in Asia between 1750 and 1850 was British India. Unlike in North America, the changes that the British fostered in Asia did not lead to political independence. Instead, India was increasingly dominated by the **East India Company**, which the crown had chartered in 1600. The company's control over India's imports and exports in the eighteenth and nineteenth centuries, however, contradicted British claims about their allegiance to a world economic system based on "free trade."

THE EAST INDIA COMPANY'S MONOPOLY Initially the British, through the East India Company, tried to control India's commerce by establishing trading posts along the

Indian Resistance to Company Rule. Tipu Sultan, the Mysore ruler, put up a determined resistance against the British. This painting by Robert Home shows Cornwallis, the East India Company's governor, receiving Tipu's two sons as hostages after defeating him in the 1792 war. The boys remained in British custody for two years. Tipu returned to fighting the British and was killed in the war of 1799.

coast but without taking complete political control. After conquering the state of Bengal in 1757, the company began to fill its coffers and its officials began to amass personal fortunes. Even the British governor of Bengal pocketed a portion of the tax revenues. Such unbridled abuse of power caused the Bengal army, along with forces of the Mughal emperor and of the ruler of Awadh, to revolt. Although the rebels were unsuccessful, British officials left the emperor and most provincial leaders in place—as nominal rulers. Nonetheless, the British secured the right for the East India Company to collect tax revenues in Bengal, Bihar, and Orissa and to trade free of duties throughout Mughal territory. In return, the emperor would receive a hefty annual pension. The company went on to annex other territories, bringing much of South Asia under its rule by the early 1800s (see Map 15-5).

To carry out its responsibilities, the East India Company needed to establish a civil administration. Rather than place Britons in these positions, the company enlisted Hindu kings and Muslim princes; they retained royal privileges while losing their autonomy. The emperor himself was now permanently under the thumb of the company's administrators. Yet the company did not depend entirely on local leaders, for it also maintained a large standing army and a centralized bureaucracy. Together, the military force, the bureaucracy, and an array of local leaders enabled the company state to guarantee security and the smooth collection of revenues.

To rule with minimal interference, however, required knowing the conquered society. This led to Orientalist scholarship: English scholar-officials wrote the first modern histories of South Asia, translated Sanskrit and Persian texts, identified philosophical writings, and compiled Hindu and Muslim law books. Through their efforts, the company state presented itself as a force for revitalizing authentic Hinduism and recovering India's literary and cultural treasures. Although the Orientalist scholars admired Sanskrit language and literature, they still supported English colonial rule and did not necessarily agree with local beliefs.

EFFECTS IN INDIA Maintaining a sizeable military and civilian bureaucracy also required taxation. Indeed, taxes on land were the East India Company's largest source of revenue. From 1793 onward, land policies required large and small landowners alike to pay taxes to the company. As a result, large estate owners gained more power and joined with the company in determining who could own property. Whenever smaller proprietors defaulted on their taxes, the company put their properties up for auction, with the firm's own employees and large estate owners often obtaining title.

MAP 15-5   THE BRITISH IN INDIA, 1767–1857

Starting from locations in eastern and northeastern India, the British East India Company extended its authority over much of South Asia prior to the outbreak of the Indian Rebellion of 1857. What type of location did the British first acquire in India? How did the company expand into the interior of India and administer these possessions? Why did it choose a strategy of direct and indirect rule over different areas within the larger region?

Company rule and booming trade altered India's urban geography as well. By the early nineteenth century, colonial cities like Calcutta, Madras, and Bombay became the new centers at the expense of older Mughal cities like Agra, Delhi, Murshidabad, and Hyderabad. As the colonial cities attracted British merchants and Indian clerks, artisans, and laborers, their populations surged. Calcutta's reached 350,000 in 1820; Bombay's jumped to 200,000 by 1825. In these cities, Europeans lived close to the company's fort and trading stations, while migrants from the countryside clustered in crowded quarters called "black towns."

Back in Britain, the debts of rural Indians and the conditions of black towns generated little concern. Instead, calls for reform focused on the East India Company's monopoly: its sole access to Indian wealth, and its protection of company shareholders and investors. In 1813 the British Parliament, responding to merchants' and traders' demands to participate in the Indian economy, abolished the company's monopoly over trade with India.

India now had to serve the interests of an industrializing Britain, so it became an importer of British textiles and an exporter of raw cotton—a reversal of its traditional pattern of trade. In the past, India had been an important textile manufacturer, exporting fine cotton goods throughout the Indian Ocean and to Europe. But its elites could not resist the appeal of cheap British textiles. As a result, India's own process of industrialization slowed down. In addition, the import of British manufactures caused unfavorable trade balances that changed India from a net importer of gold and silver to an exporter of these precious metals.

Packing Cotton Bales. This 1864 engraving of the packing of cotton bales registers the shift in cotton trade between India and Britain: from being an exporter of cotton manufactures up to the eighteenth century, India became a source of raw cotton in the nineteenth century.

PROMOTING CULTURAL CHANGE The British did more than alter the Indian economy; they also advocated far-reaching changes in Indian culture so that its people would value British goods and culture. In 1817, James Mill, a philosopher and an employee of the East India Company, condemned what he saw as backward social practices and cultural traditions. He and his son, John Stuart Mill, argued that only dictatorial rule could bring good government and economic progress to India, whose people they considered unfit for self-rule or liberalism. (See Primary Source: James Mill on Indian Tradition.)

Evangelicals and liberal reformers also tried to change Hindu and Muslim social practices, through legislation and European-style education. For example, they sought to stop the practice of *sati,* by which women burned to death on the funeral pyres of their dead husbands. Now the mood swung away from the Orientalists' respect for India's classical languages, philosophies, cultures, and texts. In 1835, when the British poet, historian, and Liberal politician Lord Macaulay was making recommendations on educational policies, he urged that English replace Persian as the language of administration and that European education replace Oriental learning. The result, reformers hoped, would be a class that was Indian in blood and color but English in tastes and culture.

This was a new colonial order, but it was not stable. Most wealthy landowners resented the loss of their land and authority. Peasants, thrown to the mercy of the market, moneylenders, and landlords, were in turmoil. The non-Hindu forest dwellers and roaming cultivators, faced with the hated combination of a colonial state and moneylenders, revolted. Dispossessed artisans stirred up towns and cities. And merchants and industrialists chafed under the British-dominated economy. However, the British continued to extend their colonial state with its commitment to free trade, combining reform with autocracy. Even though India was part of a more interconnected world and thereby supported Europe's industrialization, it was doing so as a colony. As freedom expanded in Europe, exploitation expanded in India.

PERSISTENCE OF THE QING EMPIRE

The Qing dynasty, which had taken power in 1644, was still enjoying prosperity and territorial expansion as the nineteenth century dawned. The Chinese were largely unaware of revolutionary events occurring in North America, France, and Britain. Their sense of imperial splendor continued to rest on the political structure and social order inherited from the Ming (see Chapter 11). Although some Chinese felt that the Manchu Qing were foreign occupiers, the Qing rulers carefully adapted Chinese institutions and philosophies. Thus, Chinese elites at court did not challenge the dynasty's authority (as delegates to the Estates-General in France did).

JAMES MILL ON INDIAN TRADITION

James Mill was a Scottish political economist and philosopher who believed that according to the principles of utilitarianism, law and government were essential for maximizing a people's usefulness and happiness. Thus his History of British India *(1818) criticized India's Hindu and Muslim cultures and attributed their so-called backwardness to the absence of a systematic form of law. Mill's critique was also an attack on earlier British Orientalists, whose close engagement with Indian culture and Indian texts led them to oppose interfering in traditional practices. A year after the book's publication, the East India Company appointed him as an official.*

The condition of the women is one of the most remarkable circumstances in the manners of nations. Among rude people, the women are generally degraded; among civilized people they are exalted.

———————

Nothing can exceed the habitual contempt which the Hindus entertain for their women. Hardly are they ever mentioned in their laws, or other books, but as wretches of the most base and vicious inclinations, on whose natures no virtuous or useful qualities can be engrafted. "Their husbands," says the sacred code, "should be diligently careful in guarding them: though they well know the disposition with which the lord of creation formed them; Manu allotted to such women a love of their bed, of their seat, and of ornament, impure appetites, wrath, weak flexibility, desire of mischief, and bad conduct."

———————

They are held, accordingly, in extreme degradation. They are not accounted worthy to partake of religious rites but in conjunction with their husbands. They are entirely excluded from the sacred books. . . .

———————

They [the Hindus] are remarkably prone to flattery; the most prevailing mode of address from the weak to the strong, while men are still ignorant and unreflecting. The Hindus are full of dissimulation and falsehood, the universal concomitants of oppression. The vices of falsehood, indeed, they carry to a height almost unexampled among other races of men. Judicial perjury is more than common; it is almost universal.

———————

This religion has produced a practice, which has strongly engaged the curiosity of Europeans; a superstitious care of the life of the inferior animals. A Hindu lives in perpetual terror of killing even an insect; and hardly any crime can equal that of being unintentionally the cause of death to any animal of the more sacred species. This feeble circumstance, however, is counteracted by so many gloomy and malignant principles, that their religion, instead of humanizing the character, must have had no inconsiderable effect in fostering that disposition to revenge, that insensibility to the sufferings of others, and often that active cruelty, which lurks under the smiling exterior of the Hindu.

———————

Few nations are surpassed by the Hindus, in the total want of physical purity, in their streets, houses, and persons. Mr. Forster, whose long residence in India, and knowledge of the country, render him an excellent witness, says of the narrow streets of Benares: "In addition to the pernicious effect which must proceed from a confined atmosphere, there is, in the hot season, an intolerable stench arising from the many pieces of stagnated water dispersed in different quarters of the town. The filth also which is indiscriminately thrown into the streets, and there left exposed, (for the Hindus possess but a small portion of general cleanliness) add to the compound of ill smells so offensive to the European inhabitants of this city."

———————

The attachment with which the Hindus, in common with all ignorant nations, bear to astrology, is a part of their manners exerting a strong influence upon the train of their actions. "The Hindus of the present age," says a partial observer, "do not undertake any affair of consequence without consulting their astrologers, who are always Brahmans." The belief of witchcraft and sorcery continues universally prevalent.

→ *What did James Mill hold to be the chief indicator of a civilization's accomplishment?*
→ *In what ways do Mill's views on India reflect a deep disagreement with British Orientalists?*

SOURCE: James Mill, *The History of British India* (New Delhi: Atlantic Publishers & Distributors, 1990), pp. 279, 281–82, 286–87, 288, 289, 297, 299.

EXPANSION OF THE EMPIRE The Qing had a talent for extending the empire's boundaries and settling frontier lands. Before 1750, they conquered Taiwan (the stronghold of remaining Ming forces), pushed westward into central Asia, and annexed Tibet. Qing troops then eliminated the threat of the powerful Junghars in western Mongolia and halted Russian efforts to take southern Siberia in the 1750s. To secure these territorial gains, the Qing encouraged settlement of frontier lands like Xinjiang. New crops from the Americas aided this process—especially corn and sweet potatoes, which grow well in less fertile soils.

Through rising agricultural productivity and population growth, rural life became commercialized and state revenues surged. Furthermore, despite the Chinese ideal for women to stay home while men worked the land, in reality most rural women had toiled at fieldwork for centuries—and now their labor became even more important. In the eighteenth century, rural markets participated in more interregional trade in grain, cotton, tea, and silk. As rural industries proliferated, peasant households became the backbone of early manufactures (as in Europe), especially in textiles.

Like their European counterparts, Chinese peasants were on the move. But migration occurred in Qing China for different reasons. The state-sponsored westward movement into Xinjiang, for example, aimed to secure a recently pacified frontier region through military colonization, after which

Rice Paddies. Farmers working in neatly planted rice paddy fields in late imperial China. The process was labor intensive, but it reduced wastage.

civilians would follow. So peasants received promises of land, tools, seed, and the loan of silver and a horse—all with the dual objectives of producing enough food grain to supply the troops and relieving pressure on the poor and arid northwestern part of the country. These efforts brought so much land under cultivation by 1840 that the region's ecological and social landscape completely changed.

Other migrants were on the move by their own initiative. The ever-growing competition for land even drove them into areas where the Qing regime had tried to restrict migration (because of excessive administrative costs), such as Manchuria and Taiwan. As the migrants introduced their own agricultural techniques, they reshaped the environment through land reclamation and irrigation projects and sparked large population increases.

PROBLEMS OF THE EMPIRE Despite their success in expanding the empire, the Qing faced nagging problems. As a ruling minority, they took a conservative approach to innovation. And only late in the eighteenth century did they deal with rapid population growth. On the one hand, the tripling of China's population since 1300 demonstrated the realm's prosperity; on the other, a population of over 300 million severely strained resources—especially soil for growing crops and wood for fuel.

Even as rulers recognized the problems, they had limited ability to tackle them. The taxes they levied were light (compared to the ones European monarchs levied).

Bureaucrats were understaffed. And as local authorities introduced many new taxes, the common people regarded them as corrupt. In the late eighteenth and early nineteenth centuries, uprisings inspired by mystical beliefs in folk Buddhism, and at times by the idea of restoring the Ming, engulfed northern China.

In spite of the difficulties that beset the Qing, European rulers and upper classes remained eager consumers of Chinese silks, teas, carved jade, tableware, jewelry, paper for covering walls, and ceramics. The Chinese, for their part, had little interest in most European manufactures. In 1793, Emperor Qianlong wrote in response to a request for trade by Britain's king that "as your ambassador can see for himself, we possess all things," adding, "I have no use for your country's manufactures."

By the mid-nineteenth century, however, extraordinary changes had made western European powers stronger than ever before, and the Qing could no longer dismiss their demands. The first clear evidence of an altered balance of power was not the rise of Napoleon, but a British-Chinese war over a narcotic. Indeed, the **Opium War** exposed China's vulnerability in a new era of European ascendancy.

THE OPIUM WAR AND THE "OPENING" OF CHINA Europeans had been selling staples and intoxicants in China for a long time. For example, tobacco, a New World crop, had become widely popular in China by the seventeenth century. Initially, few people would have predicted that tobacco smoking would lead to the widespread use of opium, previously used as a medicine or an aphrodisiac. But before long people in Southeast Asia, Taiwan, and China were smoking crude opium mixed with tobacco. By the late eighteenth century, opium smokers with their long-stemmed pipes were conspicuous at every level of Chinese society.

Although the Qing banned opium imports in 1729, the Chinese continued to smoke the drug and import it illegally. Sensing its economic potential, the East India Company created an opium monopoly in India in 1773. The reason was a rapid growth in the company's purchase of tea. Because the Chinese showed little taste for British goods, the British had been financing their tea imports with exports of silver to China. But by the late eighteenth century, the company's tea purchases had become too large to finance with silver. Fortunately for the company, the Chinese were eager for Indian cotton and opium, and then mostly just opium. Thus the British exported essentially no silver after 1804. Given the drug's importance, the company expanded its cultivation by offering loans to Indian peasants: they agreed to grow opium and sell it to the company's agents at a predetermined price.

The illegal opium traffic could not have flourished without the involvement of corrupt Chinese bureaucrats and a network of local brokers and distributors. Although another official ban in 1799 slowed the flow of opium into China for a while, the volume increased eightfold by 1839. The dramatic increase reflected an influx of private British merchants after the British government revoked the East India Company's monopoly over trade with China.

Opium's impact on the empire's balance of trade was devastating. In a reversal from earlier trends, silver began to flow out of instead of into China. Once silver shortages occurred, the peasants' tax burden grew heavier because they had to pay in silver (see Chapter 13). Consequently, long-simmering unrest in the countryside gained momentum. At the Qing court, some officials wanted to legalize the opium trade so as to eliminate corruption and boost revenues. (After all, as long as opium was an illegal substance, the government could not tax its traffic). Others wanted stiffer prohibitions. In 1838 the emperor sent a special commissioner to Canton, the main center of the trade, to eradicate the influx of opium. In a letter to Queen Victoria of Britain, the commissioner, Lin Zexu, claimed that China exported tea and silk for no other reason than "to share the benefit with the people of the whole world." He asked, therefore, why the British inflicted harm on the Chinese people through opium imports.

Lin demanded that foreigners hand over their opium stocks to the Chinese government (for destruction) and stop the trade. When British merchants in Canton resisted, Lin ordered the arrest of the president of the British Chamber of Commerce. After this man refused to comply, 350 foreigners were blockaded inside their own quarters. Lin ultimately convinced the foreign community to surrender 20,283 chests of opium with an estimated value of $9 million—an enormous sum in those days. But merchants had overstocked in anticipation of the trade's legalization, and the British government representative in Canton promised to compensate them for their losses. For Lin, the surrendering of the opium (which the Chinese flushed out to sea) was proof that the foreigners accepted submission. The Chinese victory, however, was short-lived. War soon broke out.

Opium. (*Left*) A common sight in late Qing China were establishments catering specifically to opium smoking. Taken from a volume condemning the practice, this picture shows opium smokers idling their day away. (*Right*) Having established a monopoly in the 1770s over opium cultivation in India, the British greatly expanded their manufacture and export of opium to China to balance their rapidly growing import of Chinese tea and silk. This picture from the 1880s shows an opium warehouse in India where the commodity was stored before being transported to China.

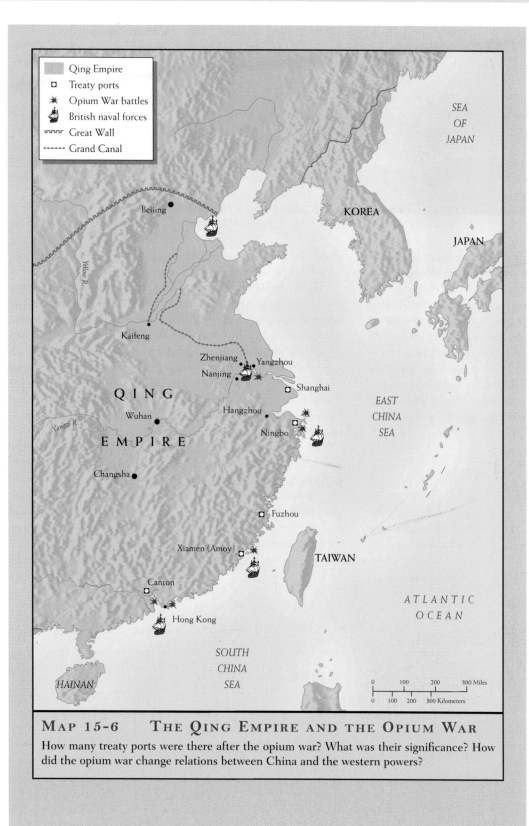

MAP 15-6   THE QING EMPIRE AND THE OPIUM WAR

How many treaty ports were there after the opium war? What was their significance? How did the opium war change relations between China and the western powers?

Though determined, the Chinese were no match for Britain's modern military technology. After a British fleet—including four steam-powered battleships—entered Chinese waters in June 1840, the warships bombarded coastal regions near Canton and sailed upriver for a short way (see Map 15-6). On land, Qing soldiers used spears, clubs, and a few imported matchlock muskets against the modern artillery of British troops, many of whom were Indians supplied with percussion cap rifles. Along the Yangzi River, outgunned Qing forces fought fiercely, as soldiers killed their own wives and children before committing suicide themselves.

FORCING MORE TRADE The British triumphed as the Qing ruling elite wanted to avoid further conflicts with the militarily superior British. With the 1842 Treaty of Nanjing, the British acquired the island of Hong Kong and the right to trade in five treaty ports, and they forced the Chinese to repay their costs for the war—and the value of the opium Lin had destroyed. British traders now won the right to trade directly with the Chinese and to live in the treaty ports.

Subsequent treaties guaranteed that the British and other foreign nationals would be tried in their own courts for crimes, rather than in Chinese courts, and would be exempt from Chinese law. Moreover, the British insisted that any privileges granted through treaties with other parties would also apply to them. Other Western nations followed the British example

Trade in Canton. In this painting, we can see the hongs, the buildings that made up the factories, or establishments, where foreign merchants conducted their business in Canton. From the mid-eighteenth century to 1842, Canton was the only Chinese port open to European trade.

in demanding the same right, and the arrangement thus guaranteed all Europeans and North Americans a privileged position in China.

Still, China did not become a formal colony. To the contrary, in the mid-nineteenth century Europeans and North Americans were trading only on its outskirts. Most Chinese did not encounter the Europeans. Daily life for most people went on as it had before the Opium War. Only the political leaders and urban dwellers were beginning to feel the foreign presence and wondering what steps China might take to acquire European technologies, goods, and learning.

CONCLUSION

During the period 1750–1850, changes in politics, commerce, industry, and technology reverberated throughout the Atlantic world and, to varying degrees, elsewhere around the globe. By 1850, the world was more integrated economically, with Europe increasingly at the center.

In the Americas, colonial ties broke apart. In France, the people toppled the monarchy. Dissidents threatened the same in Russia. Such upheavals introduced a new public vocabulary—the language of the nation—and made the idea of revolution empowering. In the Americas and parts of Europe, nation-states took shape around redefined hierarchies of class, gender, and color. Britain and France emerged from the political crises of the late eighteenth century to expand their borders. Their drive forced older empires such as Russia and the Ottoman state to make reforms.

As commerce and industrialization transformed economic and political power, European governments compelled others (including Egypt, India, and China) to expand their trade with European merchants. Ultimately, such countries had to participate in a European-centered economy as exporters of raw materials and importers of European manufactures.

Chronology

	1750	1775
THE AMERICAS		◆- - - - - - - - - - -◆ 1776–1783 *American Revolution* 1791–1804 *Haitian Rebellion* ◆- - - - - - - - - - - 1793 *Eli Whitney invents the cotton gin* ◆
EUROPE		◆ 1769 *James Watt invents steam engine* 1789–1799 *French Revolution* ◆- - - - - - - - - - -
RUSSIA AND OTTOMAN EMPIRE		
AFRICA		
SOUTH ASIA		◆ 1765 *British establish company rule in India*
EAST ASIA	◆- - - - 1736–1796 *Chinese expansion under Qianlong emperor*	

By the 1850s, many of the world's peoples became more industrious, producing less for themselves and more for distant markets. Through changes in manufacturing, some areas of the world also made more goods than ever before. With its emphasis on free trade, Europe began to force open new markets—even to the point of colonizing them. Gold and silver now flowed out of China and India to pay for European-dominated products like opium and textiles.

However, global reordering did not mean that Europe's rulers had uncontested control over other people, or that the institutions and cultures of Asia and Africa ceased to be dynamic. Some countries became dependent on Europe commercially; others became colonies. China escaped colonial rule but was forced into unfavorable trade relations with the Europeans. In sum, dramatic changes combined to unsettle systems of rulership and to alter the economic and military balance between western Europe and the rest of the world.

Review and research materials are available at StudySpace: ⓢ WWNORTON.COM/STUDYSPACE

KEY TERMS

Simón Bolívar (p. 577)
Napoleon Bonaparte (p. 570)
bourgeoisie (p. 581)
democracy (p. 562)
East India Company (p. 589)
free labor (p. 562)
free markets (p. 562)
free trade (p. 562)
industrial revolution (p. 582)

industrious revolution (p. 581)
Muhammad Ali (p. 586)
nationalism (p. 562)
nation-state (p. 563)
Opium War (p. 593)
popular sovereignty (p. 562)
republican government (p. 568)
social contract (p. 566)

STUDY QUESTIONS

1. Describe the political and social revolutions that occurred in the Atlantic world between 1750 and 1850. What ideas inspired these changes? How far did revolutionaries extend these changes?

2. Compare and contrast the way Latin American peoples achieved independence to the similar process in the United States. How similar were their goals? How well did they achieve these goals?

3. Explain Napoleon's role in spreading the ideas of political and social revolution. How did his armies spread the concept of nationalism? How did Napoleon's military pursuits affect political and social ferment in the Americas?

4. Explain how the Atlantic world's political and social revolution led to the end of the Atlantic slave trade. What economic, social, and political consequences did this development have on sub-Saharan Africa?

5. Explain the relationship between industrialization and the "industrious revolution." Where did the industrial revolution begin? What other parts of the Atlantic world did it spread to during this time?

6. Explore how industrialization altered the societies that began to industrialize during this time. What impact did this process have on the environment? How were gender roles and familial relationships altered?

7. Analyze how the two intertwined Atlantic revolutions (political and industrial) altered the global balance of power. How did the Russian, Mughal, Ottoman, and Qing dynasties respond to this change?

8. To what extent did Great Britain emerge as the leading global power between 1750 and 1850? How did the British state shape political and economic developments around the world during this time?

1800	1825	1850

◆ 1807 Robert Fulton launches first commercial steamship

◆- ◆ 1810–1824 Revolutions in South America

◆- - - - - - - - - - - - ◆ 1804–1815 Napoleon's empire   ◆ 1830 First railway launched in England

◆- ◆ 1808–1839 Reign of Mahmud II, Ottoman Empire

1825 Decembrist Revolt in Russia ◆

1829 Greek independence ◆

◆ 1798–1801 French invasion of Egypt

1803–1867 Abolition of Atlantic slave trade

1805–1848 Reign of Muhammad Ali, Egypt

◆ 1813 Abolition of company trade monopoly in India

1839–1842 Opium War, China ◆- - - - - ◆

ALTERNATIVE VISIONS OF THE NINETEENTH CENTURY

By the late nineteenth century, territorial expansion in the United States confined almost all Indians to reservations. Across the American West, many Indians fell into despair. One was a Paiute Indian named Wovoka. But in 1889, he had a vision of a much brighter future. In his dream, the "Supreme Being" told Wovoka that if Indians lived harmoniously, shunned white ways (especially alcohol), and performed the cleansing Ghost Dance, then the buffalo would return and Indians, including the dead, would be reborn to live in eternal happiness.

As word spread of Wovoka's vision, Indians from hundreds of miles around made pilgrimages to the lodge of this new prophet. Many proclaimed him the Indians' messiah or the "Red Man's Christ," an impression fostered by scars on his hands. Especially among the Shoshone, Arapaho, Cheyenne, and Sioux peoples of the northern Plains, Wovoka's message inspired new hope. Soon increasing numbers joined in the ritual Ghost Dance, hoping it would restore the good life that colonialism had extinguished. Among the hopefuls was Sitting Bull, a revered Sioux chief who was himself famous for his visions. Yet, less than two years after

Wovoka's vision, Sitting Bull died at the hands of police forces on a Sioux reservation. A few days later, on December 29, 1890, Sioux Ghost Dancers were massacred at a South Dakota creek called Wounded Knee.

Though it failed, this movement was one of many prophetic crusades that challenged an emerging nineteenth-century order. The ideals of the French and American revolutions, laissez-faire capitalism, the nation-state organization, new technologies, and industrial organizations now provided the dominant answers to age-old questions of who should govern and what beliefs should prevail. But these answers did not stamp out other views. A diverse assortment of political radicals, charismatic prophets, peasant rebels, and anticolonial insurgents put forward striking counterproposals to those that capitalists, colonial modernizers, and nation-state builders had developed. The people making these counterproposals were motivated by the impending loss of their existing worlds and were energized by visions of ideal, utopian futures.

This chapter attends to the voices and visions of those who opposed a nineteenth-century world in which capitalism, colonialism, and nation-states held sway. It puts the spotlight on challengers who shared a dislike of global capitalism and European (and North American) colonialism. Beyond that similarity they differed in significant ways, for the alternatives they proposed reflected the local circumstances in which each of them developed. Although many of the leaders and movements they inspired suffered devastating defeats, like the Ghost Dancers at Wounded Knee, the dreams that aroused their fervor did not always die with them. Some of these alternative visions of the nineteenth century endured to propel the great transformations of the twentieth.

REACTIONS TO SOCIAL AND POLITICAL CHANGE

> → *What factors accounted for the differences among alternative movements?*

The transformations of the late eighteenth and early nineteenth centuries had upset polities and economies around the globe. In Europe, the old order had been either swept aside or severely battered by the tide of political and economic revolutions. In North America, the newly independent United States began an expansion westward. Territorial growth led to the dispossession of hundreds of Indian tribes and the acquisition of nearly half of Mexico by conquest. In Latin America, fledgling nation-states that now replaced the Spanish Empire struggled to control their subject populations. And in Asia and Africa, rulers and common people alike confronted the growing might of western military and industrial power. At stake were issues of how to define and rule territories, and what social and cultural visions they would embody.

The alternatives to the dominant trends varied considerably. Some rebels and dissidents called for the revitalization of traditional religions; others wanted to strengthen village and communal bonds; still others imagined a society where there was no private property and where people shared goods equally. The actions of these dissenters depended on their local traditions and the degree of contact they had with the effects of industrial capitalism, European colonialism, and centralizing nation-states.

Focus Questions

ⓢ WWNORTON.COM/STUDYSPACE

→ *What factors accounted for the differences among alternative movements?*

→ *How did prophets and "big men" tap into Islamic and African traditions?*

→ *What prompted the Taiping Rebellion, and what changes did it envision?*

→ *What forces fueled European radicalism?*

→ *How were alternative movements in the Americas and India similar and different?*

MAIN THEMES

→ *Protest movements challenge the nineteenth-century order based on ideals of the French and American revolutions, laissez-faire capitalism, the nation-state, and industrialization.*

→ *The movements express visions of ideal, utopian futures and offer opportunities to hear the usually overlooked voices of peasants and workers, as well as those of prophets, political radicals, and anticolonial insurgents.*

→ *The movements differ markedly depending on proximity to the centers of change (Europe and the Americas) and reflect local circumstances.*

→ *Although most movements are defeated, they inspire later generations.*

FOCUS ON *Regional Variations in Alternative Visions*

Europe and the Americas—The Heartland of Modernizing Change

✦ European socialists and radicals envision a world free of exploitation and inequalities, while nationalists work to create new independent nation-states.

✦ Native American prophets in the United States imagine a world restored to its customary ways and traditional rites.

✦ Mayans in the Yucatan defy the central Mexican government in a rebellion known as the Caste War.

The Islamic World and Africa

✦ Revivalist movements in the Arabian Peninsula and West Africa demand a return to traditional Islam.

✦ A charismatic warrior, Shaka, creates a powerful state in southern Africa.

Semicolonial China

✦ An inspired prophetic figure, Hong Xiuquan, leads the Taiping Rebellion against the Qing dynasty and European encroachment on China.

Colonial India

✦ Indian troops mutiny against the British and attempt to restore Mughal rule.

This era of rapid social change, when differing visions of power and justice vied with one another, offers unique opportunities to hear the voices of the lower orders—the peasants and workers, whose perspectives the elites often ignored or suppressed. While there are few written records that capture the views of the illiterate and the marginalized, we do have traditions of folklore, dreams, rumors, and prophecies. Handed down orally from generation to generation, these resources illuminate the visions of common folk.

The alternative visions that challenged the dominance of colonialism, capitalism, and nation-states differed markedly. In Europe and the Americas, the heartlands of industrial capitalism and the nation-state, radical thinkers dreamed of far-reaching changes. They sought nothing less than an end to private property and a socialist alternative to capitalism.

In Africa, the Middle East, and China, regions not yet colonized by Europeans, dynamic religious prophets and charismatic military leaders emerged. Here, men (and sometimes women) revitalized traditional ways, rejuvenated destabilized communities, and reorganized societies in hopes of preventing the spread of unwelcome foreign ideas and institutions. Finally, in South Asia and the Americas, where indigenous groups had come under the domination of Europeans and peoples of European descent, rebellions targeted the authority of the state. A Native American prophetic leader, Wovoka, inspired a revolt against the U.S. government. Facing the domineering power of the Mexican state, Mayans fought to defend their cultural and political autonomy. So, too, did Indian peasants and old elites, who joined a fierce revolt against their colonial masters in British India.

PROPHECY AND REVITALIZATION IN THE ISLAMIC WORLD AND AFRICA

> → *How did prophets and "big men" tap into Islamic and African traditions?*

In regions that felt European and North American influence but not direct colonial rule, alternative perspectives were strongest far from the main trade and cultural routes. Persons outside the emerging capitalist world order led these movements. In the Islamic world, the margins were especially important in articulating alternative views. Such areas sharply differed from other Islamic areas where reformers were trying to refashion their societies along European lines—that is, the Islamic heartland (the Ottoman Empire), and the most western-influenced regions of sub-Saharan Africa (the western coast and the southern tip of the continent).

Even though much of the Islamic world and non-Islamic Africa had not been colonized and was only partially involved with European-dominated trading networks, these regions had reached turning points. By the late eighteenth century, the era of Islamic expansion and flowering under the Ottomans, Safavids, and Mughals was over. Their empires had extended Muslim trading orbits, facilitated cross-cultural communication, and promoted common knowledge over vast territories. Their political and military decline, however, brought new challenges to the faithful. The sense of alarm intensified as Christian Europe's power spread from the edges of the Islamic world to its centers. (See Global Connections & Disconnections: Islamic Rebels: Abd al-Qasim and Zaynab.) While this perception of danger motivated military men in Egypt and the Ottoman sultans to modernize their states (see Chapter 15), it also bred religious revitalization movements that sought to recapture the glories of past traditions. Led by prophets who feared that the Islamic faith was in trouble, these movements spoke the language of revival and restoration as they sought to establish new theocratic governments across lands in which Muslims ruled and Islamic law prevailed.

Prophecy also exerted a strong influence in non-Islamic Africa, where long-distance trade and population growth were upending the social order. Just as Muslim clerics and political leaders sought solutions to unsettling changes by rereading Islamic classics, African communities looked to charismatic leaders who drew strength from their peoples' spiritual and magical traditions. Often uniting disparate groups behind their dynamic visions, prophetic leaders and other "big men" gained power because they were able to resolve local crises—mostly caused by drought, a shortage of arable land, or some other issue related to the harsh environment.

ISLAMIC REVITALIZATION

Movements to revitalize Islam took place on the peripheries—in areas that seemed immune from the potentially threatening repercussions of the world economy. Here, religious leaders rejected westernizing influences (see Map 16-1). Instead, revitalization movements looked back to Islamic traditions and modeled their revolts on the life of Muhammad. But even as they looked to the past, they attempted to establish something new: full-scale theocratic polities. These reformers conceived of the state as the primary instrument of God's will and as the vehicle for purifying Islamic culture.

WAHHABISM One of the most powerful reformist movements arose on the Arabian Peninsula, the birthplace of the Muslim faith. In the Najd region, an area surrounded by mountains and deserts, a religious cleric named Muhammad Ibn abd al-Wahhab (1703–1792) galvanized the population by attacking what he regarded as lax religious practices. His message found a ready response among local inhabitants, who felt threatened by the new commercial activities and fresh intellectual currents swirling around them. Abd al-Wahhab demanded a return to the pure Islam of Muhammad and the early caliphs.

Although Najd was far removed from the currents of the expanding world economy, Abd al-Wahhab himself was not. Having been educated in Iraq, Iran, and the Hijaz (a region on the western end of modern Saudi Arabia, on the Red Sea), he believed that Islam had fallen into a degraded state, particularly in its birthplace. He railed against the polytheistic beliefs that had taken hold of the people, complaining that in defiance of Muhammad's tenets men and women were worshipping trees, stones, and tombs and making sacrifices to false images. Abd al-Wahhab's movement stressed the absolute oneness of Allah (hence his followers were called *Muwahhidin*, or Unitarians) and severely criticized Sufi sects for extolling the lives of saints over the worship of God.

As **Wahhabism** swept across the Arabian Peninsula, the movement posed less of a threat to European power than it did to the Ottomans' hold on the region. Wahhabism gained a powerful political ally in the Najdian House of Saud, whose followers, inspired by the Wahhabis' religious zeal, undertook a militant religious campaign. They sacked the Shiite shrines of Karbala in southern Iraq, and in 1803 they overran the holy cities of Mecca and Medina, damaging the tombs of the saints. Frightened by the Wahhabi challenge, the Ottoman sultan persuaded the provincial ruler of Egypt to send troops to the Arabian Peninsula to suppress the movement. The Egyptians defeated the Saudis, but Wahhabism and the

→ *How did prophets and "big men" tap into Islamic and African traditions?*

MAP 16-1   MUSLIM REVITALIZATION MOVEMENTS IN THE MIDDLE EAST AND AFRICA, AND THE *MFECANE* MOVEMENT IN SOUTHERN AFRICA

During the nineteenth century, a series of Muslim revitalization movements took place throughout the Middle East and North Africa. According to this map, in how many different areas did the revitalization movements occur? Based on their geographic location within their larger regions, did these movements occur in central or peripheral areas? Were any of the same factors that led to Islamic revitalization involved in the *Mfecane* developments in southern Africa?

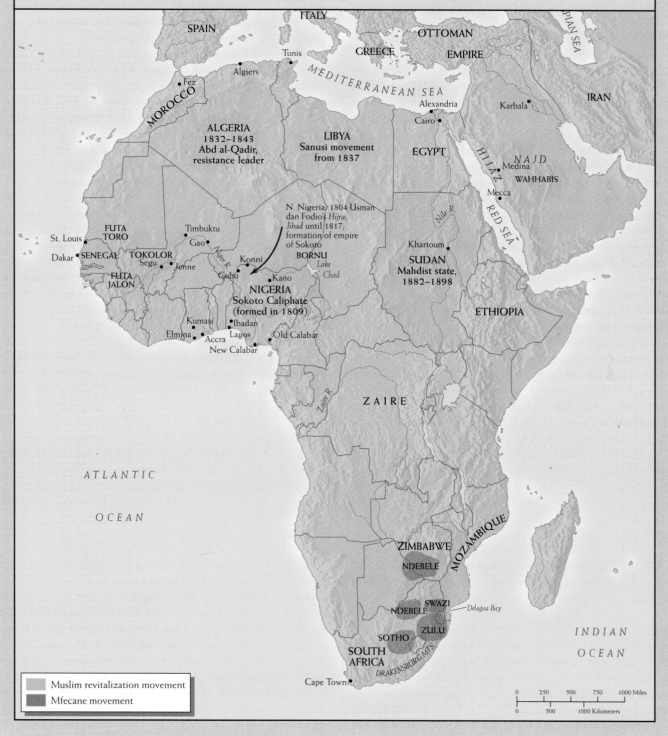

Muslim revitalization movement

Mfecane movement

ISLAMIC REBELS: ABI AL-QASIM AND ZAYNAB

Reformist ideas swirled through the Islamic world throughout the nineteenth century, producing new visions and powerful new communities across the Middle East and Africa. In no part of the Islamic world was opposition to European colonial and capitalist encroachment more strongly articulated than in Algeria. When France claimed jurisdiction over the area beginning in 1830, Algerians rose in bold and bloody revolts. The most violent uprisings were the rebellion of Abd al-Qadir in the 1830s and the revolt of 1849.

The French repressed these movements ruthlessly, resulting in heavy losses to combatants and civilians alike. The military lessons took hold: Algerian Muslims learned to use more subtle means to preserve their autonomy, fearing to challenge the French authorities openly.

A master in the art of protecting his community's religious and political autonomy was Shaykh Muhammad ibn Abi al-Qasim (1823–1897), a religious notable who lived in southern Algeria. He gained a large circle of religious devotees because his Sufi brotherhood served as a safe haven for those who did not want to live under direct French rule. When, however, al-Qasim's health deteriorated in the late 1870s, the French became embroiled in an internal struggle over his succession. Accepting the conventional wisdom that Islam was a patriarchal religion, the French supported the candidacy of the shaykh's male cousin over that of his daughter, Zaynab. Unfortunately, their calculations proved utterly wrong, for they failed to account for Zaynab's powerful personality and her religious legitimacy. When al-Qasim passed away in 1897, the French faced a situation for which their traditional dealings with Islamic leaders had not prepared them: they stood in opposition to a dynamic female religious personage.

Zaynab (1850–1904) laid claim to her father's legacy because of her exemplary piety, her understanding of her father's teachings, her vow of celibacy, and her independence from the French. Her descent from the family of the prophet Muhammad, as well as the many miracles attributed to her, soon elevated her to the status of a religious holy person and gave her a legitimacy that women did not frequently attain in Islamic religious affairs.

But as we have seen in other settings (see Global Connections & Disconnections: Joan of Arc in Chapter 11), at times when communal values were under great pressure, people were prepared to turn to a woman. This was certainly the case as the French extended their direct political influence into southern Algeria and interfered in local religious succession. Indeed, Zaynab contested French power more vigorously than her father would have advised because she realized that the French had never faced a woman leader before.

Zaynab's actions revealed how vulnerable and uncertain the French were in their response to opposition from women. Colonial authorities claimed they were protecting women from male exploitation; nonetheless, the French turned against Zaynab, describing her as "passionate to the point of hatred and bold to the point of insolence and impudence." But their opposition only heightened her appeal and her legitimacy among her followers. In spite of French opposition, Zaynab succeeded to the position that her father had occupied and thus defeated the French efforts to determine internal religious decisions within her community.

House of Saud continued to represent a pure Islamic faith that attracted clerics and common folk throughout the Muslim world.

USMAN DAN FODIO AND THE FULANI In West Africa, Muslim revolts erupted from Senegal to Nigeria, responding in part to increased trade with the outside world and the circulation of religious ideas from across the Sahara Desert. In this region, the Fulani people were decisive in religious uprisings that sought, like the Wahhabi movement, to re-create a supposedly purer Islamic past. Although the

Fulani had originated in the eastern part of present-day Senegal (and retain a powerful presence there today), they moved eastward to escape drought and, over time, set down roots across the savannah lands of West Africa. The majority were cattle-keepers, practicing a pastoral and nomadic way of life. But some were sedentary, and people in this group converted to Islam, read the Islamic classics, and communicated with holy men of North Africa, Egypt, and the Arabian Peninsula. They concluded that West African peoples were violating Islamic beliefs and engaging in irreligious practices.

The most powerful of these reform movements flourished in what is today northern Nigeria. Its leader was a Fulani Muslim cleric, **Usman dan Fodio** (1754–1817), who ultimately created a vast Islamic empire. Dan Fodio's movement had all the trappings of the Islamic revolts of this period. It sought inspiration in the life of Muhammad and demanded a return to early Islamic practices. It attacked false belief and heathenism and urged followers to wage holy war (*jihad*) against unbelievers. Usman dan Fodio's adversaries were the old Hausa rulers (city-states that emerged between 1000 and 1200 CE), who, in his view, were not sufficiently faithful to Islamic beliefs and practices. So dan Fodio withdrew from his original habitation in Konni and established a new community of believers at Gudu, citing the ancient precedent of Muhammad's withdrawal from Mecca to establish a community of true believers at Medina (see Chapter 9). The practice of withdrawal, called *hijra* in Muhammad's time, was yet another of the prophet's inspirations that religious reformers invoked at this time.

Dan Fodio was a member of the Qadiriyya, one of many Sufi brotherhoods that had helped spread Islam into West Africa. Sufism, the mystical and popular form of Islam, sought an emotional connection with God through a strict regimen of prayers, fasting, and religious exercises to obtain mystical states. Like Wovoka and Sitting Bull in North America, dan Fodio had visions that led him to challenge the West African ruling classes. In one vision, the founder of the Qadiriyya order instructed him to unsheathe the sword of truth against the enemies of Islam.

Dan Fodio won the support of devout Muslims in the area, who agreed that the people were not properly practicing Islam. He also gained the backing of his Fulani tribes and many of the Hausa peasantry, who had suffered under the rule of the Hausa landlord class. The revolt, initiated in 1804, resulted in the overthrow of the Hausa rulers and the creation of a confederation of Islamic emirates, almost all of which were in the hands of the Fulani allies of dan Fodio.

Fulani women of northern Nigeria made critical contributions to the success of the religious revolt. Although dan Fodio and other male leaders of the purification movement expected women to obey the *sharia* (Islamic law), being modest in their dress and their association with men outside the family, they also expected women to support the community's military and religious endeavors. In this effort, they cited women's important role in the first days of Islam. The best known of the Muslim women leaders was Nana Asma'u, daughter of dan Fodio. Fulani women of the upper ranks acquired an Islamic education, and Asma'u was as astute a reader of Islamic texts as any of the learned men in her society. Like other Muslim Fulani devotees, she accompanied the warriors on their campaigns, encamped with them, prepared food for them, bound up their wounds, and provided daily encouragement. According to many accounts, Asma'u inspired the warriors at their most crucial battle, hurling a burning spear into the midst of the enemy army. Her poem "Song of the Circular Journey" celebrates the triumphs of military forces that trekked thousands of miles to bring a reformed Islam to the area. (For another poem by Asma'u, see Primary Source: A Female Muslim Voice in Africa.)

Usman dan Fodio considered himself a cleric first and a political and military man second. Although his political leadership was decisive in the revolt's success, thereafter he retired to a life of scholarship and writing. He delegated the political and administrative functions of the new empire to his brother and his son. An enduring decentralized state structure, which became known as the Sokoto caliphate in 1809, developed into a stable empire that helped spread Islam through the region. In 1800, on the eve of dan Fodio's revolt, Islam was the faith of a small minority of people living in northern Nigeria; a century later, it had become the religion of the vast majority.

CHARISMATIC MILITARY MEN IN NON-ISLAMIC AFRICA

Non-Islamic Africa saw revolts, new states, and prophetic movements arise from the same combination of factors that influenced the rest of the world—particularly long-distance trade and population increase. Local communities here also looked to religious traditions and, as was so often the case in African history, expected "big men" to provide political leadership.

In southern Africa, early in the nineteenth century, a group of political revolts reordered the political map. Collectively known as the *Mfecane* **movement** ("the crushing" in Zulu), its epicenter was a large tract of land lying east of the Drakensberg Mountains, an area where growing populations and land resources existed in a precarious balance (see again Map 16-1). Compounding this pressure, trade with the Portuguese in Mozambique and with other Europeans at Delagoa Bay had disrupted the traditional social order. This set the stage for a political crisis for the northern Nguni (Bantu-speaking) peoples.

Many branches of Bantu-speaking peoples had inhabited the southern part of the African landmass for centuries. At the end of the eighteenth century, however, their political organizations still operated on a small scale, revolving around families and clans and modest chieftaincies. These tiny polities could not cope with the overpopulation and competition for land that now dominated southern Africa. A branch of the Nguni, the Zulus, produced a fierce war leader, Shaka (1787–1828), who created a ruthless warrior state. It drove other populations out of the region and forced a shift from small clan communities to large, centralized monarchies throughout southern and central Africa.

Shaka was the son of a minor chief who emerged victorious in the struggle for cattle-grazing and farming lands that

A FEMALE MUSLIM VOICE IN AFRICA

The Islamic scholar, writer, and poet Nana Asma'u was the daughter of Usman dan Fodio, the leader of the Fulani revolt in northern Nigeria at the turn of the nineteenth century. Many of her poems conveyed religious inspiration and sought to demonstrate how much her father's revolt was inspired by the life and message of the Prophet Muhammad. She was also deeply attached to her brother, Muhammad Bello, who succeeded their father as head of the Sokoto caliphate. Muhammad Bello looked to his sister to promote traditional Muslim values among the female population in his empire, and she worked to extend education to rural women. Following is an elegy, written in poetic form, that Nana Asma'u composed in praise of her brother, underlining his commitment to an Islamic way of life.

I give thanks to the King of Heaven, the One God. I invoke blessings on the Prophet and set down my poem.

The Lord made Heaven and earth and created all things, sent prophets to enlighten mankind.

Believe in them for your own sake, learn from them and be saved, believe in and act upon their sayings.

I invoke blessings on the Prophet who brought the Book, the Qur'an: he brought the *hadith* to complete the enlightenment.

Muslim scholars have explained knowledge and used it, following in the footsteps of the Prophet.

It is my intention to set down Bello's characteristics and explain his ways.

For I wish to assuage my loneliness, requite my love, find peace of mind through my religion.

These are his characteristics: he was learned in all branches of knowledge and feared God in public and in private.

He obeyed religious injunctions and distanced himself from forbidden things: this is what is known about him.

He concentrated on understanding what is right to know about the Oneness of God.

He preached to people and instructed them about God: he caused them to long for Paradise.

He set an example in his focus on eternal values: he strove to end oppression and sin.

He upheld the *shari'a*, honored it, implemented it aright, that was his way, everyone knows.

And he made his views known to those who visited him: he said to them "Follow the *shari'a*, which is sacred."

He eschewed worldly things and discriminated against anything of ill repute; he was modest and a repository of useful knowledge.

He was exceedingly level-headed and generous, he enjoyed periods of quietude: but was energetic when he put his hand to things.

He was thoughtful, calm, a confident statesman, and quick-witted.

He honored people's status: he could sort out difficulties and advise those who sought his help.

He had nothing to do with worldly concerns, but tried to restore to a healthy state things which he could. These were his characteristics.

---

arose during a severe drought. A muscular and physically imposing figure, Shaka was also a violent man who used terror to intimidate his subjects and to overawe his adversaries. His enemies knew that the price of opposition would be a massacre, even of women and children. Nor was he much kinder to his own people. Following the death of his beloved mother, for example, Shaka executed those who were not properly contrite and did not weep profusely. Reportedly, it took 7,000 lives to assuage his grief.

Shaka built a new state around his own military and organizational skills and the fear that his personal ferocity produced. He drilled his men relentlessly in the use of short stabbing spears and in discipline under pressure. Like the Mongols, he had a remarkable ability to incorporate defeated communities into the state and to absorb young men into his ultradedicated warrior forces. His army of 40,000 men comprised regiments that lived, studied, and fought together. Forbidden from marrying until they were discharged from the

He never broke promises, but faithfully kept them: he sought out righteous things. Ask and you will hear.

He divorced himself entirely from bribery and was totally scrupulous: He flung back at the givers money offered for titles.

One day Garange [chief of Mafora] sent him a splendid gift, but Bello told the messenger Zitaro to take it back.

He said to the envoy who had brought the bribe, "Have nothing to do with forbidden things."

And furthermore he said, "Tell him that the gift was sent for unlawful purposes; it is wrong to respond to evil intent."

He was able to expedite matters: he facilitated learning, commerce, and defense, and encouraged everything good.

He propagated good relationships between different tribes and between kinsmen. He afforded protection; everyone knows this.

When strangers came he met them, and taught about religious matters, explaining things: he tried to enlighten them.

He lived in a state of preparedness, he had his affairs in order and had an excellent intelligence service.

He had nothing to do with double agents and said it was better to ignore them, for they pervert Islamic principles.

He was a very pleasant companion to friends and acquaintances: he was intelligent, with a lively mind.

He fulfilled promises and took care of affairs, but he did not act hastily.

He shouldered responsibilities and patiently endured adversities.

He was watchful and capable of restoring to good order matters which had gone wrong.

He was resourceful and could undo mischief, no matter how serious, because he was a man of ideas.

He was gracious to important people and was hospitable to all visitors, including non-Muslims.

He drew good people close to him and distanced himself from people of ill repute.

Those are his characteristics. I have recounted a few examples that are sufficient to provide a model for emulation and benefit.

May God forgive him and have mercy on him: May we be united with him in Paradise, the place we aspire to.

For the sake of the Prophet, the Compassionate, who was sent with mercy to mankind.

May God pour blessings on the Prophet and his kinsmen and all other followers.

May God accept this poem. I have concluded it in the year 1254 AH [after *hijra*, the Muslim dating system].

→ *In what ways does this description convey a sense of proper Muslim values?*
→ *Identify at least ten ways in which Bello was exemplary, according to this poem.*
→ *Why would Nana Asma'u feel compelled to write a poem in praise of her brother?*

SOURCE: "Gikku Bello" from *One Woman's Jihad: Nana Asma'u, Scholar and Scribe* by Beverly B. Mack and Jean Boyd. Copyright © 2000 by Beverly B. Mack and Jean Boyd. Reprinted by permission of Indiana University Press.

army, Shaka's warriors developed an intense esprit de corps and regarded no sacrifice as too great in the service of the state. So overpowering were these forces that other peoples of the region fled from their home areas, and Shaka claimed their estates for himself and his followers.

Thus did the Zulus under Shaka create a ruthless warrior state that conquered much territory in southern and central Africa, assimilating some peoples and forcing others to fashion their own similarly centralized polities. Shaka's defeated foes adopted many of the Zulu state's military innovations. They did so first to defend themselves and then to take over new land as they fled their old areas. The new states of the Ndebele in what later became Zimbabwe and of the Sotho of South Africa came into existence in the mid-nineteenth century in this way and proved long-lasting.

In turning southern Africa from a region of smaller polities into an area with larger and more powerful ones, Shaka seemed very much a man of the modern, nineteenth-century world. Yet

Shaka and His Zulu Regiments. (*Left*) This illustration, the only one from the time, may be an exaggeration, but it does not exaggerate the view that many had of the awesome strength and power of Shaka, the leader who united the Zulu peoples into an invincible warrior state. (*Right*) Shaka's Zulu state owed its political and military successes to its young warriors, who were deeply loyal to their ruler and whose training and discipline were exemplary. Shown here is a regimental camp in which the warriors slept in huts massed in a circular pattern and trained in military drill and close combat in the inside circle.

he was, in his own unique way, a familiar kind of African leader. He shared a charismatic and prophetic style with others who emerged during periods of acute social change. He was, in this sense, one of many big men to seek dominance.

PROPHECY AND REBELLION IN CHINA

> → *What prompted the Taiping Rebellion, and what changes did it envision?*

Whereas movements promoting alternative visions in the Islamic world and Africa appeared in areas distant from western influences, China was no longer isolated. In fact, it had been conducting a brisk trade in opium with Europe. Until 1842, the Chinese had confined trade with Europeans to the port city of Canton. After the Opium War, however, westerners forced Qing rulers to open up a number of other ports to trade. To be sure, the dynasty retained authority over almost the whole realm, and western influence remained confined to a small minority of merchants and missionaries. Nevertheless, foreign gunboats and extraterritorial rights reminded the Chinese of the looming power of the West.

As in the Islamic world and other parts of sub-Saharan Africa, population increases in China—from 250 million in 1644 to around 450 million by the 1850s—were putting considerable pressure on land and other resources. Moreover, the rising consumption of opium, grown in India and brought to China by English traders, was producing further social instability and financial crisis. As banditry and rebellions spread, the Qing dynasts turned to the gentry to maintain order in the countryside. But as the gentry raised its militia to suppress these troublemakers, it whittled away at the authority of the Qing Manchu rulers. Faced with these changes, the Qing dynasty, already weakened by the humiliating Treaty of Nanjing following the Opium War, struggled to maintain control and legitimacy. Searching for an alternative present and future, beginning in 1850 hundreds of thousands of disillusioned peasants joined what became known as the Taiping Rebellion.

The uprising drew on China's long history of peasant revolts. Traditionally, these rebellions ignited within popular religious sects whose visions were egalitarian or **millenarian** (convinced of the imminent coming of a just and ideal society). Moreover, in contrast to orthodox institutions, here women played important roles. Inspired by Daoists, who revered a past golden age before the world was corrupted by human conventions, or by Buddhist sources, these sects threatened the established order. In times of political breakdown, millenarian sects could transform local revolts into large-scale rebellions. Thus did the Taiping Rebellion, which began as a local movement in southern China, tap into the millenarian tradition and spread rapidly.

THE DREAM

The story of the rebellion begins with a complex dream that inspired its founding prophet, Hong Xiuquan (1813–1864). A native of Guangdong province in the southernmost part of the country (see Map 16-2), Hong first encountered Christian missionaries in the 1830s. He was then trying, unsuccessfully, to pass the civil service examination, which would have won him entry into the elite and a po-

MAP 16-2   THE TAIPING REBELLION IN CHINA, 1851–1864

Note that the Taiping Rebellion started in the southwestern part of the country. The rebels, however, went on to control much of the lower Yangzi region and part of the coastal area. What cities did the rebels' march start and end in? Why do you think the Taiping rebels were so successful in southern China and not in northern regions? How did western powers react to the Taiping Rebellion? Would they have been as concerned if the rebellion took place farther to the north or west?

tential career in the Qing bureaucracy. Disappointed by his poor showing, Hong began to have visions, including a dream in 1837 that led him to form the Society of God Worshippers and the Taiping Heavenly Kingdom (see below).

In this dream, a ceremonial retinue of heavenly guards escorted Hong to heaven. The group included a cock-like figure that he later identified as Leigong, the Duke of Thunder, a familiar figure in Chinese mythology. When Hong reached heaven, his belly was slit open and his internal organs were replaced with new ones. As the operation for his renewal was completed, heavenly texts were unrolled for him to read. The "Heavenly Mother" then met and thoroughly cleansed him. She addressed him as "Son" before bringing him in front of the "Old Father." Although not part of the heavenly bureaucracy, Confucius and women generals from the Song dynasty were also present. Upon meeting Hong, the "Old Father" complained that human beings had been led astray by demons, as demonstrated by the vanity of their shaven heads (a practice the Manchu Qing regime imposed), their consumption of opium, and other forms of debauchery. The "Old Father" even denounced Confucius, who, after being flogged and begging for mercy before Hong's heavenly "Elder Brother," was allowed to stay in heaven but forbidden to teach again. Still, the world was not yet free of demons. So the "Old Father" instructed Hong to leave his heavenly family behind and return to earth to rescue human beings from demons.

How much of this account has been embellished with hindsight scholars will probably never know. What we do know is that Hong, after failing the civil service exam for the third time, suffered a strange "illness" in which he had visions of combating demons. He also began proclaiming himself the Heavenly King. Relatives and neighbors thought he might have gone mad, but Hong gradually returned to his normal state. In 1843, after failing the exam for the fourth time, Hong immersed himself in a Christian tract entitled *Good Words for Exhorting the Age*. Reportedly, reading this tract enabled Hong to realize the full significance of his earlier dream. All the pieces suddenly fell into place. The "Old Father," he concluded, was the Lord Ye-huo-hua (a Chinese rendering of "Jehovah"), the creator of heaven and earth. Accordingly, the cleansing ritual foretold Hong's baptism. The "Elder Brother" was Jesus the Savior, the son of God. He, Hong Xiuquan, was the younger brother of Jesus—God's other son. Just as God had previously sent Jesus to save mankind, Hong thought that God was now sending *him* to rid the world of evil. What was once a dream was now a prophetic vision.

Taiping Rebellion. A painting depicting the Taiping rebels attacking a town. Had the Taiping succeeded in overthrowing the Qing, it would have changed the course of Chinese history and profoundly affected the rest of the world.

THE REBELLION

Unlike earlier sectarian leaders whose plots for rebellion were secret before exploding onto the public arena, Hong chose a more audacious path. Once convinced of his vision, he began to preach his doctrines openly, baptizing converts and destroying Confucian idols and ancestral shrines. Such assaults on the establishment testified to his conviction that he was carrying out God's will. Hong's message of revitalization of a troubled land and restoration of the "heavenly kingdom," imagined as a just and egalitarian order, appealed to the subordinate classes caught in the flux of social change. Drawing on a largely rural social base and asserting allegiance to Christianity, the **Taiping** ("Great Peace") **Rebellion** claimed to herald a new era of economic and social justice.

Many early followers came from the margins of local society—those whose anger at social and economic dislocations caused by the Opium War was directed not at the Europeans, but at the Qing government. The Taiping identified the ruling Manchus as the "demons" and as the chief obstacle to realizing God's kingdom on earth. Taiping policies were strict: they prohibited the consumption of alcohol, the smoking of opium, or any indulgence in sensual pleasure. Men and women were segregated for administrative and residential purposes. (See Primary Source: The Taiping on the Principles of the Heavenly Nature.) At the same time, in a drastic departure from dynastic practice, women joined the army in segregated units. These female military units mostly comprised Hakka women. Hakka is an ethnic subgroup within the Han (to which Hong Xiuquan, the founder of the Taiping, belonged) with a distinct identity. An important part of their culture was that Hakka women did not bind their feet.

There were further challenges to established social and cultural norms. For example, women could serve in the Taiping bureaucracy. Also, examinations now focused on a translated version of the Bible and assorted religious and literary compositions by Hong. Finally, all land was to be divided among the families according to family size, with men and women

Primary Source

THE TAIPING ON THE PRINCIPLES OF THE HEAVENLY NATURE

In this excerpt from 1854, the Taiping leaders envision a radically new community based on values that challenge those of conventional Chinese society. Inspired by their understanding of Christianity, the Taiping leadership confronted the central role of the family and ancestral worship in Chinese society by urging all its followers to regard themselves as belonging to a single family. It also advocated the segregation of the sexes, despite striving to improve women's lives in some of its other policy proclamations.

We brothers and sisters, enjoying today the greatest mercy of our Heavenly Father, have become as one family and are able to enjoy true blessings; each of us must always be thankful. Speaking in terms of our ordinary human feelings, it is true that each has his own parents and there must be a distinction in family names; it is also true that as each has his own household, there must be a distinction between this boundary and that boundary.

Yet we must know that the ten thousand names derive from the one name, and the one name from one ancestor. Thus our origins are not different. Since our Heavenly Father gave us birth and nourishment, we are of one form though of separate bodies, and we breathe the same air though in different places. This is why we say, "All are brothers within the four seas." Now, basking in the profound mercy of Heaven, we are of one family. . . .

We brothers, our minds having been awakened by our Heavenly Father, joined the camp in the earlier days to support our Sovereign, many bringing parents, wives, uncles, brothers, and whole families. It is a matter of course that we should attend to our parents and look after our wives and children, but when one first creates a new rule, the state must come first and the family last, public interests first and private interests last.

Moreover, as it is advisable to avoid suspicion [of improper conduct] between the inner [female] and the outer [male] and to distinguish between male and female, so men must have male quarters and women must have female quarters; only thus can we be dignified and avoid confusion. There must be no common mixing of the male and female groups, which would cause debauchery and violation of Heaven's commandments. Although to pay respects to parents and to visit wives and children occasionally are in keeping with human nature and not prohibited, yet it is only proper to converse before the door, stand a few steps apart and speak in a loud voice; one must not enter the sisters' camp or permit the mixing of men and women. Only thus, by complying with rules and commands, can we become sons and daughters of Heaven.

→ *What reasons do the Taiping leaders give for telling their followers "we are of one family"?*

→ *What reasons do they give for men and women to have separate quarters?*

SOURCE: *The Principles of the Heavenly Nature*, in *Sources of Chinese Tradition*, 2nd ed., Vol. 2, compiled by Wm. Theodore de Bary and Richard Lufrano (New York: Columbia University Press, 2000), pp. 229–30.

receiving equal shares. Once each family met its own needs for sustenance, the communities would share the remaining surplus. These were all radical departures from Chinese traditions. But the Taiping opposition to the Manchus did not involve the formation of a modern nation-state. The rebellion remained caught between the modern and the traditional.

By 1850, Hong's movement had amassed a following of over 20,000, giving Qing rulers cause for concern. When they sent troops to arrest Hong and other rebel leaders, Taiping forces repelled them and then took their turmoil beyond the southwestern part of the country. In 1851, Hong declared himself Heavenly King of the "Taiping Heavenly Kingdom" (or "Heavenly Kingdom of Great Peace"). By 1853, the rebels had captured major cities. Upon capturing Nanjing, the Taiping cleansed the city of "demons" by systematically killing all the Manchus they could find—men, women, and children. Then they established their own "heavenly" capital in the city.

But the rebels could not sustain their vision. Several factors contributed to the fall of the Heavenly Kingdom: struggles within the leadership, excessively rigid codes of conduct, and the rallying of Manchu and Han elites around the embattled dynasty. Disturbed by the Taiping's repudiation of Confucianism and wanting to protect their property, landowning gentry led militias against the Taiping. Moreover, western governments also opposed the rebellion, claiming that its doctrines represented a perversion of Christianity. Thus did a mercenary army led by foreign officers take part in suppressing the rebellion. Hong himself perished as his heavenly capital fell in 1864. With the Qing victory imminent, few of the perhaps 100,000 rebels in Nanjing surrendered. Their slaughter prepared the stage for a determined attempt by imperial bureaucrats and elite intellectuals to rejuvenate the Qing state. Although the Taiping's millenarian vision vanished, the desire to reconstitute Chinese society and government did not. The rebellion, in that sense, continued to inspire reformers as well as future peasant uprisings.

Like their counterparts in the Islamic world and Africa, the Taiping rebels promised to restore lost harmony. Despite all the differences of cultural and historical background, what Abd al-Wahhab, dan Fodio, Shaka, and Hong had in common was the perception that the present world was unjust. Thus, they sought to reorganize their communities—an endeavor that involved confronting established authorities. In this regard, the language of revitalization used by prophets in Islamic areas and China was crucial, for it provided an alternative vocabulary of political and spiritual legitimacy. Although in non-Islamic Africa the impulse was not religious revitalization, it still was an appeal to tradition—to communal solidarity and to the familiar role of "big men" in stateless societies. By mobilizing masses eager to return to an imagined golden age, these prophets and charismatic leaders gave voice to those dispossessed by global change, while producing new, alternative ways of organizing society and politics.

Congress of Vienna. At the Congress of Vienna in 1815, the Austrian prime minister Clemens von Metternich took the lead in drafting a peace settlement that would balance power between the states of Europe.

SOCIALISTS AND RADICALS IN EUROPE

> → *What forces fueled European radicalism?*

Europe and North America were the core areas of capitalist activity, nation-state building, and colonialism. But there, too, the main currents of thought and activity bumped up against challenges. Prophets of all stripes—political, social, cultural, and religious—voiced antiestablishment values and dreamed of alternative arrangements. Radicals, liberals, utopian socialists, nationalists, abolitionists, and religious mavericks made plans for better worlds to come. They did so in the face of a new era dominated by conservative monarchies. This conservatism was pervasive in central Europe, where reestablished kings and aristocrats revived most of their former power and privileges (see Map 16-3). Restoration of the old regimes had occurred at the Congress of Vienna in 1815, at the end of the French Revolution and Napoleon's conquests (see Chapter 15). However, opposition to this arrangement was widespread, and radical voices confidently predicted the coming of a new day.

RESTORATION AND RESISTANCE

The social and political ferment of the **Restoration period** (1815–1848) owed a great deal to the ambiguous legacies of the French Revolution and the Napoleonic wars. Kings had been toppled and replaced by republics, and then by Napoleon and his relatives; these experiments gave Restoration-era states and radicals many political options to choose from. The revolutionaries' attempt to replace Christianity with reason resulted in the clergy's loss of power and property, but very few Europeans actually gave up their religious beliefs. In the 1820s, the reactionary powers tried to reinstitute religious orthodoxy and clerical power, hoping to use the churches to suppress radical ideas. But in the religious sphere as in the political one, ideas and forces had been unleashed that would be impossible to tame.

Europeans in the Restoration era could draw not only on revolutionary ideas, but also on longer traditions of religious radicalism and reformist thought. Like purification movements in the Islamic world and religious sects in China, fundamentalist beliefs fueled social and political rebellions in Europe. For example, the sixteenth- and seventeenth-century English Puritans and German Anabaptists had sought to remake communities from the ground up. In predicting an apocalyptic end for those who lived under sinful and oppressive rulers, these radical dissenters had established principles of both violent and passive resistance that now found application again.

MAP 16-3   CIVIL UNREST AND REVOLUTIONS IN EUROPE, 1819–1848

Civil unrest and revolutions swept Europe after the Congress of Vienna established a peace settlement at the end of the French Revolution and Napoleon's conquests. Conservative governments had to fight off liberal rebellions and demands for change. How many sites of revolutionary activity can you locate on this map? What parts of Europe appear to have been politically stable, and what parts rebellious? Can you explain the stability of some parts of Europe and the instability of others?

Radicals could also invoke the early egalitarian image of "Pansophia," an ideal republic of inquisitive Christians united in the search for knowledge of nature as a means of loving God. This idea was promoted by the Czech Protestant John Amos Comenius, who championed education for all as early as the 1620s—at a time, that is, when most believed that learning was a privilege reserved for the elite. Forced into exile by Catholic victories during the Thirty Years War, Comenius traveled widely in Protestant Europe, inspiring egalitarian movements in many countries. Alternatively, the Europeans could refer to certain Enlightenment thinkers who were confident that mankind was already well on its way to scientific, political, and even biological perfection. Critics of the old regime in the Restoration period appeared in many stripes, but all of them reflected, in one way or another, a combination of recent experience and older traditions.

Self-conscious "reactionaries" also emerged at this time. Their crusade was not just to restore privileges to kings and nobles but also to reverse all the religious and democratizing concessions that sovereigns had made during the revolutionary and Napoleonic periods. In Russia, for example, the Slavophiles touted what they regarded as "native" traditions and institutions against the excessively "westernizing" reforms introduced by Peter the Great and continued by his self-styled "enlightened despot" successors. Many Slavophiles were ardent monarchists. Their desire for a strong yet "traditional" Russia brought them into conflict with the conservative, but modernizing, tsarist state.

The liberals, in contrast, wanted their states to carry through the legal and political reforms envisioned in 1789—but not to attempt economic leveling in the manner of the radical Jacobins (see Chapter 15). Liberals were eager to curb the states' restrictions on trade, destroy the churches' stranglehold on education, and give more people the right to vote—all the while preserving the free market, the Christian churches, and the rule of law. Proponents of **liberalism** insisted on the individual's right to think, speak, act, and vote as he or she pleased, so long as no harm came to people or property. Liberals feared the corruptibility of powerful states and held that the proper role of government was to foster civil liberties and promote legal equality.

In sum, the reactionaries wanted a return to the traditionally ordered societies that existed prior to the French Revolution; the liberals wanted reforms that would limit the power of government and the church and promote the rights of individuals and free trade. Both could find elements to their taste in all the nations of the post-Napoleonic world. Indeed, it was the rivalry between these two groups that defined much of the political landscape of the era before 1848.

RADICAL VISIONS

Reactionaries and liberals did not form the only alternative groups of importance at this time. Most discontented of all—and most determined to effect grand-scale change—were the radicals. The term *radicals* refers to those who favored the total reconfiguration of the old regime's state system: going to the root of the problem and continuing the revolution, not reversing it or stopping reform. In general, radicals shared a bitter hatred for the status quo and an insistence on popular sovereignty, but beyond this consensus there was much dissension in their ranks. If some radicals demanded the equalization or abolition of private property, others (like Serbian, Greek, Polish, and Italian nationalists) were primarily interested in throwing off the oppressive overlordship of the Ottoman and Austrian empires and creating their own nation-states. It was the radicals' threat of a return to revolutions that ultimately reconciled both liberals and reactionaries to preserving the status quo.

NATIONALISTS   In the period before 1848, nationalism was a cause dear to liberals and radicals, and threatening to the conservative balance of power introduced into Europe at the Congress of Vienna in 1815. Now the idea of popular sovereignty spread, but who exactly were "the people"? In many cases, the people were imagined as the nation—those who shared a common language and what was thought to be a common history, and who therefore deserved their own state.

Each fledgling nationalist movement—whether Polish, Czech, Greek, Italian, or German—had different contours, but they all drew backers from the liberal aristocracy and the well-educated and commercially active middle classes. University students were especially active in these movements. Most nationalist movements were, at first, weak and easily crushed, such as attempted Polish uprisings inside tsarist Russia in 1830–1831 and 1863–1864. The movements' leaders instead pursued educational and cultural programs to arouse and unite their nation for eventual statehood. By contrast, the Greeks, inspired by religious revivalism and enlightened ideas, managed to wrest independence from the Ottoman Turks after a years-long series of skirmishes.

Invoking both the classical tradition and their membership in the community of Christians, Greek patriots won support among Europeans in their fight against the Muslim Ottoman Empire. However, most of this support had to come in the form of private donations or volunteer soldiers, for European rulers feared that any sympathy they might show for the oppressed Greeks would fan the flames of revolution or separatism at home. Still, the Europeans sent their ships to the Mediterranean and defeated the Ottomans at Navarino in 1827. The Ottomans finally recognized Greek independence in 1829.

In the new state, the Greeks could not resolve differences between those who wanted a small, essentially secular republic and those who wanted to reclaim Istanbul (Constantinople) for Greek Orthodoxy. So they ended up inviting Otto, a Bavarian prince, to be king of Greece. The new Greek state had won its independence from the Ottomans, but it was neither the resurrected Athens nor the revived Byzantium that the revolutionaries had envisioned.

Other nationalist movements were suppressed or at least slowed down with little bloodshed. In places like the German principalities, the Italian states, and the Hungarian parts of the Habsburg Empire, secret societies of young men—students and intellectuals—gathered to plan bright, republican futures. Regrettably for these patriots, however, organizations like Young Italy, founded in 1832 to promote national unification and renewal, had little popular or foreign support. Censorship and a few strategic executions suppressed them. Yet many of these movements would ultimately succeed in the century's second half, when conservatives and liberals alike in western Europe employed nationalist fervor to advance their own great power ambitions. However, in central Europe, nationalism pitted many claimants for the same territories against one another, like the Czechs, Serbs, Slovaks, Poles, and Ruthenians (Ukrainians). They did not understand why they could not have a nation-state too.

SOCIALISTS AND COMMUNISTS   Much more threatening to the ruling elite were the radicals who believed that the

The Phalanx. The Phalanx, as one of Fourier's German followers envisioned it. In this rendering, the idealized home for the residents of the cooperative social system is represented as a building architecturally similar to the home of the French kings, the Louvre.

French Revolution had not gone far enough. They longed for a grander revolution that would sweep away the Restoration's political *and* economic order. Early socialists and communists (the terms were more or less interchangeable at the time) insisted that political reforms offered no effective answer to the more pressing "social question": what was to be done about the inequalities that industrial capitalism was introducing? The socialists worried in particular about two things. One was the growing gap between impoverished workers and newly wealthy employers. The other concern was that the division of labor—that is, the dividing up and simplifying of tasks so that each worker performs most efficiently—might make people into soulless, brainless machines. The socialists believed that the whole free market economy, not just the state, had to be transformed to save the human race from self-destruction. Liberty and equality, they insisted, could not be separated; aristocratic privilege along with capitalism belonged on history's ash heap.

No more than a handful of radical prophets hatched revolutionary plans in the years after 1815, but they were not the only participants in strikes, riots, peasant uprisings, and protest meetings. Indeed, ordinary workers, artisans, domestic servants, and women employed in textile manufacturing all joined in attempts to answer the "social question" to their satisfaction. A few socialists and feminists campaigned for social and political equality of the sexes. In Britain in 1819, Manchester workers at St. Peter's Field demonstrated peacefully for increased representation in Parliament, but panicking guardsmen fired on the crowd, leaving 11 dead and 460 injured in an incident later dubbed the Peterloo Massacre. In 1839 and 1842, nearly half the adult population of Britain signed the People's Charter, which called for universal suffrage for all adult males, the secret ballot, equal electoral districts, and annual parliamentary elections. This mass movement, known as **Chartism**, like most such endeavors, ended in defeat. Parliament rejected the charter in 1839, 1842, and 1848.

FOURIER AND UTOPIAN SOCIALISM Despite their many defeats, the radicals kept trying. Some sense of this age of revolutionary aspirations reveals itself in one European visionary who had big grievances and even bigger plans: Charles Fourier (1772–1837). Fourier's **utopian socialism** was perhaps the most visionary and influential of all Restoration-era alternative movements. He introduced planning, whereas the revolutionaries invoked violence, and he generally rejected the equalizing of conditions, fearing the suppression of diversity. Still, he and like-minded socialists dreamed of transforming states, workplaces, and human relations in a much more thorough way than their religious or political predecessors.

Fired by the egalitarian hopes and the cataclysmic failings of the French Revolution, Fourier believed himself to be the scientific prophet of the new world to come. He was a highly imaginative, self-taught man who earned his keep in the cloth trade, an occupation that gave him an intense hatred for merchants and middlemen. Convinced that the division of labor and repressive moral conventions were destroying mankind's natural talents and passions, Fourier concluded that a revolution grander than that of 1789 was needed. But this utopian transformation of economic, social, and political conditions, he thought, could occur through organization, not through bloodshed. Indeed, by 1808 Fourier believed that the thoroughly corrupt world was on the brink of giving way to a new and harmonious age, of which he was the oracle.

First formulated in 1808, his "system" envisioned the reorganization of human communities into what he called phalanxes. In these harmonious collectives of 1,500 to 1,600 people and 810 personality types, diversity would be preserved, but efficiency maintained; best of all, work would become enjoyable. All members of the phalanx, rich and poor, would work, though not necessarily at the same tasks. All would work in short spurts of no more than two hours, so as to make labor more interesting and sleep, idleness, and overindulgence less attractive. A typical rich man's day would begin at 3:30 A.M. for eating breakfast, reviewing the previous day, and participating in an industrial parade. At 5:30 he would hunt; at 7:00 he would turn to fishing. At 8:00 he would have lunch and read the newspapers (though what news there might be in this world is hard to fathom). At 9:00 he would meet with horticulturists, and at 10:00 he would go to mass. At 10:30 he would meet with a pheasant breeder; later he would tend exotic plants, herd sheep, and attend a concert. Each man would cultivate what he wanted to eat and learn about what he wanted to know. As for unpleasant tasks, they would become less so because they would now occur in more comfortable settings, such as warmed barns and spotless factories. Truly undesirable jobs, like sweeping out stables or cleaning latrines, would fall to young adolescents, who, Fourier argued, actually liked mucking about in filth.

Fourier's phalanxes by no means constituted an Eden in which humankind lived without knowing what it was like to sweat; rather, it was a workers' paradise in which comforts and rewards made working enjoyable. However, this system of production and distribution would run without merchants. Fourier intentionally excluded middlemen like himself from his plan for paradise. He believed that they corrupted civilization and introduced unnaturalness into the division of labor.

Fourier's writings gained popularity in the 1830s, appealing to radicals who supported a variety of causes. In France, women were particularly active in spreading his ideas. Longing for social and moral reforms that would address problems such as prostitution, poverty, illegitimacy, and the exploitation of workers (including women and children), some women saw in **Fourierism** a higher form of Christian communalism. By reshaping the phalanx to accommodate monogamous families and Christian values, women helped to make his work more respectable to middle-class readers. In Russia, Fourier's works fired the imaginations of the young writer Fyodor Dostoevsky. He and fourteen others in the radical circle to which he belonged were sentenced to death for their views (though their executions were called off at the last minute). In 1835–1836, both the young Italian nationalist Giuseppe Mazzini and the Spanish republican Joaquin Abreu published important articles on Fourier's thought. Karl Marx read Fourier with great care, and there are many remnants of utopian thought in his work. In *The German Ideology* Marx describes life in an ideal communist society; in a postrevolutionary world, he predicts that "nobody has one exclusive sphere of activity but each can become accomplished in any branch he wishes, society regulates the general production and thus makes it possible for me to do one thing today and another tomorrow, to hunt in the morning, fish in the afternoon, rear cattle in the evening, [and] criticize after dinner."

Karl Marx. The author (with Friedrich Engels) of *The Communist Manifesto*, Karl Marx argued that the exploitation of wage laborers would trigger a proletarian revolution and would lead to socialism supplanting capitalism.

MARXISM Karl Marx proved to be the most important Restoration-era radical. University educated and philosophically radical, Marx (1818–1883) took up a career in journalism. Required to cover legislative debates over property rights and taxation, he was forced to deal with economics. His understanding of *capitalism*, a term he was instrumental in popularizing, deepened through his collaboration with Friedrich Engels (1820–1895). Engels was a German-born radical who, after observing conditions in the factories owned by his wealthy father in Manchester, England, published a hair-raising indictment of industrial wage-labor entitled *The Condition of the Working Class in England*.

Together, Marx and Engels developed what they called "scientific socialism," which they contrasted with the "utopian socialism" of others like Fourier. Scientific socialism was rooted, they argued, in a materialist theory of history: what mattered in history were the production of material goods and the ways in which society was organized into classes of producers and exploiters. History, they claimed, consisted of successive forms of exploitative production and rebellions against them. Capitalist exploitation of the wage worker was only the latest, and worst, version of class conflict, Marx and Engels contended. In industrialized societies, capitalists owned the means of production (the factories and machinery) and exploited the wage workers. Marx and Engels were confident that the clashes between industrial wage workers—or **proletarians**—and capitalists would end in a colossal transformation of human society and would usher in a new world of true liberty, equality, and fraternity. These beliefs constituted the fundamentals of **Marxism.** For Marx and Engels, history moved through stages: feudalism to capitalism, to socialism, and eventually to communism.

From these fundamentals, Marx and Engels issued a comprehensive critique of post-1815 Europe. They identified a whole class of the exploited—the working class. They believed

Primary Source

"BOURGEOISIE AND PROLETARIAT": FROM *THE COMMUNIST MANIFESTO*

In January 1848, Karl Marx and Friedrich Engels prepared a party program for the Communist League, a German workingman's association. Published in French as The Communist Manifesto, *the document foretold the inevitable overthrow of bourgeois-dominated capitalism by the working classes and the transition to socialism and ultimately to communism. The following excerpt demonstrates their certainty that history, driven by economic factors and class conflict, was moving unavoidably toward the revolution of the proletariat. Marx and Engels defined the bourgeoisie as capitalists, owners of the means of production and employers of wage laborers. They defined the proletariat as wage laborers who had to sell their labor to live.*

A spectre is haunting Europe—the spectre of Communism. . . .

The history of all hitherto existing society is the history of class struggles. . . .

The modern bourgeois society that has sprouted from the ruins of feudal society has not done away with class antagonisms. It has but established new classes, new conditions of oppression, new forms of struggle in place of the old ones.

Our epoch, the epoch of the bourgeoisie, possesses, however, this distinctive feature: it has simplified the class antagonisms: Society as a whole is more and more splitting up into two great hostile camps, into two great classes directly facing each other: Bourgeoisie and Proletariat. . . .

The bourgeoisie . . . has put an end to all feudal, patriarchal, idyllic relations. It has pitilessly torn asunder the motley feudal ties that bound man to his "natural superiors," and has left remaining no other nexus between man and man than naked self-interest, than callous "cash payment." . . .

The need of a constantly expanding market for its products chases the bourgeoisie over the whole surface of the globe. It must nestle everywhere, settle everywhere, establish connexions everywhere. . . .

The bourgeoisie, by the rapid improvement of all instruments of production, by the immensely facilitated means of communication, draws all, even the most barbarian, nations into civilisation. The cheap prices of its commodities are the heavy artillery with which it batters down all Chinese walls, with which it forces the barbarians' intensely obstinate hatred of foreigners to capitulate. . . .

The weapons with which the bourgeoisie felled feudalism to the ground are now turned against the bourgeoisie itself.

But not only has the bourgeoisie forged the weapons that bring death to itself; it has also called into existence the men who are to wield those weapons—the modern working class—the proletarians. . . . These labourers, who must sell themselves piece-meal, are a commodity, like every other article of commerce, and are consequently exposed to all the vicissitudes of competition, to all the fluctuations of the market. . . .

But with the development of industry the proletariat not only increases in number; it becomes concentrated in greater masses, its strength grows, and it feels that strength more. . . . Thereupon the workers begin to form combinations (Trades Unions) against the bourgeois; they club together in order to keep up the rate of wages; they found permanent associations in order to make provision beforehand for these occasional revolts. Here and there the contest breaks out into riots.

Now and then the workers are victorious, but only for a time. The real fruit of their battles lies, not in the immediate result, but in the ever-expanding union of the workers. . . .

. . . What the bourgeoisie, therefore, produces, above all, is its own grave-diggers. Its fall and the victory of the proletariat are equally inevitable.

→ *According to Marx and Engels, how does the bourgeoisie draw "all, even the most barbarian, nations into civilization"?*

→ *How does the bourgeoisie contribute to its own downfall?*

→ *Is the new social system supposed to arise automatically, or is human action required to bring it about?*

SOURCE: Karl Marx and Friedrich Engels, *The Communist Manifesto*, in *The Marx-Engels Reader*, 2nd ed., edited by Robert C. Tucker (New York: Norton, 1978), pp. 473–83, 490–91, 500.

that more and more people would fall into this class as industrialization proceeded and that the masses would not share in the rising prosperity that capitalists monopolized. Marx and Engels predicted that there would be overproduction and underconsumption, which would lead to lower profits for capitalists and, consequently, to lower wages or unemployment for workers—which would ultimately spark a proletarian revolution. This revolution would result in a "dictatorship of the proletariat" and the end of private property. With the destruction of capitalism, the men claimed, exploitation would cease and the state would wither away.

In 1848, revolutionary fervor ignited uprisings in France, Austria, Russia, Italy, Hungary, and the German states. After hearing that revolution had broken out in France, Marx and Engels published *The Communist Manifesto,* calling on the workers of all nations to unite in overthrowing capitalism. (See Primary Source: "Bourgeoisie and Proletariat": From *The Communist Manifesto.*) But the men were sorely disappointed (not to mention exiled) by the reactionary crackdowns that followed the 1848 revolutions. After 1850, Marx and Engels took up permanent residence in England, where they tried to organize an international workers' movement. In the doldrums of midcentury they turned to science, but they never abandoned the dream of total social reconfiguration. Nor would their many admirers and heirs. The failure of the 1848 revolutions did not doom prophecy itself or diminish commitment to alternative social landscapes.

INSURGENCIES AGAINST COLONIZING AND CENTRALIZING STATES

> → *How were alternative movements in the Americas and India similar and different?*

Outside Europe, for Native Americans and for Britain's colonial subjects in India, the greatest threat to traditional worlds was the colonizing process itself, not industrial capitalism and centralizing states. While European radicals looked back to revolutionary legacies in imagining a transformed society, Native American insurgents and rebels in British India drew on their traditional cultural and political resources to imagine local alternatives to foreign impositions. Like the peoples of China, Africa, and the Middle East, native groups in the Americas and India met the period's challenges with prophecy, charismatic leadership, and rebellion. Everywhere the insurgents spoke in languages of the past, but the new worlds they envisioned bore unmistakable marks of the present as well.

ALTERNATIVE TO THE EXPANDING UNITED STATES: NATIVE AMERICAN PROPHETS

Like other native peoples threatened by imperial expansion, the Indians of North America's Ohio Valley dreamed of a world in which intrusive colonizers disappeared. Taking such dreams as prophecies, in 1805 many Indians flocked to hear the revelations of a Shawnee Indian named Tenskwatawa. Facing a dark present and a darker future, they enthusiastically embraced the Shawnee Prophet's visions, which (like that of the Paiute prophet Wovoka nearly a century later) foretold how invaders would vanish if Indians returned to their customary ways and traditional rites.

EARLY CALLS FOR RESISTANCE AND A RETURN TO TRADITION Tenskwatawa's visions—and the anticolonial uprising they inspired—drew on a long tradition of visionary leaders. From the first encounters with Europeans, Indian seers had periodically encouraged native peoples to purge their worlds of colonial influences and to revitalize indigenous traditions. Often these prophets had aroused their followers not only to engage in cleansing ceremonies but also to cooperate in violent, anticolonial uprisings. In 1680, for example, previously divided Pueblo villagers in New Mexico had united behind the prophet Popé to chase Spanish missionaries, soldiers, and settlers out of that colony. After their victory, Popé's followers destroyed all things European: they torched wheat fields and fruit orchards, slaughtered livestock, and ransacked Catholic churches. For a dozen years the Indians of New Mexico reclaimed control over their lands, but soon divisions within native ranks prepared the way for Spanish reconquest in 1692.

Seventy years later and half a landmass away, the preachings of the Delaware shaman Neolin encouraged Indians of the Ohio Valley and Great Lakes to take up arms against the British, leading to the capture of several British military posts. Although the British put down the uprising, imperial officials learned a lesson from the conflict: they assumed a less arrogant posture toward Ohio Valley and Great Lakes Indians, and to preserve peace they forbade colonists from trespassing on lands west of the Appalachian Mountains. The British, however, were incapable of restraining the flow of settlers across the mountains, and the problem became much worse for the Indians once the American Revolution ended. With the Ohio Valley transferred to the new United States, American settlers crossed the Appalachians and flooded into Kentucky and Tennessee.

Despite the settlers' considerable migration, much of the territory between the Appalachian Mountains and the Mississippi River, which Americans referred to as the "western country," remained an Indian country. North and south of Kentucky and Tennessee, Indian warriors more than held their own against American forces. As in previous anticolonial campaigns, the visions of various prophets bolstered the

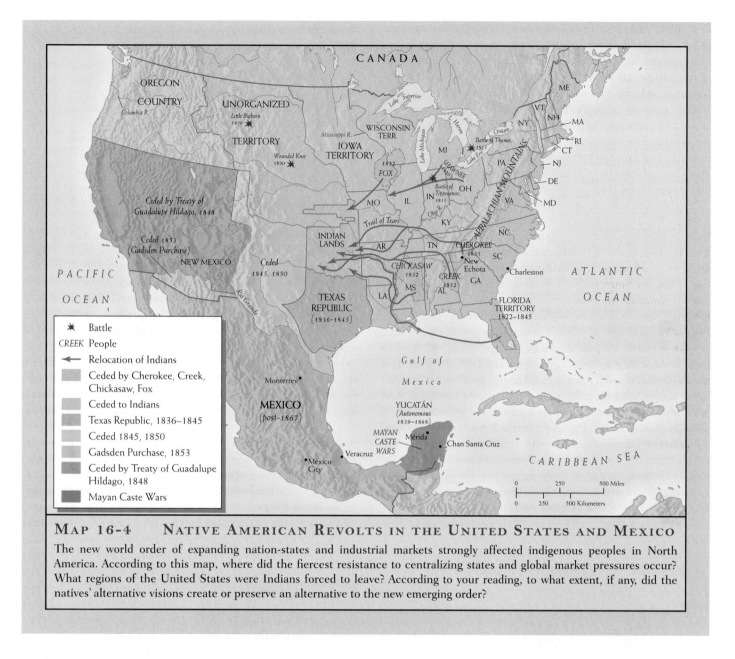

MAP 16-4   NATIVE AMERICAN REVOLTS IN THE UNITED STATES AND MEXICO
The new world order of expanding nation-states and industrial markets strongly affected indigenous peoples in North America. According to this map, where did the fiercest resistance to centralizing states and global market pressures occur? What regions of the United States were Indians forced to leave? According to your reading, to what extent, if any, did the natives' alternative visions create or preserve an alternative to the new emerging order?

confidence and unity of Indian warriors, who twice joined together to rout invading American armies. But their confederation failed in a third encounter, in 1794, and their leaders had to surrender lands in what is now the state of Ohio to the United States (see Map 16-4).

TENSKWATAWA: THE SHAWNEE PROPHET The Shawnees, who lost most of their holdings, were among the most bitter—and bitterly divided—of Indian peoples living in the Ohio Valley. Some Shawnee leaders concluded that their people's survival now required that they cooperate with American officials and Christian missionaries. This strategy, they realized, entailed wrenching changes in Shawnee culture. European reformers, after all, insisted that Indian men give

up hunting and take up farming, an occupation that the Shawnees and their neighbors had always considered "women's work." Moreover, the Shawnees were pushed to abandon communal traditions in favor of private property rights. Of course, missionaries prodded Indians to quit their "heathen" beliefs and practices and become faithful, "civilized" Christians. For many Shawnees, these demands went too far; worse, they promised no immediate relief from the dispossession and impoverishment that now marked the natives' daily lives. Young men especially grew angry and frustrated.

Among the demoralized was **Tenskwatawa** (1775–1836), whose story of overcoming personal failures through religious visions and embracing a strict moral code has uncanny parallels with that of Hong Xiuquan, the Taiping leader. In his first thirty years, Tenskwatawa could claim few accomplishments. He had failed as a hunter and as a medicine man, had blinded himself in one eye, and had earned a reputation as an obnoxious braggart. All this changed in the spring of 1805, however, after he fell into a trance and experienced a vision, which he vividly recounted to one and all. In this dream, Tenskwatawa encountered a heaven where the virtuous enjoyed the traditional Shawnee way of life and a hell where evildoers suffered punishments. Additional revelations followed, and Tenskwatawa soon stitched these together into a new social gospel that urged disciples to abstain from alcohol and return to traditional customs.

Like other prophets, Tenskwatawa exhorted Indians to reduce their dependence on European trade goods and to sever their connections to Christian missionaries. Thus he urged his audiences to replace imported cloth and metal tools with animal skins and implements fashioned from wood, stone, and bone. Livestock, too, was to be banished, as Indian men again gathered meat by hunting wild animals with bows and arrows, instead of guns and powder. If Indians obeyed these dictates, Tenskwatawa promised, the deer, which "were half a tree's length under the ground," would come back in abundant numbers to the earth's surface. Likewise, he claimed, Indians killed in conflict with colonial intruders would be resurrected, while evil Americans would depart from the country west of the Appalachians. (See Primary Source: Tenskwatawa's Vision.)

Like the Qing's response to Hong's visions, American officials initially dismissed Tenskwatawa as deluded but harmless; their concerns grew, however, as the Shawnee Prophet gathered more followers. These converts came not only from among the Shawnees but also from Delaware, Ottawa, Wyandot, Kickapoo, and Seneca villages. The spread of Tenskwatawa's message raised anew the specter of a pan-Indian confederacy. Hoping to undermine the Shawnee Prophet's claims to supernatural power, territorial governor William Henry Harrison challenged Tenskwatawa to make the sun stand still. But Tenskwatawa one-upped Harrison. Having learned of an impending eclipse from white astronomers, Tenskwatawa assembled his followers on June 16, 1806. Right on schedule, and as if on command, the sky darkened. Claiming credit for the eclipse, Tenskwatawa saw his standing soar, as did the ranks of his disciples. Now aware of the growing threat, American officials tried to bribe Tenskwatawa, hoping that cash payments might dim his vision and quiet his voice. Failing that, they wondered if one of the prophet's Indian adversaries might be encouraged to assassinate him.

In fact, Tenskwatawa had made plenty of enemies among his fellow Indians. His visions, after all, consigned drinkers to hell (where they would be forced to swallow molten metal) and singled out those who cooperated with colonial authorities for punishment in this world and the next. Indeed, Tenskwatawa condemned as witches those Indians who rejected his preaching in favor of the teachings of Christian missionaries and American authorities. (To be sure, Tenskwatawa's damnation of Christianized Indians was somewhat paradoxical, for missionary doctrines obviously influenced his vision of a burning hell for sinners and his crusade against alcohol.)

TECUMSEH AND THE WISH FOR INDIAN UNITY Although Tenskwatawa's accusations alienated some Indians, his prophecies gave heart to many more. This was particularly the case once his brother, **Tecumseh** (1768–1813), helped circulate the message of Indian renaissance among Indian villages from the Great Lakes to the Gulf Coast. On his journeys

Visions of American Indian Unification. (*Left*) A portrait of Tenskwatawa, the "Shawnee Prophet," whose visions stirred thousands of Indians in the Ohio Valley and Great Lakes to renounce dependence on colonial imports and resist the expansion of the United States. (*Right*) A portrait of his brother, Tecumseh, who succeeded in building a significant pan-Indian confederation, although it unraveled following his death at the Battle of Thames in 1813 and the end of warfare between the United States and Britain the following year.

TENSKWATAWA'S VISION

In the first decade of the nineteenth century, the Shawnee Indian leader Tenskwatawa recalled an earlier, happier time for the Indian peoples of the Great Lakes and Ohio Valley. It was a time before the coming of the Europeans. In this oration, Tenskwatawa recounts how contact with the "white men's goods" contaminated and corrupted the Indians. He urges them to spurn the ways of white Americans and return to the pure ways of a precolonial past.

Our Creator put us on this wide, rich land, and told us we were free to go where the game was, where the soil was good for planting. That was our state of true happiness. We did not have to beg for anything. Our Creator had taught us how to find and make everything we needed, from trees and plants and animals and stone. We lived in bark, and we wore only the skins of animals.

Thus were we created. Thus we lived for a long time, proud and happy. We had never eaten pig meat, nor tasted the poison called whiskey, nor worn wool from sheep, nor struck fire or dug earth with steel, nor cooked in iron, nor hunted and fought with loud guns, nor ever had diseases which soured our blood or rotted our organs. We were pure, so we were strong and happy.

For many years we traded furs to the English or the French, for wool blankets and guns and iron things, for steel awls and needles and axes, for mirrors, for pretty things made of beads and silver. And for liquor. This was foolish, but we did not know it. We shut our ears to the Great Good Spirit. We did not want to hear that we were being foolish.

But now those things of the white men have corrupted us, and made us weak and needful. Our men forgot how to hunt without noisy guns. Our women don't want to make fire without steel, or cook without iron, or sew without metal awls and needles, or fish without steel hooks. Some look in those mirrors all the time, and no longer teach their daughters to make leather or render bear oil. We learned to need the white men's goods, and so now a People who never had to beg for anything must beg for everything! . . .

And that is why Our Creator purified me and sent me down to you full of the shining power, to make you what you were before!

No red man must ever drink liquor, or he will go and have the hot lead poured in his mouth! . . .

Do not eat any food that is raised or cooked by a white person. It is not good for us. Eat not their bread made of wheat, for Our Creator gave us corn for our bread. . . .

The Great Good Spirit wants our men to hunt and kill game as in the ancient days, with the silent arrow and the lance and the snare, and no longer with guns.

If we hunt in the old ways, we will not have to depend upon white men, for new guns and powder and lead, or go to them to have broken guns repaired. Remember it is the wish of the Great Good Spirit that we have no more commerce with white men! . . .

. . . Our Creator told me that all red men who refuse to obey these laws are bad people, or witches, and must be put to death. . . .

The Great Good Spirit will appoint a place to be our holy town, and at that place I will call all red men to come and share this shining power. For the People in all tribes are corrupt and miserable! In that holy town we will pray every morning and every night for the earth to be fruitful, and the game and fish to be plentiful again.

→ *Tenskwatawa mentions many commodities and habits that the Indians had been adopting from white men. Identify at least ten.*

→ *According to Tenskwatawa, how has this dependency reduced a proud people to begging?*

→ *What rules did "Our Creator" give Tenskwatawa to help him make his people "what you were before"?*

SOURCE: Words of Tenskwatawa, in *Messages and Letters of William Henry Harrison*, edited by Logan Esarey (Indianapolis: Indiana Historical Commission, 1922). Retrieved from http://history.missouristate.edu/FTMiller/EarlyRepublic/tecandtensk.htm

after 1805, Tecumseh did more than spread his brother's visions; he also wed them to the idea of a renewed and enlarged Indian confederation. Moving around the Great Lakes and traveling across the southern half of the western country, Tecumseh preached the need for Indian unity. Always, he insisted that Indians resist any American attempts to get them to sell more land. In response, thousands of followers renounced their ties to colonial ways and prepared to combat the expansion of the United States.

By 1810, Tecumseh had emerged, at least in the eyes of American officials, as even more dangerous than his brother. Impressed by Tecumseh's charismatic organizational talents, William Harrison warned that this new "Indian menace" was forming "an Empire that would rival in glory" that of the Aztecs and the Incas. In 1811, while Tecumseh was traveling among southern tribes, Harrison had his troops attack Tenskwatawa's village, Prophet's Town, on the Tippecanoe River in what is now the state of Indiana. The resulting battle was evenly fought, but the Indians eventually gave ground and American forces burned Prophet's Town. That defeat discredited Tenskwatawa, who had promised his followers protection from destruction at American hands. Spurned by his former disciples, including his brother, Tenskwatawa fled to Canada.

Tecumseh soldiered on. Although he mistrusted the British, he recognized that only a British victory over the Americans in the War of 1812 could check further American expansion. So he aligned himself with the British. Commissioned as a brigadier general in the British army, Tecumseh recruited many Indians to the British cause, though his real aim remained the building of a pan-Indian union. But in 1813, with the war's outcome in doubt and the pan-Indian confederacy still fragile, Tecumseh perished at the Battle of the Thames north of Lake Erie.

INDIAN REMOVALS The discrediting of Tenskwatawa and the death of Tecumseh damaged the cause of Indian unity; then British betrayal dealt it a fatal blow. Following the war's end in 1814, the British withdrew their support and left the Indians south of the Great Lakes to fend for themselves against land-hungry American settlers and the armies of the United States. By 1815, American citizens outnumbered Indians in the western country by a seven-to-one margin, and this gap dramatically widened in the next few years. Recognizing the hopelessness of military resistance, Indians south of the Great Lakes resigned themselves to relocation. During the 1820s, most of the peoples north of the Ohio River were removed to lands west of the Mississippi River. During the 1830s, the southern tribes were cleared out, completing what amounted to an ethnic cleansing of Indian peoples from the region between the Appalachians and the Mississippi.

In the midst of these final removals, Tenskwatawa died, though his dream of an alternative to American expansion had faded for his people years earlier. Through the rest of the nineteenth century, however, other Indian prophets emerged, and their visions continued to inspire followers with the hope of an alternative to life under the colonial rule of the United States. But like Wovoka and the Ghost Dancers in 1890, these dreams failed to halt the expansion of the United States and the contraction of Indian lands.

ALTERNATIVE TO THE CENTRAL STATE: THE CASTE WAR OF THE YUCATAN

As in North America, the Spanish establishment of an expansionist nation-state in Mexico sparked widespread revolts by indigenous peoples. The most protracted was the Mayan revolt in the Yucatan. The revolt started in 1847, and its flames were not finally doused until the full occupation of the Yucatan by Mexican national troops in 1901.

EARLY MAYAN AUTONOMY The strength and endurance of the Mayan revolt stemmed in large measure from the unusual features of the Spanish conquest in southern Mesoamerica. Because this area was not a repository of precious metals or fertile lands, Spain and its rivals focused elsewhere—on central and northern Mexico and the Caribbean islands. As a result, the Mayan Indians escaped forced recruitment for silver mines or sugar plantations. This does not mean, however, that global processes sidestepped the Mayan Indians. In fact, the production of dyes and foodstuffs for shipment to other regions drew the Yucatan into long-distance trading networks. Nonetheless, cultivation and commerce were much less disruptive to indigenous lives in the Yucatan than elsewhere in the New World.

The dismantling of the Spanish Empire early in the nineteenth century gave way to almost a century of political turmoil in Latin America. In the Yucatan, civil strife brought the region autonomy by default, allowing Mayan ways to survive without much upheaval. Their villages still constituted the chief political domain, ruled by elders; ownership of their land was collective, the property of families and not individuals. Corn, a mere staple to white consumers, continued to enjoy sacred status in Mayan culture.

GROWING PRESSURES FROM THE SUGAR TRADE Local developments, however, encroached on the Mayan world. First, regional elites—mainly white, but often with the support of mestizo populations—bickered for supremacy so long as the central authority of Mexico City remained weak. Weaponry flowed freely through the peninsula, and some belligerents even appealed for Mayan support. At the same time, regional and international trade spurred the spread of sugar estates, which threatened traditional corn cultivation. Over the decades, plantations encroached on Mayan properties. Planters used several devices to lure independent Mayans to work, especially in the harvest. The most important device, debt peonage, involved giving small cash advances to Indian families, which obligated fathers and sons to work for meager wages to pay off the debts. In addition, Mexico's costly wars, culminating in a showdown with the United States in 1846, drove tax collectors and army recruiters into villages in search of revenues and soldiers.

The combination of spiritual, material, and physical threats was explosive. When a small band of Mayans, fed up with rising taxes and ebbing autonomy, used firearms to drive back white intruders in 1847, they sparked a war that took a half-century to complete. The rebels were primarily free Mayans who had not yet been absorbed into the sugar economy. They wanted to dismantle old definitions of Indians as a caste—a status that deprived the Indians of rights to defend their sovereignty on equal legal footing with whites and that also subjected the Indians to special taxes. Thus, local Mayan leaders, like Jacinto Pat and Cecilio Chi, upheld a republican model in the name of formal equality of all political subjects and devotion to a spiritual order that did not distinguish between Christians and non-Christians. "If the Indians revolt," one Mayan rebel explained, "it is because the whites gave them reason; because the whites say they do not believe in Jesus Christ, because they have burned the cornfield."

THE CASTE WAR Horrified, the local white elites reacted to the uprising with vicious repression and dubbed the ensuing conflict a **Caste War**. In their view, the bloody conflict was a struggle between forward-looking liberals and backward-looking Indians. At first, whites and mestizos were no match for the determined Mayans, whose forces seized town after town. They especially targeted the emblems of their subservience. With relish they demolished the whipping posts where Indians had endured public humiliation and punishment. By 1848, Indian armies controlled three-quarters of the peninsula and were poised to take the Yucatan's largest city, Mérida. Fear seized the embattled whites, who appealed for U.S. and British help, offering the peninsula for foreign annexation in return for military rescue from the Mayans.

In the end, fortune, not political savvy, saved the Yucatan's whites. The Mayan farmers, who had taken up arms to defend their world, went back to being farmers because the planting season called. When rain clouds appeared, they saw that "the time has come for us to make our planting, for if we do not we shall have no Grace of God to fill the bellies of our children." But by putting down their weapons and returning to their fields, Mayan farmers became vulnerable to reconquest by Mexican armies. Furthermore, they were unaware of international changes that had an impact on their situation: settlement of the war with the United States in 1848 enabled Mexico City to rescue local elites. With the help of a $15 million payment from Washington for giving up its northern provinces, Mexico could spend freely to build up its southern armies. The Mexican government soon fielded a force of 17,000 soldiers and waged a scorched earth campaign to drive back the depleted Mayan forces.

By 1849, the confrontation had entered a new phase in which Mexican troops engaged in mass repression of the Mayans. Mexican armies set Indian fields and villages ablaze. Slaughtering Indians became a blood sport of barbaric proportion. Between 30 and 40 percent of the Mayan population perished in the war and its repressive aftermath. The white governor even sold captured Indians into slavery to Cuban sugar planters. Indeed, the white formulation of the caste nature of the war eventually became a self-fulfilling prophecy. Entire Mayan cities pulled up stakes and withdrew to isolated districts protected by fortified villages. War between armies degenerated into guerrilla warfare between an occupying Mexican army and mobile bands of Mayan squadrons, inflicting a gruesome toll on the invaders. As years passed, the war ground to a stalemate, especially once the U.S. funds ran out and Mexican soldiers began deserting in droves.

RECLAIMING A MAYAN IDENTITY Warfare prompted a spiritual transformation that reinforced a purely Mayan identity against the invaders' "national" project. Thus, a struggle that began with demands for legal equality and relative cultural autonomy became a crusade for spiritual salvation and the complete cultural separation of the Mayan Indians. A particularly influential group under José María Barrera retreated to a hamlet called Chan Santa Cruz. There, at the site where he found a cross shape carved into a mahogany tree, Barrera had a vision of a divine encounter. Thereafter a swath of Yucatan villages refashioned themselves as moral communities orbiting around Chan Santa Cruz. Leaders created a polity, with soldiers, priests, and tax collectors pledging loyalty to the Speaking Cross. As with the followers of Hong in China's Taiping Rebellion, Indian rebels forged an alternative religion: it blended Christian rituals, faiths, and icons with Mayan legends and beliefs. At the center was a stone temple, Balam Na ("House of God"), 100 feet long and 60 feet wide. Through pious pilgrimages to Balam Na and the secular justice of Indian judges, the Mayans soon governed their autonomous domain in the Yucatan, almost completely cut off from the rest of Mexico.

This alternative to Latin American state formation, however, faced formidable hurdles. For example, disease ravaged the people of the Speaking Cross. Once counting 40,000 inhabitants, the villages dwindled to 10,000 by 1900. Also a new crop, henequen, used to bind bales for North American farms and to stuff the seats of automobiles, began to spread across the Yucatan. In place of the peninsula's mixed agrarian societies, it now became a desiccated region producing a single crop, driving the people to seek refuge farther into the interior. As profits from henequen production rose, white landowners began turning the Yucatan into a giant plantation. But Mayan villagers refused to give up their autonomy and rejected labor recruiters.

Finally, the Mexican oligarchy, having resolved its internal disputes, threw its weight behind the strong-arm ruler General Porfirio Díaz (r. 1876–1911). The general sent one of his veteran commanders, Ignacio Bravo, to do what no other Mexican could accomplish: vanquish Chan Santa Cruz and drive Mayans into the henequen cash economy. When

General Bravo finally entered the town, he found the once-imposing temple Balam Na covered in vegetation. Nature was reclaiming the territories of the Speaking Cross. Hunger and arms finally drove the Mayans to work on white Mexican plantations; the alternative vision was vanquished.

THE REBELLION OF 1857 IN INDIA

Like Native Americans, the peoples of nineteenth-century India had a long history of opposition to colonial domination. Armed revolts had occurred since the onset of rule by the English East India Company (see Chapter 15). Nonetheless, the uprising of 1857 was unprecedented in its scale, and it posed a greater threat than had any previous rebellion. Marx, with the hope for revolution dashed in Europe, cast his eyes on the revolt in British India, eagerly following the events and commenting on them in daily columns for the New York *Daily Tribune*. Though led primarily by the old nobility and petty landlords, it was a popular uprising with strong support from the lower orders of Indian society. The rebels appealed to bonds of local and communal solidarity, invoked religious sentiments, and reimagined traditional hierarchies in egalitarian terms. They did this to pose alternatives to British rule and the deepening involvement of India in a network of capitalist relationships.

INDIA UNDER COMPANY RULE When the revolt broke out in 1857, the East India Company's rule in India was a century old. During that time, the company had become an increasingly autocratic power whose reach encompassed the whole region. Mughal rule still existed in name, but the emperor lived in Delhi, all but forgotten and without any effective power. For a while, the existence of several princely states with which the British had entered into alliances prevented the British from exercising complete control over all of India. These princely domains enjoyed a measure of fiscal and judicial authority within the British Empire. They also contained landed aristocrats who held the right to shares in the produce and maintained their own militias.

Believing that the princely powers and landed aristocracies were out of date, the company instituted far-reaching changes in administration in the 1840s. These infuriated local peoples and laid the foundations for one of the world's most violent and concerted movements of protest against colonial authority. Lord Dalhousie, upon his appointment as governor-general in 1848, immediately began annexing what had been independent princely domains and stripping native aristocrats of their privileges. Swallowing one princely state after another, the British removed their former allies. The government also decided to collect taxes directly from peasants, displacing the landed nobles as intermediaries. In disarming the landed nobility, the British threw the retainers and militia of the notables into unemployment. Moreover, the company's new systems of land settlement eroded peasant rights and enhanced the power of moneylenders. Meanwhile, the company transferred judicial authority to an administration that was insulated from the Indian social hierarchy.

The most prized object for annexation was the kingdom of Awadh in northern India (see Map 16-5). Founded in 1722 by an Iranian adventurer, it was one of the first successor states to have gained a measure of independence from the Mughal ruler in Delhi. With access to the fertile resources of the Ganges Plain, its opulent court in Lucknow was one place where Mughal splendor still survived. In 1765, the company imposed a treaty on Awadh under which the ruler paid an annual tribute for British troops stationed in his territory to "protect" his kingdom from internal and external enemies. The British constantly ratcheted up their demands for tribute and abused their position to monopolize the lucrative trade in cotton, indigo, textiles, and other commodities. But the more successful they were in exploiting Awadh, the more they longed to annex it completely. Thus, Dalhousie declared in 1851 that Awadh was "a cherry which will drop into our mouths some day."

TREATY VIOLATIONS AND ANNEXATION In 1856, citing misgovernment and deterioration in law and order, the East India Company violated its treaty obligations and sent its troops to Lucknow to take control of the province. Nawab Wajid Ali Shah, the poet-king of Awadh, whom the British saw as effete and debauched, refused to sign the treaty of abdication. Instead, he came dressed in his mourning robes to meet with the British official charged to take over the province. After pleading unsuccessfully for his legal rights under the treaty, he handed over his turban to the official and then left for Calcutta to argue his case before Dalhousie. There was widespread distress at the treatment he received. Dirges were recited, and religious men rushed to Lucknow to denounce the annexation.

In fact, the annexation of princely domains and the abolition of feudal privileges formed part of the developing practices of European imperialism. To the policy of annexation, Dalhousie added an ambitious program of building railroads, telegraph lines, and a postal network to unify the disjointed territory into a single "network of iron sinew" under British control. Dalhousie saw these infrastructures as key to developing India into a productive colony—a supplier of raw materials for British industry, and a market for its manufactures.

A year after Dalhousie's departure in 1856, India went up in flames. The spark that ignited the simmering discontent into a furious rebellion—the **Rebellion of 1857**—was the "greased cartridge" controversy. At the end of 1856, the British army, which consisted of many Hindu and Muslim recruits (sepoys) commanded by British officers, introduced the new Enfield rifle to replace the old-style musket. To load the rifle, soldiers had to bite the cartridge open. Although manufacturing instructions stated that linseed oil and beeswax be used to grease the cartridge, a rumor circulated that cow and pig fat had been used. But biting into cartridges greased with animal fat meant violating the Hindu and Muslim sepoys' religious traditions. The sepoys became convinced that there was a plot afoot to defile them and to compel their conversion to Christianity. So a wave of rebellion spread among the 270,000 Indian soldiers, who greatly outnumbered the 40,000 British soldiers employed to rule over 200 million Indians.

REBELLION BREAKS OUT
The mutiny broke out on May 10, 1857, at the military barracks in Meerut. The previous day, the native soldiers had witnessed eighty-five of their comrades being manacled and shackled in irons and marched off to the prison for refusing to load their rifles. The next day, all three regiments at Meerut mutinied, killed their British officers, and marched thirty miles south to Delhi, where their comrades in regiments there welcomed them joyfully. Together, they "restored" the aging Bahadur Shah as the Mughal emperor, which lent legitimacy to the uprising.

The revolt soon turned from a limited military mutiny into a widespread civil rebellion that involved peasants, artisans, day laborers, and religious leaders. While the insurgents did not eliminate the power of the East India Company, which managed to retain the loyalty of princes and landed aristocrats in some places, they did throw the company into a crisis. Before long, the mutineers in Delhi issued a proclamation declaring that because the British were determined to destroy the religion of both Hindus and Muslims, it was the duty of the wealthy and the privileged to support the rebellion. (See Primary Source: The Azamgarh Proclamation.) To promote Hindu-Muslim unity, rebel leaders asked Muslims to refrain from killing cows in deference to Hindu sentiments.

MAP 16-5   INDIAN REBELLION OF 1857

The Indian Rebellion of 1857 broke out first among the Indian soldiers of the British army. Other groups soon joined the struggle. According to this map, how many centers of rebellion were located in British territory, and how many in dependent states? Can you speculate on why the rebellion occurred in the interior of the subcontinent rather than along the coasts? In what way was the company's expansion into formerly autonomous areas during the first half of the nineteenth century a factor in the rebellion?

Primary Source

THE AZAMGARH PROCLAMATION

The Indian leaders of the Rebellion of 1857 issued numerous proclamations. The Azamgarh Proclamation, excerpted below, is representative of these petitions. The emperor, Bahadur Shah, issued it in August 1857 on behalf of the mutineers who had seized the garrison town of Azamgarh, sixty miles north of Benares. Like other proclamations, it attacks the British for subverting Indian traditions and calls on its followers to restore the pre-British order—in this case, the Mughal Empire.

It is well known to all, that in this age the people of Hindoostan, both Hindoos and Mohammedans, are being ruined under the tyranny and oppression of the infidel and treacherous English. It is therefore the bounden duty of all the wealthy people of India, especially of those who have any sort of connection with any of the Mohammedan royal families, and are considered the pastors and masters of their people, to stake their lives and property for the well being of the public. . . .

Several of the Hindoo and Mussalman chiefs, who have long since quitted their homes for the preservation of their religion, and have been trying their best to root out the English in India, have presented themselves to me, and taken part in the reigning Indian crusade. . . . Parties anxious to participate in the common cause, but having no means to provide for themselves, shall receive their daily subsistence from me; and be it known to all, that the ancient works, both of the Hindoos and the Mohammedans, the writings of the miracle-workers and the calculations of the astrologers, pundits, and rammals, all agree in asserting that the English will no longer have any footing in India or elsewhere. . . .

Section I—Regarding Zemindars [large landholders, responsible for collecting land taxes for the government]. It is evident, that the British Government in making zemindary settlements have imposed exorbitant *Jumas* [revenue assessments], and have disgraced and ruined several zemindars. . . . Such extortions will have no manner of existence in the Badshahi Government; but on the contrary, the *Jumas* will be light, the dignity and honour of the zemindars safe, and every zemindar will have absolute rule in his own zemindary. . . .

Section II—Regarding Merchants. It is plain that the infidel and treacherous British Government have monopolized the trade of all the fine and valuable merchandise, such as indigo, cloth, and other articles of shipping, leaving only the trade of trifles to the people, and even in this they are not without their share of the profits, which they secure by means of customs and stamp fees, &c. in money suits, so that the people have merely a trade in name. . . . When the Badshahi Government is established, all these aforesaid fraudulent practices shall be dispensed with, and the trade of every article, without exception, both by land and water, shall be open to the native merchants of India. . . .

Section IV—Regarding Artisans. It is evident that the Europeans, by the introduction of English articles into India, have thrown the weavers, the cotton dressers, the carpenters, the blacksmiths, and the shoemakers, &c., out of employ, and have engrossed their occupations, so that every description of native artisan has been reduced to beggary. But under the Badshahi Government the native artisan will exclusively be employed in the services of the kings, the rajahs, and the rich. . . .

Section V—Regarding Pundits, Fakirs and other learned persons. The pundits and fakirs being the guardians of the Hindoo and Mohammedan religions respectively, and the Europeans being the enemies of both the religions, and as at present a war is raging against the English on account of religion, the pundits and fakirs are bound to present themselves to me, and take their share in the holy war.

→ *What are the main grievances against the English in India?*

→ *How will the emperor's Badshahi Government alleviate these grievous conditions?*

→ *What was the role of religion in the 1857 rebellion?*

Source: "Proclamation of Emperor Bahadur Shah," in *India in 1857: The Revolt against Foreign Rule*, edited by Ainslie T. Embree (Delhi: Chanakya Publications, 1987), pp. 3–6.

The Indian Sepoys. Pictured here are Indian soldiers, or sepoys, who were armed, drilled, and commanded by British officers. The sepoys were drawn from indigenous groups that the British considered to be "martial races." This photograph shows the Sikhs, designated as one such "race."

Triumphant in Delhi, the rebellion spread to other parts of India. In Awadh, proclamations in Hindi, Urdu, and Persian called on Hindus and Muslims to revolt. Troops at the garrison in Lucknow, Awadh's capital, did just that. Seizing control of the town, the rebels urged all classes to unite in expelling the British and succeeded in compelling the colonial forces to retreat.

Although the dispossessed aristocracy and petty landholders led the rebellion, leaders also appeared from the lower classes. Bakht Khan, who had been a junior noncommissioned officer in the British army, became commander-in-chief of the rebel forces in Delhi, replacing one of the Mughal emperor's sons. And Devi Singh, a wealthy peasant, set himself up as a peasant king. Dressed in yellow, the insignia of Hindu royalty, he constituted a government of his own, modeling it on the British administration. While his imitation of company rule showed his respect for the British bureaucracy, he defied British authority by leading an armed peasantry against the hated local moneylenders. The call to popular forces also marked the rebel career of Maulavi Ahmadullah Shah, a Muslim theologian. He stood at the head of the rebel forces in Lucknow, leading an army composed primarily of ordinary soldiers and people from the lower orders. Claiming to be an "Incarnation of the Deity," and thus inspired by divine will, he emerged as a prophetic leader of the common people. He voiced his undying hatred of the British in religious terms, calling on Hindus and Muslims to destroy British rule and warning his followers against betrayal by landed authorities.

PARTICIPATION BY THE PEASANTRY The presence of popular leadership points to the role of lower classes as historical actors. Although feudal chieftains often brought them into the rebellion, the peasantry made it their own. The organizing principle of their uprising was the common experience of oppression. Thus, they destroyed anything that represented the authority of the company: prisons, factories, police posts, railway stations, European bungalows, and law courts. Equally significant, the peasantry attacked native moneylenders and local power-holders who had purchased land at government auctions and were seen as benefiting from company rule.

Vigorous and militant as the popular rebellion was, it was limited in its territorial and ideological horizons. To begin with, the uprisings were local in scale and vision. Peasant rebels attacked the closest seats of administration and sought to settle scores with their most immediate and visible oppressors. They did not carry their action beyond the village or collection of villages. Their loyalties remained intensely local, based on village attachments and religious, caste, and clan ties. Nor did popular militants seek to undo traditional hierarchies of caste and religion.

The Rani of Jhansi. The Rani of Jhansi, who was deposed by the British, rose up during the revolt of 1857. In subsequent nationalist iconography, as this twentieth-century watercolor illustrates, she is remembered as a heroic rebel, all the more so because of her gender.

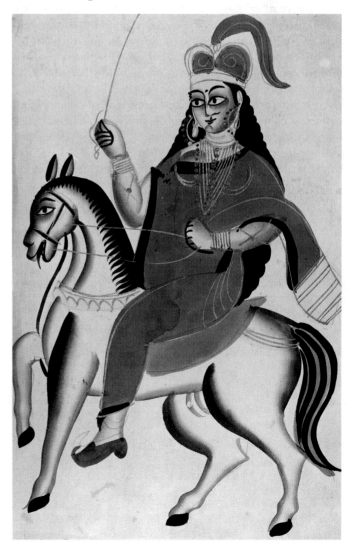

COUNTERINSURGENCY AND PACIFICATION Convinced that the rebellion was the result of plotting by a few troublemakers, the British carried out their counterinsurgency with brutal vengeance. Villages were torched, and rebels were tied to cannons and blown to bits to teach Indians a lesson in power. Delhi fell in September 1857; Lucknow in March 1858. The British exiled the unfortunate Mughal emperor to Burma, where he died, and murdered his sons. Most of the other rebel leaders were either killed in battle or captured and executed. When, at the same time, the British also moved to annex the state of Jhansi in northern India, its female leader, Lakshmi Bai, mounted a counterattack. After a two-week siege, Jhansi fell to the British, but Lakshmi Bai escaped on horseback, only to die in the fighting for control of a nearby fortress. Her intelligence, bravery, and youth (she was twenty-eight) made her the subject of many popular Indian ballads in the decades to follow.

By July 1858, the vicious pacification campaign had achieved its goal. Yet, in August, the British Parliament abolished company rule and the company itself, and transferred responsibility for the governing of India to the crown. In November, Queen Victoria issued a proclamation guaranteeing religious toleration, promising improvements, and allowing Indians to serve in the government. She promised to honor the treaties and agreements with princes and chiefs and to refrain from interfering in religious matters. The insurgents had risen up not as a nation, but as a multitude of communities acting independently, and their determination to find a new order shocked the British and threw them into a panic. Having crushed the uprising, the British resumed the work of transforming India into a modern colonial state and economy. But the desire for radical alternatives and traditions of popular insurgency, though vanquished, did not vanish.

CONCLUSION

The nineteenth century was a time of turmoil and transformation. While powerful forces reconfigured the world as a place for capitalism, colonialism, and nation-states, so too did prophets, charismatic leaders, radicals, peasant rebels, and anticolonial insurgents arise to offer alternatives. Reflecting local circumstances and traditions, the struggles of these men and women for a different future opened up spaces for the ideas and activities of subordinate classes.

Conventional historical accounts either neglect these struggles or fail to view them as a whole. These individuals were not just romantic, last-ditch resisters, as some scholars have argued. Even after defeat, their messages remained alive within their communities. Nor were their actions isolated and atypical events, for when viewed on a global scale they bring to light a world that looks very different from the one that became dominant. To see the Wahhabi movement in the Arabian Peninsula together with the Shawnee Prophet in North America, the utopians and radicals in Europe with the peasant insurgents in British India, and the Taiping rebels with the Mayans in the Yucatan is to glimpse a world of marginalized regions and groups. It was a world that more powerful groups endeavored to suppress but could not erase.

In this world, prophets and rebel leaders usually cultivated power and prestige locally; the emergence of an alternative polity in one region did not impinge on communities and political organizations in others. As much as these individuals had in common, they envisioned widely different kinds of futures. Even Marx, who called the workers of the world to unite, was acutely aware that the call for a proletarian revolution applied only to the industrialized countries of

Chronology

	1800			1820	
THE AMERICAS		◆------------◆ 1805–1811 *Preaching of Tenskwatawa (North America)*			
		1820s–1830s *American Indians moved west of Mississippi River* ◆------------------◆			
SOUTH ASIA					
EAST ASIA					
EUROPE		1814–1815 *Congress of Vienna* ◆--◆			
		1819 *Peterloo Massacre (England)* ◆			
		1821–1829 *Greek war for independence* ◆------------------◆			
		1830 *Revolutions in France, Belgium, Rhineland, Italy* ◆			
AFRICA AND THE MIDDLE EAST		◆------------◆ 1804–1809 *Dan Fodio leads revolt in West Africa*			
		◆-----◆ 1813–1815 *Wahhabis wage militant religious campaign*			
		1818–1828 *Shaka creates Zulu empire* ◆------------------◆			

Europe. Other dissenters had even more localized horizons. A world fashioned by movements for alternatives meant a world with multiple centers and different historical paths.

What gave force to a different mapping of the world was the fact that common people were at the center of these alternative visions, and their voices, however muted, gained a place on the historical stage. Egalitarianism in different forms defined efforts to reconstitute alternative worlds. In Islamic regions, the egalitarianism practiced by revitalization movements was evident in their mobilization of all Muslims, not just the elites. Even charismatic military leaders in Africa, for all their use of raw power, used the framework of community to build new polities. The Taiping Rebellion distinguished itself by seeking to establish an equal society of men and women in service of the Heavenly Kingdom. Operating under very different conditions, the European radicals imagined a society free from aristocratic privileges and bourgeois property. Anticolonial rebels and insurgents depended on local solidarities and proposed alternative moral communities. In so doing, these movements compelled ruling elites to adjust the way they governed. The next chapter explores this challenge.

Review and research materials are available at StudySpace: ⊚ WWNORTON.COM/STUDYSPACE

KEY TERMS

Caste War of Yucatan (p. 623)
Chartism (p. 615)
Usman dan Fodio (p. 605)
Fourierism (p. 616)

liberalism (p. 614)
Marxism (p. 616)
Mfecane movement (p. 605)
millenarian (p. 609)

proletarians (p. 616)
Rebellion of 1857 (p. 624)
Restoration period (p. 612)
Taiping Rebellion (p. 610)

Tecumseh (p. 620)
Tenskwatawa (p. 619)
utopian socialism (p. 615)
Wahhabism (p. 602)

STUDY QUESTIONS

1. Define the global order emerging in the nineteenth century in light of the revolutions in the Atlantic world studied in Chapter 15. How did it challenge social relations within societies?

2. Explain the goals of Islamic revitalization movements such as Wahhabism in the Arabian Peninsula and dan Fodio's movement in West Africa. How were these regions affected by the new world order? What alternative did Islamic revitalization propose?

3. Describe Hong Xiuquan's vision for China during the Taiping Rebellion. How did he propose reordering Chinese society?

4. Describe the various alternative visions to the status quo that European radicals proposed in the nineteenth century. What traditions and beliefs did they reflect?

5. Compare and contrast the Shawnee rebellion in the United States and the Caste War in Mexico. How did they reflect tensions between Native Americans and European Americans?

6. Analyze to what extent the Indian Rebellion of 1857 encouraged a new identity among its followers. What goals did participants in the rebellion share?

7. Explore the role of women in promoting alternative visions around the world in the nineteenth century. Which alternative vision movements proposed new roles for women in society?

8. List major similarities among the alternative visions explored in this chapter. Why did they all fail to achieve their objectives? Did they have any important legacies?

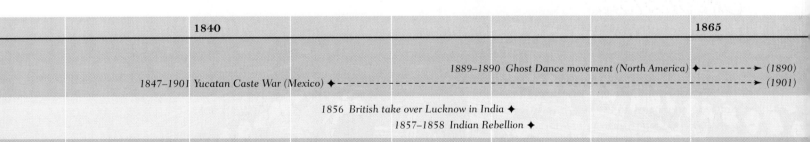

1840		1865

1889–1890 *Ghost Dance movement* (North America) ◆- - - - - - - -► (1890)

1847–1901 *Yucatan Caste War* (Mexico) ◆- -► (1901)

1856 *British take over Lucknow in India* ◆
1857–1858 *Indian Rebellion* ◆

1851–1864 *Taiping Rebellion* (China) ◆- ◆

◆- - - - - - ◆ 1831–1834 *Revolutions in Poland and Italy*
◆ 1832 *Mazzini founds "Young Italy" movement*
1839–1848 *Chartism in England* ◆- ◆ 1848 *Revolutions in France, Austria, Prussia, Italy*

empires. In Asia and Africa resisters struggled to repel their invaders, often demanding the right to govern themselves.

The second half of the nineteenth century, as this chapter details, witnessed the simultaneous—and entwined—advance of nationalism and imperialism. These decades also saw the further expansion of the industrial revolution. Taken together, the era's political and economic developments allowed western Europe and the United States to attain greater primacy in world affairs. But tensions inside these nations and their empires, as well as within other states, made the new world order anything but stable.

CONSOLIDATING NATIONS AND CONSTRUCTING EMPIRES

> → *What was the relationship between nationalism and imperialism?*

During the second half of the nineteenth century, the idea of building nation-states engulfed the globe. In the previous century a series of wars, ending with the Napoleonic Wars, had made Europeans increasingly conscious of political and cultural borders—and of the power of new bureaucracies. Enlightenment thinkers had emphasized the importance of nations, defined as peoples who shared a common past, territory, culture, and traditions. To many people it seemed natural that once absolutist rulers had fallen, the state should draw its power and legitimacy from those who lived within its borders and that the body of institutions governing each

territory should be uniquely concerned with promoting the welfare of that particular people. This seemed such a natural process that little thought was given to how nation-states arose; they were simply supposed to well up from the people's longing for liberty and togetherness.

BUILDING NATIONALISM

In practice, nations did not usually well up from people's longings for liberty and togetherness. More often than not, ruling elites themselves created nations. They did so by compelling diverse groups of people and regions to accept a unified network of laws, a central administration, time zones, national markets, and a single regional dialect as the "national" language. To overcome strong regional identities, state administrators broadened public education in the national language and imposed universal military service to build a national army. These efforts nurtured the notion of a one-to-one correspondence between a "people" and a nation-state, and they radiated the values and institutions of dominant elites outward to regions throughout each nation-state and beyond their national borders.

The world's major nation-states of the late nineteenth century were not all alike, however. They took many forms. Some had been in existence for years, such as Japan, England, France, Spain, Portugal, and the United States; here, citizens widely embraced their national identities. Two nation-states (Germany and Italy) were entirely new, forged through strategic military conquests. Elsewhere, plans for nation-states like those in central Europe, the Balkans, Poland, and the Ukraine were chiefly the inventions of local elites; their plans displeased Russian, Austrian, and Ottoman monarchs and were of little interest to the multilingual, multiethnic peasantry in these areas. In many parts of the

Focus Questions

→ *What was the relationship between nationalism and imperialism?*

→ *How did nation-building patterns compare among the United States, Canada, and Brazil?*

→ *How did European nation-states forge national identities?*

→ *How did new materials and technologies transform industry and the global economy?*

→ *What were the motives for imperialism and the practices of colonial rulers?*

→ *How did expansionism affect Japan, Russia, and China?*

MAIN THEMES

�→ *The advance of nation-state building and imperialism.*
�→ *Industrialization, science, and technology elevate states in North America and Western Europe over the rest of the world.*
�→ *European and American imperialism encounters fierce opposition in Africa and Asia.*

FOCUS ON *Nationalism, Imperialism, and Scientific/Technological Innovations*

The Americas and Europe: Consolidating Nations

+ Residents of the United States claim territory across the North American continent after fighting a bloody civil war to preserve the union and abolish slavery.
+ Canadians also build a new nation and expand across the continent.
+ Brazilians create a prosperous nation-state that excludes much of the population from the privileges of belonging to the "nation" and the "state."
+ The dynastic states of Prussia and Sardinia-Piedmont create German and Italian nation-states at the expense of France and the Austrian Empire.

Industry, Science, and Technology on a Global Scale

+ Continued industrialization, coupled with scientific research, transforms the global economy.
+ New technologies of warfare, transportation, and communication ease global economic integration.
+ Charles Darwin's *Origin of Species* overturns previous conceptions of nature, arguing that present-day life forms evolved from simpler ones over long periods.

Empires

+ After suppressing the Indian Mutiny, the British reorganize their rule in India.
+ The Dutch take over administrative responsibilities in Indonesia from the Dutch East India Company.
+ Seven European powers partition the entire African continent (except for Ethiopia and Liberia) despite intense African resistance.
+ Americans win the Spanish-American war, annex Puerto Rico, and establish a colony over the Philippines.
+ The expansionist aims of Japan, Russia, and China lead to clashes over possessions in East Asia, with Russia gaining much territory and Japan defeating the Chinese.
+ Colonial rule spurs nationalist sentiments among the colonized.

---

world, intellectuals were the primary agents agitating for new nation-states, often urging new states to break away from existing empires. That secessionist impulse posed a particularly thorny challenge to the rulers of multinational empires like Russia and Austria.

EXPANDING THE EMPIRES

In countries that became nation-states, the processes of nation building and the acquisition of new territories, often called **imperialism,** went hand in hand. Their rulers measured national strength not only by their people's unity but also by the conquest of new territories and the possession of the most modern means of production. Thus Germany, France, the United States, Russia, and Japan rivaled Britain by expanding and modernizing their industries and seizing nearby or far-off territories. By the century's end, gaining new territory had become so important that these states scrambled to colonize peoples from Africa to the Amazon, from California to Korea.

Never before had there been such a rapid reshuffling of peoples and resources. As transportation costs declined, workers left their homelands in search of better opportunities. Japanese moved to Brazil, Indians to South Africa and the Caribbean, Chinese to California, and Italians to New

York and Buenos Aires. At the same time, American capitalists invested outside the United States, and British investors financed the construction of railroads in China and India. Raw materials from Africa and Southeast Asia flowed to the manufacturing nations of Europe and the Americas.

Imperial rule facilitated a widespread movement of labor, capital, commodities, and information. As scholars studied previously unknown tribes and races, new schools taught colonized peoples the languages, religions, scientific practices, and cultural traditions of their colonizers. Publications and products from the "mother country" circulated widely among indigenous elites. Yet empire builders did not extend to non-white inhabitants of their colonies the same rights as they gave to inhabitants of their own nations; here, nation and empire were incompatible. Not only were colonial subjects prohibited from participating in government, but they were also not considered members of the nation at all. As a result, imperialism produced diametrically opposed reactions: exultation among the colonizers, and bitterness among the colonized.

EXPANSION AND NATION BUILDING IN THE AMERICAS

> → *How did nation-building patterns compare among the United States, Canada, and Brazil?*

Once freed from European control, the elites of the Americas set about creating political communities of their own. By the 1850s, they shared a desire to both create widespread loyalty to their political institutions and expand territorial domains. This required refining the tools of government to include national laws and court systems, standardized money, and national political parties. It also meant finding ways to settle hinterlands that previously belonged to indigenous populations. Having once been European colonies, New World territories became vibrant nation-states based on growing prosperity and industrialization.

Although nation-states took shape throughout the world, the Americas saw the most complete assimilation of new possessions. Instead of treating outlying areas as colonial outposts, American nation-state builders turned them into new provinces. With the help of rifles, railroads, schools, and land surveys, frontiers became strategic possessions for North and South American societies. For indigenous peoples, however, such national expansion meant the loss of traditional lands on a vast scale.

Not all national consolidations in the Americas were the same. The United States, Canada, and Brazil, for example, experienced different processes of nation building, territorial expansion, and economic development. Each one incorporated frontier regions into national polities and economies, although they used different techniques for subjugating indigenous peoples and administering their new holdings.

THE UNITED STATES

Military might, fortuitous diplomacy, and the power of numbers enabled the United States to claim territory that spanned the North American continent (see Map 17-1). At its independence, the nation had been a barely united confederation of states. Indian resistance and Spanish and British rivalry hemmed in the "Americans" (as they came to call themselves). At the same time, the disunited states threatened to fracture into northern and southern polities, for questions of slavery versus free labor intruded into national politics. Yet, rallying to the rhetoric of **Manifest Destiny**, which maintained that it was God's will for the United States to "overspread" North America, Americans pushed their boundaries westward. They acquired territories via purchase agreements and treaties with France, Spain, and Britain and via warfare and treaties with diverse Indian nations and Mexico. (See Primary Source: Manifest Destiny.)

As part of the territories taken from Mexico after the Mexican-American War (1846–1848), the United States gained California, where the discovery of gold brought migration on an unprecedented scale. As news of the find spread, hopeful prospectors raced to stake their claims. In the next few years, over 100,000 Americans took to the overland trails and to the seas in quest of California's riches.

The California gold rush, however, was not only a great American migration; it also inspired tens of thousands of individuals from Latin America, Australia, Asia, and Europe to pour into California. What had just a few years earlier been a sparsely populated corner of northwestern Mexico was transformed almost overnight into the most cosmopolitan place on earth. In the 1850s, California was truly where worlds came together.

CIVIL WAR AND STATES' RIGHTS   Ironically, California and the territories that the United States took from Mexico also spurred the coming apart of the American nation. The deeply divisive issue was whether these lands would be open to slavery or restricted to free labor. Following the 1860 election of Abraham Lincoln, who pledged to halt the expansion of slavery, the United States divided between North and South and plunged into a gruesome Civil War (1861–1865).

The bloody conflict led to the abolition of slavery, and the struggle to extend voting and citizenship rights to freed slaves qualified the Civil War as a second American Revolution. It gave the nation a new generation of heroes and martyrs such as the assassinated president, Abraham Lincoln. He had

The Canadian state also faced friction with Indians. Frontier warfare threatened to drive away investors and settlers, who could always find property south of the border instead. To prevent the kind of bloodletting that characterized the United States' westward expansion, the Canadian government signed treaties with Indians to ensure strict separation between natives and newcomers. It also created a special police force, the Royal Canadian Mounted Police, to patrol the territories.

Canadian expansion was hardly bloodless, however. Many Indians and mixed-blood peoples (*métis*) resented the treaties. Moreover, the Canadian government was often less than honest in its dealings. As in the United States, the government's Indian policy in Canada sought to turn Indians into farmers and then incorporate them into Canadian society—regardless of whether they wanted to become farmers or join the nation.

The need to accommodate resident French speakers, defensive expansionism, and a degree of legality in dealing with Indians gave the Canadian government a strong foundation. Indeed, it acquired significant powers to intervene, regulate, and mediate social conflict and relations. (These powers, in fact, were fuller than those of the U.S. government.) But even though the state was relatively strong, the sense of a national identity was comparatively weak. Expansionism helped Canada remain an autonomous state, but it did not solve the question of what it meant to belong to a Canadian nation.

LATIN AMERICA

Latin American elites also engaged in nation-state building and expanded their territorial borders. But unlike in the United States and Canada, expansion did not always create homesteader frontiers that could help expand democracy and forge national identities. Instead, civil conflict fractured certain countries in the region (see Chapters 15, 16), although one—Brazil—remained united.

Much of Latin America shared a common social history. Far more than in North America, the richest lands in Latin America went not to small farmers, but to large estate holders producing exports such as sugar, coffee, or beef. The result: privileged elites monopolized power more than in North America's young democracies. Even though territorial expansion and strong economic growth were Latin American hallmarks, these processes sidelined the poor, the Indians, and the blacks.

CONSOLIDATION VERSUS FRAGMENTATION   Indian and peasant uprisings were a major worry in new Latin American republics. Fearing insurrections, elites devised governing systems that protected private property and investments while limiting the political rights of the poor and the propertyless. Likewise, the specter of slave revolts, driven home not just by earlier, brutal events in Haiti (see Chapter 15) but also by daily rumors of rebellions, kept elites in a state of alarm. One Argentine writer echoed the concern about giving too much power to the masses, and he described the challenge of nation-state building in Latin America as a struggle between elitist "civilization" and popular "barbarism." Creating strong nations, it seemed to many Latin American elites, required excluding large groups of people from power.

BRAZIL: AN "EXCLUSIVE" NATION-STATE   Brazil illustrates the process by which Latin American rulers built nation-states that excluded much of the population from both the "nation" and the "state." Through the nineteenth century, rulers in Rio de Janeiro defused political conflict by allowing planters to retain the reins of power. Moreover, although the Brazilian government officially abolished the slave trade in 1830, it allowed illegal slave imports to continue for another two decades (until British pressure compelled Brazil to enforce the ban).

The end of the slave trade, coupled with slave resistance, began to choke the planters' system by driving up the price of slaves within the region. Sensing that the system of forced

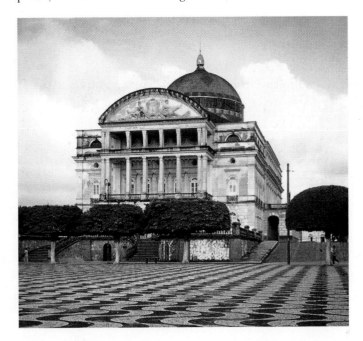

Opera House in Manaus. The turn-of-the-century rubber boom brought immense wealth to the Amazon jungle. As in many boom-and-bust cycles in Latin America, the proceeds flowed to a small elite and diminished when the rubber supply outstripped the demand. But the wealth produced was sufficient to prompt the local elite to build temples of modernity in the midst of the jungle. Pictured here is the Opera House in the rubber capital of Manaus. Like other works built by Latin American elites of the period, this one emulated the original in Paris.

labor was unraveling, slaves began to flee the sugar and coffee plantations, and army personnel refused to hunt them down. In the 1880s, even while laws still upheld slave labor, country roads in the state of São Paulo were filled with fugitive slaves looking for relatives or access to land. Finally, in 1888, the Brazilian emperor abolished slavery.

Thereafter, as in the United States, Brazilian elites followed two strategies in creating a new labor force for their estates. They retained some former slaves as gang-workers or sharecroppers, and they also imported new workers— especially from Italy, Spain, and Portugal. These laborers often came as seasonal migrant workers or indentured tenant farmers. Indeed, European and even Japanese migration to Brazil helped planters preserve their holdings in the post-slavery era. In all, two million Europeans and some 70,000 Japanese moved to Brazil.

The Brazilian state was deliberately exclusive. The constitution of 1891, which established a federal system and proclaimed Brazil a republic, separated those who could be trusted with power from the rest. After all, with the abolition of slavery, the sudden enfranchisement of millions of freedmen would have threatened to flood the electoral lists with propertyless, potentially uncontrollable voters. As in the United States, politicians responded by slapping severe restrictions on suffrage and by rigging rules to reduce political competition. However, given the greater share of the black population in Brazil, restrictions there excluded a larger share of the potential electorate than in the United States.

BRAZIL: EXPANSION AND ECONOMIC DEVELOPMENT

Like Canada and the United States, the Brazilian state extended its reach to distant areas and incorporated them as provinces. The largest land-grab occurred in the Amazon River basin, the world's largest drainage watershed and tropical forest. It had built up over millennia around the meandering tributaries that convey runoffs from the eastern slopes of the Andean mountains all the way to the Atlantic Ocean. It was a massive yet delicate habitat of balanced biomass suspended by towering trees with a canopy of leaves and vines that kept the basin ecologically diverse. Here, the Brazilian state gave giant concessions to local capitalists to extract rubber latex. When combined with sulfur, rubber was a key raw material for tire manufacturing in European and North American bicycle and automobile industries.

As Brazil became the world's exclusive exporter of rubber, its planters, merchants, and workers prospered. Rich merchants became lenders and financiers, not only to workers but also to landowners themselves. The mercantile elite of Manaus, the capital of the Amazon region, designed and decorated their city to reflect their new fortunes. Although the streets were still paved with mud, the town's elite built a replica of the Paris Opera House, and Manaus became a regular stopover for European opera singers on the circuit between Buenos Aires and New York. Rubber workers also benefited from the boom. Mostly either Indians or mixed-blood people, they sent their wages home to families elsewhere in the Amazon jungle or on the northeastern coast of Brazil.

But the Brazilian rubber boom soon went bust. One problem was the ecosystem: such a diversified biomass could not tolerate a regimented form of production that emphasized the cultivation of rubber trees at the expense of other vege-

Rubber Plantation Workers. (*Left*) Workers on rubber plantations draw latex from rubber plants by using taps that have been sunk into the plant. (*Right*) The workers collect the latex in buckets and then take it to central collection points.

tation and made the forest vulnerable to nonhuman predators. Leaf blight and ferocious ants destroyed all experiments at creating more sustainable rubber plantations. Moreover, it was expensive to haul the rubber latex out of the jungle all the way to the coast along the slow-moving Amazon River. Another problem was that Brazilian rubber faced severe competition after a British scientist smuggled rubber plant seeds out of Brazil in 1876. Following years of experimentation, British patrons transplanted a blight-resistant hybrid to the British colony of Ceylon (present-day Sri Lanka). As competition led to increased supplies and reduced prices, Brazilian producers went bankrupt. Merchants called in their loans, landowners forfeited their titles, and rubber workers returned to their subsistence economies. Tropical vines crept over the Manaus Opera House, and it gradually fell into disrepair.

Throughout the Americas, nineteenth-century societies worked to adapt obsolete elite models of politics and to satisfy popular demands for inclusion. While the ideal was to construct nation-states that could reconcile differences among their citizens and pave the way for economic prosperity, in fact political autonomy did not bring prosperity, or even the right to vote, to all. As each nation-state expanded its territorial boundaries, many new inhabitants were left out of the political realm.

CONSOLIDATION OF NATION-STATES IN EUROPE

> ↦ *How did European nation-states forge national identities?*

In Europe, no "frontier" existed into which new nations could expand. Instead, nation-states took shape out of older monarchies, and their borders were determined by diplomats or by battles between rival claimants. In the wake of the French Revolution, the idea caught on that "the people" should form the basis for the nation and that nations should be culturally homogenous—but no one could agree on who "the people" should be. Yet, over the course of the nineteenth century, as literacy, the cities, industrial production, and the number and prosperity of property owners expanded, ruling elites had no choice but to share power with a wider group of citizens. These citizens, in turn, increasingly defined themselves as, say, Frenchmen or Germans, rather than as residents of Marseilles or subjects of the King of Bavaria.

DEFINING "THE NATION"

For a very long time, in most places, "the nation" was understood to comprise kings, clergymen, nobles—and occasionally rich merchants or lawyers—and no one else. Although some peoples, such as the English and the Spanish, were already self-conscious about their unique histories, only in the late eighteenth century were the crucial building blocks of European nationalism put in place.

To begin with, intellectuals laid the ideological foundations of the nation. In 1776, Adam Smith had described the wealth of each nation as equivalent to the combined output of all its producers, not the sum in the king's treasury. Then, in 1789, the left-leaning French clergyman Emmanuel Joseph Sieyès had published a widely circulated pamphlet arguing that the nation consisted of all of those who worked to enrich it, and that those who were "parasites" (Sieyès meant the clergy and the aristocracy) did not belong. Sieyès's revolutionary Declaration of the Rights of Man and the Citizen, inspired by the American Declaration of Independence, declared that all men were equal under the law and insisted that "the principle of all sovereignty lies essentially in the nation."

Material and social conditions also prepared the way for nation-states. During the nineteenth century, a huge expansion of literacy and the periodical press made it possible for people all across Europe to read books and newspapers in their own languages. At the same time, the emerging industrial economy brought people into closer contact and made merchants anxious to standardize laws, taxation policies, and weights and measures. States invested huge sums in building roads and then railroads—and these linked provincial towns and bigger cities, laying the foundations for a closer political integration.

But who were the people, and what constituted a viable nation-state? Neither Smith's treatise nor Sieyès's pamphlet could clarify which people belonged inside which nation-state, for belonging to a nation had long been associated with the sharing of cultural or religious traditions. For some people, the nation was a collection of all those who spoke one language; for others, it was all those who lived in the domains of one prince, or who shared a religious heritage. This was a particularly acute problem in multiethnic central and southeastern Europe, where even peasants were often multilingual. But some who shared the same language objected to being lumped into one nation-state. The Irish, for example, spoke English but were predominately Catholics and wanted to be free from Anglican rule.

The Europe-wide revolutions of 1848 (see Chapters 15, 16) sought to put "the people" in power; in many cases, too, rebels sought to create unified nation-states, each of which would serve one particular cultural and linguistic group. (Examples include the Czechs and Italians, both of whom wanted states independent from the Habsburg Empire.) But

Primary Source

WHAT IS A NATION?

The French linguist and historian of religion Ernest Renan explored the concept of nationhood in an 1882 essay entitled "What Is a Nation?" Arguing with racial, religious, and language-based interpretations of nationhood, Renan offers an explicitly republican model.

. . . The principle of nations is our principle. But what, then, is a nation? . . . Why is Switzerland, with its three languages, its two religions, and three or four races, a nation, when Tuscany, for example, which is so homogeneous, is not? Why is Austria a state and not a nation? In what does the principle of nations differ from that of races? . . .

Ethnographic considerations have . . . played no part in the formation of modern nations. France is Celtic, Iberic, and Germanic. Germany is Germanic, Celtic, and Slav. Italy is the country in which ethnography finds its greatest difficulties. Here Gauls, Etruscans, Pelasgians, and Greeks are crossed in an unintelligible medley. The British Isles, taken as a whole, exhibit a mixture of Celtic and Germanic blood, the proportions of which are particularly difficult to define.

The truth is that no race is pure, and that to base politics on ethnographic analysis is tantamount to basing it on a chimera. . . .

What we have said about race, applies also to language. Language invites union, without, however, compelling it. The United States and England, as also Spanish America and Spain, speak the same language without forming a single nation. Switzerland, on the contrary, whose foundations are solid because they are based on the assent of the various parties, contains three or four languages. There exists in man a something which is above language: and that is his will. The will of Switzerland to be united, in spite of the variety of these forms of speech, is a much more important fact than a similarity of language, often attained by vexatious measures. . . .

Nor can religion provide a satisfactory basis for a modern nationality. . . . Nowadays . . . everyone believes and practices religion in his own way according to his capacities and wishes. State religion has ceased to exist; and a man can be a Frenchman, an Englishman, or a German, and at the same time a Catholic, a Protestant, or a Jew, or practice no form of worship at all.

A nation is a soul, a spiritual principle. Two things, which are really only one, go to make up this soul or spiritual principle. One of these things lies in the past, the other in the present. The one is the possession in common of a rich heritage of memories; and the other is actual agreement, the desire to live together, and the will to continue to make the most of the joint inheritance. . . . The nation, like the individual, is the fruit of a long past spent in toil, sacrifice, and devotion. . . . To share the glories of the past, and a common will in the present; to have done great deeds together, and to desire to do more—. . . These are things which are understood, in spite of differences in race and language.

. . . The existence of a nation is . . . a daily plebiscite. . . . A province means to us its inhabitants; and if anyone has a right to be consulted in the matter, it is the inhabitant. It is never to the true interest of a nation to annex or keep a country against its will. The people's wish is after all the only justifiable criterion, to which we must always come back.

→ *According to Renan, what are the two key ingredients needed to create a nation-state?*

→ *What arguments does Renan offer against basing nationhood on a common race, religion, or language?*

SOURCE: Ernest Renan, "What Is a Nation?" in *The Nationalism Reader*, edited by Omar Dahbour and Micheline R. Ishay (Atlantic Highlands, NJ: Humanities Press, 1995), pp. 143–55.

the revolutions ran into difficulties defining who "the people" were and how to fashion new nations out of Europe's multiethnic empires. Deep divisions opened among ethnic groups and between middle-class liberals and radicals, some of whom wanted to share out the nation's wealth. Monarchs took advantage of the chaos and restored their regimes. The troubling questions continued to agitate Europe for many years to come. (See Primary Source: What Is a Nation?)

UNIFICATION IN GERMANY AND ITALY

Two of Europe's fledgling nation-states came into being when the dynastic states of Prussia and Piedmont-Sardinia swallowed their smaller, linguistically related neighbors, creating the German and Italian nation-states (see Map 17-2). In both regions, conservative prime ministers—Count Otto von Bismarck of Prussia and Count Camillo di Cavour of Piedmont—exploited radical, and especially liberal, nationalist sentiment to rearrange the map of Europe.

BUILDING UNIFIED STATES The unification of Germany and Italy posed all the familiar problems of who the people were and who should be included in the new nation-states. To begin with, German-speakers were spread all across central and eastern Europe, a result of more than a millennium of eastward colonization. For centuries, they had lived in many different states. Similarly, Italian-speakers had lived separately in city-states and small kingdoms on the Italian peninsula. The historical experiences and economic developments had made Bavarian Germans (Catholic) quite different from Prussian Germans (Protestant); likewise, the Milanese (who lived in a wealthy urban industrial center) shared little with the typical Sardinian peasant. But liberal nationalists had made the case that a shared language and literature overrode all these differences, and emotional appeals by poets, composers, and orators convinced many people that this was indeed the case.

Ultimately, two conservative leaders, Bismarck and Cavour, merged nationalist rhetoric with clever diplomacy to forge united German and Italian polities. Nor did they ignore military might. In a famous address in 1862, Bismarck bellowed: "Not through speeches and majority decisions are the great questions of the day decided—that was the great mistake of 1848 and 1849—but through blood and iron." True to his word, Bismarck accomplished the unification of northern German states by war: with Denmark in 1864, Austria in 1866, and France (over the western provinces of Alsace and Lorraine) in 1870–1871. Italy also was united through a series of small conflicts, many of them engineered to prevent the establishment of more radical republics.

STATES' INTERNAL CONFLICTS These "unified" states rejected democracy. In the new Italy, which was a constitutional monarchy, not a republic, less than 5 percent of the 25 million people could vote. The new German empire (the Reich) did have an assembly elected by all adult males (the Reichstag), but it was ruled by a combination of aristocrats and bureaucrats under a monarch. Liberals dominated in many localities, but only the emperor (the kaiser) could depose the prime minister. In fact, Bismarck continued to dominate Prussian politics for twenty-eight years, until fired in 1890 by Kaiser Wilhelm II, who was even more authoritarian and bellicose.

The new states were not internally cohesive. In Italy, Piedmontese liberals in the north hoped that centralized rule would transform southern Italy into a prosperous, commercial, and industrial region like their own. But southern notables, who owned large agricultural estates, had little interest in northern customs. While the northern provinces industrialized and developed commercial links with Switzerland and France, the southern ones remained agrarian and largely isolated from modernizing processes. In Germany, many non-Germans—Poles in Silesia, French in Alsace and Lorraine, Danes in the provinces of Schleswig-Holstein—became "national minorities" whose rights remained in question. In the 1870s, Bismarck branded both Catholics and socialists as traitors to the new state; both retaliated by forming powerful political movements. By the 1890s, unification had yielded brisk economic growth, especially for the Germans, but conflict between regions and political groups continued.

Berlin, the capital of Prussia, now became the capital of the German Reich. Although Kaiser Wilhelm II remarked in 1892 that "the glory of Paris robs Berliners of their sleep," Berlin was on the rise. Its population of 1 million people in 1875 had doubled by 1910. The overall German population boomed as well, and the French, whose birthrates were dropping, worried about swelling battalions of well-drilled German soldiers.

NATION BUILDING AND ETHNIC CONFLICT IN THE AUSTRO-HUNGARIAN EMPIRE

Bismarck's wars of unification came at the expense of Habsburg supremacy in central Europe and of French territory and influence in the west. Following Germany's swift victory over the Austrian army in 1866, the Hungarian nobles who controlled the eastern Habsburg Empire forced the weakened dynasts to grant them home rule. In the Compromise of 1867, the Habsburgs agreed that their state would officially be known as the Austro-Hungarian Empire. But this move did not solve Austria-Hungary's nationality problems. In both the Hungarian and the Austrian halves of the dual state, Czechs, Poles, and other Slavs now began to clamor for their own power-sharing "compromise" or autonomous national homelands.

In 1871, the Habsburg emperor seemed prepared to accommodate the Czechs and put them politically on a par with the Hungarians. But the emperor's Hungarian partners scuttled the deal. After this point, interethnic conflict increased over divisive issues such as whether Czech (or Italian, Serbo-Croatian, Polish, Ukrainian, etc.) language could be used

MAP 17-2 ITALIAN UNIFICATION AND GERMAN UNIFICATION, 1815–1871

Italian unification and German unification altered the political map of Europe. What were the names of the two original states that grew to become Italy and Germany? Who were the big losers in these territorial transfers? According to your reading, what problems did the new Italian and German states face in creating strong national communities?

instead of German in regional administrative and educational settings and whether bureaucrats should have to be able to speak more than one language. Moreover, by the 1880s, a wave of impoverished eastern European Jews and non-Jewish Slavs migrating from the countryside entered Austria-Hungary's larger cities, stimulating anti-Semitic feeling and racist political pressure groups. Still, loyalty to the emperor was widespread and multinationalism flourished in the imperial bureaucracy, in the army officers' corps (whose members had to speak both German and the languages of the soldiers under their command), in the upper administration of the Catholic Church, and in the highly cosmopolitan cities.

DOMESTIC DISCONTENTS IN FRANCE AND BRITAIN

Although already unified as nation-states, Britain and France, too, faced major difficulties. For the French, dealing with military defeat at the hands of the Germans was the primary national concern in the decades leading up to World War I. For the British, issues of Irish separatism, the rise of the working class, and feminists' demands troubled the political arena.

DESTABILIZATION IN FRANCE   Bismarck launched the Franco-Prussian War of 1870–1871 in order to complete the unification of Germany; he did not intend to destabilize France. But the sound drubbing the French troops received, and the capture of Napoleon III early in the conflict, proved embarrassing and upsetting. Even more catastrophic for France was the German siege of Paris, which lasted for more than three months. Unprepared, Parisians had no food stocks and were compelled to eat all sorts of things, including two zoo elephants. Under terrible conditions and without effective leadership, the French capital resisted until January 1871, when the government signed a humiliating peace treaty—in the Hall of Mirrors at Versailles, formerly the residence of France's powerful "Sun King." The Germans left in place a weak provisional French government. Furious Parisians vented their rage and established a socialist commune proclaiming the city a utopia for workers. The leftist commune lasted until the provisional government's predominantly peasant army stormed Paris a few months later. At least 25,000 Parisians died in the bloody mop-up that followed.

A "Third Republic" took the place of Napoleon III's empire, but its conservative leaders were wary of the socialists and workers. They also were determined to revenge themselves for their humiliation in 1871. For the French, the years to follow would bring two unsettling developments: increasingly sharp conflict between classes over the shape of the republic, and rising anti-German nationalism. Some of this antagonism also radiated outward to target French colonial subjects, who now experienced more virulent forms of racism.

IRISH NATIONALISM IN GREAT BRITAIN   Although the English had long thought of themselves as a nation, the idea that all Britons belonged in the same state was much more problematic. Great Britain—composed of England, Wales, Scotland, and Ireland—was home to people whose historical experiences, religious backgrounds, and economic opportunities were very different. In the nineteenth century, British leaders wrestled in particular with lower-class agitation and demands for independence from Irish nationalists. England responded to these pressures by extending political rights to all men but not women. Thereafter, free trade and progress became the priorities of a middle class flush with new wealth generated by industry and empire. The long reign of Queen Victoria (r. 1837–1901), as well as England's prosperity, overseas conquests, and world power, increasingly bound both workers and owners to the nation.

Yet Ireland remained England's Achilles' heel. Although in 1836 Irish Catholics finally became equal to Protestants before the law, the two communities' political and economic conditions remained very uneven. The English were widely condemned for their failure to relieve Irish suffering during the potato famine of 1846–1849 (see Chapter 15); even though millions of poor Irish and Scottish workers made their way to England, seeking either passage to North America or work in the English mill towns, they did not assimilate easily and often got the lowliest jobs. All of this, on top of 300 years of repressive English domination, spawned a mass movement for Irish home rule.

Born in opposition to the old monarchical regimes, European nationalism by the end of the nineteenth century had become a means used by liberal and conservative leaders alike to unite "the people" behind them. In most places, aside from Russia, "the people" essentially meant all adult males—and that group had won the right to vote in national elections (though most states still had monarchs as well). The new nation-states had been shaped by increasing literacy and urbanization, but also by warfare.

INDUSTRY, SCIENCE, AND TECHNOLOGY

> → *How did new materials and technologies transform industry and the global economy?*

A powerful combination of industry, science, and technology shaped the emerging nation-states in North America and western Europe. It also reordered the relationships among different parts of the world. One critical factor was that after 1850 western Europe and North America experienced a new phase of industrial development—essentially a second industrial revolution. Japan, too, joined the ranks of industrializing nations as its state-led program of industrial development started to pay dividends. These changes transformed the global economy and intensified rivalries among industrial societies. For example, Britain now had to contend with competition from the United States and Germany.

NEW MATERIALS, TECHNOLOGIES, AND BUSINESS PRACTICES

New materials and new technologies were vital in late-nineteenth-century economic development. For example, **steel**, which was more malleable and stronger than iron, became essential for industries like shipbuilding and railways. The world output of steel shot up from half a million tons in 1870 to 28 million tons in 1900. The miracle of steel was

Eiffel Tower. Gustave Eiffel, a French engineer known for his innovative iron bridges, built this tower for the 1889 Universal Exhibition in Paris.

scientific research with capitalist enterprise: universities and corporate laboratories produced swelling ranks of engineers and scientists, as well as patents.

The breakthroughs of the second industrial revolution ushered in new business practices, especially mass production and the giant integrated firm. No longer would modest investments suffice, as they had in Britain a century earlier. Now large banks were the major providers of funds. In Europe, limited-liability joint-stock companies were as wildly successful in raising capital on stock markets as they were in the United States. Companies like Standard Oil, U.S. Steel, and Siemens mobilized capital from a large number of investors, called shareholders. The scale of these firms was awesome. U.S. Steel alone produced over half the world's steel ingots, castings, rails, and heavy structural shapes—and nearly half of all its steel plates and sheets, which were vital in the construction of buildings, railroads, ships, and the like.

INTEGRATION OF THE WORLD ECONOMY

Not only did industrial change concentrate power in North Atlantic societies, but it also reinforced their power on the world economic stage. Of course, Europe and the United States increased their exports in new products; but at the same time, they grew eager to control the importation of tropical commodities such as cocoa and coffee. While the North Atlantic societies were still largely self-sufficient in coal, iron, cotton, wool, and wheat (the major commodities of the first industrial revolution), the second industrial revolution bred a need for rubber, copper, oil, and bauxite (an ore used to make aluminum), which were not available domestically.

celebrated through the construction of the Eiffel Tower (completed in 1889) in Paris, an aggressively modern monument that loomed over the picturesque cityscape and was double the height of any other building in the world at the time. Steel was part of a bundle of innovations that included chemicals, oil, pharmaceuticals, and mass transportation vehicles like trolleys and automobiles.

The late nineteenth century witnessed major technological changes with the arrival of new organic sources of power (like oil) and new ways to get old organic sources (like coal) to processing plants. These changes freed manufacturers from having to locate their plants close to their fuel sources. Not only did the most important new source of energy—electricity—permit factories to arise in areas with plenty of skilled workers, but it also slashed production costs. Scientific research, too, boosted industrial development. German companies led the way in creating laboratories where university-trained chemists and physicists conducted research to serve industrial production. The United States likewise wedded

Railroad Workers. The construction of railroad lines across the United States was dangerous work, much of it done by immigrant laborers, including large numbers of Chinese, such as those in this photograph taken in Utah c. 1869.

→ *How did new materials and technologies transform industry and the global economy?*

Suez Canal. The Suez Canal opened to world shipping in 1869 and reduced the time it took to sail between Europe and Asian ports. Although the French and the Egyptians supplied most of the money and the construction plans and Egyptians were the main workforce, British shipping dominated canal traffic from the outset.

Equally important, large pools of money became available for investing overseas. London may have lost its industrial leadership, but it retained dominance over the world's financial operations. By 1913, the British had the huge sum of £4 billion invested overseas—funds that generated an annual income of £200 million, or one-tenth of Britain's national income.

MOVEMENTS OF LABOR AND TECHNOLOGY Because the more integrated world economy needed workers for fields, factories, and mines, vast movements of the laboring population took place. Indians moved thousands of miles to work on sugar plantations in the Caribbean, Mauritius, and Fiji, to labor in South African mines, and to build railroads in East Africa. Chinese workers constructed railroads in the western United States and toiled on sugar plantations in Cuba. The Irish, Poles, Jews, Italians, and Greeks flocked to North America to fill its burgeoning factories. Italians also moved to Argentina to harvest wheat and corn.

New technologies of warfare, transportation, and communication eased global economic integration—and strengthened European domination. With steam-powered gunboats and breech-loading rifles, Europeans opened new territories for trade and conquest. At home and in their colonial possessions, imperial powers constructed networks of railroads that carried people and goods from hinterlands to the coasts. From there, steamships bore them across the seas. Completion of the Suez Canal in 1869 shortened ship voyages between Europe and Asia and lowered the costs of interregional trade. Information moved even faster than cargoes, thanks to the laying of telegraph cables under the oceans, supplemented by overland telegraph lines.

CHARLES DARWIN AND NATURAL SELECTION Although machines were the most visible evidence that humans could master the universe, perhaps the most momentous shift in the conception of nature derived from the travels of one British scientist: **Charles Darwin** (1809–1882). Longing to see exotic fauna, in 1831 he signed on for a four-year voyage on a surveying vessel bound for Latin America and the South Seas. As the ship's naturalist, Darwin collected large quantities of specimens and recorded observations daily. After returning to England, he became convinced that the species of organic life had evolved under the uniform pressure of natural laws, not by means of a special, one-time creation as described in the Bible.

Darwin's theory, articulated in his *Origin of Species* (1859), laid out the principles of **natural selection**. Inevitably, he claimed, populations grew faster than the food supply; this condition created a "struggle for existence" among species. In later work he showed how the passing on of individual traits was also determined by what he called sexual selection—according to which the "best" mates are chosen for their strength, beauty, or talents. The outcome: the "fittest" survived to reproduce, while the less adaptable did not. The "economy of nature" was, Darwin confessed, a painful reality: people would rather behold "nature's face bright with gladness" than recognize that some animals must be others' prey and that shortages are, ultimately, part of nature's "miraculous efficiency." Although Darwin's book dealt exclusively with animals (and mostly with birds), his readers immediately wondered what his theory implied for humans. (See Primary Source: *The Origin of Species.*)

A passionate debate began among scientists and laymen, clerics and anthropologists. Some read Darwin's doctrine of

Charles Darwin. Darwin testing the speed of a tortoise in the Galapagos Islands. It was during his visit to these islands that Darwin developed many of the ideas that he would put forth in his 1859 *Origin of Species.*

the "survival of the fittest" to mean that it was natural for the strong nations to dominate the weak, or justifiable to allow disabled persons to die—something Darwin explicitly refuted. As more groups (mis)interpreted Darwin's theory to suit their own objectives, a set of beliefs known as Social Darwinism legitimated the suffering of the underclasses in industrial society: it was unnatural, Social Darwinists claimed, to tamper with natural selection. In subsequent years Europeans would repeatedly suggest that they had evolved more than Africans and Asians. Extending Darwinian ideas far beyond the scientist's intent, some Europeans came to believe that therefore nature itself gave them the right to rule others.

GLOBAL EXPANSIONISM AND AN AGE OF IMPERIALISM

> → *What were the motives for imperialism and the practices of colonial rulers?*

Increasing rivalries among nations and social tensions within them produced an expansionist wave late in the nineteenth century. Although Africa became the primary focus of interest, a frenzy of territorial conquest overtook Asia as well. The period witnessed the French occupation of Vietnam,

Cambodia, and Laos, and the British expansion in Malaya (present-day Malaysia). In China's territories, competition by foreign powers to establish spheres of influence heated up in the 1890s. And in India, imperial ambitions provoked the British to conquer Burma (present-day Myanmar). Moreover, Britain and Russia competed for preeminence from their respective outposts in Afghanistan and central Asia. In the Americas, expansion usually involved the incorporation of new territories as provinces, making them integral parts of the nation.

In Asia and Africa, however, European imperialism turned far-flung territories into colonial possessions. Here, inhabitants were usually designated as subjects of the empire without the rights and privileges of citizens. Britain's imperial regime in India provided lessons to a generation of European colonial officials in Africa and other parts of Asia on how to build this kind of empire.

INDIA AND THE IMPERIAL MODEL

Britain's successful colonial rule in India provided a model for others, but its methods of rule also were responses to popular discontent. Having suppressed the Indian Rebellion of 1857 (see Chapter 16), authorities revamped the colonial administration. Indians were not to be appeased—and certainly not brought into British public life. But they did have to be governed, and the economy had to be revived. So, after replacing East India Company rule by crown government in 1858, the British set out to make India into a more secure

THE ORIGIN OF SPECIES

Charles Darwin's Origin of Species *(1859) was the product of his many years of studying animals and plants. In addressing the question "How and why are new species created?" the book described the process of natural selection, according to which nature creates overabundance so that the "fittest" species survive and adapt themselves to their environments. Although Darwin's book said nothing about human beings, his contemporaries speculated on his theory's implications for the evolution of human beings.*

Again, it may be asked, how is it that varieties, which I have called incipient species, become ultimately converted into good and distinct species, which in most cases obviously differ from each other far more than do the varieties of the same species? How do those groups of species, which constitute what are called distinct genera, and which differ from each other more than do the species of the same genus, arise? All these results . . . follow inevitably from the struggle for life. Owing to this struggle for life, any variation, however slight and from whatever cause proceeding, if it be in any degree profitable to an individual of any species, in its infinitely complex relations to other organic beings and to external nature, will tend to the preservation of that individual, and will generally be inherited by its offspring. The offspring, also, will thus have a better chance of surviving, for, of the many individuals of any species which are periodically born, but a small number can survive. I have called this principle, by which each slight variation, if useful, is preserved, by the term of Natural Selection, in order to mark its relation to man's power of selection. We have seen that man by selection can certainly produce great results, and can adapt organic beings to his own uses, through the accumulation of slight but useful variations, given to him by the hand of Nature. But Natural Selection, as we shall hereafter see, is a power incessantly ready for action, and is as immeasurably superior to man's feeble efforts, as the works of Nature are to those of Art.

We will now discuss in a little more detail the struggle for existence. . . . I should premise that I use the term Struggle for Existence in a large and metaphorical sense, including dependence of one being on another, and including (which is more important) not only the life of the individual, but success in leaving progeny. Two canine animals in a time of dearth, may be truly said to struggle with each other which shall get food and live. But a plant on the edge of a desert is said to struggle for life against the drought, though more properly it should be said to be dependent on the moisture. . . .

A struggle for existence inevitably follows from the high rate at which all organic beings tend to increase. Every being, which during its natural lifetime produces several eggs or seeds, must suffer destruction during some period of its life, and during some season or occasional year, otherwise, on the principle of geometrical increase, its numbers would quickly become so inordinately great that no country could support the product. Hence, as more individuals are produced than can possibly survive, there must in every case be a struggle for existence, either one individual with another of the same species, or with the individuals of distinct species, or with the physical conditions of life. . . . Although some species may be now increasing, more or less rapidly, in numbers, all cannot do so, for the world would not hold them.

It may be said that natural selection is daily and hourly scrutinising, throughout the world, every variation, even the slightest; rejecting that which is bad, preserving and adding up all that is good; silently and insensibly working, whenever and wherever opportunity offers, at the improvement of each organic being in relation to its organic and inorganic conditions of life. We see nothing of these slow changes in progress, until the hand of time has marked the long lapses of ages, and then so imperfect is our view into long past geological ages, that we only see that the forms of life are now different from what they formerly were.

→ *How does Darwin explain the divergence of species?*
→ *Why does Darwin think struggle is inevitable for all living beings?*

SOURCE: Charles Darwin, *The Origin of Species*, Chapters 3 and 4.

Sinews of the Raj. (*Top*) During the second half of the nineteenth century, the British built an extensive system of railroads to develop India as a profitable colony and to maintain military security. This engraving shows the East India Railway around 1863. (*Bottom*) The British allowed several native princes to remain as long as they accepted imperial paramountcy. This photograph shows a road-building project in one such princely state. Officials of the Muslim princely ruler and British advisers supervise the workers.

and productive colony. This period of British sovereignty was known as the **Raj** ("rule").

The most urgent tasks facing the British in India were those of modernizing its transportation and communication systems and transforming the country into an integrated colonial state. These changes had begun under the governor-general of the East India Company, Lord Dalhousie, who oversaw the development of India's modern infrastructure. When he left office in 1856, he boasted that he had harnessed India to the "great engines of social improvement—I mean Railways, uniform Postage, and the Electric Telegraph." A year later, northern India exploded in the 1857 rebellion. But the rebellion also demonstrated the military value of railroads and telegraphs, for these modern systems were useful tools for rushing British troops to severely affected regions.

After the British suppressed the revolt, they took up the construction of public works with renewed vigor. Railways were a key element in this project, attracting approximately £150 million of British capital. (Though it came from British investors, Indian taxpayers paid off the debt through their taxes.) The first railway line opened in 1853, and by 1910 India had 30,627 miles of track in operation—the fourth largest railway system in the world.

Construction of other public works followed. Engineers built dams across rivers to tame their force and to irrigate lands; workers installed a grid of telegraph lines that opened communication between distant parts of the region. These public works served imperial and economic purposes: India was to become a consumer of British manufactures and a supplier of primary staples such as cotton, tea, wheat, vegetable oil seeds, and jute (used for making rope or burlap sacking). The control of India's massive rivers allowed farmers to cultivate the rich floodplains, transforming them into lucrative cotton-producing provinces. On the hillsides of the island of Ceylon and the northeastern plains of India, the British established vast plantations to grow tea—which was then marketed in England as a healthier alternative to Chinese green tea. India also became an important consumer of British manufactures, especially textiles, in an ironic turnaround to its centuries-old tradition of exporting its own cotton and silk textiles.

India recorded a consistent surplus in its foreign trade through the export of agricultural goods and raw materials. But what India gained from its trade to the world it lost to Britain, its colonial master, because it had to pay for interest on railroad loans, salaries to colonial officers (even when they went on furlough in Britain), and the maintenance of imperial troops outside India. In reality, India ended up balancing Britain's huge trade deficits with the rest of the world, especially the Americas.

Nonetheless, administrative programs made India into a unified territory and enabled its inhabitants to regard themselves as "Indians." These were the first steps to becoming a "nation"—like Italy and the United States. But there were profound differences. Indians lacked a single national language, and they were not citizens of their political community who enjoyed sovereignty. Rather, they were colonial subjects ruled by outsiders.

DUTCH COLONIAL RULE IN INDONESIA

The Dutch, like the British, joined the parade of governments trying to modernize and integrate their colonies economically without welcoming colonial peoples into the life of the nation at home. Decades before the British government took control of India away from the East India Company, Holland had terminated the rule of the Dutch East India Company over

Indonesia. Beginning in the 1830s, the Dutch government took administrative responsibility over Indonesian affairs. Holland's new colonial officials envisioned a more regulated colonial economy than that of their British counterparts in India. For example, they ordered Indonesian villagers to allocate one-third of their land for cultivating coffee beans, an important export. In return, the colonial government paid a set price (well below world market prices) and placed a ceiling on rents owed to landowners.

These policies had dreadful local consequences. For example, increased production of the export crops of coffee beans, sugar, and tobacco meant reduced food production for the local population. By the 1840s and 1850s, famine spread across Java; over 300,000 Indonesians perished from starvation. Surviving villagers voiced growing discontent, prompting harsh crackdowns by colonial forces. Back in Holland, the embarrassing spectacle of colonial oppression prompted calls for reform. Thus in the 1860s the Dutch government introduced what it called an ethical policy for governing Asian colonies: it reduced governmental exploitation and encouraged Dutch settlement of the islands and more private enterprise. For Indonesians, however, the replacement of government agents with private merchants made little difference. In some areas, islanders put up fierce resistance. On the sprawling island of Sumatra, for instance, armed villagers fought off Dutch invaders. After decades of warfare, Sumatra was finally subdued in 1904. The shipping of Indonesian staples continued to enrich the Dutch.

COLONIZING AFRICA

No region felt the impact of European colonialism more powerfully than Africa. In 1880, the only two large European colonial possessions there were French Algeria and two British-ruled South African states, the Cape Colony and Natal. But within a mere thirty years, seven European states had carved almost all of Africa into colonial possessions (see Map 17-3).

A major moment in initiating the European scramble for African colonies occurred in 1882 when the British invaded and occupied Egypt. This action provoked the French, who had regarded Egypt as their special sphere of influence ever since Napoleon's 1798 invasion. Indeed, Britain's move not only intensified the two powers' rivalry to seize additional territories in Africa, but it also alarmed the other European states, fearful that they might be left behind. As these powers joined the scramble, Portugal called for an international conference to discuss claims to Africa. Meeting in Berlin between 1884 and 1885, delegates from Germany, Portugal, Britain, France, Belgium, Spain, Italy, the United States, and the Ottoman Empire agreed to carve up Africa and to recognize the acquisitions of any European power that had achieved occupation on the ground.

PARTITIONING THE AFRICAN LANDMASS The consequences for Africa were devastating. Nearly 70 percent of the newly drawn borders failed to correspond to older demarcations of ethnicity, language, culture, and commerce—for Europeans knew little of the landmass beyond its coast and rivers. They based their new colonial boundaries on European trading centers rather than on the location of African population groups. In West Africa, for example, the Yoruba were split between the French in Dahomey and the British in southwestern Nigeria. In fact, Nigeria became an administrative nightmare, as the British attempted to integrate the politically centralized Muslim populations of the north with the city-state Yoruba dwellers and small tribes of the Ibos of the south. (See Global Connections & Disconnections: Drawing the Boundaries of Africa.)

Several motives led the European powers into their frenzied partition of Africa. Although European businesses were primarily interested in Egypt and South Africa, where their investments were lucrative, small-scale traders and investors harbored fantasies of great treasures locked in the vast uncharted interior. Politicians, publicists, and the reading public also took an interest. The writings of explorers like David Livingstone (1813–1873), a Scottish doctor and missionary, and Henry Morton Stanley (1841–1904), an adventurer in the pay of the *New York Herald*, excited readers with accounts of Africa as a continent of unlimited economic potential.

There was also the lure of building personal fortunes and reputations. In eastern Africa, Carl Peters (1856–1918) aspired to found a vast German colony, and he brought German East Africa into existence. In southern Africa, the British champion of imperialism Cecil Rhodes (1853–1902) brought the Rhodesias, Nyasaland, Bechuanaland, the Transvaal, and the Orange Free State into the British Empire. He was delighted that the Rhodesias bore his name.

Even more committed to the imperialist project was Leopold II (r. 1865–1909), king of the Belgians. Not content to be a minor monarch of a small European state, Leopold seized for himself a colonial state eighty times the size of Belgium, dubbing his possession the Congo Independent State. Leopold's agent in the Congo did not shrink from using overwhelming firepower to subdue local populations. The Congo Independent State was unique in that it belonged to a single individual, the Belgian king. It remained so until 1908, when gruesome news of the enslavement and slaughter of innocent Congolese leaked out. After international criticism mounted, the Belgian parliament took away Leopold's African property and made the Congo a Belgian colony.

Other Europeans saw Africa as a grand opportunity for converting souls to Christianity. In fact, Europe's civilizing mission was an important motive in the scramble for African territory. In Uganda, northern Nigeria, and central Africa, missionaries went ahead of European armies, begging the European statesmen to follow their lead.

MAP 17-3   PARTITION OF AFRICA, 1880–1914

The partition of Africa took place between the early 1880s and the outbreak of World War I. Which two European powers gained the most territory in Africa? Which two African states managed to remain independent? What kind of economic and political gain did European powers realize through the colonization of Africa? Did any of the European states realize their ambitions in Africa?

SPANISH MOROCCO 1912

MOROCCO 1912

SPANISH SAHARA 1912

RIO DE ORO 1885

ALGERIA

Algiers

TUNISIA 1881

Tripoli

MEDITERRANEAN SEA

LIBYA 1912

Suez Canal 1869

Alexandria

Cairo

EGYPT (British occupation 1882)

RED SEA

MAURITANIA 1903

FRENCH WEST AFRICA 1880s–1900s

St. Louis

Dakar

SENEGAL

FRENCH SUDAN

Gao

NIGER

GAMBIA

PORT. GUINEA

FRENCH GUINEA 1893

UPPER VOLTA

SIERRA LEONE

Monrovia

LIBERIA

IVORY COAST 1893

GOLD COAST 1898

TOGO 1884

DAHOMEY 1894

NIGERIA 1880s–1900, 1914

MANDARA

CHAD

FRENCH EQUATORIAL AFRICA 1880s–1900s

ANGLO-EGYPTIAN SUDAN (Condominium 1899)

Omdurman

Khartoum

Fashoda

Addis Ababa

ERITREA 1889

Adwa

ETHIOPIA

FRENCH SOMALILAND 1891

Djibouti

BRITISH SOMALILAND

CAMEROON 1884 1912

FERNANDO PO

PRINCIPE

SÃO TOMÉ

RIO MUNI 1912

GABON 1910

MIDDLE CONGO 1910

Brazzaville

Leopoldville

INDEPENDENT STATE OF THE CONGO 1885 (BELGIAN CONGO 1908)

UGANDA 1890

BRITISH EAST AFRICA 1888 (KENYA)

Mogadishu

ITALIAN SOMALILAND 1889

GERMAN EAST AFRICA 1885

PEMBA

ZANZIBAR

Dar-es-Salaam

INDIAN OCEAN

Luanda

ATLANTIC OCEAN

Benguela

ANGOLA

NYASALAND 1891

NORTHERN RHODESIA 1911

Mozambique

SOUTHERN RHODESIA 1888

PORTUGUESE EAST AFRICA (MOZAMBIQUE)

MADAGASCAR 1896

WALVIS BAY

GERMAN SOUTH-WEST AFRICA 1884

BECHUANA-LAND 1885/1896

TRANSVAAL 1900

Johannesburg

WITWATERSRAND

UNION OF SOUTH AFRICA 1910

Cape Town

SWAZILAND 1907

ORANGE FREE STATE 1900

BASUTOLAND 1868

Belgian
British
French
German
Italian
Portuguese
Spanish
British dominion
Independent state

0   500   1000 Miles

0   500   1000 Kilometers

Europeans in Africa. (*Left*) Henry Morton Stanley was one of the most famous of the nineteenth-century explorers in Africa. He first made his reputation when he located the British missionary-explorer David Livingstone, feared dead, in the interior of Africa, uttering the famous words, "Dr. Livingstone, I presume." Stanley worked on behalf of King Leopold, establishing the Belgian king's claims to territories in the Congo and often using superior weaponry to cow African opponents. (*Right*) The ardent British imperialist Cecil Rhodes endeavored to bring as much of Africa as he could under British colonial rule. He had an ambition to create a swath of British-controlled territory that would stretch from the Cape in South Africa to Cairo in Egypt, as this cartoon shows.

AFRICAN RESISTANCE Contrary to European assumptions, Africans did not welcome European "civilization." Resistance, however, was largely futile. Africans faced two unappealing options: they could capitulate to the Europeans and negotiate to limit the loss of their autonomy, or they could fight to preserve their sovereignty. Only a few chose the course of moderation. Lat Dior, a Muslim warlord in Senegal, refused to let the French build a railway through his kingdom. "As long as I live, be well assured," he wrote the French commandant, "I shall oppose with all my might the construction of this railway. I will always answer no, no, and I will never make you any other reply. Even were I to go to rest, my horse, *Malay*, would give you the same answer." Conflict was inevitable, and Lat Dior lost his life in a battle with the French in 1886.

Only Menelik II of Ethiopia repulsed the Europeans, for he knew how to play rivals off one another. By doing so, he procured weapons from the French, British, Russians, and Italians. He also had a united, loyal, and well-equipped army. In 1896, his troops routed Italian forces at the Battle of Adwa, after which Adwa became a celebrated moment in African history. Its memory inspired many of Africa's later nationalist leaders.

Most resisters were ignorant of the disparity in military technology between Africans and Europeans—especially the killing power of European breech-loading weapons and the Maxim machine gun. In addition, the European armies had better tactics and a more sustained appetite for battle. Africa's armies fought during the nonagricultural season, engaging in open battles so as to achieve quick and decisive results

DRAWING THE BOUNDARIES OF AFRICA

The political boundaries of contemporary Africa are largely those drawn by European colonizers, who knew little about the geography of the continent's interior. They characterized Africa as "the dark continent" and were utterly lacking in information about its ethnic groups, its long-distance trading networks, and its history. Lord Salisbury, who was British prime minister while the partition was under way, summed up the problem: "We have been engaged in drawing lines upon maps where no white man's feet have ever trod; we have been giving away mountains and rivers and lakes to each other, only hindered by the small impediment that we never knew exactly where the mountains and rivers and lakes were."

Salisbury's statement reveals the European boundary-making dilemma. The colonizing powers had to lay down the basic lines of partition—those that would separate the European colonies from one another—even before their armies and colonial officials, let alone their mapmakers, had arrived on the scene (see Map 17.3). European knowledge of the interior did not extend much beyond the rivers and their basins, which had attracted much attention from earlier European travelers. So European mapmakers drew the new boundaries to take account of river basins. Thus, for example, the Anglo-Egyptian Sudan and the Belgian Congo followed the river basins of the Nile and Congo rivers. The results of such mapmaking were often catastrophic for African states after they won independence. Consider West Africa, where the French colony of Senegal completely surrounded the tiny British colony of Gambia (see Map 17-4A below). This geographical anomaly

reflected prepartition conditions, since the British had been preeminent on the Gambia River, and the French everywhere else. But what a dilemma it has made for the modern leaders of Senegal and Gambia!

Nigeria is Africa's most populous state today, with a population of well over 100 million. Its tangled postcolonial history of civil war, civil violence, and frequent military coups d'état is a result of the boundary-making decisions by British, French, and Germans as they divided up the Niger River basin area before World War I. The final arrangements turned large and powerful ethnic groups like the Ibo, Yoruba, and Hausa-Fulani peoples into bitter competitors for power in a single state. The boundaries also sliced apart large communities and even small villages that had long histories of dwelling together.

Contemporary Nigeria is surrounded by four states—Benin in the west, Niger and Chad in the north, and Cameroon in the east. The primary decisions about these borders were made between 1880 and 1900 at a time when the British, French, and Germans were only just pushing into the West African interior. These original boundaries completely ignored conditions on the ground. The results were dismaying to many groups, such as the Mandara peoples of northeastern Nigeria and Cameroon (see Map 17-4B below). These peoples had formed a unified Islamic kingdom before the arrival of European colonial powers; now they were split between Nigeria and Cameroon. This was not an unusual occurrence, and the number of African states that found themselves under two or even three colonial administrations was quite substantial.

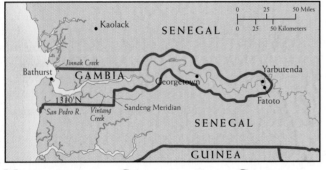

MAP 17-4A   SENEGAL AND GAMBIA

MAP 17-4B   MANDARA PEOPLES

and then returning to their farms. Such military traditions were effective in fighting neighbors, but not well-equipped invaders.

Some African forces did adapt their military techniques to the European challenge. For example, Samori Touré (1830–1900) proved a stubborn foe for the French, employing guerrilla warfare and avoiding full-scale battles in the savannah lands of West Africa. From 1882 until 1898, Touré eluded the French. Dividing his 35,000-man army, Touré had one part take over territories not yet conquered by the French and there reestablish a fully autonomous domain. A smaller contingent conducted a scorched-earth campaign in the regions from which it was retreating, leaving the French with parched and wasted new possessions. But these tactics only delayed the inevitable. The French finally defeated and captured Touré and sent him into exile in Gabon, where he died in 1900.

COLONIAL ADMINISTRATIONS IN AFRICA   Once the euphoria of partition and conquest had worn off, power fell to "men on the spot"—military adventurers, settlers, and entrepreneurs whose main goal was to get rich quick. As these individuals established near-fiefdoms in some areas, Africans (like Native Americans on the other side of the Atlantic) found themselves confined to territories where they could barely provide for themselves. To uphold such an invasive system at minimal expense, Europeans created permanent standing armies by equipping their African supporters, whom they either bribed or compelled to join their side. Such armies bullied local communities into doing the colonial authorities' bidding.

Eventually, these rough-and-ready systems led to violent revolts from aggrieved Africans, and in their aftermath the colonial rulers had to create more efficient and rational administrations. As in India, colonial powers in Africa laid the foundations for future nation-state organizations. Once information trickling out of Africa revealed that the imperial governments were not realizing their goal of bringing "civilization" to the "uncivilized," each European power implemented a new form of colonial rule, stripping the strongman conquerors of their absolute powers.

However much the colonial systems of the European states differed, all had three similar goals. First, the colony was to pay for its own administration. Second, administrators on the spot had to preserve the peace; nothing brought swifter criticism from the mother country than a colonial rebellion. Third, colonial rule was to attract other European groups, such as missionaries, settlers, and merchants. Missionaries came to convert "heathens" to Christianity, convinced that they were battling with Islam for the soul of the continent. Settlers went only to those parts of Africa that had climatic conditions similar to those in Europe. They poured into Algeria and South Africa but only trickled into Kenya,

Battle of Adwa. Portrait of King Menelik, who defeated the Italian forces at the battle of Adwa in 1896, thus saving his country from European colonization.

Southern Rhodesia, Angola, and Mozambique, attracted by advertising at home that stressed comfortable living conditions and promised that these areas would someday become white man's territories. Moreover, colonial governments' promises to construct railroads, roads, and deep-water facilities persuaded European merchants and investors to take out bigger commercial stakes in Africa.

Eventually, stabilized colonies began to deliver on their economic promise. Whereas early imperialism in Africa had relied on the export of ivory and wild rubber, after these resources became depleted the colonies pursued other exports. From the rain forests came cocoa, coffee, palm oil, and palm kernels. From the highlands of East Africa came tea, coffee, sisal (used in cord and twine), and pyrethrum (a flower used to make insecticide). Another important commodity was long-staple, high-quality cotton, grown in Egypt and the Anglo-Egyptian Sudan. Indeed, tropical commodities from all across Africa (as from India and Latin America) flowed to industrializing societies.

Thus, European colonial administrators saw Africa as fitting into the world economy in the same way that British administrators viewed India—as an exporter of raw materials

Diamond Mine. The discovery of diamonds and gold in South Africa in the late nineteenth century led to the investment of large amounts of overseas capital, the mobilization of poorly paid and severely exploited African mine workers, and the Boer War of 1899 to 1902, which resulted in the incorporation of the Afrikaner states of the Transvaal and the Orange Free State into the Union of South Africa.

and an importer of manufactures. They expected Africa to profit from this role. But, in truth, African workers gained little from participating in colonial commerce, while the price they paid in disruption to traditional social and economic patterns was substantial.

Such disruptions were particularly acute in southern Africa, where mining operations lured African men thousands of miles from their homes. Meanwhile, women had to take care of subsistence and cash crop production in the home villages. By the turn of the century the gold mines of Witwatersrand in South Africa required a workforce of 100,000, drawing miners from as far away as Mozambique, the Rhodesias, and Nyasaland, as well as from South Africa itself. Because work below ground was hazardous and health services were inadequate, workers often tried to flee. But armed guards and barbed-wired compounds kept them in the mines. Companies made enormous profits for their European shareholders, while the workers toiled in dangerous conditions and barely eked out a living wage.

To observers, the European empires in Africa seemed solid and durable, but in fact, European colonial rule there was fragile. For all of British Africa, the only all-British force was 5,000 men garrisoned in Egypt. Elsewhere, European officers depended on African military and police forces. And prior to 1914, the number of British administrative officers available for the whole of northern Nigeria was less than 500. These were hardly strong foundations for statehood. It would not take much to destabilize the European order in Africa.

THE AMERICAN EMPIRE

The United States, like Europe, was drawn into the mania of overseas expansion and empire building. Echoing the rhetoric of Manifest Destiny from the 1840s, the expansionists of the 1890s claimed that Americans still had a divine mission to spread their superior civilization and their Christian faith around the globe. However, America's new imperialists followed the European model of colonialism from Asia and Africa: colonies were to provide harbors for American vessels, supply raw materials to American industries, and purchase the surplus production of American farms and factories. These new territorial acquisitions were not intended for American settlement or statehood. Nor were their inhabitants to become American citizens, for nonwhite foreigners were considered unfit for incorporation into the American nation.

The pressure to expand came to a head in the late 1890s, when the United States declared war on Spain and invaded the Philippines, Puerto Rico, and Cuba. From 1895, Cuban patriots had been slowly pushing back Spanish troops and occupying sugar plantations—some of which belonged to American planters. Fearing social revolution off the shores of Florida, the American expansionists presented themselves as the saviors of Spanish colonials yearning for freedom, while at the same time safeguarding property for foreign interests in the Spanish-American War (1898). After defeating Spanish regulars in Cuba, American forces began disarming Cuban rebels and returning lands to their owners.

"That wicked man is going to gobble you up, my child!"

Uncle Sam Leading Cuba. In the years before the Spanish-American War, cartoonists who wished to see the United States intervene on behalf of Cuba in the islanders' struggle for independence from Spain typically depicted Cuba as a white woman in distress. By contrast, in this and other cartoons following the Spanish-American War, Cubans were drawn as black, and usually as infants or boys unable to care for themselves and in need of the benevolent paternal rule of the United States.

Although the Americans claimed that they were intervening to promote freedom in Spain's colonies, they quickly forgot their promises. The United States annexed Puerto Rico after minimal protest, but Cubans and Filipinos resisted becoming colonial subjects. Bitterness ran particularly high among Filipinos, to whom American leaders had promised independence if they joined in the war against Spain. Betrayed, Filipino rebels launched a war for independence in the name of a Filipino nation. In two years of fighting, over 5,000 Americans and perhaps 200,000 Filipinos perished. The outcome: the Philippines became a colony of the United States.

The Women of Algiers in Their Apartment. An oil painting by Eugène Delacroix (1798–1863) of Algerian women being attended by a black servant. European painters in the nineteenth century often used images of women to portray Arab Muslim society.

Colonies in the Philippines and Cuba laid the foundations for a revised model of U.S. expansionism. The earlier pattern had been to turn Indian lands into privately owned farmsteads and to extend the Atlantic market across the continent. But now, in this new era, the nation's largest corporations (with government support) aggressively intervened in the affairs of neighbors near and far. Following the Spanish-American War, the United States repeatedly sent troops to many Caribbean and Central American countries. The Americans preferred to turn these regimes into dependent client states, rather than making them part of the United States itself (as with Alaska and Hawaii) or converting them into formal colonies (as the Europeans had done in Africa and Asia). The entire world was an object for the powerful states to shape to their needs.

IMPERIALISM AND CULTURE

Imperialism gave new legitimacy to ideas of European and American racial superiority, and such ideas made imperialism seem natural and just. In literature and painting, for example, a new genre known as **Orientalism** portrayed non-western peoples as exotic, sensuous, and economically backward with respect to Europeans. But empire did not affect, or interest, all Europeans equally. In general, the extension and upkeep of colonies directly involved only a small minority of Europeans.

At least since the Crusades, Europeans had regularly written and thought about others. These images and ideas had served to inform, entertain, flatter, and criticize European culture. What was novel in the late nineteenth century was the fact that these "others" were now under European control; this seemed to solidify their status as "lower" races. Europe's relationship to them might be one of condescending sympathy or of Darwinian exploitation, but in no sense were the two parties equal. The strong sense that a cultural

The Civilizing Mission. This advertisement for Pears' Soap shamelessly tapped into the idea of Europeans bringing civilization to the people of their colonies. It said that use of Pears' Soap would teach the virtues of cleanliness to the "natives" and implied that it would even lighten their skin.

gradient ran from west to east and from north to south allowed Europeans to put Africans in native costumes on display at the Paris World's Fair of 1889, alongside the "gallery of machines" that represented European cultural progress. Working on the same assumption, European scholars refined their expertise in "oriental" languages, believing that indigenous peoples could not do justice to their own great texts. Although some individuals—including free-traders and socialists—opposed new conquests, for many people European dominance was an undisputed fact.

CELEBRATING IMPERIALISM Especially in middle- and upper-class circles, Europeans celebrated their imperial triumphs. After the invention of photographic film and the Eastman Kodak camera in 1888, imperial images surfaced in popular forms such as postcards and advertisements. Imperial themes also decorated packaging materials; tins of coffee, tea, tobacco, and chocolates featured pictures highlighting the commodities' colonial origins. Cigarettes often had names like "Admiral," "Royal Navy," "Fighter," and "Grand Fleet." Some of this served as propaganda, produced by investors in imperial commodities or by colonial pressure groups.

Propaganda promoted imperialism abroad but also inspired changes at home. For example, champions of empire argued that if the British population did not grow fast enough to fill the world's sparsely settled regions, then the population of other nations would. Population was power, and the number of healthy children provided an accurate measure of global influence. "Empire cannot be built on rickety and flat-chested citizens," warned a British member of Parliament in 1905. In addition, writers for young audiences often invoked colonial settings and themes. Whereas girls' literature stressed domestic service, childrearing, and nurturing, boys' readings depicted exotic locales, devious Orientals and savage Africans, and daring colonial exploits.

PRESSURES OF EXPANSION IN JAPAN, RUSSIA, AND CHINA

> → *How did expansionism affect Japan, Russia, and China?*

The challenge of integrating political communities and extending territorial borders was a problem not just for western Europe and the United States. Other societies also aimed to overcome domestic dissent and establish larger domains. Japan, Russia, and China provide three contrasting models; their differing forms of expansion eventually led them to fight over possessions in East Asia.

JAPAN'S TRANSFORMATION AND EXPANSION

Starting in the 1860s, Japanese rulers tried to recast their country less as an old dynasty and more like a modern nation-state. Since the early seventeenth century, the Tokugawa Shogunate had kept outsiders within strict limits and thwarted internal unrest. But after an American naval officer, Commodore Matthew Perry, entered Edo Bay in 1853 with a fleet of steam-powered ships, other Americans, Russians, Dutch, and British followed in his wake. These outsiders forced the Tokugawa rulers to sign humiliating treaties that opened Japanese ports, slapped limits on Japanese tariffs, and exempted foreigners from Japanese laws. Younger Japanese, especially among the military (samurai) elites, felt that Japan should respond by adopting, not rejecting, western practices. They respected the power demonstrated by the intruding ships and weaponry; yet in adapting Western technology, they expected to remain true to their own culture.

In 1868, a group of reformers toppled the Tokugawa Shogunate and promised to return Japan to its mythic greatness. Then Emperor Mutsuhito—the Meiji ("Enlightened Rule") Emperor—became the symbol of a new Japan. His reign (1868–1912) was called the **Meiji Restoration**. By founding schools, initiating a propaganda campaign, and revamping the army to create a single "national" fighting force, the Meiji government promoted a political community that stressed linguistic and ethnic homogeneity, as well as superiority compared to others. In this way the Meiji leaders overcame age-old regional divisions, subdued local political authorities, and mobilized the country to face the threat from powerful Europeans.

Perry Arrives in Japan. A Japanese woodblock print portraying the uninvited arrival into Edo (Tokyo) Bay on August 7, 1853, of a tall American ship, which was commanded by Matthew Perry. This arrival marked the end of Japan's ability to fully control the terms of its interactions with foreigners.

ECONOMIC DEVELOPMENT One of the Meiji period's remarkable achievements was the nation's economic transformation. After 1871, when the government banned the feudal system and allowed peasants to become small landowners, farmers improved their agrarian techniques and saw their standard of living rise. Some business practices that underlay the economic transformation had taken shape under the Tokugawa Shogunate, but the Meiji government was far more activist in terms of internal modernization. For example, stressing the slogan "rich country, strong army," the energetic new government unified the currency around the yen, created a postal system, introduced tax reforms, laid telegraph lines, formed compulsory foreign trade associations, launched savings and export campaigns, established an advanced civil service system, began to build railroads, and hired thousands of foreign consultants. In 1889, the Meiji government introduced a constitution (based largely on the German model). The following year, 450,000 people—about 1 percent of the population—elected Japan's first parliament, the Imperial Diet.

As the government sold valuable enterprises to the people it knew best, it created private economic dynasties. The new large companies (such as Sumitomo, Yasuda, Mitsubishi, and Mitsui) were family organizations. Fathers, sons, cousins, and uncles ran different parts of large integrated corporations—some in charge of banks, some running the trade wing, some overseeing factories. Women played a crucial role, not just as custodians of the home but also as cultivators of important family alliances, especially among potential marriage partners. In contrast to American limited-liability firms, which issued shares on stock markets to anonymous buyers, Japan's version of large-scale managerial capitalism was a personal affair.

EXPANSIONISM AND CONFLICT WITH NEIGHBORS As in many other emerging nation-states, expansion in Japan was a tempting prospect. It offered the promise of more markets for selling goods and obtaining staples, and it was a way to burnish the image of national superiority and greatness. Japanese ventures abroad were initially spectacularly successful. The Meiji moved first to take over the kingdom of the Ryūkyūs, southwest of Japan (see Map 17-5). A small show of force, only 160 Japanese soldiers, was enough to establish the new Okinawa Prefecture there in 1879. The Japanese regarded the people of the Ryūkyūs as an ethnic minority and refused to incorporate them into the nation-state on equal terms. In contrast with the British in India or the Americans in Puerto Rico, the Japanese conquerors refused to train a native Ryūkyū governing class. Meiji intellectuals insisted that the "backward" Okinawans were unfit for local self-rule and representation.

In 1876, the Japanese fixed upon Korea, which put their plans on a collision course with China's sphere of influence. In a formal treaty, the Japanese recognized Korea as an independent state, opened Korea to trade, and won extraterritorial rights. As a result, the Chinese worried that soon the Japanese would try to take over Korea. These fears were well founded, for Japanese designs on Korea eventually sparked the Sino-Japanese War of 1894–1895, in which the Chinese suffered a humiliating defeat.

![legend-dark]	Japanese Empire, 1870
![legend-mid]	Japanese acquisition, 1874–1895
→	Japanese attacks in Sino-Japanese War, 1894–1895
→	Japanese attacks in Russo-Japanese War, 1904–1905
![legend-light]	Japanese acquisition, 1905–1910

MAP 17-5   JAPANESE EXPANSION, 1870–1910

Under the Meiji Restoration, the Japanese state built a strong national identity and competed with foreign powers for imperial advantage in East Asia. According to the map, what were the first areas that the Japanese Empire acquired as it started to expand? What two empires' spheres of influence were affected by Japan's aggressive attempts at expansion? What were the new Japanese state's objectives? How were they similar to or different from European expansionism of the same period?

Economic Transformation of Japan. During the Meiji period, the government transformed the economy by building railroads, laying telegraph lines, founding a postal system, and encouraging the formation of giant firms known as *zaibatsu*, which were family organizations consisting of factories, import-export businesses, and banks. Here we see a raw-silk-reeling factory that was run by one of the *zaibatsu*.

The Sino-Japanese War accelerated Japan's rapid transformation to a nation-state and a colonial power with no peer in Asia. Having lost the war, China ceded the province of Taiwan to the Japanese. Japan also annexed Korea in 1910 and converted Taiwan and Korea into the twin jewels of its young empire. The colonial administration built transportation networks and established educational and health institutions—while keeping the colonized people out of top managerial and technical positions. Like the British in India, the Japanese regarded their colonial subjects as racially inferior and unworthy of the privileges of citizenship. And like other imperial powers, the Japanese expected their possessions to serve the metropolitan center. Densely populated and short of land, Japan wanted these colonies to become granaries, sending rice to the mother country. Moreover, the Meiji regime exploited Taiwanese sugar exports to relieve a Japanese economy heavily dependent on imports. Indeed, by serving as staple-exporting regions, Korea and Taiwan were a source of foreign exchange that helped defray Japan's trade deficits. They had grown huge as a result of massive imports to build up new industries.

RUSSIAN TRANSFORMATION AND EXPANSION

Russia expanded out of a sense of mission and a need to defend against other countries expanding along its immense border. Facing an emerging Germany, a British presence in the Middle East and Persia, a consolidating China, and an ascendant Japan, Russia knew it would have to enlarge its ter-

ritorial domain. So it established a number of expansionist fronts simultaneously: southwest to the Black Sea, south into the Caucasus and Turkestan, and east into Manchuria (see Map 17-6). Success depended on annexing territories and establishing protectorates over vulnerable conquered peoples.

Looking west and south, Russia invaded the Ottoman territories of Moldavia (present-day Moldova) and Walachia (present-day Romania) in 1853. The invasion provoked opposition from Britain and France, who joined with the Ottomans to defeat Russia in the Crimean War (1853–1856). By exposing Russia's lack of modern weapons and its problems in supplying troops without a railway system, the defeat spurred a course of aggressive modernization and expansion.

MODERNIZATION AND INTERNAL REFORM In the 1860s, Tsar Alexander II launched a wave of "Great Reforms" to make Russia more competitive. Autocratic rule continued, but officials reintegrated the society. In 1861, for example, a decree emancipated peasants from serfdom. Other changes included a sharp reduction in the duration of military service, a program of education for the conscripts, and the beginnings of a mass school system to teach children reading, writing, and Russian culture. Starting in the 1890s, as railroads and factories expanded, so did the steel, coal, and petroleum industries. But while the reforms strengthened the state, they did not enhance the lives of common people. Workers in Russia were brutally exploited, even by the standards of the industrial revolution. Also, large landowners had kept most of the empire's fertile land, and the peasants had to pay substantial redemption fees for the poorer-quality plots they received.

MAP 17-6 RUSSIAN EXPANSION, 1801–1914

The Russian state continued to expand in the nineteenth century. According to this map, what lands did Russia acquire during the period 1796–1855? What lands did it acquire next? Compare this map on Russian expansion with Map 13-7 (p. 515). How did the direction of Russia's expansion change in the nineteenth century? Which states did the expanding Russian Empire more resemble in this era, western Europe (such as Great Britain) or American states (such as the United States)?

The reforms revealed a fundamental problem: the rulers were eager to reform society, but not the basis of government (autocracy). This caused liberals, conservatives, and malcontents alike to question the state-led modernizing mission. Before long, in the press, courtrooms, and streets, men and women denounced the regime. Revolutionaries engaged in terror and assassination. In 1881, a terrorist bomb blew the tsar to pieces. In the 1890s, following another famine, the radical doctrines of Marxism (see Chapter 16) gained popularity in Russia. Even aristocratic intellectuals, such as the author of *War and Peace,* Count Leo Tolstoy, lamented their despotic government.

TERRITORIAL EXPANSION Yet the critics of internal reform did not hold back the Russian expansionists, who be-

lieved they had to take over certain lands to keep them out of rivals' hands. So they conquered the highland people of the Caucasus Mountains to prevent Ottomans and Persians from encroaching on Russia's southern flank. And they battled the British over areas between Turkestan and British India, such as Persia (Iran) and Afghanistan. Although some Russians moved to these lands, they never became a majority there. The new provinces were multiethnic, multireligious communities that were only partially integrated into the Russian state. (See Primary Source: Two Faces of Empire.)

Perhaps the most impressive Russian expansion occurred in East Asia, where the underpopulated Amur River basin boasted rich lands, mineral deposits, and access to the Pacific Ocean. The Chinese also wanted to colonize this area,

TWO FACES OF EMPIRE

Russification (forced assimilation) was one of the Russian Empire's responses to the challenge of the nation-state idea. In 1863 the tsar prohibited publication of the Bible in the Little Russian (Ukrainian) language, alienating many otherwise loyal Slavic subjects. By contrast, most non-Christians, such as the Muslims of newly annexed Turkestan (central Asia), were exempted from Russification because they were considered "aliens" who should be ruled separately. The excerpts below present an 1876 edict prohibiting the use of Ukrainian, and a celebration of colonialism by a member of the Russian governor-general's office in Turkestan.

Russification in Ukraine

In order to halt what is, from the state's point of view, the dangerous activity of the Ukrainophiles, it is appropriate to take the following measures immediately: 1. To prohibit the import into the empire of any books published abroad in the Little Russian dialect [Ukrainian], without the special permission of the Chief Press Administration. 2. To prohibit the printing inside of the empire of any original works or translations in this dialect, with the exception of historical documents. . . . 3. Equally to prohibit any dramatic productions, musical lyrics and public lectures (which at present have the charter of Ukrainophile demonstrations) in this dialect. . . . 6. To strengthen supervision by the local educational administration so as not to allow any subjects in primary schools be taught in the Little Russian dialect. . . . 7. To clear the libraries of all primary and secondary schools in the Little Russian provinces of books and pamphlets prohibited by paragraph 2. . . . 8. . . . To demand from the heads of these districts a list of teachers with a note as to their reliability in relation to Ukrainophile tendencies. Those noted as unreliable or doubtful should be transferred to Great Russian provinces.

Colonialism in Turkestan

Our battalion arrived in Tashkent four years after Turkestan had been annexed to the empire. Tashkent at that time looked more like a military settlement than the chief city of the region, that is the capital of Russian Central Asia. The majority of the inhabitants were soldiers, either resting after some campaign or else about to go out on a new expedition. Civilians and women were a rarity. Now, thirty-six years later, looking proudly at the path we have followed, I can see the colossal results achieved by the Russian government, always humane to the vanquished, but insistently pursuing its civilising mission. Of course, there have been many mistakes, there have been abuses, but this has not halted the rational and expedient intentions of the government. We went into a region which had a population alien to us. . . . They had for many centuries been accustomed to submitting humbly to the barbaric and cruel despotism of their rulers, but they nevertheless came to terms with their position because their rulers were of their own faith. . . . The fanatical mullahs began rumours amongst the mass of the population that, instead of true believer khans, they were to be ruled by heathens who would convert them to Christianity, put crosses around their necks, send them to be soldiers, introduce their own laws, revoke the Sharia [the fundamental law of Islam] and make their wives and daughters uncover their faces.

. . . Frequent outbursts, uprisings and disorders took place and repression followed. But at the same time the natives saw that the very first steps of the first Governor-General proved the complete falseness of the mullahs. . . . It was announced solemnly everywhere to the local population, that as subjects of the Russian monarch, the population would keep its faith, its national customs, its courts and its judges, that all taxes demanded by the previous collectors were illegal and burdensome in the extreme and would be revoked, and that instead just taxes would be imposed, and that the position of women would remain inviolable. All this of course soon calmed the population and an industrious people settled down to a peaceful life.

→ Based on the "Russification in Ukraine" document, explain how important the arts and education can be in maintaining a people's identity—and in subverting a foreign power's authority.

→ According to the "Colonialism in Turkestan" document, what steps did the Russians take to calm the Muslims' fears of colonial domination?

SOURCE: Martin McCauley and Peter Waldron, *The Emergence of the Modern Russian State, 1855–1881* (Totowa, NJ: Barnes and Noble Books, 1988), pp. 209, 211–12.

The Trans-Siberian Railroad. Russia's decision to build a railway across Siberia to the Pacific Ocean derived from a desire to expand the empire's power in East Asia and to forestall British advances in Asia. The colossal undertaking, which claimed the lives of thousands of workers, reached completion just as Russia clashed militarily with Japan. The new railroad ferried Russian troops over long distances to battles, such as the one at Mukden, in Manchuria, which was then the largest land battle in the history of warfare.

which lay just north of Manchuria. After twenty years of struggle, Russia claimed the land north and south of the Amur River and in 1860 founded Vladivostok, a port on the Pacific Ocean whose name signified "Rule the East." Deciding to focus on these areas in Asia, the Russian government sold its one territory in North America (Alaska) to the United States. Then, to link the capital (Moscow) and the western part of the country to its East Asian spoils, the government began construction of the Trans-Siberian Railroad. When it was completed in 1903, the new railroad bridged the east and the west. Russia then began to eye the Korean peninsula, on which Japan, too, had set its sights.

GOVERNING A DIVERSE NATION   Russia was a huge empire whose rulers were only partially effective at integrating its diverse parts into a political community. In 1897, during the first complete population census, ethnographers struggled over what to call all the empire's peoples: nations or tribes. In the end, authorities chose the term *nationalities,* recognizing 104 of them, speaking 146 languages and dialects. Ethnic Russians accounted for slightly more than half the population.

Counting and categorizing peoples formed part of the state's attempts to figure out how to govern this diverse realm. As the United States did, Russia made conquered regions into full parts of the empire. But unlike the United States, Russia was suspicious of decentralized federalism, fearing it would lead groups to demand secession. Moreover, the tsars were terrified by the idea of popular sovereignty. Preferring the tried-and-true method of centralized autocracy, they divided most of the empire into governorships ruled by appointed civilian or military governors who were supposed to function like local tsars or autocrats.

Unlike the United States, which displaced or slaughtered native populations during its expansion across an entire continent, Russia mostly assimilated the new peoples. In this daunting task, the state's approach ranged from outright repression (of Poles and Jews) to favoritism (toward Baltic Germans and Finns), although the beneficiaries of favoritism often later lost favor if they became too strong. Further, unlike the United States, which managed to pacify borders with its weaker neighbors, Russia faced the constant suspicions of Persians and Ottomans and the menace of British troops in Afghanistan. (The troops were there to prevent Russia from cutting off the overland route to India.) In East Asia, a clash with expansionist Japan loomed on the horizon.

Such expansionism was a constant fiscal drain and a heavy burden on the population. To promote the image of a great Russian Empire, rulers leaned more heavily on the rural poor and pursued intensive modernization, but that generated instability. For the time being, Moscow's main threat did not come from within Russia's borders. It came from the outside.

CHINA UNDER PRESSURE

While the Russians and Japanese scrambled to copy European models of industrialism and imperialism, the Qing were slower to mobilize against threats from the west. Even as the European powers were dividing up China into spheres of influence, Qing officials were much more worried about internal revolts and threats from their northern borders. Into the 1850s and 1860s, many Qing officials still regarded the increasing European incursions and demands as a lesser danger by comparison.

ADOPTING WESTERN LEARNING AND SKILLS A growing number of Chinese officials, however, recognized the superior armaments and technology of rival powers and were deeply troubled by the threat posed by European military might. Starting in the 1860s, reformist bureaucrats sought to adopt elements of western learning and technological skills—but with the intention of keeping the core Chinese culture intact.

This so-called **Self-Strengthening movement** included a variety of new ventures: arsenals, shipyards, coal mines, a steamship company to contest the foreign domination of coastal shipping, and schools for learning foreign ways and languages. Most interesting was the dispatch abroad of about 120 schoolboys under the charge of Yung Wing. The first Chinese graduate of an American college (Yale University, 1854), Yung believed that western education would greatly benefit Chinese students, so he took his charges to Connecticut in the 1870s to attend school and live with American families. Conservatives at the Qing court were soon dismayed by reports of the students' interest in Christianity and aptitude for baseball. In 1881, after the U.S. government refused to admit the boys into military academies, they summoned the students home.

Yung Wing's abortive educational mission was not the only setback for the Self-Strengthening movement, for skepticism about western technology was rife among conservative officials. Some insisted that the introduction of machinery would lead to unemployment; others worried that railways would facilitate western military maneuvers and lead to an invasion; still others complained that the crisscrossing tracks disturbed the harmony between humans and nature. The first short railway track ever laid in China was torn up in 1877 shortly after being built, and the country had only 288 kilometers of track prior to 1895.

Although they did not acknowledge the railroad's usefulness, the Chinese did adopt other new technologies to access a wider range of information. For example, by the early 1890s there were about a dozen Chinese-language newspapers (as distinct from the foreign-language press) published in major cities, with the largest ones having a circulation of 10,000 to 15,000. To avoid government intervention, these papers sidestepped political controversy; instead, they featured commercial news and literary contributions. In 1882, the newspaper *Shenbao* made use of a new telegraph line to publish dispatches within China.

INTERNAL REFORM EFFORTS China's defeat by Japan in the Sino-Japanese War (1894–1895), sparked by quarrels over Korea, prompted the first serious attempt at reform by the Qing. Known as the Hundred Days' Reform, the episode lasted only from June to September 1898. The force behind it was a thirty-seven-year-old scholar named Kang Youwei and his twenty-two-year-old student Liang Qichao. Citing rulers such as Peter the Great of Russia and the Meiji Emperor of Japan as their inspiration, the reformers urged Chinese leaders to develop a railway network, a state banking system, a modern postal service, and institutions to foster the development of agriculture, industry, and commerce.

The reformers' opportunity to accelerate change came in the summer of 1898 when the twenty-seven-year-old Guangxu Emperor decided to implement many of their ideas, including changes in the venerable civil service examination system. But the effort was short-lived, for conservative officials rallied behind Guangxu's aunt, the Empress Dowager Cixi, who emerged from retirement to overturn the reforms. The young emperor was put under house arrest. Kang and Liang fled for their lives and went into exile. It would take still more military defeats to finally jolt the Qing court into action, but by then it was too late to save the regime.

The reforms of the Self-Strengthening movement were too modest and poorly implemented. Very few Chinese acquired new skills. Despite talk of modernizing, the civil service examination remained based on Confucian classics and still opened the only doors to government service. Governing elites were not yet ready to reinvent the principles of their political community, and they adhered instead to the traditional dynastic structure.

By the late nineteenth century, the success of the Qing regime in expanding its territories a century earlier seemed like a distant memory, as various powers repeatedly forced it to make economic and territorial concessions. Unlike Japan or Russia, however, the Qing government resisted any comprehensive social reforms (until after the turn to the twentieth century), and its policies left the country vulnerable to both external aggression and internal instability.

 CONCLUSION

Between 1850 and 1914, most of the world's people lived not in nation-states but in landed empires or in the colonies of nation-states. But as reformers sought a new political framework in response to popular upheavals and economic changes, the nation-state became a desirable form of governance.

Although the ideal of "a people" united by territory, history, and culture grew increasingly popular worldwide, it was not easy to make it a reality. Official histories, national heroes, novels, poetry, and music helped, but central to the process of nation formation were the actions of bureaucrats. Asserting sovereignty over what it claimed as national territory, the state "nationalized" diverse populations by creating a unified system of law, education, military service, and government.

Colonization beyond borders was another part of nation building in many societies. In these efforts, territorial conquests took place under the banner of nationalist endeavors. In Europe, the Americas, Japan, and to some extent Russia, the intertwined processes of nation building and territorial expansion were most effective. The Amazon River basin, Okinawa, and especially the North American West became important provinces of integrated nation-states, populated with settlers who produced for national and international markets.

However, the integrating impulses of emerging nations did not wipe out local differences, mute class antagonisms, or eliminate gender inequalities. Even as Europeans and Americans came to see themselves as chosen—by God or by natural selection—to rule the rest, they suffered deep divisions. Not everyone identified with the nation-state or the empire, or agreed on what it meant to belong or to conquer. But by the century's end, racist advocates and colonial lobbyists seem to have convinced many that their interests and destinies were bound up with their nations' unity, prosperity, and global clout.

Ironically, nation building had an unintended consequence, for self-determination could also apply to racial or ethnic minorities at home and in the colonies. Armed with the rhetoric of progress and uplift, colonial authorities tried to subjugate distant people, but colonial subjects themselves often asserted the language of "nation" and accused imperial overlords of betraying their own lofty principles. As the twentieth century opened, Filipino and Cuban rebels used Thomas Jefferson's Declaration of Independence to oppose American invaders, Koreans defined themselves as a nation crushed under Japanese heels, and Indian nationalists made colonial governors feel shame for violating English standards of "fair play."

Review and research materials are available at StudySpace: ⓖ WWNORTON.COM/STUDYSPACE

KEY TERMS

Charles Darwin (p. 647)
imperialism (p. 633)
limited-liability joint-stock company (p. 637)
Manifest Destiny (p. 634)
Meiji Restoration (p. 658)

natural selection (p. 647)
Orientalism (p. 657)
Raj (p. 650)
Self-Strengthening movement (p. 665)
steel (p. 645)

Chronology

1850

THE AMERICAS		1861–1865 U.S. Civil War 1867 Canada gains self-rule ♦ 1867 Russia sells Alaska to the U.S.♦
EUROPE	♦ 1859 Publication of Darwin's Origin of Species 1870–1871 Franco-Prussian War ♦--♦	
RUSSIA	♦----------♦ 1853–1856 Crimean War 1860s "Great Reforms" to modernize Russia ♦------------------------------♦	
EAST AND SOUTHEAST ASIA	♦ 1853 Commodore Perry "opens" Japan 1860s–1890s Self-Strengthening movement (China) ♦-------- 1860s–1890s French occupation of Vietnam, Cambodia, and Laos ♦-------- 1868–1912 Meiji Era in Japan ♦--------- 1872 Japan takes over Ryūkyūs ♦ 1870s–1880s British expansion in Southeast Asia ♦---------	
AFRICA	1869 Opening of Suez Canal ♦	
SOUTH ASIA	♦ 1858 "The Raj" begins in India	

STUDY QUESTIONS

1. Explain the process of nation building that occurred in the nineteenth century. What polities initiated these efforts, and what different strategies were involved?

2. Identify where strong nation-states emerged during this period. How did the nation-state idea challenge certain polities and other organized groups?

3. Define imperialism. Why did state-directed efforts at nation building often lead to imperialist efforts and other forms of territorial expansion?

4. List and explain several major sources of the new wave of imperialism that occurred in the second half of the nineteenth century. To what extent did these ideas find support among the populations of imperialist states?

5. Analyze to what extent different colonized societies resisted imperialist efforts. How successful were their actions?

6. Describe the policies that imperial powers used to govern their overseas colonies. What were the goals of imperial administrations, and how successful were they in achieving them?

7. Analyze the cultural impact of imperialist ambitions on imperialist nations themselves. How did colonization and territorial expansion shape notions of race and ethnicity there?

8. Analyze how the spread of nationalism and imperialism shaped state behavior in China, Russia, and Japan. To what extent did each state adapt to these new patterns?

9. Explain how nation-state building, territorial expansion, and imperialism reshaped the global economy. How would you describe the relationship between industrial regions and the rest of the world's societies?

1875   1900

1888 Brazil abolishes slavery ◆

1898 Spanish-American War ◆

1887–1889 Construction of the Eiffel Tower ◆-------◆

1891–1903 Russia constructs Trans-Siberian Railroad ◆--------------------→

1894–1895 Sino-Japanese War

1882 British occupy Egypt ◆

1884–1885 Berlin Conference on Africa ◆---◆

◆ 1877 Victoria crowned empress of India

An Unsettled World, 1890–1914

*I*n 1905 a young African man, Kinjikitile Ngwale, began to move among various ethnic groups in German East Africa, spreading a message of opposition to German colonial authorities. In the tradition of visionary prophets (see Chapter 16), Kinjikitile claimed that by anointing his followers with blessed water (*maji* in Swahili), he could protect them from European bullets and drive the Germans from East Africa. Kinjikitile's reputation spread rapidly, drawing followers from across 100,000 square miles of territory. Although German officials soon executed Kinjikitile, they could not prevent a broad uprising, called the Maji-Maji Revolt. The Germans brutally suppressed the revolt, killing between 200,000 and 300,000 Africans.

The Maji-Maji Revolt and its aftermath revealed the intensity of opposition to the world of nations and their empires. In Europe and North America, critics who felt deprived of the full benefits of industrializing nation-states—especially women, wage workers, and frustrated nationalists—demanded far-reaching reforms. In Asia, Africa, and Latin America, anticolonial critics and exploited classes protested European domination. In the face of so much unrest from within their nations and from their colonies, Europeans' faith in the idea of progress and the superiority of their "civilization" was shaken. Ironically, this occurred at the very moment when Europeans and people of European descent seemed to have established preeminence in world affairs.

This chapter tackles the anxieties and insecurities that unsettled the world around the turn of the twentieth century. It ties them in particular to several key factors: (1) the uprooting of millions of people from countryside to city and from one continent to another, (2) discontent with the poverty that many suffered even as economic production leaped upward, (3) frustration with the incomplete expansion of rights within nation-states and the incomplete realization of national aspirations, and, (4) in Asia and Africa, resentment of and resistance to European domination. Around the globe, this tumult caused a questioning of old ideas that led to a flowering of new thinking and fresh artistic expression under the label of "modernism." This unsettling movement was a defining feature of the era.

PROGRESS, UPHEAVAL, AND MOVEMENT

> → *How did an unsettled world produce new opportunities and anxieties?*

The decades leading up to 1914 were a time of unprecedented possibility for some, and social disruption and economic frustration for others. They were also years of anxiety worldwide. Rapid economic progress brought challenges to the established order and the people in power. In Europe and the United States, radicals and middle-class reformers agitated for political and social change. In areas colonized by European countries and the United States, resentment focused on either colonial rulers or indigenous elites. Even in nations such as China, which had not been formally colonized but which faced repeated intrusions, popular discontent targeted domination by Europeans. In China, Mexico, and Russia, angry peasants and workers allied with frustrated reformers to topple autocratic regimes.

In the late nineteenth century, whole new industries fueled economic growth, especially in the industrial countries and in territories that exported vital raw materials to Europe and the United States. But industrial capitalism also spurred inequalities within industrial countries and, especially, between the world's industrial and nonindustrial regions. It also brought unwelcome changes in how and where people worked and lived. Rural folk flocked into the cities, hoping to escape the poverty that encumbered most people in the countryside. In the cities, even though public building projects produced sewer systems, museums, parks, and libraries, the poor had little access to them. Anxieties intensified when economic downturns left thousands out of work. This led, in some cases, to organized opposition to authoritarian regimes or to the free market system.

In Europe and North America, as industrialization expanded, a generation of younger artists, writers, and scientists known as **modernists** broke with older conventions and sought new ways of seeing and describing the world. In Asia, Africa, and South America as well, many modernists were energized by the idea of moving beyond traditional forms of art, literature, music, and science. But the modernist generation's exuberance worried those who were not ready to give up their cultural traditions and institutions. In the colonized world, and in areas threatened by colonial domination, "modernism" seemed to some to mean full-on "westernization" and with it, the loss of cultural autonomy. The acceleration of cultural change, like that of economic advances, sparked new conflicts and new anxieties both within states and across the globe.

PEOPLES IN MOTION

If the world was being *unsettled* by political, economic, and cultural changes, it was also being *resettled* by mass emigration (see Map 18-1). Consider what historian Alfred Crosby

Focus Questions

◎ WWNORTON.COM/STUDYSPACE

→ *How did an unsettled world produce new opportunities and anxieties?*

→ *How did Africans and Chinese show their opposition to imperialism?*

→ *What were the sources of unease around the world?*

→ *How did different fields reflect cultural modernism?*

→ *How did conceptions about race and nation change during this era?*

called the "Caucasian tsunami": the emigration of throngs of Europeans to North America, Australia, Argentina, Africa, and Cuba. The "tsunami" began after the Napoleonic wars and gathered momentum in the 1840s, when the Irish fled their starving communities to seek better lives in North America. After 1870, the flow of Europeans became a torrent. The United States was the favored destination, with European migrants exceeding by sixfold the number of Europeans who migrated to Argentina (the second-place receiving country) between 1871 and 1920. The high point occurred between 1901 and 1910, when over 6 million Europeans entered the United States. This was nothing less than a demographic revolution.

EMIGRATION, IMMIGRATION, INTERNAL MIGRATION Europeans were not the only peoples on the move. Between the 1840s and the 1940s, 29 million South Asians migrated into the Malay Peninsula and Burma (British colonies), the Dutch Indies (Indonesia), East Africa, and the Caribbean. Most were recruited to labor on plantations, railways, and mines in British-controlled territories. Merchants followed laborers, and soon the South Asian migrant populations became more diverse. Meanwhile, the Chinese, too, emigrated in significant numbers. Between 1845 and 1900, forces such as population pressure, a shortage of cultivable land, and social turmoil drove 800,000 Chinese to seek new homes in North and South America, New Zealand, Hawaii, and the West Indies. Close to four times as many settled in Southeast Asia.

Moreover, industrial changes caused millions to migrate *within* their own countries or to neighboring ones, seeking employment in the burgeoning cities or other opportunities in frontier regions. In North America, hundreds of thousands headed west, while millions relocated from the countryside to the cities. In Asia, about 10 million Russians went east to Siberia and central Asia, and 2 million Koreans moved northwest to Manchuria. In Africa, small numbers of South Africans moved north into Northern and Southern Rhodesia in search of arable land and precious metals. Across the world, gold rushes, silver rushes, copper rushes, and a diamond rush took people across landmasses and across oceans. Mostly men, these emigrants were hell-bent on profit and often willing to destroy the land in order to extract precious commodities as quickly as possible.

People traveled with varying credentials and goals. Some went as colonial officials or soldiers; some as missionaries or big-game hunters—most of these folks did not plan to stay. Merchants and traders were more likely to settle in for the long term. Several million East Asians (mostly Chinese) went to the Philippines and South Africa, California and Cuba, British Columbia and Singapore, Guyana and Trinidad, replacing freed slaves on plantations or doing construction. Japanese laborers migrated to Peru to mine guano for fertilizer and to Hawaii to harvest sugar.

Migrants took big risks. Travel was often hazardous, and leaving behind native cultures and kin groups was painful. Many experienced conflicts with resident populations, as did Chinese migrants who ventured into Taiwan and other frontier regions. In the cities, tensions mounted as migrant workers faced low wages, poor working and living conditions, and barriers to higher-paying positions. In China, women without male relatives to protect them sometimes suffered abuse or exploitation. And yet, the economic rewards were substantial enough that the risks of sending the men abroad seemed worth taking.

Until 1914, governments imposed almost no controls on immigration or emigration. The Qing government tried to restrict emigration into the Manchus' northeastern homelands, but it failed. The United States allowed entry to anyone who was not a prostitute, a convict, or a "lunatic"; but in 1882, racist reactions spurred legislation that barred entry to almost all Chinese. Travel within Europe required no passports or work permits; foreign-born criminals were subject to deportation, but that was the extent of immigration policy. In fact, there generally was no reason to have an immigration policy, because immigration seemed doubly good: emigrants allowed large productivity gains in the countries they *left* (because low-productivity populations departed), and immigrants fueled economic growth in the countries they *entered*. This was especially true in North America, where funds were flowing for building railroads and other infrastructure, and where a growing population meant growing consumer markets. Overall, immigration to the New World prompted enormous leaps in productivity.

URBAN LIFE AND CHANGING IDENTITIES Cities boomed, with both positive and negative repercussions. Tokyo's population climbed from 500,000 in 1863 to 1,750,000 in 1908, and London's passed 6.5 million. Major cities faced housing shortages, despite governments' massive rebuilding and beautification projects. This was the era in which city planning came into its own—to widen and regularize thoroughfares for train and streetcar traffic, and to make crowded city life attractive to new inhabitants. City governments in New York, Cairo, Buenos Aires, and Brussels spent lavishly on opera houses, libraries, sewers, and parks, hoping to ward off disease and crime and to impress others with their modernity. Still, modern amenities did not yet make much difference for the vast majority of city dwellers, who labored long (if they could find steady work) for low wages and lived in overcrowded and unsanitary conditions.

Life in the metropolis at the turn of the century was different from city life in the mid-1800s. Workplaces were farther away from residences, and different social classes lived in separate districts. The lives of western women in particular were transformed. They had long worked as domestic servants, textile workers, or agricultural laborers, but now some

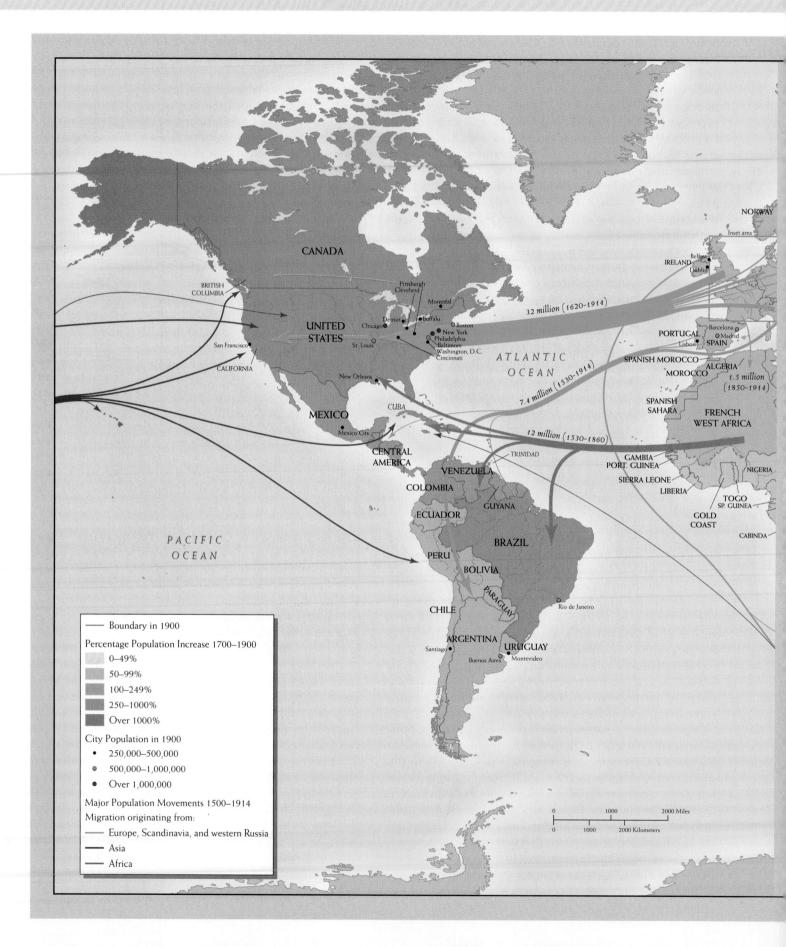

CANADA

BRITISH
COLUMBIA

Pittsburgh
Cleveland
Montréal
Detroit Buffalo
Chicago Boston
UNITED New York
STATES Philadelphia
St. Louis Baltimore
Washington, D.C.
Cincinnati

San Francisco

CALIFORNIA

New Orleans

MEXICO

Mexico City

CENTRAL
AMERICA

CUBA

VENEZUELA

COLOMBIA

ECUADOR

TRINIDAD

GUYANA

PERU

BRAZIL

BOLIVIA

PARAGUAY

CHILE

Rio de Janeiro

ARGENTINA

Santiago

URUGUAY

Buenos Aires Montevideo

ATLANTIC
OCEAN

32 million (1620–1914)

7.4 million (1530–1914)

12 million (1530–1860)

NORWAY

Inset area

IRELAND Belfast
Dublin

PORTUGAL Barcelona
Lisbon Madrid
SPAIN

SPANISH MOROCCO ALGERIA
MOROCCO 1.5 million
(1850–1914)

SPANISH
SAHARA FRENCH
WEST AFRICA

GAMBIA
PORT. GUINEA
SIERRA LEONE NIGERIA
LIBERIA

TOGO
SP. GUINEA
GOLD
COAST

CABINDA

PACIFIC
OCEAN

Boundary in 1900

Percentage Population Increase 1700–1900
- 0–49%
- 50–99%
- 100–249%
- 250–1000%
- Over 1000%

City Population in 1900
- • 250,000–500,000
- ◉ 500,000–1,000,000
- ● Over 1,000,000

Major Population Movements 1500–1914
Migration originating from:
- —— Europe, Scandinavia, and western Russia
- —— Asia
- —— Africa

0   1000   2000 Miles
0   1000   2000 Kilometers

→ *How did an unsettled world produce new opportunities and anxieties?*

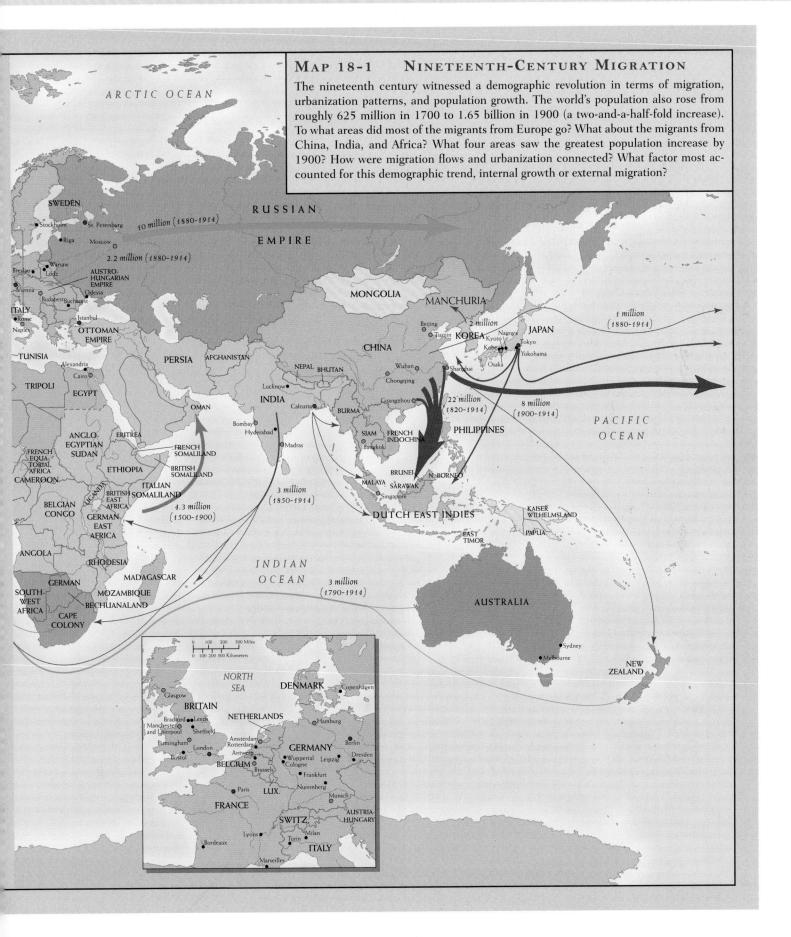

MAP 18-1   NINETEENTH-CENTURY MIGRATION
The nineteenth century witnessed a demographic revolution in terms of migration, urbanization patterns, and population growth. The world's population also rose from roughly 625 million in 1700 to 1.65 billion in 1900 (a two-and-a-half-fold increase). To what areas did most of the migrants from Europe go? What about the migrants from China, India, and Africa? What four areas saw the greatest population increase by 1900? How were migration flows and urbanization connected? What factor most accounted for this demographic trend, internal growth or external migration?

took positions as shop girls, secretaries, or—thanks to educational opportunities—teachers. Increasing female literacy and the falling price of books and magazines gave western women access to new models of acceptable behavior. In cities it became respectable, even fashionable, for women to be seen on the boulevards. The availability in some places of ready-made clothes and packaged goods offered relief from household drudgery (provided one could afford them). Yet, for most women, leisure time and luxury consumption were still dreams more than realities.

Personal and national identities now came under scrutiny, not just in cities but in entire nations. In response to political and economic upheaval, social disruption, massive migration, and modern thinking, western notions of race became key in defining identities and justifying inequalities. Seeking to unify nations internally, many writers, artists, and political leaders created mythic histories that aimed to give diverse groups a common story of nationhood. Such inventions were crucial in nation building, but they also fueled conflict among nations that in 1914 erupted in the Great War—an event that would generate another huge wave of emigration, much of it involuntary.

DISCONTENT WITH IMPERIALISM

> → *How did Africans and Chinese show their opposition to imperialism?*

In the decades before the Great War, opposition to European domination in Asia and Africa gathered strength. During the nineteenth century, as Europeans touted imperialism as a "civilizing mission," local prophets had voiced alternative visions contesting European supremacy (see Chapter 16). Although these movements were quashed, opposition did not stop. While imperialists consolidated their hold, suppression of unrest in the colonies required ever more force and bloodshed. As the cycle of resistance and repression escalated, many Europeans back home questioned the harsh means of controlling their colonies. By 1914, these questions were intensifying as colonial subjects across Asia and Africa challenged imperial domination. In China, too, where Europeans

Urban Transportation. (*Left*) Streetcars in Tokyo, Japan's capital, are watched over by sword-bearing patrolmen in 1905, during the Russo-Japanese War. The first electric streetcar began running in Japan in 1895. Note the elevated electricity lines, which dated from the 1880s. (*Right*) Heavy traffic in London, about 1910, points to an urban population on the move. Note the many kinds of transportation—motor buses as well as horse-drawn wagons; the railings in the foreground mark the entrance to the Underground, or subway.

MAIN THEMES

→ *Numerous factors lead to global anxieties: vast population movements, deep-seated poverty, failure of nation-states to achieve important goals, and hatred of colonial domination.*
→ *The tumult challenges Europeans' faith in "progress."*
→ *Turmoil promotes new scientific thinking and artistic expression, known as cultural modernism.*

FOCUS ON *Sources of Global Anxieties and Expressions of Cultural Modernism*

Global Trends
◆ Mass migrations and unprecedented urban expansion challenge national identities.

Africa and China: Anti-Colonialism
◆ The Anglo-Boer War and violent uprisings against colonial rule in Africa call Europe's imperializing mission into question.
◆ The Chinese rise up against European encroachments in the Boxer Rebellion.

Europe and North America: Mounting Tensions
◆ Intense political rivalries, financial insecurities and crises, rapid industrialization, feminism, and class conflict roil Europe and spread to the rest of the world.

Mexico: Resentment toward Elites
◆ The most widespread revolution from below takes place in Mexico.

Cultural Modernism
◆ Popular culture comes of age.
◆ Elite culture explores new forms in painting, architecture, music, literature, and science in order to break with the past and differentiate itself more dramatically from popular culture.
◆ New ideas of race emerge, as does a renewed emphasis on the nation-state and nationalism.

---

were scrambling for trading opportunities without actually establishing formal colonial power, local populations were resisting foreign influences.

UNREST IN AFRICA

Africa witnessed many anticolonial uprisings in the first decades of colonial rule (see Map 18-2). Violent conflicts embroiled not only the Belgians and the Germans, who ruled autocratically, but also the British, whose colonial system left traditional African rulers in place. These uprisings made Europeans uneasy: why were Africans resisting regimes that had huge advantages in firepower and transport and that were bringing medical skills, literacy, and other fruits of European civilization? Some Europeans concluded that Africans were too stubborn or unsophisticated to appreciate Europe's

generosity. Others, shocked by colonial cruelty, called for reform. A few radicals even demanded an end to imperialism.

African opposition was too spirited to ignore. Across the continent, organized armies and unorganized villagers rose up to challenge the European conquest. The resistance of villagers in the central highlands of British East Africa (Kenya) was so intense that the British mounted savage punitive expeditions to bring the area back under their control. Nonetheless, Africans continued to revolt against imperial authority— especially in areas where colonial rulers imposed forced labor, increased taxes, and appropriated land.

THE ANGLO-BOER WAR The continent's most devastating anticolonial uprising occurred in South Africa. This unique struggle pitted two white communities against each other: the British in the Cape Colony and Natal against the Afrikaners, descendants of original Dutch settlers who lived

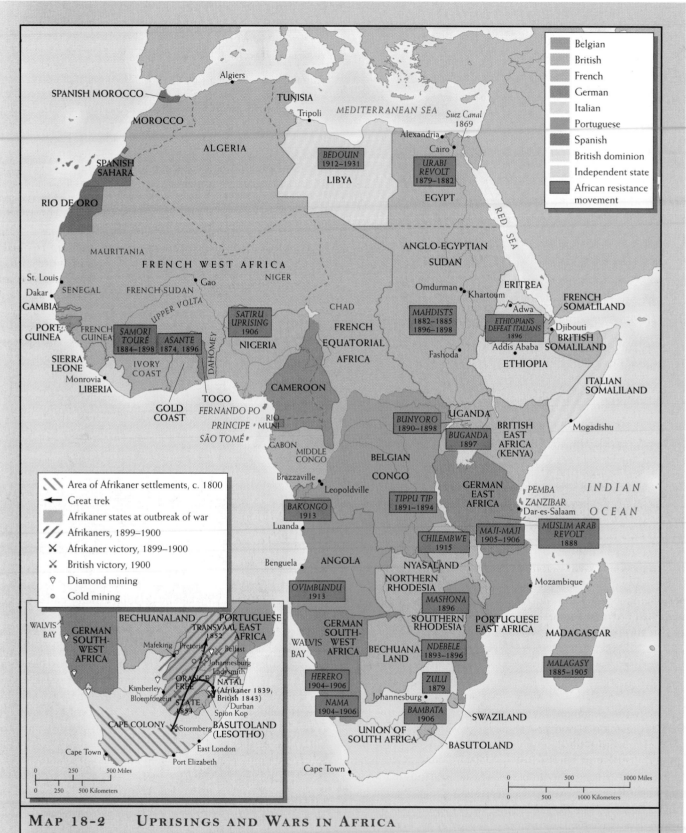

Legend:
- Belgian
- British
- French
- German
- Italian
- Portuguese
- Spanish
- British dominion
- Independent state
- African resistance movement

Inset legend:
- Area of Afrikaner settlements, c. 1800
- Great trek
- Afrikaner states at outbreak of war
- Afrikaners, 1899–1900
- Afrikaner victory, 1899–1900
- British victory, 1900
- Diamond mining
- Gold mining

MAP 18-2   UPRISINGS AND WARS IN AFRICA

The European partition and conquest of Africa were violent affairs. How many separate African resistance movements can you count on this map? Where was resistance the most prolonged? According to your reading, why were Ethiopians, who sustained their autonomy, able to do what other African opponents of European armies were not?

The Anglo-Boer War. The British sent a large contingent of troops to South Africa to deal with the resistance of the two Boer republics—the Orange Free State and the Transvaal. The loss of life and the cruelties inflicted on soldiers and civilians alike during the war, which lasted from 1899 to 1902, did much to undermine the British people's views of their imperial mission. Transvaal and the Orange Free State fought valiantly to keep from becoming part of the British Empire. In the end, they lost.

civilian population led the British to institute a terrifying innovation: the concentration camp. At one moment in the war, at least 155,000 captured men, women, and children were held in camps surrounded by barbed wire. Nor were the camps restricted to Afrikaners. The British also rounded up Africans whom they feared would side with the "anticolonial" Dutch descendants. The suffering and loss in these camps were appalling; by the war's end, 28,000 Afrikaner women and children, as well as 14,000 black Africans, had perished there. (The atrocities did not go unnoticed, however, as newspaper reports and photographs brought the misery of the Anglo-Boer War back to Europe.) Ultimately, the British won

in the Transvaal and the Orange Free State (see Map 18-2 inset). Although two white regimes were the main adversaries, the **Anglo-Boer War** (1899–1902) involved the area's 4 million black inhabitants as fully as its 1 million whites. Its horrors particularly traumatized the British at home, who regarded themselves as Europe's most enlightened and efficient colonial rulers.

The war's origins lay in the discovery of gold in the Transvaal in the mid-1880s. As the area rapidly became Africa's richest state, the prospect that Afrikaner republics might become the powerhouse in southern Africa was more than British imperialists could accept. Joseph Chamberlain, colonial secretary in London, and Cecil Rhodes, the leading politician in the Cape Colony, found allies in the British population living in the Afrikaner republics. Lacking voting rights and experiencing other forms of discrimination, these outsiders protested the Afrikaner governments' policies and pressed the British government to intervene. For their part, Afrikaner leaders emphasized the rights of a free people to resist.

Fearing that war was inevitable, the president of the Transvaal launched a preemptive strike against the British. In late 1899, Afrikaner forces crossed into South Africa. Fighting a relentless guerrilla campaign, Afrikaners waged a war that would last three years and cost Britain 20,000 soldiers and £200 million. Britain's frustrated attempts to respond to Afrikaner hit-and-run tactics and contain the local

Extermination of the Herero. The Germans carried out a campaign of near-extermination against the Herero population in German Southwest Africa in 1904–5. Nearly 90 percent of the Herero were killed.

the war, bringing the Transvaal and the Orange Free State—with their vast gold reserves—into their empire.

OTHER STRUGGLES IN COLONIZED AFRICA The revulsion that the Anglo-Boer War sent through western public opinion deepened after Germany's activities in Africa also went brutally wrong. Germany had established colonies in Southwest Africa (present-day Namibia), Cameroon, and Togo in 1884 and in East Africa in 1885. In German Southwest Africa, the Herero and San people resisted the Germans, and in German East Africa (modern-day Tanzania), the Muslim Arab peoples rebelled. Between 1904 and 1906, fighting in German Southwest Africa escalated to such an extent that the German commander issued a genocidal extermination order against the Herero population. Equally troubling was the Maji-Maji Revolt in German East Africa of 1905–1906, described at the beginning of this chapter.

Apologists for imperial violence tried to dampen public outcries. Journalists portrayed the Maji-Maji rebels as fanatics in the thrall of a demonic African witch doctor, Kinjikitile Ngwale, and the Afrikaners as uncouth ruffians who deserved what they got. According to defenders, the unjustifiable horrors of Leopold's Belgian Congo (see Chapter 17) were an exception, created by a dissolute and reckless monarch who had no scruples when it came to enhancing his own wealth and political power. Apologists from all the European powers argued that these incidents did not represent the reality of empire—at least not *their* nation's empire. Thus, the British denounced the Belgians to highlight their own benevolence, while the French spread gory images of German repression to underscore their own success at uplifting Africans. Portraying Africans as either accepting subjects or childlike primitives, the European powers sought to redouble their coercive

efforts and, in many cases, the number of officials and soldiers stationed in the colonies.

THE BOXER UPRISING IN CHINA

At the turn of the century, forces from within and without also unsettled China. Although China's turmoil differed from Africa's, it, too, arose from concern about European intrusions. As the population swelled to over half a billion and outstripped the country's resources, problems of landlessness, poverty, and peasant discontent (constants in China's modern history) led many to mourn the decay of political authority. In response, in 1898 the Qing emperor tried to modernize industry, agriculture, commerce, education, and the military. But opponents blocked the emperor's designs. Before long the emperor faced house arrest in the palace, while the Empress Dowager Cixi, whom conservatives supported, actually ruled.

EXTERNAL FACTORS The breakdown of dynastic authority originated largely with foreign pressure. For one thing, China's defeat in the Sino-Japanese War of 1894–1895 (see Chapter 17) was deeply humiliating. Although Japan, which acquired Taiwan as its first major colony, was the immediate beneficiary of the war, Britain, France, Germany, and Russia quickly scrambled for additional concessions from China. They demanded that the Qing government grant them specific areas within China as their respective "spheres of influence" (see Map 18-3). The United States argued instead for maintaining an "open door" policy that would keep access available to all traders. But the Americans also wanted the Qing to accept western norms of political and economic

Cixi's Allies. The Empress Dowager Cixi emerged as the most powerful figure in the Qing court in the last decades of the dynasty, from the 1860s until her death in 1908. Highly able, she approved many of the early reforms of the Self-Strengthening movement, but her commitment to the preservation of the Manchu Qing dynasty made her suspicious of more fundamental and wide-ranging changes. Here she is shown surrounded by court eunuchs. Early Qing rulers were very conscious of the danger of the meddling of eunuchs in court affairs. Yet, as a woman whose power relationships with orthodox officials were often ambivalent, Cixi was perhaps particularly compelled to ally herself closely with the eunuchs as a counterweight to the other official factions.

MAP 18-3   FOREIGN SPHERES OF INFLUENCE IN CHINA, 1842–1907
While technically independent, the Qing dynasty could not prevent foreign penetration and domination of its economy during the nineteenth century. Which five powers established spheres of influence in China? At what time was the greatest number of treaty ports established? According to your reading, what did the foreign powers hope to achieve within their spheres of influence? What kinds of local opposition did the foreign influence inspire?

exchange and to acknowledge the superiority of Christian civilization. In response, some Chinese elites developed an anti-European stance while advocating the use of European ideas and technology to strengthen China itself.

The most explosive reaction to these pressures, the **Boxer Uprising,** started within the peasantry. Like colonized peoples in Africa, the Boxers violently resisted European meddling in their communities. And like the Taiping Rebellion decades earlier (see Chapter 16), the story of the Boxers was tied to missionary activities. Whereas in earlier centuries Jesuit missionaries had sought to convert the court and the elites, by the mid-nineteenth century the missionary goal was to convert commoners. After the Taiping Rebellion, Christian missionaries had streamed into China, impatient to make new converts in the hinterlands and confident of their governments' backing. With the Qing dynasty in a weakened state, Christian missionaries became more aggressive.

An incident in 1897, in which Chinese residents killed two German missionaries in the northern province of Shandong, brought tensions to a boil. In retribution, the German government demanded the right to construct three cathedrals, to remove hostile local officials, and to seize the northeastern port of Jiaozhou. As tensions mounted, martial arts groups in the region began to attack the missionaries and converts, calling for an end to the Christians' privileges. In early 1899, several of these groups united under the name Boxers United in Righteousness and adopted the slogan "Support the Qing, destroy the foreign." Like the African followers of Kinjikitile, the Boxers believed that divine protection made them immune to all earthly weapons: "We requested the gods to attach themselves to our bodies. When they had done so, we became Spirit Boxers, after which we were invulnerable to swords and spears, our courage was enhanced, and in fighting we were unafraid to die and dared to charge straight ahead."

INTERNAL FACTORS The Boxer movement flourished especially where natural disasters and harsh economic conditions spread hardships. Shandong province had suffered floods throughout much of the decade, followed by prolonged drought in the winter of 1898. Idle, restless, and often hungry, many peasants, boatmen, and peddlers turned to the Boxers for support. They also liked the Boxers' message that the gods were angry over the foreign presence in general and Christian activities in particular.

As these activists, many of them young men, swelled the Boxers' ranks, women also found a place in the movement. The so-called Red Lanterns were mostly teenage girls and unmarried women who announced their loyalty by wearing red garments. Although the Red Lanterns were segregated from the male Boxers—they worshipped at their own altars and practiced martial arts at separate boxing grounds—they were important to the movement in counteracting the influence of Christian women. Indeed, one of the Boxers' greatest fears was that cunning Christian women would use their guile to weaken the Boxers' spirits. The rebels believed that their invulnerability came from spirit possession and that the inherent polluting power of women threatened their "magic." However, they claimed that the "purity" of the Red Lanterns could counter this threat. The Red Lanterns were supposedly capable of incredible feats: they could walk on water or fly through the air. Belief in their magical powers provided critical assistance for the uprising.

As the movement gained momentum, the Qing vacillated between viewing the Boxers as a threat to order and embracing them as a force to check foreign intrusion. Early in 1900, Qing troops clashed with the Boxers in an escalating cycle of violence. By spring, however, the Qing could no longer control the tens of thousands of Boxers roaming the vicinities of Beijing and Tianjin. Embracing the Boxers' cause, the

The Boxer Uprising in China. The Boxer Uprising was eventually suppressed by a foreign army made up of Japanese, European, and American troops that arrived in Beijing in August 1900. The picture here shows fighting between the foreign troops and the combined forces of Qing soldiers and the Boxers. After a period of vacillation, the Qing court, against the advice of some of its officials, finally threw its support behind the quixotic struggle of the Boxers against the foreign presence, laying the ground for the military intervention of the imperialist powers.

empress dowager declared war against the foreign powers in June 1900.

FOREIGN INVOLVEMENT AND AFTERMATH Acting without any discernible plan or leadership, the Boxers went after Christian and foreign symbols and persons. They harassed and sometimes killed Chinese Christians in parts of northern China, destroyed railroad tracks and telegraph lines, and attacked owners of foreign objects such as lamps and clocks. In Beijing, the Boxers besieged foreign embassy compounds where diplomats and their families cowered in fear. The Boxers also reduced the Southern Cathedral to ruins and then besieged the Northern Cathedral, where more than 3,000 Catholics and 40 French and Italian marines had sought refuge. Those inside were rescued only with the arrival of a foreign expeditionary force.

In August 1900, a foreign army of 20,000 troops crushed the Boxers. About half came from Japan; the rest came primarily from Russia, Britain, Germany, France, and the United States. Thereafter, the victors forced the Chinese to sign the punitive Boxer Protocol. Among other punishments, it required the regime to pay an exorbitant compensation in gold (about twice the empire's annual income) for damages to foreign life and property. The protocol also authorized western powers to station troops in Beijing. Furthermore, although the defeat prompted the Qing to make a last-ditch effort at reform, it dealt another blow to the dynasty's standing both internally and externally.

Even in defeat, the Boxers' anti-western uprising showed how much had changed in China since the Taiping Rebellion. Although the Boxers were primarily peasants, even they had felt the unsettledness generated by European inroads into China. Indeed, the Europeans' commercial and spiritual reach, once confined to elites and port cities, had extended across much of China. Whereas the Taiping Rebellion had mobilized millions against the Qing, the Boxers remained loyal to the dynasty and focused their wrath on foreigners and Chinese Christians. The Boxer Rebellion, like the Maji Maji Revolt in East Africa, revealed the widespread political opposition to westernization and the willingness of local disaffected populations to resist western programs.

WORLDWIDE INSECURITIES

→ *What were the sources of unease around the world?*

Protests against European intrusion in Africa and China were distant movements that most Europeans could disregard. News of unrest in the colonies and in China generally did not lead them to question their ways. Instead, it reinforced their belief in the inferiority of other cultures. In Africa, for example, unrest in a rival's empire was taken as a sign of poor management. Anxiety here reflected the difficulty of the "civilizing mission," although a few did begin to question imperial ethics. At the same time, however, conflicts closer to home tore at European and North American confidence. These included rivalries among western powers, the booms and busts of expanding industrial economies, new types of class conflict, challenges about the proper roles of women, and problems of uncontrolled urbanization (see again Map 18-1).

IMPERIAL RIVALRIES AT HOME

The rise of a European-centered world deepened rivalries within Europe and promoted instability there. Numerous factors fostered conflict, including France's smoldering resentment at its defeat in the Franco-Prussian War (see Chapter 17), but tension increased as the European states competed for raw materials and colonial footholds. Even as these powers built up their supply of weapons, as well as ships and railroads to transport troops, not everyone supported the buildup. Many Europeans, for example, disapproved of spending on massive steam-powered warships. Others warned that the arms race would end in a devastating war.

Intra-European rivalry had powerful effects on Germany and Russia. In fact, the unifications of Germany and Italy at the expense of France and the Austrian Empire had smashed the old balance of power in Europe. New alliances began to crystallize after 1890, as German–French hostility persisted and German–Russian friendship broke down. This left Germany surrounded by foes: Britain and France to the west, Russia to the east. Adding to the instability was the weakening of the Ottoman and the Habsburg empires. Flanking these empires were the Balkans, where a series of small wars and the rise of Slavic nationalism destabilized the area. Sensing conflict on the horizon, Britain, Germany, France, Austria-Hungary, and Russia entered into a massive arms race.

FINANCIAL, INDUSTRIAL, AND TECHNOLOGICAL INSECURITIES Economic developments helped make powers "great," but they could also unsettle societies. Indeed, pride about wealth and growth coincided with laments about changes in national and international economies. To begin with, Americans and Europeans recognized that the small-scale, laissez-faire capitalism championed by Adam Smith (see Chapter 14) was giving way to an economic order dominated by huge, heavily capitalized firms. Gone, it seemed, was Smith's vision of many small producers in vigorous competition with one another, all benefiting from efficient—but not exploitative—divisions of labor.

Labor Disputes. The late nineteenth century witnessed a surge in industrial strife, worker strikes, and violent suppression of labor movements. (*Left*) One of the deadliest confrontations in the United States occurred in May 1892, when a strike against the Carnegie Steel Company escalated into a gunfight, which left ten dead and many more wounded. Here, a group of striking workers keeps watch over the steel mill in Homestead, Pennsylvania. (*Right*) Striking dock workers rally in London's Trafalgar Square, 1911. By this time, residents of European cities were used to seeing crowds of protesters pressing for improved working conditions or political reform.

Instead of smooth progress, the economy of the West in the nineteenth century bounced between booms and busts: long-term business cycles of rapid growth followed by counter-cycles of stagnation. Late in the century, the pace of economic change accelerated. Large-scale steel production, railroad building, and textile manufacturing expanded at breakneck speed, while waves of bank closures, bankruptcies, and agricultural crises ruined many small property owners, including farmers. By the century's end, European and North American economies were dominated as never before by a few large-scale firms.

GLOBAL FINANCIAL AND INDUSTRIAL INTEGRATION
These were years of heady international financial integration. More and more countries joined the world system of borrowing and lending; more and more countries were linked financially because their national currencies were all backed by gold. At the hub of this world system were the banks of London, which since the Napoleonic wars had been a major source of capital for international borrowers.

The rise of giant banks and huge industrial corporations caused alarm, for it seemed to signal an end to free markets and competitive capitalism. In the United States, an entire generation of journalists cut their teeth exposing the skullduggery (shady dealings) of financial and industrial giants. These "muckrakers" portrayed the captains of finance like J. P. Morgan and John D. Rockefeller as bent on amassing private power at the expense of working families and public authorities. In Europe, too, critics lamented a similar trend in which lack of competition created greater disparities of wealth between the owners of firms and the workforce.

Rather than longing for the return of truly free markets, many critics sought reforms that would protect people from economic instability. Indeed, starting in the 1890s, the reaction against economic competition gathered steam. Producers, big and small, grew unhappy with supply and demand mechanisms. To cope with an unruly market, farmers created cooperatives. For their part, big industrialists fashioned monopolies, or cartels, in the name of improving efficiency, correcting failures in the market, and heightening profits. At the same time, government officials and academic specialists worried that modern economies were inherently unstable, prone to overproduce, and vulnerable to bankruptcy and crisis. The solution, many economists thought, was for the state to manage the market's inefficiencies.

FINANCIAL CRISES Banking especially seemed in need of closer government supervision. Many industrial societies already had central banks, and London's Bank of England had long since overseen local and international money markets. But public institutions did not yet have the resources to protect all investments during times of economic crisis. Between 1890 and 1893, fully 550 American banks collapsed, and only the intervention of J. P. Morgan prevented the depletion of the nation's gold reserves.

The road to regulation, however, was hardly smooth. In 1907, a more serious crisis threatened, caused by a panic on Wall Street that led to a run on the banks. Once again, it fell to J. P. Morgan to rescue the American dollar from financial panic—by compelling financier after financier to commit unprecedented funds (eventually $35 million) to protect banks and trusts against depositors' panic. Morgan himself lost $21 million and emerged from the bank panic convinced that some sort of public oversight was needed. By 1913, the U.S. Congress ratified the Federal Reserve Act, creating boards to monitor the supply and demand of the nation's money.

The crisis of 1907 showed how national financial matters could quickly become international affairs. The sell-off of the shares of banks and trusts in the United States also led American investors to withdraw their funds from other countries that relied on American capital. As a result, Canada, for instance, suffered a bank crisis of its own. Countries like Egypt and Mexico, far apart geographically yet linked through international capital, also suffered either withdrawal of investors' funds or a suspension of new investments and a string of bankruptcies. Although the head of Mexico's government, General Porfirio Díaz, tried to regain investors' confidence and their funds, Mexico fell into a severe recession as U.S. capital dried up. In turn, Mexicans lost faith in their own economic—and political—system. Unemployed and suffering new hardships, many Mexicans flocked to Díaz's political opponents, who eventually raised the flag of rebellion in 1910. A year later, the entire regime collapsed in revolution (see below).

INDUSTRIALIZATION AND THE MODERN ECONOMY Just as financial circuits linked nations as never before, so did industrialization. Backed by big banks, industrialists could afford to extend their enterprises physically and geographically. So heavy industries now came to new places. In Russia,

for example, industrial activity quickened. With loans from European (especially French, Belgian, and British) investors, Russia built railways, telegraph lines, and factories and developed coal, iron, steel, and petroleum industries. By 1900, Russia was producing half of the world's oil and a considerable amount of steel. Yet industrial development remained uneven: southern Europe and the American South continued to lag behind northern regions. The gap was even more pronounced in colonial territories, which contained few industrial enterprises aside from railroad building and mining.

By 1914, the factory and the railroad had become global symbols of the modern economy—and of its positive and negative effects. Everywhere, the coming of the railroad to one's town or village was a big event: for some, it represented an exhilarating leap into the modern world; for others, a terrifying abandonment of the past. Ocean liners, automobiles, and airplanes, likewise, could be both dazzling and disorienting. The older conservative elite found technological development more worrisome than did urban liberals, who increasingly set state policies.

For ordinary people, the new economy brought benefits and drawbacks. Factories produced cheaper goods, but they belched clouds of black smoke. Railways offered faster transport, but they ruined small towns unlucky enough to be left off the branch line. Machines (when operating properly) were more efficient than human and animal labor, but workers who used them felt reduced to machines themselves. Indeed, the American Frederick Winslow Taylor proposed a system of "scientific management" to make human bodies perform more like machines, maximizing the efficiency of workers' movements. But workers did not want to be managed or to cede control of the pace of production to employers. Labor's resistance to "Taylorization" led to numerous strikes. For strikers, as for conservatives, the course of progress had taken an unsettling turn.

THE "WOMAN QUESTION"

Complicating the situation was turmoil about the politics of domesticity, or the "woman question." In the West, female activists demanded that women be given more rights as citizens, and more radical voices called for fundamental changes to the family and the larger society. At the same time, imperial architects claimed that colonial rule was bringing great improvements to women in Asia and Africa. But the "woman question" was no more easily settled there than elsewhere.

WOMEN'S ISSUES IN THE WEST In western countries, for most of the nineteenth century, a belief in "separate spheres" had supposedly confined women to domestic matters, while leaving men in charge of public life and economic undertakings. (In practice, only women from middle- and upper-class families avoided working outside the home for wages.)

Woman Suffrage in Finland. The British and then the French introduced the concept of citizenship with universal rhetoric, but in practice the category of citizen was generally restricted to property-holding males. Only gradually were all men, and then women, recognized as citizens, with the right to own property, associate in public, and vote. Finland granted its women the right to vote in 1906, earlier than most countries. In the photo, the Finnish woman casts her ballot in the election of 1906.

Moreover, as economic developments created new jobs for women and greater access to education, women increasingly found work as teachers, secretaries, typists, department store clerks, social workers, and telephone operators. These jobs offered greater economic and social independence. Some educated women spearheaded efforts to improve conditions for the urban poor and to expand the government's role in regulating economic affairs. Much of the population, however, continued to think that higher education and public activism were not suitable for women.

In one very important change, many women began to assert control over reproduction. Although in numerous countries the use of contraceptive devices was illegal, women still found ways to limit the number of children they bore. Early in the twentieth century, the birthrate in America was half of what it had been a century before. By having fewer children, families could devote more income to education, food, housing, and leisure activities. And declining birthrates, along with improved medicine, meant that fewer women died in childbirth and more would see their children reach adulthood.

Still, changes in women's social status did not translate into electoral reform at the national level. By midcentury, several women's suffrage movements had appeared, but these campaigns bore little immediate fruit. In 1868, women received the right to vote in local elections in Britain. Within a

few years, Finland, Sweden, and some American states allowed single, property-owning women the right to cast ballots—again, only in local elections. Women obtained the right to vote in national elections in New Zealand in 1893, in Australia in 1902, in Finland in 1906, and in Norway in 1913. Despite these gains, male alarmists portrayed women's suffrage and women's rights as the beginning of civilization's end.

VARYING VIEWS ON FEMINISM Most middle-class women in Europe and the Americas were not seeking to make women equal to men. Indeed, many bourgeois women recoiled from the close relationships between socialism and feminism. In Latin America, for example, anarchists championed a version of feminism arguing that the abolition of private property would liberate women from their misery and that the traditional family was a bourgeois convention. Other women feared becoming too "mannish," and a few worried that equality would destroy female sensuality. (See Primary Source: Viragoes or Temple Courtesans?) Most, probably, looked to reform less in terms of voting rights and more in terms of better treatment within families and local communities.

Radical women met stiff repression wherever they challenged the established order. This was especially true outside Europe and the Americas, where the feminist movement was not strong and where women's education and entry into the professions lagged far behind those of men. In 1903, China's Qiu Jin (1875–1907) left her husband and headed to Japan to study. There she befriended other radicals and made a name for herself by dressing in men's clothing, carrying a sword, and trying her hand at bomb-making. Returning to China in 1906, she founded the *Chinese Women's Journal* (*Zhongguo nübao*) and wrote articles urging women to fight for their rights and to leave home if necessary. (See Primary Source: A Chinese Feminist Condemns Injustices to Women.) Qing authorities executed Qiu Jin after she participated in a failed attempt to topple the dynasty.

WOMEN'S STATUS IN COLONIES In the colonial world, the woman question was a contentious issue—but it was mainly argued among men. European authorities liked to boast that colonial rule improved women's status. Citing examples of traditional societies' subordination of women, they criticized as barbaric the veiling of women in Islamic societies, the binding of women's feet in China, widow burning (*sati*) in India, and female genital mutilation in Africa. Europeans believed that prohibiting such acts was a justification for colonial intervention.

And yet, for women in Africa, the Middle East, and India, colonialism added to their burdens. As male workers headed into the export economy, formerly shared agricultural work fell exclusively on women's shoulders. In Africa, for example, the opening of vast gold and diamond mines drew thousands of men away to work in the mines, leaving women to fend for themselves. Similarly, the rise of European-owned agricultural

Primary Source

VIRAGOES OR TEMPLE COURTESANS?

The German novelist Franziska von Reventlow was one of the more radical proponents of women's rights in Europe. In her 1899 essay excerpted below, she attacks the feminist "viragoes" (aggressive women) for wanting to make women too much like men. Instead of pressing for political and economic rights, Reventlow—who was notorious for having affairs—recommends a return to the promiscuity enjoyed by temple courtesans in ancient Greece, the freeing of women from oppressive work, and an end to the sensuality-stifling conventions of middle-class Christian culture.

The most fanatical members of the women's movement have put forward the claim: women can do everything men can do. . . . We don't want to deny that there are many achievements of which both sexes are equally capable. . . . But when it comes to heavy physical labor, that is a different question. One has only to look at these hard-working women of the lower classes, who, in addition to their jobs: bring a child into the world every year, to see that the female body is not made for this, and that it in this way loses its form and gradually is ruined. . . .

The man has the role that he has been given by nature, he is everywhere the dominant, the attacker, in all areas of life, in all professions. . . . The woman is not made for the harder things of this world, but for ease, for joy, for beauty. . . .

But perhaps a women's movement will arise in this sense, one that frees the woman as a sexual being, and which teaches her to demand what it is proper to demand, full sexual freedom, that is, full control over her body, which publicly sanctioned promiscuity will bring back. Please, no cries of indignation! The temple courtesans of antiquity were free, highly cultivated, and respected women, and no one took offense when they gave their love and their bodies to whom and as often as they liked and at the same time took part in the intellectual life enjoyed by men. Instead of this, Christianity created monogamy—and prostitution. The latter is a proof that marriage is a flawed institution. While, by means of Christian moral education, there is an attempt to kill the sexual feelings of one part of womankind . . . at the same time, prostitution is institutionalized, and thereby another part of womankind is compelled to be polygamous in order to service men for whom marriage is unsatisfying. . . .

To return to the women's movement: it is the declared enemy of all erotic culture, because it wants to make women into men. . . .

Darwin tells us that the English sheep breeders weed out the sexual mutants from their herds because they don't produce either beautiful wool or good mutton chops. Nature has already done the same among humans; the newest textbooks on anatomical pathologies show that hermaphrodites are dying out. The viragoes, who want to do away with our men, are for the most part just hermaphroditic ghosts who will soon be banished by the healthy erotic spirit of the new paganism whose triumph we await in the next century.

→ *How does Reventlow define a woman's freedom?*

→ *What are her criticisms of Christianity?*

→ *Reventlow mentions Charles Darwin, whose work influenced late-nineteenth-century thought. Look up the word* hermaphrodite, *and then explain whether you find the reference to this term and Darwin's work appropriate in a discussion of the women's movement.*

→ *How does Reventlow's vision for women's freedom compare to "lipstick" feminism today?*

SOURCE: Franziska von Reventlow, "Viragines oder Hetaere," in *Autobiographisches: Novellen, Schriften, Selbstzeugnisse*, edited by Else Reventlow, translated by Suzanne Marchand. Reprinted with the permission of Suzanne Marchand.

estates in Kenya and Southern Rhodesia depleted surrounding villages of male family members, who went to work on the estates. In these circumstances, women kept the local, food-producing economy afloat.

Nor did colonial "civilizing" rhetoric improve women's political or cultural circumstances. In fact, European missionaries preached a message of domesticity to Asian and African families, emphasizing that women's place was in the home

A CHINESE FEMINIST CONDEMNS INJUSTICES TO WOMEN

Although a small minority, Chinese feminists of the early twentieth century were vocal in condemning the injustices inflicted on women in China. In this essay from 1904, directed to her countrywomen, Qiu Jin compares the treatment of Chinese women to slavery. She also displays a strong nationalistic streak as she ties the future of Chinese women to the fate of the Chinese nation.

Alas! The greatest injustice in this world must be the injustice suffered by our female population of two hundred million. If a girl is lucky enough to have a good father, then her childhood is at least tolerable. But if by chance her father is an ill-tempered and unreasonable man, he may curse her birth: "What rotten luck: another useless thing." Some men go as far as killing baby girls while most hold the opinion that "girls are eventually someone else's property" and treat them with coldness and disdain. In a few years, without thinking about whether it is right or wrong, he forcibly binds his daughter's soft, white feet with white cloth so that even in her sleep she cannot find comfort and relief until the flesh becomes rotten and the bones broken. What is all this misery for? Is it just so that on the girl's wedding day friends and neighbors will compliment him, saying, "Your daughter's feet are really small"? Is that what the pain is for?

But that is not the worst of it. When the time for marriage comes, a girl's future life is placed in the hands of a couple of shameless matchmakers and a family seeking rich and powerful in-laws. A match can be made without anyone ever inquiring whether the prospective bridegroom is honest, kind, or educated. On the day of the marriage the girl is forced into a red and green bridal sedan chair, and all this time she is not allowed to breathe one word about her future. . . .

When Heaven created people it never intended such injustice because if the world is without women, how can men be born? Why is there no justice for women? We constantly hear men say, "The human mind is just and we must treat people with fairness and equality." Then why do they greet women like black slaves from Africa?

How did inequality and injustice reach this state? . . .

I hope that we all shall put aside the past and work hard for the future. Let us all put aside our former selves and be resurrected as complete human beings. Those of you who are old, do not call yourselves old and useless. If your husbands want to open schools, don't stop them; if your good sons want to study abroad, don't hold them back. Those among us who are middle-aged, don't hold back your husbands lest they lose their ambition and spirit and fail in their work. After your sons are born, send them to schools. You must do the same for your daughters and, whatever you do, don't bind their feet. As for you young girls among us, go to school if you can. If not, read and study at home. Those of you who are rich, persuade your husbands to open schools, build factories, and contribute to charitable organizations. Those of you who are poor, work hard and help your husbands. Don't be lazy, don't eat idle rice. These are what I hope for you. You must know that when a country is near destruction, women cannot rely on the men any more because they aren't even able to protect themselves. If we don't take heart now and shape up, it will be too late when China is destroyed.

Sisters, we must follow through on these ideas!

→ *Identify at least three ways in which Chinese women suffer injustice, according to Qiu Jin.*
→ *In what way does the author's comparison of Chinese women to "black slaves from Africa" reveal a growing global awareness within the Chinese population?*
→ *Why is nationalism an important part of Qiu Jin's message?*

SOURCE: Qiu Jin, "An Address to Two Hundred Million Fellow Countrywomen." Reprinted with the permission of The Free Press, a division of Simon & Schuster, Inc., from *Chinese Civilization: A Sourcebook*, Second Edition, revised and expanded by Patricia Buckley Ebrey. Copyright © 1993 by Patricia Buckley Ebrey. All rights reserved.

raising children and that women's education should be different from men's. Thus males overwhelmingly dominated the new schools that Europeans built. Moreover, customary law in colonial Africa, as interpreted by chiefs who collaborated with colonial officials, favored men. As a result, African women often lost landholding and other rights that they had enjoyed before the Europeans' arrival. (See Primary Source: Industrialization and Women's Freedom in Egypt.)

CLASS CONFLICT IN A NEW KEY

Capitalism's volatility shook confidence in free market economies and sharpened conflicts between classes; the tone of political debates was transformed as new, more strident voices called for radical change. Although living conditions for European and North American workers improved over time, widening inequalities in income and the slow pace of reform led to frustration. Most workers remained committed to peaceful agitation, but some radicals turned to violence. Often, especially in eastern Europe and Russia, the closed character of political systems fueled frustration—and radicalism. This was also the case in Latin America, where even the middle classes were largely shut out of politics until new parties offered fresh opportunities for political expression. In Argentina, for example, urban workers found outlets for protest within movements known as **syndicalism** (the organization of workplace associations that included unskilled laborers), socialism, and **anarchism** (the belief that society should be a free association of members, not subject to government, laws, or police).

STRIKES AND REVOLTS   In the Americas and in Europe, radicals adopted numerous tactics for asserting the interests of the working class. In Europe, the franchise was gradually expanded in hopes that the lower classes would prefer voting to revolution—and indeed, most of the new political parties that catered to workers had no desire to overthrow the state. But conservatives feared them anyway, especially as they gained electoral clout. The Labour Party, founded in Britain in 1900, quickly boasted a large share of the vote. By 1912, the German Social Democratic Party was the largest party in the Reichstag. But it was not the legally sanctioned parties that sparked violent street protests and strikes in the century's last decades. A whole array of syndicalists, anarchists, radical royalists, and revolutionary socialists sprang up in this period, making work stoppages everyday affairs.

Although the United States did not have similarly radical factions or successful labor parties, American workers were also organizing. The labor movement's power burst forth dramatically in 1894 when the American Railway Union launched a strike that spread across the nation. Spawned by wage cuts and firings following an economic downturn, the Pullman Strike (directed against the maker of railway sleeping cars, George Pullman) involved approximately 3 million workers. The strike's conclusion, however, revealed the enduring power of the status quo. After hiring replacement workers to break the strike, Pullman requested federal troops to protect his operation. When the troops arrived, infuriated strikers reacted with violence—which led to a further crackdown by the government against the union. After its leaders were jailed, the strike collapsed.

A few upheavals from below did succeed, at least briefly. In 1905, in the wake of the Russo-Japanese War (in which the Russians lost to the Japanese), revolt briefly shook the tsarist state and yielded a fledgling form of representative government. The revolutionaries tried some new forms, most notably workers' soviets, which were groups of delegates representing particular industries. Ultimately, however, the army put down both urban and rural unrest. Autocracy was reestablished. Liberals and radicals were excluded from power.

The Pullman Strike. In 1894, in response to wage cuts and layoffs by the Pullman Company, the American Railway Union organized a nationwide strike that brought 3 million workers onto the picket lines. That year's labor unrest often turned violent, as in the incident pictured here, showing strikers setting fire to several hundred freight cars.

INDUSTRIALIZATION AND WOMEN'S FREEDOM IN EGYPT

In this selection, taken from a 1909 lecture in Cairo open only to women, an educated upper-class Egyptian woman insists that female confinement is unnatural and absurd. She demands a place for women in the workplace. The writer, Bahithat al-Badiya, criticizes the effect of traditional religious practices on women's freedom and blames men for not allowing women to enter the professions and enjoy the freedoms that men take for granted.

Men say when we become educated we shall push them out of work and abandon the role for which God created us. But isn't it rather men who have pushed women out of work? Before, women used to spin and to weave cloth for clothes for themselves and their children, but men invented machines for spinning and weaving and put women out of work. . . . Since male inventors and workers have taken away a lot of our work should we waste our time in idleness or seek other work to occupy us? Of course, we should do the latter. . . . Obviously, I am not urging women to neglect their home and children to go out and become lawyers or judges or railway engineers. But if any of us wish to work in such professions our personal freedom should not be infringed. . . .

Men say to us categorically, "You women have been created for the house and we have been created to be bread-winners." Is this a God-given dictate? How are we to know this since no holy book has spelled it out? Political economy calls for a division of labor but if women enter the learned professions it does not upset the system. The division of labor is merely a human creation. . . . If men say to us that we have been created weak we say to them, "No it is you who made us weak through the path you made us follow." After long centuries of enslavement by men, our minds rusted and our bodies weakened. . . .

Men criticize the way we dress in the street. They have a point because we have exceeded the bounds of custom and propriety. . . . [But:] veiling should not prevent us from breathing fresh air or going out to buy what we need if no one can buy it for us. It must not prevent us from gaining an education nor cause our health to deteriorate. When we have finished our work and feel restless and if our house does not have a spacious garden why shouldn't we go to the outskirts of the city and take the fresh air that God has created for everyone and not just put in boxes exclusively for men.

→ *How has al-Badiya's Muslim faith influenced her views on the role of women in society? Find two places in the reading where these influences are apparent.*

→ *How have western influences affected her views on the role of women in society? Find at least two places in the reading where these influences are evident.*

SOURCE: Bahithat al-Badiya, "A Public Lecture for Women Only in the Club of the Umma Party," from "Industrialization and Women's Freedom in Egypt," in *Opening the Gates: A Century of Arab Feminist Writing*, edited by Margot Badran and Miriam Cooke. Copyright © 1990. Reprinted with permission of Indiana University Press.

REVOLUTION IN MEXICO Perhaps the most successful turn-of-the-century revolution occurred in Mexico. A peasant uprising, it thoroughly transformed the country. Fueled by the unequal distribution of land and by disgruntled workers, the **Mexican Revolution** erupted in 1910 when political elites split over the succession of General Porfirio Díaz after decades of his strong-arm rule. Dissidents balked when Díaz refused to step down, and peasants and workers rallied to the call to arms.

What destroyed the Díaz regime and its powerful army was the swelling flood of peasants, farmers, cattlemen, and rural workers who were desperate for a change in the social order. From the north (led by the charismatic Pancho Villa) to the south (under the legendary Emiliano Zapata), rural folk helped topple the Díaz regime. In the name of providing land for farmers and ending oligarchic rule, peasant armies defeated Díaz's troops and then proceeded to destroy many large estates. The fighting lasted for ten brutal years, during which almost 10 percent of the country's population perished.

Thereafter political leaders had to accept popular demands for democracy, respect for the sovereignty of peasant communities, and land reform. As a result the Constitution

The Mexican Revolution. (*Left*) By 1915, Mexican peasants, workers, and farmers had destroyed much of the old elitist system. This was the first popular, peasant revolution of the twentieth century. Among the most famous leaders were Pancho Villa and Emiliano Zapata. They are pictured here in the presidential office in the capital. Villa took the president's chair jokingly. Zapata, carrying the broad hat typical of his people, refused to wear military gear and glowered at the camera suspiciously. (*Right*) By the 1920s, Mexican artists and writers were putting recent events into images and words. Pictured here is one of the muralist Diego Rivera's paintings of the Mexican Revolution. Notice the nationalist interpretation: Porfirio Díaz's troops defend foreign oil companies and white aristocrats against middle-class and peasant (and darker-skinned) reformers who call for a "social revolution." Observe also the absence of women in this epic mural.

of 1917 incorporated widespread reform, and by 1920 an emerging generation of politicians recognized the power of a militarized peasantry and initiated deep-seated changes in Mexico's social structure. These leaders also realized that their new regime had to appeal ideologically to common folk. Revolutionaries gave trade unions sweeping rights to organize. They paved the way for nationalizing the country's mines and oil industries. But perhaps their most lasting legacy was the creation of rural communes for Mexico's peasantry, especially for indigenous people or villagers who had taken on collective ways. These communal village holdings, called *ejidos*, sought to harken back to a precolonial heritage. The revolution thus spawned a set of new national myths, based on the heroism of rural peoples, Mexican nationalism, and a celebration of the Aztec past.

PRESERVING ESTABLISHED ORDERS Although the Mexican Revolution succeeded in toppling the old elite, elsewhere in Latin America the ruling establishment remained united against assaults from below. Already in 1897, the Brazilian army had mercilessly suppressed a peasant movement in the northeastern part of the country. Moreover, in Cuba, the Spanish and then the American armies crushed tenant farmers' efforts to reclaim land from sugar estates. In Guatemala, Mayan Indians lost land to coffee barons.

Much the same occurred in Europe and the United States, where the preservation of established orders did not rest on repression alone. Here, too, elites grudgingly agreed to gradual change. Indeed, by the century's end, left-wing agitators, muckraking reporters, and middle-class reformers began to win meaningful social improvements. Unable to suppress the socialist movement, Otto von Bismarck, the German chancellor, defused the appeal of socialism by enacting social welfare measures in 1883–1884 (as did France in 1904 and England in 1906). He enacted legislation insuring workers against illness, accidents, and old age and establishing maximum working hours. In the United States, it took lurid journalistic accounts of unsanitary practices in Chicago slaughterhouses (including tales of workers falling into lard vats and being rendered into cooking fat) to spur the federal government into action. In 1906, President Theodore Roosevelt signed a Meat Inspection Act that provided for government supervision of meatpacking operations. In other cases (banking, steel production, railroads), the federal government's enhanced supervisory authority served corporate interests as well.

These consumer and family protection measures reflected a broader reform movement, one dedicated to creating a more efficient society and correcting the undesirable consequences of urbanization and industrialization. At local and state levels, **progressive reformers** attacked corrupt city governments that had allegedly fallen into the hands of immigrant-dominated "political machines." The progressives also attacked other vices, such as gambling, drinking, and prostitution—all associated with industrialized, urban settings. The creation of city parks preoccupied urban planners, who hoped parks' green spaces would serve as the city's "lungs" and offer healthier forms of entertainment than houses of prostitution, gambling dens, and bars. In Europe and the United States, thousands of associations took shape against capitalism's excesses. From Scandinavia to California, the proponents of old-age pensions and public ownership of utilities put pressure on lawmakers, and they occasionally succeeded in changing state policies. Intervening in the market and supporting the poor, the aged, the unemployed, and the sick in ways never dreamed of in classical liberal philosophy, progressive reform movements laid the foundations for the modern welfare state.

CULTURAL MODERNISM

> → *How did different fields reflect cultural modernism?*

As revolutionaries and reformers wrestled with the problems of progress, intellectuals, artists, and scientists also had insecurities and uncertainties. What we call modernism—the sense of having broken with tradition—came to prominence in many fields, from physics to architecture, from painting to the social sciences. The movement largely originated from the experimental thinking shaped by turn-of-the-century anxieties. Emblematic of the new ideas was the work of Sigmund Freud (1856–1939), a physician in Vienna who emphasized the power of sexual drives in the formation of individual character.

Modernist movements were notably international. Egyptian social scientists read the works of European thinkers, while French and German painters flocked to museums to inspect artifacts from Egypt and artworks from other parts of Africa, Asia, and Oceania. These museums, as well as international exhibitions held in the second half of the century, reflected a change in the meaning of "culture": it was gradually becoming less elitist and more democratic. (See Global Connections & Disconnections: Modernist Pressures on German and Egyptian Universities.)

The European elites did not give up their opera houses and paintings, however, in favor of arts and entertainments that were popular among urban workers or colonized peoples. Instead, elite culture became even more elitist. For example, modern musicians abandoned the comfort of harmonic and diatonic sound (the eight-tone scale standard in classical western music at the time) and left representational art behind. Many artists demonstrated their cutting-edge originality by spurning sales figures for loftier ambitions. "Art for art's sake" became their motto; their aim was to speak to posterity.

Above all, modernism in arts and sciences replaced the certainties of the Enlightenment with the unsettledness of the new age. No longer confident about civilizing missions or urban and industrial "progress," artists and scientists struggled to make sense of a world in which older beliefs and traditional faiths had given way. What would come next, however, no one could say.

POPULAR CULTURE COMES OF AGE

By the late nineteenth century, production and consumption of the arts, books, music, and sports were much different from what they had been a century earlier. The change derived mainly from new urban settings, technological innovations, and increased leisure time. As education (especially in America and Europe) became nearly universal, there were many more readers and museum-goers. At the same time, cultural works now found their way down to nonelite members of society. Middle-class art lovers who could not afford original paintings eagerly purchased lithographs and mass-produced engravings; millions who could not attend operas and formal dress balls attended dance halls and vaudeville shows (entertainment by singers, dancers, and comedians). For the first time, sports attracted mass followings. Soccer in Europe, baseball in the United States, and cricket in India had wildly devoted middle-class and working-class fans. Thus did a truly **popular culture** emerge, delivering affordable and accessible forms of art and entertainment to "the masses."

By the century's close, the press stood as a major form of popular entertainment and information. This was partly because publishers were offering different wares to different classes of readers and partly because many more people could read, especially in Europe and the Americas. The yellow press was full of stories of murder and sensationalism that appealed to the urban masses. By now, the English *Daily Mail* and the French *Petit Parisien* boasted circulations of over 1 million. In the United States, urban dwellers, many of whom were immigrants, avidly read newspapers—some in English, others in their native languages. Here, too, banner headlines, sensational stories, and simple language drew in readers with little education or poor English skills. Books, too, proliferated and fell in price; penny novels about cowboys, murder, and romance became the rage. The Mexican printmaker and artist José Guadalupe Posada produced an early form of comics. In fliers, new songs, cooking recipes, and gory news stories, Posada criticized the Díaz regime and revolutionary excess and parodied Mexican life.

By now the kind of culture one consumed had become a reflection of one's real (or desired) status in society, a central part of one's identity. For many Latin American workers, for example, reading one's own newspaper or comic strip was

MODERNIST PRESSURES ON GERMAN AND EGYPTIAN UNIVERSITIES

Stages of Development in German Universities

In the late eighteenth and early nineteenth centuries, sweeping reforms transformed the universities of German-speaking Europe. No longer polishing schools for aristocrats, these centers for higher learning became respected institutions for the collection and dissemination of knowledge. Striving to combine research with teaching, the German universities produced such pathbreaking scholarship that other Europeans and Americans looked to them as models.

These institutions were places where researchers, students, and teachers exchanged ideas and information, supposedly on an equal basis (though in most cases, one still had to be male, and middle class or above, to attend). For most of the nineteenth century, such institutions stressed the humanities—languages (especially classical languages), history, philosophy, and religion. Indeed, educated Europeans still looked to classical antiquity for the origins of their advanced "civilization," as opposed to what they considered the nonculture of the Americas and Africa

and the decadent culture of Asia. Their focus on the classics produced a wealth of insights—but it was extremely narrow. And by the century's end, these institutions were under siege, both from within and from without.

From within, natural scientists and specialists in modern subjects (such as the social sciences, and modern European history and languages) claimed a greater share of the universities' budget and curriculum. Their demands suited Germany's modernizing aims, and by the end of the century "modern" laboratories, lecture courses, and scholarly institutes had become central to the institutions' mission. It took longer (until the 1920s) to accommodate the demands of women and workers, who insisted that they, too, should be allowed to attend courses. And, increasingly, reformers argued that universities should address non-European subjects, especially to prepare businessmen and state officials for service in the colonies.

Modernizing Higher Learning in Egypt

As the university became the hallmark of modern learning, colonial and semicolonial regions struggled to adapt their traditional scholarly institutions. In Egypt, the approach to higher learning followed two pathways. First, a group of Egyptian reformers sought to imitate institutions of higher learning in Europe. Calling for a purely secular and modern Egyptian university, they finally overcame the opposition of British officials and, in 1908, celebrated the opening of the Egyptian University. It was an immediate success, attracting the cream of Egypt's student population and featuring in its early days a staff of top European academics. Its curriculum hardly differed from that of European and North American universities.

The second pathway was more difficult. Egypt's religious elite, not wishing to be left behind, adapted their own center of higher religious learning, al-Azhar, to modern purposes. Founded in the tenth century during the Fatimid conquest of Egypt, the mosque of al-Azhar had become the leading center of learning throughout the Islamic world as well as a venerable place of worship. But the secular and westernizing tendencies that swept through Egypt in the nineteenth century threatened to make it irrelevant. In response, its advocates introduced modern and secular subjects alongside traditional religious subjects, improved the faculty's training, regularized coursework, instituted regular examination procedures, and expanded the library. In short, they introduced features of the modern western university while keeping the traditional training in Islamic learning. Thus al-Azhar retained an important place in the hierarchy of Egyptian schools in the twentieth century.

Egyptian religious university al-Azhar. An image from an 1898 stereograph showing students gathered around a teacher, probably at al-Azhar University in Cairo, Egypt. At al-Azhar, religious leaders attempted to blend features of the modern western university with traditional Islamic learning.

Díaz and the Liberal Party. In this 1910 print, the Mexican satirist José Guadalupe Posada portrays the leaders of the popular Liberal Party as being literally under the feet of the elitist followers of General Porfirio Díaz.

part of the business of being a worker. Argentina's socialist newspaper, *La Vanguardia*, was one of Buenos Aires's most prominent periodicals, read and debated at work and in the cafés of working-class neighborhoods. Anyone seen reading the bourgeois paper, *La Prensa*, faced heckling and ridicule by proletarian peers.

As the community of cultural consumers broadened, and as ideas from across the globe flooded in, writers, artists, and scholars struggled to adapt. Their attempts to confront the brave new world in the making resulted in the remarkable innovations that characterize modernism—the breaking with tradition.

MODERNISM IN EUROPEAN CULTURE

In intellectual and artistic terms, Europe at the turn of the twentieth century experienced perhaps its richest age since the Renaissance. A desire to understand social and imperial maladies laid the foundations for the twentieth century's social sciences. The French scholar Emile Durkheim (1858–1917), for example, pioneered the field of sociology by studying a characteristic affliction of his age—suicide. In 1895, the French social psychologist Gustave Le Bon (1841–1931) wrote a treatise on crowd behavior that became a classic in Europe and beyond; he equated the unconscious volatility of crowds with the irrationality of women and "primitives." Le Bon's work became wildly popular, appealing even to Benito Mussolini in Italy and Vladimir Lenin in Russia.

Artists' work reflected their ambivalence about the modern, as represented by the railroad, the big city, and the factory. While the impressionists and realists of the mid-nineteenth century had largely celebrated progress, the painters and novelists of the century's end took a darker view. They turned away from enlightened clarity and descriptive prose, searching for more instinctual truths. Now the primitive came to symbolize both Europe's lost innocence and the forces that reason could not control, such as sexual drives, religious fervor, or brute strength. The painter who led the way in incorporating these themes into modern art was Pablo Picasso (1881–1973), who found in African art forms a radically new way of expressing human sentiments that was shocking to most European and American observers. Against conservative criticism, Picasso and his contemporaries claimed that African and Oceanic forms were both beautiful and more instinctual than overly refined western forms.

Now Europeans began to see the world in a fundamentally different way, aided by the experience of nonwestern visual arts. Through this lens, classical and Christian images and forms seemed outdated. The experience of seeing other cultures' artwork was essential to this revolutionary change. But other artists were inspired by the sleekness and syncopation of machines, or by the irrational content of dreams. And painting was not the only art form that displayed a modern style. Arnold Schönberg (1874–1951) composed the first piece of music that dispensed with traditional western tonality. World-famous dancers like Isadora Duncan (1877–1927) pioneered the expressive, free-form movements that laid the foundations for modern dance.

However, the arts alone did not undermine older views of the world. Even science, in which the Enlightenment had placed so much faith, worked a disenchanting magic on the midcentury bourgeois worldview. After the century's turn, pioneering physicists and mathematicians like Albert Einstein (1879–1955) took apart the Enlightenment's conviction that man could achieve full knowledge of, and control over, nature. In a series of papers published between 1905 and 1915, Einstein worked out the special and general theories of relativity, which demonstrated that measurements of speed and gravitational pull were not purely objective, but always conditioned by the "relative" position and conditions of the observer. In his later work, Einstein drew on the previously ridiculed work of the Indian physicist Satyendra Nath Bose

Impressionism. These two paintings, Claude Monet's *The Gare St-Lazare* (*left*) and Camille Pissarro's *Sunset over the Boieldieu Bridge at Rouen* (*right*), exemplify the impressionists' celebration of nineteenth-century progress.

Pablo Picasso. The Franco-Spanish artist Pablo Picasso was one of the first to incorporate "primitive" artistic forms into his work, as displayed in two works from 1907: *Les Demoiselles d'Avignon* (The Courtesans of Avignon), which was inspired by the artist's study of African sculpture and masks, and "Head of a Sleeping Woman (Study for Nude Drapery)."

Sigmund Freud, at Work in His Study in Vienna. Freud surrounded himself not only with books but also with Egyptian figurines and African masks, expressions of universal artistic prowess—and irrational psychological drives.

(1894–1974), who understood light to be a gas composed of particles. These particles were too tiny to be distinguished by any microscope, but their existence could be hypothesized through the application of statistics. The work of Einstein, Bose, and other scholars of their generation laid the foundations for today's quantum physics. In this modernist form of science, probabilities took the place of certainties. Although most scientists continued to collect data feeling certain that they could plumb nature's depths, some of their colleagues began to question the arrogance of this view.

From the time of the Enlightenment, Europeans had prided themselves on their "reason." To be rational was to be civilized; respectable, middle-class nineteenth-century men were thought to embody these virtues. But in the late nineteenth century, faith in rationality began to falter. Perhaps reason was *not* man's highest attainment, said some; perhaps reason was too hard for man to sustain, said others. Friedrich Nietzsche (1844–1900) claimed that conventional European attempts to assert The Truth—including science and Judeo-Christian moral codes—were nothing more than life-destroying quests for power; individuals would do better to dispense with the old forms and invent new forms of truth to live by. Sigmund Freud began to excavate layers of the human subconscious, where irrational desires and fears lay buried. For Freud, human nature was not as simple as it had seemed to Enlightenment thinkers. Instead, he asserted, humans were driven by sexual longings and childhood traumas, some

revealed only as neuroses, in dreams, or during extensive psychoanalysis. Neither Nietzsche nor Freud was well loved among nineteenth-century liberal elites. But in the new century, Nietzsche would become the prophet for many antiliberal, antirational causes, from nudism to Nazism; and Freud's dark vision would become central to the twentieth century's understanding of the self.

CULTURAL MODERNISM IN CHINA

What it meant to be modern sparked debate beyond western Europe and North America. The Europeans provided one set of answers; thinkers elsewhere offered quite different answers. For example, Chinese intellectuals articulated their own perspectives. As in Europe, Chinese artists and scientists at the turn of the century did much experimentation and innovation, including selectively importing western ideas. Indeed, some scholars have described the late Qing period as a time of competing cultural *modernities*, in contrast to the post-Qing era, which pursued a single, western-oriented *modernity*. These forms of modernity involved critical reflection on Chinese traditions and ambivalent reactions to western culture.

In literature, late Qing writers explored topics such as the self, technology, and sexuality. And, as in the West, Chinese writers now had a wider readership. By the late nineteenth century, more than 170 presses in China were serving a potential readership of 2 to 4 million concentrated mostly in the urban areas. These cities were more economically vibrant and culturally fluid than the hinterlands. Not only was there an expanding body of readers, but newly rich beneficiaries of the treaty-port economy now patronized the arts.

In the late nineteenth century, for example, painters from the lower Yangzi region congregated in Shanghai. Collectively known as the **Shanghai School**, they symbolized the vitality of the artistic scene. The Shanghai painters adopted elements from both indigenous and foreign sources for their innovations in compositional structure, coloring, figural rendering, and spatial conception. Although classically trained, they appropriated western technical novelties into their artistic practice. Consider the self-portrait of the artist Ren Xiong (1820–1857): bareheaded and legs apart, he stands upright and stares straight at the viewer. Ren Xiong's work reflected the influence of photography, a new visual medium.

Similarly, fantasy novels drew on both western science and indigenous supernatural beliefs. Some experimental writers explicitly addressed Chinese–western relations. The novel *New Era* (1908), for example, put its opening scenes in the year 1999, by which time the story envisioned China as a supreme world power and a constitutional monarchy. Depicting China at war with western powers, *New Era* celebrated conventional military themes but also introduced inventions such as electricity-repellent clothing and bulletproof satin. More visionary still was the *The Stone of Goddess Nüwa*

Ren Xiong, Self-Portrait. This famous self-portrait of Ren Xiong was most likely produced in the 1850s. Ren Xiong was probably familiar with the new practice of portrait photography in the treaty ports. Although his self-portrait reproduced some old conventions of Chinese scholarly art, such as the unity of the visual image with a lengthy self-composed inscription, it is also clear that, through its rather unconventional pose and image, Ren Xiong had pointed to the establishment of a new kind of subject position characteristic of the trend of cultural modernism in China during this period.

(1905), whose male author imagined a technologically advanced feminist utopia. Its female residents studied subjects ranging from the arts to physics, drove electric cars, and ate purified liquid food extracts. Their mission was to save China by eliminating corrupt male officials. Such works, combining the fanciful with the critical, offered a new and provocative vision of China.

Yet the integration of western science into Chinese culture was an intellectual challenge. Did being modern mean giving up China's scholarly traditions and values? The nineteenth century had seen Christian missionaries use their scientific knowledge to attract followers. For example, John Fryer, an English missionary and translator, founded *The Science Journal* (*Gezhi huibian*) in 1876. Other publications in the same period included *The Universal Gazette* (*Wanguo gongbao*). Recognizing the usefulness of western science, many Chinese scholars helped missionaries promote it—although they considered it mostly as a way to acquire national wealth and power, rather than as a way of understanding the world.

It is not surprising that the Chinese scholars took this stance, for western visitors to China also presented science as a means to material betterment. Thus, although steamships, telegraphs, and railroads captured public attention, there was little interest in changing fundamental Chinese beliefs. Indeed, even as Chinese intellectuals recognized new modes of knowledge, many of the elite insisted that Chinese learning remain the principal source of all knowledge. What kind of balance should exist between western thought and Chinese learning, or even whether the ancient classics should keep their fundamental role, was an issue that would haunt generations to

come. In this respect, the Chinese dilemma reflected a worldwide challenge to accepting the impulses of modernism.

RETHINKING RACE AND REIMAGINING NATIONS

→ *How did conceptions about race and nation change during this era?*

Ironically, at this time of huge population transfers and shared technological modernization, individuals and nations became passionate defenders of the idea that identities were deeply rooted and unchangeable. Although physical characteristics had always played *some* role in identifying persons, by the late nineteenth century the Linnaean classifications (see Chapter 14) had become the means for ranking the worth of whole nations.

Race now defined who could belong to the nation and enjoy its rights and privileges; by the century's close, racial roots had also become a crucial part of cultural identity. This was the era of ethnographic museums, folkloric collectors, national essence movements, and racial genealogies. People wanted to know who they (and their neighbors) were—especially in terms of *biological* ancestry. Now the idea of inheritance took on new weight, in both cultural and biological forms. Doctors, officials, and novelists described the genetic inheritance of madness, alcoholism, criminality, and even homosexuality; nationalists spoke of the uniqueness of the Slavic soul, the German mind, Hindu spirituality, the Hispanic race. The preoccupation with race reflected a worldwide longing for fixed roots in an age that seemed to be burning all its bridges to the past.

Nationalist and racial ideas were different in different parts of the world. In Europe and America, debates about race and national purity reflected several concerns: fear of losing individuality in a technological world, rising tensions among states, and fear of being overrun by the brown, black, and yellow peoples beyond the borders of "civilization." By contrast, in India these ideas were part of the anticolonial debate, and they helped to mobilize people politically. This was also the case in China, Latin America, and the Islamic world, where discussions of identity went hand in hand with opposition to western domination and corrupt indigenous elites. Especially in the colonial world, racial identity was primarily a question about the community's coherence and endurance, not about the races of humankind in general.

These new impulses produced a variety of national movements, from China's anti-Qing campaign to India's Swadeshi movement (see below). At the same time, panethnic movements looked beyond the nation-state, envisioning communities based on ethnicity. Behind these movements was the notion that political communities should be built on racial purity or unsullied indigenous traditions. These views indicated just how unsettled the world was by the century's end and how urgent the questions of identity and belonging had become.

NATION AND RACE IN NORTH AMERICA AND EUROPE

In the United States, the changing mood was striking. Americans greeted the end of the century with a combination of chest-beating pride and shoulder-slumping pessimism. In the early 1890s, for example, Americans flocked to extravagant commemorations of the four hundredth anniversary of Christopher Columbus's discovery. The largest was the Columbian Exposition in Chicago. Such events displayed the most modern machinery and celebrated the nation's marvelous destiny. Yet, at the same time, Americans feared for their future. They especially worried that America had exhausted its supposedly infinite supply of new land and resources—as evidenced by the disappearance of the buffalo, the erosion of soils, and the depletion of timber stands by aggressive logging companies. Conservationists' alarm grew more intense with the Census Bureau's 1890 announcement that the American frontier had "closed."

The Columbian Exposition. More than 27 million people attended the Columbian Exposition in Chicago in 1893. Like many of the era's world's fairs, this one celebrated technological progress, including the spread of electricity, as evidenced by the General Electric Tower of Light.

PRESERVING NATURAL RESOURCES When Theodore Roosevelt became president in 1901, he translated concerns about conserving natural resources into government policy. Fearing a world without conquerable frontiers, Roosevelt agonized about the fate of market economies and the decline of America's spirit of pioneer individualism. The market, insisted Roosevelt and like-minded conservationists, could not be trusted to protect "nature." Instead, federal regulation was necessary. This led to the creation in 1905 of the National Forest Service, to manage the development of millions of acres of permanent public lands.

Roosevelt also worried about a nation dominated by impersonal corporations and populated primarily by urban-dwelling factory workers. He was particularly concerned that modern comforts would deprive men of the tests of rough-and-ready manhood that generations of pioneers had found in conquering Indians and taming wilderness. So Roosevelt pushed for lands to be designated as wildlife reserves and national parks, where he hoped that future generations would continue to experience "the strenuous life."

RESTRICTING IMMIGRATION Most white Americans did not agonize about what the African American intellectual W. E. B. Du Bois (1868–1963) predicted would be "the problem of the twentieth century"—that is, "the problem of the color line." Rather, white Americans were busily drawing new color lines, initiating new forms of racial discrimination where old forms (like slavery) had broken down. In the American West, animosity toward Chinese workers led to the 1882 Exclusion Act, which prohibited almost all immigration from China. In the American South, where most of the nation's 7 million African Americans resided, a system of "Jim Crow" laws upheld racial segregation and inequality.

White Americans grew even more anxious as throngs of "swarthy" immigrants entered the United States. These people came primarily from southern and eastern Europe, but to the champions of "Anglo-Saxonism" they were not "white." Even more threatening were darker peoples who were colonial subjects in the Philippines, Puerto Rico, and Cuba. Talk of the end of white America fueled support for more restrictive immigration policies.

Across the North Atlantic, European elites engaged in similar discussions. For them, the final divvying up of Africa was in many respects equivalent to the closing of the American frontier. The Germans and Italians, in particular, complained about the lack of new territories on which to plant their flags. The French and British began to worry about how to preserve their empires, especially in light of the anticolonial sentiments seething in their colonies.

FACING NEW SOCIAL ISSUES Like Americans, Europeans also expressed concerns about trends at home. For example, intellectuals suggested that mechanization deprived men of their vitality. At the same time, Darwinist theory

The Conservation Movement. Recognizing that certain vital resources were being rapidly depleted and concerned that urban men were losing the vitality of their pioneer forebears, a conservation movement gathered political strength in the United States in the late nineteenth century. Among the notable early victories for conservationists was the setting aside of California's Yosemite Valley as a national park.

provoked new anxieties about inherited diseases, racial mixing, and the dying out of white "civilizers." Sexual relations between European colonizers and indigenous women—and their mixed offspring—had almost always been a part of European expansionism, but as racial identities hardened, such relations now seemed to threaten the moral fiber of the whole nation. Talk of virility arose, partly provoked by doctors' and scientists' involvement in treating social problems. Before long, English and American schoolboys were encouraged to play sports, to avoid becoming too weak to defend the nation. In addition, medical attention focused on homosexuality, regarding it as a disease and a threat to Anglo-Saxon civilization. In France, the falling birthrate seemed to signal a period of decadence characterized by weak, sickly men and irrational women.

Some people tied decadence to debates about whether Jews—defined by religious practice or, increasingly, by ethnicity—could be fully assimilated into European society. Even though Jews had gained rights as citizens in most European nations by the late nineteenth century, powerful prejudices persisted. In the 1880s and 1890s, violent pogroms, often involving police complicity, targeted the large Jewish populations in the Russian Empire's western territories and pushed the persecuted farther westward. These emigrants'

presence, in turn, stirred up fear and resentment, especially in Austria, Germany, and France. Reactionaries began to talk about the "pollution" of the European races by mixing with Semites and to circulate rumors about Jewish bankers' conspiratorial powers. Perhaps because nothing else seemed stable and enduring, wealthy white male Europeans (like their American counterparts) promoted programs of racial purity to shore up the civilizations they saw coming apart at the seams.

RACE-MIXING AND THE PROBLEM OF NATIONHOOD IN LATIN AMERICA

In Latin America, debates about identity chiefly addressed ethnic intermixing and the legacy of a system of government that, unlike much of the North Atlantic world, excluded rather than included the populace. After all, social hierarchies reaching back to the sixteenth century ranked white Iberians at the top, creole elites in the middle, and indigenous and African populations at the bottom. Thus, the higher on the social ladder, the more likely the people were to be white.

CONTESTED MIXTURES It is important to note that "mixing" did not lead to a shared heritage. Nor did it necessarily lead to homogeneity. In fact, the "racial" order did not stick, since some Iberians occupied the lower ranks, while a few people of color did manage to ascend the social ladder. Moreover, starting in the 1880s, the racial hierarchy saw further disruption by the deluge of poor European immigrants; they were flooding into prospering Latin American countrysides or into booming cities like Buenos Aires in Argentina and São Paulo in Brazil. Latin American societies, then, did not easily become homogeneous "nations." Indeed, many Latin American observers wondered whether national identities could survive these transformations at all.

In an age of acute nationalism, the mixed racial composition of Latin Americans generated special anxieties. In the 1870s in Mexico, it was common to view Indians as obstacles to change. One demographer, Antonio García Cubas, considered indigenous people "decadent and degenerate." According to him, their presence deprived the republic of the right kind of citizens. In Cuba and Brazil, observers made the same claims about blacks. According to many modernizers, Latin America's own people were holding it back. The solution, argued some writers, was to attract white immigrants and to establish educational programs that would uplift Indians, blacks, and people of mixed descent. Thus, many intellectuals joined the crusade to modernize and westernize their populations.

PROMOTING NATIONHOOD BY CELEBRATING THE PAST For their part, Latin American leaders began to exalt bygone glories as a way to promote national selfhood. Inventing successful myths could make a government seem more legitimate—as the heir to a rightful struggle of the past. Thus

Diego Rivera's History of Mexico. This is one of the most famous works of Mexican art, a portrait of the history of Mexico by the radical nationalist painter Diego Rivera. In this chapter, and in previous chapters, we have shown parts of this mural. In stepping back to view the whole work, which is in the National Palace in Mexico City, we can see how Rivera envisioned the history of his people generally. Completed in 1935, this work seeks to show a people fighting constantly against outside aggressors, from their glorious preconquest days (lower center), winding like a grand epic through the conquest, colonial exploitation, the revolution for independence, nineteenth-century invasions from France and the United States, to the popular 1910 Revolution. It culminates in an image of Karl Marx, framed by a "scientific sun"—pointing to a future of progress and prosperity for all, as if restoring a modern Tenochtitlán of the Aztecs. This work captured many Mexicans' efforts to return to the indigenous roots of the nation and to fuse them with modern scientific ideas.

in Mexico, General Díaz placed the bell that Father Hidalgo had tolled on September 16, 1810, to mark the beginning of the war against Spain (see Chapter 15), in the National Palace in Mexico City. In the month of that centennial in 1910, grand processions wound through the capital. Many of the parades celebrated Aztec grandeur, thereby creating a mythic arc from the greatness of the Aztec past to the triumphal story of Mexican independence—and to the benevolence and progress of the Díaz regime. As the government glorified the Aztecs with pageants, statues, and pavilions, however, it continued to ignore modern Aztec descendants, who lived in squalor.

Some thinkers now began to celebrate ancient heritages as a basis for modern national identities. For example, in Mexico and eventually in the Andes, the pre-Spanish past became a crucial foundation stone of the nation-state. The young Mexican writer José Vasconcelos (1882–1959) grew disenchanted with the brutal rule of Díaz and his westernizing ambitions. Nonetheless, he endorsed Díaz's celebration of the Indian past, for he believed that Mexicans were capable of a superior form of civilization. He insisted that if they had

fewer material concerns, their combined Aztec and Spanish Catholic origins could create a spiritual realm of even higher achievement. In Vasconcelos's view, Mexico's greatness flowed not in spite of, but because of, its mixed nature.

SUN YAT-SEN AND THE MAKING OF A CHINESE NATION

Just as Latin American thought celebrated an authentic past, so did Chinese writers emphasize the power and depth of Chinese culture—in contrast to the Qing Empire's failing political and social strength. Here, writers used race to emphasize the superiority of the Han Chinese. Here, too, the pace of change generated a desire to trace one's roots back to secure foundations. Moreover, traditions were reinvented in the hope of saving the Chinese soul threatened by modernity.

In China, as elsewhere, scholars and political mobilizers took up the challenge of redefining identities. By the century's end, prominent members of both groups had abandoned their commitment to preserving the old order but were not ready to fully adopt western practices. Their attempts at combining traditions and values from home and abroad gave rise to the modern Chinese intelligentsia and modern Chinese nationalism.

PROMOTING HAN NATIONALISM Symbolizing the challenge of nation building were the endeavors of **Sun Yat-sen** (1866–1925), who was part of an emerging generation of critics of the old regime. Like his European counterparts, Sun dreamed of a political community reshaped along national lines. Born into a modest rural household in southern China, he studied medicine in the British colony of Hong Kong and then turned to politics during the Sino-Japanese War. When the Qing government rejected his offer of service to the Chinese cause, he became convinced that China's rulers were out of touch with the times. Subsequently he established an organization based in Hawaii to advocate the Qing downfall and the cause of republicanism. The cornerstone of his message was Chinese—specifically, Han—nationalism.

Sun blasted the feeble rule by outsiders, the Manchus, and trumpeted a sovereign political community of "true" Chinese. No ruler, he argued, could enjoy legitimacy without the nation's consent. He envisioned a new China free of Manchu rule, building a democratic form of government and an economic system based on equalized land rights. In this fashion, Sun claimed, China would join the world of nation-states and have the power to defend its borders.

Sun's nationalism did not catch on immediately in China itself, partly because the Qing regime persecuted all dissenters. His ideas fared better among the hundreds of thousands of Chinese who had emigrated in the second half of the nineteenth century. Often facing discrimination in their adopted homelands, these overseas communities applauded Sun's racial nationalism and democratic ideas. In addition, Chinese students studying abroad found inspiration in his message.

REPLACING THE QING AND RECONSTITUTING A NATION Sun's nationalist and republican call resonated more powerfully as the Qing Empire grew weaker early in the twentieth century. Military defeat at the hands of the Japanese was especially humiliating, coming from those whom the Chinese had historically considered a "lowly" folk. Realizing that reforms were necessary, the Manchu court began overhauling the administrative system and the military in the aftermath of the Boxer Uprising. Yet these changes came too late. The old elites grumbled, and the new class of urban merchants, entrepreneurs, and professionals (who often benefited from business with westerners) regarded the government as outmoded. Peasants and laborers resented the high cost of the reforms, which seemed to help only the rulers.

A mutiny, sparked in part by the government's nationalization of railroads and its low compensation to native Chinese investors, broke out in the city of Wuchang in central China in 1911. As it spread to other parts of the country, Sun Yat-sen hurried home from traveling in the United States.

Sun Yat-sen. Through the medium of clothing, these two images of Sun Yat-sen, the man generally known as the "father of the Chinese nation," epitomize the evolving cultural ambiguities of China in the late nineteenth and early twentieth centuries. *(Left)* As a young man studying medicine in the British colony of Hong Kong in the late 1880s, Sun and his friends dressed in the conventional Qing garb of Chinese gentlemen. *(Right)* Two decades later, in early 1912, Sun and the officials of the new republic appeared in public in full western-style jackets and ties. Clothing, like so many parts of the cultural arena in China during this period, had become a contested ground in the battle to forge a new nation's identity.

Few people rallied to the emperor's cause, and the Qing dynasty collapsed—an abrupt end to a dynastic tradition of more than 2,000 years. In the provinces, coalitions of gentry, merchants, and military leaders ran the government.

China would soon be reconstituted, and Sun's ideas, especially those regarding race, would play a central role. The original flag of the republic, for example, consisted of five colors representing the citizenry's major racial groups: red for the Han, yellow for the Manchus, blue for the Mongols, white for the Tibetans, and black for the Muslims. But Sun had reservations about this multiracial flag, believing there should be only one Chinese race. The existence of different groups in China, he argued, was the result of incomplete assimilation—a problem that the modern nation now had to confront.

NATIONALISM AND INVENTED TRADITIONS IN INDIA

British imperial rule persisted in India, but the turn of the century saw cracks in its stranglehold. Four strands had woven the territory together: the consolidation of colonial administration, the establishment of railways and telegraphs, the growth of western education and ideas, and the development of colonial capitalism. Now it was possible to speak of India as a single unit. And it was also possible for anticolonial thinkers to imagine seizing and ruling India by themselves. Thus a new form of resistance emerged, different from peasant rebellions of the past. Now, dissenters talked of Indians as "a people" who had both a national past and national traditions.

A MODERNIZING ELITE   Leaders of the nationalist opposition were western-educated intellectuals from colonial cities and towns. Although a tiny minority of the Indian population, they gained influence through their access to the official world and their familiarity with European knowledge and history. This elite group used their knowledge to develop modern cultural forms. For example, they turned colloquial languages (such as Hindi, Urdu, Bengali, Tamil, and Malayalam) into standardized, literary forms for writing novels and dramas. Now the publication of journals, magazines, newspapers, pamphlets, novels, and dramas surged, facilitating communication throughout British India. (See Primary Source: A Muslim Woman Dreams of Secluding Men from the World.)

Along with print culture came a growing public sphere where intellectuals debated social and political matters. By 1885, voluntary associations in big cities had united to establish a political party, the Indian National Congress. Lawyers, prominent merchants, and local notables dominated its early leadership. The congress demanded greater representation of Indians in administrative and legislative bodies, criticized the government's economic policies, and encouraged India's industrialization.

Underlying this political nationalism, embodied by the Indian National Congress, was cultural nationalism. The nationalists claimed that Indians might not be a single race but were at least a unified people, because of their unique culture and common colonial history. Indeed, nationalism in India (unlike in Europe) developed with an acute awareness of Indians as colonial subjects. The critical question was: could India be a modern nation *and* hold on to its Indian identity?

BUILDING A MODERN IDENTITY ON REWRITTEN TRADITIONS   The recovery of traditions became a way to establish a modern Indian identity without acknowledging the recent subjugation by British colonizers. So Indian intellectuals (like those in Latin America) turned to the past and rewrote the histories of ancient empires and kingdoms. In this way, Indian intellectuals promoted the idea of the nation-state even though the region had no integrated, national history prior to colonization.

To portray Indians as a people with a unifying religious creed, intellectuals reconfigured Hinduism so that it resembled western religion. This was no easy task, for traditional Hinduism did not have a supreme textual authority, a monotheistic God, an organized church, or an established creed. Nonetheless, nationalist Hindu intellectuals combined various philosophical texts, cultural beliefs, social practices, and Hindu traditions into a mix that they labeled the authentic Hindu religion. Other Indian revivalists, too, explored the roots of a national culture. Some researched ancient Indian contributions to astronomy, mathematics, algebra, chemistry, and medicine and called for a national science. In the fine arts, intellectuals constructed an imaginary line of continuity to the glorious past to promote a specifically Indian art and aesthetics (sense of beauty).

While fashioning hybrid forms, revivalists also narrowed the definition of Indian traditions. As Hindu intellectuals looked back, they identified Hindu traditions and the pre-Islamic past as the only sources of India's culture. Other contributors to the region's mosaic past were forgotten; the Muslim past, in particular, had no prominent role. However, the Muslims and other religious, ethnic, and linguistic groups also attempted to mobilize their communities for modern, secular purposes. The Indian National Muslim League, for example, which formed in 1906, advanced the *political* interests of Muslims, not the Islamic religion.

HINDU REVIVALISM   Hindu revivalism became a powerful political force in the late nineteenth century, when the nationalist challenge to the colonial regime took a militant turn. New leaders rejected constitutionalism and called for militant agitation. The British decision to partition Bengal in 1905 into two provinces—one predominantly Muslim, the other Hindu—drew militants into the streets to urge the

Primary Source

A MUSLIM WOMAN DREAMS OF SECLUDING MEN FROM THE WORLD

Though international in breadth, the women's movement addressed different issues in different national contexts. In the Muslim world, many women demanded an end to their seclusion and the right to appear in public without being fully veiled. In this selection Rokeya Sakhawat Hossain, a Muslim Bengali woman, uses satire to highlight the injustices of confining women to the zenana (the harem). Hossain's story appeared in 1905 in The Indian Ladies Magazine, *an English journal in Madras, India. The heroine, Sultana, dreams of a world in which women fill the streets and lock away the men.*

One evening I was lounging in an easy chair in my bedroom and thinking lazily of the condition of Indian womanhood. I am not sure whether I dozed off or not. But, as far as I remember, I was wide awake. I saw the moonlit sky sparkling with thousands of diamondlike stars, very distinctly.

All of a sudden a lady stood before me; how she came in, I do not know. I took her for my friend, Sister Sara. . . .

I used to have my walks with Sister Sara, when we were at Darjeeling. Many a time did we walk hand in hand and talk lightheartedly in the botanical gardens there. I fancied Sister Sara had probably come to take me to some such garden, and I readily accepted her offer and went out with her.

When walking I found to my surprise that it was a fine morning. The town was fully awake and the streets alive with bustling crowds. I was feeling very shy, thinking I was walking in the street in broad daylight, but there was not a single man visible.

Some of the passersby made jokes at me. Though I could not understand their language, yet I felt sure they were joking. I asked my friend, "What do they say?"

"The women say you look very mannish."

"Mannish?" said I. "What do they mean by that?"

"They mean that you are shy and timid like men."

"Shy and timid like men?" It was really a joke. . . .

"I feel somewhat awkward," I said, in a rather apologizing tone, "as being a *purdahnishin* woman I am not accustomed to walking about unveiled."

"You need not be afraid of coming across a man here. This is Ladyland, free from sin and harm. Virtue herself reigns here." . . .

I became curious to know where the men were. I met more than a hundred women while walking there, but not a single man.

"Where are the men?" I asked her.

"In their proper places, where they ought to be."

"Pray let me know what you mean by 'their proper places.'"

"Oh, I see my mistake, you cannot know our customs, as you were never here before. We shut our men indoors."

"Just as we are kept in the *zenana*?"

"Exactly so."

"How funny." I burst into a laugh. Sister Sara laughed too.

"But, dear Sultana, how unfair it is to shut in the harmless women and let loose the men. . . . Why do you allow yourselves to be shut up?"

"Because it cannot be helped as they are stronger than women."

"A lion is stronger than a man, but it does not enable him to dominate the human race. You have neglected the duty you owe to yourselves, and you have lost your natural rights by shutting your eyes to your own interests."

"But my dear Sister Sara, if we do everything by ourselves, what will the men do then?"

"They should not do anything, excuse me; they are fit for nothing. Only catch them and put them into the *zenana*."

→ *What do you learn (indirectly) about the customary treatment of Muslim women by reading this excerpt?*

→ *What does Hossain believe to be the fundamental difference between men and women?*

SOURCE: Rokeya Sakhawat Hossain, "Sultana's Dream" from *Sultana's Dream: A Feminist Utopia and Selections from The Secluded Ones*, edited and translated by Roushan Jahan. Translation copyright © 1988 by Roushan Jahan. Reprinted with permission of the publishers, The Feminist Press at the City University of New York, www.feministpress.org. All rights reserved.

Rabindranath Tagore. The Bengali writer, philosopher, and teacher Rabindranath Tagore became the poet laureate of the Swadeshi Movement in Bengal in 1903–1908. The first Asian Nobel laureate, he became disenchanted with nationalism, viewing it as narrow and not universalistic. The photo shows Tagore reading to a group of his students in 1929.

boycott of British goods. Rabindranath Tagore, a famous Bengali poet and future Nobel laureate, composed stirring nationalist poetry. Activists formed voluntary organizations, called Swadeshi ("one's own country") Samitis, that championed indigenous enterprises for manufacturing soap, cloth, medicine, iron, and paper, as well as schools for imparting nationalist education. Although few of these ventures succeeded, the efforts reflected the nationalist desire to assert Indians' autonomy as a people.

The Swadeshi movement swept aside the moderate leadership of the Indian National Congress and installed a radical leadership that broadened the nationalist agitation. Although the people did not topple the colonial regime, Indian mass mobilization was enough to alarm the British rulers, who turned to force to keep the colony intact. When the movement slipped into a campaign of terrorism in 1908, the government responded by imprisoning militant leaders. However, the colonial administrators also annulled their partition of Bengal in 1911.

Late-nineteenth-century Indian nationalism posed a different kind of challenge to the British than the suppressed 1857 rebellion. Back then, insurgents had wanted to preserve local identities against the encroaching modern state and colonial economy. Now, in contrast, nationalist leaders imagined a modern national community. Invoking religious and ethnic symbols, they formed modern political associations to operate in a national public arena. Unlike the insurgents of 1857, they did not seek a radical alternative to the colonial order; instead, they fought for the political rights of Indians as a secular, national community. In these new nationalists, British rulers discovered an enemy not so different from themselves.

THE PAN MOVEMENTS

India and China were not the only places where activists dreamed of founding new states. Across the globe, groups had begun to imagine new communities based on ethnicity or, in some cases, religion. **Pan movements** (from the Greek *pan*, "all") sought to link people across state boundaries. The grand aspiration of all these movements—which included pan-Asianism, pan-Islamism, pan-Africanism, pan-Slavism, pan-Turkism, pan-Arabism, pan-Germanism, and Zionism—was the rearrangement of borders in order to unite dispersed communities. But such remappings posed a threat to rulers of the Russian, Austrian, and Ottoman empires, as well as to overseers of the British and the French colonial empires.

PAN-ISLAMISM Within the Muslim world, intellectuals and political leaders begged their coreligionists to put aside sectarian and political differences so that they could unite under the banner of Islam in opposition to European incursions. The leading spokesman for pan-Islamism was the well-traveled Jamal al-Din al-Afghani (1839–1897). Born in Iran and given a Shiite upbringing, he nonetheless called on Muslims worldwide to overcome their Sunni and Shiite differences so that they could work together against the West. Afghani called for unity and action, for an end to corruption and stagnation, and for acceptance of the true principles of Islam. During a sojourn in Egypt, he joined with a young Egyptian reformer, Muhammad Abduh (1849–1905), to inspire an Islamic protest against Europe. Later, Afghani and Abduh (then living in Paris) published a pan-Islamic newspaper. Afghani subsequently made his way to Istanbul, where he supported the pan-Islamic ambitions of Sultan Abdul Hamid II, who promoted the defense of Islam as a way to thwart European schemes to divide up the Ottoman Empire.

The pan-Islamic appeal only added to Muslims' confusion as they confronted the West. Indeed, Arab Muslims living as Ottoman subjects had many calls on their loyalties. Should they support the Ottoman Empire to resist European encroachments? Or should they embrace the Islamism of Afghani? Most decided to work within the fledgling nation-states of the Islamic world, looking to a Syrian or Lebanese identity as the way to deal with the West and gain autonomy. But Afghani and his disciples had struck a chord in Muslim culture, and their Islamic message has long retained a powerful appeal.

The Birth of the Turkish Nation. Sultan Abdul Hamid II bestows a constitution on the Turkish people.

PAN-GERMANISM AND PAN-SLAVISM Pan-Germanism found followers across central Europe, where it often competed with a pan-Slavic movement that sought to unite all Slavs against their Austrian, German, and Ottoman overlords. This area had traditionally been ruled by German-speaking elites, who owned the land farmed by Poles, Czechs, Russians, and other Slavs. German elites began to feel increasingly uneasy as Slavic nationalisms (spurred by the mid-century revivals of traditional Czech, Polish, Serbian, and Ukrainian languages and cultures) became more popular. Even more threatening was the fact that the Slavic populations were growing faster than the German. As pogroms in the Russian Empire's borderlands in the 1880s, as well as economic opportunities, drove crowds of eastern European Jews westward, German resentment toward these newcomers also increased.

What made pan-Germanism a movement, however, was the intervention of a former liberal, Georg von Schönerer (1842–1921). In 1882, Schönerer, outraged by the Habsburg Empire's failure to favor Germans, founded the League of German Nationalists. It comprised students, artisans, teachers, and small businessmen. Schönerer detested the Jews, defining them by their "racial characteristics" rather than by their religious practices. After his election to the Austrian upper house, he attempted to pass anti-Jewish legislation modeled on the American Chinese Exclusion Act of 1882. Schönerer's subsequent campaigns to promote German interests within the Habsburg Empire sought to break what he regarded as Austria's anti-German dependency on the pope. Ultimately, he wanted German Austria to unite with the Germans in Bismarck's empire, thus forming a huge, racially unified state that would dominate central Europe. Although Schönerer's plans were too radical for most German Austrians, his anti-Semitism found echoes in a milder form by Viennese mayor Karl Lueger in the late 1890s and in a stronger form by Adolf Hitler after 1933.

The rhetoric of pan-Germanism motivated central Europeans to think of themselves as members of a German *race*, their identities determined by blood rather than defined by state boundaries. This, too, was the lesson of pan-Slavism. Both movements led fanatics to take actions that were dangerous to existing states. The organization of networks of radical southern Slavs, for example, unsettled Serbia and Herzegovina (annexed by the Austrians in 1908). Indeed, it was a Serbian proponent of plans to carve an independent Slav state out of Austrian territory in the Balkans who assassinated the heir to the Habsburg throne in June 1914. By August, the whole of Europe had descended into mass warfare, bringing much of the rest of the world directly or indirectly into the conflict as well. Eventually, the war would fulfill the pan-Slav, pan-German, and anti-Ottoman Muslim nationalist longing to tear down the Ottoman and Habsburg empires.

CONCLUSION

Ever since the Enlightenment, Europeans had put their faith in "progress." Through the nineteenth century, educated elites took pride in their booming industries, bustling cities, and burgeoning colonial empires. Yet by the century's end, urbanization and industrialization seemed more disrupting than uplifting, more disorienting than reassuring. Moreover, colonized people's resistance to the "civilizing mission" fueled doubts about the course of progress.

Especially unsettling to the ruling elite was the realization that "the people" not only were against them but also were developing ways to unseat them. In colonial settings, nationalists learned how to mobilize large populations. In Europe, socialist and right-wing leaders challenged liberal political power. By contrast, old elites, whose politics relied on closed-door negotiations between "rational" gentlemen, were unprepared to deal with modern ideas and identities.

Nor were the elites able to control the scope of change, for the expansion of empires had drawn ever more people into an unbalanced global economy. Everywhere, disparities in wealth appeared—especially in Africa, Asia, and Latin America. Moreover, the size and power of industrial operations threatened small firms and made individuals seem insignificant. Even some cities seemed too big and too dangerous. All these social and economic challenges stretched the capacities of gentlemanly politics.

Yet anxieties stimulated creative energy. Western artists borrowed nonwestern images and vocabularies; nonwestern intellectuals looked to the West for inspiration, even as they formulated anti-western ideas. The upheavals of modern experience propelled scholars to study the past and to fabricate utopian visions of the future.

Revivals and dislocations, as well as cultural and political movements, influenced the reformulating of identities. However, this was an incomplete process. For even as these changes unsettled the European-centered world, they intensified rivalries among Europe's powers themselves. Thus, this order was unstable at its center—Europe itself. And in the massive conflict that destroyed this era's faith in progress, Europe would ravage itself. The Great War would yield an age of even more rapid change—and even more violent consequences.

Review and research materials are available at StudySpace: Ⓢ WWNORTON.COM/STUDYSPACE

KEY TERMS

anarchism (p. 687)
Anglo-Boer War (p. 677)
Boxer Uprising (p. 679)
Mexican Revolution (p. 688)
modernists (p. 670)
pan movements (p. 702)

popular culture (p. 690)
progressive reformers (p. 689)
Shanghai School (p. 695)
Sun Yat-sen (p. 699)
syndicalism (p. 687)

Chronology

	1870	1880	1890
THE AMERICAS		1880s–1910s Labor unrest ✦------ ✦ 1882 Chinese Exclusion Act (United States)	
EUROPE		1883–1884 Social welfare laws (Germany) ✦--✦ 1880s–1910s Labor unrest ✦--------------	
SOUTH ASIA		1885 Indian National Congress established ✦	
EAST ASIA			1894–1895 Sino-Japanese War ✦--
RUSSIA			
AFRICA			✦ 1886 Discovery of gold in the Transvaal
MIDDLE EAST			

STUDY QUESTIONS

1. Explain why westerners used the term *progress* to describe the world at the end of the nineteenth and beginning of the twentieth centuries. What did they believe were the sources of this progress?
2. List and explain various examples of worldwide anxieties that challenged the idea of progress during this time. Which groups protested the status quo?
3. Describe the armed uprisings against western imperialism in Africa and China during this era. How similar were these movements to other alternative visions to the new world order explored in Chapter 16?
4. Compare and contrast revolutionary and reform movements in Latin America and China during this era. How were their goals and methods similar and different?
5. Analyze how anxieties about progress shaped cultural developments around the world. What was cultural modernism, and how did it challenge traditional assumptions about art and science?
6. Define the term *popular culture*. Why did it become so powerful during this time, and how did it shape individuals' identity?
7. Analyze to what extent new ideas of race and nation created tension within and between states. What new forms of nationalism emerged during this time?

1900	1910	1920

1910–1920 Mexican Revolution ◆--------------------------◆

◆ 1900 Paris Exhibition
◆ 1900 British Labour Party founded

◆ 1904 Social welfare laws (France)
◆ 1906 Social welfare laws (Great Britain)
◆ 1906 Women vote in national elections in Finland

◆ 1905 British partition of Bengal
◆ 1906 Indian National Muslim League founded

◆--◆ 1899–1900 Boxer Uprising (China)
1904–1905 Russo-Japanese War ◆--◆
◆ 1911 Chinese Republican Revolution

◆--◆ 1904–1905 Russo-Japanese War
◆ 1905 Revolt in Russian Empire

◆----------◆ 1899–1902 South African (Boer) War
◆------◆ 1904–1906 Herero Revolt
◆--◆ 1905–1906 Maji-Maji Revolt

◆ 1923 Birth of the Turkish state

19

OF MASSES AND VISIONS OF THE MODERN, 1910–1939

he last guns of the Great War (World War I) fell silent not on the bloody battlefields of Europe, but in a remote corner of East Africa. It took a full day for news of the armistice to reach that region where African soldiers, under British and German officers, were battling for control of German East Africa. Here, 10,000 German-led African soldiers used guerrilla tactics to thwart the efforts of over 300,000 British-led African soldiers. Thousands of African troops died in these battles, beyond the spotlight of international opinion. Thus did this world conflagration come to a close outside Europe.

Raging from August 1914 to November 1918, World War I shook the foundations of the European-centered world. Although most major battles occurred on European soil, multitudes of American, African, and Asian soldiers were ferried across oceans to join the killing and maiming there. Campaigns also bloodied the soil in Turkey, Egypt, Syria, and sub-Saharan Africa. This was the first modern war involving whole societies. Its impact was thoroughly global. In addition to involving countless soldiers from Europe's colonies, its aftermath fostered notions of freedom and self-determination and a growing disillusionment with European rule in these locations. Elsewhere, nations grappled with competing visions for building a viable, modern society.

This chapter deals with the Great War and its global impact. First, because the war was fought on a worldwide scale and to utter exhaustion in Europe, it required the resources of a large part of the world. Therefore it prompted production and consumption on a mass scale. These in turn became defining features of economic modernity. Wartime leaders used new media such as radio and film to promote national loyalties and to discredit enemies—and thereby helped to spread a mass culture. Second, the harsh terms of the peace settlement unbalanced the global economy and led directly to the Great Depression. Third, political turmoil surrounding the war inflamed disputes over how to manage mass societies and build a better world. To this end, three strikingly different visions arose: liberal democratic, authoritarian, and anticolonial. These ideologies competed for preeminence in the decades leading up to World War II.

THE QUEST FOR THE MODERN

> → *What were the different forms of political modernity?*

When people spoke of "being modern" in the 1920s and 1930s, they disagreed on what it meant. Most agreed, however, that in economic terms modernity involved mass production and mass consumption. In the West, for example, the automobile, the gramophone (a record player), the cinema, and the radio reflected the benefits of economic and cultural modernism. In terms of political issues, being modern meant the involvement of the masses in politics. Everywhere people favored strong leadership to reinvigorate their societies; some wanted more democracy to replace monarchical and colonial rule. Following the Great Depression in the 1930s, even more intense debates arose. These debates led to bitter divisions on how to build modern societies.

The first political vision of modernism—the *liberal democratic* one—confronted economic failings without sacrificing market economies or parliamentary democracy. It did so through widened participation in governance but also greater power for state regulatory bureaucracies. However, after the Great Depression spread hard times and unemployment, this predominantly American and western European model linking capitalism and democracy no longer seemed so promising. Around the world, people considered alternatives that might better deliver the promises of modernity. Although many rejected the parliamentary or liberal perspective, the system survived in the United States, parts of western Europe, and several Latin American nations.

For many observers, liberal democracies failed to match the astonishing dynamism of a second perspective—*authoritarianism*. Authoritarian regimes rejected parliamentary rule, subordinated the individual to the state, managed and often owned most aspects of the production process, used censorship and terror to enforce loyalty, and exalted an all-powerful leader. Authoritarianism was evident in both right-wing dictatorships (Fascist Italy, Nazi Germany, dictatorial Spain and Portugal, and militaristic Japan) and a left-wing dictatorship (the Soviet Union).

The third vision—*anticolonial*—also questioned the liberal democratic order, primarily because of its connection to colonialism. However, most anticolonialists did not reject parliaments or private enterprise. Resentful of European rulers who preached democracy but practiced despotism, anticolonial leaders sought to oust their colonial rulers and then find their own path to modernity. They generally favored mixing western ideas with indigenous traditions.

Focus Questions

→ *What were the different forms of political modernity?*

→ *In what ways did the Great War change the world?*

→ *How did different political systems utilize mass culture?*

→ *How did different political systems respond to economic, political, and social disorder?*

MAIN THEMES

→ *The Great War (World War I) engulfs the entire globe, exhausts Europe, and promotes production and consumption on a mass scale.*

→ *The harsh terms of the peace settlement unbalance the global economy and lead directly to the Great Depression.*

→ *Three strikingly different visions for building a better world arise: liberal democratic, authoritarian, and anticolonial.*

FOCUS ON *World War I and Its Aftermath*

The Great War

+ The war destroys empires, starting with the Bolshevik Revolution against the tsarist regime in Russia, followed by the defeat and dissolution of the German, Austro-Hungarian, and Ottoman empires.

+ Mass mobilization sees almost 70 million men join the fighting, undermines traditional gender boundaries, and forces states to recognize their peoples' demands for compensation afterward.

+ Mass culture spreads as leaders use the new media of radio and film to promote national loyalties and discredit enemies.

The Aftermath

+ Liberal democracies in France, Britain, and the United States survive the Great Depression by enacting far-reaching changes in their political systems and free-market economies.

+ Authoritarian (communist and fascist) dictatorships with many political similarities emerge in the Soviet Union, Italy, Germany, Spain, and Portugal.

+ Latin American leaders devise hybrid solutions that combine democratic and authoritarian elements.

+ Peoples living under colonial rule in Asia and Africa mobilize traditional values to oppose imperial rulers.

+ Key individuals emerge in the struggle to define newly independent nations: Kenyatta, Gandhi, Chiang Kai-shek, and Ataturk.

THE GREAT WAR

> → *In what ways did the Great War change the world?*

Few events were more decisive in drawing men and women worldwide into national and international politics than the **Great War**. For over four years, millions of soldiers from Europe, as well as from its dominions and colonies, killed and mutilated one another. Such carnage damaged European claims to civilized superiority and encouraged colonial subjects to break from imperial masters. Among Europeans, too, the war's effects shook the hierarchies of prewar society. Above all, the war made clear how much the power of the state now depended on the support of the people.

The war's causes were complex. The bedrock cause was the combustible rivalry between Great Britain and Germany. Through most of the nineteenth century, Britain had been the preeminent power. By the century's end, however, German industrial output had surpassed Britain's, and Germany had begun building a navy. For the British, who controlled the world's seas, the German navy was an affront; for the Germans, it was a logical step in their expanding ambitions. This Anglo-German antagonism drew in the other powers in rival alliances. Germany joined Austria-Hungary to form the **Central Powers**; Britain affiliated itself with France and Russia in the Triple Entente (later called the **Allied Powers** after Italy joined).

Well armed and secretly pledged to defend their partners, the rivals lacked only a spark to ignite open hostilities. That came in August 1914, when the heir to the Habsburg throne was assassinated in Sarajevo, the capital of Austrian Bosnia. The assassin hoped to trigger an independence movement that would detach South-Slav territories from the Austro-Hungarian Empire (see Chapter 18) and unite them with independent Serbia. But as the Ottoman Empire was pushed out of the Balkans, Russia and Austria-Hungary competed for influence and territory there. Russia backed the Serbs against Austria-Hungary, and the British, French, and Germans were drawn into the conflict in support of their partners. The world war that followed dragged in Europe's colonies, too.

THE FIGHTING

The declarations of war drew cries of jubilation from those who anticipated a short triumphal conflict for their side. Dreams of glory inspired tens of thousands of men to enlist. But the fighting did not go as expected.

BATTLE FRONTS, STALEMATE, AND CARNAGE Despite hopes for a swift resolution, the war became infamous for its duration and horrors. The initial German offensive, which intended to thrust through neutral Belgium, stalled thirty miles outside Paris at the battle of the Marne in September 1914 (see Map 19-1). A stalemate ensued. Instead of a quick war, vast land armies dug trenches along the Western Front—from the English Channel through Belgium and France to the Alps—installing barbed wire and setting up machine-gun posts. The troops became immobilized. Anything but glorious, life in the trenches mixed boredom, dampness, dirt, vermin, and disease, punctuated by the terror of being ordered to "go over the top" to attack the enemy's entrenched position. Doing so meant running across a "no man's land" in which machine guns mowed down almost all attackers.

On the other side of Europe, Russian troops advanced into East Prussia and Austria-Hungary along the Eastern Front. Although the Russians defeated Austro-Hungarian troops in Galicia (between present-day Poland and Ukraine) and scored initial victories in eastern Germany, they suffered devastating reversals in East Prussia once the Germans threw in well-trained divisions that were better armed and better provisioned than the Russian troops.

By 1915, the war had ground to a gruesome standstill. Along the Western Front, neither the Allies nor the Central Powers could advance. On the Eastern Front, the Russians had been driven back and had lost much of Poland. At Ypres in 1915, the Germans tried to break the stalemate by introducing poison gas, but a countermove of equipping soldiers with gas masks nullified that advantage. In July 1916, the British launched an offensive along the Somme River in northeastern France. By November, when the futile attack halted, approximately 600,000 British and French and 500,000 Germans had perished. Yet the battle lines had hardly budged. Attempts to win by opening other fronts—in Turkey, the Middle East, and Africa—failed and added to the war's carnage (see Map 19-2).

The death toll forced governments to call up more men than ever before. Nearly 70 million men worldwide fought in the war, including almost all of Europe's young adult males. From 1914 to 1918, 13 million served in the German army. In Russia, more than 15 million men took up arms. The British mobilized 5.25 million troops, almost half the prewar population of men age fifteen to forty-nine, and in France around 8 million served, nearly 80 percent of the same prewar age-group population.

Mass mobilization also undermined traditional gender boundaries. Tens of thousands of women served at or near the front as doctors, nurses, and technicians. Even more women mobilized on the "home front," taking on previously male occupations—especially in munitions plants. But women could also turn against the state. Particularly in central Europe and Russia, the war's demands for soldiers and supplies left farms untended and caused food shortages. Bread riots and peaceful protests by women, traumatized by loss and desperate to feed their children, put states on notice that their citizens expected compensation for their sacrifices. Indeed, civilian pressure forced many states to make promises they would have to fulfill after the war, in the form of welfare provisions, expanded suffrage, and pensions for widows and the wounded.

In the four years of war, military deaths exceeded 8 million. Another 20 million soldiers were wounded. Vast numbers of survivors bore artificial limbs. Naval blockades and aerial bombardments had aggravated civilian food shortages and left people susceptible to epidemics, like influenza. As

Trenches in World War I. The anticipated war of mobility turned out to be an illusion; instead, armies dug trenches and filled them with foot soldiers and machine guns. To advance entailed walking into a hail of machine-gun fire. Life in the trenches meant cold, dampness, rats, disease, and boredom.

Western Front

← Allied advance
← German advance
— The Western Front, November 1914
•••• German offensive, spring 1918
--- The Western Front, March 1918
— Armistice Line, November 1918
✳ Major battle

Eastern Front

← Russian advance
← German advance
— Limit of Russian advance, 1914–1915
--- Limit of Austro-German advances, 1915–1916
— German penetration into Russia, June 1918
✳ Major battle

Allies and colonies
Neutral nations that joined Allies
Central Powers
Neutral nations and empires that joined Central Powers and colonies
Neutral nations
← Allied advance
← Central Powers' advance
--- Maximum German Advance, 1918
— Armistice line, Nov. 11, 1918
— Armistice line, Treaty of Brest-Litovsk, 1918

MAP 19-1   WORLD WAR I: THE EUROPEAN AND MIDDLE EASTERN THEATERS

Most of the fighting in World War I, despite its designation as a world war, occurred in Europe. Although millions of soldiers fought on both sides, the territorial advances were relatively small. Look at the maps above, and identify all the countries where Allies and Central Powers made advances. Which countries had to fight a two-front war? Did the armies of the Central Powers or the Allies gain the most territory during the war? According to your reading, how did this factor affect the war's outcome?

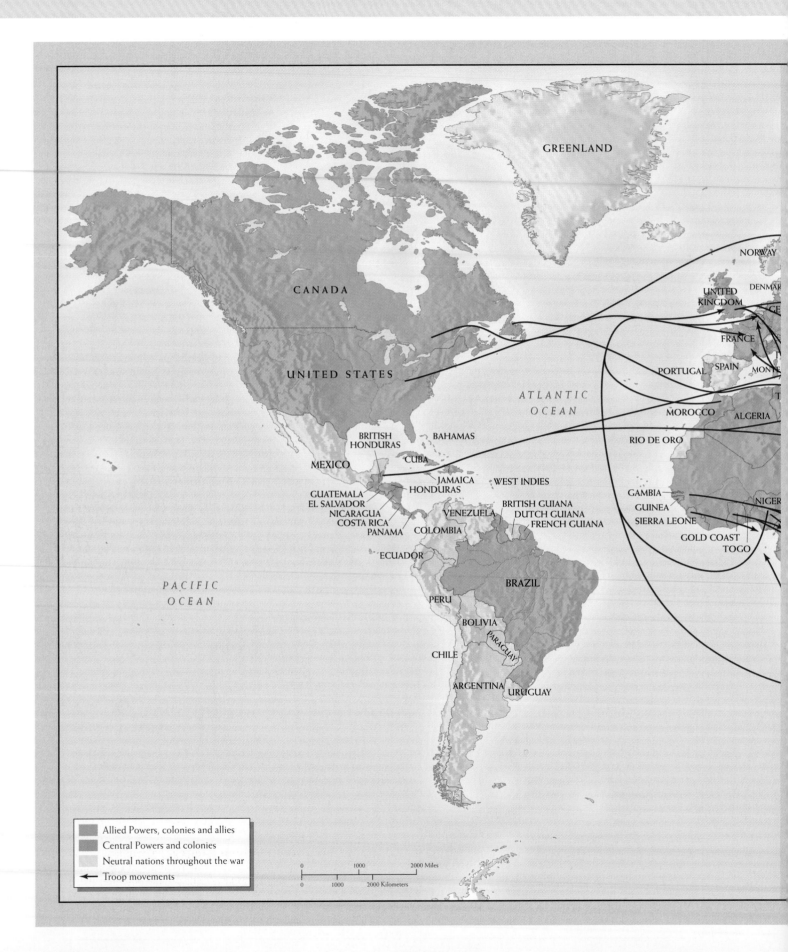

GREENLAND

NORWAY

DENMARK

UNITED
KINGDOM

GE

FRANCE

PORTUGAL   SPAIN   MONTE

CANADA

MOROCCO   ALGERIA

UNITED STATES

*ATLANTIC
OCEAN*

RIO DE ORO

BRITISH
HONDURAS   BAHAMAS

CUBA

MEXICO   JAMAICA
            HONDURAS   WEST INDIES   GAMBIA

GUATEMALA   GUINEA   NIGER
EL SALVADOR   SIERRA LEONE
NICARAGUA   VENEZUELA   BRITISH GUIANA
COSTA RICA   DUTCH GUIANA   GOLD COAST
PANAMA   COLOMBIA   FRENCH GUIANA   TOGO

ECUADOR

*PACIFIC
OCEAN*

BRAZIL

PERU

BOLIVIA

PARAGUAY

CHILE

ARGENTINA   URUGUAY

Allied Powers, colonies and allies
Central Powers and colonies
Neutral nations throughout the war
Troop movements

0   1000   2000 Miles

0   1000   2000 Kilometers

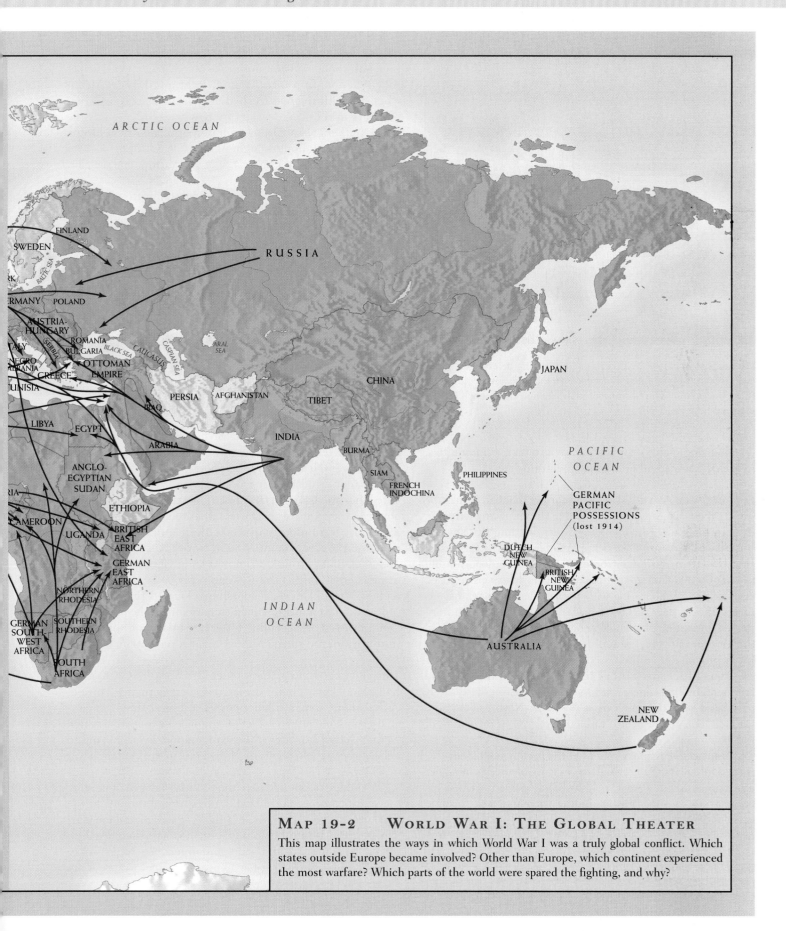

MAP 19-2   WORLD WAR I: THE GLOBAL THEATER

This map illustrates the ways in which World War I was a truly global conflict. Which states outside Europe became involved? Other than Europe, which continent experienced the most warfare? Which parts of the world were spared the fighting, and why?

Women's War Effort. With armies conscripting nearly every able-bodied man, women filled their places in factories, especially in those that manufactured war materials, such as the French plant pictured here in 1916.

demobilizing soldiers spread disease into their communities, influenza claimed 50 million people worldwide.

EMPIRE AND WAR   The war's horrors reached across the world's regions (see again Map 19-2). The sprawling Ottoman Empire sided with the Central Powers, battling British- and Russian-led forces in Egypt, Iraq, Anatolia, and the Caucasus. In 1915–1916, Ottoman forces massacred or deported between 800,000 and 1.3 million Armenians, who were accused en masse of collaborating with the Russians. Many analysts regard these attacks as the world's first genocide, the intentional elimination of a whole people. To increase their forces, the British and the French conscripted colonial subjects: India provided 1 million soldiers; over 1 million Africans fought in Africa and Europe for their colonial masters, and another 3 million transported war supplies. Even the sparsely populated British dominions of Australia, New Zealand, and Canada dispatched over a million loyal young men to fight for the empire.

Despair and disillusionment at the prolonged, bloody war turned into revolt and revolution. In British-ruled Nyasaland, a mission-educated African, John Chilembwe, directed his compatriots to refuse British military demands and to stand up for "Africa for the Africans." Although the British suppressed the insurrection and executed the rebel leader, Chilembwe's death did not stop the growing desire to undo bonds to the mother country.

Controlling the mobilized masses proved even more difficult in Europe. In 1916, after the second winter of deprivation, antiwar demonstrations broke out. The next year, strikes roiled Germany, France, Britain, Italy, and Russia. Meanwhile, in trying to break the battlefield stalemate, Allied commanders introduced devastating new weapons such as the tank. Neither civilian protest nor new armaments could stop the war's devastation, though. As a result, Europe's postwar leaders reaped a bitter harvest of anger, sorrow, and despair.

THE RUSSIAN REVOLUTION   The war destroyed entire empires. The first to go was Romanov Russia. In February 1917, Tsar Nicholas II stepped down under pressure from his generals. They wanted to quash the mass unrest in the capital, which, they believed, threatened the war effort along the Eastern Front. Some members of the Russian parliament formed a provisional government; at the same time, grass-roots councils (soviets) sprang up in factories, garrisons, and towns. The irony of Russia's February Revolution, which brought an end to the monarchy, was that the military and civilian elites wanted to restore order, not encourage a revolution. With the tsar removed, millions of peasants seized land, soldiers and sailors abandoned the front, and borderland nationalities declared autonomy from the crumbling Russian Empire.

In October 1917, left-wing Socialists calling themselves **Bolsheviks** seized power. Led by Vladimir Lenin and Leon Trotsky, the Bolsheviks drew support among radicalized soldiers, sailors, and factory workers organized in the soviets. Arresting provisional government members and claiming power in the name of the soviets, the Bolsheviks proclaimed a socialist revolution to overtake the February "bourgeois" revolution. Several months later, Soviet Russia signed the Treaty of Brest-Litovsk, acknowledging German victory on the Eastern Front as the Russian army collapsed. For protection, the Bolshevik leadership relocated the capital to Moscow and set up a so-called dictatorship of the proletariat. Lenin insisted on accepting the peace treaty and the loss of vast territories to safeguard the socialist revolution.

THE FALL OF THE CENTRAL POWERS   On April 2, 1917, the United States declared war on Germany. This occurred after German submarines sank several American merchant ships and after a secret telegram came to light in which German officials sought Mexican support by promising to help Mexico regain territories it had lost to the United States in 1848.

With U.S. troops added to the fray, the balance of military power in Europe changed. The Allies turned the tide at the Second Battle of the Marne in July 1918 and forced the Germans to retreat into Belgium. German troops then began to surrender en masse, and some announced a soldiers' strike as hunger and influenza became unbearable. Before long,

THE GREAT WAR | 715

The Russian Revolution. (*Left*) The July 1917 demonstrations in Petrograd were among the largest in the Russian Empire during that turbulent year of war and revolution. In this photo, marchers carry banners, "Down with the Ministers-Capitalists" and "All Power to the Soviets of Worker, Soldier and Peasant Deputies." (*Right*) Vladimir Lenin died just six years and three months after the October 1917 revolution, but he lived on in his writings and images, such as in this painting by Pavel Kuznetsov. Artists and propagandists helped make Lenin a ubiquitous icon of the new Soviet order.

Germany tottered on the edge of civil war as the Allied blockade caused food shortages. Faced with defeat and civil strife, the Central Powers fell in succession. Although most of Austria-Hungary's troops remained at the front, German generals agreed to an armistice in November 1918. After Kaiser Wilhelm II slipped into exile, the German empire became a republic. The last Habsburg emperor also abdicated, and Austria-Hungary dissolved into several new states. With the collapse of the Ottoman Empire, the war claimed a fourth dynasty among its casualties.

THE PEACE SETTLEMENT AND THE IMPACT OF THE WAR

To decide the fate of vanquished empires and the future of the modern world, the victors convened five peace conferences, one for each of the Central Powers. Most important was the conference to negotiate peace with Germany, held at Versailles, France, in January 1919. Delegates drew many of their ideas from American President Woodrow Wilson's "Fourteen Points," a blueprint he had devised for making peace in Europe. Wilson especially insisted that postwar borders be redrawn by following the principle of "self-

determination of nations" and that an international **League of Nations** be set up to negotiate further quarrels. Such high-minded ideas were appealing, but once delegates got down to the business of carving up Europe and doling out Germany's colonies, negotiations became tense and difficult. Over the objections of the Americans and British, the French insisted on a punitive treaty that assigned Germany sole blame for the war and forced it to pay reparations.

Applying the principle of self-determination was much more difficult in practice than Wilson had understood. Suddenly, 60 million people in central and eastern Europe now emerged as inhabitants of new nation-states (see Map 19-3). The patchwork nature of the old multiethnic empires here meant that as many as 25 million now lived in states in which they were ethnic minorities and vulnerable to persecution in the tumultuous years after the armistice. The limits of self-determination were even more telling in terms of non-Europeans' rights, for the peacemakers were not prepared to extend self-determination beyond Europe.

Instead of granting independence to the inhabitants of Germany's former colonies in Africa, the treaty parceled them out to the French, the British, the Belgians, and the South Africans. They were assigned as mandates under the oversight of the League of Nations. The same was true of the Arab

MAP 19-3   OUTCOMES OF WORLD WAR I IN EUROPE, NORTH AFRICA, AND SOME OF THE MIDDLE EAST

The political map of Europe and the Middle East changed greatly after the peace treaty of 1919. Comparing this map with Map 19-1, which shows the European and Middle Eastern theaters of war, identify the European countries that came into existence after the war. What happened to the Ottoman Empire, and what powers gained control over many territories of the Ottoman state? What states emerged from the Austro-Hungarian Empire?

provinces of the Ottoman Empire (Syria, Lebanon, Palestine, Jordan, and Iraq), which were turned over to the British and the French.

Whatever idealism survived the peacemaking process absorbed another blow when the U.S. Senate, reflecting a resurgence of isolationism, turned down the Treaty of Versailles and kept the United States out of the League of Nations. Russia, too, was outside the league. For Britain, France, Japan, and the United States, keeping Communist "Red" Russia isolated became a postwar priority.

Demobilization hit societies hard, especially working women; when soldiers hobbled home, women faced layoffs from their wartime jobs. Still, they did not retreat entirely. Within a few years, women gained the vote in Russia, Britain, Germany, and the United States. France held out until 1944, partly because the left feared that French women were under the thumb of the conservative Catholic Church. Nonetheless, in all these nations women claimed new privileges. Young, unmarried women went out in public unescorted, dressed as they saw fit, and maintained their own apartments. Such behavior shocked cultural conservatives, but young women and men alike were determined to enjoy the new, modern world.

MASS SOCIETY: CULTURE, PRODUCTION, AND CONSUMPTION

> → *How did different political systems utilize mass culture?*

The war also contributed to another modern phenomenon: the making of mass societies. Even before World War I mobilized entire societies to produce and to fight, parliamentary regimes had begun to democratize, in many cases granting non–property holders and women the right to vote. Authoritarian regimes, meanwhile, had begun to mobilize the people via rallies and mass organizations. And new technologies, such as radio, were helping to create mass cultures that spanned geographic and class divides.

MASS CULTURE

Indicative of the modern world were new forms of mass communication and entertainment. These were partially wartime products. In an effort to mobilize populations for total war, leaders had disseminated propaganda as never before—through public lectures, theatrical productions, musical com-

positions, and (censored) newspapers. Indeed, the war's impact had politicized cultural activities while broadening the audience for nationally oriented information and entertainment. Together with new media, the war was instrumental in fostering mass culture.

Postwar **mass culture** was distinctive. First, it differed from elite culture (opera, classical music, paintings, literature) because it reflected the tastes of the working and the middle classes, who now had more time and money to spend on entertainment. Second, mass culture relied on new technologies, especially film and radio, which could reach an entire nation's population and consolidate their sense of being a single state.

RADIO Radio entered its golden age after World War I. Invented early in the twentieth century, it made little impact until the 1920s, when powerful transmitters permitted stations to reach much larger audiences—often with nationally syndicated programs. Radio "broadcasts" gave listeners a sense of intimacy with newscasters and stars, addressing consumers as personal friends and drawing them into the lives of serial heroes. Special programs targeted children and women, making radio listening something for the whole family. Even the illiterate could enjoy the programs, such as *The Lone Ranger.* By the late 1920s, nearly two-thirds of homes in the United States had at least one radio. Britain achieved similar radio saturation a decade later.

Radio also was a way to mobilize the masses, especially in authoritarian regimes. For example, the Italian dictator Benito Mussolini pioneered the radio address to the nation. Later, Soviet and Nazi propagandists used this format with great regularity and effect. In Japan, too, radio became a tool to promote the right-wing government's goals. But even dictatorships could not exert total control over mass culture. Although the Nazis regarded jazz as racially inferior music and the Soviets regarded it as "bourgeois," neither could prevent young or old from tuning in to foreign radio broadcasts, smuggling gramophone records over the borders, or creating their own jazz bands.

FILM AND ADVERTISING Film, too, had profound effects. For traditionalists, Hollywood by the 1920s signified vulgarity and decadence because the silver screen prominently displayed modern sexual habits. And like radio, film served political purposes. Here, again, antiliberal governments took the lead. German filmmaker Leni Riefenstahl's movie of the Nazi Nuremberg rally of 1934, *Triumph of the Will,* is a key example of propagandistic cinema. Nazi-era films were comedies, musicals, melodramas, detective films, and adventure epics—sometimes framed by racial stereotypes and political goals. Soviet film studios also produced Hollywood-style musicals alongside didactic pictures about Socialist triumphs.

In market economies, radio and film grew into big businesses, and with expanded product advertising they promoted

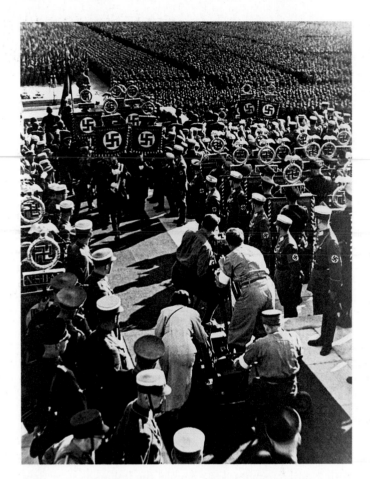

Triumph of the Will. The shooting of *Triumph of the Will*, perhaps the greatest propaganda film ever, directed by Leni Riefenstahl. The film, later denounced, won gold medals in Venice in 1935 and at the World's Fair in 1937.

other enterprises as well. Especially in the United States, advertising became a major industry, with radio commercials shaping national consumer tastes. Increasingly, too, American-produced entertainment, radio programs, and cinematic epics reached an international audience. Thanks to new media, America and the world began to share mass-produced images and fantasies.

MASS PRODUCTION AND MASS CONSUMPTION

The same factors that promoted mass culture also enhanced production and consumption on a mass scale. In fact, World War I paid perverse tribute to the power of industry, for machine technologies produced war materials with abundant and devastating effect.

Never before had armies had so much firepower at their disposal. Whereas in 1809 Napoleon's artillery had discharged 90,000 shells over two days during the largest battle

waged in Europe to that point, by 1916 German guns were firing 100,000 rounds of shells per hour over the full twelve hours of the Battle of Verdun. To sustain military production, millions of men and women worked in factories at home and in the colonies. Producing huge quantities of identical guns, gas masks, bandage rolls, and boots, these factories reflected the modern world's demands for greater volume, faster speed, reduced cost, and standardized output—key characteristics of **mass production**.

The war reshuffled the world's economic balance of power, boosting the United States as an economic powerhouse. As its share of world industrial production climbed above one-third in 1929 (roughly equal to that of Britain, Germany, and Russia combined), people around the globe regarded the United States as a "working vision of modernity" in which not only production but also consumption boomed.

THE AUTOMOBILE ASSEMBLY LINE   The most outstanding example of the relationship between mass production and consumption in the United States was the motor car. It symbolized the machine age and the American road to modernization. Before World War I, the automobile had been a rich man's toy. Then came Henry Ford, who founded the Ford Motor Company in 1903. Five years later, he began production of the Model T, a car that at $850 was within the reach of middle-class consumers. Soon popular demand outstripped supply. Seeking to make more cars faster and cheaper, Ford used mechanized conveyors to send the auto frame along a track, or assembly line, where each worker performed one simplified, repetitive task. By standardizing the manufacturing process, subdividing work, and substituting machinery for manual labor, Ford's assembly line brought a new efficiency to the mass production of automobiles.

By the 1920s, a finished car rolled off Ford's assembly line every ten seconds. Although workers complained about becoming "cogs" in a depersonalized labor process, the system boosted output and reduced costs. The effects reverberated throughout the nation's economy. Ford's factory near Detroit employed 68,000 workers—the largest factory in the world. In addition, millions of cars required millions of tons of steel alloys, as well as vast amounts of glass, rubber, textiles, and petroleum. Cars also needed roads to drive on and service stations to keep them running. Altogether, nearly 4 million jobs related directly or indirectly to the automobile—an impressive total in a labor force of 45 million workers.

After World War I, automobile ownership became more common among Americans. By the 1920s, assembly-line production had dropped the Model T's price to $290. Ford further expanded the market for cars by paying his own workers $5 per day—approximately twice the average manufacturing wage in the United States. He understood that without **mass consumption**, increased purchasing power in the middle classes, and appetite for goods there could be no

Car Assembly Line. Mass production was made possible by the invention of the electric motor in the 1880s, and it enacted three principles: the standardization of core aspects of products, the subdivision of work on assembly lines, and the replacement of manual labor by machinery as well as by reorganizing flow among shops. The greatest successes occurred in the auto plants of Henry Ford, shown here in 1930. With each worker along the line assigned a single task, millions of automobiles rolled off the Ford assembly line, and millions of Americans became owners of automobiles.

mass production. Whereas in 1920 Americans owned 8 million motor cars, a decade later they owned 23 million. The automobile's rapid spread seemed to demonstrate that mass production worked. (See Primary Source: Bruce Barton's Gospel of Mass Production.)

THE GREAT DEPRESSION Not all was easy listening or smooth motoring in countries where mass societies were taking root. During the 1920s, many producers of foodstuffs, coal, and ores faced sagging prices because of overproduction. As staple prices declined in proportion to manufactured goods, farmers throughout the United States, Canada, Australia, and Latin America lamented their dwindling fortunes compared to those of their urban cousins.

On October 24, 1929—Black Tuesday—the American stock market collapsed, plunging not only the American economy but also international financial and trading systems into crisis. This event led the world into the **Great Depression**. Its causes went back to the Great War, which had left European nations in deep debt as they struggled to rebuild their economies and pay off war debts. To restore stability, Europeans borrowed heavily from the United States. When wobbly governments and small investors defaulted on their loans, the U.S. Federal Reserve reacted by raising interest rates. Starting in central Europe, financial institutions began to collapse. As banks fell, other lenders scrambled to call in their loans. Companies, governments, and private borrowers were soon floating in a sea of debt. The panic then spread to the world's stock markets, which led to the Wall Street crash of 1929, which spurred more bank closures.

Financial turmoil produced a major contraction of world trade. Striving to protect workers and investors from the

Stock Traders after the Crash. On October 24, 1929, the American stock market crashed. Here traders are pictured congregating in the financial district of New York City, on what came to be known as "Black Tuesday." As stock values plummeted, panic gripped Wall Street and soon spread across the nation. The market crash was followed by even more devastating bank runs as the Great Depression overtook the world.

BRUCE BARTON'S GOSPEL OF MASS PRODUCTION

In 1925, the journalist (and, later, advertising executive) Bruce Barton published The Man Nobody Knows, *which became a best-seller. In the book, Barton interpreted the life and teachings of Jesus as a gospel for success in modern business. In the excerpt below, Barton uses Henry Ford, whose Model T automobile reigned as the era's marvel of mass production, to show the profitable connections between religion and commerce.*

"If you're forever thinking about saving your life," Jesus said, "you'll lose it; but the man who loses his life shall find it."

Because he said it and he was a religious teacher, because it's printed in the Bible, the world has dismissed it as high minded ethics but not hard headed sense. But look again! . . .

What did Henry Ford mean, one spring morning, when he tipped a kitchen chair back against the whitewashed wall of his tractor plant and talked about his career?

"Have you ever noticed that the man who starts out in life with a determination to make money, never makes very much?" he asked. It was rather a startling question; and without waiting for my comment he went on to answer it: "He may gather together a competence, of course, a few tens of thousands or even hundreds of thousands, but he'll never amass a really great fortune. But let a man start out in life to build something better and sell it cheaper than it has ever been built or sold before—let him have *that* determination, and, give his whole self to it—and the money will roll in so fast that it will bury him if he doesn't look out.

"When we were building our original model, do you suppose that it was money we were thinking about? Of course we expected that it would be profitable, if it succeeded, but that wasn't in the front of our minds. We wanted to make a car so cheap that every family in the United States could afford to have one. So we worked morning, noon and night, until our muscles ached and our nerves were so ragged that it seemed as if we just couldn't stand it to hear anyone mention the word automobile again. One night, when we were almost at the breaking point I said to the boys, 'Well, there's one consolation,' I said, 'Nobody can take this business away from us unless he's willing to work harder than we've worked.' And so far," he concluded with a whimsical smile, "nobody has been willing to do that."

→ *What are the key ingredients to success, according to Ford?*
→ *What was foremost on Ford's mind when he set out to build "our original model"?*
→ *How do the lessons from the Bible and Henry Ford relate to each other? Do you think the indirect analogy is effective? Explain why or why not.*

SOURCE: Bruce Barton, *The Man Nobody Knows: A Discovery of the Real Jesus*, in Loren Baritz, ed., *The Culture of the Twenties* (Indianapolis: Bobbs-Merrill, 1925), pp. 241–42.

influx of cheap foreign goods, governments raised tariff barriers against imports. After the United States enacted protective tariffs, other governments abandoned free trade in favor of protectionism. Manufacturers cut back production, laid off millions of workers, and often went out of business. By 1935, world trade had shrunk to one-third of its 1929 level. Primary producers felt the harshest effects, for their international markets shut down almost completely. World prices for Argentine beef, Chilean nitrates, and Indonesian sugar all dropped sharply. The combination of shrinking markets and drastic shortages of credit forced industries and farms worldwide into bankruptcy.

The Great Depression soon spawned rethinking of the tenet that markets should govern themselves, the core of laissez-faire liberalism (see Chapter 14). By the late 1930s, the exuberant embrace of private mass production had ceded to a new conviction: state intervention to regulate the economy was critical to prevent disaster. In 1936, the British economist John Maynard Keynes published a landmark treatise, *The General Theory of Employment, Interest, and Money.* He argued that the market could not always adjust to its own failures and that sometimes the state had to stimulate it by increasing the money supply and creating jobs. Although the "Keynesian Revolution" took years to transform economic policy and to produce the welfare state, many governments were determining that capitalism had to be saved from itself. This unsettling realization called into question political liberalism.

MASS POLITICS: COMPETING VISIONS FOR BUILDING MODERN STATES

> → *How did different political systems respond to economic, political, and social disorder?*

World War I heightened the prewar unsettling of class, gender, and colonial relations, further challenging the liberal vision of technological progress, free markets, and societies guided by the educated few. On battlefronts and home fronts, countless workers, peasants, women, and colonial subjects had sacrificed and now expected to share in the fruits of peace. Many, even in victorious nations, lost confidence in traditional authorities who had failed to prevent the cataclysm and allowed it to go on so long.

Politics, no longer contained in genteel chambers, shifted to the street. Everywhere except in the United States, variants of socialism gained throngs of new adherents. In the Soviet Union, the Bolsheviks began to construct a society whose rules defied capitalist principles. Elsewhere mass movements sought to replace imperiled liberal democratic states, as in Germany, Italy, and Spain. Even liberal democratic empires such as Britain and France faced challenges to square their rule over colonial subjects with their rhetoric of freedom. And a hybrid political order, mixing democratic and authoritarian institutions, emerged in Latin America. Meanwhile, the Great Depression further undermined capitalism and parliaments.

Authoritarian solutions to problems like mass unemployment grew increasingly popular, especially as the Communist Soviet Union, Nazi Germany, Fascist Italy, dictatorial Portugal and Spain, and militaristic Japan projected images of national strength and pride. Outside Europe, anticolonial movements gathered steam; here, liberal models could not cope with the scale and diversity of the new politics. Thus, by the late 1930s, the states that retained democracy and capi-

talism in some form appeared weak and vulnerable. Dictators seemed to be riding the wave of the future, and colonies were threatening to go their own separate ways.

LIBERAL DEMOCRACY UNDER PRESSURE

In Europe of the 1920s, anxiety about modernization increased. Reacting to the war's carnage, elite Europeans looked longingly for supposedly pristine worlds that their own corrupting civilization had not destroyed. This trend found expression in the arts. For example, Josephine Baker, an African American dancer who performed nude, wild dances on the Parisian stage, enjoyed colossal popularity. So did Oswald Spengler's *The Decline of the West* (1919), a best-seller whose title seemed to capture the trajectory of liberal modernity.

The demands of fighting a total war had offered European states the opportunity to experiment with illiberal policies.

Josephine Baker. The African American entertainer Josephine Baker was a sensation on the stage in interwar Paris. Many of her shows exoticized or even caricatured her African descent.

Indeed, the war brought both the suspension of parliamentary rule and an effort by governments to manage industry and distribution. States on both sides of the conflict jailed many individuals who opposed the war. Governments regulated both production and, through rationing, consumption. Above all, the war revolutionized the size and scope of the state.

BRITISH AND FRENCH RESPONSES TO ECONOMIC CRISES At the war's end, liberal democratic elites wished to return to free-market policies, but women, veterans, and workers insisted that the states for which they had fought address their needs—for jobs, housing, and compensation for war wounds. Recurrent economic crises, especially the Great Depression, forced most liberal democrats to rethink their ideas. By 1930, even Britain had given up on free trade, and other countries were seeking economic self-sufficiency.

Britain and France retained their parliamentary systems, but even here, old-fashioned liberal democracy was on the run. Strife rippled across the British Empire, and in the home isles Britain gave independence to what became the Republic of Ireland in 1922. Britain's working-class Labour Party came to power twice between 1923 and 1931; but either alone or in coalition with Liberals and Conservatives, Labour could not lift the country out of its economic crisis. In 1926, 162 million working days were lost to strikes. Still, despite hard times, the British retained their commitment to parliamentarianism and capitalism.

Disorder was even more pronounced in France, which had lost 10 percent of its young men and seen the destruction of vast territory. In 1932–1933, six government coalitions came and went over the course of just nineteen months. Against the threat of a rightist coup, a coalition of the moderate and radical left, including the French Communist Party, formed the Popular Front government (1936–1939). It introduced the right of collective bargaining, a forty-hour workweek, two-week paid vacations, and minimum wages.

THE AMERICAN NEW DEAL In the United States, too, markets and liberalism faced challenges. When the Great Depression shattered the nation's fortunes, pressure intensified to create a more secure political and economic system.

In contrast to postwar Europe, where labor parties and Socialist movements were surging, the 1920s saw a conservative tide engulf American politics. Calling for a "return to normalcy" (a retreat from the government activism that had characterized the presidencies of Theodore Roosevelt and Woodrow Wilson), Warren Harding won the presidency in 1920 with a resounding 60 percent of the popular vote. Four years later, Calvin Coolidge scored an even greater landslide; his remark that the "business of America is business" reflected his dislike of government interference in free enterprise. With the election of Herbert Hoover in 1928, Republicans continued their string of presidential triumphs.

Largely left behind was the nation's African American population. In the rural American South, "Jim Crow" laws enforced social segregation, economic inequality, and political disenfranchisement. Like rural whites, millions of blacks quit the countryside and moved to northern cities such as

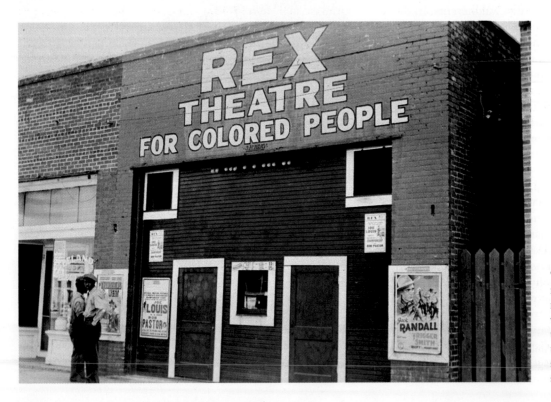

"Jim Crow." "Jim Crow" laws mandated the segregation of races in the American South, with African Americans forced to use separate, and usually unequal, facilities, including schools, hotels, and theaters, such as this one in Mississippi.

New York and Chicago. Here they found some relief from the legal barriers that had limited their opportunities and rights, but discrimination continued to hold them down and to restrict their residences to urban ghettos. Still, within black neighborhoods, most famously New York City's Harlem, a vibrant cultural scene blossomed. The New Negro Movement, or Harlem Renaissance, showcased black novelists, poets, painters, and musicians, many of whom used their art to protest racial subordination.

With the Great Depression came deeper challenges to liberal modernity. By the end of 1930, more than 4 million American workers had lost their jobs. As President Hoover insisted that citizens' thrift and self-reliance, not government handouts, would restore prosperity, the economic situation worsened. By 1933, industrial production had dropped a staggering 50 percent since 1929. The hard times were even worse in the countryside, where farm income plummeted by two-thirds between 1929 and 1932.

In the 1932 presidential election, a Democrat, Franklin Delano Roosevelt, won by a landslide. He promptly launched what came to be called the **New Deal**, a set of programs and regulations that dramatically expanded the scope of the American national government and its role in the nation's economic life. In his first hundred days in office, Roosevelt obtained legislation to provide relief for the jobless and to rebuild the shattered economy. Among his administration's experiments were the Federal Deposit Insurance Corporation to guarantee bank deposits up to $5,000, the Securities and Exchange Commission to monitor the stock market, and the Federal Emergency Relief Administration to help states and local governments assist the needy. Subsequently, in 1935, the Works Progress Administration put nearly 3 million people to work building roads, bridges, airports, and post offices. In addition, the Social Security Act inaugurated old-age pensions supported by the federal government.

Never before had the U.S. federal government expended so much on social welfare programs or intervened so directly in the national economy. Yet the Depression lingered, and before long unemployment again climbed—from 7 million in 1937 to 11 million in 1938.

The persistence of hard times opened the New Deal to attacks from both the left and the right. Emboldened labor leaders, resurgent radicals, and populist demagogues claimed that the New Deal was not addressing the problems of the poor and the unemployed. But Roosevelt continued on a moderate course. The New Deal did not substantially redistribute national income. Likewise, although Roosevelt's administration established public agencies to build dams and to oversee the irrigation of arid lands and the electrification of rural districts, these were exceptions. Privately owned enterprises continued to dominate American society. Roosevelt's aim was not to destroy capitalism, but to save it. In this regard the New Deal succeeded, for it staved off authoritarian solutions to modern problems.

AUTHORITARIANISM AND MASS MOBILIZATION

Like the liberal systems they challenged, authoritarian regimes came in various stripes. On the right arose dictatorships in Italy, Germany, and Japan. Although differing in important respects, all disliked the left-wing dictatorship of the Soviet Union. The Soviets had no liking for the Fascists. Yet all the postwar dictatorships were forged principally in opposition to the liberal democracies. In place of liberal inertia, these regimes touted their success in mobilizing the masses to create dynamic yet orderly societies. They also had charismatic leaders, who personified the power and unity of the societies over which they ruled.

Although rejecting liberal democracy, post–World War I dictators insisted that they had their people's support. True, they treated their people as a mass conscript army that needed firm leadership to build new societies and guarantee well-being. But their demands, the leaders maintained, would yield robust economies, restore order, and renew pride. In addition, dictators gained support by embracing public welfare programs. They also vowed to deliver on all of modernity's promises (prosperity, national pride, technology) without having to endure any of its costs (class divisions, unemployment, urban-industrial squalor, moral breakdown). For a time, many of the globe's inhabitants believed them.

THE SOVIET UNION AND SOCIALISM   The most dramatic blow against liberal capitalism occurred in Russia when the highly radical Bolshevik Party seized power. The coup aroused opposition inside and outside the country. Fearing the spread of socialist revolution, Britain, France, Japan, and the United States sent armies to Russia to contain Bolshevism. But after executing the tsar and his family, the Bolsheviks rallied support by defending the homeland against its invaders. They also mobilized people to fight (and win) a civil war (1918–1921) in the name of defending the revolution. The conflict pitted an array of disunified forces (former tsarist supporters but also some social democrats and independent peasant armies) against the Bolsheviks and their supporters (many soldiers, sailors, workers, and state functionaries).

In the all-out mobilization against those whom they labeled the Whites, or counterrevolutionaries, the Bolsheviks, calling themselves the Reds, began to rebuild state institutions. Amid this turmoil, the need to requisition grain from the peasantry as well as the extensive military operations weighed heavily on the population and interfered with the harvest. From 1921 to 1923, Russia suffered a severe famine in which some 7 to 10 million people died from hunger and disease.

To revive the economy, the Bolsheviks grudgingly legalized private trade and private property. In 1924, with the country still recovering from civil war, the undisputed leader of the revolution, Lenin, died. No one had done more to

Stalin. Joseph Stalin posing at the Allies' "Big Three" conference in Yalta, on Soviet soil, February 1945. Much had changed since Stalin became leader of the Communist Party of the Soviet Union in 1922.

shape the institutions of the revolutionary regime, including creating expectations for a single ruler. After eliminating his rivals, **Joseph Stalin** (1878–1953) emerged as the new leader of the Communist Party and the country, which soon became the Union of Soviet Socialist Republics (U.S.S.R.), or Soviet Union.

THE SOVIETS BUILD SOCIALISM   Since socialism as a fully developed social and political order did not exist anywhere in the 1920s, no one was sure how it would actually work. Stalin resolved this dilemma by defining Soviet or revolutionary socialism in opposition to capitalism. Since capitalism had "bourgeois" parliaments serving the interests of the rich, socialism, as elaborated by Stalinist leaders, would have soviets (councils) of worker and peasant deputies. Since capitalism had unregulated markets, which led to inefficiency and unemployment, socialism would have economic planning and full employment. And since capitalism relied on the "exploitation" of private ownership, socialism would outlaw private trade and private property. In short, socialism would

eradicate capitalism and then invent socialist forms in housing, culture, values, dress, and even modes of reasoning.

The efforts to build a noncapitalist society required class war, and these began in the heavily populated countryside. Peasants already lived in village communes, leasing the land together while working it individually (as households). Stalin wanted to combine the farms into larger units owned and worked collectively, and run by regime loyalists. Tens of thousands of urban activists and Red Army soldiers led a drive to establish these collective farms and to compel farmers to sell all their grain and livestock at state-run collection points for whatever price the state was willing to pay (often very little).

In protest, many peasants burned their crops, killed their livestock, and destroyed their farm machinery. The government responded by deporting these protesters, along with many bystanders, to remote areas. Villages had to fill quotas for deportation; often those selected were people who had slept with someone's wife rather than those whose cows produced the most milk. Thus, "class warfare" reflected personal animosities, greed, and ambition. Meanwhile harvests again declined, and a second famine claimed millions more lives. Grudgingly, the regime conceded household plots to the collectivized peasants. Here they could grow their own food and take some of their produce to approved markets. But few escaped the collectives, which depended on the state for seed, fertilizers, and machinery.

The late 1920s saw the beginning of a frenzied Five-Year Plan to "catch and overtake" the leading capitalist countries. Now millions of enthusiasts (as well as deported peasants) set about building a Socialist urban utopia founded on advanced technology, almost all of it purchased from the Depression-mired capitalist countries. More than 10 million people helped build or rebuild hundreds of factories, hospitals, and schools. Huge hydroelectric dams, automobile and tractor factories, and heavy machine-building plants symbolized the promise of Soviet-style modernity, which eliminated unemployment during the capitalist Great Depression.

Soviet authorities also started building socialism in the borderlands. In 1922, the U.S.S.R. joined the independent states of Ukraine, Belorussia (Belarus), and the Transcaucasian Federation with Soviet Russia to form a single federal state. The U.S.S.R. also soon included several new republics, such as those in central Asia; eventually there were fifteen (see Map 19-4), all of which acquired their own institutions—but under centralized rule from Moscow. In the 1930s, collectivization and mass arrests devastated the

Collectivized Agriculture. Soviet plans for the socialist village envisioned the formation of large collectives supplied with advanced machinery, thereby transforming peasant labor into an industrial process. The realities behind the images of smiling farmers—such as in this poster, exhorting "Let's Achieve a Victorious Harvest"—were low productivity, enormous waste, and often broken-down machinery.

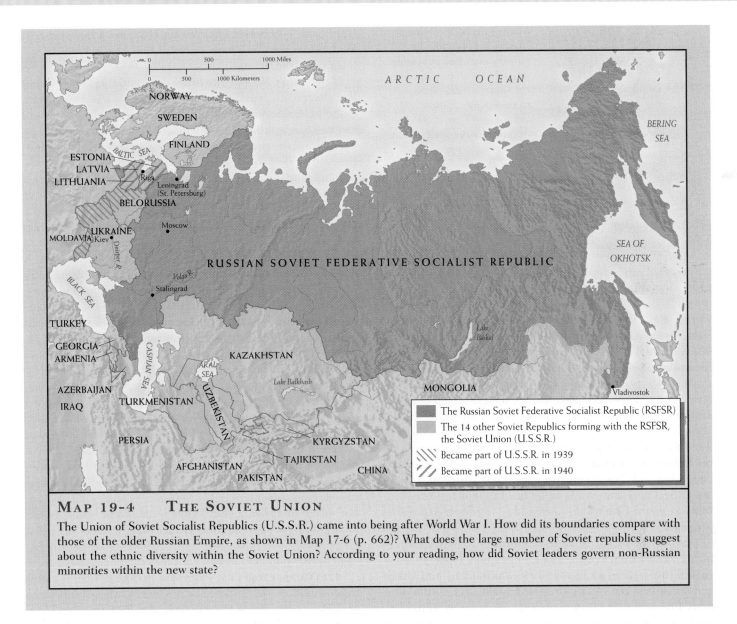

MAP 19-4   THE SOVIET UNION

The Union of Soviet Socialist Republics (U.S.S.R.) came into being after World War I. How did its boundaries compare with those of the older Russian Empire, as shown in Map 17-6 (p. 662)? What does the large number of Soviet republics suggest about the ethnic diversity within the Soviet Union? According to your reading, how did Soviet leaders govern non-Russian minorities within the new state?

peasants and nomads as well as the officials of the republics, but industrialization and urbanization strengthened local elites.

MASS TERROR AND STALIN'S DICTATORSHIP   The Soviet political system became more despotic as the state expanded. Police power grew the most, partly from forcing peasants into collectives and organizing mass deportations. As the party's ranks swelled, ongoing loyalty verifications also led to the removal of party members, even when they professed absolute loyalty. From 1936 to 1938, trials of supposedly treasonous "enemies of the people" resulted in the execution of around 750,000 people and the arrest or deportation of several million more. They were sent to forced labor camps, collectively known as the Gulag. Such purges decimated the loyal Soviet elite—party officials, state officials, intelligentsia, army officers, and even members of the police who had enforced the terror.

Behind this mass terror loomed fear, a sense of omnipresent conspiracies, and the Soviet leader's overpowering personal dictatorship. Although Stalin initiated mass terror against the elite, his motives remain unclear. Neither he nor the regime was under threat, and the leaders' loyalty was not in doubt. What is clear is that the political police, given sizeable arrest quotas, often exceeded them. In addition, millions of ordinary people helped implement the terror. Some reluctantly turned in neighbors; some did so to try to save themselves; many showed fanatical zeal in fingering "enemies." In the end, the terror manifested highly petty motives as well as a desire to participate in the violent crusade of building socialism in a hostile world, full of internal and external enemies.

ITALIAN FASCISM   Long before the Soviets had created a new anticapitalist model, the political situation in capitalist societies had begun to change. Two key factors were

Mussolini. Benito Mussolini liked to puff out his chest, particularly when appearing in public. *Il Duce* pioneered the leader's radio address to the people, and he encouraged Fascist versions of the mass spectacles that also became common in Soviet Russia.

disillusionment with the costs of the Great War, and lessons drawn from the Bolshevik takeover in Russia. In Italy, for example, mass strikes, occupations of factories, and peasant land seizures swept the country in 1919 and 1920. Amid this disorder, rightists seized power. Their leader was **Benito Mussolini** (1883–1945), a former Socialist journalist.

In 1919, Mussolini sought to organize disaffected veterans into a mass political movement called **fascism.** His early programs mixed nationalism with social radicalism and revealed a yearning to sweep away all the institutions discredited by the war. Fascist supporters demanded the annexation of "Italian" lands in the Alps and on the Dalmatian coast and called for female suffrage, an eight-hour workday, a share of factory control for workers, a tax on capital, land redistribution, and a constituent assembly—in short, a populist program.

Fascists attracted numerous followers. Their violence-prone shock troops wore black shirts and loose trousers tucked into high black leather boots and saluted with a dagger thrust into the air. In 1920, the squads received money from landowners and factory owners to beat up Socialist leaders, after which Italian fascism became fully identified with the right. Still, the Fascists saw themselves as champions of the little guy, of peasants and workers, as well as of war veterans, students, and white-collar types.

In 1922, Mussolini announced a march on Rome. The march was a bluff, yet it intimidated the king, who opposed Fascist ruffians but feared bloodshed. So he withheld use of the army against the lightly armed marchers. When the Italian government resigned in protest, the monarch invited Mussolini to become prime minister, despite the fact that Fascists had won only a small minority of seats in the 1921 elections.

The 1924 elections, in which Fascists won 65 percent of the vote, took place in an atmosphere of intimidation and fraud. Mussolini dealt with other challenges by mobilizing the squads and police for crackdowns on the liberal and Socialist opposition. Soon a series of decrees transformed

Italy from a constitutional monarchy into a dictatorship. Within two years, all parties except that of the Fascists had been dissolved.

Mussolini's dictatorship made deals with big business and the church, thus falling short of a total social revolution. Nonetheless, it was skilled at using parades, films, radio, and visions of recapturing Roman imperial grandeur to boost support during the troubled times of the Depression. The cult of the leader, *Il Duce,* also provided cohesion. As the first antiliberal, anti-socialist alternative, Italian fascism served as a model for other countries.

GERMAN NAZISM   In Germany, too, fear of Bolshevism and anger over the war's outcome propelled the right to power. Here, the dictator was **Adolf Hitler** (1889–1945). After a small nationalist workers' organization took shape in Munich, dedicated to winning workers over from socialism, the army high command ordered a young demobilized corporal to infiltrate the group. That corporal, Hitler, soon dominated the nationalist workers' movement, whose name he changed to the National Socialist German Workers' Party (*National-Sozialistische Arbeits-Partei,* or **Nazis**).

Unlike Mussolini, the young Hitler was never a Socialist. The first Nazi Party platform, set forth in 1920, combined nationalism with anticapitalism and anti-Semitism. It also called for the renunciation of the Treaty of Versailles. It was an assertion of Germany's grievances against the world and of the small man's grievances against the rich. At first, Hitler and the Nazis were unsuccessful, and Hitler himself was arrested. He was sentenced to five years in prison for treason, but served less than a year. While in prison he wrote an autobiographical and fanatically anti-Semitic treatise called *Mein Kampf* (My Struggle, 1925), which subsequently became wildly popular among Nazis.

The Weimar Republic enjoyed a period of stability after hyper-inflation was curtailed by the intervention of American bankers, and in the 1926 elections the Nazi Party received only 2.6 percent of the votes. It only gained popularity after the collapse of the American stock market in 1929, when short-term loans were called in. As more and more people lost their jobs, farms, and small businesses, Germans considered radical alternatives. In this atmosphere, fearing popular support of the Communist and Socialist parties and convinced that he could control Hitler, Germany's president appointed Hitler chancellor (prime minister) in 1933. Initially, Hitler pledged that traditional conservatives would dominate the government. Thus, like Mussolini, Hitler came to power peacefully and legally.

Hitler's first step as chancellor was to heighten fear of a Communist conspiracy to take power. The burning of the Reichstag building in Berlin the following month provided the opportunity. The Nazis blamed the fire on the Communists, immediately suspended civil liberties "as a defensive measure against the Communists," and forced the left-wing press out

Hitler. Adolf Hitler and his advisors mastered the staging of mass rallies. These rallies and marches projected an image of dynamism and collective will, which Hitler claimed to embody.

of business. The latter move robbed opponents of the ability to criticize the regime publicly. Hitler then proposed legislation that would enable him to promulgate laws on his authority as chancellor without the parliament's approval.

Within a month Hitler was free from the control of parliament and the conservative elites. Soon the government seized the offices, banks, and newspapers of trade unions and arrested their leaders. The Socialist and Communist parties were outlawed; others were dissolved. By July 1933, the Nazis were the only legal party and Hitler was dictator of Germany. He aggressively curbed dissent and banned strikes, jailing political opponents and building the first concentration camps (initially to house political prisoners) when the jails overflowed.

He also unleashed a campaign of persecution against the Jews, believing that assimilated Jews controlled the banks and that Eastern Jewish emigrants carried disease. Like many other right-wing Germans, Hitler also believed that a Jewish-socialist conspiracy had stabbed the German army in the back, causing its surrender in World War I, and that intermarriage with Jews was destroying the supposed purity of the Aryan race (which included northern, white, Europeans). Hitler and the Nazis did not believe that religious practice defined Jewishness; instead, they held, it was transmitted biologically from parents to children. Once he became dictator, Hitler instituted legal measures that excluded Jews from the civil service and the professions, forced them to sell their property, deprived them of citizenship, and forbade them to marry or have sex with Aryans. Hitler also encouraged the use of terror against Jews, destroying their businesses, homes, and marriages with non-Jews, frightening them into leaving

Germany, and ultimately eliminating all traces of Jewish life and culture in Nazi-dominated central Europe.

Although some Germans opposed Hitler's illiberal activism, the Nazis won popular support for restoring order and reviving the economy. In 1935, defying the Treaty of Versailles, Hitler began a vast rearmament program that absorbed the unemployed. Now economic despair and national disgrace turned into fierce pride and impressive national power. The state also financed public works including reforestation and swamp drainage projects; organized leisure, entertainment, travel, and vacations; and built highways and public housing. Anti-Semitism mixed with full employment and social welfare programs that privileged racially approved groups.

Germany reemerged as a great power with expansionist aspirations. Hitler called his state the Third Reich (the first being the Holy Roman Empire, or Reich, and the second the Reich created by Bismarck in 1871). He claimed that, like the Holy Roman Empire, his empire would last 1,000 years. Hitler also harbored grand aspirations to impose racial purity and German power in Europe and perhaps beyond. (See Primary Source: Cult of the Dynamic Leader.)

DICTATORSHIPS IN SPAIN AND PORTUGAL As authoritarian regimes spread across Europe, the military took over and instituted dictatorships in Spain and Portugal. Their effort to seize power in Spain provoked a brutal civil war from 1936 to 1939, which left 250,000 dead.

The Spanish civil war was, from the start, an international war. When the Spanish republican government introduced reforms to break the hold of the church and landlords on the

Primary Source

CULT OF THE DYNAMIC LEADER

Nazi political theorists offered no apologies for dictatorship. On the contrary, they bragged about it as the best way of mobilizing the masses and directing the state. The Führer, or Leader, stood above the Nazi Party and all government institutions and embodied the supposed will of the German nation. He also decided who belonged, or did not belong, to the nation. The following excerpt, taken from the writings of Ernst Rudolf Huber, Germany's major constitutional expert of the 1930s, elaborated on the awesome powers being conferred on Hitler as Führer.

The office of Führer has developed out of the National Socialist movement. In its origins it is not a State office. This fact must never be forgotten if one wishes to understand the current political and legal position of the Führer. The office of Führer has grown out of the movement into the Reich, firstly through the Führer taking over the authority of the Reich Chancellor and then through his taking over the position of Head of State. Primary importance must be accorded to the position of "Führer of the movement"; it has absorbed the two highest functions of the political leadership of the Reich and thereby created the new office of "Führer of the Nation and of the Reich." . . .

The position of Führer combines in itself all sovereign power of the Reich; all public power in the State as in the movement is derived from the Führer power. If we wish to define political power in the Third Reich correctly, we must not speak of "State power" but of "Führer power." For it is not the State as an impersonal entity which is the source of political power but rather political power is given to the Führer as the executor of the nation's common will. Führer power is comprehensive and total; it unites within itself all means of creative political activity; it embraces all spheres of national life; it includes all national comrades who are bound to the Führer in loyalty and obedience. Führer power is not restricted by safeguards and controls, by autonomous protected spheres, and by vested individual rights, but rather it is free and independent, exclusive and unlimited.

→ *How did the office of Führer arise, according to Huber?*
→ *What are the source and scope of "Führer power"?*

SOURCE: Ernst Rudolf Huber, "Führergewalt," from *Nazism 1919–1945: A Documentary Reader; Volume 2: State, Economy, and Society, 1933–1939*, pp. 198–99, edited by J. Noakes and G. Pridham. Reprinted by permission of University of Exeter Press.

---

state, the military intervened and all of Europe's major powers got involved. The military's attack against the republic at first failed, but with the help of German and Italian weapons (above all, airplanes) Generalissimo Francisco Franco gained the upper hand. Meanwhile, Britain and France dithered and only Stalin's Russia supported the republican government, allowing Franco to establish a dictatorship.

MILITARIST JAPAN Unlike authoritarian regimes, Japan did not suffer wounded power and pride during World War I. In fact, because wartime disruptions reduced European and American competition, Japanese products found new markets in Asia. Japan expanded production, exporting munitions, textiles, and consumer goods to Asian and western markets. During the war, the Japanese gross national product (GNP) grew 40 percent, and the country built the world's third largest navy. After a devastating earthquake and fire in 1923, Tokyo was rebuilt with steel and reinforced concrete, symbolizing the new, modern Japan.

Initially, post–World War I Japan seemed headed down the liberal democratic road. When Japan's Meiji Emperor died in 1912, his third son succeeded him and oversaw the rise of mass political parties. Suffrage expanded in 1925, increasing the electorate roughly fourfold. But along with democratization came repressive measures. Although the Meiji Constitution remained in effect, a new Peace Preservation Law specified up to ten years' hard labor for any member of an organization advocating change in the political system or abolition of private property. The law served as a club against the mass leftist parties.

RUSSIA

AMUR
PROVINCE

SAKHALIN

SEA OF
OKHOTSK

KURILE ISLANDS

MANCHURIA
(MANCHUKUO, 1932)

OUTER
MONGOLIA

EZO
(HOKKAIDŌ)

INNER
MONGOLIA

JEHOL

Vladivostok

Beijing

Mukden

SEA OF
JAPAN

JAPAN

Tianjin

Dalian
Lüshun
(Port Arthur)
Weihaiwei

Seoul

KOREA

Tokyo

HONSHŪ

Kyoto

Qingdao

Pusan

SHIKOKU

CHINA

YELLOW
SEA

Nagasaki

KYŪSHŪ

Nanjing

Shanghai

EAST
CHINA
SEA

PACIFIC
OCEAN

BONIN
ISLANDS

VOLCANO
ISLANDS

RUSSIAN BALTIC FLEET

Fuzhou

OKINAWA

RYŪKYŪ ISLANDS

Xiamen
(Amoy)

TAIWAN

Guangzhou (Canton)

PESCADORES

Hong Kong
Macao

	Japanese acquisitions as of 1895
	Japanese acquisitions, 1905–1910
	Japanese area of influence before 1914
→	Japanese attack, 1914
	Occupied by Japan after 1918
	Occupied by Japan, 1920–1925
	Japan forms puppet state of Manchukuo, 1932
	Occupied by Japan, 1933

0   100   200   300 Miles

0 100 200 300 Kilometers

Map 19-5   The Japanese Empire in Asia, 1933

Hoping to become a great imperial power like the European states, Japan established numerous colonies and spheres of influence early in the twentieth century. What were the main territorial components of the Japanese Empire? How far did the
Japanese succeed in extending their political influence throughout East Asia? According to your reading, what problems did
the desire to extend Japanese influence in China present to Japanese leaders?

Hirohito. A portrait of Crown Prince Hirohito of Japan in 1925, the year before he ascended the Japanese throne. Hirohito presided over Japan's war in Asia, beginning with the 1931 seizure of Manchuria and culminating in the 1945 surrender, but he remained emperor for another four decades. When he died in 1989, his wartime responsibility was still a difficult subject for many.

Japan veered still further from the liberal democratic road after Emperor Hirohito came to power in 1926. In Japan, as in Germany, the Great Depression spurred the eventual shift to dictatorship. Japan's trade with the outside world had more than tripled between 1913 and 1929, but after 1929 China and the United States imposed barriers on Japanese exports in preference for domestic products. These measures contributed to a 50 percent decline in Japanese exports. Unemployment surged.

Such turmoil invited calls for stronger leadership, which military commanders were eager to provide. Already beyond civilian control, in 1927 and 1928 the army flexed its muscles by twice forcing prime ministers out of office. New "patriotic societies" used violence to intimidate political opponents. Violence culminated in the assassination of Japan's prime minister, accompanied by an uprising of young naval officers and army cadets. Their coup failed, but it further eclipsed the power of political parties.

It was in the Japanese Empire that militarism and expansionism received a boost. In 1931, a group of army officers arranged an explosion on the Japanese-owned South Manchurian Railroad as a pretext for taking over Manchuria. In 1932, adding Manchuria to its Korean and Taiwanese colonies (see Map 19-5), Japan oversaw the proclamation of the puppet state of Manchukuo. In 1933, the Japanese army seized the Chinese province of Jehol to use as a buffer zone between China proper and Manchukuo. Later, they annexed it to the Empire of Manchukuo. Meanwhile, at home, "patriots" continued a campaign of terror against uncooperative businessmen and critics of the military. As in Italy and Germany, the state in Japan took on a sacred aura. This occurred through the promotion of an official religion, Shinto, and of Emperor Hirohito's divinity. By 1940, the clique at the top had merged all political parties into the Imperial Rule Assistance Association, ending even the semblance of parliamentary rule.

COMMON FEATURES OF AUTHORITARIAN REGIMES Despite important differences, the major authoritarian regimes of this period—communist Soviet Union, Fascist Italy, Nazi Germany, and militarist Japan—shared many traits. All rejected parliamentary rule and sought to revive their countries' power through authoritarianism, violence, and a cult of the leader.

All claimed that modern economies required state direction. In Japan, the government fostered huge business conglomerates; in Italy, it encouraged big business to form cartels. The German state also regarded the private sector as the vehicle of economic growth, but it expected entrepreneurs to support the Nazis' racial, antidemocratic, and expansionist aims. The most thorough form of economic coordination occurred in the Soviet Union, which adopted American-style mass production while eliminating private enterprise. Instead, the Soviet state owned and managed all the country's industry. Here, as elsewhere, state-organized labor forces replaced independent labor unions.

Another common feature involved using mass organizations for state purposes. Russia, Italy, and Germany had single mass parties; Japan had various rightist groups until the 1940 merger. All promoted dynamic youth movements, such as the Hitler Youth and the Union of German Girls, the Soviet Communist Youth League, and the Italian squads marching to the anthem "Giovinezza" (Youth).

Three of the states adopted extensive social welfare policies. The Nazis emphasized full employment, built public housing, and provided assistance to needy Aryan families. The Italian National Agency for Maternity and Infancy provided services for unwed mothers and infant care. Soviet programs addressed maternity, disability, sickness, and old age. In fact, the Soviet state viewed welfare assistance as an ongoing program that distinguished socialism from capitalism. Although Japan did not enact innovative social welfare legislation, its Home Affairs Ministry enlisted helpmates among civic groups, seeking to raise savings rates and improve childrearing practices.

A fourth common feature was ambivalence about women in public roles—the Soviet Union excepted. But even that state eventually promoted higher rates of reproduction, rewarding mothers who had many children and restricting abortion. State officials were eager to honor new mothers as a way to repair the loss of so many young men during the Great War. Yet, many more women were also entering professional careers, and some were becoming their families' primary wage earners. In Italy, Fascist authorities had to accept the existence of *la maschietta*—the new woman, or flapper, who wore short skirts, bobbed her hair, smoked cigarettes, and engaged in freer sex. In Japan, the *moga* or *modan gāru* ("modern girl") phenomenon provoked considerable negative comment, but

Hitler Youth. Like the Communists in the Soviet Union, the Nazis organized and indoctrinated boys and girls in the hopes of making them strong supporters of the regime. Pictured here are members of the Hitler Youth, about 1939.

authorities could not suppress it. The Soviets demonstrated the most contradictory behavior. In 1918, they declared men and women equal, legalized (and subsidized) abortion, and eased divorce laws. However, by 1935–1936 new laws made divorce nearly impossible, drove abortion underground, and rewarded "hero mothers" of multiple children. Nonetheless, the rapidly industrializing Soviets had the highest percentage of women in the paid workforce.

Finally, all the dictatorships used violence and terror against their own citizens, colonial subjects, and "foreigners" living within their state borders. These tools served as levers for remaking the sociopolitical order. The Italians and the Japanese were not shy about arresting political opponents, particularly in their colonies. However, it was the Nazis and especially the Soviets who filled concentration and labor camps with alleged enemies of the state, whether Jews or supposed counterrevolutionaries.

Still, brutal as these regimes were, their successes in mastering the masses drew envious glances even from those trying to stay on the liberal democratic road. They also attracted imitators. British and French Fascists and communists, though they never came to power, formed national parties and proclaimed support for foreign models. Certain politicians, intellectuals, and labor organizers in South and North America admired Hitler, Lenin, and Stalin. Many also hoped to use the methods of mass mobilization and mass violence for their own ends. This was particularly true of anticolonial movements.

THE HYBRID NATURE OF LATIN AMERICAN CORPORATISM

Latin American nations felt the same pressures that produced liberal democratic and authoritarian responses in Europe, Russia, and Japan. However, the Latin American leaders devised solutions that combined democratic and authoritarian elements.

ECONOMIC TURMOIL Latin American countries had stayed out of the fighting in World War I, but their export economies had suffered. As trade plummeted, popular confidence in oligarchic regimes fell, and radical agitation surged. During the war years, trade unionists in the port of Buenos Aires took control of the city's docks, and the women of São Paulo's needle trades inspired Brazil's first general strike. Bolivian tin miners, inspired by events in Russia, proclaimed a full-blown Socialist revolution.

The Great Depression brought even sharper challenges from workers' groups. More than in any other region, the Depression battered Latin America's trading and financial systems because they were most dependent on the exports of basic staples, from sugar to wheat, and faced stiff protection or evaporating demand for their commodities. The region, in fact, suffered a double whammy because it had borrowed so much money to invest in infrastructure and expansion. When world money markets went belly-up, creditors called in their loans from Latin America. This move drove borrowers to

Getúlio Vargas. This cartoon of Vargas, governor of the southern state of Rio Grande do Sul, portrays him as a country bumpkin even as he leads the overthrowing of Brazil's Old Republic.

Ruling as a patriarch enabled Vargas to squelch dissent and build new lines of loyalty. When he revamped the constitution in 1937, he banned competitive political parties and created forms of national representation along corporatist lines. Each social sector or class would be represented by its function in society (for example, as workers, industrialists, or educators), and each would pledge allegiance to the all-powerful state. Although his opponents complained about losing their democratic rights, Vargas also created rights for previously excluded groups like trade unions, who now could use their corporatist representatives to press for demands. To bolster the system, he employed a small army of modern propagandists using billboards, loudspeakers, and radio to broadcast the benevolence of "Father" Vargas.

default. In response, Latin American governments—with enthusiastic backing from the middle classes, nationalist intellectuals, and urban workers—turned to their domestic rather than foreign markets as the main engine of growth. Here, too, the state took on a more interventionist role in market activity.

After the war, Latin American elites confronted the mass age by establishing mass parties and encouraging interest groups to associate with them. Collective bodies such as chambers of commerce, trade unions, peasant associations, and organizations for minorities like blacks and Indians all operated with state sponsorship. This form of modern politics, often labeled corporatist, used social groups to bridge the gap between ruling elites and the general population.

CORPORATIST POLITICS IN BRAZIL Corporatist politics took hold especially in Brazil, where the old republic collapsed in 1930. In its place, a coalition led by the skilled politician Getúlio Vargas (1883–1954) cultivated a strong following by enacting socially popular reforms.

Dubbing himself the "father of the poor," Vargas encouraged workers to organize, erected monuments to national heroes, and supported the building of schools and the paving of roads. He made special efforts to appeal to Brazilian blacks, who had been excluded from public life since the abolition of slavery. Thus he legalized many previously forbidden Afro-Brazilian practices, such as the ritual "candomblé" dance, whose African and martial overtones seemed threatening to white elites. Vargas also supported samba schools, organizations that not only taught popular dances but also raised funds for public works. (See Global Connections & Disconnections: Samba: Mass Culture from the Bottom Up.) Moreover, Vargas addressed maternity and housing policies and enfranchised women (although they had to be able to read, as did male voters). Although he condemned the old elites for betraying the country to serve the interests of foreign consumers and investors, he also arranged foreign funding and technical transfers to build steel mills and factories. However, he took this step to create domestic industry so that Brazil would not be so dependent on imports.

ANTICOLONIAL VISIONS OF MODERN LIFE

Debates over liberal democratic versus authoritarian models engaged the world's colonial and semicolonial regions as well. But here there was a larger concern: what to do about colonial authority? Throughout Asia, most educated members of these communities wanted to roll back the European and American imperial presence. Some Asians even accepted Japanese imperialism as an antidote, under the slogan "Asia for the Asians." In Africa, however, where the European colonial presence was more recent, intellectuals still questioned the real meaning of colonial rule: were the British and the French sincerely committed to African improvement, or were they obstacles to African peoples' well-being?

World War I crippled Europe but gave it more colonies than ever before. Ottoman territories, in particular, wound up in Allied hands. Great Britain emerged with an empire that straddled one-quarter of the earth. Rechristened as the British Commonwealth of Nations, Britain conferred dominion status on white-settler colonies in Canada, Australia, and New Zealand. This meant independence in internal and external affairs in exchange for continuing loyalty to the crown. But no such privileges went to possessions in Africa and India, where nonwhite peoples were the vast majority. Here the British fell back on an old line: nonwhite peoples were not yet ready for self-government.

In Africa as well as Asia, then, the search for the modern encompassed demands for power sharing or full political independence. Anticolonialism was the preeminent vision. To overcome the contradictions of European democratic liberalism, educated Asians and Africans proposed various incarnations of nationalism.

Behind the Asian and African nationalist movements were profound disagreements about how best to govern nations once they gained independence and how to define citizenship. For many intellectuals, the democratic ethos of the imperial powers was appealing. Others liked the radical

SAMBA: MASS CULTURE FROM THE BOTTOM UP

The evolution and dissemination of the musical and dance form known as samba in Brazil illustrates the ways in which mass culture could emerge in poorer societies and then spread upward to elite consumers and outward across national borders. Radio especially helped to diffuse such distinctly regional cultural products throughout Latin America.

Samba originated in Rio de Janeiro's shantytowns as a mixture of popular Spanish fandangos and the 2/4 meter of slave songs. Samba's lyrics extolled the freeing of the slaves in 1888 and the benevolence of the old monarchs. But mostly samba celebrated the idea that life was not all squalor. Samba was not high culture (though many in the elite had joined the audiences and even the dance troupes by the 1920s), and it was not the culture of any race or ethnic group (though it had African roots). Nor was it simply popular culture. Rather, it became a mass culture uniting the people of Rio de Janeiro and soon thereafter other parts of Brazil, and eventually it found an international audience as well.

What transformed the samba musical form from a local into a national and then international mass cultural phenomenon was the invention of the phonograph and long-playing records. These allowed samba to be broadcast on the new medium, radio. The movie house helped disseminate samba, too. Brazilian samba musical films brought fame to a Portuguese-born dancer, Carmen Miranda, whose fruit-decorated hats made her a household symbol of the tropics in the United States. Records and radio also spread the tango of Argentina, boleros of Mexico, and salsa, the New York musical creation of Cuban and Puerto Rican émigrés.

The content and influence of musical mass culture were internationalized, but music and dance were also instrumental in fostering "national" cultures in Latin America. Songs and artists transcended physical barriers and regional accents, and as such, they did the work of nation building, creating cultural links between disparate people.

Samba took on new political implications during the 1920s when dance organizations began to create "schools" to instruct neighbors and to raise funds to help with public works in the face of the Brazilian state's neglect. By the 1930s, samba schools were often the largest benefactors of schools, roads, and utilities in Rio de Janeiro. They also became patronage machines for local political bosses. For many years, the Brazilian government banned these organizations as potentially subversive, although they continued to operate illegally. But President Getúlio Vargas, eager to induct the schools into his own political network, legalized the schools in 1935 and allowed them to occupy an ever more prominent place in the capital's cultural landscape. Thereafter, the annual festival of Mardi Gras evolved from a boisterous parade and religious celebration to an occasion for Rio's proliferating samba schools to strut their colorful and highly choreographed stuff. The belated efforts by the authorities to harness samba for their own purposes demonstrated its power as a mass culture from and for the people.

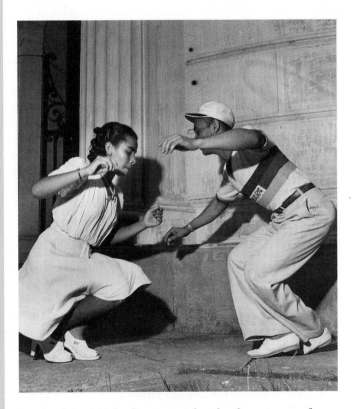

Samba dancers. The dance started in the shanty towns of Rio de Janeiro and eventually became popular throughout the world, thanks to films, photographs, and long-playing records that featured samba music.

authoritarianism of fascism and communism, with their promises of rapid change to modernity. Whatever their political preferences, most literate colonials also regarded their own religious and cultural traditions as sources for political mobilization. Thus Muslim, Hindu, Chinese, and African values became vehicles for galvanizing the rank and file. The colonial figures involved in political and intellectual movements insisted that the societies they sought to establish were going to be modern *and* at the same time retain their indigenous characteristics.

AFRICAN STIRRINGS   Africa contained the most recent territories to come under the Europeans' control, so anticolonial nationalist movements there were quite young. The region's fate remained very much in the hands of Europeans. After 1918, however, African peoples probed more deeply for the meaning of Europe's imperial presence.

In some parts of Africa, environmental degradation contributed to resentment. In the peanut belt of Senegal, for example, African cultivators pushed into more arid regions, cutting down trees and eventually exhausting the soil. Across the continent, in Kenya, where African peoples were confined to specific locations so as to make land available to European settlers, Africans began to overgraze and overcultivate their lands. A severe problem occurred among the Kamba people living near Nairobi. Their herds had become so large that the government attempted to implement a forcible campaign of culling. Refusing to cooperate, the Kamba joined the chorus of African protesters against British authority.

There was some room (but not much) for voicing African interests under colonialism. The French had long held to a vision of assimilating their colonial peoples into French culture. In France's primary West African colony, Senegal, four coastal cities had traditionally elected one delegate (of mixed African and European ancestry) to the French National Assembly. This practice lasted until 1914, when Blaise Diagne (1872–1934), an African candidate, ran for office and won, invoking his African origins and garnering the African vote. While the British allowed Africans to elect delegates to municipal bodies, they refused to permit colonial representatives to sit in Parliament. Committed to democracy at home, the European powers were steadfastly against it in their colonies.

Excluded from representative bodies, Africans experimented with various forms of protest. For example, in southeastern Nigeria in 1929, Ibo and Ibibio women responded to a new tax by breaking off contact with the local colonial chiefs. Moving beyond boycotts of local officials, women burned down chiefs' huts, as well as European and Lebanese trading establishments, to protest their exploitation.

Opposition was still not widespread in Africa, for protests ran up against not only colonial administrators but also western-educated African elites. These individuals often built western-style homes, drove automobiles, wore western clothing, and consumed western foods. Yet, even this privileged group began to reconsider its relationship to colonial authorities. In Kenya, immediately after World War I, a small contingent of mission-educated Africans called on the British to provide more and better schools and to return lands they claimed European settlers had stolen. Although they enlisted the support of liberal missionaries, their pleas fell on deaf ears and their leader was arrested. Although defeated in this instance, the young nationalists drew important lessons from their confrontation with the authorities. They now viewed colonialism in a more combative light. Their new spokesperson, Jomo Kenyatta (1898–1978), invoked their precolonial Kikuyu traditions as a basis for resisting colonialism. (See Primary Source: *Facing Mount Kenya*.)

IMAGINING AN INDIAN NATION   As Africans explored the use of modern politics against Europeans, opposition in India took on a more advanced form. The war and its aftermath brought full-blown challenges to British rule. Indeed, the Indian nationalist challenge provided inspiration for other anticolonial movements.

For over a century, Indians had heard British authorities extol the virtues of parliamentary government, yet they were excluded from participation. In 1919, the British did slightly enlarge the franchise in India and allowed more local self-government, but these moves did not satisfy Indians' nationalist longings. During the 1920s and 1930s, the nationalists, led by **Mohandas Karamchand (Mahatma) Gandhi** (1869–1948), laid the foundations for an alternative, anticolonial movement.

GANDHI AND NONVIOLENT RESISTANCE   Gandhi had studied law in England and had worked in South Africa on behalf of Indian immigrants before returning to India in 1915. Thereafter, he assumed leadership in local struggles.

Blaise Diagne. Diagne was the first African elected to the French National Assembly. He won the election to the French Parliament in 1914, beating white and mixed-race candidates by appealing to the majority black African population that lived in the four communes of Senegal.

FACING MOUNT KENYA

Jomo Kenyatta, one of Kenya's leading nationalists, wrote a moving account of his own Kikuyu community in Facing Mount Kenya *(1937). The book demonstrated the cohesion and strong tribal bonds of precolonial Kikuyu society, as well as the destructive elements of the colonial assault on African traditions. The excerpt below is from the conclusion.*

And it is the culture which he inherits that gives a man his human dignity as well as his material prosperity. It teaches him his mental and moral values and makes him feel it worth while to work and fight for liberty.

But a culture has no meaning apart from the social organisation of life on which it is built. When the European comes to the Gikuyu country and robs the people of their land, he is taking away not only their livelihood, but the material symbol that holds family and tribe together. In doing this he gives one blow which cuts away the foundations from the whole of Gikuyu life, social, moral, and economic. When he explains, to his own satisfaction and after the most superficial glance at the issues involved, that he is doing this for the sake of the Africans, to "civilise" them, "teach them the disciplinary value of regular work," and "give them the benefit of European progressive ideas," he is adding insult to injury, and need expect to convince no one but himself.

There certainly are some progressive ideas among the Europeans. They include the ideas of material prosperity, of medicine, and hygiene, and literacy which enables people to take part in world culture. But so far the Europeans who visit Africa have not been conspicuously zealous in imparting these parts of their inheritance to the Africans, and seem to think that the only way to do it is by police discipline and armed force. They speak as if it was somehow beneficial to an African to work for them instead of for himself, and to make sure that he will receive this benefit they do their best to take away his land and leave him with no alternative. Along with his land they rob him of his government, condemn his religious ideas, and ignore his fundamental conceptions of justice and morals, all in the name of civilisation and progress.

If Africans were left in peace on their own lands, Europeans would have to offer them the benefits of white civilisation in real earnest before they could obtain the African labour which they want so much. They would have to offer the African a way of life which was really superior to the one his fathers lived before him, and a share in the prosperity given them by their command of science. They would have to let the African choose what parts of European culture would be beneficially transplanted, and how they could be adapted. He would probably not choose the gas bomb or the armed police force, but he might ask for some other things of which he does not get so much today. As it is, by driving him off his ancestral lands, the Europeans have robbed him of the material foundations of his culture, and reduced him to a state of serfdom incompatible with human happiness. The African is conditioned, by the cultural and social institutions of centuries, to a freedom of which Europe has little conception, and it is not in his nature to accept serfdom for ever. He realises that he must fight unceasingly for his own complete emancipation; for without this he is doomed to remain the prey of rival imperialisms, which in every successive year will drive their fangs more deeply into his vitality and strength.

✦ *According to Kenyatta, why is it so devastating when European imperialists rob African people of their land?*

✦ *Why do you think the Europeans were not zealous in imparting "progressive ideas" to the Africans?*

✦ *Why does Kenyatta think the Africans would not choose to adopt "the gas bomb or the armed police force" from European culture?*

SOURCE: Excerpt from *Facing Mount Kenya: The Tribal Life of the Gikuyu* by Jomo Kenyatta, published by Vintage Books, a division of Random House, Inc. Used by permission of Alfred A. Knopf, a division of Random House, Inc.

He also spelled out the moral and political philosophy of *satyagraha,* or **nonviolent resistance**, which he had developed while in South Africa. His message to Indians was simple: Develop your own resources and inner strength and control the instincts and activities that encourage participation in colonial economy and government, and you shall achieve *swaraj* ("self-rule"). Faced with Indian self-reliance and self-control pursued nonviolently, Gandhi claimed, the British eventually would have to leave. (See Primary Source: India and Self-Government.)

A crucial event in rising opposition to British rule was a massacre in 1919 of Indian civilians protesting British policies in the Punjab. The incident, in which a British general ordered soldiers to fire on the protesters, left 379 Indian civilians dead and more than 1,200 wounded. As news of the massacre spread, many Indians were infuriated—especially when they learned that British authorities were not punishing the general.

This and other conflicts spurred the nationalists to oppose cooperation with government officials, to boycott goods made in Britain, to refuse to send their children to British schools, and to withhold taxes. Gandhi added his voice, calling for an all-India *satyagraha.* He also formed an alliance with Muslim leaders and began turning the Indian National Congress from an elite organization of lawyers and merchants into a mass organization open to anyone who paid dues, even the illiterate and poor.

When the Depression struck India in 1930, Gandhi singled out salt as a testing ground for his ideas on civil disobedience. Every Indian used salt, whose production was a heavily taxed government monopoly. Thus, salt symbolized the Indians' subjugation to an alien government. To break the colonial government's monopoly, Gandhi began a 240-mile march from western India to the coast to gather sea salt for free. Accompanying him were seventy-one followers representing different regions and religions of India. News wire services and mass circulation newspapers worldwide reported on the drama of the sixty-one-year-old Gandhi, wooden staff in hand, dressed in coarse homespun garments, leading the march. Thousands of people gathering en route were moved by the sight of the frail apostle of nonviolence encouraging them to embrace independence from colonial rule. The air thickened with tension as observers speculated on the British reaction to Gandhi's arrival at the sea. After nearly three weeks of walking, Gandhi waded into the surf, picked up a lump of natural salt, held it high, confessed that he had broken the salt law, and invited every Indian to do the same.

Inspired by Gandhi's example, millions of Indians joined strikes, boycotted foreign goods, and substituted indigenous hand-woven cloth for imported textiles. Many Indian officials in the colonial administration resigned in solidarity. The colonizers were taken aback by the mass mobilization. Yet, British denunciations of Gandhi only added to his personal aura and to the anticolonial crusade. By insisting that Indians follow

Gandhi and the Road to Independence. *(Left)* Gandhi launched a civil disobedience movement in 1930 by violating the British government's tax on salt. Calling it "the most inhuman poll tax the ingenuity of man can devise," Gandhi, accompanied by his followers, set out on a month-long march on foot covering 240 miles to Dandi on the Gujarat coast. The picture shows Gandhi arriving at the sea, where he and his followers broke the law by scooping up handfuls of salt. *(Right)* Gandhi believed that India had been colonized by becoming enslaved to modern industrial civilization. Indians would achieve independence, he argued, when they became self-reliant. Thus, he made the spinning wheel a symbol of *swaraj* and handspun cloth the virtual uniform of the nation.

Primary Source

INDIA AND SELF-GOVERNMENT

The following excerpt is from Mohandas (Mahatma) Gandhi's Hind Swaraj, *a pamphlet that he wrote in 1909 to explain why India needed self-government. Gandhi wrote it as a dialogue between a newspaper editor and a reader. Taking the role of the editor, he criticized modernity as represented by modern western civilization, which was based on industry and materialism. In contrast, Gandhi's imagined civilization of India derived from religion and harmonious village life. According to Gandhi, India demanded modern nationhood (or self-rule,* swaraj*) so that it could restore the best elements of its age-old civilization.*

READER: . . . I would now like to know your views on Swaraj. . . .

EDITOR [GANDHI]: It is quite possible that we do not attach the same meaning to the term. You and I and all Indians are impatient to obtain Swaraj, but we are certainly not decided as to what it is. . . .

Why do we want to drive away the English?

READER: Because India has become impoverished by their Government. They take away our money from year to year. The most important posts are reserved for themselves. We are kept in a state of slavery. They behave insolently towards us, and disregard our feelings.

EDITOR: Supposing we get self-government similar to what the Canadians and the South Africans have, will it be good enough?

READER: . . . We must own our navy, our army, and we must have our own splendour, and then will India's voice ring through the world.

EDITOR: . . . In effect it means this: that we want English rule without the Englishman. You want the tiger's nature, but not the tiger; that is to say, you would make India English, and, when it becomes English, it will be called not Hindustan but Englistan. This is not the Swaraj that I want.

READER: Then from your statement I deduce that the Government of England is not desirable and not worth copying by us.

EDITOR: . . . If India copies England, it is my firm conviction that she will be ruined.

READER: To what do you ascribe this state of England?

EDITOR: It is not due to any peculiar fault of the English people, but the condition is due to modern civilisation. It is a civilisation only in name. Under it the nations of Europe are becoming degraded and ruined day by day.

READER: . . . I should like to know your views about the condition of our country.

EDITOR: . . . India is being ground down not under the English heel but under that of modern civilisation. It is groaning under the monster's terrible weight. . . . India is becoming irreligious. Here I am not thinking of the Hindu, the Mahomedan, or the Zoroastrian religion, but of that religion which underlies all religions. We are turning away from God.

READER: You have denounced railways, lawyers and doctors. I can see that you will discard all machinery. What, then, is civilisation?

READER: . . . The tendency of Indian civilisation is to elevate the moral being, that of the Western civilisation is to propagate immorality. The latter is godless, the former is based on a belief in God. So understanding and so believing, it behooves every lover of India to cling to the old Indian civilisation even as a child clings to its mother's breast.

READER: . . . What, then, . . . would you suggest for freeing India?

EDITOR: . . . Those alone who have been affected by Western civilisation have become enslaved. . . . If we become free, India is free. And in this thought you have a definition of Swaraj. It is Swaraj when we learn to rule ourselves.

➤ *What are Gandhi's complaints about English colonial rule?*
➤ *Why does Gandhi reject modern civilization?*
➤ *According to Gandhi, what are the best aspects of "the old Indian civilisation"?*

SOURCE: M. K. Gandhi, *Hind Swaraj and Other Writings*, edited by Anthony J. Parel (Cambridge: Cambridge University Press, 1997), pp. 26–91.

their conscience (always through nonviolent protest), by exciting the masses through his defiance of colonial power, and by using symbols like homespun cloth to counter foreign, machine-spun textiles, Gandhi instilled in the people a sense of pride, resourcefulness, and Indian national awareness.

A DIVIDED ANTICOLONIAL MOVEMENT   Unlike the charismatic authoritarians who dominated Italy, Germany, and Russia, Gandhi did not aspire to dictatorial power. Moreover, his program met opposition from within, for many in the Indian National Congress Party did not share his vision of community as the source of public life. Cambridge-educated Jawaharlal Nehru (1889–1964), for example, believed that only by embracing science and technology could India develop as a modern nation.

Even less enamored were radical activists who wanted a revolution, not peaceful protest. In the countryside, these radicals sought to organize peasants to overthrow colonial domination. Other activists galvanized the growing industrial proletariat by organizing trade unions. Their stress on class conflict ran against Gandhi's ideals of national unity.

Religion, too, threatened to fracture Gandhi's hope for anticolonial unity. The Hindu-Muslim alliance crafted by nationalists in the early 1920s splintered over who represented them and how to ensure their political rights. The gulf widened after the Government of India Act of 1935 conceded substantial provincial autonomy and enlarged the franchise. The Muslim community found an impressive leader in Muhammad Ali Jinnah, who set about making the Muslim League the sole representative organization of the Muslim community. In 1940, the Muslim League passed a resolution demanding independent Muslim states in provinces where they constituted a majority, on the grounds that Muslims were not a religious minority of the Indian nation, but a nation themselves.

Hindus also sought a political role on the basis of religious identity. Movements to revitalize Hinduism began organizing Hindus as a religious nation. Indeed, the influence of Hindu culture on Indian nationalism was broad. Hindu symbols and a Hindu ethos colored the fabric of Indian nationalism woven by Gandhi and the Indian National Congress Party.

A further challenge came from women. Long-standing efforts to "uplift" women now escalated into a demand for women's rights, including suffrage. Following the formation of the All India Women's Conference in 1927, activists took up issues relating to women workers, health, employment, education, and literacy and demanded legislative seats for women. The Indian National Congress Party, however, elevated its nationalist agenda above women's demands, just as it had done in dealing with the lower castes and the relations between Hindus and Muslims.

In 1937, the British belatedly granted India provincial assemblies, a bicameral (having two chambers or bodies) national legislature, and a self-governing executive. By then, however, India's people were deeply politicized. The Congress Party, which inspired the masses to overthrow British rule, struggled to contain the different ideologies and new political institutions, such as labor unions, peasant associations, religious parties, and communal organizations. Seeking a

Gandhi and Nehru Sharing a Light Moment. Despite their divergent views on modernity, Gandhi was personally close to Nehru, who was his chosen political heir.

path to economic modernization, Gandhi, on one side, envisioned independent India as an updated collection of village republics organized around the benevolent authority of male-dominated households. Nehru, on another side, hoped for a socioeconomic transformation powered by science and state-sponsored planning. Both believed that India's traditions of collective welfare and humane religious and philosophical practices set it apart from the modern West. By the outbreak of World War II, India was well on its way toward political independence, but British policies and India's divisions foretold a violent end to imperial rule (see Chapter 20).

CHINESE NATIONALISM Unlike India and Africa, China was never formally colonized. But foreign powers' "concession areas" on Chinese soil compromised its sovereignty. Indeed, foreign nationals living in China enjoyed many privileges, including immunity from Chinese law. Furthermore, unequal treaties imposed on the Qing government had robbed China of its customs and tariff autonomy. Thus, the Chinese nationalists' vision of a modern alternative echoed that of the Indian nationalists: ridding the nation of foreign domination was the initial condition of national fulfillment. For many, the 1911 Revolution (as the fall of the Qing dynasty came to be known; see Chapter18) symbolized the first step toward transforming a crumbling agrarian empire into a modern nation.

Despite high hopes, the new republic could not establish legitimacy. For one thing, factional and regional conflicts made the government little more than a loose alliance of gentry, merchants, and military leaders. Its intellectual inspiration came from the ideas of the nationalist leader Sun Yat-sen. In 1912, after the Qing emperor stepped down, a military strongman, Yuan Shikai, forced Sun Yat-sen to concede the presidency to him. Although Sun had organized his followers into a political party, the Guomindang, Yuan dismissed all efforts to further democracy and dissolved the parliament. Only Yuan's death in 1916 ended his attempt to establish a new personal dynasty.

The republic endured another blow when the Treaty of Versailles awarded Germany's old concession rights in the Shandong peninsula to Japan. On May 4, 1919, thousands of Chinese students demonstrated in Beijing. As the protests spread to other cities, students appealed to workers and merchants to join their ranks. In what became known as the May Fourth movement, workers went on strike and merchants closed shops. Across the country, the Chinese boycotted Japanese goods.

As the Guomindang, still led by Sun Yat-sen, tried to rejuvenate itself, it looked to students and workers as well as the Russian Revolution for inspiration. In 1923, Sun reached an agreement with the Russians and admitted Chinese Communists to the Guomindang as individual members. Under the banner of anti-imperialism, the reorganized party sponsored mass organizations of workers' unions, peasant leagues, and women's associations.

Chiang. Riding the current of anti-imperialism, Chiang Kai-shek, shown here in 1924 in military dress, led the Guomindang on a military campaign in 1926–1928 and seized power, establishing a new national government based in Nanjing.

In 1926, amid a renewed tide of antiforeign agitation, **Chiang Kai-shek** (1887–1975) seized control of the party following Sun's death. Chiang launched a partially successful military campaign to reunify the country and established a new national government with its capital in Nanjing. However, he broke with the Soviets and the Chinese communists, whom he viewed as more threat than ally. Furthermore, his regime, despite its anti-imperialist platform, honored the treaty rights and concessions gained by foreigners in the late Qing era.

Still, Chiang acknowledged that China needed to change in order to succeed as a modern nation. He believed that the Chinese masses had to be mobilized. The New Life movement, launched with a torchlight parade in 1934 in Nanchang, exemplified his aspiration for a new Chinese national consciousness. Drawing on diverse ideas (from Confucian precepts to Social Darwinism) and fascist practices such as the militarization of everyday life in the name of sacrificing for the nation, the New Life movement aimed to instill discipline and moral purpose into a unified citizenry. It promoted dress codes for women, condemned casual sexual liaisons, and campaigned against spitting, urinating, or smoking in public.

PEASANT POPULISM IN CHINA: WHITE WOLF For many Guomindang leaders, the peasant population represented a backward class. Thus, the leadership failed to see the revolutionary potential of the countryside, which was alive with grassroots movements such as that of White Wolf.

From late 1913 to 1914, Chinese newspapers circulated reports about a roving band of armed men led by a mysterious figure known as White Wolf. This figure terrified members of the elite with his almost magical power. It is unlikely that the band, rumored to have close to a million followers, had more than 20,000 members even at its height. But the mythology surrounding White Wolf was so widespread that the movement's impact reverberated well beyond its physical presence.

Popular myth depicted White Wolf as a Chinese Robin Hood with the mission to restore order. The band's objective was to rid the country of the injustices of Yuan Shikai's government. Raiding major trade routes and market towns, White Wolf's followers gained a reputation for robbing the rich and aiding the poor. It was said that once the band captured a town, "cash and notes were flung out to the poor." Such stories won the White Wolf army many followers in rural China, where local peasants joined temporarily as fighters and then returned home when the band moved on.

Although the White Wolf army lacked the power to restore order to the countryside, its presence reflected the changes that had come to China. The army struck areas where inhabitants were feeling the effects of the new market forces. In the northwestern province of Shaanxi (Shensi), for example, where the band made its most famous march, markets that formerly flourished with trade in Chinese cotton now awaited camels carrying cotton bales shipped from Fall River, Massachusetts. The fact that the Guomindang never managed to bridge the differences between themselves and a rural-based movement such as that of White Wolf showed the limits of their nationalist vision. The challenge fell to the Chinese communists, who had fled to the countryside to escape Chiang's persecution. They learned that the rural population could indeed become a mass political force—a lesson that served them well during the subsequent war and Japanese occupation in the 1930s and 1940s.

A POST-IMPERIAL TURKISH NATION Of all the postwar anticolonial movements, none was more successful or more committed to European models than that of **Mustafa Kemal Ataturk** (1881–1938), who helped forge the modern Turkish nation-state. Until 1914, the Ottoman Empire was a colonial power in its own right. But having fought on the losing German side, it saw its realm shrink to a part of Anatolia under the Treaty of Sèvres, which ended the war between the Allies and the Ottoman Empire.

Some of its former territories, such as those in southern Europe, became independent states; others, such as those in the Middle East, came under British and French administration as mandates of the League of Nations. Fearing that the rest of the empire would be colonized, Ottoman military leaders, many of whom had resisted Turkish nationalism, now embraced the cause. What made modern Turkish nationalism so successful was its ability to convert the mainstay of the old regime, the army, to the goal of creating a Turkish nation-state. These men, in turn, mobilized the masses and launched a state-led drive for modernity.

In 1920, an Ottoman army officer and military hero named Mustafa Kemal harnessed this groundswell of Turkish nationalism into opposition to Greek troops who had been

Ataturk. In the 1920s, Mustafa Kemal, known as Ataturk, introduced the Latin alphabet for the Turkish language as part of his campaign to modernize and secularize Turkey. He underscored his commitment to change by being photographed while giving instruction in the use of the new alphabet.

sent to enforce the peace treaty. Rallying his own troops to defend the fledgling Turkish nation, Kemal reconquered most of Anatolia and the area around Istanbul and secured international recognition for the new state in 1923 at the Treaty of Lausanne. Thereafter, a vast, forcible exchange of populations occurred. Approximately 1.2 million Greek Christians left Turkey to settle in Greece, and 400,000 Muslims relocated from Greece to Turkey.

With the Ottoman Empire gone, Kemal and his followers moved to build a state based on Turkish national consciousness. First they deposed the sultan. Then they abolished the Ottoman caliphate and proclaimed Turkey a republic, whose supreme authority would be an elected House of Assembly. Later, after Kemal insisted that the people adopt European-style surnames, the assembly conferred on Kemal the mythic name Ataturk, "father of the Turks."

In forging a Turkish nation, Kemal looked to construct a European-like secular state and to eliminate Islam's hold over civil and political affairs. The Turkish elite replaced Muslim religious law with the Swiss civil code, instituted the western (Christian) calendar, and abolished the once-powerful dervish religious orders. They also suppressed Arabic and Persian words from Turkish, substituted Roman script for Arabic letters, forbade polygamy, made wearing the fez (a brimless cap) a crime, and instructed Turks to wear European-style hats. The veil, though not outlawed, was denounced as a relic. In 1934, the government enfranchised Turkish women, granted them property rights in marriage and inheritance, and allowed them to enter the professions. Schools, too, were taken out of the hands of Muslim clerics, placed under state control, and, along with military service, became the chief instrument for making the masses conscious of belonging to a Turkish nation. Yet, many villagers did not accept Ataturk's non-Islamic nationalism, remaining devoted to Islam and resentful of the prohibitions against dervish dancing.

In imitating Europe, Kemal borrowed its antidemocratic models. Inspired by the Soviets, he inaugurated a five-year plan for the economy emphasizing centralized coordination. During the 1930s, Turkish nationalists also drew on Nazi examples by advocating racial theories that posited central Asian Turks as the founders of all civilization. In another authoritarian move, Kemal occasionally rigged parliamentary elections, while using the police and judiciary to silence his critics. The Kemalist revolution in Turkey was the most far-reaching and enduring transformation that had occurred outside Europe and the Americas up to that point. It offered an important model for the founding of secular, authoritarian states in the Islamic world.

NATIONALISM AND THE RISE OF THE MUSLIM BROTHERHOOD IN EGYPT Elsewhere in the Middle East, where France and Britain expanded their holdings at the Ottomans' expense, anticolonial movements borrowed from European models while putting their own stamp on nation-making and modernization campaigns. In Egypt, British occupation predated the fall of the Ottoman Empire, but here, too, World War I energized the forces of anticolonial nationalism.

When the war ended, Sa'd Zaghlul (1857–1927), an educated Egyptian patriot, pressed for an Egyptian delegation to be invited to the peace conference at Versailles. He hoped to present Egypt's case for national independence. Instead, British officials arrested and exiled him and his most vocal supporters. When news of this action came out, the country burst into revolt. Rural rebels broke away from the central government, proclaiming local republics. Villagers tore up railway lines and telegraph wires, the symbols of British authority.

After defusing the conflict, British authorities tried to mollify Egyptian sensibilities. In 1922, Britain proclaimed Egypt independent, though it retained the right to station British troops on Egyptian soil. Ostensibly, this provision would protect traffic through the Suez Canal and foreign populations residing in Egypt, but it also enabled the British to continue to influence Egyptian politics. Two years later, elections placed Zaghlul's nationalist party, the Wafd, in office. But the British prevented the Wafd from exercising real power.

This subversion of independence and democracy provided an opening for antiliberal variants of anticolonialism. During the Depression years, a fascist group, Young Egypt, garnered wide appeal. So did an Islamic group, the Muslim Brotherhood, which attacked liberal democracy as a facade for middle-class, business, and landowning interests. The Muslim Brotherhood was anticolonial and anti-British, but its members considered mere political independence insufficient. Egyptians, they argued, must also renounce the lure of the West (whether liberal capitalism or godless communism) and return to a purified form of Islam. For the Muslim Brotherhood, Islam offered a complete way of life. A "return to Islam" through the nation-state created yet another model of modernity for colonial and semicolonial peoples.

CONCLUSION

The Great War and its aftermath accelerated the trend toward mass society and the debate over how to organize it. Because mass society meant production and consumption on a staggering scale, satisfying the populace became a pressing concern for rulers worldwide. Competing programs vied for ascendancy in the new, broader, public domain.

Most programs fell into one of three categories: liberal democratic, authoritarian, or anticolonial. Liberal democracy defined the political and economic systems in western Europe and the Americas. Resting on faith in free enterprise and representative democracy (with a restricted franchise), liberal regimes had already been unsettled before the Great War. Turn-of-the-century reforms broadened electorates and brought government oversight and regulation into private economic activity. But during the Great Depression, dissatisfaction again deepened. Only far-reaching reforms, introducing greater regulation and more aggressive government intervention to provide for the citizenry's welfare, saved capitalist economies and democratic political systems from collapse.

Still, through the 1930s, liberal democracy was in retreat. Authoritarianism seemed better positioned to satisfy the masses while representing the dynamism of modernity. While authoritarians differed about the faults of capitalism, they joined in the condemnation of electoral democracy. Authoritarians mobilized the masses to put the interests of the nation above the individual. That mobilization often involved brutal repression, yet it seemed also to restore pride and purpose to the masses.

Meanwhile, the colonial and semicolonial world searched for ways to escape from European domination. In Asia and Africa, anticolonial leaders sought to eliminate foreign rule while turning colonies into nations and subjects into citizens. Some looked to the liberal democratic West for models of nation building, but others rejected liberalism because it was associated with colonial rule. Instead, socialism, fascism, and a return to religious traditions offered more promising paths.

The two decades after the end of World War I brought great political upheavals and deep economic dislocations. At times, the competition among liberal democracy, authoritarianism (both right and left), and anticolonial nationalism grew heated. Yet the traumas were tame compared to what followed with the outbreak in 1939 of World War II.

Review and research materials are available at StudySpace: Ⓢ WWNORTON.COM/STUDYSPACE

KEY TERMS

Allied Powers (p. 709)	League of Nations (p. 715)
Mustafa Kemal Ataturk (p. 740)	mass consumption (p. 718)
Bolsheviks (p. 714)	mass culture (p. 717)
Central Powers (p. 709)	mass production (p. 718)
Chiang Kai-shek (p. 739)	Mohandas Karamchand (Mahatma) Gandhi (p. 734)
fascism (p. 726)	Benito Mussolini (p. 726)
Great Depression (p. 719)	Nazis (p. 726)
Great War (World War I) (p. 709)	New Deal (p. 723)
	nonviolent resistance (p. 736)
Adolf Hitler (p. 726)	Joseph Stalin (p. 724)

Chronology

	1910		1920
AMERICAS		◆ 1917 United States enters World War I	
EUROPE	◆ 1914 The Great War begins -	◆ 1918 Dissolution of German and Austro-Hungarian Empi◆ ◆ 1919 Treaty of Versailles ends World War I 1922 Mussolini and Fascists march on Rome ◆	
RUSSIA (SOVIET UNION)		◆ 1917 Bolshevik Revolution 1918–1921 Russian Civil War ◆ - - - - - - - - - - - - - - - - ◆	
EAST ASIA		◆ 1919 May Fourth movement (China)	
SOUTH ASIA		◆ 1919 Massacre at Amritsar	
MIDDLE EAST		◆ 1918 Dissolution of Ottoman Empire 1922 Ottoman sultan deposed ◆ 1923 Mustafa Kemal leads Turkey to nationhood	

STUDY QUESTIONS

1. List and explain the numerous ways in which World War I changed the world. How did it usher in a new age for diverse societies?

2. Define the terms *mass culture*, *mass production*, and *mass consumption*. How did World War I help to diffuse these concepts across the world's cultures?

3. Analyze how the Great Depression challenged political establishments after World War I. How were the two events linked? What values and assumptions did the Great Depression challenge?

4. Explain competing visions of modernity that emerged across the globe during the period covered in this chapter. How were they similar and how were they different?

5. Compare and contrast the liberal democratic and authoritarian visions of modernity as epitomized by various states in the 1930s. What features did they have in common?

6. List and explain various anticolonial visions of modern life that emerged in the first half of the twentieth century. To what extent did they reflect borrowed developments versus native traditions and ideas?

7. Describe how Latin American societies adjusted to modern ideas at this time. How did visions of modernity affect states and societies in that region of the world?

1930   **1940**

◆ 1929 Great Depression begins

◆ 1930 Getúlio Vargas becomes leader of Brazil

1933–1941 American "New Deal" ◆ - ◆

◆ 1929 Great Depression begins

◆1933 Hitler becomes dictator of Germany

1936–1939 Spanish Civil War ◆ - - - - - - - - - - - - - - ◆

1936–1939 Popular Front rules France ◆ - - - - - - - - - - - - - - ◆

1929–1935 Collectivization in Russia ◆ - ◆　　◆ - - - - - - - - - ◆ 1936–1938 Great Purge in the Soviet Union

◆ 1928 Chiang Kai-shek becomes leader of China

◆ 1932 Japan annexes Manchuria

◆ 1930 Gandhi's March to the Sea

◆ 1928 Muslim Brotherhood established (Egypt)

20

THE THREE-WORLD ORDER, 1940–1975

*I*n February 1945, the three leaders of the World War II Allies—President Franklin Delano Roosevelt of the United States, Prime Minister Winston Churchill of Great Britain, and Premier Joseph Stalin of the Soviet Union—met to prepare for the postwar world. By then, Germany, Italy, and Japan were losing the war. But the world's re-ordering was a source of deep contention, for the three leaders had profoundly different visions. Roosevelt, who envisioned independent nation-states kept at peace by an international body, had no interest in restoring the old European empires. Churchill, however, resisted liquidation of the British Empire. Stalin's negotiations left no doubt that he intended to secure influence in eastern Europe and Asia and to weaken Germany so that it could never again menace the Soviet Union.

When the fighting finally stopped, it was clear that the European-centered order, shocked by World War I, had been shattered by World War II. Empires either lay in ruins or faced dismantling by colonial independence movements. The nation-state had emerged as the prevailing political organization. Moreover, the state's reach had expanded as it took on new functions related to postwar reconstruction. Meanwhile, with the weakening of Great Britain, France, and Germany, a new three-world order emerged.

This chapter explores the development of the three-world order in the wake of World War II. Heading the "First World" was the United States, which with its allies championed capitalism and democracy as bringing unprecedented prosperity in the decades after 1945. Leading the "Second World" was the Soviet Union, which turned from ally of the United States during World War II to its chief adversary in the protracted cold war that followed. As leader of the communist bloc, the Soviet Union contested capitalist societies' claims and trumpeted socialism's accomplishments. Caught in between (and sometimes literally caught in the crossfire when the cold war turned hot) were formerly colonized and semicolonized people. Lumped together as the "Third World," they struggled through the postwar period to find their own third way.

COMPETING BLOCS

> → *What challenges did each world bloc face?*

The roots of the world's division into three blocs lay in the breakup of Europe's empires and the demise of European world leadership. The destruction of Europe and the defeat of Japan left a power vacuum, which the United States and the Soviet Union rushed to fill. Both believed that their respective systems—capitalism and communism—had universal application. They were now **superpowers** because of their size, their possession of the atomic bomb, and the fact that each embodied a model of civilization applicable to the whole world. As their spheres of influence expanded, they engaged in bitter rivalry and an arms race that threatened a potential World War III.

While the capitalist and communist blocs embarked on a cold war, conflicts in the Third World got very hot. (The **cold war** was an ideological battle for influence in which no direct military conflict occurred between the superpowers.) In Asia and Africa, anticolonial leaders intensified their campaigns for independence. Winning popular support by mobilizing deep-seated desires for justice and autonomy, they swept away foreign rulers and asserted their claims for national independence. Latin American countries, too, sought progress and nationhood. But newfound political freedom did not easily translate into economic development or social equity. Moreover, as the two superpowers looked for allies and client states, they militarized rival states and factions within the Third World.

Each superpower also faced internal problems. Even as the United States maintained that its booming industrial economy, abundant consumer goods, liberal democracy, and entertaining popular culture were proof of capitalism's superiority, the nation also wrestled with racism and became involved in unpopular wars to stop the spread of communism—most notably in Vietnam. The Soviet Union celebrated its own economic prowess and social welfare policies, but its continued authoritarianism, political prisoners, and use of military force to crush socialist reform efforts within the Soviet bloc undermined communism's allure.

By the 1960s and the early 1970s, tensions were simmering in the three-world order. The United States and the Soviet Union faced discontent within their societies and opposition within their respective blocs. At the same time, the rising economic might of Japan and the other Pacific economies, the emerging clout of oil-rich states, and the specter of radical revolution in Africa, Asia, and Latin America suggested a shift in the balance of wealth and power away from the First and Second worlds.

Focus Questions

→ *What challenges did each world bloc face?*

→ *In what ways was World War II a global conflict?*

→ *How did the United States try to rebuild Europe and contain the spread of communism?*

→ *To what extent did decolonization involve large-scale violence?*

→ *What were the successes and failures of each world bloc?*

→ *What major fissures developed in the three-world order?*

MAIN THEMES

✦ *World War II shatters the European-centered order and lays the groundwork for a world divided into three camps: an American-led liberal democratic order; a communist world led by the Soviet Union; and newly independent, decolonized states in Asia, Africa, and Latin America.*

✦ *War and postwar reconstruction enhance the reach and functions of the modern nation-state.*

✦ *Allies during World War II, the United States and the Soviet Union engage in an ideological cold war, each touting the superiority of its views on how best to organize societies, while decolonized states in Asia, Africa, and Latin America struggle to find a "third way" but find themselves caught between rival superpowers.*

FOCUS ON *World War II and a New Global Order*

World War II

✦ World War II grows out of unresolved problems connected to World War I, especially the aggressive plans of Germany and Japan to expand their political and economic influence.

✦ The war brings unheard-of human and material costs and ushers in an age of nuclear weapons.

✦ At war's end, the United States, fearing the spread of communism and Soviet influence, rebuilds war-torn Europe and Japan and creates military and political alliances to contain Soviet expansionist ambitions.

A New Global Order

✦ The Soviet Union and the United States become superpowers.

✦ Japan emerges as an economic powerhouse and a U.S. ally.

✦ A weakened Europe cannot resist demands for independence from Asian and African nationalists.

✦ Chinese communists engineer a revolution, while Indian nationalists and many African leaders achieve independence through negotiations.

✦ Elsewhere, decolonization is violent (Palestine, Israel, Egypt, Algeria, and Kenya) or incomplete (southern Africa).

✦ Actions by Latin American reformers and revolutionary insurgents spark counterinsurgency efforts by the United States and its regional allies.

✦ An insecure three-world order emerges after most Asian and African states achieve independence.

WORLD WAR II AND ITS AFTERMATH

> ✦ *In what ways was World War II a global conflict?*

World War II grew out of unresolved problems connected to the Great War. World War I had not been, as many had prophesied, "the war to end all wars." It became instead merely the *First* World War after the *Second* World War began in 1939. Especially influential were the resentments bred by the harsh provisions and controversial state boundaries set out in the treaties signed at the war's end.

World War II also resulted from the aggressive ambitions and racial theories of Germany and Japan. Both states sought to impose racial hierarchy (master and inferior races) through conquest and coerced labor. By the late 1930s, German and Japanese ambitions to become colonial powers brought these conservative dictatorships (which along with Italy constituted the **Axis powers**) into conflict with France, Britain, the Soviet Union, and eventually the United States (the **Allied powers**).

Even more than its predecessor, World War II was truly a world conflict, and a devastatingly total one. Fighting occurred in Europe, Africa, and Asia, the Atlantic and the Pacific, and the Northern and Southern hemispheres. Warring nations mobilized millions of people into armed forces and placed enormous demands on civilians. Noncombatants had to produce far more to support the war effort, and they had to consume far less. Moreover, as aerial bombardment of cities caused colossal civilian casualties, the total war erased the old distinction between soldiers and civilians. Women—as victims and as collaborators, as volunteers and as forced laborers, as workers behind the scenes and as witnesses to the conflict—were involved as never before. They, together with children, the infirm, and the elderly, also swelled the enormous population of refugees seeking safety in the midst of worldwide chaos.

World War II also completed the decline of European world dominance that World War I had set in motion. The unspeakable acts of barbarism perpetrated during the Second World War, including the Nazi genocides directed against Jews and others, robbed Europe of its lingering claims as a superior civilization. In the war's wake, anticolonial movements demanded national self-determination from exhausted and battered European powers.

THE WAR IN EUROPE

Although Hitler had annexed Austria and parts of Czechoslovakia in 1938, World War II officially began in Europe in September 1939, with Germany's invasion of Poland and the British and French decision to oppose it. Before it was all over in 1945, much of Europe, including Germany, had been leveled.

BLITZKRIEG AND RESISTANCE   Hitler's early success was staggering. His troops overran Poland, France, Norway, Denmark, Luxembourg, Belgium, and Holland. In 1940 he signed the Tripartite Pact with Italy and Japan, formalizing an alliance among the Axis powers. Within less than two years, the Germans controlled virtually all of Europe from the English Channel to the Soviet border (see Map 20-1). Only Britain escaped Axis control, although Nazi bombers pulverized British cities. In the east, Germany had a nonaggression pact with the Soviet Union, but in 1941 the German army invaded the Soviet Union with 170 divisions, 3,000 tanks, and nearly 4 million men—an invasion force of a size unmatched before or since. Here, as elsewhere, the Germans fought a *blitzkrieg* ("lightning war") of tank-led assaults followed by motorized infantrymen and then foot soldiers. Already by October 1941, the Germans had reached the outskirts of Moscow. The Soviet Union seemed on the verge of a monumental defeat.

The Nazi war was not just a grab for land and raw materials; it was also a crusade for a new order based on race. Nazi racial occupation policies created massive social, economic, and political upheavals throughout Europe. Hitler established puppet governments that complied with deportation orders against Jews and dissidents. Hitler's police and the puppet states turned Europe into a giant police state and spawned both collaborators and resistance fighters. Even the resistance movements represented many different points of view—from nationalists (who opposed German domination) to communists (who wanted to defeat both Fascism and capitalism). Here, the seeds for postwar enmities were sown.

In the east, the tide turned against the Germans and their collaborators after the ferocious battles of Stalingrad in 1942–1943 and Kursk in 1943. Once the Soviet army blunted

The Devastation of War. (*Left*) In the Battle of Britain, Nazi warplanes strafed British cities in an effort to break British morale. But the devastating bombing raids, such as this one in Coventry in November 1940, helped rally the British, who refused to give in. (*Right*) In November 1942, Nazi troops entered Stalingrad, some 2,000 miles from Berlin. Hitler wanted to capture the city not only to exploit the surrounding wheat fields and the oil of the Caucasus but also for its very name. With handheld flamethrowers and sometimes just their fists, Soviet troops drove out the Germans in February 1943.

MAP 20-1　WORLD WAR II: THE EUROPEAN THEATER

The Axis armies enjoyed great success during the early stages of World War II. Look at the map. Which states were within the Axis territory when World War II began in September 1939? What were the territorial boundaries when the Axis powers reached their greatest extent? When did the military balance begin to turn against Germany and Italy? Where do you think the outcome of the conflict was decided, eastern Europe or western Europe?

the initial German assault, it launched a massive counter-offensive. This move initiated the defeat of the German war effort on the Eastern Front, but full retreat took another two years as the Soviets drove Hitler's army slowly westward. Before 1944 the Soviets bore the brunt of the fighting, causing more than 85 percent of all German casualties, although the

British attacked the Nazis in the air and on the sea and, along with American troops, stopped a German advance across North Africa into Egypt. The spectacular D-Day landing of western Allied forces in Normandy on June 6, 1944 (when the Germans had a mere 15 divisions in France, against more than 300 on the Eastern Front), brought the Germans face to face with American and British troops also determined to fight their way to Germany. On April 30, 1945, as Soviet and Anglo-American forces converged on Berlin, Hitler committed suicide. Days later, Germany surrendered unconditionally. Still, what the postwar European map would look like remained unclear.

THE BITTER COSTS OF WAR   The war in Europe had devastating human and material costs. This was particularly the case in eastern Europe, where German forces leveled more than 70,000 Soviet villages, obliterated one-third of the Soviet Union's wealth, and inflicted 7 million Soviet military deaths (by contrast, the Germans lost 3.5 million soldiers) and up to 20 million civilian deaths. German bombing of British cities, such as London, inflicted a heavy toll on civilians and buildings, as did Allied bombing of war plants and Axis cities like Dresden and Tokyo. Urban casualties were perhaps greatest in Leningrad, a city that was surrounded and besieged for nine hundred days; 900,000 people lost their lives during this struggle. By the war's end, Poland had lost 6 million people and Great Britain had lost 400,000. Tens of millions in the east and west were left homeless.

Europe's Jews paid an especially high price. Hitler had long talked of "freeing" Europe of all Jews. At the war's outset, the Nazis herded Jews into ghettos and labor camps and then seized their property. As the German army moved eastward, more and more Jews came under their control. At first the Nazi bureaucrats contemplated deportation but then ruled out transporting "subhumans" as too costly. By 1940 special troops had begun mass shootings of communists and Jews. Soon this came to be considered a waste of ammunition, and shootings gave way to the use of mobile gas vans. By fall 1941, Hitler and the S.S. (the *Schutzstaffel*, a security police force) were building a series of killing centers. The largest concentration camp was Auschwitz-Birkenau in Poland.

Cattle cars shipped Jews from all over Europe to the extermination sites in the east, where Nazis used the latest technology to kill men, women, and children. The deliberate racial extermination of the Jews, known as the **Holocaust**, claimed around 6 million European Jews. Most died in the gas chambers of concentration camps; many others perished from starvation or exhaustion. The Nazis also turned their mass killing apparatus against gypsies, homosexuals, communists, and Slavs, with deportations to the death camps continuing to the very end of the war.

THE PACIFIC WAR

Like the war in Europe, the conflict in the Pacific transformed the military and political landscape (see Map 20-2). The war broke out when Japan's ambitions to dominate Asia targeted American interests and might.

JAPAN'S EFFORTS TO EXPAND   Japan's expansionist aims became clear when its military invaded and occupied Manchuria in 1931 and then launched an offensive against the rest of China in 1937. Although the Japanese did not achieve China's complete submission, the invaders exacted a terrible toll on the population. Most infamous was the so-called rape of Nanjing, in which Japanese aggressors slaughtered at least 100,000 civilians and raped thousands of women in the Chinese city between December 1937 and February 1938.

Meanwhile, events in Europe opened opportunities for further Japanese expansion in Asia. Germany's swift occupation of western Europe left defeated nations' colonies at the mercy of Japanese forces. After concluding a pact with Germany in 1940, the Japanese occupied French Indochina in 1941 and made demands on the Dutch East Indies for oil

Japanese Aggression. The brutal Battle of Shanghai (August–November 1937) marked the beginning of what turned out to be World War II in Asia. Claiming to be "protecting" China from European imperialists and expecting a relatively easy victory, the Japanese instead met with stiff resistance from the Chinese troops under Chiang Kai-shek. Here we see Japanese marines parading through the streets of the city after they finally broke through Chinese defenses. About a quarter of a million Chinese soldiers, close to 60 percent of Chiang's best troops, were killed or wounded in the campaign, a blow from which Chiang's regime never recovered. The Japanese sustained more than 40,000 casualties.

MAP 20-2   WORLD WAR II: THE PACIFIC THEATER

Like Germany and Italy, Japan experienced stunning military successes in the war's early years. In what directions did the Japanese direct their military offensives? Analyzing this map, why do you think the Japanese were so concerned about an American presence in East Asia, when the United States was so geographically distant? According to your reading, how did the Allied strategies to defeat the Japanese Empire shape postwar relations in the region?

and rubber. Now the chief obstacle to further expansion in the Pacific was the United States, which already had imperial interests in places like China and the Philippines, as well as other Pacific islands. Hoping to strike the United States before it was prepared for war, the Japanese launched a surprise air attack on the American naval base at Pearl Harbor in Hawaii on December 7, 1941. As the United States entered the war, Germany and Italy also declared war on America.

Now Japan's expansion shifted into high gear. During 1942, its military racked up victory after victory over the tottering western armies. With French Indochina already under their control, the Japanese turned against the American colony of the Philippines and against the Dutch East Indies, both of which fell in 1942. By coordinating their army, naval, and air force units and using tactical surprise, the Japanese seized a huge swath of territory that included British-ruled Hong Kong, Singapore, Malaya, and Burma, while threatening the British Empire's hold on India as well.

Japan justified its aggression on the grounds that it was anticolonial and pan-Asian; Japan promised to drive out the European imperialists and to build a new order reflecting "Asia for Asians." In practice, however, the Japanese made terrible demands on fellow Asians for resources, developed myths of Japanese racial purity and supremacy, and treated Chinese and Koreans with brutality. During the war, Japan put up to 4 million Koreans to work for its empire, forcibly imported another 700,000 Korean men as laborers, and pressed up to 200,000 young women into service as prostitutes for Japanese soldiers. (In a similar move, the Nazi war effort in Europe involved forcing 12 million foreign laborers—including 2 million prisoners of war—to settle and work in Germany.)

ALLIED ADVANCES AND THE ATOMIC BOMB Like the Germans in their war against Russia, the Japanese could not sustain their military successes against the United States. By mid-1943, U.S. forces had put the Japanese on the defensive. Fighting from island to island, American troops recaptured the Philippines, and a combined force of British, American, and Chinese troops returned Burma to Britain. The Allies then moved toward the Japanese mainland. By summer 1945, American bombers had all but devastated the major cities of Japan. Yet Japan did not surrender.

Anticipating that an invasion of Japan would cost hundreds of thousands of American lives, U.S. president Harry Truman unleashed the Americans' secret weapon. It was the work of a team of scientists who were predominantly European refugees. On August 6, 1945, an American plane dropped an atomic bomb on the city of Hiroshima, killing or maiming over 100,000 people. Three days later, the Americans dropped a second atomic bomb on Nagasaki. Within days, Emperor Hirohito announced Japan's surrender.

But the bombs' work was not over, for air, soil, and groundwater were irradiated, poisoning the sources of sustenance. This was not the first time (nor would it be the last) that human-made technologies not only clinched victory for one army but also altered the chemical composition of the land itself.

The Aftermath of the Atomic Bomb. (*Left*) A view of Nagasaki less than half a mile from "ground zero" after the atomic bomb was dropped in August 1945. A few reinforced concrete buildings still stand. (*Right*) Thousands of people were immediately crushed or burned to death in the blast. Many died later from horrendous burns and radiation poisoning.

THE BEGINNING OF THE COLD WAR

> → *How did the United States try to rebuild Europe and contain the spread of communism?*

World War II left much of Europe in ruins. Charred embers lay where great cities had once stood. Major bridges lay crumbled at the bottom of rivers; railway lines were twisted scrap; sunken ships blocked harbors. Scarcity and hunger were widespread. Millions had died; tens of millions more were wounded, displaced, widowed, and orphaned. "What is Europe now?" mused British prime minister Winston Churchill. "A rubble heap, a charnel house, a breeding ground of pestilence and hate."

Postwar Planning at Yalta. The "Big Three" allies confer about the end of the war at the Black Sea resort of Yalta in February 1945. On the left is British prime minister Winston Churchill; at the center is American president Franklin Roosevelt; and on the right is Soviet premier Joseph Stalin.

REBUILDING EUROPE

The task of political rebuilding was daunting, for the old order had been discredited. By contrast, communism gained new appeal because its credo promised a clean slate. Many eastern Europeans, following the horrors of Fascism and not knowing the extent of Stalin's crimes, looked to the Soviets for answers. Even many of those opposed to the Soviets saw some form of Socialism as a way to create powerful, modern, egalitarian societies in Europe.

Europe's leftward tilt alarmed U.S. policymakers. They feared that the Soviets would use their ideological influence and the territory conquered by the Red Army to spread communism. They also worried that Stalin might seize Europe's overseas possessions and create communist regimes outside Europe. American and British governments had mistrusted Stalin during the war, but they had depended on the Soviet Union's strength against Germany. With a common enemy gone, however, misgivings evolved into a

The Berlin Airlift. In summer 1948, a new currency was issued for the united occupation zones of West Germany. It began to circulate in Berlin at more favorable exchange rates than the eastern zone's currency, and Berlin seemed poised to become an outpost of the West inside the Soviet occupation zone. The Soviets responded by blocking western traffic into Berlin; the West countered with an airlift, forcing the Soviets to back down in May 1949 but hastening the division of Germany into two countries.

determination to block further Soviet influence. An American journalist popularized the term *cold war* in 1946 to describe the new struggle.

President Truman advocated a policy of containing Soviet communism. This policy soon faced a test in Germany, which had been partitioned into British, French, American, and Soviet zones of occupation. Although Berlin, the capital, was technically in the Soviet occupation zone, postwar agreements stipulated that all four powers administer it jointly. In 1948, the Soviets attempted to seize all of Berlin for themselves by blocking western routes to the capital. The Allies responded with the Berlin Airlift, which involved transporting supplies in planes to western Berlin to keep the population from capitulating to the Soviets. This crisis lasted for almost a year, until Stalin allowed trucks to roll through the eastern zone in May 1949.

Stalin and his successors did not, however, relax their hold on eastern Germany. In 1949, occupied Germany was split into two hostile states: the democratic Federal Republic of Germany in the west, and the communist German Democratic Republic in the east. In 1961, leaders in the German Democratic Republic built a wall around West Berlin to insulate the east from capitalist propaganda and to halt a flood of émigrés fleeing communism. The **Berlin Wall** soon symbolized a divided Europe and the cold war.

U.S. policymakers wanted to shore up democratic governments in Europe, so Truman promised American military and economic aid. Containing the spread of communism meant securing a capitalist future for western Europe, a job that fell to Truman's secretary of state, General George C. Marshall. He launched the Marshall Plan, an ambitious program that provided over $13 billion in grants and credits to reconstruct Europe and facilitate an economic revival. U.S. policymakers hoped the aid would dim communism's appeal by fostering economic prosperity, muting class tensions, and integrating western European nations into an alliance of capitalist democracies.

Stalin saw the Marshall Plan as a threat to the Soviet Union. He felt the same about the formation in 1949 of the **North Atlantic Treaty Organization (NATO)**, a military alliance between countries in western Europe and North America. He believed that the Soviet Union, having sacrificed millions of people to the war against Fascism, deserved to be dominant in eastern Europe. Soviet troops had occupied eastern European nations at the war's end, and both communists and leftist members of other parties formed Soviet-backed coalition governments there. By tricking their moderate leftist allies and repressing their critics and opponents, the communists established dictatorships in Bulgaria, Romania, Hungary, and Czechoslovakia in 1948. With these communist nations the Soviets formed the **Warsaw Pact,** a military alliance of their own, in 1955. As the Warsaw Pact nations of eastern Europe faced off against NATO's forces in western Europe (see Map 20-3), the 1950s and 1960s witnessed tense

confrontations that brought the world to the brink of an atomic World War III.

THE NUCLEAR AGE

The cold war changed military affairs forever. When the Americans dropped atomic bombs on Japan in 1945, they had a decisive technological edge. In 1949, however, the Soviets tested their first nuclear bomb. Thereafter, each side rushed to stockpile nuclear weapons and update its military technologies. In so doing, they shifted from explosives using nuclear fission to those using nuclear fusion.

The weapon that destroyed Hiroshima, a fission bomb, was calculated in kilotons (each the equivalent of 1,000 tons of TNT). But fusion, or hydrogen, bombs were calculated in megatons (one *million* tons of TNT, or 1,000 kilotons). Thus, by 1960, it was possible that nuclear war might lead to the world's destruction without a soldier firing a single shot. This sobering realization changed the rules of the game. Each side now possessed the power to inflict total destruction on the other, a circumstance that caused great anxiety but also inhibited direct confrontations.

The confrontation between capitalist and communist blocs turned into open military struggle in parts of Asia where the postwar settlement was murky. The French wanted to restore their Indochinese empire, but they met fierce resistance from Vietnamese nationalists. China descended into a civil war that the communists won in 1949, forcing remnants of

Atom Bomb Anxiety. Schoolchildren taking shelter under their desks during an A-bomb drill in Brooklyn, New York, 1951. The Soviets had exploded their first test bomb in 1949. Underground bomb shelters were built in many American urban areas as places in which to survive a doomsday attack.

U.S. and Canada are also part of NATO

ICELAND

ATLANTIC OCEAN

FINLAND

NORWAY $236 million

SWEDEN $107 million

NORTH SEA

DENMARK $273 million

BALTIC SEA

SOVIET UNION

IRELAND $148 million

GREAT BRITAIN $3190 million

NETHERLANDS $1084 million

BELGIUM

EAST GERMANY

POLAND

Luxembourg and Belgium together receive $546 million

LUXEMBOURG

WEST GERMANY 1955 $1391 million

CZECHOSLOVAKIA

FRANCE $2714 million

SWITZERLAND

AUSTRIA $678 million

HUNGARY

ROMANIA

PORTUGAL $51 million

SPAIN 1982

BALEARIC ISLANDS

CORSICA

SARDINIA

ITALY $1509 million

ADRIATIC SEA

YUGOSLAVIA

ALBANIA until 1968

BULGARIA

BLACK SEA

GREECE 1952 $707 million

AEGEAN SEA

TURKEY 1952 $225 million

SICILY

MEDITERRANEAN SEA

CRETE

RHODES

NATO
Warsaw Pact
Neutral
U.S. $ Marshall aid recipient

MAP 20-3   NATO AND WARSAW PACT COUNTRIES

The cold war divided Europe into two competing blocs: those joined with the United States in the North Atlantic Treaty Organization (NATO) and those linked to the Soviet Union under the Warsaw Pact. Which nations had borders with nations belonging to the opposite bloc? Comparing this map with Map 20-1, explain how combat patterns in World War II shaped the dividing line between the two blocs. According to the map, where would you expect cold war tensions to be the most intense?

the American-backed regime to flee to Taiwan. Korea was divided up, having been liberated by the Soviets from the north, who then stopped and allowed their wartime allies, the Americans, to occupy the south.

In 1950, North Korean troops backed by the Soviet Union invaded U.S.-backed South Korea, setting off the **Korean War** (see Map 20-4). Claiming this violated the Charter of the United Nations, which had been established in 1945 to safeguard world peace and protect human rights, President Truman ordered American troops to drive back the North Koreans. The U.N. Security Council, thanks to a Soviet boycott, also sent troops from fifteen nations to restore peace. Within a year, the invaders had been routed and were near collapse. When U.N. troops advanced to the Chinese border, however, Stalin maneuvered his communist Chinese allies into rescuing the communist regime in North Korea and driving the South Korean and U.N. forces back to the old boundary. Across the Korean isthmus, communist and American-led U.N. troops waged a seesaw war. The fighting continued until 1953, when an armistice divided the country at roughly the same spot as at the start of the war. Nothing had been gained. Losses, however, included 33,000 Americans, at least 250,000 Chinese, and up to 3 million Koreans.

The Korean War energized America's anticommunist commitments and spurred a rapid increase in NATO forces. U.S. policy shifted because Japan now was seen as a bulwark against communism. Although Japan renounced war in its postwar constitution, a 1951 treaty with the United States stipulated that the Japanese could rearm for self-defense and that American troops could be stationed in Japan. Moreover, the United States resolved to rebuild Japanese economic power. Like West Germany, Japan went from being the enemy in World War II to being a valued ally during the cold war.

DECOLONIZATION

> ⟶ *To what extent did decolonization involve large-scale violence?*

The unsettling of all empires during the war inspired colonial peoples to reconsider their political futures. Rid of the Japanese, the liberated Asian territories had no desire to restore colonial or quasi-colonial rule. Africa, too, felt increasing pressure for decolonization. A weakened Europe emboldened anticolonial leaders to dismantle the European order and create a world of their own.

The process of **decolonization** and nation building followed three patterns: civil war, negotiated independence, and incomplete decolonization. The first occurred principally in China, where the ousting of Japanese occupiers led to a civil war that ended in a communist triumph. Here, national independence was associated with a Socialist revolution. The second pattern, involving negotiated independence, played out in India and much of Africa. Algeria and South Africa illustrate the third pattern, in which the presence of sizeable European settler populations complicated the path from colony to nation.

THE CHINESE REVOLUTION

Although the Japanese defeat left China politically independent, some of China's leaders, notably the Chinese communists, rejected any restoration of the prewar regime. Their campaign reflected a worldwide movement to achieve autonomy from the western powers. Painfully aware of China's long semicolonial subordination, the communists vowed to free themselves from colonialism.

The Long March. In China, the Long March of 1934–1935 has been commemorated by the ruling communists as one of the most heroic episodes in the party's history. This picture shows communist partisans crossing the snow-covered mountains in the western province of Sichuan in 1935. Despite their efforts, the ranks of the party were decimated by the end of the 6,000-mile journey from the southeastern to the northwestern part of the country—fewer than one in eight reached their destination.

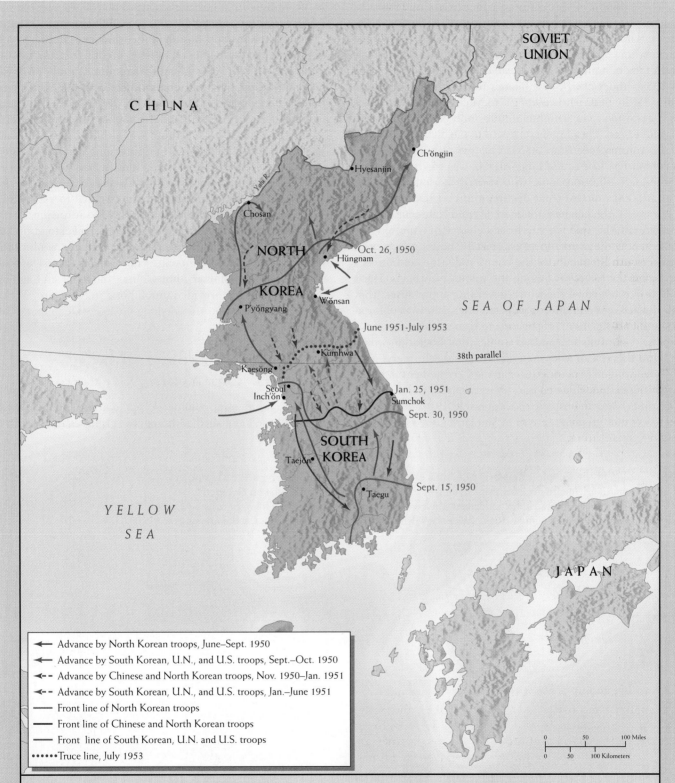

MAP 20-4 THE KOREAN WAR

The Korean War was an early confrontation between the capitalist and communist blocs during the cold war era. What were the dates of each side's farthest advance into the other side's territory? Why was this peninsula strategically important? According to your reading, how did the outcome of the war shape political affairs in East Asia for the next several decades?

The triumph of the Chinese communists in 1949 had been in the making for decades. Back in 1927, Chiang Kai-shek's Nationalist regime had driven outgunned communist forces from China's cities into remote, mountainous refuges. There, the communists had established bases called soviets. In 1934, under attack by Chiang's forces, the communists, led by **Mao Zedong,** (1893–1976), abandoned their bases and undertook an arduous 6,000-mile journey through rugged terrain. They finally retreated to the distant northwest of the country (see Map 20-5). This great escape, glorified in communist lore as the Long March, was costly: of the approximately 80,000 people who started the journey, fewer than 10,000 reached their destination. Fortunately for the communists, the Japanese invasion diverted Nationalist troops and offered Mao and the survivors a chance to regroup.

When the Japanese invaders seized China's major cities but were unable to control the countryside, the communists expanded their support among the vast peasantry. As Mao's followers established their own governing apparatuses, they emphasized rent reduction, graduated taxes, cooperative farming, and anti-Japanese propaganda to gain popular support.

The communists promised women that liberation would apply to them, too. Like many anticolonial reformers, Mao regarded women's emancipation as a key component in building a new nation, since he considered their oppression to be both unjust and an obstacle to progress. In 1931, a new marital law, a more radical version of similar legislation enacted by the Nationalists, forbade arranged marriages and allowed either partner to initiate divorce proceedings.

The communist expansion in the rural areas during World War II swelled its membership from 40,000 in 1937 to over a million in 1945. After Japan's surrender, China's civil war between nationalists and communists resumed. But communist forces now had the numbers, the guns (mostly supplied by the Soviet Union), and the popular support to assault Nationalist strongholds. By contrast, although the Nationalist government had weapons and financing from the United States, as well as control of the cities, it had not recovered from its defeat at the hands of the Japanese. No match for the invigorated communists, the nationalists fled to establish a rival Chinese state on the island of Taiwan.

In 1949, Mao proclaimed that China had "stood up" to the world and had experienced a "great people's revolution." Subsequently, many of his ventures proved disastrous failures (see later in this chapter), but China's model of an ongoing people's revolution provided much hope in the Third World. (See Primary Source: Mao Zedong on "New Democracy.")

NEGOTIATED INDEPENDENCE IN INDIA AND AFRICA

In India and most of colonial Africa, gaining independence involved little bloodshed, although the aftermaths were often

The Founding of the People's Republic of China. (*Left*) Mao Zedong standing atop the reviewing stand at Tiananmen Square declares the founding of the People's Republic of China on October 1, 1949. Although most Chinese knew little about the communist party, many had high hopes for a new, independent, and liberated China. (*Right*) With flags flying, the crowd celebrates the dawn of a new era.

MAP 20-5   THE LONG MARCH, 1934–1935

During the Long March, which took place during the struggle for power between the Guomindang (Nationalists) and the communists within China, communist forces traveled over 6,000 miles to save their lives and their movement. What route did the communist forces take? Why did the communists take this particular route? How did this movement affect the outcome of this internal struggle in the long run?

MAO ZEDONG ON "NEW DEMOCRACY"

Many twentieth-century Chinese political and intellectual leaders, including the communists, believed that the rejuvenation of China required changing its culture. The key question was what to embrace and what to discard. Here we find Mao in 1940 explaining the New-Democratic culture—nationalistic, scientific, and mass-based—that he regarded as a transitional stage to communism. He cautions against the wholesale importation of western values and practices, including Marxism, and emphasizes instead the specific conditions of the Chinese revolution.

New-Democratic culture is national. It opposes imperialist oppression and upholds the dignity and independence of the Chinese nation. . . . China should absorb on a large scale the progressive cultures of foreign countries as an ingredient for her own culture; in the past we did not do enough work of this kind. We must absorb whatever we today find useful, not only from the present socialist or New-Democratic cultures of other nations, but also from the older cultures of foreign countries, such as those of the various capitalist countries in the age of enlightenment. However, we must treat these foreign materials as we do our food, which should be chewed in the mouth, submitted to the working of the stomach and intestines, mixed with saliva, gastric juice, and intestinal secretions, and then separated into essence to be absorbed and waste matter to be discarded—only thus can food benefit our body; we should never swallow anything raw or absorb it uncritically.

So-called wholesale Westernization is a mistaken viewpoint. China has suffered a great deal in the past from the formalist absorption of foreign things. Likewise, in applying Marxism to China, Chinese Communists must fully and properly unite the universal truth of Marxism with the specific practice of the Chinese revolution; that is to say,

the truth of Marxism must be integrated with the characteristics of the nation and given a definite national form before it can be useful; it must not be applied subjectively as a mere formula. . . .

Communists may form an anti-imperialist and anti-feudal united front for political action with certain idealists and even with religious followers, but we can never approve of their idealism or religious doctrines. A splendid ancient culture was created during the long period of China's feudal society. To clarify the process of development of this ancient culture, to throw away its feudal dross, and to absorb its democratic essence is a necessary condition for the development of our new national culture and for the increase of our national self confidence; but we should never absorb anything and everything uncritically.

→ *How does Mao expect to integrate Marxism with the Chinese revolution?*

→ *What does Mao think of China's "splendid ancient culture"? In this regard, how does he differ from previous rulers of China?*

SOURCE: Mao Zedong, *Selected Works*, in *Sources of Chinese Tradition*, 2nd ed., vol. 2, edited by Wm. Theodore de Bary and Richard Lufrano (New York: Columbia University Press, 2000), pp. 422–23.

---

extremely violent. The British, realizing that they could no longer rule India without coercion, bowed to the inevitable and withdrew. Much the same happened in Africa, even though British and French colonial officials knew that African territories were much less ready for independence than India.

INDIA   Unlike China, India achieved political independence without an insurrection. But it did veer dangerously close to civil war. As anticolonial elites in the Indian National Congress Party negotiated a peaceful transfer of power from British rule, they disagreed about what kind of state an

independent India should have. Should it, as Gandhi wished, be a nonmodern utopia of self-governing village communities, or should it emulate western and Soviet models with the goal of establishing a modern nation-state? Even more pressing was the question of relations between a Hindu majority and the Muslim minority.

For the most part, the congress leadership retained tight control over the mass movement that it had mobilized in the 1920s and 1930s. Even Gandhi hesitated to leave the initiative to the common people, believing that they had not yet assimilated the doctrine of nonviolence. Accordingly, Gandhi and the leadership worked hard to convince the British that they, the middle-class leaders, spoke for the nation. At the same time, the threat of a mass peasant uprising with radical aims (as was occurring in China) encouraged the British to transfer power quickly.

As negotiations moved forward, Hindu-Muslim unity deteriorated. Whose culture would define the new nation? The Indian nationalism that had existed in the late nineteenth century reflected the culture of the Hindu majority. Yet this movement masked the multiplicity of regional, linguistic, caste, and class differences *within* the Hindu community, just as Muslim movements that arose in reaction to Hindu-dominated Indian nationalism overlooked divisions within their own ranks. Now the prospect of defining "India" created a grand contest between newly self-conscious communities. Riots broke out between Hindus and Muslims in 1946, which increased the mutual distrust between congress and Muslim League leaders. The leader of the Muslim League demanded that British India be partitioned into separate Hindu and Muslim states if there were no constitutional guarantees for Muslims. The specter of civil war haunted the proceedings, as outgoing colonial rulers decided to divide the subcontinent into two states: India and Pakistan.

On August 14, 1947, Pakistan gained independence from Britain; a day later, India did the same. The euphoria of decolonization, however, drowned in a frenzy of brutality. Shortly after independence, up to 1 million Hindus and Muslims killed one another. Fearing further violence, 12 million Hindus and Muslims left their homes to relocate in the new countries where they would be in the majority. Distraught by the rampage, Gandhi fasted, refusing sustenance until the killings stopped. The violence abated. This was perhaps Gandhi's finest hour. But animosity and fanaticism remained. Less than six months later, a Hindu zealot shot Gandhi dead as he walked to a prayer meeting.

Had Gandhi lived, he would not have approved of the direction independent India took. He had already voiced disapproval of industrialization and of equipping the Indian state with army and police forces. But India's first prime minister and leader of the Indian National Congress Party, Jawaharlal Nehru, and other leaders in the congress were committed to state-directed modernization. Inspired by Soviet-style planned development, on the one hand, and by western democratic institutions, on the other, Nehru sought a "socialistic pattern of society" based on a mixed economy of public and private sectors. Declaring that he wanted to give India the "garb of modernity," Nehru asked Indians to consider hydroelectric dams and steel plants the temples of modern India. His watchwords were education and economic development, believing that these would loosen the hold of religion on Muslims and encourage them to join the national mainstream. He also hoped that the diminished role of religious traditions would improve women's condition. Such a vision allowed Nehru, until his death in 1964, to guide Indian modernization

Jawaharlal Nehru. Nehru, the leader of independent India, sought to combine a "mixed economy" of private and public sectors with democracy to chart an independent path for India. The photo shows him at a public meeting in 1952.

along a third path. (See Primary Source: Nehru on Building a Modern Nation.)

AFRICA FOR AFRICANS   Shortly after Indian independence, most African states also gained their sovereignty. Except for southern Africa, where minority white rule persisted, the old colonial states ceded to indigenous rulers. One reason for this rapid decolonization was the fact that nationalist movements had made gains during the interwar period. These years had taught a generation of nationalists to seek wider support for their political parties. World War II, then, swelled the ranks of anticolonial political parties, as many African soldiers expected tangible rewards for serving in imperial armies.

The postwar years also saw throngs of Africans flock to the cities in search of a better life. As expanding educational systems produced a wave of primary and secondary school graduates, these educated young people and other new urban dwellers became disgruntled when attractive employment opportunities were not forthcoming. The three groups—former servicemen, the urban unemployed or underemployed, and the educated—led the nationalist agitation that began in the late 1940s and early 1950s (see Map 20-6).

Faced with rising nationalist demands, European powers agreed to decolonize. The new world powers, the Soviet Union and the United States, for their own reasons, also favored decolonization. Thus decolonization in most of Africa

Primary Source

NEHRU ON BUILDING A MODERN NATION

The following excerpt, written by Jawaharlal Nehru in 1940, documents the centrality of planning in the desire to build a modern nation. Although the idea of planning derived from the Soviet experience, Nehru did not want India to adopt communism. He saw planned development as a scientific instrument for achieving rapid economic growth and fundamental social changes. Planning would avoid the excesses and inequalities of capitalism and provide a "third way"—equally distanced from both communism and capitalism.

The octopus of war grips and strangles the world and the energy of mankind is more and more directed to destroying what man has built up with infinite patience and labour. Yet it is clear that war by itself cannot solve any problem. It is by conscious, constructive and planned effort alone that national and international problems can be solved. In India many people thought, with reason, that it was premature to plan, so long as we did not have the power to give effect to our planning. The political and economic freedom of India was a prerequisite to any planning, and till this was achieved our national and international policy would continue to be governed, as heretofore, in the interests of the City of London and other vested interests. And yet we started, wisely I think, a National Planning Committee and we are trying, even in these days of world conflict and war, to draw up a picture of planned society in the free India of the future.

Our immediate problem is to attack the appalling poverty and unemployment of India and to raise the standards of our people. That means vastly greater production which must be allied to juster and more equitable distribution, so that the increased wealth may spread out among the people. That means a rapid growth of industry, scientific agriculture and the social services, all co-ordinated together, under more or less state control, and directed towards the betterment of the people as a whole. The resources of India are vast and if wisely used should yield rich results in the near future.

We do not believe in a rigid autarchy, but we do want to make India self-sufficient in regard to her needs as far as this is possible. We want to develop international trade, importing articles which we cannot easily produce and exporting such articles as the rest of the world wants from us. We do not propose to submit to the economic imperialism of any other country or to impose our own on others. We believe that nations of the world can co-operate together in building a world economy which is advantageous for all and in this work we shall gladly co-operate. But this economy cannot be based on the individual profit motive, nor can it subsist within the framework of an imperialist system. It means a new world order, both politically and economically, and free nations cooperating together for their own as well as the larger good.

→ *According to Nehru, what are the key problems that India faces?*

→ *How does Nehru's vision of India compare to Gandhi's (see Chapter 19, p. 737)?*

SOURCE: Jawaharlal Nehru, "A Note to the Members of the National Planning Committee," May 1, 1940, in *Jawaharlal Nehru: An Anthology,* edited by Sarvepalli Gopal (Delhi: Oxford University Press, 1980), pp. 306–7.

was a rapid and relatively sedate affair. In 1957, the Gold Coast (renamed Ghana) under Prime Minister Kwame Nkrumah became tropical Africa's first independent state. Other British colonial territories followed in rapid succession, so that by 1963 all of British-ruled Africa except for southern Rhodesia was independent. In these former colonial possessions, charismatic nationalist leaders became the authorities to whom the British ceded power. Many of the new rulers had obtained western educations but were committed to returning Africa to the Africans.

Decolonization in much of French-ruled Africa followed a similarly smooth path, although the French were initially resistant. Believing their own culture to be unrivaled, the French treated decolonization as assimilation: instead of negotiating independence, they tried first to accord fuller voting rights to their colonial subjects, even allowing Africans and

→ *To what extent did decolonization involve large-scale violence?*

Legend:
- Date of independence
- Former colonial power
  - British
  - French
  - Portuguese
  - Spanish
  - Belgian
  - Italian
  - Former German colony, mandate of League of Nations after W.W. I
  - Independent state
  - ✳ Anti-colonial revolt or war since 1945

MOROCCO 1956
ATLAS MOUNTAINS
TUNISIA 1956
MEDITERRANEAN SEA
ALGERIA 1962 ✳ 1954–1962
LIBYA 1951
Suez crisis ✳ 1956
EGYPT 1922 with severe restrictions 1954 British withdraw troops
WESTERN SAHARA 1975
SAHARA DESERT
NUBIAN DESERT
RED SEA
MAURITANIA 1960
MALI 1960
NIGER 1960
CHAD 1960
SUDAN 1956
ERITREA 1993
Nile R.
SENEGAL 1960
Senegal R.
GAMBIA 1965
Gambia R.
GUINEA BISSAU 1974 ✳ 1961–1974
GUINEA 1958
UPPER VOLTA (BURKINA FASO) 1960
Niger R.
DAHOMEY (BENIN) 1960
NIGERIA 1960
DJIBOUTI 1977
ETHIOPIAN HIGHLANDS
SIERRA LEONE 1961
LIBERIA
IVORY COAST 1960
GHANA 1957
TOGO 1960
CENTRAL AFRICAN REPUBLIC 1960
CAMEROON 1960
ETHIOPIA
SOMALIA 1960 ✳ 1950–1960
EQUATORIAL GUINEA 1968
SÃO TOMÉ & PRINCIPE 1975
GABON 1960
CONGO R.
Congo Basin
RWANDA 1962
UGANDA 1962
KENYA 1963 ✳ 1952–1957
CONGO 1960
CONGO (ZAIRE) 1960
BURUNDI 1962
Lake Victoria
TANZANIA (TANGANYIKA) 1961
INDIAN OCEAN
Lake Tanganyika
ATLANTIC OCEAN
ANGOLA 1975 ✳ 1961–1974
Lake Nyasa
ZAMBIA 1964
MALAWI 1964
Zambezi
SOUTH-WEST AFRICA (NAMIBIA) (controlled by South Africa) 1990 ✳ 1966–1990
RHODESIA 1965
ZIMBABWE 1980 ✳ 1965–1980
BOTSWANA 1966
KALAHARI DESERT
MOZAMBIQUE 1975 ✳ 1964–1974
MADAGASCAR 1960 ✳ 1947–1948
SOUTH AFRICA 1910–1961 1994 whole population votes ✳ 1948–1994
SWAZILAND 1968
LESOTHO 1966

0   500   1000 Miles
0   500   1000 Kilometers

MAP 20-6   DECOLONIZATION IN AFRICA

African decolonization occurred after World War II, largely in the 1950s, 1960s, and 1970s. Find at least four areas that won independence in the 1950s, and identify which former colonial power had ruled each area. What areas took longer to gain independence? According to your reading, what problems and tensions contributed to this uneven process across Africa?

Kwame Nkrumah. West Africa's leading nationalist, Kwame Nkrumah mobilized the peoples of the Gold Coast and, through electoral successes, convinced the British to confer independence on the Gold Coast, which was renamed Ghana in 1957.

Asians to send delegates to the French National Assembly. In the end, however, the French electorate had no desire to share the privileges of French citizenship with overseas populations. Nor did African leaders wish to submerge their identities in a Greater France. Thus, France dissolved its political ties with French West Africa and French Equatorial Africa in 1960, having given protectorates in Morocco and Tunisia their independence in 1956. Algeria, always considered an integral part of France overseas, was a different matter. Its independence did not come quickly or easily (see below).

The leaders of African independence believed that Africa's precolonial traditions would enable the region to move from colonialism right into a special African form of socialism, escaping the ravages of capitalism. Without rejecting western

Léopold Sédar Senghor. Senghor combined sharp intellect with political savvy. An accomplished poet and essayist and one of the founders of the Negritude movement among Francophone intellectuals, he became Senegal's first president when the country gained full independence in 1960.

culture completely, they vaunted the so-called African personality, exemplified by the idea of "Negritude" developed by Senegal's first president, Léopold Sédar Senghor. Negritude, they claimed, was steeped in communal solidarities and able to embrace social justice and equality, while rejecting the naked individualism that Africans felt lay at the core of European culture. (See Primary Source: Senghor's View of Political Independence.)

VIOLENT AND INCOMPLETE DECOLONIZATIONS

Although transfers of power in most of Africa and Asia ultimately occurred peacefully, there were notable exceptions. In Palestine, Algeria, and southern Africa, the presence of European immigrant groups created violent conflicts that aborted any peaceful transfer of power—or left the process incomplete. In Vietnam, the process was also violent and delayed, partly because of France's desire to reimpose colonial control and partly from the power politics of cold war competition.

PALESTINE, ISRAEL, EGYPT In Palestine, Arabs and Jews had been on a collision course since the end of World War I. Before that war, a group of European Jews, known as Zionists, had argued that only an exodus from existing states to their place of origin in Palestine could lead to Jewish self-determination. **Zionism** combined a yearning to realize the ancient biblical injunction to return to the holy lands with a fear of anti-Semitism and anguish over increasing Jewish assimilation. Zionists wanted to create a Jewish state, and they won a crucial victory during World War I when the British government, under the Balfour Declaration, promised a homeland for the Jews in Palestine. This encouraged the immigration of Jewish settlers into the country. But the Balfour Declaration also guaranteed the rights of indigenous Palestinians.

The immigration of Jews to Palestine set the stage for a conflict between fledgling Jewish and Arab nations. Contrary to Zionist assertions, a substantial Arab population already lived in Palestine, and the Palestinian Arabs joined with their Arab neighbors to oppose a Jewish political entity. In due course, they proclaimed their own right to self-determination as Palestinians. When Hitler came to power in Germany, European Jews looked to Palestine as a haven; but the British, mindful of Arab opposition and the Arab states' strategic oil wealth, vacillated over supporting Zionist demands for greater immigration. How to reconcile the conflicting aspirations of Jewish settlers and indigenous Palestinians was not clear to anyone. Moreover, the pressure to allow more immigration increased after World War II as hundreds of thousands of concentration camp survivors clamored for entry into Palestine. Arabs resented the presence of Jews, who continued to

SENGHOR'S VIEW OF POLITICAL INDEPENDENCE

One of the most striking visions of African independence as a "third way" came from the pen of Léopold Sédar Senghor, a Senegalese nationalist leader who became the first president of Senegal. The first excerpt, drawn from an essay published in 1959, differentiates the socialism of Africa from Marxism. The second excerpt, taken from a speech delivered in 1961, develops the idea of "Negritude," or black civilization, markedly different from but not inferior to European cultural forms.

African Socialism

In the respective programs of our former parties, all of us used to proclaim our attachment to socialism. This was a good thing, but it was not enough. Most of the time, we were satisfied with stereotyped formulas and vague aspirations, which we called scientific socialism—as if socialism did not mean a return to original sources. Above all, we need to make an effort to rethink the basic texts in the light of the Negro African realities. . . .

Can we integrate Negro African cultural values, especially religious values, into socialism? We must answer that question once and for all with an unequivocal "Yes." . . .

We are not Communists for a practical reason. The anxiety for human dignity, the need for freedom—man's freedom, the freedoms of collectivities—which animate Marx's thought and provide its revolutionary ferment—this anxiety and this need are unknown to Communism, whose major deviation is Stalinism. The "dictatorship of the proletariat," which was to be only temporary, becomes the dictatorship of the part and state by perpetuating itself. . . .

The paradox of socialistic construction in Communist countries—in the Soviet Union at least—is that it increasingly resembles capitalistic construction in the United States, the American way of life, with high salaries, refrigerators, washing machines, and television sets. And it has less art and freedom of thought. Nevertheless, we shall not be won over by a regime of liberal capitalism and free enterprise. We cannot close our eyes to segregation, although the government combats it; nor can we accept the elevation of material success to a way of life.

We stand for a middle course, for a *democratic socialism* which goes so far as to integrate spiritual values, a socialism which ties in with the old ethical current of the French socialists. . . . In so far as they are idealists, they fulfill the requirements of the Negro African soul, the requirements of men of all races and countries. . . .

A third revolution is taking place, as a reaction against capitalistic and Communistic materialism—one that will integrate moral, if not religious, values with the political and economic contributions of the two great revolutions. In this revolution, the colored peoples, including the Negro African, must play their part; they must bring their contribution to the construction of the new planetary civilization.

"What Is Negritude?"

Assimilation was a failure; we could assimilate mathematics or the French language, but we could never strip off our black skins or root out black souls. And so we set out on a fervent quest for the "holy grail": our collective soul. And we came upon it. . . .

Negritude is the *whole complex of civilized values—cultural, economic, social, and political—which characterize the black peoples*, or, more precisely, the Negro-African world. All these values are essentially informed by intuitive reason, because this sentient reason, the reason which comes to grips, expresses itself emotionally, through that self-surrender, that coalescence of subject and object; through myths, by which I mean the archetypal images of the collective soul; and, above all, through primordial rhythms, synchronized with those of the cosmos. In other words, the sense of communion, the gift of mythmaking, the gift of rhythm, such are the essential elements of Negritude, which you will find indelibly stamped on all the works and activities of the black man.

→ *What is African socialism for Senghor?*
→ *In what way, according to Senghor, does Negritude express Negro Africans' "collective soul"?*

SOURCE: Léopold Sédar Senghor, excerpts from *African Socialism* (New York: American Society of African Culture, 1959), trans. Mercer Cook. Reprinted by permission of Moorland-Spingarn Research Center, Howard University, Washington, DC.

The Creation of the State of Israel. Standing beneath a portrait of Theodore Herzl, the founder of the Zionist movement, David Ben Gurion, the first Israeli prime minister, proclaimed independence for the state of Israel in May 1948.

buy land and displace farmers who had lived on the land for generations.

In 1947, after the British announced that they would leave negotiations over the area's fate to the United Nations, that body voted to partition Palestine into Arab and Jewish territories. The Arab states rejected the partition, and the Zionist Agency only reluctantly accepted it. When the British withdrew their troops in 1948, a Jewish provisional government proclaimed the establishment of the state of Israel. Although the Jews were delighted to have an independent state, they were unhappy about its small size, its indefensible borders, and the fact that it did not include all the lands that had belonged to ancient Israel. For their part, the Palestinians were shocked at the partition, and they looked to their better-armed Arab neighbors to regain the territories set aside for the new state of Israel.

The ensuing **Arab-Israeli War** of 1948–1949 shattered the legitimacy of Arab ruling elites. Arab states entered the war poorly prepared to take on the well-run and enthusiastically supported Israeli Defense Force. By the time the United Nations finally negotiated a truce, Israel had extended its boundaries and more than 1 million Palestinians had become refugees in surrounding Arab countries.

Embittered by this defeat, a group of young officers in the Egyptian army plotted to overthrow a regime that they felt had not yet shed its colonial subordination. Although Egypt had acquired legal independence from Britain in 1936, the plotters believed that incompetent leaders were squandering the nation's sovereignty. One of the officers, Gamal Abdel Nasser, became the head of a secret organization of junior military officers—the Free Officers Movement. These men

had ties with communists and other dissident groups, including the Muslim Brotherhood, which favored a return to Islamic rule.

Nasser and his colleagues devised a program to address the maladies of Egyptian society. First they launched a successful coup in 1952, forcing the king to abdicate and leave the country. Then they enacted a land reform scheme that deprived large estate owners of lands in excess of 200 acres and redistributed these lands to the landless and smallholders, who instantly became ardent supporters of the new regime. The new regime also dissolved the parliament, banned political parties, and enacted a new constitution. Moreover, it banned the communists and the Muslim Brotherhood and stripped the old elite of its wealth.

Israel now feared that a strengthened Egypt would become the focal point of Arab opposition to the Zionist state. In 1956, shortly after Nasser nationalized the Suez Canal Company (an Egyptian company, mainly run by French businessmen and experts), the Israelis, the British, and the French invaded Egypt. They seized territory along the Suez Canal but had to agree to a ceasefire before they could control all of it. Opposition by the United States and the Soviet Union forced them to withdraw, providing Nasser with a spectacular diplomatic triumph. As Egyptian forces reclaimed the canal, Nasser's reputation as leader of the Arab world soared. He became the chief symbol of a pan-Arab nationalism that swept across the Middle East and North Africa and especially through the camps of Palestinian refugees.

The Anglo-Egyptian Treaty. The photo shows Egyptian president Nasser signing the Anglo-Egyptian Treaty with the British minister of state in 1954. The agreement ended the stationing of British troops on Egyptian soil and called for the withdrawal of British troops stationed at the Suez Canal military base. But shortly after the last British soldiers left Egypt in early 1956, Britain invaded the country in a vain effort to block Nasser's nationalization of the Suez Canal Company and to remove the Egyptian leader from power.

THE ALGERIAN WAR OF INDEPENDENCE The appeal of Arab nationalism was particularly strong in Algeria, where a sizeable French settler population (the *colons*) stood in the way of a complete and peaceful decolonization. Indeed, French leaders claimed that Algeria was an integral part of France, an overseas department that was legally no different from Brittany or Normandy. Although the *colons* were a minority, they held the best land and lived in wealthy residential quarters in the major cities. Also, although all residents of Algeria were supposedly entitled to the same rights as the French citizenry, in fact the *colons* reserved these advantages to themselves.

As elsewhere, anticolonial nationalism in Algeria gathered force after World War II. When the French military responded with harsh countermeasures, the independence movement gained strength. The Front de Libération Nationale (FLN), the leading nationalist party, used violence to provoke its opponents and to make the local population choose between supporting the nationalist cause or the *colons*. The full-fledged revolt that erupted in 1954 pitted FLN troops and guerrillas against thousands of French troops. Atrocities and terrorist acts occurred on both sides.

The war dragged on for eight years, at a cost of perhaps 300,000 lives. At home, French society was torn asunder, for many French citizens had accepted the myth that Algeria was not a colonial territory but part of France itself. The *colons* insisted that they had emigrated to Algeria in response to their government's promises and that yielding power to the nationalists would be a betrayal. After an insurrection led by *colons* and army officers brought down the French government in 1958, the new French president, Charles de Gaulle, negotiated a peace accord.

Shortly after handing over power to FLN leaders, more than 300,000 *colons* left Algeria. By late 1962, over nine-tenths of the European population had departed. At independence, then, Algeria had a population mix no different from that of the other North African countries.

EASTERN AND SOUTHERN AFRICA The bloody conflict in Algeria highlights a harsh reality of African decolonization: the presence of European settlers prevented the smooth transfer of power. Even in British-ruled Kenya, where the European settler population had never been large, a violent war of independence broke out between European settlers and African nationalists. Employing secrecy and intimidation, the Kikuyu peoples, Kenya's largest ethnic group, organized a revolt. This uprising, which began in 1952, forced the British to fly in troops to suppress it, but ultimately the British government conceded independence to Kenya in 1963. Decolonization proved even more difficult in the southern third of the continent, where Portuguese Angola, Portuguese Mozambique, and British Southern Rhodesia (present-day Zimbabwe) did not gain independence until the 1970s.

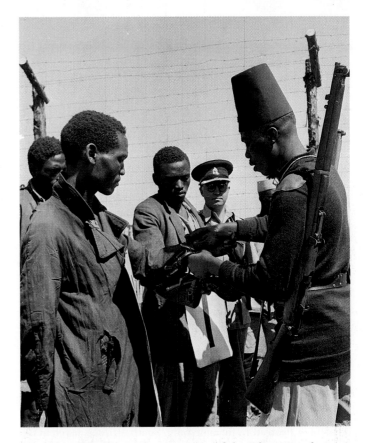

Mau Mau Rebellion. A large segment of the Kikuyu population rose up against the British colonial occupation of Kenya. This revolt, which began in 1952, was finally suppressed by British arms and Kikuyu "loyalists." Nonetheless, the Mau Mau Revolt led to Kenya's independence from British rule.

Women played vital roles in these decolonization struggles. In Egypt, for example, the leading nationalists were all men, but they gained crucial support from educated and modernizing women, many of whom organized impressive demonstrations on their behalf. The wife of Sa'd Zaghlul, Egypt's most dynamic nationalist figure after World War I, gained a large following and a reputation as mother of the nation. Moreover, during Kenya's battle against British colonial rule, women supplied the fighters with food, medical resources, and information about the British. Those who were caught ended up in concentration camps and suffered brutal treatment from their prison guards. Yet, once independence was achieved, most women reverted to their traditional subordinate status.

South Africa, which held the continent's largest and wealthiest settler population (a mixture of Afrikaan- and English-speaking peoples of European descent), defied black majority rule longer than other African states. After winning the elections of 1948, the Afrikaner-dominated National Party enacted an extreme form of racial segregation known as **apartheid**. Under apartheid, laws stripped Africans, Indians,

Apartheid Protest. In Johannesburg, South Africans march in the street to protest the new restrictions on African citizens, soon to be known worldwide as apartheid, implemented by the white minority government of Daniel Malan. During the Malan administration (1948–1954), informal discrimination was systematically made law, and all electoral, housing, civil, and employment rights of African citizens were dismantled.

and colored persons (those of mixed descent) of their few political rights. Racial mixing of any kind was forbidden, and schools were strictly segregated. The Group Areas Act, passed in 1950, divided the country into separate racial and tribal areas and required Africans to live in their own racial areas, called homelands. Pass laws prohibited Africans from traveling outside their homelands without special work or travel passes.

The ruling party tolerated no protest. Nelson Mandela, one of the leaders of the African National Congress (ANC) who campaigned for an end to discriminatory legislation, was repeatedly harassed, detained, and tried by the government, even though he urged peaceful resistance. After the Sharpeville massacre in 1960, in which police killed demonstrators who were peacefully protesting the pass laws, Mandela and the ANC decided to oppose the apartheid regime with violence. Subsequently the government announced a state of emergency, banned the ANC, and arrested those of its leaders who had not fled the country or gone underground.

A South African court sentenced Mandela to life imprisonment. Other black leaders were tortured or beaten to death. Despite such human rights violations, the whites retained external support. After all, through the 1950s and 1960s, western powers (especially the United States) saw South Africa as a bulwark against the spread of communism in Africa.

VIETNAM   The same concern to contain communism also drew the United States into support for a regime in South Vietnam. Vietnam had come under French rule in the 1880s, and by the 1920s approximately 40,000 Europeans were living among and ruling over roughly 19 million Vietnamese. To promote an export economy of rice, mining, and rubber, the colonial rulers granted vast land concessions to French companies and local collaborators, while leaving large numbers of peasants landless.

The colonial system also generated a new intelligentsia. Primarily schooled in French and Franco-Vietnamese schools, educated Vietnamese worked as clerks, shopkeepers, teachers, and petty officials. Yet they had few opportunities for advancement in the French-dominated colonial system. Thus, discontented, they turned from the traditional ideology of Confucianism to modern nationalism. Vietnamese intellectuals overseas, notably Ho Chi Minh, took the lead in imagining a new Vietnamese nation-state.

Ho had left Vietnam at an early age and found his way to London and Paris. During the interwar period he read the writings of Marx, Engels, and Lenin, and he discovered not only an ideology for opposing French exploitation but also a vision for transforming the common people into a political force. He was a founding member of the French communist party and subsequently founded the Indochinese communist party. After the Japanese occupied Indochina, he traveled to China, embraced the idea of an agrarian revolution, and established the Viet Minh, a liberation force, in 1941. Back in Vietnam, the communist-led Viet Minh became a powerful nationalist organization as it mobilized the peasantry.

When the French tried to restore their rule in Vietnam after Japan's defeat in 1945, Ho appealed to the United States (for whom he had been an intelligence agent during the war) for diplomatic and moral support. His appeals fell on deaf ears, but the Viet Minh declared independence anyway. War with France followed (1946–1954), featuring guerrilla tactics to undermine French positions. The Viet Minh were most successful in the north, but even in the south their campaign bled the French. Finally, in 1954, the anticolonial forces won a decisive military victory. At the Geneva Peace Conference, Vietnam (like Korea) was divided into two zones. Ho controlled the north, while a government with French and American support took charge in the south.

Although the French departed, decolonization in Vietnam was incomplete. North Vietnam supported the Viet Cong—communist guerrillas—who were determined to overthrow

Ho Chi Minh. Ho Chi Minh's formation of the League for the Independence of Vietnam, or Viet Minh, in 1941 set the stage for Ho's rise at the end of World War II. Here he attends a youth rally in October 1955, just over a year after the victory of his forces at Dien Bien Phu, which resulted in the ousting of the French from Vietnam.

the noncommunist government in South Vietnam and to unite the north and south. Equally determined to contain the spread of communism in Southeast Asia, the United States began smuggling arms to the regime in the south. During the early 1960s, U.S. involvement escalated. In 1965, large numbers of American troops entered the country to fight on behalf of South Vietnam, while communist North Vietnam turned to the Soviet Union for supplies. Over the next several years, the United States sent more and more soldiers. Yet even the deployment of 500,000 troops in the **Vietnam War** could not prevent the spread of communism in Southeast Asia.

Combining anti-imperialist nationalism with a radical land reform program, the communists won crucial support from the peasants. This support enabled Viet Cong insurgents to carry out a fierce guerrilla war against the United States and its South Vietnamese puppet regime. Despite bombing of villages and directing counterinsurgency operations, the United States became mired in an unwinnable war. Faced with antiwar opposition at home and ferocious resistance from the Vietnamese, the U.S. government adopted the policy of "Vietnamization"—that is, placing the responsibility of fighting the communists on the South Vietnamese puppet government. Vietnamization was a convenient fiction spun to enable the United States to withdraw without losing face. In 1975, just two years after the final withdrawal of American troops, the South Vietnamese government collapsed.

THREE WORLDS

→ *What were the successes and failures of each world bloc?*

World War II made the Soviet Union and the United States into superpowers. Possessing nuclear weapons, superior armies, and industrial might, they vied for global influence. As decolonization spread, the two cold war belligerents offered new leaders their models for modernization. On one side, the United States, together with its western European allies and Japan, had developed democratic forms of governance and a dynamic capitalist economy that produced immense quantities of affordable consumer goods. The Soviet Union, on the other side, trumpeted the communist party's egalitarian ideology and its rapid transition from being "backward" to highly industrialized. Both the First World and the Second World expected the decolonized Third World to adopt their models.

The decolonized, however, had their own ideas. With the communist takeover in 1949, China had shrugged off semicolonial status, but Mao soon broke from Soviet direction. Other decolonized nations in Asia and Africa had underdeveloped economies and could not leap into capitalist or communist industrial development. Moreover, in some places decolonization remained incomplete. Most problematic for Third World nations was the expanding cold war. In Europe, First and Second worlds coexisted uneasily alongside one another, but in the Third World the conflict often turned hot—and bloody.

THE FIRST WORLD

As the cold war spread in the early 1950s, western Europe and North America became known as the **First World**, or "the free world." Later on, Japan joined this group. Following the principles of liberal modernism, First World states sought to organize the world on the basis of capitalism and democracy. Yet, in struggling against communism, the free world sometimes aligned with Third World dictators, thereby sacrificing its commitment to freedom and democracy for the sake of political expediency.

WESTERN EUROPE   The reconstruction of western Europe after World War II was a spectacular success. By the late 1950s, most nations' economies there were thriving, thanks in part to massive American economic assistance. Improvements in agriculture were particularly impressive. With increased mechanization and the use of pesticides, fewer farmers were feeding more people. In 1950, for example, each French farmer had produced enough food for seven people; by 1962, one farmer could feed forty. And as industrial production boomed and wages rose, goods that had been luxuries before the war—refrigerators, telephones, automobiles, indoor plumbing—became commonplace. Prosperity allowed governments to expand social welfare systems, such that by the late 1950s education and health care were within the reach of virtually all citizens.

Western Europe's economic recovery blunted the appeal of socialist and communist programs. Moreover, the cold war slowed down efforts to punish Fascists, Nazis, and collaborators. Although war crimes trials brought the conviction of a number of prominent Nazis, the fear was that a complete de-Nazification would deprive Germany of political and economic leaders, leaving it susceptible to communist subversion.

THE UNITED STATES   While Europe lay in ruins, the United States enjoyed economic expansion and a rising standard of living. Americans could afford more consumer goods than ever before—almost always U.S. manufactures. Home ownership became more common, especially in the burgeoning suburbs. Stimulating suburban development was a baby boom that reversed more than a century of declining

birth rates. Indeed, in contrast to the gloomy 1930s, in the 1950s Americans enjoyed unprecedented prosperity.

Yet, even as suburbanites basked in the affluence that they credited to free enterprise, anxieties about the future of the free world abounded. Following the Soviet Union's explosion of an atomic bomb, the Communist Revolution in China, and the outbreak of the Korean War, fear of the communist threat prompted increasingly harsh rhetoric. In fact, anticommunist hysteria led the Republican senator from Wisconsin, Joseph McCarthy, to initiate a campaign to uncover closet communists in the State Department and in Hollywood. Televised congressional hearings broadcast his views to the entire nation. Although by late 1954 the tide had turned against him, McCarthyism persisted in American foreign policy. Now almost all elected officials, not wanting to seem "soft" on communism, voted to spend more money on American armies and armaments.

Postwar American prosperity did not benefit all citizens equally. During the prosperous 1950s, nearly a quarter of the American population lived in poverty. But many African Americans, a group disproportionately trapped below the poverty line, participated in a powerful movement for equal rights and the end of racial segregation. The National Association for the Advancement of Colored People (NAACP) won court victories that mandated the desegregation of

Levittown. In the decades after World War II, the American population shifted from the cities to the suburbs. To satisfy the demand for single-family homes, private developers, assisted by government policies, built thousands of new communities on the outskirts of urban centers. Places like Long Island's Levittown (pictured here), made affordable by the use of standard designs and construction, enabled many middle-class Americans to own their own homes.

Anticommunism. As the cold war heated up, anticommunist fervor swept the United States. Leading the charge against the "communist conspiracy" was Wisconsin senator Joseph McCarthy, pictured here with his aide, the attorney Roy Cohn.

Civil rights movement. The 1955 arrest of Rosa Parks (*left*), for refusing to relinquish her seat on a Montgomery, Alabama, bus, led to a boycott that brought Martin Luther King to prominence and galvanized the challenge to legal racial segregation in the American South. (*Right*) Borrowing from Gandhi's tactics of nonviolent civil disobedience, protesters staged "sit-ins" across the southern United States in the 1950s and early 1960s, as in this photograph of black and white students seated together at a segregated lunch counter in Jackson, Mississippi.

schools. Boycotts, too, became a weapon of the growing **civil rights movement**, with **Martin Luther King Jr.** (1929–1968) leading a successful strike against injustices in the bus system of Montgomery, Alabama. Here and in subsequent campaigns against white supremacy, King borrowed his most effective weapon—the commitment to nonviolent protest and the appeal to conscience—from Gandhi. As the civil rights movement spread, the federal government gradually supported programs for racial equality.

THE JAPANESE "MIRACLE" An impressive triumph for the western liberal capitalist vision was the emergence of Japan as a postwar economic powerhouse. The war had ended with Japan's unconditional surrender in 1945, its dreams of dominating East Asia dashed, and its homeland devastated. As in war-wrecked Europe, socialism and communism were enticing options for rebuilding. Yet by the mid-1970s, Japan, formerly a dictatorship, was a politically stable civilian regime with a thriving economy. As with West Germany, Japan owed some of this momentous change to American military protection, investment, and transfers of technology—benefits of being incorporated into the First World.

Even more important than military protection was economic support. To facilitate recovery, the United States opened its enormous domestic market to Japanese goods. Moreover, because the Americans transferred considerable

technology, Japan rebuilt its devastated industries with more up-to-date equipment than any other country except perhaps West Germany. The Japanese government guided this economic development through directed investment, partnerships with private firms, and protectionist policies. To promote an export-driven economy, the government encouraged its citizens to save, not spend. It also erected import barriers that allowed certain industries to grow without foreign competition. Together, these factors yielded an unprecedented boom from the 1950s into the 1970s.

THE SECOND WORLD

The scourge of World War II and the shadow of the cold war fell heavily on the Soviet Union, which with its satellites in eastern and central Europe as well as Mongolia and North Korea constituted the **Second World**. Having suffered more deaths and more damage than any other industrialized nation, the Soviet Union was determined to insulate itself from future aggression from the West. That meant turning eastern Europe into a bloc of communist buffer states.

THE APPEAL OF THE SOVIET MODEL The Soviet model's egalitarian ideology and success with rapid industrialization made it seem a worthy alternative to capitalism. Here, there was no private property and thus, in Marxist terms, no

ПУСТЬ ЗДРАВСТВУЕТ
И ПРОЦВЕТАЕТ НАША РОДИНА!

Soviet Propaganda. Amid the brick-by-brick reconstruction efforts following World War II, a 1949 Soviet poster depicts a youth in a red scarf with a fatherly Stalin and the slogan "May Our Motherland Live Long and Flourish."

exploitation. Workers "owned" the factories and worked for themselves. The Soviet state promised full employment, boasting that a state-run economy would be immune from upturns and downturns in business cycles. Freedom from exploitation, combined with security, was contrasted with the capitalist model of owners hoarding profits and suddenly firing loyal workers when they were not needed.

The Soviet system touted protections for workers, inexpensive mass transit, paid maternity leave, free health care, and universally available education. Whereas under the tsarist regime less than one-third of the Russian Empire's population had been literate, by the 1950s the literacy rate soared above 80 percent. True, Soviet policies did not provide material abundance of the sort that First World nations were enjoying. But if consumer goods were often scarce, they were always cheap. Likewise, while it sometimes took ten years to obtain a small apartment through waiting lists at work, when one's turn finally came the apartment carried low annual rent and could be passed on to one's children.

Critical to the Soviet system's attractiveness was the fact that few among the population knew how their counterparts lived in the capitalist world. Government censors skewed news about the First World and suppressed unfavorable information about the Soviet Union and the communist bloc. Yet, even when people learned about the prosperity of western Europe and the United States (usually from western films and radio), they still contended that the Soviet Union was the more just society. Theirs, they believed, was a land with no racial or class divisions at all. If members of the Soviet elite lived in privileged circumstances, their luxurious lifestyles were well concealed. Indeed, socialism's internal critics did not typically seek to overthrow the system and restore capitalism. Rather, they wanted the Soviet regime to introduce reforms that would create "socialism with a human face."

REPRESSION OF DISSENT Few outside the Soviet sphere knew just how inhuman Soviet communism was, and few within knew the extent of the brutality. After the war, the leadership tightened its grip. Surviving soldiers who had been prisoners of war in Germany and civilians who had survived being slave laborers for the Germans were sent to special screening camps, simply because they had been abroad; many disappeared. By the time of Stalin's death in 1953, the vast Gulag (labor camp complex) confined several million people, who dug for gold and uranium and survived on hunks of bread and gruel.

Stalin's successors had to face hard questions: What to do with so many prisoners? How to explain the existence of the labor camp system? This problem became acute when strikes rocked the camps. In 1956, the new party leader, Nikita Khrushchev, delivered a speech at a closed session of the Communist Party Congress in which he attempted to separate Stalin's crimes from true communism. The speech was never published in the Soviet Union, but party members distributed it to party organizations abroad. The crimes that Khrushchev revealed came as a terrible shock.

Repercussions were far-reaching. Eastern European leaders interpreted Khrushchev's speech as an endorsement for political liberation and economic experimentation. Right away, Polish intellectuals began a drive to break free from the communist ideological straitjacket. Soon Polish workers organized a general strike in Poznan—first over bread and wages, then against Soviet occupation. Emboldened by these events, Hungarian intellectuals and students held demonstrations demanding an uncensored press, free elections with genuine alternative parties, and the withdrawal of Soviet troops. The Hungarian Party leader joined with the rebels.

But the seeming liberalization promised by Khrushchev's speech proved short-lived. Rather than let eastern Europeans stray or allow the Soviet people to call for changes, the Soviet leadership crushed dissent. In Poland, the security police massacred strikers. In Hungary, tanks from the Soviet Union

The Gulag. The Soviet labor camp system was an integral part of the Soviet economy. At any given time, around three million prisoners labored in camps, like this one in Perm, Siberia, felling timber, building railroads, or digging for gold. Several million more were forced into exile in isolated locales. During World War II, the Gulag population fell drastically, as inmates were sent to certain death at the front or perished from starvation. Between the war's end and Khrushchev's destalinization in the 1950s, the Gulag system reached its peak, with German and Japanese POWs, the deportation of entire nations, and the Soviet internment of its own returnees from German camps.

and other Warsaw Pact members invaded and installed a new government that aimed to smash all "counterrevolutionary" activities. After the revolts, Hungary and Poland did win some economic and cultural autonomy; but unquestionably, the Second World remained very much the dominion of the Soviet Union.

Despite its repressive policies, the Soviet Union was undeniably a superpower. In fact, its status surged after the launching of Sputnik, the first satellite, into space in 1957. Students from Third World countries flocked to the Soviets' excellent education system for training as engineers, scientists, army commanders, and revolutionaries. The updated 1961 communist party program predicted euphorically that within twenty years the Soviet Union would surpass the United States and eclipse the First World.

THE THIRD WORLD

In the 1950s, French intellectuals coined the term **Third World** (*tiers monde*) to describe those countries that, like the "third estate" in the 1789 French Revolution, represented the majority of the population but was oppressed. By the early 1960s, the term characterized a large bloc of countries in Asia, Africa, and Latin America. All had experienced colonial domination and now aimed to create more just societies than those of the First and Second worlds. Their leaders believed

Hungarian Revolt. Khrushchev's secret 1956 speech denouncing Stalin's crimes unintentionally destabilized the communist bloc. Tanks of the Soviet-led Warsaw Pact crossed into Hungary to put down a revolt that year, restoring the Soviet-style system but damaging Soviet prestige. Some American officials and especially American-supported radio had encouraged the Hungarians to rise up but then did nothing to support them, damaging U.S. prestige. The upshot was a turn to "national communism" in the Soviet satellites as a way to promote stability and loyalty.

that they could build strong democratic societies, like those in the West, and promote rapid economic development, as the Soviet Union had done. All this could occur, they felt, without the empty materialism of western capitalism or the state oppression of communist regimes.

The early 1960s were years of heady optimism in the Third World. Ghanaian prime minister Kwame Nkrumah trumpeted pan-Africanism as a way to reach a par with the rest of the world. Egyptian president Gamal Abdel Nasser boasted that his democratic socialism was neither western nor Soviet and that Egypt would remain neutral in the cold war struggle. Indian prime minister Jawaharlal Nehru blended democratic politics and vigorous state planning to promote India's quest for political independence and economic autonomy.

LIMITS TO AUTONOMY Charting a third way proved difficult. Both the Soviets and the Americans saw the Third World as "underdeveloped," and Americans especially wanted to ensure that market structures and private property underlay modernization. The western powers looked to two new instruments of global capitalism, the World Bank and the International Monetary Fund (IMF), to provide crucial economic guidance in the Third World. The World Bank funded loans for projects to lift poor societies out of poverty (such as providing electricity in India and building roads in Indonesia), while the IMF supported the new governments' monetary systems when they experienced economic woes (as in Ghana, Nigeria, and Egypt). Yet both institutions also intruded on these states' autonomy.

Another force that threatened Third World economic autonomy was the multinational corporation. In the rush to acquire advanced technology, Africans, Asians, and Latin Americans struck deals with multinationals to import their know-how. Owned primarily by American, European, and Japanese entrepreneurs, firms such as United Fruit, Firestone, and Volkswagen expanded cash cropping and plantation activities and established manufacturing branches worldwide. But such corporations impeded the growth of indigenous firms. Although the world's nations were more economically interdependent, the West still made the decisions—and reaped most of the profits.

Whether dealing with the West or the Soviet Union, Third World leaders had limited options because neither side welcomed neutral parties. To create more client states, the Soviet Union backed communist insurgencies around the globe, while the United States supported almost any leaders who declared their anticommunism. Indeed, to contain communist expansion, the United States formed a number of military alliances. Following the 1949 creation of NATO, similar regional arrangements took shape in Southeast Asia (SEATO) and in the Middle East (the Baghdad Pact). These organizations brought many Third World nations into American-led alliances and allowed the United States to establish military bases in foreign territories. The Soviet Union countered by positioning its own forces in other Third World countries.

Nowhere was the militarization of Third World countries more threatening to economic development than in Africa. Whereas in the colonial era African states had spent little on military forces, this trend ended abruptly once the states became independent and were drawn into the cold war. Civil wars, like the one that splintered Nigeria between 1967 and 1970, were opportunities for the great powers to wield influence. When the West refused to sell weapons to the Nigerian government so it could suppress the breakaway eastern province of Biafra, the Soviets supplied MIG aircraft and other vital weapons. A similar situation occurred in Egypt, a strategic region to both superpowers. After the founding of Israel, Egypt's new military rulers insisted that their country never again be caught militarily unprepared. Aware of the West's support for Israel, the Egyptians turned to the Soviet bloc. The resulting arms race between Egypt and Israel left the region bristling with modern weaponry.

Thus, Third World nations now confronted "neocolonial" problems. How were they to apply liberal or Socialist models to their own situations? How were they to deal with economic relations that seemed to reduce their autonomy and limit their development? And how might they escape being puppets of the West or the Soviet Union? No wonder Third World nations grew frustrated about prospects for an alternative way to modernity.

By the mid-1960s, as the euphoria of decolonization evaporated and new states became mired in debt and dependency, many Third World nations fell into dictatorship and authoritarian rule. Although some dictators still spoke about forging a third way, they did so mainly to justify their own corrupt regimes. They had forgotten the democratic commitments that were promised at independence. Most also had been drawn into the cold war, the better to extract arms and assistance from one or the other superpower.

REVOLUTIONARIES AND RADICALS   Against the background of blasted expectations, Third World radicalism emerged as a powerful force. Revolutionary movements in the late 1950s and the 1960s sought to transform their societies. But while some radicals seized power, they, too, had trouble cracking the existing world order.

Third World revolutionaries drew on the pioneering writings of Frantz Fanon (1925–1961). While serving as a psychiatrist in French Algeria, Fanon (who was born in a French Caribbean colony) became aware of the psychological damage of European racism. He subsequently joined the Algerian Revolution and became a radical theorist of liberation. His 1961 book *The Wretched of the Earth* urged Third World peoples to achieve catharsis through violence against their European oppressors. The book also scathingly criticized those Third World nationalists who wished merely to replace European masters without making radical social changes.

THE MAOIST MODEL   While Fanon moved people with his writings, others did so by building radical political organizations and undertaking revolutionary social experiments. One model was Mao Zedong. In 1958, Mao introduced the Great Leap Forward—an audacious attempt to unleash the people's energy. Mao's program organized China into 24,000 social and economic units, called communes. Peasants took up industrial production in their own backyards. The campaign aimed to catapult China past the developed countries, but the communes failed to feed the people and the industrial goods were inferior. Thus China took an economic leap backward. Some 20 million subsequently perished from famine and malnutrition, forcing the government to abandon the experiment.

Fearing that China's revolution was losing spirit, in 1966 Mao launched the Great Proletarian Cultural Revolution. This time Mao turned against his associates in the communist party and appealed to China's young people. They enthusiastically responded. Organized into "Red Guards," over 10 million of them journeyed to Beijing to participate in huge

The Cultural Revolution in China. (*Left*) Young women were an important part of the Red Guards during the Cultural Revolution. Here female Red Guards, armed with their "little red books," march in the front row of a parade in the capital city of Beijing under a sign that reads "Rise." (*Right*) In their campaign to cleanse the country of undesirable elements, the Red Guards often turned to public denunciation as a way to rally the crowd. Here a senior provincial party official is made to stand on a chair wearing a dunce's cap, while the young detractors chant slogans and wave their fists in the air.

rallies. Chanting, crying, screaming, and waving the little red book of Mao's quotations, they pledged to cleanse the party of its corrupt elements and to thoroughly remake Chinese society.

With help from the army, the Red Guards set out to rid society of the "four olds"—old customs, old habits, old culture, and old ideas. They ransacked homes, libraries, museums, and temples. They destroyed classical texts, artworks, and monuments. With its rhetoric of struggle against American imperialism and Soviet revisionism, the Cultural Revolution also targeted anything foreign. Knowledge of a foreign language was enough to compromise a person's revolutionary credentials. The Red Guards attacked government officials, party cadres, or just plain strangers in an escalating cycle of violence. Even family members and friends were pressured to denounce one another; all had to prove themselves faithful followers of Chairman Mao. As chaos mounted, in late 1967 the army moved in to quell the disorder and reestablish control. To forestall further disruption, the government created an entire "lost generation" when, between 1967 and 1976, it deprived some 17 million Red Guards and students of their formal education and relocated them to the countryside "to learn from the peasants."

Given the costs of the Great Leap Forward and the Cultural Revolution, many of Mao's revolutionary policies were hard to celebrate. But radicals in much of the Third World were unaware of these costs and found the style of rapid and massive—if deeply undemocratic—uplift of the populace attractive. At least rhetorically, such policies aimed to transform poor countries within a generation.

LATIN AMERICAN REVOLUTION   Most Third World radicals did not go as far as Mao, but they still dreamed of overturning the social order. In Latin America, such dreams excited those who wished to throw off the influence of U.S.-owned multinational corporations and local elites.

Reform programs in Latin America addressed numerous concerns. Economic nationalists urged greater protection for domestic industries and sought to curb the multinationals. Liberal reformers wanted to democratize political systems and redistribute land, lest discontent erupt into full-blown revolutions like China's. But when liberals and nationalists joined forces, as in Guatemala in the 1950s, their reforms met resistance from local conservatives and from the United States. In Guatemala, the banana-producing American multinational United Fruit Company (which was the largest landowner and controlled the country's railroads and its major port) opposed land reform. Still, the progressive and nationalist regime of Jacobo Arbenz persevered with plans for agrarian reform and proposed taking over uncultivated land owned by United Fruit. Despite Arbenz's intention of compensating the company for its land, the U.S. Central Intelligence Agency (CIA) plotted with sectors of the Guatemalan army to put an end to reform, culminating in a coup d'état.

Through moves such as this, the United States warned other governments that Washington would not tolerate assaults on its national interests in what it deemed its backyard.

In Cuba, the failure to address political, social, and economic concerns spurred a revolution. Since the Spanish-American War of 1898, Cuba had been ruled by governments better known for their compliance with U.S. interests than with popular sentiment. In 1933, during the crisis resulting from the Great Depression, Sergeant Fulgencio Batista emerged as a strongman, and in 1952 he led a military coup that deposed a corrupt civilian government and made him dictator.

The Batista dictatorship did little to clean up public affairs, while continuing to serve the wishes of North American investors. Although sugar planters and casino operators prospered, middle- and working-class Cubans did not. The latter demanded a voice in politics and a new moral bond between the people and their government. University students, especially, called for revolution. In 1953, a group of young men and women launched a botched assault on a military garrison. One of the leaders, a law student named Fidel Castro, gave a stirring speech at the rebels' trial, which made him a national hero. After his release from prison in 1955, he fled to Mexico. Several years later, he returned and started organizing guerrilla raids.

Batista's fortunes nose-dived when the U.S. Congress suspended military supplies and aid in response to newspaper reports about his thuggery. Deprived of American support, his regime crumbled in 1958. Entire regiments of his army defected to the rebels. On New Year's Day 1959, Batista announced that he was leaving Cuba. Within days, guerrillas seized the capital.

As **Fidel Castro** began to consolidate power, his regime grew increasingly radical. He elbowed aside rivals and wrested control of the economy from the wealthy elite, who fled to exile. Soon American leaders began to plot his demise. When Castro announced a massive redistribution of land and the nationalization of foreign oil refineries, the United States ended all aid and sealed off the American market to Cuban sugar. Then, in 1961, the CIA mounted an invasion by Cuban exiles, landing at the Bay of Pigs. The invasion not only failed to overthrow Castro but further radicalized his ambitions for Cuba. He now declared himself a socialist and aligned himself with the Soviet Union. (See Global Connections & Disconnections: Radicalizing the Third World: Che Guevara.)

It was over Cuba and its radicalizing revolution that the world came closest to nuclear Armageddon in the Cuban Missile Crisis of 1962. To deter further U.S. attacks, Castro appealed to the Soviet Union to install nuclear weapons in Cuba—a mere ninety miles off the coast of Florida. When U.S. intelligence detected the weapons, President John F. Kennedy ordered a blockade of Cuba just as weapons-bearing Soviet ships were heading toward Havana. For several weeks, the world was paralyzed with anxiety as Kennedy, Khrushchev, and Castro matched threats. In the end, Kennedy succeeded in getting the Soviets to withdraw their nuclear missiles from Cuba.

If radicals could make a revolution ninety miles off the coast of the United States, what did this spell for the rest of the hemisphere? To combat the germ of revolution, the Kennedy administration sent American advisers throughout Latin America to dole out aid, explain how to reform local land systems, and demonstrate the benefits of liberal capitalism. But to most Latin American radicals, these were inadequate band-aids. Instead, inspired by the Cuban Revolution, peasants in Colombia and Venezuela seized estates; workers in Argentina occupied factories. And in Chile, a leftist alliance led by President Salvador Allende triumphed at the ballot box in 1970.

Reacting to revolutionary insurgency, the United States and its allies in the region bolstered their own counterinsurgency program. Working with American advisers, Latin American militaries were trained to root out radicalism. They learned that gaining the support of indigent civilians was the key to defeating the guerrillas. Even Salvador Allende's democratically elected socialist government in Chile was not spared; the CIA and U.S. policymakers aided General Augusto Pinochet's military coup against the regime in 1973 and looked the other way while political opponents were butchered. By 1975, rebel

Fidel Castro and Cuba's National Liberation. The Cuban Revolution of 1958–1959 was a powerful model for many national liberation movements elsewhere in the world. No sooner did Cuban rebels force a break with the United States in 1959 than they discovered that they needed outside support to survive. The Soviet Union, eager to lay a toehold for communism close to the United States, began to provide economic and military subsidies to their Caribbean ally. Here Castro grasps the hand of Nikita Khrushchev atop the Lenin Mausoleum for the May Day parade in 1963.

RADICALIZING THE THIRD WORLD: CHE GUEVARA

The Cuban Revolution was a turning point in the making of the Third World. After 1959, the Castro regime championed liberation for the Third World from the First World and embraced Socialism as a radical solution to underdevelopment. By rejecting the power of capitalist industrial societies, Castro and his followers promoted revolution, not reform, as a way to achieve Third World liberation. The symbol of this new spirit was Castro's closest lieutenant, Ernesto "Che" Guevara (1928–1967).

THE GUERRILLA FIGHTER "El Che" grew up in Argentina and traveled widely around Latin America as a student. Shortly after receiving his medical degree in 1953, he arrived in Guatemala in time to witness the CIA-backed overthrow of the progressive Jacobo Arbenz government. Thereafter, Guevara became increasingly bitter about American influences in Latin America. He joined Castro's forces and helped topple the pro-American regime of Fulgencio Batista in Cuba in 1958. After 1959, he held several posts in the Cuban government but grew restive for more action. Latin America, he felt, should challenge the world power of the United States. Soon his casual military uniform, his patchy beard, his cigar, and his moral energy became legendary symbols of revolt.

The image of the guerrilla fighter as savior appealed to young people worldwide. Che Guevara published a manual in 1960, *Guerrilla Warfare,* on how to mount a successful revolution. Although Mao Zedong and North Vietnamese general Vo Nguyen Giap had also published blueprints for peasant-based revolutions, Che drew on the more recent and successful experiences of the Cuban struggle. He told his radical readers to blend in with the urban and especially the rural poor to create a "people's army" and to strike at the weakest points in the established order. He enjoined men in particular to lead the crusade to show the poor that their misery could be reversed through heroic violence. Women, too, had a role to play in revolution: they could cook for, nurse, and serve as helpmates for fighters. Despite Guevara's radicalism, he did not transcend conventional models of relations between the sexes. Not surprisingly, the image of the armed freedom fighter for Third World liberation appealed mainly to young men.

SPREADING THE IDEA OF REVOLUTION The idea of revolution as a way to overcome underdevelopment and to free Third World societies spread beyond Latin America. Che became Castro's envoy to world meetings and summits of Third World state leaders, where he celebrated the Cuban road to freedom. Soviet premier Nikita Khrushchev recognized the power of Che's message. Che himself exported his model to Africa, seeking to link Africa and Latin America in a common front against American and European capitalism. For example, he led a group of Cuban guerrillas to support Congolese rebels in south-central Africa. Although the expedition failed, Cuban forces remained involved in African struggles into the 1980s.

Returning to Latin America, Che set up his center of operations in highland Bolivia in 1966, among South America's most downtrodden Indians. "We have to create another Vietnam in the Americas with its center in Bolivia," he proclaimed. Guevara did not, however, know the local Indian language, and he had little logistical support. He and his two dozen fighters launched their region-wide war in absolute isolation. Thus it took little time for the Bolivian army and CIA operators to capture the rebels. After a brief interrogation, Bolivian officers ordered that the guerrilla commander be killed on the spot.

Third World governments continued to block radical options just as they had done with Che Guevara's movement. Only in Nicaragua—twenty years after Castro's victory—would rebels ever take control. In Africa and Asia, too, Third World revolution became a rarity. Militaries in Latin America, Asia, and Africa learned to fight guerrillas with new technology and new counterinsurgency techniques. And all too often, poor people found guerrilla commanders as despotic as their governments.

Che Guevara. Ernesto "Che" Guevara, shown here addressing a conference in Uruguay in 1961 at which he denounced U.S. interventions in Latin America, was a chief lieutenant to Cuba's Fidel Castro and a fierce champion of Third World radicalism.

Nor did oil revenues help overcome poverty and dependency in the Third World as a whole. To the contrary, most revenue surpluses from OPEC simply flowed back to First World banks or boosted real-estate holdings in Europe and the United States. Some of it was in turn re-loaned to the world's poorest countries in Africa, Asia, and Latin America, at high interest rates, to pay for more expensive imports—including oil! The biggest bonanza went to multinational petroleum firms whose control over production, refining, and distribution yielded enormous profits.

For all the talk in the mid-1970s of changing the balance of international economic relations between the world's rich and poor countries, fundamental inequalities persisted. Those nations that appeared to break out of the cycle of poverty, like South Korea and Taiwan, did not achieve success through international markets. Rather, these states regulated markets, nurtured new industries, educated the populace, and required multinationals to work collaboratively with local firms. These were exceptions that proved the general rule: the international economy reinforced existing structures.

CONCLUSION

The three-world order arose on the ruins of European empires and their Japanese counterpart. First, the Soviet Union and the United States became superpowers. Second, World War II affirmed the nation-state rather than the empire as the primary form for organizing communities. Third, in spite of the rhetoric of individualism and the free market, the war and postwar reconstruction enhanced the reach and functions of the modern state. In the Third World, too, leaders of new nations saw the state as the primary instrument for promoting economic development.

The organization of the world into three blocs lasted into the mid-1970s. This arrangement fostered the economic recovery of western Europe and Japan from the wounds inflicted by war. These nations' recovery grew out of a cold war alliance with the United States, where anticommunist hysteria accompanied an economic boom. The cold war also cast a shadow over the citizens of the Soviet Union and eastern Europe. Gulags and political surveillance became widespread, while the Soviets and their satellite regimes mobilized resources for military purposes. The Third World, squeezed by its inability to reduce poverty, on the one hand, and superpower rivalry, on the other, struggled to pursue a "third way." While some states maintained democratic institutions and promoted economic development, many tumbled into dictatorships and authoritarian regimes.

In this context Third World revolutionaries sought radical social and political transformation, seeking paths different from both western capitalism and Soviet communism. Though not successful, they energized considerable tensions in the three-world order. These tensions intensified in the late 1960s and early 1970s as Vietnamese communists defeated the United

Chronology

	1935	1940	1945	1950
AMERICAS		1941 U.S. enters World War II ✦		
			1950s–1960s American civil rights movement ✦- - - - - - - -	
EUROPE		1939–1945 World War II ✦- ✦	1948–1952 Marshall Plan ✦- - - - - - - - - - - ✦	
			1948–1949 Berlin blockade and airlift ✦- - - ✦	
				✦ 1949 NATO formed
SOVIET UNION				1953 Stalin dies ✦
AFRICA			✦ 1948 Apartheid begins in South Africa	
			1950s–1970s African countries gain independence ✦- - - - - - - - - - - -	
				1954–1962 Algerian War
SOUTH ASIA			✦ 1947 India and Pakistan gain independence	
MIDDLE EAST			✦- - - ✦ 1948–1949 Arab-Israeli War	
EAST AND SOUTHEAST ASIA		✦ 1937 Japan invades China		1954–1975 Vietnam War
		1945–1949 Nationalists fight Communists in China ✦- - - - - - - - - - - - ✦		
			1950–1953 Korean War ✦- - - - - - - - - - - ✦	

States, an oil crisis struck the West, and protests escalated in the First and Second worlds. Thirty years after the war's end, the world order forged after 1945 was beginning to give way.

Review and research materials are available at StudySpace: Ⓢ WWNORTON.COM/STUDYSPACE

KEY TERMS

Allied powers (p. 747)
apartheid (p. 767)
Arab-Israeli War (p. 766)
Axis powers (p. 747)
Berlin Wall (p. 754)
Fidel Castro (p. 776)
civil rights movement (p. 771)
cold war (p. 746)
decolonization (p. 756)
First World (p. 769)
Holocaust (p. 750)
Martin Luther King Jr. (p. 771)
Korean War (p. 756)

Mao Zedong (p. 758)
North Atlantic Treaty Organization (NATO) (p. 754)
Prague Spring (p. 781)
Second World (p. 771)
sexual revolution (p. 779)
superpowers (p. 746)
Third World (p. 773)
Vietnam War (p. 769)
Warsaw Pact (p. 754)
Zionism (p. 764)

STUDY QUESTIONS

1. Analyze how World War II was a truly global war and why it led to the end of a European-dominated world. How did the war challenge the ideological justifications for imperialism?
2. Define the term *cold war*. How did the task of rebuilding Europe and Asia after World War II lead to this intense global rivalry between the Soviet Union and the United States?
3. Describe the other process that dominated world affairs during these years—decolonization. What forms did it take?
4. Compare and contrast the three worlds of the postwar order. What was each world attempting to achieve? How successful was each one in achieving these goals?
5. List and explain tensions among the three worlds of the postwar era. How did cold war rivalries affect the Third World?
6. List and explain various successes and failures in the three competing worlds as they struggled to create "modern societies." What problems did the Third World face?
7. Evaluate the impact of Third World revolutionaries and radicals in transforming their societies. How successful were Mao and Castro in challenging the international status quo?
8. Assess the impact of nuclear weapons on state rivalries and relations after World War II. How did the proliferation of these weapons affect Soviet–American relations?
9. What tensions emerged between 1945 and 1975 to challenge the three-world order? What challenges did they present for various states?

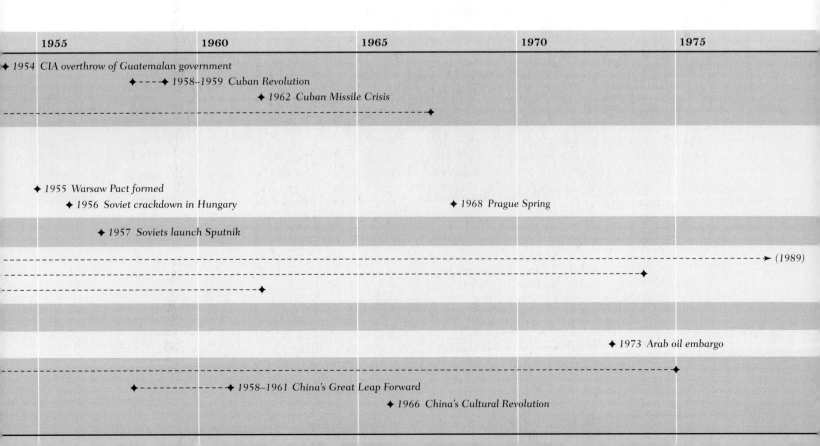

| 1955 | 1960 | 1965 | 1970 | 1975 |

◆ 1954 CIA overthrow of Guatemalan government
◆----◆ 1958–1959 Cuban Revolution
◆ 1962 Cuban Missile Crisis

◆ 1955 Warsaw Pact formed
◆ 1956 Soviet crackdown in Hungary
◆ 1968 Prague Spring
◆ 1957 Soviets launch Sputnik

→ (1989)

◆ 1973 Arab oil embargo

◆------------◆ 1958–1961 China's Great Leap Forward
◆ 1966 China's Cultural Revolution

21

GLOBALIZATION, 1970–2000

onsider the following comparison. In the thirteenth century, few people could imagine moving beyond their local regions. Venetian explorer Marco Polo, who traveled through China, and Arab scholar Ibn Battuta, who traversed the Islamic world, were rare exceptions. In contrast, in the late twentieth century people could traverse in a matter of hours the distances that it took Marco Polo and Ibn Battuta years to cover. Many others staying at home could "travel" the world via the Internet, books, newspapers, and televisions.

But not all travelers moved about so comfortably. Many migrants—desperate to escape political chaos, religious persecution, or poverty—slipped across borders in the dark of night, traveled as human cargo inside containers, or used their own feet to flee their homelands. Billions of others still had no access to the global age's technological wonders and economic opportunities. Thus, while **globalization** (the development of integrated worldwide cultural and economic structures) created possibilities for some, it also caused deeper disparities.

Moreover, consider two different settings: a fishing village in the Amazon River basin, and cosmopolitan Los Angeles. Picture an elderly Amazonian fisherman trying to teach his children their parents' tongue, Cocama-Cocamilla, but to no avail. All his children speak Spanish instead. "I tried to teach them. It's like paddling against the current." Seven centuries ago, over 500 languages rang throughout the Amazon River basin. As of 2000, only 57 languages survived there. Evidently, one effect of globalization is to reduce diversity. But it can also increase local diversity. For example, Los Angeles, once the emblem of white, suburban America, became a cacophonous city with over 100 languages spoken in its public schools.

This chapter observes the impact of globalization in several ways: (1) the movement of families and groups, as well as goods and ideas, across boundaries that once divided religious, ethnic, and national communities; (2) the role of international financial organizations in addressing world financial issues; (3) the power of multinational corporations in transforming local markets into international ones; and (4) unexpected effects such as galvanizing discontent, sparking a revival of traditional religions (to counter secular and materialist influences), and driving deeper divisions among and within the world's regions—even while bringing them closer together.

GLOBAL INTEGRATION

> → *How did globalization change the nation-state?*

The full impact of globalization remains unknown. Clearly, though, by the late twentieth century the forces driving global integration—and inequality—were no longer the political empires of old. By the mid-twentieth century, the European empires had lost their sway. The cold war and decolonization movements that had produced the three-world order lost their salience. Power structures in the First World, under such stress in the 1970s, did not crack. But those in the Second World did. Thus did the cold war end with the implosion of the Soviet bloc. The Third World also splintered, with some areas becoming highly advanced and others falling into deep poverty; the term **developing world** obscured these differences. Now a new architecture of power organized the world into a unified marketplace with unhindered flows of capital, commerce, culture, and labor. By 2000, most societies had endorsed electoral systems and adopted some form of market economy.

Because the United States promoted these changes, globalization has looked to some like Americanization. The United States unquestionably stood as the world's most influential society, with its music, food, principles of representative government, and free markets spreading worldwide. Yet the process did not run one way. The world also came to America and shaped its society: people living in the United States, their inventions, sports stars, and musical inspirations increasingly came from elsewhere.

Nor was the United States immune from transnational forces challenging the power of the nation-state itself. In the United States, as elsewhere, globalization functioned through networks of investment, trade, and migration that operated relatively independently of nation-states. In the process, globalization shook entrenched forms of political and social identification, from religious to military authority. Members of societies now often identified more with local, subnational, or international movements or cultures, rather than with nation-states. To be sure, nation-states remained essential for establishing democratic institutions and protecting human rights, but supranational institutions like the European Union and the International Monetary Fund (see later discussion) often impinged on their autonomy.

Focus Questions

→ *How did globalization change the nation-state?*

→ *What were the major obstacles to globalization?*

→ *What were the agents of globalization?*

→ *What were the characteristics of the new global order?*

→ *How did citizenship in the global world create new problems and responses?*

MAIN THEMES

→ *A new architecture of power organized around electoral systems and market economies after the collapse of the three-world order creates large disparities between those who participate in the networks of globalization and those who do not.*

→ *The United States emerges as the most influential society in the world, with its cultures and institutions spreading to most corners of the globe, while the world also comes to America and shapes its texture.*

→ *Transnational forces like migration, investment networks, and trade begin to operate independently of the nation-state via international organizations like the United Nations and the International Monetary Fund, which erode the power of the nation-state.*

FOCUS ON *Globalization*

Removing Obstacles to Globalization

✦ Communism's fall and the end of the cold war improve prospects for global exchange of peoples, ideas, and resources.

✦ Final decolonization in Angola and Mozambique and the end of apartheid in South Africa return self-rule throughout Africa.

Unleashing Globalization

✦ Financial deregulation and the end of gold and silver standards allow money to move freely across borders but lead to a Third World debt crisis.

✦ Widespread migrations occur as people in Africa, Asia, and Latin America move to Europe and America, following the tracks of their former colonizers.

✦ Revolutions in culture and communications spread American culture worldwide, but also make cultural diversity more possible for those who can afford it.

The New Global Order

✦ Globalization leads to dramatic population expansion, requiring greater agricultural and industrial output.

✦ Family structure changes, life spans increase, and more goods are available, yet inequalities deepen as decent education and good health determine social status as never before.

✦ As globalization erodes the power of the nation-state, greater violence occurs between and within states. Nongovernmental organizations (NGOs) and religion become resources for dealing with violence and inequality and for reimagining the nation-state.

REMOVING OBSTACLES TO GLOBALIZATION

→ *What were the major obstacles to globalization?*

In the mid-1970s, political practices and institutions associated with the three-world order started to deteriorate. By the late 1980s, the communist Second World was disintegrating. The collapse of the Soviet Union brought the cold war to an end. At the same time, the capitalist First World gave up its last colonial possessions, and the remnants of white settler supremacy disintegrated. But as this occurred, the formerly colonized Third World's dream of a "third way" also vanished. As empires withdrew, they revealed a world integrated by ties other than forced loyalties to imperial masters.

ENDING THE COLD WAR

A world divided between two hostile factions limited the prospects for a global exchange of peoples, ideas, and resources. There was widespread exchange within the rival blocs—that is, among socialist countries and among capitalist countries—but for other countries the pressure from the Soviet Union and the United States to align with a superpower imposed limits to interaction, even with neighboring nations. A few countries, like Egypt, managed to switch sides (from the Soviets to the Americans), opening up some new global links while closing off others. Pushing against the cold war superpower framework, however, were strong nationalist aspirations and religious movements, which the cold war order tried to control, or in some cases inflame, at great cost.

MOUNTING COSTS   The many regional conflicts of the cold war era (Vietnam, Afghanistan, Nicaragua) were costly for countries caught in the ideological crossfire. Vietnam became a battleground for Russian, Chinese, and American ambitions. This war spilled over into Laos and Cambodia, dragging them to ruin along with Vietnam. China attracted several client states in the competition for influence in the Third World and within the communist bloc. In Afghanistan, Moscow propped up a puppet regime, only to fall into a bloody war against Islamic and tribal guerrillas financed and armed by the United States, Saudi Arabia, and Pakistan. In Central America, U.S. president Ronald Reagan and his advisers opposed the victory of the left-leaning Nicaraguan Sandinista coalition in 1979. During the 1980s the U.S. government pumped millions of dollars to the Contras (right-wing opponents of the left-wing Sandinistas) and lent military and monetary assistance to other Central American anti-communist forces. Thus, for much of the world, the cold war was a real confrontation with tremendously high costs for local powers.

Rivalry was costly to the superpowers, too, for the 1970s and 1980s saw the largest peacetime accumulation of arms in history. Despite myriad treaties and summits, the United States and the Soviet Union stockpiled nuclear and conventional weaponry. Furthermore, in 1983 Reagan unveiled the Strategic Defense Initiative ("Star Wars"), a plan to use satellites and space missiles to insulate the United States from incoming nuclear bombs. For both sides, military spending sprees brought economic troubles. The U.S. national debt increased; Soviet life expectancy began to decline and infant mortality to rise.

Cracks on either side of the conflict appeared in the 1970s. The intelligence organizations of both the Soviet Union and the United States produced secret memos questioning whether the Soviet bloc could sustain its global position. As stalemate in Afghanistan undermined the image of the mighty Soviet armed forces, mothers of Soviet soldiers protested their government's involvements abroad. The eastern European satellites became dependent on western European loans and consumer goods. At the same time, the western alliance itself faced internal tensions. In Europe and North America, the antinuclear movement rallied millions to the streets. Western industrialists worried about competition from Japan, which had been plowing money into rapid industrialization rather than arms. Political leaders also grappled with distressingly high unemployment rates. Thus, both sides shared a common crisis: fatigue from the cold war, and an economic challenge from East Asia.

THE SOVIET BLOC COLLAPSES   In the end, the Soviet bloc collapsed (see Map 21-1). Even though planned economies employed the entire Soviet population, they failed to fill stores with sufficient consumer goods. Socialist health care and benefits lagged behind those of the capitalist welfare states. Authoritarian political structures relied on deception and coercion rather than elections and civic activism. Although the communist party had promised to beat capitalism by building socialism on the way to achieving full communism, the latter paradise was nowhere on the horizon. The gap between socialism and capitalism was growing.

One catalyst in socialism's undoing was Poland. A critical event was the naming of a Polish archbishop as pope in 1978. The first non-Italian pope in 455 years, John Paul opposed the Soviet form of socialism. In 1979, he made a pilgrimage to his native Poland, holding enormous outdoor masses; in 1980, he supported mass strikes at the Gdansk shipyard, which led to the formation of the Soviet bloc's first independent trade union, Solidarity. As communist party members in Poland defected to its side, the union became a society-wide movement; it aimed not to reform socialism (as in Czechoslovakia in 1968; see Chapter 20) but to overcome it. A crackdown by the Polish military and police put most of Solidarity's leadership in prison and drove the movement

Lech Walesa. A Polish electrician from the Lenin Shipyard in the Baltic port city of Gdansk, Walesa spearheaded the formation of Solidarity, a mass independent trade union of workers who battled the communist regime that ruled in their name. He later was elected president of post-communist Poland.

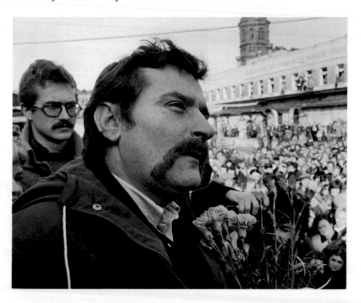

→ *What were the major obstacles to globalization?*

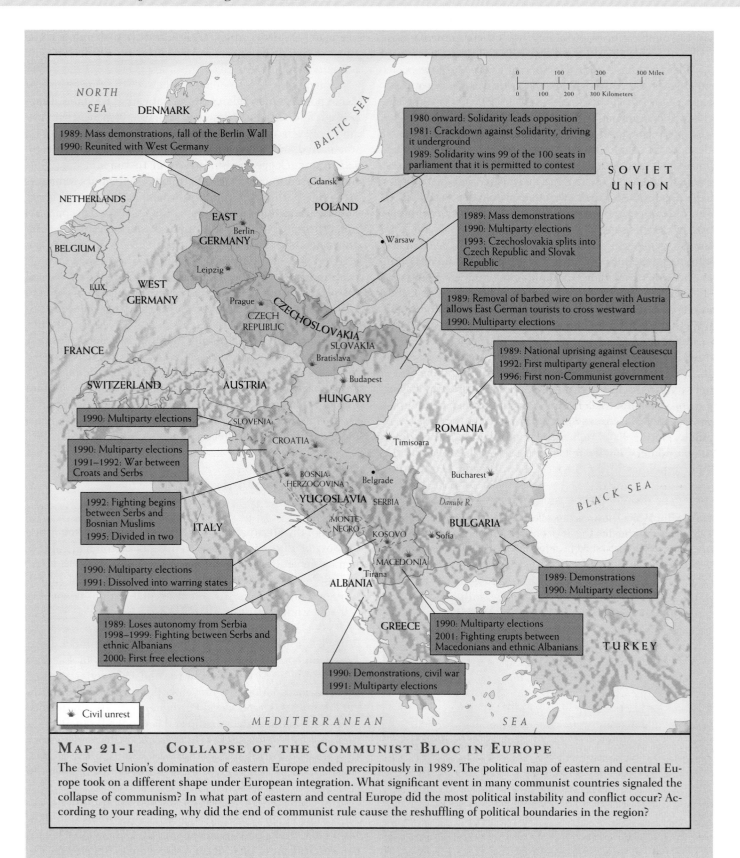

MAP 21-1   COLLAPSE OF THE COMMUNIST BLOC IN EUROPE

The Soviet Union's domination of eastern Europe ended precipitously in 1989. The political map of eastern and central Europe took on a different shape under European integration. What significant event in many communist countries signaled the collapse of communism? In what part of eastern and central Europe did the most political instability and conflict occur? According to your reading, why did the end of communist rule cause the reshuffling of political boundaries in the region?

underground, but Soviet intelligence officials secretly worried that Solidarity could not be easily eradicated.

The most consequential factor in the collapse of the Soviet superpower was Mikhail Gorbachev, who became general secretary of the Soviet communist party in 1985 and launched an effort to reform the Soviet system. Under this effort (*perestroika*, "reconstruction"), Gorbachev permitted contested elections for communist party posts, relaxed censorship, sanctioned civic associations, legalized small nonstate businesses, granted autonomy to state firms, and encouraged the republics to be responsible for their own affairs within the Soviet Union. These reforms were linked with dramatic arms control initiatives to ease the superpower burden on the Soviet Union. Gorbachev then began withdrawing troops from Afghanistan and informed eastern European leaders that they could not count on Moscow's armed intervention to prop up their regimes.

Having set out to improve socialism, however, Gorbachev instead destabilized it. Civic groups called not for reform of the system, but for its liquidation. Eastern Europe declared its intention to leave the Soviet orbit, and some of the union republics began to push for independence. In response, disgruntled factions within the communist party and the Soviet military tried to preserve the destabilized old order by staging a coup attempt in 1991. However, the former communist party boss of Moscow and elected president of the Russian republic, Boris Yeltsin, rallied the opposition and faced down the hard-liners. Under Yeltsin, Russia, like Ukraine and the other republics of the Soviet Union, became a refuge for

The Berlin Wall. The breaching of the Berlin Wall in November 1989 spelled the end of the Soviet bloc. Decades of debate over whether communism could be reformed turned out to be moot. In the face of competition from the richer, consumer-oriented West, communism collapsed.

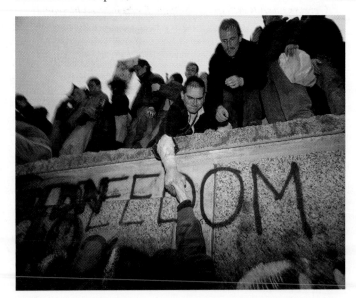

beleaguered Soviet elites. Thereafter they abandoned the cause of the Soviet Union and socialism and divided up state property among themselves.

When communist regimes collapsed, the European and Asian political maps changed dramatically. Old states disappeared, and new ones emerged. In Asia, although the division between North and South Korea remained, Vietnam was united and, along with China, welcomed western capitalism under communist party rule. In Europe, East Germany ceased to exist; West Germany absorbed its remnants after the Berlin Wall came down in 1989. (See Primary Source: Tidal Pull of the West: East Germany Disappears.) Soon thereafter the Soviet empire dissolved into independent states (see Map 21-2). But the end of Soviet-style socialism was not entirely peaceful. The worst carnage occurred in the former Yugoslavia, which suffered wars of dissolution as leaders exploited ethnic fears. Serbs and Croats, in particular, engaged in savage struggles over territories in the Balkans.

By historical standards the cold war had been relatively brief, spanning four decades. But communism had played a major role in the military conflicts and the headlong modernization of Russia and China, and it exercised important influence on India. However, it could not keep up the cold war *and* deliver the good life to its adherents *and* survive in a more competitive world economy.

AFRICA AND THE END OF WHITE RULE

Although the aftermath of World War II saw the dismantling of most of Europe's empires, remnants of colonial rule remained in southern Africa (see Map 20-6 on p. 763). Here, whites clung to centuries-old notions of their racial superiority over non-Europeans. Final decolonization meant that self-rule would return to all of Africa.

THE LAST HOLDOUTS The last fortresses under direct European control were the Portuguese colonies of southern and western Africa. However, by the mid-1970s efforts to suppress African nationalist movements had exhausted Portugal's resources. Demoralized Portuguese officers now pushed aside their nation's dictatorship and began the Portuguese experiment with democracy. As African nationalist demands led to a hurried Portuguese withdrawal from Guinea-Bissau, Angola, and Mozambique, formal European colonialism in Africa came to an end.

But white rule still prevailed elsewhere in Africa. In Rhodesia, a white minority resisted all international pressure to allow black rule. In the end, independent African neighbors helped support a liberation guerrilla movement under Robert Mugabe. Surrounded, Rhodesian whites finally capitulated. Mugabe

TIDAL PULL OF THE WEST: EAST GERMANY DISAPPEARS

After Soviet premier Mikhail Gorbachev instituted a series of reforms to save socialism, dissenters in eastern Europe saw their chance to throw off Russian dominance. The Berlin Wall (erected in 1961) was the most visible symbol of Soviet oppression. Here journalist Ann Tusa recalls the November 1989 press conference that accidentally led to the opening of the Berlin Wall. As both the wall and East Germany fell, Russia kept its nearly 400,000 troops that were on East German soil confined to their barracks.

At about 7 o'clock on the evening of November 9, 1989, some 300 journalists from all over the world are crammed into a room in East Berlin for a routine press conference. . . . For the first time since the foundation of a separate Communist East German state in 1946, the German Democratic Republic, there have been massive demonstrations against the regime. . . .

East Germans, who have not known a free election since 1933, have been voting with their feet. From January to October 1989, some 200,000 people had left their country. By early November the figure was up to 250,000—and that was out of a total population of 16.7 million. At first, many East Germans went out on "holiday visas" to Iron Curtain countries [European states under Soviet domination], then claimed asylum in West German embassies in Warsaw, Budapest or Prague. Thousands more have driven or walked round the East German frontiers looking for an undefended crossing or a guard with a blind eye, wriggled across, then headed for Austria and a refugee camp. . . .

The November 9 press conference is handled by Günter Schabowski. . . . This evening he feeds the press a startling hint that there might soon be free elections. Good story. Everyone wants to go out and file it. But then Schabowski turns up a sheet from the bottom of the pile of papers on his table. "This will be interesting for you." And in a style that suggests it is all news to him, slowly reads aloud: "Today the decision was taken to make it possible for all citizens to leave the country through the official border crossing points. All citizens of the GDR can now be issued with visas for the purposes of travel or visiting relatives in the West. This order is to take effect at once. . . ."

The news is broadcast on an East German television bulletin at 7:30 P.M. The station's switchboard is immediately jammed with callers. "Is it true? I can't believe it."

They always believed West German television, though, and it is soon flashing the announcement. A few East and West Berliners go to the Wall to see what is happening. . . . Then at 10:30 a discussion program on Sender Freies Berlin, the West Berlin television station, is interrupted by a live broadcast from the Wall. No preamble, just shots of a small crowd milling round a checkpoint, then a man runs toward the camera: "They've opened the crossing at Bornholmer Strasse." After that the news spreads like wildfire, by radio, television, telephone, shouts in the street. The trickle across the Wall swells to a flood. That weekend 2 million East Germans are reckoned to have stood in West Berlin. One reaction is common to them all: "We've seen the West on TV, of course. But this is real."

. . . The fatal piece of paper had been hurriedly swept up as he left for the press conference. It had never been intended for publication. It was a draft based on a recent Politburo decision: unable to control the tide of refugees, thrashing around for ways to quiet the demonstrators on the streets, they had decided that in their own good time they would ease travel restrictions, having first made arrangements for a limited issue of visas under carefully controlled circumstances.

→ *The Berlin Wall (and other border defenses) kept East Germans and West Germans apart for twenty-eight years. How did some East Germans try to circumvent the barriers during that time?*

→ *Why didn't the 400,000 Soviet troops in East Germany intervene during the collapse of the Berlin Wall?*

→ *What does this piece tell us about the state of mind of the East German government at this time?*

SOURCE: Ann Tusa, "A Fatal Error" from *Media Studies Journal*, Fall 1999, pp. 26–29. Copyright © 1999. Reprinted by permission of *Media Studies Journal*.

MAP 21-2   THE BREAKUP OF THE SOVIET UNION

The Soviet Union broke apart in 1991. Compare this map with Map 17-6 (see p. 662), which illustrates Russian expansion in the nineteenth century. Which parts of the old Russian Empire remained under Russian rule, and which territories established their own states? In what areas did large migrations accompany the breakup, and for what reasons? According to your reading, how did the breakup of the Soviet Union change Russia's status in Europe and Asia?

The End of Apartheid. (*Left*) Nelson Mandela, running for president in 1994 as the candidate of the African National Congress, here casts a ballot in the first all-races election in South Africa. This election ended apartheid and saw the African National Congress take control of the Republic of South Africa. (*Right*) After the overwhelming electoral triumph of Mandela, F. W. de Klerk, leader of the once-powerful Afrikaner-dominated National Party, shakes hands with his successor.

swept to power with massive electoral support in 1979. The new constitutional government renamed the country Zimbabwe, erasing from Africa's map the name of the long-deceased British expansionist Cecil Rhodes (see Chapter 17).

SOUTH AFRICA AND NELSON MANDELA   The final outpost of white rule was South Africa, where a European minority was larger, richer, and more entrenched than elsewhere in the region—and highly invulnerable to outside pressures. Although powerful international firms operated there, they were reluctant to risk their investments by boycotting the racist regime. In addition, the U.S. government regarded South Africa's large army as a useful tool to fight Soviet allies elsewhere in southern Africa. In any case the ruling Afrikaner-led National Party used ruthless tactics against internal critics. Yet, in the countryside and cities, defiance of white rule was growing. Africans lobbed rocks and crude bombs (Molotov cocktails) at tanks and organized mass strikes in the multinational-owned mines.

At the same time, pressures from abroad were mounting. The International Olympic Committee banned South African athletes starting in 1970. American students insisted that their universities divest themselves of companies with investments in South Africa. As international pressures grew, foreign governments—even that of the United States, once South Africa's staunchest ally—applied economic sanctions against South Africa. A swelling worldwide chorus demanded that **Nelson Mandela**, the imprisoned leader of the African National Congress (ANC), be freed. The white political elite eventually realized that it was better to negotiate new arrangements than to endure international ostracism and years of

internal warfare against a majority population. In 1990, President F. W. de Klerk (of the National Party) released Mandela from prison and legalized the ANC and the communist party of South Africa. Ensuing negotiations produced South Africa's first free, mass elections in 1994. These brought an overwhelming victory to the ANC, with Nelson Mandela elected as president. Majority rule had finally come to South Africa, and for the first time in centuries Africans ruled over all of Africa.

In Nelson Mandela, South Africa's white rulers found a man of exceptional integrity and political savvy. He had spent more than two decades in prison, much of it at hard labor. But he looked beyond past injustices to ease the transition to full democracy. Besides, he was aware that, with the country veering toward civil war, only a negotiated change would preserve South Africa's industries, wealth, and educational system.

Still, the leaders of independent Africa faced immense problems in building stable political communities. Although they set out to destroy the vestiges of colonial political structures and to erect African-based public institutions, local contests for political power impeded this process. Ethnic and religious rivalries, held in check during the colonial period, now blazed forth. Civil wars erupted in many countries (most violently in Nigeria, Sudan, and Zaire), and military leaders were drawn into politics. Coups d'état were common. Nigeria, for instance, had six military coups between 1966 and 1999. The ruling elements increasingly maintained power by using the state's resources to reward their clients and to punish their enemies. By the 1990s, the continent was aflame with civil strife—armed conflicts that started with the cold war and lasted well after it ended.

UNLEASHING GLOBALIZATION

> → *What were the agents of globalization?*

As obstacles to international integration began to dissolve, capital, commodities, people, and culture crossed borders with ever-greater freedom. Even though trade, foreign investment, migration, and cultural borrowing had long been hallmarks of modern history, the global age has changed their scale. At the same time, never had there been such unequal access to the fruits of globalization. Several factors contributed to increasing integration and to new power arrangements: international banking, expanded international trade, population migrations, and technical breakthroughs in communications.

FINANCE AND TRADE

The increased international flow of goods and capital was well under way in the 1970s, but the end of the cold war removed many impediments to globalization. During the 1990s, even the strongest nation-states felt the effects of economic globalization.

GLOBAL FINANCIAL TRANSFERS AND DEREGULATED MARKETS   Major transformations occurred in the world's financial system in the 1970s. America's budget and trade deficits prompted President Richard Nixon to take the dollar off the gold standard, an action that enabled the yen, the lira, the pound, the franc, and other national currencies to cut their ties to the American dollar. Now international financiers enjoyed greater freedom from national regulators and found fresh business opportunities. A new system of informal money management across borders replaced an older system of formal management within borders. Where formal management of world financial relations existed, it fell increasingly under international authorities such as the World Bank and the International Monetary Fund.

The primary agents of the heightened global financial activity were banks. Based mainly in London, New York, and Tokyo, big, highly diversified financial banks became conduits for mobile capital looking for lucrative ventures. Revenues from oil producers provided a large infusion of cash into the global economy in the 1970s. At the same time, banks joined forces to issue mammoth loans to developing nations.

International financial firms found academic allies who outlined the economic rules of fiscal sobriety for a global economic environment. These intellectuals were primarily North American–trained economists whose new framework minimized the welfare concerns of the Keynesian approach (see Chapter 19). Instead, these economists emphasized unfettered markets and profit motivations as the cornerstone of capitalist economic development. Employed in banks and ministries worldwide, they argued that the old regulatory policies of nation-states prevented rather than promoted economic growth. Working as advisers in many governments (especially under Margaret Thatcher in Britain and Ronald Reagan in the United States), these economists guided public policy to deregulate market life.

No international financial organization was more influential than the **International Monetary Fund (IMF)**. During the 1980s it emerged as a central player, especially in response to the so-called debt crisis in Third World and eastern-bloc countries. Throughout the 1970s, European, Japanese, and North American banks had loaned money on very easy terms to cash-strapped Third World and eastern-bloc borrowers. But what was once good business soon turned sour. In 1982, a wave of defaults threatened to overrun Latin America in particular. Throughout the 1980s, international banks and the IMF kept heavily indebted customers solvent. The IMF offered short-term loans to governments on condition that recipients adopt new fiscal ways and compel civilian populations to tighten their belts. Latin Americans pioneered the process of merging their domestic markets with international ones. Trade barriers crumbled, state enterprises became private firms, and foreign investors called the former debtors "emerging markets." Eastern Europe and Asia followed suit in the 1990s, and emerging-market mania buoyed a boom in international finance.

EFFECTS OF INTEGRATED NETWORKS   New technologies and institutions enabled many more financial investors and traders to participate in the integrated networks of world finance. The Internet and online trading accelerated the mobility—and volatility—of capital across borders. Volatility soon created problems, however. In the 1990s, currency devaluations in Mexico, in Russia, and across East Asia shocked financiers. When the Mexican economy went into paralysis in 1994, the crisis was so extreme that not even the IMF could bail it out; the U.S. Treasury had to issue the largest international loan in history to pull Mexico out of its economic tailspin. Despite acting as the lender in that instance, the United States emerged in the new financial order as the world's largest borrower. Early in the new millennium, its net foreign debt soared past $2 trillion—a 700 percent increase since the early 1990s. Much of this debt was owed to Asian, especially Chinese, bankers.

Globalization increased commercial, as well as financial, interdependence. The total value of world trade increased nearly tenfold between 1973 and 1998, and trade in Asia grew even faster. In 1960, trade accounted for 24 percent of the world gross domestic product (GDP; the total value of all goods and services produced in a country in a single year). By 1995,

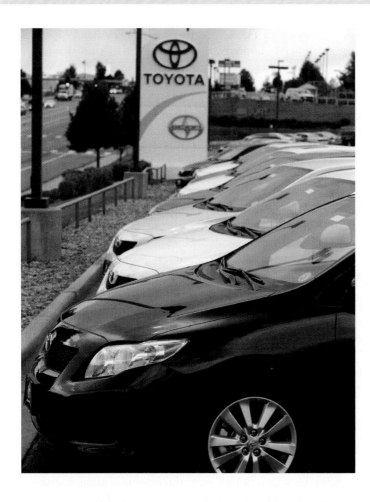

Globalization. In the past, Americans mostly bought products, such as cars, that were manufactured domestically. Now, Americans often buy products made abroad.

started to become an economic powerhouse. For the next two decades, China chalked up astounding 10 percent annual growth rates, swelling its share of world GDP from 5 percent to 12 percent.

For East Asia as a whole, the share of world exports doubled in the same period, with smaller countries like Singapore, Taiwan, South Korea, and Hong Kong becoming mini-powerhouses. By the early 1990s, these countries and Japan were major investors abroad. Overall, East Asia's share of world production rose from 13.6 percent to 25.3 percent between 1965 and 1989. By contrast, over the same period, the U.S. and European shares decreased.

REGIONAL TRADE BLOCS AND GROWING DISPARITIES Industrialization of previously less developed countries, combined with lower trade barriers, increased the pressures of world competition on national economies. Some areas responded by creating regional blocs. In North America, much trade and finance flowed back and forth across the U.S.-Canadian border. By the 1980s, fearing competition from inexpensive Asian manufactures, the two countries admitted Mexico into the trading bloc to encourage plants to locate within the region. They negotiated a North American Free Trade Agreement (NAFTA) in 1992.

Meanwhile, the most complete regional integration occurred in Europe. Indeed, Europeans slashed trade barriers and harmonized their commercial policies toward the rest of the world. In 1991, the Maastricht Treaty paved the way for creating a single European currency, the euro. Maastricht became, in effect, the constitution for the **European Union (EU)**. Although the EU was conceived as a trading and financial bloc, rather than a political union, increasingly its legislative and judicial bodies (the European Parliament and the Court of Justice of the European Union) made political and legal decisions that were binding for all member nations. To a remarkable degree, states within the EU gave up aspects of their sovereignty in the hopes of establishing permanent peace and prosperity.

Trade integration and interdependence coincided with a transformation in traded commodities. Pharmaceuticals, computers, software, and services from insurance to banking became key exports and imports. High technology, in particular, now occupied an ever-greater share of the manufacturing and exports of the world's richest countries.

Competition and the shift to producing sophisticated goods affected world incomes. For "rich" countries as a whole, about half of total GDP reflected the production and distribution of such goods and services, giving those countries a competitive advantage. In general, where global incomes were

that share had almost doubled. Where an American would once have worn American-made clothes (Levi's), driven an American car (a Ford), and watched an American television (Zenith), such was rarely the case by century's end. Increasingly, consumers bought foreign goods and services and sold a greater share of their own output abroad. This pattern had always been true of smaller regions like Central America and southern Africa. But in the 1980s it intensified, with Hong Kong and Singapore prospering through expanding world trade.

International trade also shifted the international division of labor. After World War II, Europeans and North Americans dominated manufacturing, while Third World countries supplied raw materials. But by the 1990s this was no longer the case. Brazil became a major airplane maker, South Korea exported millions of automobiles, and China emerged as the world's largest source of textiles, footwear, and electronics.

The most remarkable global shift involved East Asian industry and commerce. Manufactured goods, including high-technology products, now issued from the eastern fringe of Afro-Eurasia as often as from its western fringe. Japan blazed the Asian trail: between 1965 and 1990, its share of world trade doubled to almost 10 percent. China, too, flexed its economic muscle. When Deng Xiaoping took power in 1978, China was already a growing economy. Under Deng, China lower and people were less educated, the share of knowledge as a contributor to wealth was also lower. Poor nations remained, with few exceptions, locked in the production of low-tech goods and the export of raw materials. Increasingly, technology and knowledge now divided the world into affluent, technically sophisticated countries and poor, technically underdeveloped regions.

MIGRATION

Migration, a constant feature of world history, became more pronounced in the twentieth century (see Map 21-3). Although after 1970 fewer Europeans were on the move, many more Asians, Africans, and Latin Americans were. By 2000, there were 120 million migrants scattered across 152 countries, up from 75 million in 1965. Most left poorer countries for richer destinations.

PATTERNS OF MIGRATION Migratory flows often followed the contours of existing political relations. Where North America and Europe had had colonies or dependencies, their political withdrawal left tracks for migrants to follow. Indians and Pakistanis moved to Britain. Dominicans, Haitians, and Mexicans went to the United States. Algerians and Vietnamese moved to France. And where emerging rich societies cultivated close diplomatic ties, these relations opened migratory gates. This was true of Germany's relationship with Turkey, of Japan's with South Korea, and of Canada's with Hong Kong. In most cases, economic factors propelled migrants across national borders.

International migration was often an extension of regional and national migration from poorer, rural areas to urban centers. In Nigeria, for example, rural-urban migration intensified after 1970. In 1900, Nigeria's capital, Lagos, had a population of 41,847. At the century's end, Lagos had more than 10 million people, with predictions that it would double by 2025. The key to Lagos's boom in the 1970s was the existence of large oil reserves inside the country and the high prices that oil fetched in international markets. When the Organization of Petroleum Exporting Countries (OPEC) sent oil prices soaring, money poured into Nigeria. The government kept most of it in its largest city. That, in turn, spurred people to move to Lagos. This rural-urban migration increased Lagos's population by 14 percent per year in the 1970s and 1980s. No government—least of all a new, weakly supported one like Nigeria's—could cope with such a huge influx. Electricity supplies failed regularly. There were never enough schools, teachers, or textbooks. But the city burst with the vitality of new arrivals, prompting one immigrant to exclaim: "It's a terrible place; I want to go there!"

The search for opportunities also pushed people to move from less developed to more developed nations. Although many corporations relocated their manufacturing plants in poorer countries, where unskilled labor was abundant and government regulations were few, these jobs remained less attractive than even the lowest-wage positions available in richer nations. Thus, the possibility for better wages—and the hope for better lives—inspired millions to leave their homelands.

TEMPORARY MIGRANTS Some migrants moved for temporary sojourns. At least that was the original intent. In the 1950s and 1960s, southern Europeans moved northward; but when Spain, Portugal, Greece, and Italy also became wealthy societies, not only did the exodus decline, but these countries became magnets for Middle Eastern, North African, and (more recently) eastern European migrants. However, Europeans' strong identification with their nations did not permit the easy integration of foreigners. Nor did European states support the permanent settlement of immigrants. Most migrants from Asia and Africa went initially to Europe in search of temporary jobs as guest workers. With time they settled in their host countries, often living in urban squalor (for example, Pakistanis in Britain's city of Leeds, and Algerians in impoverished suburbs of Paris).

In Japan, too, immigrants were not easily incorporated. Tokyo's policy in the 1970s resembled the European guest worker program. Discouraging permanent settlement and immigration, Japan encouraged mainly itinerant workers to move to the country, yet its economy required increasing numbers of these sojourners. Indeed, Japan's deep reluctance to integrate migrants led to dire labor shortages.

After Japan, the economic tigers of Hong Kong, Taiwan, and Malaysia all became hosts for temporary migrants. So millions of guest workers moved there, but ultimately the migrants sank deeper roots, especially once their children entered schools. This presented a challenge to host societies that were accustomed to thinking of their national communities as ethnically homogeneous. At times, discrimination led to violent conflicts among recent immigrants, long-time residents, and the state's security forces. Governments also

Lagos, Nigeria. During the twentieth century, Lagos was one of the fastest-growing and most crowded cities in Africa.

grappled with the challenge of extending citizenship rights to and culturally assimilating newcomers who wanted to dress according to religious custom, as in the case of Muslims in France (10 percent of that country's population).

DEMOGRAPHIC CHANGES IN THE UNITED STATES
One society that had fewer problems integrating migrants, and that attracted the lion's share of international migrants, was the United States. Long a magnet for Europeans, the United States enacted an immigration reform in 1965 that opened its gates to the world's migrants. By 2000, 27 million immigrants lived there, accounting for almost 10 percent of the population—double the share in 1970.

The profile of migration also changed. In 1970, there were more Canadians or Germans living in the United States than Mexicans. Over the next thirty years, the Mexican influx rose tenfold and by 2000 accounted for almost one-third of immigrants in the United States. The numbers migrating from Asia also surged, accounting for over 40 percent of all immigrants to the United States in the 1990s. But it was above all from south of the Rio Grande that the American demographic landscape changed.

RESIDENT NONCITIZENS AND REFUGEES
Arguments in Los Angeles over schools and health care for resident noncitizens became part of a global debate. In Argentina, up to 500,000 undocumented Peruvians, Bolivians, and Paraguayans also lived without rights as citizens. Even more staggering, between 3 and 8 million migrants moved from Mozambique, Zimbabwe, and Lesotho to South Africa. In some Middle Eastern countries, like Saudi Arabia and Kuwait, foreign-born workers constituted over 70 percent of the workforce. In general, migrants were only partially accommodated, while many were fully excluded from host societies. Thus, even though population movements flowed across political, kinship, and market networks, demographic reshuffling heightened national concerns about the ethnic makeup of political communities.

Finally, forced migrations remained a hallmark of the modern world. In contrast to earlier centuries' forced migration of slaves from Africa, recent involuntary flows involved refugees fleeing civil war and torture. Many suffered for weeks, months, or years in refugee camps on the periphery of violence. The greatest concentration of refugees occurred in the world's poorest region—Africa. Those Africans unable to reach wealthier areas were often caught up in ethnic and religious conflicts that generated vast refugee camps, where survival depended on the generosity of host governments and international contributions.

CULTURE

Migrations and new technologies helped create a more global entertainment culture. In this domain, globalization often equated with Americanization. Yet American entertainments

African Refugees. During the late twentieth century, Africa became a continent of displaced persons and refugee camps. Pictured here is a camp in Chad for Sudanese driven out of the Darfur region by government-sponsored raids.

themselves reflected artistic practices from across the globe, as one mass culture met another. On the global scale, there was less diversity in 2000 than in 1300; but in terms of individuals' everyday experience, the potential for experiencing cultural diversity (if one could afford the technology to do so) increased.

NEW MEDIA
Technology was key in diffusing entertainment. In the 1970s, for example, cassette tapes became the dominant medium for popular music, sidelining the long-playing record and the short-lived eight-track tape. Bootleggers illegally mass-reproduced cassette tapes and sold them cheaply to young consumers. Television was another globalizing force, as American producers bundled old dramas and situation comedies to stations worldwide. Likewise, American movie distributors sent movies and videocassettes of movies across borders.

But Americans were not the only entertainment exporters. Brazilian soap operas began to penetrate Spanish-language American TV markets in the 1980s, often inducing Mexican viewers to rush home from work to catch the latest episode. Latin American television shows and music were distributed in the United States in areas with large Spanish-speaking populations. Bombay also produced its fair share of programs for viewers of British television. Movies and actors from New Zealand, Australia, France, Italy, China, India, and Iran found audiences in Europe and the United States.

In the early 1980s, a new form of television programming spread rapidly: cable. Once again, the United States pioneered the medium, but the innovation soon caught on elsewhere. Increasingly, viewers had access to dozens, even

MAP 21-3 WORLD MIGRATION, 1918–1998

The world's population continued to grow and move around in the twentieth century. Looking at this map, identify the countries that had the greatest increase in foreign-born as a percentage of total population. Then compare the areas of most rapid population growth during the nineteenth century with those parts of the world that, according to the map shown here, had the highest percentage of foreign-born in the twentieth century. What are the similarities and differences? During the twentieth century, which parts of the world were the sending areas, and which were the receiving territories? See Map 18-1, p. 672.

Foreign-born people as percentage of total population (latest available year)

- Less than 1.5%
- 1.5%–2.9%
- 3.0%–7.5%
- More than 7.5%
- Data not available
- ← Migration

ARCTIC OCEAN

Poles and Baltic peoples to Siberia 1939–1940

RUSSIA

1930s and 1940s

POLAND

UKRAINE

1918–1922

Russian Jews to Israel 1980s and 1990s

GEORGIA 1922

1945

1922

TURKEY

SYRIA

2003

2003

IRAQ 1947–

AFGHANISTAN 1979

BANGLADESH

CHINA

NORTH KOREA

1950–1954

SOUTH KOREA

JAPAN

ISRAEL JORDAN EGYPT

1945

PAKISTAN

1947

1947

INDIA 1972

HONG KONG

to Canada and USA 1980–

PACIFIC OCEAN

LIBYA

1947

1970–

1970–

SAUDI ARABIA

Falashas to Israel 1991

1980

THAILAND

VIETNAM

to UK

to USA

SUDAN mid 1980s

to Western Europe and USA

1975

to USA 1990–

ETHIOPIA 1980s

1975

MALAYSIA

CONGO

RWANDA 1994

to France

INDONESIA

TANZANIA

INDIAN OCEAN

Southeast Asians to Australia 1970s

MOZAMBIQUE

BOTSWANA 1960–

1960–

AUSTRALIA

SOUTH AFRICA

Europeans to Australia/New Zealand 1918–

NEW ZEALAND

hundreds, of specialized channels, challenging the dominance of traditional national networks. Cable TV networks like MTV featured pop music and introduced music videos, both a musical and a visual product.

Television's globalizing effects were especially evident in sports. In many parts of the globe, American sports made particularly deep inroads as more foreigners participated in them and as television broadcast American games in other countries. The National Basketball Association (and the athletic footwear firm Nike) was particularly successful in international marketing; in the process, it made Michael Jordan the world's best-known athlete in the late twentieth century. Soccer (known as football outside the United States) became an international passion, with devoted national followings for national teams. Indeed, by the 1980s soccer was *the* world sport, with television ratings increasingly determining its schedule. Organizers of the 1986 World Cup in Mexico insisted that big soccer matches take place at midday so that games could be televised live at prime time in Europe, despite teams' having to play under the scorching sun.

GLOBAL CULTURE Technology was not the only driving force of world cultures, for migration and exchange were also important. For example, as people moved around they brought their own musical tastes and borrowed others. Reggae, born in the 1960s among Jamaica's Rastafarians, became a hit sensation in London and Toronto, where large West Indian communities had migrated. Reggae lyrics and realist imagery invoked a black countercultural sensibility and a redemptive call for a return to African roots. Soon, Bob Marley and the Wailers, reggae's flagship band, played to audiences worldwide. In northeast Brazil, where African culture emerged from decades of disdain, Bob Marley became a folk hero. In Soweto, South Africa, populated by black workers, he was a symbol of resistance.

Reggae propelled a shift in black American music. In broadcasting reggae, DJs merged sounds and chant lyrics over a beat, a "talkover" form that soon characterized rap music as well. This was a disruptive concept in the late 1970s, but within ten years rap had become a club favorite—and a nonconventional provocation. Rap lyrics emulated reggae realism by focusing on black problems, but they also opened a new domain of controversies involving gang worldviews. On the world stage, Latino rappers stressed multicultural themes, often in "Spanglish." Asian rap stressed the genre as a vehicle for cross-cultural sharing.

The effects of migration on global music were also evident in Latin American transformations of North American genres. Latin music came into its own thanks to Latin American migrants to the United States. In New York and New Jersey, Puerto Ricans and Dominicans popularized boogaloo, salsa, and merengue. In Los Angeles, Mexican *corridos* (ballads) became pop hits.

What reinforced cross-cultural borrowing was not just the medium of production and distribution of entertainment

Bob Marley. In the 1970s, young Europeans and North Americans began to listen to music from the Third World. Among the most popular was Jamaican-based reggae, and its most renowned artist, Bob Marley. Marley's music combined rock and roll with African rhythms and lyrics about freedom and redemption for the downtrodden of the world.

across borders, but also the message. Increasingly, world popular culture was youth culture—especially its message of generational opposition. Consider Egypt's popular TV serial *The School of Troublemakers*, which carried a resolutely antiestablishment message: it showed schoolboys challenging their teachers' authority and then reveling in the chaos that resulted. In Argentina, rock and roll was crucial to the counterculture during the military dictatorship of the 1970s and 1980s. Charlie García urged Buenos Aires audiences to defy authorities by daring to dream of a different order. Indeed, in countries where repressive regimes quashed public cultures, pop culture was usually counterculture.

The same globalizing effects influenced sports. Consider the staple of American identity, baseball, whose major league teams took on a more global cast. Beginning in the 1960s, the number of Latin Americans playing in North American professional leagues grew steadily. Notable in the 1980s was the Mexican pitcher Fernando Valenzuela, whose exploits as a member of the Los Angeles Dodgers made him a hero to that city's Mexican population and in his native land as well. The Dodgers also took the lead in reaching for Asian talent. In the 1990s, as Los Angeles experienced a growing Asian immigrant population, the Dodgers signed the Japanese pitcher Hideo Nomo. Meanwhile, in the Dominican Republic, baseball fans were riveted by their favorite players in the big leagues: slugger Sammy Sosa and ace pitcher Pedro Martínez.

LOCAL CULTURE World cultures may have become more integrated and homogeneous, but they did not completely replace national and local cultures. Indeed, technology and

Baseball Goes International. The 1980s and 1990s saw an influx of ballplayers from Latin America and quite a few from Asia as well. (*Left*) Boston Red Sox slugger David Ortiz hails from the Dominican Republic. (*Right*) Seattle Mariner superstar Ichiro Suzuki is from Japan.

migration often reinforced the appeal of "national" cultural icons, as national celebrities gained popularity among immigrant groups abroad. Inexpensive new technology introduced these stars to more and more people. In Egypt, the most popular singer of the Nasser years was Umm Kalthum, who became the favorite of the middle classes via radio. In 1975 she was given a state funeral, the likes of which had rarely been seen. Egypt's more liberal policies under Nasser's successor, President Anwar al-Sadat, created new national pop stars. Some, like Muhammad Abd al-Wahhab, blended western and eastern musical themes. Educated in Quranic schools, he fused Quranic vocals and chants with western synthesizers and beats to become a national sensation.

As the market for world cultures grew increasingly competitive, there was more room for acceptable performance. Among the breakthroughs that occurred since the 1970s was the triumph of black performers (Bob Marley, Whitney Houston), black athletes (Pelé, Michael Jordan), and black writers (Toni Morrison, Chinua Achebe). Competition also shattered some sexual biases. Female performers like Madonna became popular icons. So did gay performers, starting with the Village People, whose campy multicultural anthem "YMCA" created a place for a new generation of homosexual or bisexual artists. Of course, beyond Europe and North America, flirting with sexual conventions had its limits. In the Middle East, female video artists continued to wear veils—but they still swung their hips.

Because globalization introduced world consumers to a set of common icons—athletic, musical, and performing—it promoted a more homogeneous world culture. Mass culture from the United States became an especially important purveyor of products worldwide, even as local cultures became more diverse. Relatively homogeneous national cultures, often dominated by men representing the ethnic majority, gave way to a wide variety of entertainers and artists who broke loose of confining local cultures.

COMMUNICATIONS

Migration, markets, and mass entertainment were not the only forms that now enjoy global networks; even more important was a revolution in communications. By the 1970s, satellites relayed telecommunications into living rooms worldwide. Television brought the world home—but it was not interactive. Starting in the 1970s and early 1980s, however, engineers based primarily in California's Santa Clara Valley (so-called **Silicon Valley**) tinkered with the idea of computers for personal use. (Computers had served government and corporate needs since the 1940s.) At first these big, underpowered machines had little memory, but with the invention of the silicon chip, the computer weighed less and gained enormous memory capacity. On the heels of this hardware revolution, a software revolution enabled people to process words, run businesses, play games, and eventually communicate with one another via computer terminals.

Computer technology galvanized interactive communications. In the late 1980s, while working in Switzerland, the British physicist Tim Berners-Lee devised a means to pool data stored on various computers. Whereas previous electronic links had existed only between major universities and research stations, Berners-Lee made data more accessible by creating the World Wide Web. With each use and each connection, and as people entered more data, however, the Web grew unmanageably crowded. The early 1990s saw the first commercial browsers used in navigating the so-called Internet. Within a few years, the computer revolution had achieved a fully interactive form of communications and storage with the clarity and resolution of a television. Suddenly people were communicating across global networks more easily than with neighbors and more inexpensively than with local phone calls.

The change created a new generation of wealth. CEOs of top companies like General Motors, Royal Dutch Shell, and

BOMBAY/MUMBAI

Bombay has always been connected to the world economy. Acquired by the Portuguese in the sixteenth century, who then transferred its control to the East India Company, Bombay developed as a port city for colonial commerce. It profited from the cotton trade, developed a vibrant textile industry, attracted migrants, and acquired a cosmopolitan image. The twentieth century brought it unprecedented growth as Indian-owned economic institutions achieved dominance and nationalist politics won popular support. After India's independence in 1947, Bombay epitomized the modern face of the nation, and its heterogeneous population symbolized the Indian melting pot.

Beginning in the 1980s, however, the nature and effects of the city's integration into the world economy started to change. The cotton textile industry, Bombay's economic backbone, went into a decline. Industrial employment fell sharply, and the era of trade unions ended. Moreover, the share of informal household enterprises, small shops, petty subcontractors, and casual laborers rose, along with the role of banking and insurance. Economic liberalization removed hurdles against foreign businesses and brought the city directly into the global economy.

Today Bombay occupies a strategic place in transnational geography. This is evident in the increasing presence of financial institutions, trading organizations, insurance companies, telecommunications corporations, and information technology enterprises with worldwide operations. Even the city's vibrant film industry addresses a global, not just national, audience of Indians. In addition, many of the most successful productions are "placeless"; that is, the narrative occurs not in a definable place but in a global

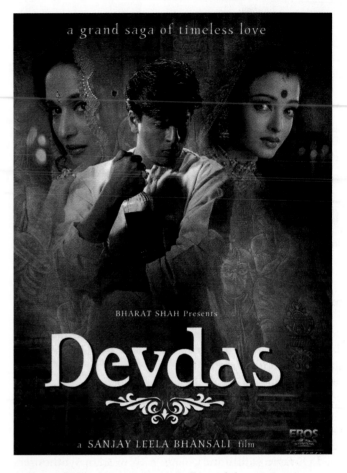

Bollywood. Bombay cinema, or Bollywood, has an increasing global presence. This is the poster for *Devdas*, a three-hour romance that won awards in India and around the world.

Merck had smaller net worths than Michael Dell (hardware maker), Bill Gates (software maker), and Jeff Bezos (creator of Amazon.com). Shares of Internet firms, known as dot-coms, swept the world's stock markets. Money from these companies flowed globally as they established offices worldwide. Software and Internet technologies developed enormous economies of scale and thus became prone to monopolization. Monoliths emerged by taking over small companies.

Hardware, software, and the Internet were not purely American innovations. Within a few years of their invention, personal computers were being made in Mexico and computer chips mass-produced in Taiwan. The brains behind the Internet were likely to be students from Indian institutes of technology. Originally engineering schools, these institutes trained a whole generation of pioneering computing engineers, many of whom resettled in California's Silicon Valley. By 1996, Indians held half of the 55,000 temporary work visas issued by the U.S. government for high-tech employees. Roughly half of Silicon Valley start-up companies in the late 1990s were the brainchildren of Indian entrepreneurs.

Computers and India. Programmers trained by Indian educational institutions became commonplace in the computer industry worldwide, and many became successful as entrepreneurs in Silicon Valley.

locale. Reflecting its increasingly global nature, Bombay cinema has acquired the nickname "Bollywood."

A striking effect of the concentration of global economic operations in the city is the high economic value of these activities. Finance, banking, telecommunications, the software industry, and corporate headquarters operations generate profits and employee wages on a much richer scale than other sectors of the economy. However, low-skilled and unskilled workers, lacking union organization, receive low wages. The city still attracts a large number of poor migrants who live in slums or call the pavements their home. The legendary gap between Bombay's rich and poor

has grown alarmingly. Millions who eke out a miserable living stand in stark contrast to a tiny elite enriched by the global economy. This inequality also affects governance. The government prevents squatters and pavement dwellers from encroaching on the wealthy districts and from acquiring too many municipal services.

Globalization has also affected the city's name and its residents' identity. In 1996, Mumbai became the official name of Bombay, the capital of the Maharashtra province. The political party then in power in Maharashtra was the Shiv Sena, a nativist regional party named after a seventeenth-century Maratha chieftain who opposed the Mughal Empire. Since its inception, the Shiv Sena has campaigned militantly for jobs and other economic opportunities for Marathi speakers, who constitute over 40 percent of the city's population. Starting in the 1980s, when the city's economy and society began to change, the Shiv Sena grew rapidly. As the industrial economy and trade unions gave way to the service sector and unorganized labor, and as globalization uprooted identities based on the secular nation-state, a space opened for alternative mobilizations. In this context the Shiv Sena emerged triumphant, by utilizing the social and political fluidity produced by deindustrialization and globalization to win support for its nativist and Hindu ideology. Bombay's cosmopolitan image went up in smoke in 1992–1993, when the Shiv Sena led pogroms against the city's Muslim residents.

Bombay/Mumbai today illustrates the uneven effects of globalization. The society is sharply divided, economic disparities are great, and the city's politics is a cauldron of conflicting identities. These are the local forms in which this vast and influential city experiences globalization.

While this revolution provided new means to share and sell information, it also reinforced hierarchies between haves and have-nots. Great swathes of the world's population living outside big cities had no access to the Internet. According to World Bank calculations, in the late 1990s countries with low-income economies had, on average, 26 phone lines per 1,000 people; countries with high-income economies had 550 lines per 1,000 people. The biggest losers were the billions living in rural areas or towns neglected by state and private communications providers.

The have-nots were poor not just from lack of capital but from lack of access to knowledge and new media. The result: a widening gap between rich and poor. In 1870, the average American made nine times what the average African earned; by 1990, an American earned forty-five times the income of someone in Chad or Ethiopia. From 1990, as globalization intensified, world inequities became massive. Paradoxically, globalization both integrated the world's peoples more tightly and intensified disparities among them. (See Global Connections & Disconnections: Bombay/Mumbai.)

CHARACTERISTICS OF THE NEW GLOBAL ORDER

> → *What were the characteristics of the new global order?*

By 2000, globalization had promoted recognizable social and economic characteristics. Populations expanded dramatically, requiring greater industrial and agricultural output from all parts of the world. Families changed, and life spans increased. Decent education and good health determined one's status in society as never before. In general, while providing access to an unimaginable array of goods and services, globalization also deepened world inequalities.

THE DEMOGRAPHY OF GLOBALIZATION

It took 160 years (1800–1960) for the world's population to increase from 1 billion to 3 billion; over the next 40 years (1960–2000) it jumped from 3 billion to over 6 billion. Behind this steepening curve were two important developments: a decline in mortality, especially among children, and a rise in life expectancy.

Population growth was hardly equal worldwide (see Map 21-4). In Europe, population growth peaked around 1900, and it moved upward only gradually from 400 million to 730 million during the twentieth century, with little growth after the 1970s. North America's population quadrupled over the same period, mainly because of immigration. The population booms in the twentieth century occurred in Asia (400 percent), Africa (550 percent), and Latin America (700 per-

cent). China and India each passed the billion-person mark. Increases were greatest in the cities. By the 1980s, the world's largest cities were Asian, African, and Latin American. Greater Tokyo-Yokohama had 30 million inhabitants, while Mexico City had 20 million, São Paulo 17 million, Cairo 16 million, Calcutta 15 million, and Jakarta 12 million.

Population growth slowed most dramatically in richer societies. For some, like Italy, the growth rate declined to zero. More recently enriched societies like Korea, Taiwan, and Hong Kong also had fewer births. Societies that did not see their birthrates decline by the same rate (much of Africa, southern Asia, and impoverished parts of Latin America) had difficulty raising income levels. But even among poor nations, birthrates declined after the 1970s.

The most remarkable turnaround occurred in China, where the government instituted a "one-child family" policy with rewards for compliance and penalties for transgression. Inducements included cash subsidies, preferential access to nurseries and kindergartens, priority in medical care, and the promise of favored treatment in housing, education, and employment. The policy also prompted an imbalance in sex ratio at birth. The bias in favor of sons (long a feature of China's patrilineal system, which emphasized descent through the male line), together with the availability of ultrasound scanners, promoted the widespread—albeit illegal—practice of prenatal sex selection.

In general, however, declining family size resulted from choice. In rich countries, more women deferred having children as education, career prospects, and birth control devices provided incentives to postpone starting a family. In addition, love became a precondition to marriage and family formation in societies that had traditionally emphasized arranged marriages.

FAMILIES   The legal definition of families became more fluid in this period. Here again, the change reflected women's choices and the relationship between love and marriage. First, couples chose to end their marriages at unprecedented rates. In the United States, for example, the divorce rate doubled between 1970 and 1998; by the century's end, one in two marriages ended in divorce. In Belgium and Britain late in the twentieth century, fewer than half of all marriages survived. China's divorce rate soared too. In Beijing, by century's

Family Planning in China. To control China's burgeoning population, the government tried to enforce a "one-child family" policy after 1979. While the policy was generally effective, its impact varied in different places and times, and disparity was often found between urban and rural areas. Market reforms since the policy was enacted further eroded government control. Shown on this billboard from the city of Wuhan in 1996 is a propaganda slogan: "Family planning is the need of mankind." Beneath the slogan is the image of an ideal family, with its single child being, significantly, a girl.

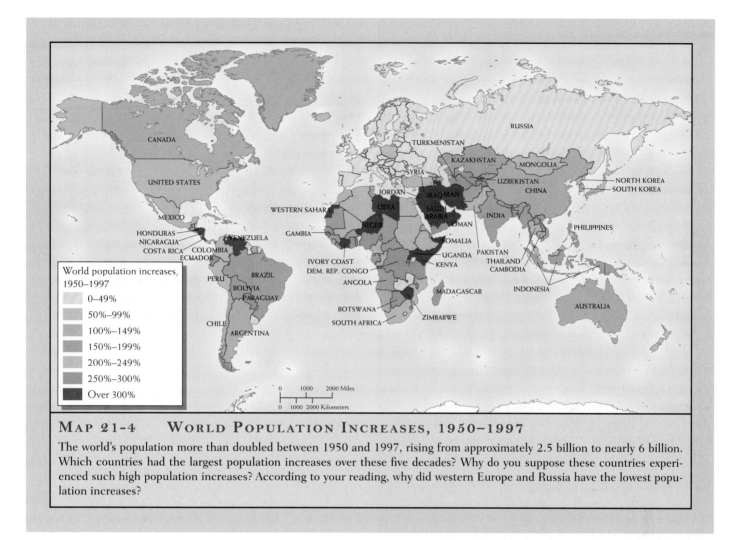

MAP 21-4   WORLD POPULATION INCREASES, 1950–1997
The world's population more than doubled between 1950 and 1997, rising from approximately 2.5 billion to nearly 6 billion. Which countries had the largest population increases over these five decades? Why do you suppose these countries experienced such high population increases? According to your reading, why did western Europe and Russia have the lowest population increases?

end it approached 25 percent—double the 1990 rate. As of 2000, women initiated more than 70 percent of divorces.

As marriages became shorter-lived, new forms of child-rearing proliferated. In the United States, out-of-wedlock childbirths constituted one-third of all births in the late 1990s, with only about half of American children living in households with both parents (compared with nearly three-quarters of children in the early 1970s). Europeans, too, including the supposedly more traditional Italians and Greeks, abandoned nuclear family conventions. In those European countries where divorce remained difficult, more couples lived together without getting married.

AGING   Longer life spans also affected family fortunes, as more infants survived childhood and lived to be old. Also, along with other industrialized nations, the U.S. population "grayed" considerably. Fewer children and longer-living adults caused a marked increase in the median age of the American population: whereas in 1970 half of all Americans were twenty-eight or under, by 1990 the median age had risen to thirty-four. Likewise, the percentage of Americans over age sixty-five grew from 8 percent in 1950 to 13 percent in 1990. In western Europe and Japan, graying rates were even more marked. Japan's birthrate plummeted, and the citizenry aged at such a rate that the country began to depopulate. From a population of 127 million in 2000, estimates forecast a decline to 105 million by 2050.

The aging population presented new challenges for families. For centuries, being a parent meant providing for children until they could be self-sufficient. Old age, the years of relatively unproductive labor, was brief. Communities and households absorbed the cost of caring for the elderly. Household savings became family bequests to future, not older, generations. But as populations aged, retirees needed society's savings to survive. So public and private pension funds swelled to accumulate future pools of money for the retired. In Germany, over 30 percent of the government's social policy spending went into the state pension fund. Chinese demographers warned that the "one-child family" policy might create an unbalanced population structure. In a society in

Wedding Ceremonies. (*Left*) At this Hindu ceremony in northern India, the union of bride and groom is symbolized by the knot between their clothes. (*Right*) South Korean Kim Jong-bok hugs his bride, Song Hee-jung, during their wedding ceremony on the Tokto islets off the Korean peninsula in 2005. Traditional martial arts performer Kim and stage actress Song held their wedding on Tokto to protest Japan's claim over the islets.

which the family still largely provided the safety net, many people worried about having to support two parents and four grandparents.

In Africa, where publicly supported pension funds were rare, the aged faced bleaker futures. Whereas in earlier times the elderly were respected founts of wisdom, colonial rule and the postcolonial world elevated the young—especially those with western educations and lifestyles. Then, in the 1970s, as birthrates soared, the demand on family resources to care for infants and children rose at the very moment when society's resource base began to shrink. The elderly could no longer work, but neither could they rely on the household's support.

HEALTH   The distribution of contagious diseases also reflected inequities in the globalized world. Although microbes have no respect for borders, the effects of public health regulations, antibiotics, and vaccination campaigns reduced the spread of contagions. By the late twentieth century, not only did nutrition and healthy habits count (as they always had), but access to medicines did too.

What used to be universal afflictions in previous centuries (such as the Black Death) now just affected certain peoples. Water treatment and proper sewerage, for example, had banished cholera from most urban centers by the mid-twentieth century. More recently, however, its deadly grip again reached across Asia and into the eastern Mediterranean, parts of Latin America, and much of sub-Saharan Africa. From the 1970s, Africa suffered frequent outbreaks. The crucial cause of the re-spread of cholera was urban developers' failure to keep sanitation systems growing apace with the demand for water. Thus, diseases proliferated where urban squalor was most acute—in cities with the greatest post-1970s population growth.

In the 1970s, entirely new diseases began to devastate the world's population. Consider **AIDS (Acquired Immunodeficiency Syndrome)**, which in its first two decades killed 12 million people. Transmitted through contact with the semen or blood of an infected person, AIDS compromises the ability of the infected person's immune system to ward off disease. First detected in 1981, AIDS was initially stigmatized as

→ *What were the characteristics of the new global order?*

a "gay cancer" (it appeared primarily in homosexual men) and received little attention. But as it spread to heterosexuals and public awareness about it increased, a new campaign urged the practice of safe sex, control of blood supplies, and restrictions on sharing hypodermic needles. In Europe and North America, where the campaigns intensified and new drugs kept the virus under control, AIDS rates stabilized.

New treatments were very expensive, however, leaving the poor and disadvantaged still vulnerable to infection. By 2000, 33 million people had AIDS (the vast majority in poor countries) and even more were infected with HIV, the human immunodeficiency virus that causes AIDS (see Map 21-5). At least two-thirds of those with AIDS lived in Africa below the Sahara. In India, 7 million carried the virus; in China, the figure topped 1 million.

Other factors behind the geographic and demographic prevalence of AIDS were schooling and literacy. Better education led to safer sexual practices. Worldwide, more educated men and women showed higher use of condoms. One Tanzanian survey showed that 20 percent of women with four to five years of education insisted that their sexual partners use condoms, whereas only 6 percent of women with no education insisted on using condoms during sex with a casual partner.

EDUCATION Access to decent education increasingly separated the haves from the have-nots. Moreover, because educational opportunities usually favored men, schooling shaped differences between males and females. In sub-Saharan Africa and in India, for example, literacy rates were, respectively, 63 and 64 percent for men and only 39 and 40 percent for women as of 2000. In the Arab world, the gap between men and women decreased somewhat by the end of the twentieth century. Yet low levels of literacy overall and the depressed levels for women continued to impede each region's efforts to combat poverty. (See Primary Source: Education and Inequality: Why Gender Matters.)

Gender bias also remained in rich societies. For decades, however, women and girls pressed for equal access, with some astounding results. In the United States, by the late 1980s, more than half of all college degrees went to women (up from 38 percent in 1960). More dramatic was the proportion of

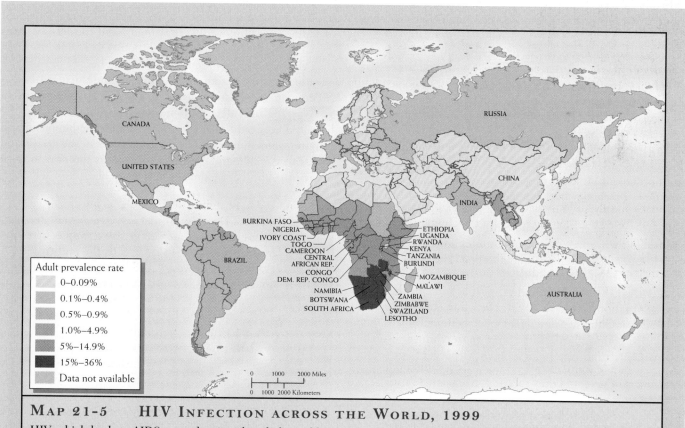

MAP 21-5   HIV INFECTION ACROSS THE WORLD, 1999

HIV, which leads to AIDS, spread across the whole world, providing further evidence of global interconnectedness. The outbreak began in Africa. Where in Africa have the highest rates of HIV infection occurred? Which countries *outside* the African continent have had the highest rates of infection, and why is this so? Why have Egypt, North Africa, and much of the rest of the Islamic world, despite their close connections with Africa below the Sahara, thus far been little affected?

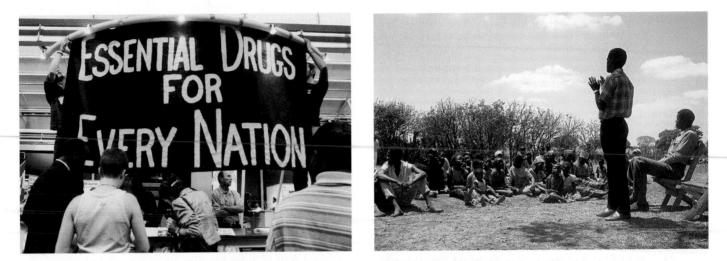

AIDS Treatment and Education. (*Left*) At the Thirteenth International AIDS Conference in Durban, South Africa, in July 2000, AIDS activists express their displeasure at the high prices and unavailability of life-saving drugs for most of those in the Third World who are affected by AIDS. (*Right*) African governments did not tackle the problem of AIDS in their severely affected continent with the energy that it warrants. Pictured here, however, a doctor seeks to impress on the youth of a local community how they should conduct their social and sexual lives in light of the AIDS crisis.

women earning postgraduate degrees (up from 3 percent to 35 percent). Chinese women made even greater strides, although roadblocks persisted. Ironically, with China's recent market reforms women's access to basic education regressed, as families, particularly in rural areas, reverted to spending their limited resources on educating sons. Thus, in 2000, up to 70 percent of China's 140 million illiterates were female.

WORK   Although more women held jobs outside the home, they lacked full equity at work. Limited by job discrimination and burdens of child-rearing, women's participation in the workforce reached a fairly stable level by the 1980s. However, in Russia and Mexico, middle-class women pursuing professional careers often encountered informal obstacles and found themselves channeled into feminized professions such as nursing, teaching, and marketing. The percentage of women at the top of the corporate pyramid was considerably smaller than their proportion in the labor force or their college graduation rates. In 1995, the Chinese government claimed that Chinese women had made better advances than their U.S. counterparts: there were more Chinese women (10 percent) than American women (3 percent) in senior managerial posts. Still, Chinese women graduates complained

of discrimination in the job market. In 2000, some 60 percent of China's unemployed were women, and the number was growing. Women worldwide had difficulties breaking through the "glass ceiling"—a seemingly invisible barrier to women's advancement. Consequently, while income disparities between men and women narrowed, a significant gap persisted.

Working outside the home led to problems inside the home. Who would take care of the children? Jamaican and Filipino women migrated by the thousands in the 1970s and 1980s to Canada and Australia to work as nannies to raise money to send back home, where they had often left their

African Women and Education. Though women's education lagged behind that of men in Africa, a number of women, like Stella Kenyi, pictured here, graduated from African high schools and attended universities at home or abroad. Kenyi taught business skills to men and women in Sudan after completing an undergraduate degree at Davidson College in North Carolina.

EDUCATION AND INEQUALITY: WHY GENDER MATTERS

In the 1970s, aid agencies recognized that reducing world poverty means improving educational opportunities. So international organizations urged national governments to plow resources into schools. The results were stunning. But a disparity appeared: the beneficiaries were mainly boys. Thus, beginning in the 1980s, aid organizations became especially active in trying to channel educational opportunities to girls. In the World Bank study excerpted here, researchers found that development among the poor improves not just with better education, but especially with better education for girls.

Evaluations of recent initiatives that subsidize the costs of schooling indicate that demand-side interventions can increase girls' enrollments and close gender gaps in education. A school stipend program established in Bangladesh in 1982 subsidizes various school expenses for girls who enroll in secondary school. In the first program evaluation girls' enrollment rate in the pilot areas rose from 27 percent, similar to the national average, to 44 percent over five years, more than twice the national average. . . . After girls' tuition was eliminated nationwide in 1992 and the stipend program was expanded to all rural areas, girls' enrollment rate climbed to 48 percent at the national level. There have also been gains in the number of girls appearing for exams and in women's enrollments at intermediate colleges. . . . While boys' enrollment rates also rose during this period, they did not rise as quickly as girls'.

Two recent programs in Balochistan, Pakistan, illustrate the potential benefits of reducing costs and improving physical access. Before the projects there were questions about whether girls' low enrollments were due to cultural barriers that cause parents to hold their daughters out of school or to inadequate supply of appropriate schools. Program evaluations suggest that improved physical access, subsidized costs, and culturally appropriate design can sharply increase girls' enrollments.

The first program, in Quetta, the capital of Balochistan, uses a subsidy tied to girls' enrollment to support the creation of schools in poor urban neighborhoods by local NGOs. The schools admit boys as long as they make up less than half of total enrollments. In rural Balochistan the second program has been expanding the supply of local, single-sex primary schools for girls by encouraging parental involvement in establishing the schools and by subsidizing the recruitment of female teachers from the local community. The results: girls' enrollments rose 33 percent in Quetta and 22 percent in rural areas. Interestingly, both programs appear to have also expanded boys' enrollments, suggesting that increasing girls' educational opportunities may have spillover benefits for boys.

→ *What does this excerpt reveal about the ways that organizations like the World Bank promote change in developing countries?*

→ *Why do you think there was a spillover effect for boys that coincided with these programs?*

Source: Reproduced with permission of the World Bank from "Using Subsidies to Close Gender Gaps in Education," *World Development Report 2000–2001*, p. 122, Box 7.2. Copyright 2000 by World Bank. Permission conveyed through Copyright Clearance Center, Inc.

own children. In South Africa and Brazil, local women served as domestic servants and nannies. They were doing the jobs that once belonged to middle- and upper-class homemakers, women who now wanted the same rights as men: to parent *and* to work.

FEMINISM The deeply ingrained inequality between men and women prompted calls for change. **Feminist movements** arose mainly in Europe and in North America in the 1960s and then become global in the 1970s. In 1975, the first truly international women's forum took place in Mexico City. But

becoming global did not necessarily imply overturning local customs. What feminists called for was not the abolition of gender differences, but equal treatment—equal pay and equal opportunities for obtaining jobs and advancement.

Women took increasingly active stances against discrimination in government and in the workplace. Indeed, as economic integration intensified with regional trade pacts (usually negotiated by men in the interest of male-owned and male-run firms), women struggled to ensure that globalization did not cut them out of new opportunities. For instance, after Argentina, Uruguay, Paraguay, and Brazil negotiated the

Forum on Women. Women representing different cultures of the world hold a "peace torch" during the opening ceremony of the Non-Governmental Organizations Forum for Women in Beijing in 1995.

Mercosur free trade pact, traffic across South American borders soared. But as trade grew, so did government efforts to monitor illegal commerce and foster approved trade along new highways and bridges. Women were responsible for one kind of illicit commerce, because for generations they had transported goods across the river separating Argentina and Paraguay. When customs officers tried to stop this practice in the mid-1990s, Argentine and Paraguayan women locked arms to occupy the new bridge that male truckers used to ship Mercosur products, protesting the restrictions on their age-old enterprise.

The rising tide of global feminism culminated in a conference in Beijing in 1995. Government delegates from more than 180 countries attended the Fourth World Conference on Women to produce "a platform for action" regarding women's rights in politics, business, education, and health. Alongside the official conference was a parallel conference for nearly 30,000 representatives at the NGO Forum for Women. These grassroots activists represented 2,000 nongovernmental organizations from every corner of the globe. Representatives planned strategies and coordinated programs on how to improve women's living and working conditions. What emerged from the conference were associations and groups that pledged to lobby for the rights of women and girls worldwide.

PRODUCTION AND CONSUMPTION IN THE GLOBAL ECONOMY

The growing world population, the desire for more education and better health, the entry of women into paid employment, and the promise of rising standards of living spurred unprecedented production and consumption of the world's resources. The most immediate challenge was how to feed so many people while developing sustainable practices that do not use up limited natural resources.

AGRICULTURAL PRODUCTION Changing agrarian practices made a huge difference in increasing food production. Starting in the 1950s, chemistry increased outputs dramatically. The "green revolution," largely involving nonfarm inputs such as chemical fertilizers, herbicides, and pesticides, produced dramatically larger harvests. Then, in the 1970s, biologists began offering genetically engineered crops that multiplied yields at an even faster rate.

But these breakthroughs were not evenly distributed. American farmers, the biggest innovators, were the greatest beneficiaries. For example, by century's end they produced approximately one-ninth of the world's wheat and two-fifths of its corn. From this output, American exports accounted for about one-third of the world's international wheat trade and four-fifths of all corn exports. At the heart of the innovation was political power, for farmers had the clout to force officials to maintain roads, subsidize credit and prices, and mop up surplus supply. But Asian rice farmers made impressive innovations, too. In Taiwan and Korea, chemical and biological breakthroughs allowed rice yields to jump by 53 and 132 percent, respectively, between 1965 and 1985. And as Indian wheat farmers deployed chemical fertilizers, new seed varieties, and irrigation systems to double their output, the Ganges River basin supported an ever-larger urban population. The most miraculous transformation occurred in China. Beginning in the late 1970s, the Chinese government broke up some of the old collective farms and restored the individual household as the basic economic unit in rural areas. Thereafter, agricultural output surged by roughly 9 percent per year between 1978 and 1986.

Other agricultural producers also replied to world demand, but sometimes their added production was disruptive. While biology and chemistry allowed some farmers to get more out of their land, others simply opened up new lands to cultivation. Lacking access to credit, seed, and good land, small farmers had to go where land was cheap. In Java, farmers cleared sloping woodland to make way for coffee plantings. In southern Colombia, peasants moved into semitropical woodlands to cultivate coca bushes (the source of cocaine) at profits that other cultivators could never realize.

The most notorious frontier expansion occurred in the Amazon River basin. Populations flocked to the Amazon frontier, largely from impoverished areas in northeastern Brazil. They cleared (by fire) cheap land, staked their claims, and, like nineteenth-century American homesteaders, tried to climb the social ladder by cultivating crops and raising livestock. But the promise of bounty failed: the soils were poor and easily eroded, and land titles provided little security, especially once large speculators moved into the area. So the frontiersmen moved

Saving the Amazon. The rise of an international environmental movement in the 1970s led to alliances with local indigenous and environmental leaders, especially in the Amazon. (*Left*) One of the most prominent advocates of the rights of indigenous people and the need to protect imperiled jungles was the British musician Sting. Here he is pictured alongside one of the Amazon's foremost Indian leaders, Bep Koroti Paiakan. (*Right*) Farmers and ranchers cut and burned the Amazon at a ferocious rate in pursuit of frontier lands. In these remote regions, it was hard for local authorities to enforce conservation laws.

farther inland to repeat the cycle. By the 1980s, migrants to the Amazon River basin had burned away much of the jungle, contaminated the biosphere (the environment in which life exists), reduced the stock of diverse plant and animal life, and fostered social conflict in the Brazilian hinterland.

Nor were breadbaskets always able to feed exploding populations. This was especially true in Africa from the 1970s onward, when domestic food production could not keep pace with population growth (see Map 21-6). Food shortages thereafter increased in frequency and duration, wiping out large numbers of sub-Saharan peoples. The protruding ribs on African children became a clichéd image of the region.

What explained Africa's famines? As the Indian Nobel Prize–winning economist Amartya Sen observed, famines—and their increasing frequency—are not natural disasters; they are man-made. Food shortages in Africa stemmed largely from governments that ignored the rural sector and its politically unorganized farmers. Unable to persuade their governments to raise prices for their crops, the farmers lacked incentives to expand production. Food shortages were also by-products of global inequities. African countries, earmarking hefty chunks of their economies to agrarian exports to repay debts incurred in the 1970s, could not produce enough foodstuffs domestically and thus became food importers.

NATURAL RESOURCES   While American farmers now produced a large share of the world's food, Americans also consumed a high proportion of its natural resources. By 2000, they were using water at a per-capita rate three times the world's average. Indeed, extensive irrigation was crucial to California's agricultural sector, the most productive and prof-

itable in the world. Gathering more water also allowed a desert metropolis like Los Angeles to grow.

Energy consumption presented a similar story, although America's enormous appetite for fossil fuels generated a domestic debate about reliance on foreign sources and pollution of the environment. In the United States and Canada, attempts to curb energy consumption saw little success, and the United States grew more dependent on imported oil. In the late 1990s, North American demand for fuel-guzzling sport utility vehicles intensified oil imports. Dependence on foreign sources locked oil importers into recurring clashes with oil exporters. In the 1970s, OPEC raised the price of crude oil (see Chapter 20). The cartel weakened in the 1980s, partly because new oil fields opened elsewhere in the world and partly because internal struggles divided the exporters.

The harshest conflict over oil occurred in the mid-1980s between Iran and Iraq, followed by the 1990 Iraqi invasion of Kuwait. Iraq was poised to become dominant in the area and thus to control oil policies. The conquest of Kuwait would have given Iraq control over about 7 percent of world oil supplies and nearly 20 percent of the world's known reserves. Only Iraq's neighbors Saudi Arabia and Iran would have been larger oil exporters, and Iraq would have been in a position to menace both. As the situation threatened to unsettle the regional balance of power, the U.S. government moved to restore it. Rallying a coalition of other nations, the Americans and their allies launched a military invasion called Operation Desert Storm. The ensuing Gulf War, which ended with Iraq's expulsion from Kuwait, restored an order in which the global distribution of power favored oil consumers over producers and preserved a regional balance of power.

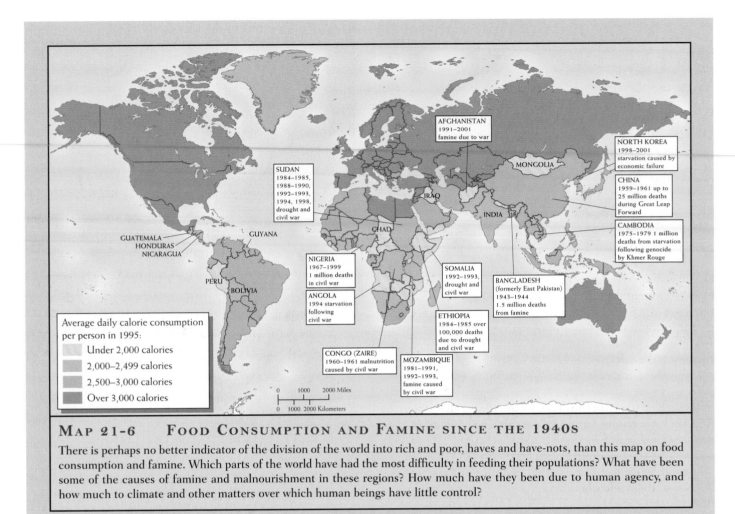

MAP 21-6   FOOD CONSUMPTION AND FAMINE SINCE THE 1940S

There is perhaps no better indicator of the division of the world into rich and poor, haves and have-nots, than this map on food consumption and famine. Which parts of the world have had the most difficulty in feeding their populations? What have been some of the causes of famine and malnourishment in these regions? How much have they been due to human agency, and how much to climate and other matters over which human beings have little control?

ENVIRONMENTAL EFFECTS   The consumption of water, oil, and other natural resources became matters of international concern late in the twentieth century. So did pollution control and the disposal of waste products. Part of this internationalization reflected the recognition that individual nations could not solve environmental issues on their own. Air and water, after all, do not stop flowing at political boundaries.

As Canadians saw their northern lakes fill up with acid rain (precipitation laced with sulfur, mainly from coal-fired plants), they urged their southern neighbor to curb emissions. Thus, reciprocal agreements between Canada and the United States took shape in the 1980s. Europeans, also beset by acidification, likewise negotiated regional environmental treaties. But some polluters simply moved overseas to poorer and less powerful nations. As the West cleaned up its environment, the rest of the world paid the price.

Other problems crossed man-made borders as well. These included the greenhouse effect and **global warming** (release into the air of human-made carbons that contribute to rising temperatures worldwide), ocean pollution, and declining bi-

ological diversity. International meetings addressed these threats inconclusively. After all, it was difficult to enforce an international solution on all national authorities when the forces of globalization compelled some of them to rely on energy-intensive industries, which generated massive emissions, in order to produce exports to pay off their debts. In 1992, the world's governments flocked to the first Earth Summit in Rio de Janeiro. But eco-friendly fanfare yielded only ineffective accords. Several years later, world leaders again met (in Kyoto, Japan) to draft a plan to enforce compliance. Even the grumblers agreed that it was necessary to reverse the emission of gases that led to global warming. However, when the administration of George W. Bush came to power in Washington in 2001, it revoked U.S. support for the Kyoto Treaty, which led others to defect as well. As a result, global climate change did not gain a global accord.

The relationship between power and resources was especially stark in dealing with contaminants. Increasing numbers of automobiles, emitting carbon fumes, caused serious air pollution in cities like Los Angeles, Tokyo, Mexico City, and Jakarta. But where environmentalists acquired political power, they forced regulators to curb emissions. Starting in the late 1960s, Japanese local governments slapped pollution controls on coal plants. Japan pioneered what one historian has called an "environmental miracle," spreading its regulations to many contaminating activities. By 1978, Japanese cars discharged only 10 percent as much pollution as in 1968. In 1987, Japan banned leaded gas altogether. But controls on fossil fuel emissions depended on power and wealth, for it was hard to impose restrictions in societies where high energy use seemed a necessity of economic life. Even the Japanese pioneers of clean fuel were polluters in other spheres. With increasing controls at home, Japanese industrialists went abroad to unload hazardous waste. U.S. industrialists did the same, sending hazardous waste to Mexico. Argentina and Canada sent their nuclear waste not abroad, but to poor provinces desperate for jobs.

Environmental problems gained new urgency after the meltdown of a Soviet nuclear reactor in Chernobyl in 1986. Initially, communist authorities tried to cover up the disaster; but when the fallout reached Sweden, they had to accept responsibility. The delayed response was disastrous for Ukraine and Belarussia (present-day Belarus). Being relatively powerless under a centralized authoritarian regime, they had no political voice to cry out for help in addressing the contamination. As Chernobyl and global warming demonstrated, environmental concerns did not observe boundary lines. Yet at the end of the twentieth century, global guidelines for regulating the impact of human activities on the environment had eluded the world's leaders.

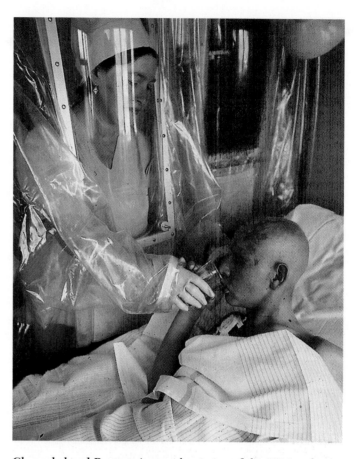

Chernobyl and Protest. Among the victims of the 1986 explosion at the Chernobyl power plant, history's worst nuclear meltdown, were firefighters, such as the man pictured here, sent in to put out the blaze. Chernobyl turned Mikhail Gorbachev's *glasnost*, or openness, into more than a slogan, and it became a rallying cry for the populace, which hoped for political change and improvements in daily life.

CITIZENSHIP IN THE GLOBAL WORLD

> ↠ *How did citizenship in the global world create new problems and responses?*

Globalization distributed its benefits unequally. In general, people with access to better education and more opportunities profited from the border-crossing freedoms that the new order permitted. For most of the world's population, however, the new power structure was not so kind. Finding little opportunity in the globalized world, disadvantaged groups often invoked older religious and nationalist ideals. As globalization fostered human rights, environmental and labor standards, and women's rights worldwide, critics claimed that the language of international rights and standards was promoting neocolonial power in the form of a new "civilizing mission."

In particular, globalization posed massive problems for the nation-state. Since the nineteenth century, nation-states were supposed to be key in defining the rights of citizens. But now the rapid movement of ideas, goods, capital, and people across national boundaries undercut the authority of even the most powerful nations. Accordingly, other political spheres emerged to define and defend citizens. After the 1970s, people realized that international organizations often had more influence over their lives than did their own national governments. These organizations became increasingly important in shaping the meaning of citizenship. This was true especially in the Third World, where nation-states struggled hardest to accommodate globalization.

SUPRANATIONAL ORGANIZATIONS

Various organizations with international responsibilities took shape after World War II for the purpose of facilitating global activities. Although these **supranational organizations** often successfully managed crisis situations, they also impinged on the autonomy of all but the most powerful states.

The most prominent supranational organizations were the World Bank and the International Monetary Fund, which provided vital economic assistance to poorer nations. Indeed, these bodies financed and offered technical information for some of the largest development programs in the Third World. The **World Bank** made available funds for the Volta River Project in Ghana to create an electrical power grid, as well as a system of national parks in the Philippines to help indigenous people manage rain forests, coral reefs, and other threatened ecological zones. Nonetheless, the World Bank required that recipient governments implement far-reaching economic reforms, which were often unpopular. Not infrequently, World Bank– and IMF-imposed programs required local governments to abolish subsidies for essential foodstuffs, leading to riots and charges that these international groups were agents of a new kind of imperialism.

Another set of supranational bodies, **nongovernmental organizations (NGOs),** also stepped forward late in the twentieth century. Many championed human rights or highlighted environmental problems. Others, like the International Committee of the Red Cross, once dedicated to war relief, became more active in peacetime, sheltering the homeless or providing food for famine victims. What united NGOs was not so much their goals but the way they pursued them: autonomously from state power. NGOs created a layer of international forces that rivaled the political power of nation-states.

International NGOs reached a new level of influence in the 1970s because most nation-states at that time were still not democracies. Of the 121 countries in 1980, only 37 were democracies, accounting for only 35 percent of the world population. People found it difficult to rely on authoritarians to uphold their rights as citizens. Indeed, the United Nations itself was a latecomer to enforcing human rights provisions, largely because its own members were the self-same authoritarians.

NGOs, then, took the lead in trying to make the language of human rights stick. The brutality of military regimes in Latin America inspired the emerging network of international human rights organizations to take action. After the overthrow of Chile's Salvador Allende in 1973, solidarity groups proliferated to protest the military junta's harsh repression. When the Argentine military began killing tens of thousands of innocent civilians in 1976 and news of their torture techniques leaked out, human rights movements again took action. Prominent among them was Amnesty International. Formed in 1961 to defend prisoners of conscience (detained for their beliefs, color, sex, ethnic origin, language, or religion), Amnesty International catalogued human rights violations worldwide. The organization became one of the most influential human rights organizations in the world. Moreover, even American foundations recognized NGOs' importance. The biggest one, the Ford Foundation, initiated support for human rights groups and research. By 2000, an extensive network of associations was informing the public, lobbying governments, and pressuring U.N. member nations to live up to commitments to respect the rights of citizens.

VIOLENCE

International organizations and NGOs could play only a limited role in preserving peace and strengthening human rights. The end of the cold war left entire regions in such turmoil that even the most effective humanitarian agencies could not prevent mass killings.

Consider the Balkans in the 1990s. In the territorial remains of Yugoslavia, groups of Serbs, Croats, Bosnians, ethnic Albanians, and others fought for control. Former neighbors, fueled by opportunistic leaders' rhetoric, no longer saw themselves as citizens of pluralistic political communities. Instead, demagogues trumpeted the superiority of ethnically defined states. Serbians took up arms against their Croat neighbors, and vice versa. When international agencies moved in to try to bolster public authority, they failed as Yugoslavia's ethnic mosaic imploded into civil war. The Dayton Accords of 1995 ended the bloodshed by partitioning Bosnia and assigning several international organizations to maintain peace. But in 1999 Serbian president Slobodan Milosevic sent troops to suppress unrest in the province of Kosovo; only NATO air strikes on Serbia's capital, Belgrade, convinced Milosevic to back down. Subsequently Milosevic was found guilty of war crimes and crimes against humanity.

The most gruesome political violence occurred in Africa, where nation-states capable of upholding the rule of law for all citizens were weakest. Here, tension often erupted in

Bosnia in the Midst of War. Despite extensive destruction and perpetual sniper fire, the multiethnic population of Sarajevo refused to abandon their city. With the help of U.N. soldiers and aid workers, they kept alive the hope for the peaceful coexistence of Muslims, Serbs, and Croats in Bosnia.

Rwandan Refugees. Perhaps as many as 800,000 Tutsis were killed in 1994 as the Hutus turned against the local Tutsi population while Rwanda was being invaded by a Tutsi-led army from Uganda. Not surprisingly, the massacre led to an enormous refugee crisis.

conflict between ethnic groups. The failure of African agriculture to sustain growing populations, as well as unequal access to resources like education, made ethnic rivalries worse. Droughts, famine, and corruption ignited the rivalries into riots and killings—even into bitter civil war and the breakdown of centralized authority.

Rwanda reflected Africa's horrifying experience with political violence. Friction grew between the majority Hutus (agrarian people, often very poor) and the minority Tutsis (herders, often with better education and more wealth) after the two peoples had intermarried and lived side by side for many generations. Some resentful Hutus blamed the Tutsis for all their woes. As tensions mounted, the United Nations dispatched peacekeeping troops. Moderate Hutus urged peaceful coexistence, only to be shouted down by government forces in command of radio stations and a mass propaganda machine. Although alerted to the impending problem, U.N. forces, fearing a clash and uncertain of their mandate, failed to prevent the violence.

The failure on the part of the international community, including the United States, which did not have troops on the ground and which had no clear policy toward Rwanda, gave the Hutu government a green light to wipe out opponents. In one hundred days of carnage in 1994, Hutu militias massacred 800,000 Tutsis and moderate Hutus. This was not, as many proclaimed, the militarization of ancient ethnic rivalries, for many Hutus were butchered as they tried to defend Tutsi friends, relatives, and neighbors. Meanwhile, the ensuing refugee crisis destabilized neighboring countries. The civil war in Rwanda sent riptides across eastern and central Africa, creating a whole new generation of conflicts.

Some societies, however, tried to put political violence behind them. In Argentina, El Salvador, Guatemala, and South Africa, the transition to democracy compelled elected rulers to establish inquiries into past rulers' human rights abuses. These **truth commissions** were vital for creating a new aura of legitimacy for democracies and for promising to uphold the rights of individuals. In South Africa, many blacks backed the new president, Nelson Mandela, but also demanded a reckoning with the punitive experience of the apartheid past. To avoid a backlash against the former white rulers, the South African leadership opted to record the past events rather than avenge them. Truth, the new leaders argued, would be powerful enough to heal old wounds. The Truth and Reconciliation Commission, chaired by Nobel Peace Prize winner and long-time opponent of apartheid Bishop Desmond Tutu, called on all who had been involved in political crimes, whites as well as blacks, to come before its tribunal and speak the truth. Although the truth alone did not fully settle old scores, a more open discussion of basic liberties fostered new bonds between public authority and citizens.

RELIGIOUS FOUNDATIONS OF POLITICS

Secular concerns for human rights and international peace were not the only foundations for politics after the cold war. In many regions, people wanted religion to define the moral fabric of political communities. Very often, religion provided a way to re-imagine the nation-state, just as globalization was undermining national autonomy.

HINDU NATIONALISM In India, Hindu nationalism offered a communal identity for a country being rapidly transformed by globalization. In the 1980s, India freed market forces, privatized state firms, and withdrew from its role as welfare provider. Economic reforms under the ruling Congress Party sparked economic growth, thereby creating Asia's largest, best-educated, and most affluent middle class. But because these changes also widened the gap between rich and poor, lower classes and castes formed political parties to challenge the traditional elites. With established hierarchies and loyalties eroding, Hindu nationalists argued that religion could now fill the role once occupied by a secular state. Claiming that the ideology of Hindutva ("Hinduness") would bring the help that secular nationalism had failed to give, Hindu militants trumpeted the idea of India as a nation of Hindus (the majority), with minorities relegated to a lesser status.

The chief beneficiary of the politics established by economic liberalization was a Hindu nationalist party, the Bhartiya Janata Party (BJP), or Indian People's Party. It was the political arm of an alliance of Hindu organizations devoted to establishing India as a Hindu state. By the late 1980s, the BJP and other like-minded parties were advancing an anti-minority (chiefly anti-Muslim) ideology. Claiming that the state had systematically appeased the minorities and trampled on the rights of the majority, they urged Hindus to overthrow "pseudo secularism." This communal ideology was a winning formula, and by 1998 a BJP coalition came to power. Hindu nationalists sought to transform the secular nation-state into a moral community, but without challenging the economic forces of globalization.

ISLAMIC CONSERVATISM In some cases, religion provided a way to resist seemingly American-dominated globalization. One of the most spirited challenges arose in the Islamic Middle East. Here, many people believed that modernizing and westernizing programs were leading their societies toward rampant materialism and unchecked individualism. Critics included traditional clerics and young western-educated elites whose job prospects seemed bleak and who felt that the promise of modernization had failed. Having criticized modernizing processes since the nineteenth century, Islamic conservatives flourished once more in the 1970s, as global markets and social dislocations undermined the moral foundations of secular leadership.

The most revolutionary Islamic movement arose in Iran, where clerics forced the shah from power in 1979. The revolt pitted a cadre of religious officials possessing only pamphlets, tracts, and tapes against the military arsenal and the vast intelligence apparatus of the Iranian state. Shah Mohammad Reza Pahlavi had enjoyed U.S. technical and military support since the Americans had helped place him on the throne in 1953. His bloated army and police force, as well as his brutally effective intelligence service, had crushed all challenges to his authority. The shah also had benefited from oil revenues after 1973. Yet the uneven distribution of income, the oppressive police state, and the royal family's ostentatious lifestyle fueled widespread discontent. As discontent rose, so did repression. And as repression intensified, so did the feeling that the government had abandoned the people.

The most vociferous critique came from the mullahs (Muslim scholars or religious teachers), who found in the **Ayatollah Ruhollah Khomeini** a courageous leader. Khomeini used his traditional Islamic education and his training in Muslim ethics to accuse the shah's government of gross violations of Islamic norms. He also identified the shah's ally, America, as the great Satan. With opposition mounting, the shah fled the country in 1979. In his wake, Khomeini established a theocratic state ruled by a council of Islamic clerics. Although some Iranians grumbled about aspects of this return to Islam (women's reduced status, leaders' arbitrariness, ruptured relations with the West, and the failure to institute democratic procedures), they prided themselves on having

American Hostage Crisis in Iran. The United States was stunned in 1979 by Iran's Islamic Revolution, which overthrew the shah and brought the exiled cleric Ayatollah Ruhollah Khomeini to power. After radical students captured the U.S. embassy, as well as fifty-three hostages, an American rescue raid failed, leading to celebration by Iranians, as shown here.

inspired a revolution based on principles other than those drawn from the West.

RELIGIOUS CONSERVATISM IN THE UNITED STATES

The search for moral foundations of politics in the global age reached beyond nonwestern societies. Indeed, in the United States, religion became a potent force after the 1970s as the membership and activism of conservative, fundamentalist Protestant churches eclipsed mainline denominations. Insisting on literal interpretation of the Bible, Protestant fundamentalists railed against secularizing trends in American society. This traditionalist crusade took up a broad range of cultural and political issues. Religious conservatives (predominantly evangelical Protestants, but including some Catholics and Orthodox Jews) attacked many of the social changes that had emerged from liberation movements of the 1960s. Shifting sexual and familial relations were sore points, but the religious conservatives especially targeted public leaders who, they felt, had abandoned the moral purpose of authority by legalizing abortion and supporting secular values.

ACCEPTANCE OF AND RESISTANCE TO DEMOCRACY

New sources of power and new social movements drastically changed politics in the global age. Increasingly, international organizations were decisive in defining the conditions of democratic citizenship.

Perhaps most remarkable was how much democracy spread toward the end of the twentieth century. In South Africa, Russia, and Guatemala, elections now decided politicians' fate. In this sense, the world's societies embraced the idea that people have a right to choose their own representatives. Nevertheless, democracy did not triumph everywhere. An important holdout was China. Mao died in 1976, and within a few years his successor, Deng Xiaoping, opened the nation's economy to market forces. But Deng and other Chinese communist party leaders resisted multiparty competition. Instead of capitalism and western-style democracy, they maintained that China should follow its own path to modernity.

By the late 1980s, economic reforms had produced spectacular increases in production and rising standards of living for most of China's people. But the widening gap between rich and poor, together with increasing public awareness of corruption within the party and the government, triggered popular discontent. Worker strikes and slowdowns, peasant unrest, and student activism spread. On April 22, 1989, some 100,000 people gathered in **Tiananmen Square** at the heart of Beijing in silent defiance of a government ban on assembling. The following month brought a greater show of defiance when television cameras and world journalists converged on China to

Tiananmen Square. This white plaster and styrofoam statue, inspired in part by the Statue of Liberty and dubbed the Goddess of Democracy, was created by students in Beijing in the spring of 1989. It was brought to Tiananmen Square and unveiled at the end of May in an attempt to reinvigorate the democracy movement and the spirits of the protesters. For five days it captured worldwide attention, until it was toppled by a tank on June 4 and crushed as the Chinese People's Liberation Army cleared the square of its democracy advocates.

cover the historic visit of Soviet leader Mikhail Gorbachev. Several hundred students, flanked by thousands of supporters, began a hunger strike at the square to demand democratic reform. Tiananmen Square was now their stage and the world their audience. Within days, the strike spread to other cities. In Beijing, where well over a million people filled the city center, a carnivalesque atmosphere prevailed as the students sang and danced to rock songs and folk ballads.

The regime responded by declaring martial law. Two huge protest demonstrations followed, and residents erected barricades to defend the city against government troops. As the protest's momentum waned, a twenty-eight-foot icon, partly inspired by the Statue of Liberty, was unveiled at the square, capturing the imagination of the crowd and the attention of the cameras. But by then the government had assembled troops to crush the movement. In a night of terror that began at dusk on June 3, the People's Liberation Army turned their guns against the people. Most students in the square negotiated a safe passage; those who lost their lives—estimates vary from 2,000 to 7,000—were the nameless people who wielded Molotov cocktails, sticks, or bricks in a futile attempt to repel the troops.

The Chinese government weathered the storm. It continued to suppress unofficial social organizations; to control access to information, including that obtained over the Internet; and to crack down on dissidents. But it could not completely control the forces of globalization. Some organizations, like the quasi-religious group Falun Gong, eluded authorities and even used the Internet to enlist international support. At the dawn of the twenty-first century, signs of change were apparent. A visible urban entrepreneurial class had emerged, whose top echelon conducted its global businesses over nearly ubiquitous cellular phones. Rural dwellers paid what little they had to be smuggled abroad, at great risk and often with lethal consequences, so that they could make a better living in America or Europe. Within China, tens of millions of people lived a transient existence, with tens of thousands daily leaving the countryside for the cities. There they often suffered economic and social exploitation, as well as police and other government abuse. Existing at the margins of the new prosperity, they, too, served as reminders of the uneven effects of globalization.

In Mexico, democracy finally triumphed, as the single party that had dominated the country for seventy-one years fell after the election of Vicente Fox in 2000. Until that time, Mexican rulers had combined patronage and rigged elections to stay in office. By the 1980s, corruption and abuse permeated the system. The abuse of democratic rights fell hardest on poor communities, especially those with large numbers of indigenous people.

Consider the state of Chiapas. An impoverished area with many Mayan descendants, Chiapas had trouble coping with social and economic change in the 1980s. The president stripped Indians of their right to communal land and let the ruling party run Chiapas like a fiefdom. By the early 1990s, the province was demanding material betterment, cultural recognition of Indian rights, and local democracy. When one group of rebels, the Zapatistas, rose up in Mexico City against the government in 1994, the government prepared to crush the insurgents. (See Primary Source: Indigenous People in Mexico Speak Out.) But no one anticipated how supranational forces would play a role in helping local democracy: Cable News Network (CNN) broadcast the clash worldwide, and the rebel leader created a Web site that drew thousands of "hits." Thereafter, international news media flooded Chiapas, filming Indians waving flags and pronouncing victory. Leaders in Mexico City, deeply embarrassed, asked local church authorities to negotiate peace and spearhead a commission to hear the villagers' concerns. In 2000, national elections toppled the ruling party (including its

Protests in Mexico. (*Left*) After generations of oppression and exclusion, peasants of Chiapas, in southern Mexico, called for democracy and respect for their right to land. When Mexican authorities refused to bend, peasants took up arms. While they knew that they posed no military threat to the Mexican army, the Zapatista rebels used the world media and international organizations to embarrass the national political establishment into allowing reforms. (*Right*) Among the great Mexican muralists of the twentieth century, David Alfaro Siqueiros most advocated class struggle. In this 1957 mural image, *The People in Arms*, Siqueiros portrays Mexican peasants as they pick up arms in 1910 to fight for a new order. Paintings such as these provided inspiration for movements such as the Chiapas Rebellion.

Primary Source

INDIGENOUS PEOPLE IN MEXICO SPEAK OUT

In late 1993, peasants of Chiapas rejected the false promises of the Mexican national government. Mostly Indians living in a jungle region, they had seen their land rights taken away and had tired of living under oppressive authorities. On January 1, 1994, they took up arms against the government, calling for a restoration of the principles of the Mexican Revolution: land for the hungry, democracy, and an end to centuries of neglect and oppression of Indians across the Americas. They formed the Zapatista Army for National Liberation (EZLN), mounted a brilliant public relations campaign, and enlisted massive international support. Here is an excerpt from their declaration of war against the Mexican government.

We are a product of 500 years of struggle: first against slavery, during the War of Independence against Spain led by the insurgents; afterward to avoid being absorbed by American imperialism; then to promulgate our constitution and expel the French Empire from our soil; and later the Porfirista dictatorship denied us just application of the Reform laws, and the people rebelled, forming their own leaders; . . . we have nothing, absolutely nothing, not even a decent roof over our heads, no land, no work, no health care, no food, or education; without the right to freely and democratically elect our authorities; without independence from foreigners, without peace or justice for ourselves and our children.

But TODAY WE SAY, ENOUGH! We are the heirs of those who truly forged our nationality. We the dispossessed are millions, and we call on our brothers to join in this call as the only path in order not to die of hunger in the face of the insatiable ambition of a dictatorship for more than 70 years led by a clique of traitors who represent the most conservative and sell-out groups in the country. They are the same as those who opposed Hidalgo and Morelos, who betrayed Vicente Guerrero, the same as those who sold over half our territory to the foreign invader, the same as those who brought a European prince to rule us, the same as those who formed the dictatorship of the Porfirista "scientists," the same as those who opposed the Oil Expropriation, the same as those who massacred the railroad workers in 1958 and the students in 1968, the same as those who today take everything from us, absolutely everything.

To prevent this, and as our last hope, after having tried everything to put into practice the legality based on our Magna Carta, we resort to it, to our Constitution, to apply Constitutional Article 39, which says:

"National sovereignty resides essentially and originally in the people. All public power emanates from the people and is instituted for the people's benefit. The people have, at all times, the unalienable right to alter or modify the form of their government."

Therefore, according to our Constitution, we issue this statement to the Mexican federal army, the basic pillar of the Mexican dictatorship that we suffer . . .

In conformity with this Declaration of War, we ask the other branches of the Nation's government to meet to restore the legality and the stability of the Nation by deposing the dictator. . . .

PEOPLE OF MEXICO: We, upright and free men and women, are conscious that the war we declare is a last resort, but it is just. The dictators have been applying an undeclared genocidal war against our people for many years. Therefore we ask for your decided participation in support of this plan of the Mexican people in their struggle for work, land, housing, food, health care, education, independence, liberty, democracy, justice, and peace.

→ *In what other periods in this book have we encountered the ancestors of the Chiapas peasants?*

→ *What does this declaration of war suggest about current and past Mexican governments?*

SOURCE: General Council of the EZLN, Declaración de la Selva Lacandona, 1993 (www.ezln.org, January 1, 1994).

representatives in Chiapas), and Mexico dismantled its one-party ruling system.

Mexico, South Africa, and China were powerful examples of how men and women in every corner of the earth yearned to choose their own leaders. In 1994, millions of previously disenfranchised South Africans lined up for hours to cast a vote for their new black African president, Nelson Mandela. In 2000, the Mexican electorate turned out the ruling party, while in China the ruling communist party had to call in the army to prevent regime change and democratic reforms.

 CONCLUSION

In the thirteenth century (as long before), a few travelers like Ibn Battuta and Marco Polo ventured over long distances to trade, to explore, and to convert souls; yet communications technology was rudimentary, making long-distance mobility and exchange expensive, rare, and perilous. The world was much more a series of communities set apart than a world bound together by culture, capital, and communication networks.

By the late twentieth century, that balance had changed. Food, entertainment, clothing, and even family life were becoming more similar worldwide. To be sure, some local differences remained. In 2000, the local lived on, and in some cases was revived, through challenges to the authority of nation-states. No longer did the nation-state or any single level of community life define collective identities. At the same time, worldwide purveyors of cultural and commercial resources offered local communities the same kinds of products, from aspirin to Nike shoes. Exchanges across local and national boundaries became easier. For the first time, many of the world's peoples felt they belonged to a global culture.

New technologies, new methods of production and investment, and the greater importance of personal health and education for human betterment created new possibilities and greater inequalities. Indeed, the disparities between haves and have-nots in 2000 were astonishing. For as humanity harnessed new technologies to accelerate exchanges across and within cultures, an ever-larger gulf separated those who participated in global networks from those who languished on the margins. This disparity produced divergent political and cultural forms, despite the collapse of the three-world order. Thus, as the world became more integrated, it also grew apart along ever-deeper lines.

Chronology

	1975	1980	1985
THE AMERICAS	1979 Nicaraguan Revolution ✦	✦ 1981 AIDS first detected 1983 Strategic Defense Initiative authorized (U.S.) ✦	
EUROPE			
THE SOVIET UNION	1979–1989 Soviet war in Afghanistan ✦------	1986 Chernobyl nuclear accident (Soviet Union) ✦ --------------------------------- 1985 Gorbachev becomes general secretary of Communist Party (Soviet Union) ✦	
AFRICA			
THE MIDDLE EAST		✦------✦ 1979–1980 American hostage crisis in Iran ✦------✦ 1979–1980 Khomeini establishes theocratic state in Iran 1980–1988 Iran-Iraq War ✦------	----------------------
SOUTH ASIA			
EAST ASIA			

Review and research materials are available at StudySpace: Ⓢ WWNORTON.COM/STUDYSPACE

KEY TERMS

AIDS (Acquired Immunodeficiency Syndrome) (p. 806)
developing world (p. 786)
European Union (p. 795)
feminist movements (p. 809)
globalization (p. 785)
global warming (p. 812)
International Monetary Fund (IMF) (p. 794)
Ayatollah Ruhollah Khomeini (p. 816)

Nelson Mandela (p. 793)
nongovernmental organizations (NGOs) (p. 814)
Silicon Valley (p. 801)
supranational organizations (p. 813)
Tiananmen Square (p. 817)
truth commissions (p. 815)
World Bank (p. 814)

STUDY QUESTIONS

1. To what extent did the three-world order discussed in Chapter 20 not exist by 1975? What architecture of power was replacing it?
2. What led to the end of the cold war? How did U.S. containment policies contribute to the Soviet Union's demise?
3. Describe the process through which apartheid was dismantled in South Africa. Why was the process relatively nonviolent?
4. Analyze how globalization transformed popular culture. To what extent does global popular culture reflect American culture?
5. Explain how globalization transformed world demography. What patterns emerged in terms of international migration?
6. Discuss how globalization affected women. How did new patterns in trade, production, and finance help or hinder opportunities for women worldwide?
7. Explain trends in agricultural production and natural resource consumption over the last several decades. Who produced the goods, and who consumed them?
8. Analyze how globalization affected the world's environment. How effectively has the global community addressed new environmental concerns?
9. Explain how globalization altered people's sense of identity. How did globalization challenge national identity and the idea of the nation-state?

1990	1995	2000

- ✦ 1992 *North American Free Trade Agreement (NAFTA) negotiated*
- ✦ 1992 *Earth Summit (Rio de Janeiro)*
- ✦ 1994 *Chiapas Revolt begins (Mexico)*

- ✦ 1989 *Berlin Wall falls*
- ✦ 1989 *Eastern European Communist regimes topple*
- ✦ - ✦ 1989–1995 *Secession wars in former Yugoslavia*
- ✦ 1990 *Germany reunited*
- ✦ 1991 *Maastricht Treaty (Europe)*

- - - - - - - - ✦

- ✦ 1991 *Dissolution of Soviet Union*

- ✦ 1990 *Mandela released from prison*
- ✦ 1994 *Free elections in South Africa*
- ✦ - ✦ 1990–1998 *Civil war in Rwanda (Africa)*

- ✦ 1991 *Gulf War (Middle East)*

- ✦ 1998 *BJP Party becomes majority in ruling coalition in India*

- ✦ 1989 *Tiananmen Square demonstrations (China)*
- ✦ 1995 *Fourth World Conference on Women (Beijing)*

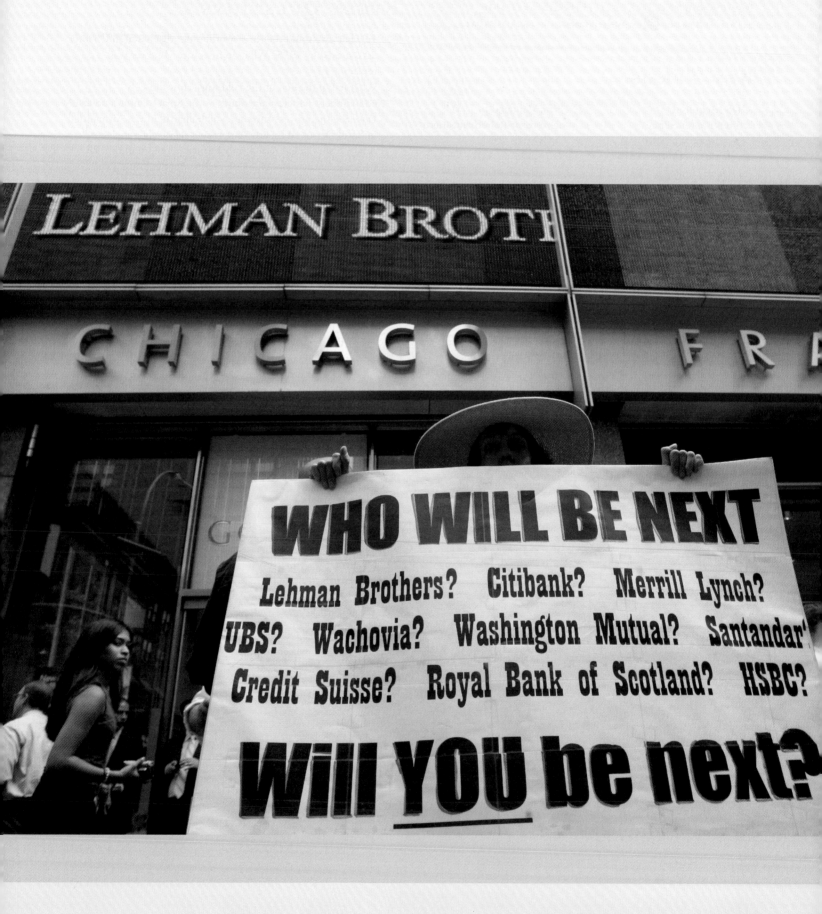

2001–THE PRESENT

On December 31, 1999, people worldwide celebrated the beginning of a new millennium. It did not matter that the twentieth century technically would not end for another year. Largely forgotten as well were fears that had circulated in the months leading up to the big night about a possible terrorist attack or about how computer systems would handle, or fail to handle, the turn from 1999 to 2000 (the Y2K problem). Instead, revelers greeted the turn in a spirit of exultation and expectation. Thanks to satellite television coverage, viewers in Australia, Asia, Africa, Europe, and the Americas could watch midnight come to each time zone and see fireworks light up the night again and again.

With the cold war over, optimists hoped for an end to the history of ideological conflict that had bloodied the twentieth century. They looked forward to an era of peace and prosperity. But in the first decade of the new millennium, it became painfully clear that conflict had not ended, that economic booms and busts had not disappeared, and that while technologies had brought the world together as never before, divergent ideals could still blow things apart.

THE UNITED STATES, THE EUROPEAN UNION, AND JAPAN

Barely nine months into the twenty-first century, terrorist violence shattered the exuberance that had welcomed the new millennium. On September 11, 2001, nineteen hijackers commandeered four airplanes. The hijackers slammed two of the planes into the World Trade Center in New York City and a third into the Pentagon Building (home of the U.S. Department of Defense) in Washington, D.C. The fourth hijacked plane was deterred from its intended target—the White House or the Capitol—by the courageous actions of its passengers and crashed in a field in southwestern Pennsylvania. As on the millennium eve, television captured the event live for global viewers, recording the horrifying, almost surreal, images of the Trade Center's twin towers engulfed in flames, then crumbling one after the other into a heap of ash and twisted metal.

COMBATING TERRORISM

Across the United States, grief unified the nation. Anger focused on Osama bin Laden and al-Qaeda, the militant Islamist group that had organized the terrorist attack. The militants claimed that it was a response to America's imperialist policies in the Middle East and retribution for American troops' presence in Saudi Arabia (during the first Iraq War). Many Americans likened "9/11" to the Japanese bombing of Pearl Harbor sixty years earlier. George W. Bush, who had become president after a close and disputed election the year before, gained broad public support for his tough talk about bringing terrorists to justice and for his insistence that the events of September 11 had introduced a divide between the "pre-9/11 world" and the "post-9/11" one. Domestically, Bush pushed for security measures to curb future terrorist violence, protect freedom, and secure the American homeland.

Internationally, President Bush declared a "global war on terrorism." With the nearly unanimous backing of the American people, as well as strong support from many nations, Bush sent American forces to Afghanistan to hunt down bin Laden, destroy al-Qaeda training camps, and topple the Taliban government that had provided a haven for the terrorists. Although the United States achieved this last goal, it failed to capture bin Laden. Expanding the battlefront of the war on terror, in 2003 Bush ordered an invasion of Iraq, whose brutal dictator, Saddam Hussein, reputedly had abetted terrorists and allegedly was developing weapons of mass destruction. As in Afghanistan, the initial offensive went well: the United States and a military coalition representing Britain, Spain, Italy, and several eastern European nations quickly overthrew Hussein's regime. But defeating the Iraqi

9/11. (*Left*) The North Tower already aflame, this photograph captures a second hijacked jet, an instant before it crashes into the South Tower of New York's World Trade Center on September 11, 2001. (*Right*) Firefighters search for survivors in the smoldering ruins.

army and finding Hussein proved easier than restoring order to the country, improving living standards, and persuading the population to rally around the American vision of a democratic polity.

Moreover, the failure to find weapons of mass destruction or to uncover indisputable links between Hussein and al-Qaeda, together with mounting American losses from an ongoing insurgency, left many U.S. citizens questioning the wisdom of this war. Although Bush won re-election in 2004, the national unity so evident right after September 11 seemed increasingly distant—as was the sense that the new century would be one of peace and prosperity under an American-led world order.

In Afghanistan, the situation shifted noticeably. U.S.-led coalition forces started to find themselves in a quagmire like the one that the Soviets had fallen into two decades earlier (see Chapter 21). Early successes to maintain stability became more challenging as local warlords exercised personal power toward achieving their own goals and as the revitalized Taliban received support from warlords in neighboring Pakistan. Following the U.S. elections of 2008, in which Barack Obama secured the presidency and the Democratic Party took over both houses of Congress, the Americans increased their military presence in Afghanistan, assaulting Taliban strongholds in the countryside.

A CHANGING WESTERN EUROPE

The American invasion of Iraq also created fractures in the alliance between the United States and western Europe. During the 1990s, the collapse of the Soviet Union and the development of the European Union (EU) had caused some rumblings about the future of NATO, but disagreements remained muted prior to the American military's entrance into Iraq. In fact, in the immediate wake of September 11, European allies rallied behind the United States. But before and after the invasion of Iraq, leaders in France and Germany sharply criticized U.S. foreign policy. Their criticism led Donald Rumsfeld, then the American secretary of defense, to disparage these countries as representatives of the "old Europe."

Although Rumsfeld suggested that a twenty-first-century split between "old" and "new" had supplanted the cold war division between west and east in Europe, more striking from a historical standpoint was the region's continuing integration. By 2010, the European Union had widened its membership to twenty-seven, including ten nations that formerly had been part of the Soviet bloc. True, this unification faced some reversals, most notably when voters in France and the Netherlands rejected the EU constitution. Still, viewed against the backdrop of twentieth-century total wars and attempts at ethnic cleansing, it is remarkable that member states could bind themselves together in a union to which each relinquished significant degrees of sovereignty.

DEMOGRAPHIC ISSUES

Looking forward, the greater threat to European integration—and to Europe's future peace and prosperity—remains the interlocking issues of aging and immigration. Roughly speaking, to maintain its population of 500 million people, each female in the European Union would have to bear a mean of 2 children, but women in the union now average only 1.5 offspring. Adding to the demographic and labor pressures is the aging of the population. With the percentage of elderly Europeans rising rapidly, sustaining the present workers-to-retirees ratio and paying for the region's burgeoning number of pensioners will require the European Union to attract around 15 million immigrants annually.

Although these numbers have not been reached, European populations have been boosted by millions of immigrants, many of them Muslims. As of 2010, Europe was home to 38 million Muslims, of whom 25 million (roughly 5 percent of the total population) resided within the European Union. Islam now represents the fastest-growing religion in Europe. In France, the figure has topped 10 percent. These immigrants often live in impoverished circumstances, and in many countries their status as guest workers (see Chapter 21) denies them the full benefits of citizenship. Their presence in Europe's larger cities threatens those who still equate Europe with Christendom and challenges those who believe that European integration requires complete assimilation of all inhabitants.

Europe is not alone in confronting the problems of an aging population and the integration of immigrants. As its baby boom generation ages, the United States faces a similar imbalance between retirees and workers that endangers its Social Security system. Likewise, the flood of immigrants, particularly from Asia and Latin America, continues to shift the nation's ethnic composition. According to U.S. Census Bureau projections, in 2010 people of Latin American descent in the United States will number nearly 48 million (about 15.5 percent of the population). The presence of so many Spanish-speakers troubles those who think the United States should remain an English-only country, and the degree to which immigrants should be required to assimilate remains a contentious issue. More heated still are debates about illegal immigration. (For a global look at population growth and life expectancies, see Maps E-1 and E-2.)

In many respects, the twin dilemmas of aging and immigration press hardest today on Japan. Like Europeans and North Americans, the Japanese are marrying later and having fewer children. Japan's female population now averages barely 1.37 children, compared with nearly 3.7 in 1950. At the same time, Japanese life expectancy has reached eighty-five, the highest in the world, which further tilts the nation's age pyramid. In 1970 the elderly (those over age sixty-five) represented around 7 percent of the population; their

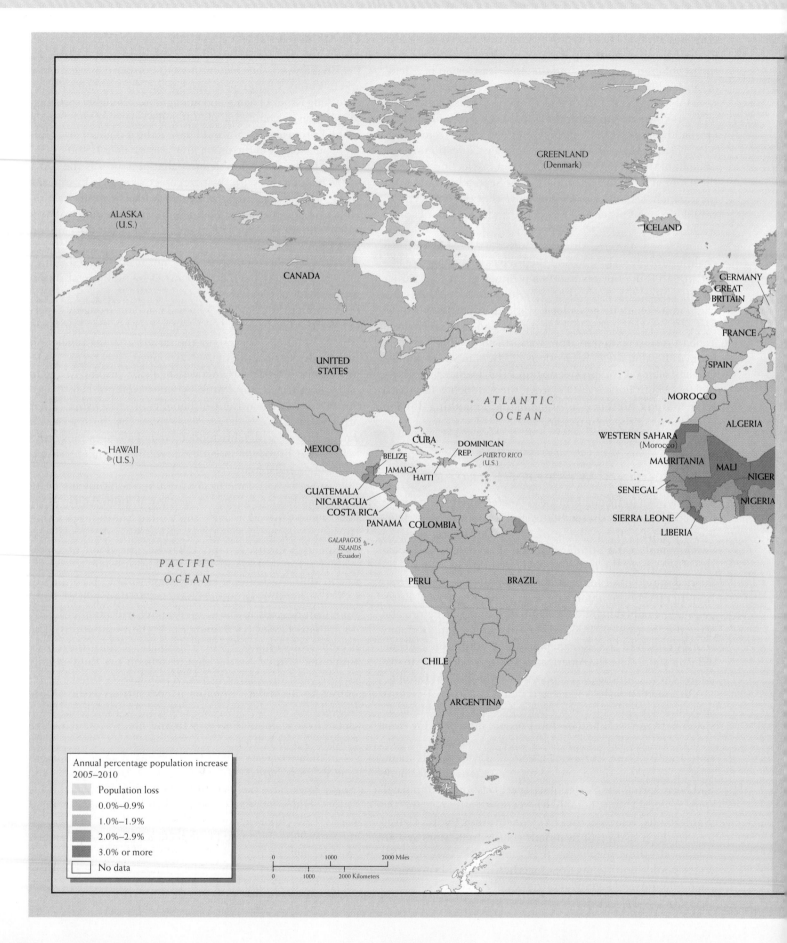

Annual percentage population increase
2005–2010

Population loss

0.0%–0.9%

1.0%–1.9%

2.0%–2.9%

3.0% or more

No data

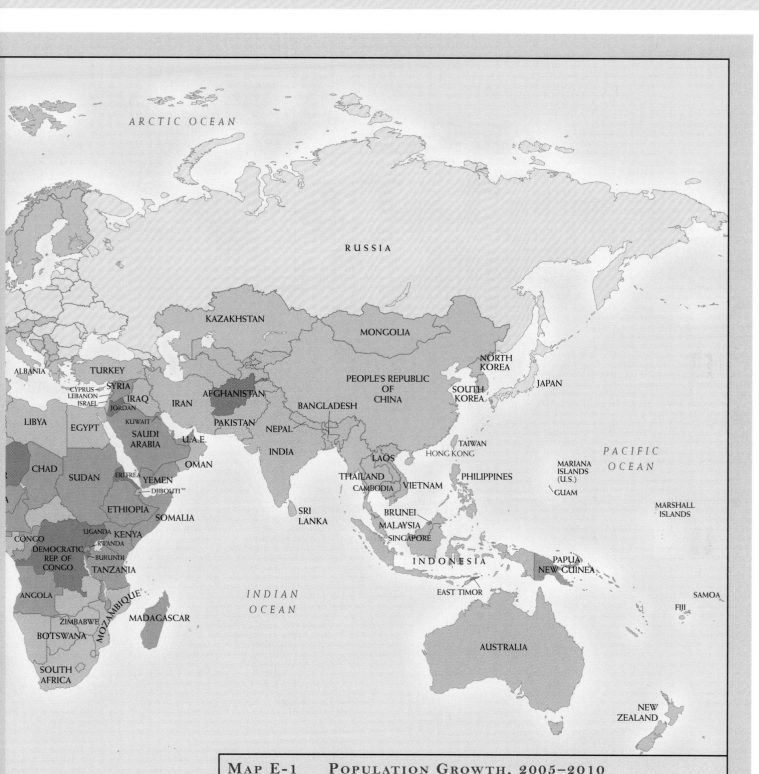

MAP E-1   POPULATION GROWTH, 2005–2010

Strong demographic patterns at the beginning of the twenty-first century pose major problems for the industrialized societies of western Europe, North America, and Japan. As life expectancy increases and population growth slows, these regions' economies face labor shortages that have fueled immigration. According to this map and Map E-2, which regions of the world are prime candidates for sending migrants to the industrialized world? What cultural and political dilemmas does this phenomenon create? Which states within the industrialized world do you think have created the best environment for immigrant residents?

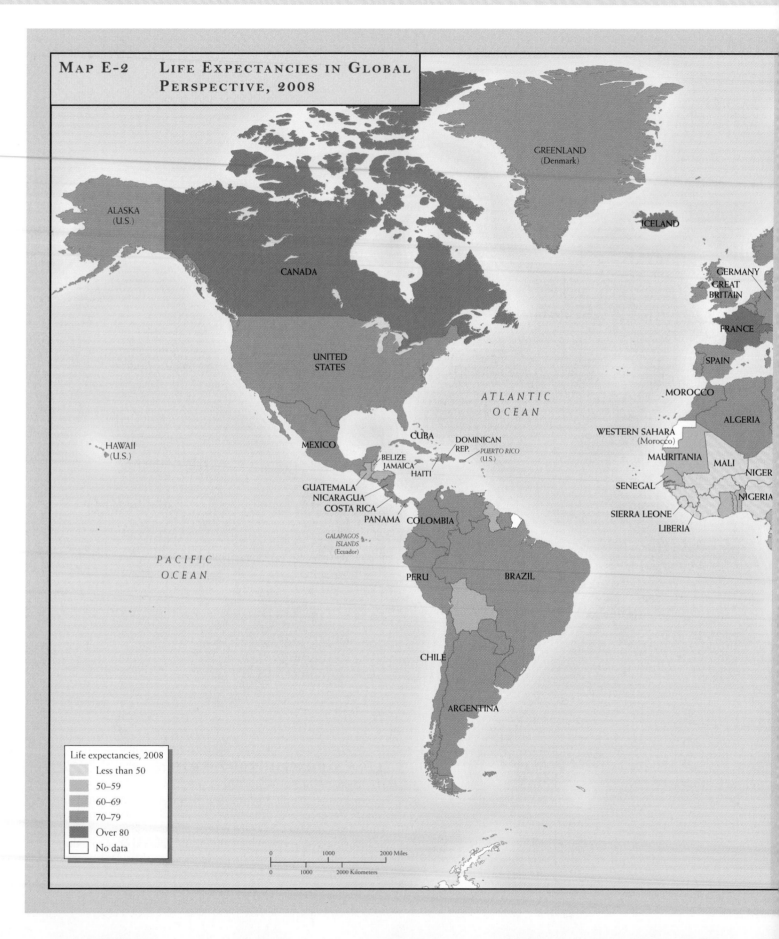

MAP E-2 LIFE EXPECTANCIES IN GLOBAL PERSPECTIVE, 2008

Life expectancies, 2008

Less than 50
50–59
60–69
70–79
Over 80
No data

São Paulo, Brazil. An aerial view of one of São Paulo's biggest slums, Favela Morumbi; Favela Morumbi borders one of the city's richest neighborhoods, also called Morumbi.

proportion reached 20 percent in 2005, and it is expected to hit 40 percent by 2050. Analysts surmise that Japan's population peaked at around 128 million and might decline to perhaps 90 million by 2050. Such a downturn bodes ill for Japan's dynamic economy, which is currently the world's second largest (although China's economy is poised to overtake it).

As in Europe and North America, Japan relies on immigrants to fill out its labor force. In the 1960s, the nation's booming economy experienced labor shortages, but neither the government nor major corporations chose then to invite in foreign laborers. They preferred automation or recruitment of workers of Japanese descent from abroad. By the 1980s, however, deepening labor shortages and the yen's rising value led to an expanded dependence on immigrant workers. Recent estimates put the number of foreign nationals in Japan at nearly 2 million, or around 1.5 percent of the total population. Most of them hail from the Korean peninsula, the Philippines, Indochina, Brazil, and Iran.

ANTI-IMMIGRANT SENTIMENTS

In Europe, where unemployment rates remain higher than in Japan or North America, the political reaction against immigration has been sharpest. Far right groups have demanded that immigration be halted or "foreigners" expelled. Support levels vary in each country, but across Europe the far right's electoral base appears to be around 15 percent; in some countries it is above 25 percent. The Freedom Party in Austria and the Northern League and National Alliance in Italy regularly place cabinet representatives in coalition governments. Ultra-right forces such as France's National Front, Denmark's People's Party, and the League of Polish Families sometimes pressure governing coalitions to slow EU integration and immigration, especially from Muslim countries.

In recent years, anti-immigrant sentiments in general and anti-Muslim ones in particular have risen in the wake of violent episodes. In Holland, the precipitant was the grisly murder of filmmaker Theo Van Gogh by Mohammed Bouyeri in 2004. Bouyeri claimed he was fulfilling his duty as a Muslim by killing Van Gogh, who had made a film about the abuse of Muslim women. Following the assassination, many in Holland questioned the nation's traditional tolerance of diversity and expressed concern that Muslims were too alien in their values to ever fit in Dutch society. Such questions about the assimilation (and assimilability) of Muslims arose again in 2006 after the publication of anti-Islamic cartoons in a Dutch newspaper generated violent demonstrations across Europe and throughout the Muslim world.

France confronted similar dilemmas after rioting rocked the mostly Muslim suburbs of Paris in 2005. This unrest highlighted the desperate plight of unemployed and alienated immigrants, but it also fed fears about Muslims' loyalties and led some politicians to take a harder line against foreigners. Nicolas Sarkozy, who was interior minister at the time, ordered the deportation of immigrants convicted of rioting, while Jean-Marie Le Pen, leader of the far right National Front, demanded that even naturalized rioters be stripped of their citizenship. In the 2007 race for the French presidency, Sarkozy defeated Le Pen (as well as the first French woman to run for the seat, Ségolène Royal).

But the question of how to include the 4 to 5 million Muslims into the republic continued to roil the country. In 2004 the French government passed a law forbidding the wearing of "conspicuous religious symbols" in French public primary and secondary schools. Although the law did not specify what such symbols were, it clearly targeted Muslim girls, many of whom wore head scarves, or *hijabs*. Many French officials believed these scarves undermined the basic secular norms that were at the heart of French culture. So, too, in Switzerland, anti-Muslim sentiment was on the rise. In 2009, 57 percent of voters there approved a plebiscite that banned minarets (the towers over mosques).

Still more alarming to Europeans' sense of well-being were several deadly terrorist bombings. In 2004, a series of bombings of commuter trains in Madrid killed 191 people and wounded more than 2,000; in 2005, terrorists struck London's subways, leaving 52 dead and 700 injured. In both cases, authorities pinned responsibility on al-Qaeda. But investigators also alleged that the operations were the work of Muslims who had resided in Spain or Britain for some time, which sparked doubts about the integration of all immigrants into European society.

In just a few years, then, the mood of the world's most advanced industrial societies has shifted decisively. The triumphant atmosphere that ushered in the new millennium has given way to a pessimistic outlook. Whereas in 2000 talk of the blessings of global integration dominated the political and economic scene, prognosticators now warn about the dangers emanating from disaffected members of their societies and from radicals, especially Islamic radicals, willing and able to unleash terror anywhere in the world.

Child Labor. Girls in a Javanese village work in a factory transferring bundles of cotton yarn to bobbins to be used in handlooms.

RUSSIA, CHINA, AND INDIA

Fueling anti-immigrant fires in Europe, Japan, and North America is the increasing number of jobs being "outsourced." In the past, businesses had turned to immigrants to fill low-wage positions (and to keep all wages down). But at the end of the twentieth and the beginning of the twenty-first centuries, it has become more economical to relocate manufacturing in places where cheap labor is already available. To compete successfully in the global market, businesses need to be agile, to take advantage of differences in prevailing wages.

ECONOMIC GLOBALIZATION AND POLITICAL EFFECTS

In the new millennium, business mobility is not limited to low-skilled and low-wage jobs. As *New York Times* columnist Thomas Friedman observed in a best-selling book, "the world" has become "flat." In other words, technological advances—particularly in computers and communication—have truly brought the world together by virtually erasing distances and enabling all sorts of enterprises to operate from almost any point on the globe. No longer do educated workers have to leave India and China for employment in Europe or North America, because it is increasingly cost-effective for more corporations to shift certain operations to those countries. The playing field has been leveled in the globalized market economy, although countries with vast labor reserves such as China, India, and Russia still have a long way to go to achieve the per capita income levels enjoyed in the older capitalist societies like the United States, Europe, and Japan.

Certainly, Russia, China, and India each boasted healthy economic growth in the first years of the new century. With the price of oil regularly topping $60 per barrel and spiking at $140 per barrel in 2008, Russia enjoyed windfall energy revenues that boosted budget and trade surpluses and expanded personal incomes. Between 1999 and 2008, Russia's gross domestic product climbed at an average rate of more than 7 percent per year—an impressive achievement after the steep economic decline that followed the Soviet Union's dissolution in 1991.

At the same time that Russia's economy is opening to the world, however, its political system seems to be closing in on itself. In addressing the anarchy of the Yeltsin era (see Chapter 21), President Vladimir Putin presided over the repossession of television stations from billionaires and the reassignment of other private properties to the state (or to his colleagues from the former KGB). He also eliminated elections for regional executives and restricted non-governmental

Chinese Environmental Concerns. Despite its prosperity, Hong Kong, like other major Chinese cities, suffers from severe air pollution, which threatens its future as a hub of international commerce. This picture shows part of the city's waterfront shrouded in smog.

organizations receiving foreign financing. In short, Russia's economy is now more firmly connected to the capitalist world, but its political system remains dominated by the executive branch. This situation has dashed hopes for the eventual consolidation of a real legislature and an independent judiciary that the Gorbachev-Yeltsin era seemed to promise.

The Chinese have followed a similar path, encouraging market economic reforms while quashing the possibilities for political liberalization. Their economic strategies seem to be successful. Over the last three decades, China's economy has grown at a breathtaking rate of over 9 percent annually, a spectacular ascent that shows no sign of abating. Consumer goods made in China dominate so many markets that it is virtually impossible, as several newspaper reporters have found, to supply an American family's needs on a "China-free" diet. As of 2010, China's economy was the third largest in the world, and projections—if current growth rates can be sustained—suggest that China will have the world's largest economy by midcentury (although its per capita income will still lag behind that of the United States).

In many ways, China's fortunes illustrate both the promises and the pitfalls of the economic reforms undertaken by many developing countries—what used to be called the Third World—in the era of globalization. On the one hand, despite the continued monopoly of political power by the Chinese communist party at home, China's entry into the World Trade Organization (WTO) in 2001 signified its full integration into the global capitalist economy. On the other hand, the reforms have caused political, social, and environmental problems that defy easy solutions. The disparity between the relatively prosperous coastal areas and the poor interior of the country—a problem that the communist government pledged to redress after it came to power in 1949—has once again become a glaring challenge.

At the same time, the gap between rich and poor in China's more economically developed urban areas has widened at an alarming rate. Government statistics indicate that the richest 10 percent of households own 45 percent of private urban wealth, while the poorest tenth command less than 1.4 percent of the wealth in the cities. Also, at home and abroad, there are concerns about the environmental impact of China's economic development. China's homes and factories, for instance, use 40 percent more coal than those in the United States, and Chinese city dwellers suffer from some of the world's worst smog and least healthy air quality.

As its energy consumption and economy have soared, so has China's global standing. In the period after 1949, China was the eager junior partner to the Soviet Union, slavishly imitating the Stalinist developmental model until the Sino-Soviet split of the 1960s (see Chapter 20). Subsequently, Richard Nixon and Henry Kissinger's courting of Mao in 1972 opened up a global option for China that Mao's successors have exploited. China's shift in foreign policy orientation from an alliance with the Soviet Union to a partnership with the United States has arguably been the most important geopolitical realignment in the contemporary world.

Moreover, China has become the number one trading partner with almost every country in Asia, displacing the United States. It has even become the top trading partner with Brazil as well as many countries in Africa. China has also replaced the United States as the number one customer for Saudi Arabian oil. China-India economic relations have strengthened, too. In parallel, the Chinese government has invested mightily in building an ocean-going navy. Although China faces numerous challenges, from environmental degradation to an aging population, it has regained the enormous global weight it held for centuries up to the eighteenth century. In fact, commentators have begun to speculate that China's authoritarian capitalism could be a model for other countries seeking rapid economic development without political liberalization.

INTERNAL DIVISIONS, EXTERNAL RIVALRIES

Like China, India seems to be one of the success stories of economic globalization, yet long-standing divisions between Hindus and Muslims threaten to undo many benefits. The success has been evident in spectacular economic growth. The tensions, though, were appallingly visible in 2008 when a small band of rebels, based in Pakistan, carried out raids around the city of Mumbai, slaughtering many civilians and security personnel before being subdued.

After coming to power in 1998, a coalition led by the Bharatiya Janata Party (BJP), the Hindu nationalist party, embraced market liberalization. Over the next five years, the government opened India to the global market economy with spectacular economic results. Growth rates topped 7 percent annually, and India's stock market boomed. India is now a favorite destination for the flow of international capital, particularly in the information technology sector. Bangalore, Hyderabad, Mumbai, and Delhi have prospered as hot spots in the global economy.

At the same time that the BJP-led government promoted market reforms, it also championed *Hindutva* (Hinduness) as the bedrock of Indian identity. Nowhere were the effects of this twin strategy of economic liberalism and Hindu nationalism more visible than in the western state of Gujarat. Home to merchant communities for centuries, Gujarat has been in the forefront of capitalist manufactures and commerce. While aggressively participating in the global economy, the state has also been a fertile ground for Hindu nationalism.

The dark side of that nationalism erupted in February 2002 after sixty Hindus perished in a fire that consumed a train compartment. Although the circumstances of the fire remain disputed, a rumor immediately spread, authenticated by the BJP government in Gujarat, that Muslims and a "foreign hand" were responsible. For the next few months, Hindu mobs went on a rampage, burning Muslim homes and hacking the residents to death. Newspapers reported that government leaders and the police force assisted in this carnage or looked the other way as over 2,000 Muslims lost their lives. Faced with widespread condemnation of the violence against Muslims, BJP leaders justified it as an understandable Hindu response to Muslim provocation. In the provincial elections of December 2002, the BJP aggressively projected itself as a Hindu nationalist and pro-business party. This strategy paid rich dividends, and the BJP was reelected to power with a commanding majority.

Still more dangerous was the ongoing tension between India and Pakistan. Flexing its nationalist muscles, the Indian government exploded a nuclear device in 1998. Pakistan then built its own bomb, casting an ominous shadow over the two nations' unresolved conflict over Kashmir. In that contested province, terrorist violence repeatedly disturbed the peace and brought nuclear-armed neighbors close to a potentially devastating war.

Presently, India and Pakistan appear to have taken a step away from that brink, in part because national elections in 2004 returned a coalition headed by the Congress Party to power in India. Led by the Italian-born Sonia Gandhi (wife of the deceased Rajiv Gandhi, Nehru's grandson), the coalition included diverse caste, regional, and ideological interests. Its victory represented a setback to the Hindu nationalist effort to define India's identity in singular terms—at least for the time being. In 2009 the Congress Party again won national elections, and its leader, Manmohan Singh, became prime minister of a coalition government.

Projecting recent trends into the future, many observers forecast a rearrangement of the world's economic order, with China and India especially moving to the fore during the twenty-first century. Yet China, India, and Russia, like other parts of the world, have not escaped from the past. These societies, too, struggle with widening internal divisions and potentially devastating external rivalries. Here as well, the impulse toward greater global integration conflicts with the desire to preserve local, regional, and national autonomy. (For a global look at hunger and disparities in income, see Maps E-3 and E-4.)

Hindu-Muslim Tensions. In 2002, Gujarat was consumed by sectarian riots, set off by a train fire in which fifty-nine Hindu pilgrims died. Although an Indian government investigation concluded that the fire was accidental, the incident sparked an orgy of violence by Hindu mobs against Muslims. Shown here is an angry right-wing Hindu party activist.

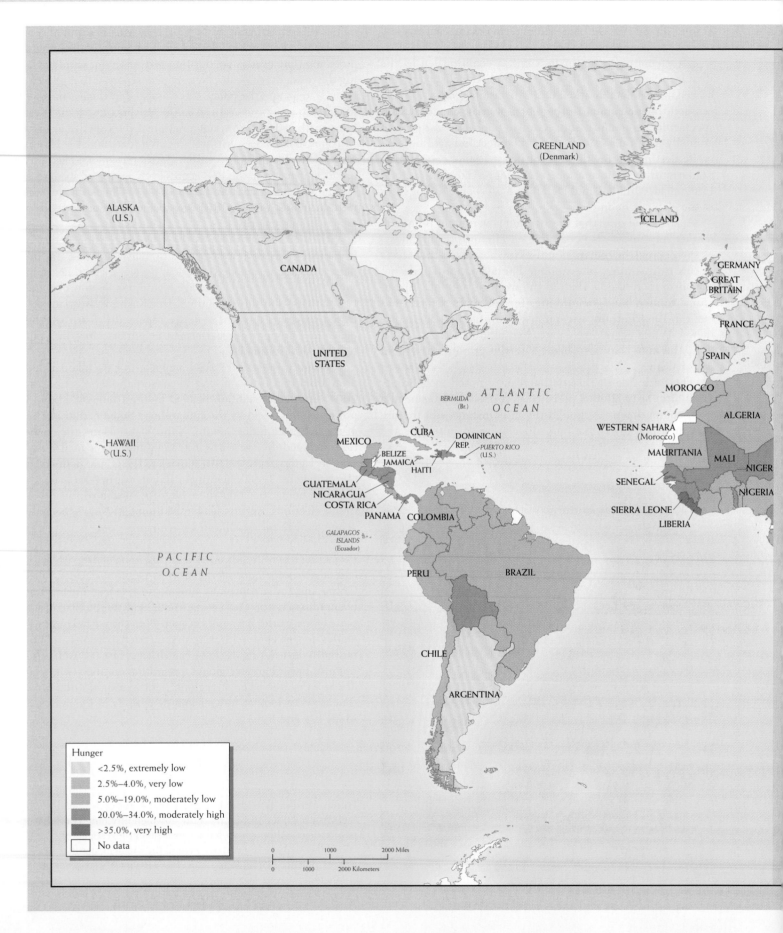

Hunger

<2.5%, extremely low

2.5%–4.0%, very low

5.0%–19.0%, moderately low

20.0%–34.0%, moderately high

>35.0%, very high

No data

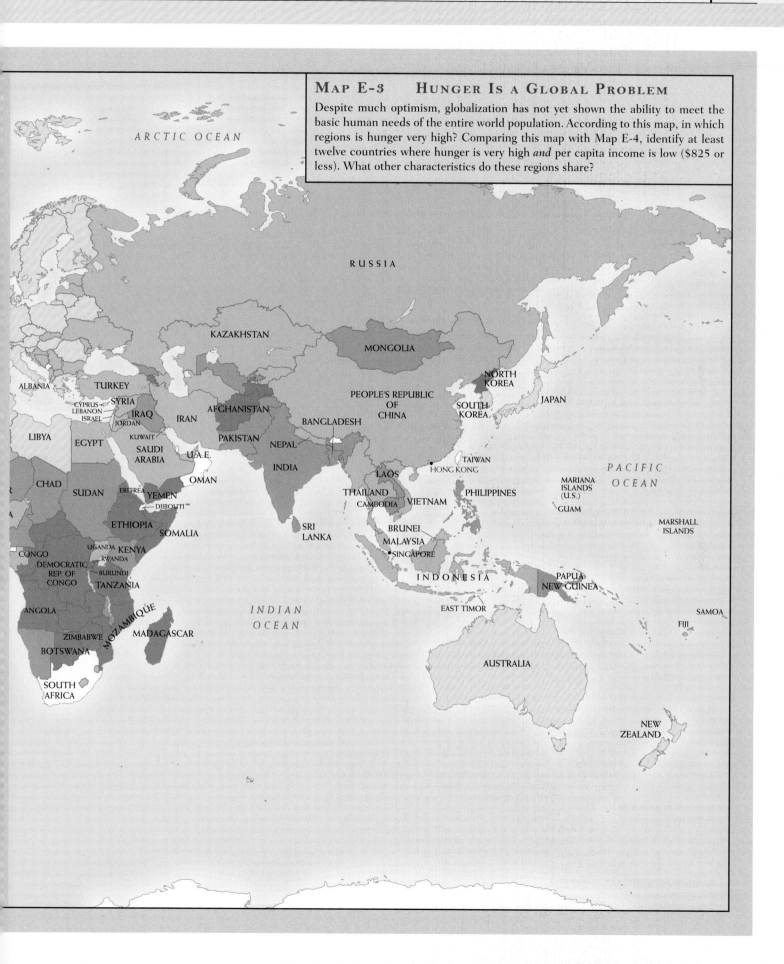

MAP E-3   HUNGER IS A GLOBAL PROBLEM

Despite much optimism, globalization has not yet shown the ability to meet the basic human needs of the entire world population. According to this map, in which regions is hunger very high? Comparing this map with Map E-4, identify at least twelve countries where hunger is very high *and* per capita income is low ($825 or less). What other characteristics do these regions share?

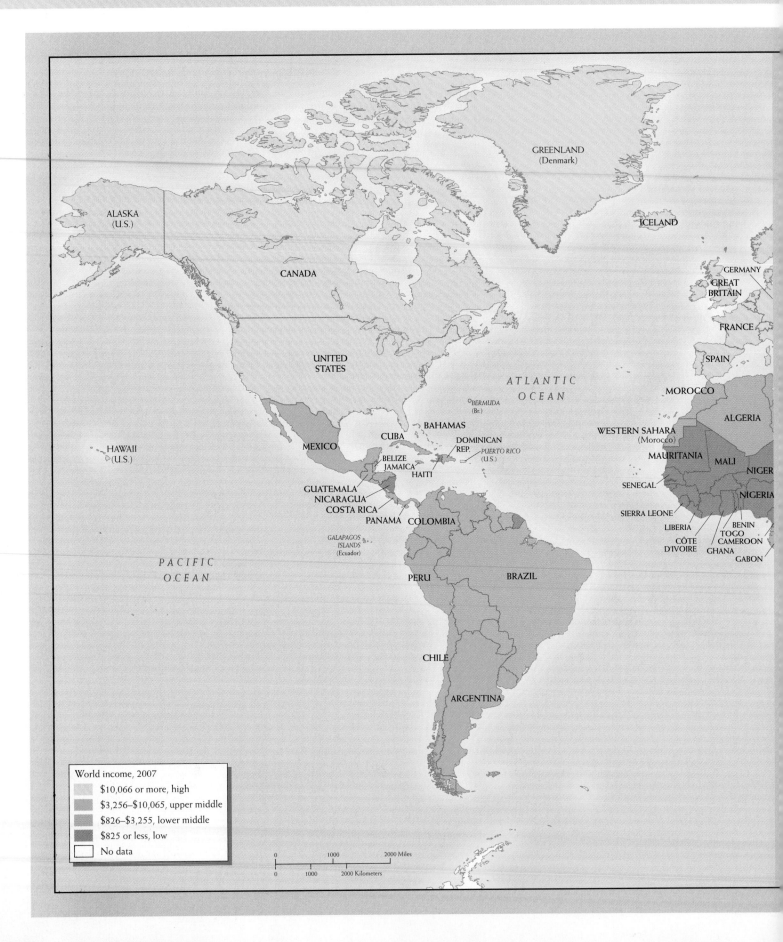

GREENLAND
(Denmark)

ICELAND

ALASKA
(U.S.)

CANADA

GERMANY
GREAT
BRITAIN

FRANCE

SPAIN

UNITED
STATES

ATLANTIC
OCEAN

MOROCCO

BERMUDA
(Br.)

ALGERIA

BAHAMAS

WESTERN SAHARA
(Morocco)

CUBA

DOMINICAN
REP.

MEXICO

PUERTO RICO
(U.S.)

MAURITANIA

MALI

HAWAII
(U.S.)

BELIZE
JAMAICA

HAITI

NIGER

SENEGAL

NIGERIA

GUATEMALA
NICARAGUA
COSTA RICA

SIERRA LEONE

PANAMA

COLOMBIA

LIBERIA

BENIN
TOGO
CAMEROON

CÔTE
D'IVOIRE

GHANA

GABON

GALAPAGOS
ISLANDS
(Ecuador)

PACIFIC
OCEAN

PERU

BRAZIL

CHILE

ARGENTINA

World income, 2007

- $10,066 or more, high
- $3,256–$10,065, upper middle
- $826–$3,255, lower middle
- $825 or less, low
- No data

| 0 | 1000 | 2000 Miles |
| 0 | 1000 | 2000 Kilometers |

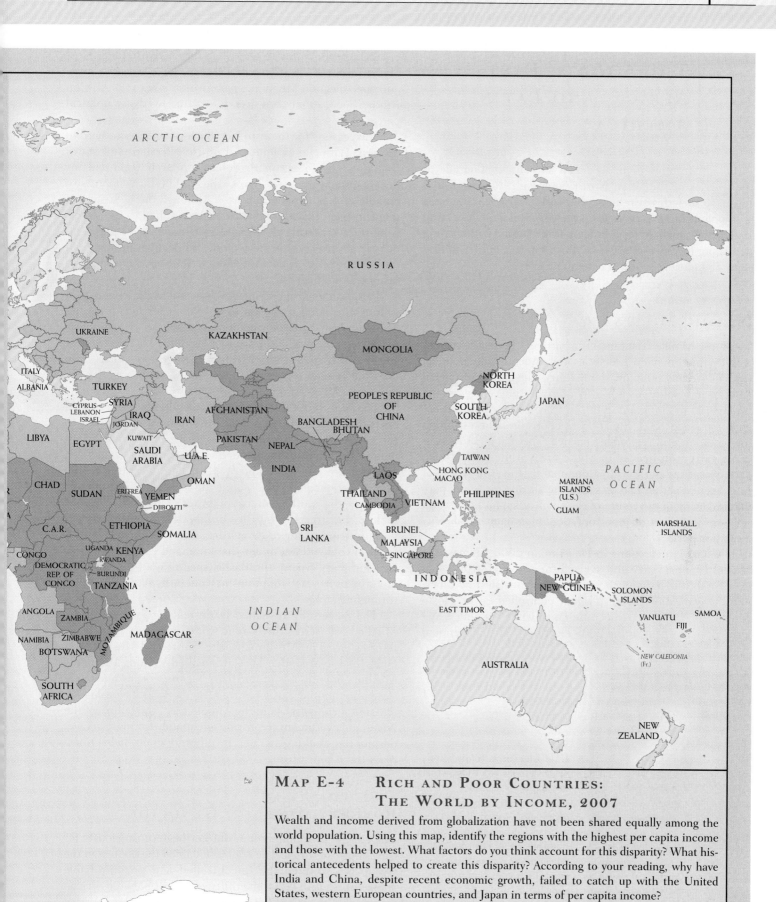

MAP E-4   RICH AND POOR COUNTRIES: THE WORLD BY INCOME, 2007

Wealth and income derived from globalization have not been shared equally among the world population. Using this map, identify the regions with the highest per capita income and those with the lowest. What factors do you think account for this disparity? What historical antecedents helped to create this disparity? According to your reading, why have India and China, despite recent economic growth, failed to catch up with the United States, western European countries, and Japan in terms of per capita income?

THE MIDDLE EAST, AFRICA, AND LATIN AMERICA

Although anxieties about terrorism and immigration add to the worries of the West, North American, European, and Japanese societies still boast the world's largest economies and longest life expectancies. Likewise, Russia, China, and India have benefited from bulging trade surpluses and rising per capita incomes. Elsewhere, however, it is harder to find signs of enduring peace or general prosperity.

ISLAMIC MILITANCY

Today, the Middle East remains a particularly volatile region, with dysfunctional civil societies and undemocratic political regimes feeding militant Islamist fury. The appeal of radical and religious solutions was evident in elections all across the Arab world in 2005 and 2006. In Iraq, under American occupation since 2003, the 2005 elections brought a triumph for sectarian and regionalist parties. The major Shiite religious party won heavily in Shiite areas while the Kurdish party swept the northern, predominantly Kurdish, region of Iraq. Secular parties had no success at all, and the Sunni population, living in the center of the country, supported its own religious party, but its representation in parliament was only a small majority.

Similarly, in elections in Palestine in 2006, Hamas, the radical Islamist party and avowed foe of Israel, triumphed over Fatah, the party of the once-dominant Palestine Liberation Organization. Even in rigidly controlled Egypt, Hosni Mubarak's National Democratic Party, while winning a majority in parliament in the 2005 elections, saw independent

Iraqi Elections. Iraqis voted on December 15, 2005, while the country was under American and allied military occupation. Voters' fingers were stained after voting so that they could not vote twice; many walked away from the polling booths showing their stained fingers with pride.

candidates gain far more seats than they had ever held. Most observers of the Egyptian political scene believe that in a free and open election Mubarak's party would lose to the Muslim Brotherhood, which, however, is still outlawed as a political party.

The reasons for the turn to radical Islam are not hard to discern. With the exception of oil-rich Persian Gulf states that are awash in petroleum-dollars, the Arab world remains deeply mired in poverty. Across the Middle East, oppressive and dictatorial regimes dominate. Although the U.S. government insisted that the invasion of Iraq aimed to free Iraqis from the tyrannical rule of Saddam Hussein and bring democratic governance to the region, the occupation has bred new resentments against the United States and has failed to bring real political reform.

Perhaps the most chilling development in the Middle East is Iran's declared intention to develop a nuclear program. Although Iran's president maintains that Iran seeks nuclear power for only peaceful purposes, his fiery diatribes against Israel and the West suggest more belligerent motives. So does the Iranian regime's defiance of efforts to monitor the program.

The June 12, 2009, presidential election in Iran revealed deep divisions and widespread resentment within Iran to the rule of the ayatollahs. Although the incumbent, Mahmoud Ahmadinejad, proclaimed victory over his challenger, Mir-Hossein Mousavi, and was inaugurated later in the year, questions abounded about the legitimacy of the election and the stuffing of ballot boxes. Opposition groups took to the streets in massive numbers to protest the election's outcome, only to be met by armed tough guys known as Basijis. Operating under the command of the repressive Revolutionary Guard, the Basijis sped around the cities on motorbikes in search of protestors and intimidated dissidents through beatings.

The power of a revivified Islam reaches far beyond the Middle East. Across the Islamic world, pressures to institute reforms based on Muslim law (the *sharia*) and Muslim principles of social justice have intensified. Among the many Muslim communities of northern Nigeria, for instance, one state after another has embraced the *sharia* as its legal guide and moral compass. As in the Middle East, the failure of the Nigerian government to provide adequately for most people, despite the wealth generated by oil production, helps to explain the Islamist turn.

POVERTY, DISEASE, GENOCIDE

Indeed, the new millennium did not begin auspiciously for the peoples of Africa. The region remained the poorest in the world and suffered the uncontrolled and uncontrollable spread of HIV/AIDS. Of the thirty-eight sub-Saharan African countries surveyed in the World Bank *Annual Development*

Report for 2009, all but seven were low-income countries. The poorest of the poor (Burundi, the Republic of the Congo, and Liberia) reported per capita incomes of $150 or less. Botswana, which enjoyed the second-highest per capita income level at $6,120 (behind only mineral-rich Gabon), was so devastated by HIV/AIDS that life expectancy, once the highest in Africa at close to seventy years, had tumbled to fifty-one years in 2007 and was one of the lowest in the world. (For a global look at HIV incidence, see Map E-5.)

To be sure, there are a few promising signs. Ghana embraced parliamentary and presidential elections. Civil strife ended in Mozambique and Angola. South Africa convened a Truth and Reconciliation Commission to put the trauma of apartheid behind it and to stay on the course of parliamentary democracy while addressing the gross disparities of income between whites and blacks that were legacies of the twentieth century.

But these have been exceptions to the rule in which political instability wrought misery and devastation. Three of West Africa's most important countries (Liberia, Sierra Leone, and the Ivory Coast) were torn asunder because of ethnic and personal rivalries and required foreign interventions. Nigeria finally rid itself of unwanted military dictatorial control and moved to a civil, parliamentary system. But Nigeria's democratically elected presidents have barely been able to hold the country together. The northern, mostly Muslim territories continue to fear and resent the southern, mainly Christian communities.

In 2003, just when Africa's longest-running civil war, pitting the animist and Christian southern Sudanese against the northern Muslim peoples, had been resolved, a new dispute broke out in the western Sudan. In the region of Darfur the state allowed local horse-riding, nomadic tribesmen to carry out ethnic cleansing campaigns against settled agriculturalists. This has led to perhaps the worst case of displaced peoples in the early twenty-first century, with over two million refugees having fled government terror and civil war to huddle in vast, miserable camps. As in Rwanda in the 1990s (see Chapter 21), genocide has once more visited Africa. But there is some hope. In the West African country of Liberia, after

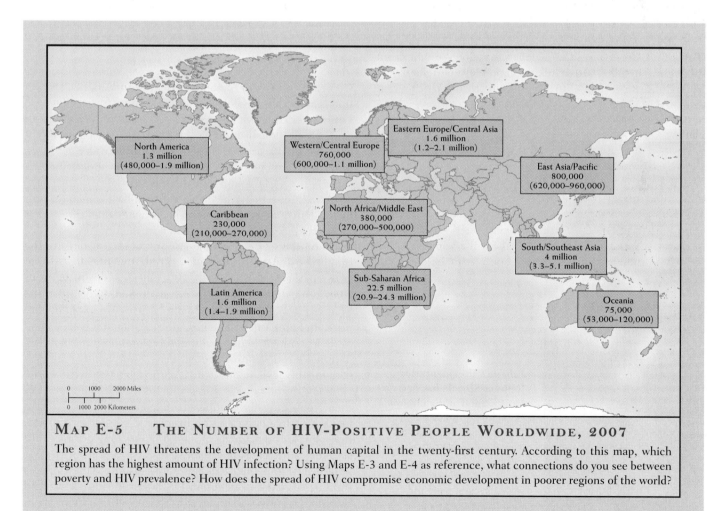

MAP E-5   THE NUMBER OF HIV-POSITIVE PEOPLE WORLDWIDE, 2007

The spread of HIV threatens the development of human capital in the twenty-first century. According to this map, which region has the highest amount of HIV infection? Using Maps E-3 and E-4 as reference, what connections do you see between poverty and HIV prevalence? How does the spread of HIV compromise economic development in poorer regions of the world?

AIDS Awareness. (*Left*) A Gambian health worker offers AIDS awareness literature. (*Right*) Due, in part, to the high cost of medicines, AIDS has taken a deadly toll on Africans, prompting this memorial in the Netherlands on December 1, 2009, which was designated World AIDS Day. The crosses represented the millions of Africans unable to gain access to AIDS medications.

years of pitiless civil war the belligerents agreed to put down their guns in 2004. In 2005, remarkable elections swept Ellen Johnson-Sirleaf into office there to be Africa's first woman president.

Liberia's President. Ellen Johnson-Sirleaf after her inauguration at the Capitol Building in Monrovia, on January 16, 2006. Johnson-Sirleaf is Africa's first elected woman president; she enjoys strong U.S. support and has vowed to fight graft and rebuild her country after years of war.

DEEPENING INEQUALITIES

Compared with sub-Saharan Africa, Latin America's situation is not so bleak. Globalization has had profound effects on Latin America, but it has not created an entirely new age. In some areas, globalization has changed the way Latin Americans see their worlds and their place in the wider world. In other domains, globalization has deepened underlying features of the social and political landscape.

Across the region, the divide between haves and have-nots has widened what already had been historically the world's most unequal region. The very rich in Buenos Aires live like the very rich in Boston; magnates of Mexico City drive the same cars, eat the same food, read the same books, and vacation in the same spots as their social cousins from Moscow. They send their children to private schools in the United States and the United Kingdom to join a cosmopolitan elite class. To Latin American elites, globalization has been a boon to their wealth and has facilitated integration into the international circulation of goods, ideas, and people. Many, in fact, identify less and less with a particular place in the world.

Some of the same features hold for the social bottom. For them, too, being disadvantaged and poor in southern Mexico looks a lot like being on the losing end in southern Africa: they cling to tiny parcels of land, migrate long distances for seasonal jobs, and fight against insensitive authorities for basic needs to be met. Globalization has offered few opportunities to make it at home. Old factories have closed in Rosario, Argentina, when faced with competition from Japan; maize farmers in Mexico have to contend with imports from

Latin American Inequality. (*Left*) Latin America's wealthy are in many ways hard to distinguish from the rich of North America. This picture is of a suburb of Santiago, Chile, called Providencia, where the well-heeled live and shop just as they do in Beverly Hills. (*Right*) Since the 1960s, millions of Latin Americans have moved from rural provinces to booming cities. But the promised jobs and services were very often not to be found. The result has been sprawling shantytowns, like this one in Rio de Janeiro, Brazil.

Iowa. In many cases, thanks to globalization, the main solution to the problem is to leave—to move to the city or across borders in search of opportunities elsewhere.

To these challenges Latin Americans have responded in many ways. One sweeping trend is for voters to elect left-wing governments. Most of these are not like the rebel firebrands of the 1960s. Instead, in Brazil, Chile, Argentina, and Uruguay, left-wing governments offer policies designed to soften the blows of globalization and meet basic needs for land, schools, and decent housing. Here the same pressures of globalization that contribute to leftist electoral triumphs limit what these fledgling governments can do. Elsewhere a more nationalist and populist brand of politics has emerged, one that decries globalization altogether. Rather than softening its effects, leaders here promise to reverse them. In Venezuela, Ecuador, and Bolivia, presidents criticize imperialism and challenge American influence. Their message is that Latin America is better off being a world apart; being together, especially if it means cozying up to the United States, implies a future of subservience and impoverishment. But as many of these leaders also stifle criticism at home, being apart does not ensure empowerment and prosperity for all, either.

The appeal of anti-globalist politics is not limited to Latin America, or even to the underdeveloped world. In the most advanced industrial societies, as well as in rapidly rising nations like China and India, programs to check globalization or buffer people from its destabilizing effects have found receptive audiences. Still, opposition to deeper global integration continues to be greatest in the poorest parts of the world, where globalization's benefits are least apparent and its costs are often so lethal.

 ## SHARED CONCERNS

While the appeal of anti-globalist politics varies from region to region, there is widespread concern about the effects of large-scale problems like global warming and the global economic crisis. Of course, many differences of opinion remain regarding the best approaches to dealing with these issues.

GLOBAL WARMING

Protests against globalization were on display in 2007 at a meeting of the Group of Eight (G8), a forum of leaders from Canada, France, Germany, Italy, Japan, Russia, the United

Global Financial Crisis. When the major investment firm Lehman Brothers declared bankruptcy in September 2008, the world's increasingly integrated financial system teetered on the brink of collapse. Although massive government interventions kept the system afloat, they did not prevent severe downturns and sharply rising unemployment rates.

Kingdom, and the United States. The summit was hosted by German chancellor Angela Merkel, one of a new generation of women to try their hand at leadership on the world stage. A key topic of the summit was global warming, which—along with fear of Islamic fundamentalism and concerns over the U.S. armed involvements in other regions—has emerged as one of the primary concerns of this new millennium.

Researchers confirm that mankind is contributing to, if not causing, the increase in temperatures and that climate change, if not curbed, will bring catastrophic storms, severe droughts, famine, and flooding. Hurricane Katrina in 2005, for example, left much of New Orleans and the Mississippi Gulf Coast in ruins. As always, the impact of these changes may be uneven, but if the warnings are correct, global warming will reshape the lives of everyone on the planet. Indeed, global warming affirms just how integrated the world has become.

Global warming is just one of numerous environmental issues that have gained prominence in the new millennium. As world population continues to grow and as more areas industrialize, the pressure on vital natural resources (especially oil and water) has inspired calls for greater conservation and more environmentally sustainable economic development. But the U.S. government's resistance to global regulations, as well as a rising demand for resources (especially by China and India), has made the future of the earth's environment uncertain.

THE GLOBAL ECONOMIC CRISIS

If the global environment was a specter of uncertainty, there was no uncertainty about another crisis: the nosedive of the

world economy beginning in 2007. The problem began in the financial sector, the most globally interlinked of all. Investors from around the world poured their money into riskier and riskier investments—many of which were so complex that not even the regulators in charge of monitoring the financial sector could understand them.

One of the most enticing of these risky bets was real estate in the United States, whose bubble burst, leading to a plunge in property values. This meant not only that banks and financial agencies were stuck with increasingly worthless assets but also that millions of homeowners went bellyup. Massive defaults on loans ripped through the world financial system and led to a seizure of credit. By the summer of 2008, there was a worldwide panic. The elaborate banking system collapsed with a series of high-profile failures like Northern Rock (in Britain), Lehman Brothers (in the United States), and several European institutions. As credit dried up and consumers stopped spending, factories shut down and stores went bankrupt. Between 2000 and 2007, the United States had accounted for fully one-third of the world's consumption. So, when the financial crisis blew a massive hole in American wallets, it dragged much of the rest of the world down, too. Germany and Japan each saw their gross domestic product sink by 15 percent; Mexico's and Russia's dropped by almost one-quarter in the first half of 2009.

The world had not seen a contraction of production, employment, and trade of this magnitude since the 1930s (see Chapter 19). But how times have changed! In the 1930s, countries often tried to solve their economic problems through strategies that hurt their neighbors. By contrast, nowadays the degree of interdependence is so great that governments

Anti-Globalization. Anti-globalization activists target annual summits of the leaders of the eight most industrialized countries. This one, in Germany in June 2007, saw riot police drive back protesters. Notice the New York baseball cap on one of the protesters.

generally avoid protectionism and instead try to fix the sources of the problem, or at least to put Band-Aids on them. Of course, there have been exceptions. China, for instance, halted the process of gradual appreciation of its currency in 2007, in order to keep its exports cheap and stem the inflow of foreign goods. This may have kept up Chinese jobs, but it inflated huge trade surpluses with neighbors and with the United States, which has led to a howl of protest against China's economic nationalism. But on the whole, governments in North America and Europe have stepped in to prevent the complete collapse of the financial system and have injected "stimulus" spending to prop up local economies. There is now talk—although it is very premature—of a more coordinated global monitoring system of world finance.

The result has been to stabilize the crisis—but with some major political changes. Most obvious were the election of Barack Obama to the presidency of the United States and the enlargement of Democratic Party majorities in the U.S. Senate and House of Representatives. But Washington, D.C., is hardly the only world capital where the financial crisis has brought signs of gathering discontent and political change. In Riga, massive rioting led to the downfall of the Latvian government. Greece was also seized by waves of violent unrest. Likewise Moldova. To forestall the same, a desperate Argentine government nationalized the private pension system for revenues in 2008, and in 2009 it made a grab at the Central Bank's reserves.

Historians, it must be said, are better at interpreting the past than at forecasting the future. What seems certain, though, is that economic, cultural, political, and environmental developments will continue in the new millennium to encourage exchange and interaction, fostering the integration of peoples and cultures. But cultural and religious diversity, local political institutions and prerogatives, economic competition and environmental particularities will also persist. And so will the dynamic tensions that both link our worlds together and keep our worlds apart.

Chapter 15 Reordering the World, 1750–1850

Allen, Robert C., *The British Industrial Revolution in Global Perspective* (2009). The most recent and authoritative study of the industrial revolution in Britain and its implications around the world.

Anderson, Fred, *Crucible of War: The Seven Years' War and the Fate of Empire in British North America, 1754–1766* (2000). The best synthesis of the "great war for empire" that set the stage for the American Revolution.

Bayly, C. A., *Indian Society and the Making of the British Empire* (1998). A useful work on the early history of the British conquest of India.

Blackburn, Robin, *The Overthrow of Colonial Slavery, 1776–1848* (1988). Places the abolition of the Atlantic slave trade and colonial slavery in a large historical context.

Cambridge History of Egypt: Modern Egypt from 1517 to the End of the Twentieth Century, Vol. 2 (1998). Volume 2 contains authoritative essays on all aspects of modern Egyptian history, including the impact of the French invasion and the rule of Muhammad Ali.

Chaudhuri, K. N., *The Trading World of Asia and the East India Company, 1660–1760* (1978). An authoritative economic history of the East India Company's operations.

Crafts, N. F. R., *British Economic Growth during the Industrial Revolution* (1985). A pioneering study that emphasizes a long-term, more gradual process of adaptation to new institutional and social circumstances.

de Vries, Jan, *Industrious Revolution: Consumer Behavior and the Household Economy, 1650 to the Present* (2008). A book on the lead-up to the industrial revolution, written by the leading economic historian who coined the term industrious revolution.

Doyle, William, *The Oxford History of the French Revolution* (1990). A highly detailed discussion of the course of events.

Drescher, Seymour, *Abolition: A History of Slavery and Anti-Slavery* (2009). A recent and authoritative overview of slavery and its opponents.

Elvin, Mark, *The Retreat of the Elephants: An Environmental History of China* (2004). A study of the different ways in which China's natural environment was shaped.

Fick, Carolyn E., *The Making of Haiti: The Saint Domingue Revolution from Below* (1990). Provides a detailed account of the factors that led to the great slave rebellion on the island of Haiti at the end of the eighteenth century.

Findley, Carter, *Bureaucratic Reform in the Ottoman Empire: The Sublime Porte, 1789–1922* (1980). A useful guide to Ottoman reform efforts in the nineteenth century.

Hevia, James, *Cherishing Men from Afar: Qing Guest Ritual and the Macartney Embassy of 1793* (1995). Offers a definitive interpretation of the nature of Sino-British conflict in the Qing period.

Hobsbawm, Eric, *Nations and Nationalism since 1780* (1990). An important overview of the rise of the nation-state and nationalism around the world.

Howe, Daniel Walker, *What Hath God Wrought: The Transformation of America, 1815–1848* (2007). A Pulitzer Prize–winning interpretation of how new technologies and new ideas reshaped the economy, society, culture, and politics of the United States in the first half of the nineteenth century.

Hunt, Lynn, *Politics, Culture and Class in the French Revolution* (1984). Examines the influence of sociocultural shifts as causes and consequences of the French Revolution, emphasizing the symbols and practice of politics invented during the revolution.

Inikori, Joseph, *Africans and the Industrial Revolution in England* (2002). Author demonstrates the important role that Africa and Africans played in facilitating the industrial revolution.

Isset, Christopher Mills, *State, Peasant, and Merchant in Qing Manchuria, 1644–1862* (2007). A study of the relationships between the sociopolitical structures and peasant lives in a key region during the Qing.

Jones, E. L., *Growth Recurring* (1988). Discusses the controversy over why the industrial revolution took place in Europe, stressing the unique ecological setting that encouraged long-term investment.

Kinsbruner, Jay, *Independence in Spanish America* (1994). A fine study of the Latin American revolutions that argues that the struggle was as much a civil war as a fight for national independence.

Mokyr, Joel, *Enlightened Economy: An Economic History of Britain, 1700–1850* (2009). Perspectives on the evolution of the British economy in the era that produced the industrial revolution.

———, *The Lever of Riches* (1990). An important study of the causes of the industrial revolution that emphasizes the role of small technological and organizational breakthroughs.

Naquin, Susan, and Evelyn Rawski, *Chinese Society in the Eighteenth Century* (1987). A survey of mid-Qing society.

Neal, Larry, *The Rise of Financial Capitalism* (1990). An important study of the making of financial markets.

Nikitenko, Aleksandr, *Up from Serfdom: My Childhood and Youth in Russia, 1804–1824* (2001). One of the very few recorded life stories of a Russian serf.

Pomeranz, Kenneth, *The Great Divergence: Europe, China, and the Making of the Modern World Economy* (2000). Offers explanations of why Europe and not some other place in the world, like parts of China or India, forged ahead economically in the nineteenth century.

Rudé, George, *Europe in the Eighteenth Century* (1972). Emphasizes the rise of a new class, the bourgeoisie, against the old aristocracy, as a cause of the French Revolution.

Wakeman, Frederic, Jr., "The Canton Trade and the Opium War," in John K. Fairbank (ed.), *The Cambridge History of China*, Vol. 10 (1978), pp. 163–212. The standard account of the episode.

Wong, R. Bin, *China Transformed: Historical Change and the Limits of European Experience* (2000). Draws attention to the relative autonomy of merchant capitalists in relation to dynastic states in Europe compared to China.

Wood, Gordon S., *Empire of Liberty: A History of the Early Republic, 1789–1815* (2009). An excellent synthesis of the history of the United States in the tumultuous years between the ratification of the Constitution and the War of 1812.

Wortman, Richard, *Scenarios of Power: Myth and Ceremony in Russian Monarchy*, 2 vols. (1995–2000). Examines how dynastic Russia confronted the challenges of the revolutionary epoch.

Chapter 16 Alternative Visions of the Nineteenth Century

Anderson, David M., *Revealing Prophets: Prophets in Eastern African History* (1995). Good discussion of the prophets in eastern Africa.

Beecher, Jonathan, *The Utopian Vision of Charles Fourier* (1983). A fine biography of this important thinker.

Boyd, Jean, *The Caliph's Sister: Nana Asma'u, 1793–1865, Teacher, Poet, and Islamic Leader* (1988). A study of the most powerful female Muslim leader in the Fulani religious revolt.

Clancy-Smith, Julia, *Rebel and Saint: Muslim Notables, Populist Protest, Colonial Encounter (Algeria and Tunisia, 1800–1904)* (1994). Examines Islamic protest movements against western encroachments in North Africa.

Clogg, Richard, *A Concise History of Greece* (1997). A good introduction to the history of Greece in its European context.

Dowd, Gregory E., *A Spirited Resistance: The North American Indian Struggle for Unity, 1745–1815* (1992). Emphasizes the importance of prophets like Tenskwatawa in the building of pan-Indian confederations in the era between the Seven Years' War and the War of 1812.

Guha, Ranajit, *Elementary Aspects of Peasant Insurgency in Colonial India* (1983). Not specifically on the Indian Rebellion of 1857 but includes it in its pioneering "subalternist" interpretation of South Asian history.

Hamilton, Carolyn (ed.), *The Mfecane Aftermath: Reconstructive Debates in Southern African History* (1995). Debates on Shaka's *Mfecane* movement and its impact on southern Africa.

Hiskett, Mervyn, *The Sword of Truth: The Life and Times of the Shehu Usman dan Fodio* (1994). An authoritative study of the Fulani revolt in northern Nigeria.

Johnson, Douglas H., *Nuer Prophets: A History of Prophecy from the Upper Nile in the Nineteenth and Twentieth Centuries* (1994). Deals with African prophetic and charismatic movements in eastern Africa.

Michael, Franz, and Chung-li Chang, *The Taiping Rebellion: History and Documents*, 3 vols. (1966–1971). The basic source for the history of the Taiping.

Mukherjee, Rudrangshu, *Awadh in Revolt 1857–58* (1984). A careful case study of the Indian Rebellion.

Omer-Cooper, J. D., *The Zulu Aftermath: A Nineteenth-Century Revolution in Bantu Africa* (1966). A good place to start in studying Shaka's *Mfecane* movement, which greatly rearranged the political and ethnic makeup of southern Africa.

Ostler, Jeffrey, *The Plains Sioux and U.S. Colonialism from Lewis and Clark to Wounded Knee* (2004). Uses the lens of colonial theory to track relations between the Sioux and the United States, offering fresh insights about the Ghost Dance movement.

Peires, J. B. (ed.), *Before and After Shaka* (1981). Discusses elements in the debate over Shaka's *Mfecane* movement.

Pilbeam, Pamela, *French Socialists Before Marx: Workers, Women and the Social Question in France* (2001). Describes the development of a variety of socialist ideas in early nineteenth-century France.

Reed, Nelson, *The Caste War of Yucatan* (1964). A classic narrative of the Caste War of the Yucatan.

Restall, Matthew, *The Maya World* (1997). Describes in economic and social terms the origins of the Yucatan upheaval in southern Mexico.

Rugeley, Terry, *Yucatán's Peasantry and the Origins of the Caste War* (1996). Explains the combination of economic and cultural pressures that drove the Mayans in the Yucatan to revolt in the Caste War.

Spence, Jonathan, *God's Chinese Son: The Taiping Heavenly Kingdom of Hong Xiuquan* (1996). A fascinating portrayal of the Taiping through the prism of its founder.

Wagner, Rudolf, *Reenacting the Heavenly Vision: The Role of Religion in the Taiping Rebellion* (1982). A brief but insightful analysis of the religious elements in the Taiping's doctrines.

White, Richard, *The Middle Ground: Indians, Empires, and Republics in the Great Lakes Region, 1650–1815* (1991). A pathbreaking exploration of intercultural relations in North America that offers a provocative interpretation of the visions of Tenskwatawa and the efforts of Tecumseh to resist the expansion of the United States.

Chapter 17 Nations and Empires, 1850–1914

Cain, P. A., and A. G. Hopkins, *British Imperialism: Innovation and Expansion, 1688–1914* (1993). An excellent discussion of British imperialism, especially British expansion into Africa.

Cronon, William, *Nature's Metropolis: Chicago and the Great West* (1991). Makes connections among territorial expansion, industrialization, and urban development.

Davis, John, *Conflict and Control: Law and Order in Nineteenth-Century Italy* (1988). A superb study of the north-south and other rifts after Italian political unification.

Friesen, Gerald, *The Canadian Prairies* (1984). The most comprehensive account of Canadian westward expansion.

Gluck, Carol, *Japan's Modern Myths: Ideology in the Late Meiji Period* (1985). A study of how states fashion useful historical traditions to consolidate and legitimize their rule.

Headrick, Daniel R., *The Tools of Empire: Technology and European Imperialism in the Nineteenth Century* (1981). A useful general study of the relationship between imperialism and technology.

Herbst, Jeffrey, *States and Power in Africa: Comparative Lessons in Authority and Control* (2000). An overview of the impact of colonial rule on contemporary African states.

Hine, Robert V., and John Mack Faragher, *The American West: A New Interpretive History* (2000). Presents an excellent synthesis of the conquests by which the United States expanded from the Atlantic to the Pacific.

Hobsbawm, Eric J., *Nations and Nationalism since 1780: Programme, Myth, Reality* (1993). An insightful survey of the origins and development of nationalist thought throughout Europe.

Lee, Leo Ou-fan, and Andrew Nathan, "The Beginnings of Mass Culture: Journalism and Fiction in the Late Ch'ing and Beyond," in David Johnson, Andrew Nathan, and Evelyn Rawski (eds.), *Popular Culture in Late Imperial China* (1985), pp. 360–95. An important article on the emergence of a mass-media market in late-nineteenth- and early-twentieth-century China.

Lieven, Dominic, *Empire: The Russian Empire and Its Rivals* (2000). A comparison of the British, Ottoman, Habsburg, and Russian empires.

Mackenzie, John M., *Propaganda and Empire* (1984). Contains a series of useful chapters showing the importance of the empire to Britain.

Mamdani, Mahmood, *Citizen and State: Contemporary Africa and the Legacy of Late Colonialism* (1996). A survey of the impact of European colonial powers on African political systems.

McClintock, Anne, *Imperial Leather: Race, Gender and Sexuality in the Colonial Contest* (1995). A study of the imperial relationship between Victorian Britain and South Africa from the point of view of cultural studies.

McNeil, William, *Europe's Steppe Frontier: 1500–1800* (1964). An excellent study of the definitive victory of Russia's agricultural empire over grazing nomads and independent frontier people.

Montgomery, David, *The Fall of the House of Labor: The Workplace, the State, and American Labor Activism, 1865–1925* (1987). An excellent discussion of changes in work in the late nineteenth century.

Myers, Ramon, and Mark Peattie (eds.), *The Japanese Colonial Empire, 1895–1945* (1984). A collection of essays exploring different aspects of Japanese colonialism.

Needell, Jeffrey, *A Tropical Belle Epoque: Elite Culture and Society in Turn of the Century Rio de Janeiro* (1987). Shows the strength of the Brazilian elites at the turn of the century.

Pan, Lynn (ed.), *The Encyclopedia of Chinese Overseas* (1999). A comprehensive coverage of the history of the Chinese diaspora.

Porter, Bernard, *The Absent-Minded Imperialists: What the British Really Thought about Empire* (2004). A careful dissection of the ways in which empire changed the British—and did not.

Topik, Steven, *The Political Economy of the Brazilian State, 1889–1930* (1987). An excellent discussion of the Brazilian state, and especially of its elites.

Walker, Mack, *German Home Towns: Community, State, and the General State, 1648–1871* (1971, 1998). A brilliant, street-level analysis of the Holy Roman Empire (the First Reich) and the run-up to the German unification of 1871 (the Second Reich).

Wasserman, Mark, *Everyday Life and Politics in Nineteenth-Century Mexico* (2000). Wonderfully captures the way in which people coped with social and economic dislocation in late-nineteenth-century Mexico.

Weeks, Theodore R., *Nation and State in Late Imperial Russia: Nationalism and Russification on the Western Frontier, 1863–1914* (1996). A good discussion of the Russian Empire's responses to the concept of the nation-state.

Yung Wing, *My Life in China and America* (1909). The autobiography of the first Chinese graduate of an American university.

Chapter 18 An Unsettled World, 1890–1914

Bayly, C. A., *The Birth of the Modern World, 1780–1914: Global Connections and Comparisons* (2004). A general study of the key political, economic, social, and cultural features of the modern era in world history.

Bergère, Marie-Claire, *Sun Yat-sen* (1998). Originally published in French in 1994, this is a judicious biography of the man generally known as the father of the modern Chinese nation.

Chatterjee, Partha, *The Nation and Its Fragments* (1993). One of the most important works on Indian nationalism by a leading scholar of "Subaltern Studies."

Conrad, Joseph, *Heart of Darkness* (1899). First published in a magazine in 1899, this novella contained a searing critique of King Leopold's oppressive and exploitative policies in the Congo and was part of a growing concern for the effects that European empires were having around the world, especially in Africa.

Esherick, Joseph, "How the Qing became China," in Joseph W. Esherick, Hasan Kayali, and Eric Van Young, eds., *Empire to Nation: Historical Perspectives on the Making of the Modern World* (2006). A study of the processes through which the Qing Empire became the nation-state of China.

———, *The Origins of the Boxer Uprising* (1987). The definitive account of the episode.

Everdell, William R., *The First Moderns: Profiles in the Origins of Twentieth-Century Thought* (1997). A rich account of the many faces of modernism, focusing particularly on science and art.

Finnane, Antonia, *Changing Clothes in China: Fashion, History, Nation* (2008). An exploration of changing Chinese identities from the perspective of clothing.

Gay, Peter, *The Cultivation of Hatred* (1994). A provocative discussion of the violent passions of the immediate pre–Great War era.

Gilmartin, Christina, Gail Hershatter, Lisa Rofel, and Tyrene White (eds.), *Engendering China: Women, Culture, and the State* (1994). Analyzes politics and society in modern China from the perspective of gender.

Hochschild, Adam, *King Leopold's Ghost: A Story of Greed, Terror, and Heroism in Colonial Africa* (1998). A well-written account of the violent colonial history of the Belgian Congo under King Leopold in the late nineteenth century.

Katz, Friedrich, *The Life and Times of Pancho Villa* (1998). An exploration of the Mexican Revolution that shows how Villa's armies destroyed the forces of Díaz and his followers.

Kern, Stephen, *The Culture of Time and Space 1880–1918* (1986). A useful study of the enormous changes in the experience of time and space in the age of late industrialism in Europe and America.

Kuhn, Philip, *Chinese among Others: Emigration in Modern Times* (2008). An overview of the history of Chinese migration.

McKeown, Adam, *Melancholy Order: Asian Migration and the Globalization of Borders* (2008). An examination of global migration patterns since the mid-nineteenth century and how regulations designed to restrict Asian migration to other parts of the world led to the modern regime of migration control.

Meade, Teresa, *"Civilizing" Rio: Reform and Resistance in a Brazilian City, 1889–1930* (1997). A wonderful study of cultural and class conflict in Brazil.

Pick, Daniel, *Faces of Degeneration: A European Disorder, c. 1848–c. 1918* (1993). A study of Europe's fear of social and biological decline, particularly focusing on France and Italy.

Pretorius, Fransjohn (ed.), *Scorched Earth* (2001). A study of the Anglo-Boer War in terms of its environmental impacts.

Sarkar, Sumit, *The Swadeshi Movement in Bengal* (1973). A comprehensive study of an early militant movement against British rule.

Schorske, Carl E. *Fin-de-Siècle Vienna: Politics and Culture* (1980). The classic treatment of the birth of modern ideas and political movements in turn-of-the-century Austria.

Trachtenberg, Alan, *The Incorporation of America: Culture and Society in the Gilded Age* (1982). A provocative synthesis of changes in the American economy, society, and culture in the last decades of the nineteenth century.

Wang, David Der-wei, *Fin-de-Siècle Splendor: Repressed Modernities of Late Qing Fiction, 1849–1911* (1997). A fine work that attempts to locate the "modern" within the writings of the late Qing period.

Warren, Louis, *Buffalo Bill's America: William Cody and the Wild West Show* (2005). A superb portrait of William F. Cody, the person; of Buffalo Bill, the persona Cody (and others) created; and of the popular culture his Wild West shows brought to audiences in Europe and North America.

Warwick, Peter, *Black People and the South African War, 1899–1902* (1983). An important study that reminds readers of the crucial involvement of black South Africans in this bloody conflict.

Womack, John, Jr., *Zapata and the Mexican Revolution* (1968). A major work on the Mexican Revolution that discusses peasant struggles in the state of Morelos in great detail.

Chapter 19 Of Masses and Visions of the Modern, 1910–1939

Brown, Judith, *Gandhi: Prisoner of Hope* (1990). A biography of Gandhi as a political activist.

De Grazia, Victoria, and Ellen Furlough (eds.), *The Sex of Things: Gender and Consumption in Historical Perspective* (1996). Pathbreaking essays on how gender affects consumption.

Dumenil, Lynn, *The Modern Temper: America in the 1920s* (1995). A general discussion of American culture in the decade after World War I.

Fainsod, Merle, *Smolensk under Soviet Rule* (1989). The most accessible and sophisticated interpretation of the Stalin revolution in the village.

Friedman, Edward, *Backward toward Revolution: The Chinese Revolutionary Party* (1974). An insightful look at the failure of liberalism in early republican China through the prism of the short-lived Chinese Revolutionary Party.

Gelvin, James, *Divided Loyalties: Nationalism and Mass Politics in Syria at the Close of Empire* (1998). Offers important insights into the development of nationalism in the Arab world.

Horne, John (ed.), *State, Society, and Mobilization during the First World War* (1997). Essays on what it took to wage total war among all the belligerents.

Johnson, G. Wesley, *The Emergence of Black Politics in Senegal* (1971). A useful examination of the stirrings of African nationalism in Senegal.

Kennedy, David M., *Freedom from Fear: The American People in Depression and War, 1929–1945* (1999). A wonderful narrative of turbulent years.

Kershaw, Ian, *Hitler*, 2 vols. (1998–2000). A masterpiece combining biography and context.

Kimble, David, *A Political History of Ghana* (1963). An excellent discussion of the beginnings of African nationalism in Ghana.

Kotkin, Stephen, *Magnetic Mountain: Stalinism as a Civilization* (1995). Recaptures the atmosphere of a time when everything seemed possible, even creating a new world.

LeMahieu, D. L., *A Culture for Democracy: Mass Communication and the Cultivated Mind in Britain between the Wars* (1988). One of the great works on mass culture.

Lyttelton, Adrian, *The Seizure of Power: Fascism in Italy, 1919–1929* (1961). Still the classic account.

Marchand, Roland, *Advertising the American Dream: Making Way for Modernity, 1920–1945* (1985). An excellent discussion of the force of mass production and mass consumption.

Mazower, Mark, *Dark Continent: Europe's Twentieth Century* (1999). A wide-ranging overview of Europe's tempestuous twentieth century.

Morrow, John H., Jr., *The Great War: An Imperial History* (2004). Places World War I in the context of European imperialism.

Nottingham, John, and Carl Rosberg, *The Myth of "Mau Mau": Nationalism in Kenya* (1966). Dispells the myths in describing the roots of nationalism in Kenya.

Taylor, Jay, *The Generalissimo: Chiang Kai-shek and the Struggle for Modern China* (2009). The first serious biographical study of Chiang Kai-shek in English, although its reliance on Chiang's own diary as a source does raise some questions of historical interpretation.

Thorp, Rosemary (ed.), *Latin America in the 1930s* (1984). An important collection of essays on Latin America's response to the shakeup of the interwar years.

Tsin, Michael, *Nation, Governance, and Modernity in China: Canton, 1900–1927* (1999). An analysis of the vision and social dynamics behind the Guomindang-led revolution of the 1920s.

Vianna, Hermano, *The Mystery of Samba* (1999). Discusses the history of samba, emphasizing its African heritage as well as its persistent popular content.

Wakeman, Frederic, Jr., *Policing Shanghai, 1927–1937* (1995). An excellent account of Guomindang rule in China's largest city during the Nanjing decade.

Winter, J. M., *The Experience of World War* (1988). A comprehensive presentation of the many sides of the twentieth century.

Young, Louise, *Japan's Total Empire: Manchuria and the Culture of Wartime Imperialism* (1998). An innovative case study of Japanese imperialism and mass culture with broad implications.

Chapter 20 The Three-World Order, 1940–1975

Aburish, Said K., *Nasser: The Last Arab* (2004). A recent and impressive look at Egypt's most powerful political leader in the 1950s and 1960s.

Anderson, Jon Lee, *Che Guevara: A Revolutionary Life* (1997). A sweeping study of the radicalization of Latin American nationalism.

Bayly, Christopher, and Tim Harper, *Forgotten Armies: Britain's Asian Empire and the War with Japan* (2004). A brilliant social and military history of the Second World War as fought and lived in South and Southeast Asia.

Chatterjee, Partha, *Nationalist Thought and the Colonial World: A Derivative Discourse?* (1986). An influential interpretation of the ideological and political nature of Indian nationalism and the struggle for a postcolonial nation-state.

Crampton, R. J., *Eastern Europe in the Twentieth Century and After* (2nd ed., 1997). Comprehensive overview covering all Soviet-bloc countries.

Dower, John W., *Embracing Defeat: Japan in the Wake of World War II* (1999). A prize-winning study of the transformation of one of the war's vanquished.

Elkins, Caroline, *Imperial Reckoning: The Untold Story of Britain's Gulag in Kenya* (2005). Pulitzer Prize–winning study of the brutal war to suppress the nationalist uprising in Kenya in the 1950s that ultimately led to independence for that country.

Gao Yuan, *Born Red: A Chronicle of the Cultural Revolution* (1987). A gripping personal account of the Cultural Revolution by a former Red Guard.

Gordon, Andrew (ed.), *Postwar Japan as History* (1993). Essays covering a wide range of topics on postwar Japan.

Hargreaves, John D., *Decolonization in Africa* (1996). A good place to start when exploring the history of African decolonization.

Hasan, Mushirul (ed.), *India's Partition: Process, Strategy and Mobilization* (1993). A useful anthology of scholarly articles, short stories, and primary documents on the partition of India.

Iriye, Akira, *Power and Culture: The Japanese-American War, 1941–1945* (1981). A discussion that goes beyond the military confrontation in Asia.

Jackson, Kenneth T., *Crabgrass Frontier: The Suburbanization of the United States* (1985). An insightful and influential consideration of the movement of the American population from cities to suburbs.

Jalal, Ayesha, *The Sole Spokesman: Jinnah, the Muslim League and the Demand for Pakistan* (1985). A study of the high politics leading to the violent partition of British India.

Keep, John L. H., *Last of the Empires: A History of the Soviet Union 1945–1991* (1995). A detailed overview of the core of the "Second World."

Morris, Benny, *Righteous Victims: A History of the Zionist-Arab Conflict, 1881–1999* (2000). On the Arab-Israeli War of 1948.

Patterson, James T., *Grand Expectations: The United States, 1945–1974* (1996). Synthesizes the American experience in the postwar decades.

Patterson, Thomas, *Contesting Castro* (1994). The best study of the tension between the United States and Cuba. Culminating in the Cuban Revolution, it explores the deep American misunderstanding of Cuban national aspirations.

Roberts, Geoffrey, *Stalin's Wars: From World War to Cold War, 1939–1953* (2007). A reassessment of Stalin's wartime leadership that conveys the vast scale of what took place.

Ruedy, John, *Modern Algeria: The Origins and Development of a Nation* (1992). Gives the history of the Algerian nationalist movements and provides an overview of the Algerian war for independence.

Saich, Tony, and Hans van de Ven (eds.), *New Perspectives on the Chinese Communist Revolution* (1995). A collection of essays reexamining different aspects of the Chinese communist movement.

Schram, Stuart, *The Thought of Mao Tse-tung* (1989). Standard work on the subject.

Tignor, Robert L., *W. Arthur Lewis and the Birth of Development Economics* (2006). An intellectual biography of the Nobel Prize–winning, West Indian–born economist, who proposed formulas to promote the economic development of less developed societies and then sought to implement them in Africa and the West Indies.

Wright, Gordon, *The Ordeal of Total War, 1939–1945* (1968). A superb treatment of the many dimensions of the war in Europe.

Zubkova, Elena, *Russia after the War: Hopes, Illusions, and Disappointments, 1945–1957* (1998). Uses formerly secret archives to catalogue the devastation and difficult reconstruction of one of the war's victors.

Chapter 21 Globalization, 1970–2000

Collier, Paul, *The Bottom Billion: Why the Poorest Countries Fail and What Can Be Done About It* (2007). Shows that despite the world's advancing prosperity, more than a billion people have been left behind in abject poverty.

Davis, Deborah (ed.), *The Consumer Revolution in Urban China* (2000). A look at the different aspects of the recent, profound social transformation of urban China.

Davis, Mike, *City of Quartz: Excavating the Future in Los Angeles* (1990). Offers provocative reflections on the recent history, current condition, and possible future of Los Angeles.

Dutton, Michael, *Streetlife China* (1999). A fascinating portrayal of the survival tactics of those inhabiting the margins of society in modern China.

Eichengreen, Barry, *Globalizing Capital: A History of the International Monetary System* (1996). An insightful analysis of how international capital markets changed in the period from 1945 to 1980.

Gourevitch, Philip, *We Wish to Inform You That Tomorrow We Will Be Killed with Our Families: Stories from Rwanda* (1999). A volume that reveals the hatreds that culminated in the Rwanda genocide.

Guillermoprieto, Alma, *Looking for History: Dispatches from Latin America* (2001). A collection of articles by the most important journalist reporting on Latin American affairs.

Han Minzhu (ed.), *Cries for Democracy: Writings and Speeches from the 1989 Chinese Democracy Movement* (1990). A collection of documents from the events leading up to the incident in Tiananmen Square on June 4, 1989.

Herbst, Jeffrey, *States and Power in Africa: Comparative Lessons in Authority and Control* (2000). Explores the political dilemmas facing modern African polities.

Honig, Emily, and Gail Hershatter, *Personal Voices: Chinese Women in the 1980's* (1988). A record of Chinese women during a period of rapid social change.

Huang, Yasheng, *Capitalism with Chinese Characteristics: Entrepreneurship and the State* (2008). A sharp, unsentimental inside look at China's market economy and its future prospects.

Klitgaard, Robert, *Tropical Gangsters* (1990). On the intimate connections between corrupt native elites and international aid agencies.

Kotkin, Stephen, *Armageddon Averted: The Soviet Collapse, 1970–2000* (2001). Places the surprise fall of the Soviet Union in the context of the great shifts in the post–World War II order.

Mamdani, Mahmood, *When Victims Become Killers: Colonialism, Nativism, and the Genocide in Rwanda* (2001). Discusses the genocide in Rwanda in light of the legacy of colonialism.

Mehta, Suketu, *Maximum City: Bombay Lost and Found* (2005). Examines one of the great, and contradictory, cities in the era of globalization.

Mottahedeh, Roy, *The Mantle of the Prophet: Religion and Politics in Iran* (2nd ed., 2008). Perhaps the best book on the 1979 Iranian Revolution and its aftermath.

Nathan, Andrew, and Perry Link, *The Tiananmen Papers* (2002). An inside look at the divisions within the Chinese elite in connection with the 1989 crackdown.

Portes, Alejandro, and Rubén G. Rumbaut, *Immigrant America* (2nd ed., 1996). A good comparative study of how immigration has transformed the United States.

Prunier, Gerald, *Africa's World War: Congo, the Rwandan Genocide, and the Making of a Continental Catastrophe* (2009). A chilling discussion of the spillover effects of the Rwandan genocide on central, eastern, and southern Africa.

Reinhart, Carmen, and Kenneth Rogoff, *This Time Is Different: Eight Centuries of Financial Folly* (2009). Explains the latest financial crash using historical perspective.

Van Der Wee, Hermann, *Prosperity and Upheaval: The World Economy, 1945–1980* (1986). Describes very well the transformation and problems of the world economy, particularly from the 1960s onward.

Westad, Odd Arne, *The Global Cold War: Third World Interventions and the Making of our Times* (2007). A genuinely global perspective on the cold war and its consequences.

Winn, Peter, *Americas: The Changing Face of Latin America and the Caribbean* (1992). A useful portrayal of Latin America since the 1970s.

Abd al-Rahman III Islamic ruler in Spain who held a countercaliphate and reigned from 912 to 961 CE.

aborigines Original, native inhabitants of a region, as opposed to invaders, colonizers, or later peoples of mixed ancestry.

absolute monarchy Form of government where one body, usually the monarch, controls the right to tax, judge, make war, and coin money. The term *enlightened absolutists* was often used to refer to state monarchies in seventeenth- and eighteenth-century Europe.

acid rain Precipitation containing large amounts of sulfur, mainly from coal-fired plants.

adaptation Ability to alter behavior and to innovate, finding new ways of doing things.

African National Congress (ANC) Multiracial organization founded in 1912 in an effort to end racial discrimination in South Africa.

Afrikaners Descendants of the original Dutch settlers of South Africa; formerly referred to as Boers.

Agones Athletic contests in ancient Greece.

Ahmosis Egyptian ruler in the southern part of the country who ruled from 1550 to 1525 BCE; Ahmosis used Hyksos weaponry—horse chariots in particular—to defeat the Hyksos themselves.

Ahura Mazda Supreme God of the Persians believed to have created the world and all that is good and to have appointed earthly kings.

AIDS (Acquired Immunodeficiency Syndrome) Virus that compromises the ability of the infected person's immune system to ward off disease. First detected in 1981, AIDS was initially stigmatized as a "gay cancer," but as it spread to heterosexuals, public awareness about it increased. In its first two decades, AIDS killed 12 million people.

Akbarnamah Mughal intellectual Abulfazl's *Book of Akbar*, which attempted to reconcile the traditional Sufi interest in the inner life within the worldly context of a great empire.

Alaric II Visigothic king who issued a simplified code of innovative imperial law.

Alexander the Great (356–323 BCE) Leader who used novel tactics and new kinds of armed forces to conquer the Persian Empire, which extended from Egypt and the Mediterranean Sea to the interior of what is now Afghanistan and as far as the Indus River valley. Alexander's conquests broke down barriers between the Mediterranean world and Southwest Asia and transferred massive amounts of wealth and power to the Mediterranean, transforming it into a more unified world of economic and cultural exchange.

Alexandria Port city in Egypt named after Alexander the Great. Alexandria was a model city in the Hellenistic world. It was built up by a multiethnic population from around the Mediterranean world.

Al-Khwarizmi Scientist and mathematician who lived from 780 to 850 CE and is known for having modified Indian digits into Arabic numerals.

Allied powers Name given to the alliance between Britain, France, Russia, and Italy, who fought against Germany and Austria-Hungary (the Central powers) in World War I. In World War II the name was used for the alliance between Britain, France, and America, who fought against the Axis powers (Germany, Italy, and Japan).

allomothering System by which mothers relied on other women, including their own mothers, daughters, sisters, and friends, to help in the nurturing and protecting of children.

alluvium Area of land created by river deposits.

American Railway Union Workers' union that initiated the Pullman Strike of 1894, which led to violence and ended in the leaders' arrest.

Amnesty International Non-governmental organization formed to defend "prisoners of conscience"—those detained for their beliefs, race, sex, ethnic origin, language, or religion.

Amorites Name that Mesopotamian urbanites called the transhumant herders from the Arabian desert. Around 2300 BCE, the Amorites, along with the Elamites, were at the center of newly formed dynasties in southern Mesopotamia.

Amun Once insignificant Egyptian god elevated to higher status by Amenemhet (1991–1962 BCE). *Amun* means "hidden" in Ancient Egyptian; the name was meant to convey the god's omnipresence.

Analects Texts that included the teachings and cultural ideals of Confucius.

anarchism Belief that society should be a free association of its members, not subject to government, laws, or police.

Anatolia Now mainly the area known as modern Turkey; in the sixth millennium BCE, people from Anatolia, Greece, and the Levant took to boats and populated the Aegean. Their small villages endured almost unchanged for two millennia.

Angkor Wat Magnificent Khmer Vaishnavite temple that crowned the royal palace in Angkor. It had statues representing the Hindu pantheon of gods.

Anglo-Boer War (1899–1902) Anticolonial struggle in South Africa between the British and the Afrikaners over the gold-rich Transvaal. In response to the Afrikaners' guerrilla tactics and in order to contain the local population, the British instituted the first concentration camps. Ultimately, Britain won the conflict.

animal domestication Gradual process that occurred simultaneously with or just before the domestication of plants, depending on the region.

annals Historical records. Notable annals are the cuneiform inscriptions that record successful Assyrian military campaigns.

Anti-Federalists Critics of the U.S. Constitution who sought to defend the people against the power of the federal government and insisted on a bill of rights to protect individual liberties from government intrusion.

Apartheid Racial segregation policy of the Afrikaner-dominated South African government. Legislated in 1948 by the Afrikaner National Party, it had existed in South Africa for many years.

Arab-Israeli War of 1948–1949 Conflict between Israeli and Arab armies that arose in the wake of a U.N. vote to partition Palestine into Arab and Jewish territories. The war shattered the legitimacy of Arab ruling elites.

Aramaic Dialect of a Semitic language spoken in Southwest Asia; it became the lingua franca of the Persian Empire.

Aristotle (384–322 BCE) Philosopher who studied under Plato but came to different conclusions about nature and politics. Aristotle believed in collecting observations about nature and discerning patterns to ascertain how things worked.

Aryans Nomadic charioteers who spoke Indo-European languages and entered South Asia in 1500 BCE. The early Aryan settlers were herders.

Asante state State located in present-day Ghana, founded by the Asantes at the end of the seventeenth century. It grew in power in the next century because of its access to gold and its involvement in the slave trade.

ascetic One who rejects material possessions and physical pleasures.

Asiatic Society Cultural organization founded by British Orientalists who supported native culture but still believed in colonial rule.

Aśoka Emperor of the Mauryan dynasty from 268 to 231 BCE; he was a great conqueror and unifier of India. He is said to have embraced Buddhism toward the end of his life.

Assur One of two cities on the upper reaches of the Tigris River that were the heart of Assyria proper (the other was Nineveh).

Aśvaghosa First known Sanskrit writer. He may have lived from 80 to 150 CE and may have composed a biography of the Buddha.

Ataturk, Mustafa Kemal (1881–1938) Ottoman army officer and military hero who helped forge the modern Turkish nation-state. He and his followers deposed the sultan, declared Turkey a republic, and constructed a European-like secular state, eliminating Islam's hold over civil and political affairs.

Atlantic system New system of trade and expansion that linked Europe, Africa, and the Americas. It emerged in the wake of European voyages across the Atlantic Ocean.

Atma Vedic term signifying the eternal self, represented by the trinity of deities.

Atman In the Upanishads, an eternal being who exists everywhere. The atman never perishes but is reborn or transmigrates into another life.

Attila Sole ruler of all Hunnish tribes from 433 to 453 CE. Harsh and much feared, he formed the first empire to oppose Rome in northern Europe.

Augustus Title meaning "Revered One," assumed in 27 BCE by the Roman ruler Octavian (63–14 BCE). This was one of many titles he assumed; others included *imperator*, *princeps*, and *Caesar*.

Australopithecines Hominid species that appeared 3 million years ago and, unlike other animals, walked on two legs. Their brain capacity was a little less than one-third of a modern human's or about the size of the brain capacity of today's African apes. Although not humans, they carried the genetic and biological material out of which modern humans would later emerge.

Austro-Hungarian Empire Dual monarchy established by the Habsburg family in 1867; it collapsed at the end of World War I.

authoritarianism Centralized and dictatorial form of government, proclaimed by its adherents to be superior to parliamentary democracy and especially effective at mobilizing the masses. This idea was widely accepted in parts of the world during the 1930s.

Avesta Compilation of holy works transmitted orally by priests for millennia and eventually recorded in the sixth century BCE.

Axis powers The three aggressor states in World War II: Germany, Japan, and Italy.

Aztec Empire Mesoamerican empire that originated with a league of three Mexica cities in 1430 and gradually expanded through the Central Valley of Mexico, uniting numerous small, independent states under a single monarch who ruled with the help of counselors, military leaders, and priests. By the late fifteenth century, the Aztec realm may have embraced 25 million people. In 1521, they were defeated by the conquistador Hernán Cortés.

baby boom Post–World War II upswing in U.S. birth rates; it reversed a century of decline.

bactrian camel Two-humped animal domesticated in central Asia around 2500 BCE. The bactrian camel was heartier than the one-humped dromedary and became the animal of choice for the harsh and varied climates typical of Silk Road trade.

Baghdad Capital of the Islamic Empire under the Abbasid dynasty, founded in 762 CE (in modern-day Iraq). In the medieval period, it was a center of administration, scholarship, and cultural growth for what came to be known as the Golden Age of Islamic science.

Baghdad Pact (1955) Middle Eastern military alliance between countries friendly with America who were also willing to align themselves with the western countries against the Soviet Union.

Balam Na Stone temple and place of pilgrimage for the Mayan people of Mexico's Yucatan peninsula.

Balfour Declaration Letter (November 2, 1917) by Lord Arthur J. Balfour, British foreign secretary, that promised a homeland for the Jews in Palestine.

Bamboo Annals Shang stories and foundation myths that were written on bamboo strips and later collected.

Bantu Language first spoken by people who lived in the southeastern area of modern Nigeria around 1000 CE.

Bantu migrations Waves of rapid population movement from West Africa into eastern and southern Africa during the first millennium CE that brought advanced agricultural practices to these regions and absorbed most of the preexisting hunting-and-gathering populations.

barbarian Derogatory term used to describe pastoral nomads, painting them as enemies of civilization; the term *barbarian* used to have a more neutral meaning than it does today.

barbarian invasions Violent migration of people in the late fourth and fifth centuries into Roman territory. These migrants had long been used as non-Roman soldiers.

basilicas Early church buildings, based on old royal audience halls.

Battle of Adwa (1896) Battle in which the Ethiopians defeated Italian colonial forces; it inspired many of Africa's later national leaders.

Battle of Wounded Knee (1890) Bloody massacre of Sioux Ghost Dancers by U.S. armed forces.

Bay of Pigs (1961) Unsuccessful invasion of Cuba by Cuban exiles supported by the U.S. government. The invaders intended to incite an insurrection in Cuba and overthrow the communist regime of Fidel Castro.

Bedouins Nomadic pastoralists in the deserts of the Middle East.

Beer Hall Putsch (1923) Nazi intrusion into a meeting of Bavarian leaders in a Munich beer hall; the Nazis were attempting to force support for their cause; Adolf Hitler was imprisoned for a year after the incident.

Beghards (1500s) Eccentric European group whose members claimed to be in a state of grace that allowed them to do as they pleased—from adultery, free love, and nudity to murder; also called Brethren of Free Speech.

bell beaker Ancient drinking vessel, an artifact from Europe, so named because its shape resembles an inverted bell.

Berenice of Egypt Egyptian "queen" who helped rule over the Kingdom of the Nile from 320 to 280 BCE.

Beringia Prehistoric thousand-mile-long land bridge that linked Siberia and North America (which had not been populated by hominids). About 18,000 years ago, *Homo sapiens* edged into this landmass.

Berlin Airlift (1948) Supply of vital necessities to West Berlin by air transport primarily under U.S. auspices. It was initiated in response to a land and water blockade of the city instituted by the Soviet Union in the hope that the Allies would be forced to abandon West Berlin.

Berlin Wall Wall built by the communists in Berlin in 1961 to prevent citizens of East Germany from fleeing to West Germany; torn down in 1989.

Bhakti Religious practice that grew out of Hinduism and emphasizes personal devotion to gods.

Bhakti Hinduism Popular form of Hinduism that emerged in the seventh century. The religion stresses devotion (*bhakti*) to God and uses vernacular languages (not Sanskrit) spoken by the common people.

big men Leaders of the extended household communities that formed village settlements in African rain forests.

big whites French plantation owners in Saint Domingue (present-day Haiti) who created one of the wealthiest slave societies.

Bilad al-Sudan Arabic for "the land of the blacks"; it consisted of the land lying south of the Sahara.

bilharzia Debilitating water-borne illness. It was widespread in Egypt, where it infected peasants who worked in the irrigation canals.

Bill of Rights First ten amendments to the U.S. Constitution; ratified in 1791.

bipedalism Walking on two legs, thereby freeing hands and arms to carry objects such as weapons and tools; one of several traits that distinguished hominids.

Black Death Great epidemic of the bubonic plague that ravaged Europe, East Asia, and North Africa in the fourteenth century, killing large numbers, including perhaps as many as one-third of the European population.

Black Jacobins Nickname for the rebels in Saint Domingue, including Toussaint L'Ouverture, a former slave who led the slaves of this French colony in the world's largest and most successful slave insurrection.

Black Panthers Radical African American group in the 1960s and 1970s; they advocated black separatism and pan-Africanism.

black shirts Fascist troops of Mussolini's regime; the squads received money from Italian landowners to attack socialist leaders.

Black Tuesday (October 29, 1929) Historic day when the U.S. stock market crashed, plunging the United States and international trading systems into crisis and leading the world into the "Great Depression."

Blitzkrieg "Lightning war"; type of warfare in which the Germans, during World War II, used coordinated aerial bombing campaigns along with tanks and infantrymen in motorized vehicles.

Bodhisattvas In Mahayan Buddhism, enlightened demigods who were ready to reach *nirvana* but delayed so that they might help others attain it.

Bolívar, Simón (1783–1830) Venezuelan leader who urged his followers to become "American," to overcome their local identities. He wanted the liberated countries to form a Latin American confederation, urging Peru and Bolivia to join Venezuela, Ecuador, and Colombia in the "Gran Colombia."

Bolsheviks Former members of the Russian Social Democratic Party who advocated the destruction of capitalist political and economic institutions and started the Russian Revolution. In 1918 the Bolsheviks changed their name to the Russian Communist Party.

Book of the Dead Ancient Egyptian funerary text that contains drawings and paintings as well as spells describing how to prepare the jewelry and amulets that were buried with a person in preparation for the afterlife.

bourgeoisie The middle class. In Europe, they sought to be recognized not by birth or title, but by capital and property.

Boxer Protocol Written agreement between the victors of the Boxer Uprising and the Qing Empire in 1901 that placed western troops in Beijing and required the regime to pay exorbitant damages for foreign life and property.

Boxer Uprising (1899–1900) Chinese peasant movement that opposed foreign influence, especially that of Christian missionaries; it was put down after the Boxers were defeated by an army composed mostly of Japanese, Russians, British, French, and Americans.

Brahma One of three major deities that form a trinity in Vedic religion. Brahma signifies birth. *See also* Vishnu *and* Siva.

Brahmans Vedic priests who performed rituals and communicated with the gods. Brahmans provided guidance on how to live in balance with the forces of nature as represented by the various deities. The codification of Vedic principles into codes of law took place at the hands of the Brahmans. They memorized Vedic works and compiled commentaries on them. They also developed their own set of rules and rituals, which developed into a full-scale theology. Originally memorized and passed on orally, these may have been written down sometime after the beginning of the Common Era. Brahmanism was reborn as Hinduism sometime during the first half of the first millennium CE.

British Commonwealth of Nations Union formed in 1926 that conferred "dominion status" on Britain's white settler colonies in Canada, Australia, and New Zealand.

British East India Company *See* East India Company.

bronze Alloy of copper and tin brought into Europe from Anatolia; used to make hard-edged weapons.

brown shirts Troops of German men who advanced the Nazi cause by holding street marches, mass rallies, and confrontations and by beating Jews and anyone who opposed the Nazis.

bubonic plague Acute infectious disease caused by a bacterium that is transmitted to humans by fleas from infected rats. It ravaged Europe and parts of Asia in the fourteenth century. Sometimes referred to as the "Black Death."

Buddha (Siddhartha Gautama; 563–483 BCE) Indian ascetic who founded Buddhism.

Buddhism Major South Asian religion that aims to end human suffering through the renunciation of desire. Buddhists believe that removing the illusion of a separate identity would lead to a state of contentment (nirvana). These beliefs challenged the traditional Brahmanic teachings of the time and provided the peoples of South Asia with an alternative to established traditions.

bullion Uncoined gold or silver.

Cahokia Commercial center for regional and long-distance trade in North America. Its hinterlands produced staples for urban consumers. In return, its crafts were exported inland by porters and to North American markets in canoes. *See also* Mound people.

Calaveras Allegorical skeleton drawings by the Mexican printmaker and artist José Guadalupe Posada. The works drew on popular themes of betrayal, death, and festivity.

caliphate Institution that arose as the successor to Muhammad's leadership and became both the political and religious head of the Islamic community. Although the caliphs exercised political authority over the Muslim community and were the head of the religious community, the *ummah,* they did not inherit Muhammad's prophetic powers and were not authorities in religious doctrine.

Candomblé Yoruba-based religion in northern Brazil; it interwove African practices and beliefs with Christianity.

canton system System officially established by imperial decree in 1759 that required European traders to have Chinese guild merchants act as guarantors for their good behavior and payment of fees.

caravan cities Set of networks at long-distance trade locations where groups of merchants could assemble during their journeys. Several of these developed into full-fledged cities, especially in the deserts of Arabia.

caravans Companies of men who transported and traded goods along overland routes in North Africa and central Asia; large caravans consisted of 600–1,000 camels and as many as 400 men.

caravansarais Inns along major trade routes that accommodated large numbers of traders, their animals, and their wares.

caravel Sailing vessel suited for nosing in and out of estuaries and navigating in waters with unpredictable currents and winds.

carrack Ship used on open bodies of water, such as the Mediterranean.

Carthage City in what is modern-day Tunisia; emblematic of the trading aspirations and activities of merchants in the Mediterranean. Pottery and other archaeological remains demonstrate that trading contacts with Carthage were as far-flung as Italy, Greece, France, Iberia, and West Africa.

cartography Mapmaking.

caste system Hierarchical system of organizing people and distributing labor.

Caste War of Yucatan (1847–1901) Conflict between Mayan Indians and the Mexican state over Indian autonomy and legal equality, which resulted in the Mexican takeover of the Yucatan peninsula.

Castro, Fidel (1926–) Cuban communist leader whose forces overthrew Batista's corrupt regime in early January 1959. Castro became increasingly radical as he consolidated power, announcing a massive redistribution of land and the nationalization of foreign oil refineries; he declared himself a socialist and aligned himself with the Soviet Union in the wake of the 1961 CIA-backed Bay of Pigs invasion.

Çatal Hüyük Site in Anatolia discovered in 1958. It was a dense honeycomb of settlements filled with rooms whose walls were covered with paintings of wild bulls, hunters, and pregnant women. Çatal Hüyük symbolizes an early transition into urban dwelling and dates to the eighth millennium BCE.

Cathedra Bishop's seat, or throne, in a church.

Catholic Church Unifying institution for Christians in western Europe after the collapse of the Roman Empire. Rome became the spiritual capital of western Europe and the bishops of Rome emerged as popes, the supreme head of the church, who possessed great moral authority.

Cato the Elder (234–149 BCE) Roman statesman, often seen as emblematic of the transition from a Greek to a Roman world. Cato the Elder wrote a manual for the new economy of slave plantation agriculture, invested in shipping and trading, learned Greek rhetoric, and added the genre of history to Latin literature.

Caudillos South American local military chieftains.

cave drawings Images on cave walls. The subjects are most often large game, although a few are images of humans. Other elements are impressions made by hands dipped in paint and pressed on a wall or abstract symbols and shapes.

Celali revolts (1595–1610) Peasant and artisan uprisings against the Ottoman state.

Central powers Defined in World War I as Germany and Austria-Hungary.

Chan Chan City founded between 850 and 900 CE by the Moche people in what is now modern-day Peru. It had a core population of 30,000 inhabitants.

Chan Santa Cruz Separate Mayan community formed as part of a crusade for spiritual salvation and the complete cultural separation of the Mayan Indians; means "little holy cross."

Chandra Gupta II King who reigned in South Asia from 320 to 335 CE. He shared his name with Chandragupta, the founder of the Mauryan Empire.

Chandravamsha One of two main lineages (the lunar one) of Vedic society, each with its own creation myth, ancestors, language, and rituals. Each lineage included many clans. *See* Suryavamsha.

chapatis Flat, unleavened Indian bread.

chariots Horse-driven carriages brought by the pastoral nomadic warriors from the steppes that became the favored mode of transportation for an urban aristocratic warrior class and for other men of power in agriculture-based societies. Control of chariot forces was the foundation of the new balance of power across Afro-Eurasia during the second millennium BCE.

charismatic Person who uses personal strengths or virtues, often laced with a divine aura, to command followers.

Charlemagne Emperor of the West and heir to Rome from 764 to 814 CE.

chartered companies Firms that were awarded monopoly trading rights over vast areas by European monarchs (e.g., Virginia Company, Dutch East India Company).

Chartism (1834–1848) Mass democratic movement to pass the Peoples' Charter in Britain, granting male suffrage, secret ballot, equal electoral districts, and annual parliaments, and absolving the requirement of property ownership for members of the parliament.

chattel slavery Form of slavery that sold people as property, the rise of which coincided with the expansion of city-states. Chattel slavery was eschewed by the Spartans, who also rejected the innovation of coin money.

Chavín A people who lived in what is now northern Peru from 1400 to 200 BCE. They were united more by culture and faith than by a unified political system.

Chernobyl (1986) Site in the Soviet Union (in Ukraine) of the meltdown of a nuclear reactor.

Chiang Kai-shek (1887–1975) Leader of the Guomindang following Sun Yat-sen's death who mobilized the Chinese masses through the New Life movement. In 1949 he lost the Chinese Revolution to the communists and moved his regime to Taiwan.

Chimu Empire South America's first empire; it developed during the first century of the second millennium in the Moche Valley on the Pacific coast.

chinampas Floating gardens used by Aztecs in the 1300s and 1400s to grow crops.

China's Sorrow Name for the Yellow River, which, when it changed course or flooded, could cause mass death and waves of migration.

chinoiserie Chinese silks, teas, tableware, jewelry, and paper; popular among Europeans in the seventeenth and eighteenth centuries.

Christendom Entire portion of the world in which Christianity prevailed.

Christianity Religion that originated at the height of the Roman Empire and in a direct confrontation with Roman imperial authority: the trial of Yeshua ben Yosef (Joshua son of Joseph; we know him today by the Greek form of his name, Jesus). Jesus was condemned for sedition and crucified. His followers believed that he was resurrected and that his teachings were not that of a man, but a god who had walked among human beings. At first, the Roman Empire refused to recognize Christianity and persecuted its followers, but in the fourth century CE Christianity was officially recognized as the Roman state religion.

Church of England Established form of Christianity in England dating from the sixteenth century.

city Highly populated concentration of economic, religious, and political power. The first cities appeared in river basins, which could produce a surplus of agriculture. The abundance of food freed most city inhabitants from the need to produce their own food, which allowed them to work in specialized professions.

city-state Political organization based on the authority of a single, large city that controls outlying territories.

Civil Rights Act (1964) U.S. legislation that banned segregation in public facilities, outlawed racial discrimination in employment, and marked an important step in correcting legal inequality.

civil rights movement Powerful movement for equal rights and the end of racial segregation in the United States that began in the 1950s with court victories against school segregation and nonviolent boycotts.

civil service examinations The world's first written civil service examination system, instituted by the Tang dynasty to recruit officials and bureaucrats. Open to most males, the exams tested a candidate's literary skills and knowledge of the Confucian classics. They helped to unite the Chinese state by making knowledge of a specific language and Confucian classics the only route to power.

Civil War, American (1861–1865) Conflict between the northern and southern states of

America; this struggle led to the abolition of slavery in the United States.

clan A social group comprising many households, claiming descent from a common ancestor.

clandestine presses Small printing operations that published banned texts in the early modern era, especially in Switzerland and the Netherlands.

Clovis people Early humans in America who used basic chipped blades and pointed spears in pursuing prey. They extended the hunting traditions they had learned in Afro-Eurasia, such as establishing campsites and moving with their herds. They were known as "Clovis people" because the arrowhead point that they used was first found by archaeologists at a site near Clovis, New Mexico.

codex Early form of book, with separate pages bound together; it replaced the scroll as the main medium for written texts. The codex emerged around 300 CE.

cognitive skills Skills such as thought, memory, problem-solving, and—ultimately—language. Hominids were able to use these skills and their hands to create new adaptations, like tools, which helped them obtain food and avoid predators.

Cohong Chinese merchant guild that traded with Europeans under the Qing dynasty.

coins Form of money that replaced goods, which previously had been bartered for services and other products. Originally used mainly to hire mercenary soldiers, coins became the commonplace method of payment linking buyers and producers throughout the Mediterranean.

cold war (1945–1990) Ideological conflict in which the Soviet Union and eastern Europe opposed the United States and western Europe.

colonies Regions under the political control of another country.

Colons French settler population in Algeria.

colosseum Huge amphitheater completed by Titus and dedicated in 80 CE. Originally begun by Flavian, the structure is named after a colossal statue of Nero that formerly stood beside it.

Columbian exchange Movements between Afro-Eurasia and the Americas of previously unknown plants, animals, people, diseases, and products that followed in the wake of Columbus's voyages.

commanderies Provinces. Shi Huangdi (First August Emperor) divided China into commanderies (*jun*) to enable the Qin dynasty to rule the massive state effectively. The thirty-six commanderies were then subdivided into counties (*xian*).

Communist Manifesto Pamphlet published by Karl Marx and Friedrich Engels in 1848 at a time when political revolutions were sweeping Europe. It called on the workers of all nations to unite in overthrowing capitalism.

Compromise of 1867 Agreement between the Habsburgs and the peoples living in Hungarian parts of the empire that the Habsburg state would be officially known as the Austro-Hungarian Empire.

concession areas Territories, usually ports, where Chinese emperors allowed European merchants to trade and European people to settle.

Confucian ideals The ideals of honoring tradition, emphasizing the responsibility of the emperor, and respect for the lessons of history, promoted by Confucius, which the Han dynasty made the official doctrine of the empire by 50 BCE.

Confucianism Ethics, beliefs, and practices stipulated by the Chinese philosopher Kong Qiu, or Confucius, which served as a guide for Chinese society up to modern times.

Confucius (551–479 BCE) Influential teacher, thinker, and leader in China who developed a set of principles for ethical living. He believed that coercive laws and punishment would not be needed to maintain order in society if men following his ethics ruled. He taught his philosophy to anyone who was intelligent and willing to work, which allowed men to gain entry into the ruling through education.

cong tube Ritual object crafted by the Liangzhu. A cong tube was made of jade and was used in divination practices.

Congo Independent State Large colonial state in Africa created by Leopold II, king of Belgium, during the 1880s, and ruled by him alone. After rumors of mass slaughter and enslavement, the Belgian parliament took the land and formed a Belgian colony.

Congress of Vienna (1814–1815) International conference to reorganize Europe after the downfall of Napoleon. European monarchies agreed to respect each other's borders and to cooperate in guarding against future revolutions and war.

conquistadors Spanish military leaders who led the conquest of the New World in the sixteenth century.

Constantine Roman emperor who converted to Christianity in 312 CE. In 313, he issued a proclamation that gave Christians new freedoms in the empire. He also founded Constantinople (at first called "New Rome").

Constantinople Capital city, formerly known as Byzantium, which was founded as the New Rome by Constantine the Great.

Constitutional Convention (1787) Meeting to formulate the Constitution of the United States of America.

Contra rebels Opponents of the Sandinistas in Nicaragua; they were armed and financed by the United States and other anticommunist countries (1980).

Conversion of Constantine A significant political and religious turning point in the Roman Empire. Before the decisive battle for Rome in 312 CE, Constantine supposedly had a dream in which he was told to place a sign with the opening letters of Christ's name on his soldiers' shields. Constantine won the ensuing battle; he soon issued a proclamation giving privileges to Christian bishops. The edict spread Christianity through the institutions and across the byways of the Roman Empire.

Conversos Jewish and Muslim converts to Christianity in the Iberian Peninsula and the New World.

Coptic Form of Christianity practiced in Egypt. It was doctrinally different from Christianity elsewhere, and Coptic Christians had their own views of Christology, or the nature of Christ.

Corn Laws Laws that imposed tariffs on grain imported to Great Britain, intended to protect British farming interests. The Corn Laws were abolished in 1846 as part of a British movement in favor of free trade.

cosmology Branch of metaphysics devoted to understanding the order of the universe.

Council of Nicaea Church council convened in 325 CE by Constantine and presided over by him as well. At this council, a Christian creed was articulated and made into a formula that expressed the philosophical and technical elements of Christian belief.

Counter-Reformation Movement to counter the spread of the Reformation; initiated by the Catholic Church at the Council of Trent in 1545. The Catholic Church enacted reforms to attack clerical corruption and it placed a greater emphasis on individual spirituality. During this time, the Jesuits were founded to help revive the Catholic Church.

coup d'état Overthrow of established state by a group of conspirators, usually from the military.

creed Formal statement of faith or expression of a belief system. A Christian creed or "credo" was formulated by the Council of Nicaea in 325 CE.

creoles Persons of full-blooded European descent who were born in the Spanish American colonies.

Crimean War (1853–1856) War waged by Russia against Great Britain and France. Spurred by Russia's encroachment on Ottoman territories, the conflict revealed Russia's military weakness when Russian forces fell to British and French troops.

crossbow Innovative weapon used at the end of the Warring States period that allowed archers to shoot their enemies with accuracy, even from a distance.

Crusades Wave of attacks launched in the late eleventh century by western Europeans. The First Crusade began in 1095, when Pope Urban II appealed to the warrior nobility of France to free Jerusalem from Muslim rule. Four subsequent Crusades were fought over the next two centuries.

Cuban Missile Crisis (1962) Diplomatic standoff between the United States and the Soviet Union that was provoked by the Soviet Union's attempt to base nuclear missiles in Cuba; it brought the world close to a nuclear war.

cult Religious movement, often based on the worship of a particular god or goddess.

cultigen Organism that has diverged from its ancestors through domestication or cultivation.

cuneiform Wedge-shaped form of writing. As people combined rebus symbols with other visual marks that contained meaning, they became able to record and transmit messages over long distances by using abstract symbols or signs to denote concepts; such signs later came to represent syllables, which could be joined into words. By impressing these signs into wet clay with the cut end of a reed, scribes engaged in cuneiform.

Cyrus the Great Founder of the Persian Empire. This sixth-century ruler (559–529 BCE) conquered the Medes and unified the Iranian kingdoms.

Daimyo Ruling lords who commanded private armies in pre-Meiji Japan.

dan Fodio, Usman (1754–1817) Fulani Muslim cleric whose visions led him to challenge the Hausa ruling classes, whom he believed were insufficiently faithful to Islamic beliefs and practices. His ideas gained support among those who had suffered under the Hausa landlords. In 1804, his supporters and allies overthrew the Hausa in what is today northern Nigeria.

Daoism School of thought developed at the end of the Warring States period that focused on the importance of following the Dao, or the natural way of the cosmos. Daoism emphasized the need to accept the world as it was rather than trying to change it through politics or the government. Unlike Confucianism, Daoism scorned rigid rituals and social hierarchies.

Dar al-Islam Arabic for "the House of Islam"; it describes a sense of common identity.

Darius I (521–486 BCE) Leader who put the emerging unified Persian Empire onto solid footing after Cyrus's death.

Darwin, Charles (1809–1882) British scientist who became convinced that the species of organic life had evolved under the uniform pressure of natural laws, not by means of a special, one-time creation as described in the Bible.

D-Day (June 6, 1944) Day of the Allied invasion of Normandy under General Dwight Eisenhower to liberate western Europe from German occupation.

Dear Boy Nickname of an early human remain discovered in 1931 by a team of archaeologists named the Leakeys. They discovered an almost totally intact skull. Other objects discovered with Dear Boy demonstrated that by the time of Dear Boy, early humans had begun to fashion tools and to use them for butchering animals and possibly for hunting and killing smaller animals.

Decembrists Russian army officers who were influenced by events in revolutionary France and formed secret societies that espoused liberal governance. They were put down by Nicholas I in December 1825.

Declaration of Independence U.S. document stating the theory of government on which America was founded.

Declaration of the Rights of Man and Citizen (1789) French charter of liberties formulated by the National Assembly that marked the end of dynastic and aristocratic rule. The seventeen articles later became the preamble to the new constitution, which the assembly finished in 1791.

decolonization End of empire and emergence of new independent nation-states in Asia and Africa as a result of the defeat of Japan in World War II and weakened European influence after the war.

Delhi Sultanate (1206–1526) Turkish regime of Northern India. The regime strengthened the cultural diversity and tolerance that were a hallmark of the Indian social order, which allowed it to bring about political integration without enforcing cultural homogeneity.

democracy The idea that people, through membership in a nation, should choose their own representatives and be governed by them.

Democritus Thinker in ancient Greece who lived from 470 to 360 BCE; he deduced the existence of the atom and postulated that there was such a thing as an indivisible particle.

demotic writing The second of two basic forms of ancient Egyptian writing. Demotic was a cursive script written with ink on papyrus, on pottery, or on other absorbent objects. It was the most common and practical form of writing in Egypt and was used for administrative record keeping and in private or pseudo-private forms like letters and works of literature. *See also* Hieroglyphs.

developing world Term applied to countries collectively called the Third World during the cold war and seeking to develop viable nation-states and prosperous economies.

Devshirme System of taking non-Muslim children in place of taxes in order to educate them in Ottoman Muslim ways and prepare them for service in the sultan's bureaucracy.

Dhamma Moral code espoused by Aśoka in the Kalinga edict, which was meant to apply to all—Buddhists, Brahmans, and Greeks alike.

Dhimmis Followers of religions, other than Islam, that were permitted by Ottoman law: Armenian Christians, Greek Orthodox Christians, and Jews.

dhows Ships used by Arab seafarers; the dhow's large sails were rigged to maximize the capture of wind.

Dien Bien Phu (1954) Defining battle in the war between French colonialists and the Viet Minh that secured North Vietnam for Ho Chi Minh and his army and left the south to form its own government to be supported by France and the United States.

Din-I-llahi "House of worship" in which the Mughal emperor Akbar engaged in religious debate with Hindu, Muslim, Jain, Parsi, and Christian theologians.

Diogenes Greek philosopher who lived from 412 to 323 BCE and who espoused a doctrine of self-sufficiency and freedom from social laws and customs. He rejected cultural norms as out of tune with nature and therefore false.

Directory Temporary military committee that took over the affairs of the state of France in 1795 from the radicals and held control until the coup of Napoleon Bonaparte.

divination The interpretation of rituals used to communicate the wishes of gods or royal ancestors to foretell future events. Divination was used to legitimize royal authority and demand tribute.

Djoser Ancient Egyptian king who reigned from 2630 to 2611 BCE. He was the second king of the Third Dynasty and celebrated the Sed festival in his tomb complex at Saqqara.

domestication Bringing a wild animal or plant under human control.

Dominion in the British Commonwealth Canadian promise to keep up the country's fealty to the British crown, even after its independence in 1867. Later applied to Australia and New Zealand.

Dong Zhongshu Emperor Wu's chief minister, who advocated a more powerful view of Confucius by promoting texts that focused on Confucius as a man who possessed aspects of divinity.

double-outrigger canoes Vessels used by early Austronesians to cross the Taiwan Straits and colonize islands in the Pacific. These sturdy canoes could cover over 120 miles per day.

Duma Russian parliament.

Dutch learning Broad term for European teachings that were strictly regulated by the shoguns inside Japan.

dynastic cycle Political narrative in which influential families vied for supremacy. Upon gaining power, they legitimated their authority by claiming to be the heirs of previous grand dynasts and by preserving or revitalizing the ancestors' virtuous governing ways. This continuity conferred divine support.

dynasty Hereditary ruling family that passed control from one generation to the next.

Earth Summit (1992) Meeting in Rio de Janeiro between many of the world's governments in an effort to address international environmental problems.

East India Company (1600–1858) British charter company created to outperform Portuguese and Spanish traders in the Far East; in the eighteenth century the company became, in effect, the ruler of a large part of India.

Eastern Front Battlefront between Berlin and Moscow during World War I and World War II.

Edict of Nantes (1598) Edict issued by Henry IV to end the French Wars of Religion. The edict declared France a Catholic country but tolerated some Protestant worship.

Egyptian Middle Kingdom Period of Egyptian history lasting from about 2040 to1640 BCE, characterized by a consolidation of power and building activity in Upper Egypt.

Eiffel Tower Steel monument completed in 1889 for the Paris Exposition. It was twice the height of any other building at the time.

eight-legged essay Highly structured essay form with eight parts, required on Chinese civil service examinations.

Ekklesia Church or early gathering committed to leaders chosen by God and fellow believers.

Ekpe Powerful slave trade institution that organized the supply and purchase of slaves inland from the Gulf of Guinea in West Africa.

Elamites A people with their capital in the upland valley of modern Fars who became a cohesive polity that incorporated transhumant people of the Zagros Mountains. A group of Elamites who migrated south and west into Mesopotamia helped conquer the Third Dynasty of Ur in 2400 BCE.

empire Group of states or different ethnic groups under a single sovereign power.

Enabling Act (1933) Emergency act passed by the Reichstag (German parliament) that helped transform Hitler from Germany's chancellor, or prime minister, into a dictator following the suspicious burning of the Reichstag building and a suspension of civil liberties.

enclosure A movement in which landowners took control of lands that traditionally had been common property serving local needs.

Encomenderos Commanders of the labor services of the colonized peoples in Spanish America.

Encomiendas Grants from European Spanish governors to control the labor services of colonized people.

Endeavor Ship of Captain James Cook, whose celebrated voyages to the South Pacific in the late eighteenth century supplied Europe with information about the plants, birds, landscapes, and people of this uncharted territory.

Engels, Friedrich (1820–1895) German social and political philosopher who collaborated with Karl Marx on many publications, including *The Communist Manifesto*.

English Navigation Act of 1651 Act stipulating that only English ships could carry goods between the mother country and its colonies.

English Peasants' Revolt (1381) Uprising of serfs and free farm workers that began as a protest against a tax levied to raise money for a war on France. The revolt was suppressed but led to the gradual emergence of a free peasantry as labor shortages made it impossible to keep peasants bound to the soil.

enlightened absolutists Seventeenth- and eighteenth-century monarchs who claimed to rule rationally and in the best interests of their subjects and who hired loyal bureaucrats to implement the knowledge of the new age.

Enlightenment Intellectual movement in eighteenth-century Europe stressing natural laws and reason as the basis of authority.

entrepôts Trading stations at the borders between communities, which made exchange possible among many different partners. Long-distance traders could also replenish their supplies at these stations.

Epicurus Greek philosopher who espoused emphasis on the self. He lived from 341 to 279 BCE and founded a school in Athens called The Garden. He stressed the importance of sensation, teaching that pleasurable sensations were good and painful sensations bad. Members of his school sought to find peace and relaxation by avoiding unpleasantness or suffering.

Estates-General French quasi-parliamentary body called in 1789 to deal with the financial problems that afflicted France. It had not met since 1614.

Etruscans A dominant people on the Italian peninsula until the fourth century BCE. The Etruscan states were part of the foundation of the Roman Empire.

eunuchs Loyal and well-paid men who were surgically castrated as youths and remained in service to the caliph or emperor. Both Abbasid and Tang rulers relied for protection on a cadre of eunuchs.

Eurasia The combined area of Europe and Asia.

European Union (EU) International body organized after World War II as an attempt at reconciliation between Germany and the rest of Europe. It initially aimed to forge closer industrial cooperation. Eventually, through various treaties, many European states relinquished some of their sovereignty, and the cooperation became a full-fledged union with a single currency, the euro, and with a somewhat less powerful common European parliament.

evolution Process by which the different species of the world—its plants and animals—made changes in response to their environment that enabled them to survive and increase in numbers.

Exclusion Act of 1882 U.S. congressional act prohibiting nearly all immigration from China to the United States; fueled by animosity toward Chinese workers in the American West.

Ezo Present-day Hokkaido, Japan's fourth main island.

Fascism Mass political movement founded by Benito Mussolini that emphasized nationalism, militarism, and the omnipotence of the state.

Fascists Radical right-wing group of disaffected veterans that formed around Mussolini in 1919 and a few years later came to power in Rome.

Fatehpur Sikri Mughal emperor Akbar's temporary capital near Agra.

Fatimids Shiite dynasty that ruled parts of the Islamic Empire beginning in the tenth century CE. They were based in Egypt and founded the city of Cairo.

February Revolution (1917) The first of two uprisings of the Russian Revolution, which led to the end of the Romanov dynasty.

Federal Deposit Insurance Corporation (FDIC) Organization created in 1933 to guarantee all bank deposits up to $5,000 as part of the New Deal in the United States.

Federal Republic of Germany (1949–1990) Country formed of the areas occupied by the Allies after World War II. Also known as West Germany, this country experienced rapid demilitarization, democratization, and integration into the world economy.

Federal Reserve Act (1913) U.S. legislation that created a series of boards to monitor the supply and demand of the nation's money.

Federalists Supporters of the ratification of the U.S. Constitution, which was written to replace the Articles of Confederation.

feminist movements Movements that called for equal treatment for men and women—equal pay and equal opportunities for obtaining jobs and advancement. Feminism arose mainly in Europe and in North America in the 1960s and then became global in the 1970s.

Ferangi Arabic word meaning "Frank" that was used to describe Crusaders.

Fertile Crescent Site of the world's first agricultural revolution; an area in Southwest Asia, bounded by the Mediterranean Sea in the west and the Zagros Mountains in the east.

feudalism System instituted in medieval Europe after the collapse of the Carolingian Empire (814 CE) whereby each peasant was under the authority of a lord.

fiefdoms Medieval economic and political units.

First World Term invented during the cold war to refer to western Europe and North America (also known as the "free world" or the West); Japan later joined this group. Following the principles of liberal modernism, First World states sought to organize the world on the basis of capitalism and democracy.

Five Pillars of Islam The five tenets, or main aspects, of Islamic practice: testification or bearing witness that there is no God other than God (Allah, in Arabic) and that Muhammad is the messenger of God; praying five times a day; fasting from sunup to sundown every day during Ramadan (a month on the Islamic calendar); giving alms; and making a pilgrimage to Mecca.

Five-Year Plan Soviet effort launched under Stalin in 1928 to replace the market with a state-owned and state-managed economy, to promote rapid economic development over a five-year period of time and thereby "catch and overtake" the leading capitalist countries. The First Five-Year Plan was followed by the Second Five-Year Plan (1933–1937), and so on, until the collapse of the Soviet Union in 1991.

Flagellants European social group that came into existence during the bubonic plague in the fourteenth century; they believed that the plague was the wrath of God.

floating population Poor migrant workers in China who supplied labor under Emperor Wu.

Fluitschips Dutch shipping vessels that could carry heavy bulky cargo with relatively small crews.

flying cash Letters of exchange—early predecessors of paper cash instead of coins—first developed by guilds in the northwestern Shanxi. By the thirteenth century, paper money had eclipsed coins.

Fondûqs Complexes in caravan cities that included hostels, storage houses, offices, and temples.

Forbidden City Palace city of the Ming and Qing dynasties.

Force Publique Colonial army used to maintain order in the Belgian Congo; during the early stages of King Leopold's rule, it was responsible for bullying local communities.

Fourierism Form of utopian socialism based on the ideas of Charles Fourier (1772–1837). Fourier envisioned communes where work was made enjoyable and systems of production and distribution were run without merchants. His ideas appealed to middle-class readers, especially women, as a higher form of Christian communalism.

free labor Wage-paying rather than slave labor.

free markets Unregulated markets.

Free Officers Movement Secret organization of Egyptian junior military officers who came to power in a coup d'état in 1952, forced King Faruq to abdicate, and consolidated their own control through dissolving the parliament, banning opposing parties, and rewriting the constitution.

free trade Domestic and international trade unencumbered by tariff barriers, quotas, and fees.

Front de Libération Nationale (FLN) Algerian anticolonial, nationalist party that waged an eight-year war against French troops, beginning in 1854, that forced nearly all of the 1,000,000 colonists to leave.

Fulani Muslim group in West Africa that carried out religious revolts at the end of the eighteenth and the beginning of the nineteenth centuries in an effort to return to the pure Islam of the past.

fur trade Trading of animal pelts (especially beaver skins) by Indians for European goods in North America.

Gandhi, Mohandhas Karamchand (Mahatma) (1869–1948) Indian leader who led a nonviolent struggle for India's independence from Britain.

garrison towns Stations for soldiers originally established in strategic locations to protect territorial acquisition. Eventually, they became towns. Alexander the Great's garrison towns evolved into cities that served as centers from which Hellenistic culture was spread to his easternmost territories.

garrisons Military bases inside cities; often used for political purposes, such as protecting rulers and putting down domestic revolts or enforcing colonial rule.

gauchos Argentine, Brazilian, and Uruguayan cowboys who wanted a decentralized federation, with autonomy for their provinces and respect for their way of life.

Gdansk shipyard Site of mass strikes in Poland that led in 1980 to the formation of the first independent trade union, Solidarity, in the communist bloc.

gendered relations A relatively recent development that implies roles emerged only with the appearance of modern humans and perhaps Neanderthals. When humans began to think imaginatively and in complex symbolic ways and give voice to their insights, perhaps around 150,000 years ago, gender categories began to crystallize.

genealogy History of the descent of a person or family from a distant ancestor.

Geneva Peace Conference (1954) International conference to restore peace in Korea and Indochina. The chief participants were the United States, the Soviet Union, Great Britain, France, the People's Republic of China, North Korea, South Korea, Vietnam, the Viet Minh party, Laos, and Cambodia. The conference resulted in the division of North and South Vietnam.

Genoa One of two Italian cities (the other was Venice) that linked Europe, Africa, and Asia as nodes of commerce in 1300 CE. Genoese ships linked the Mediterranean to the coast of Flanders through consistent routes along the Atlantic coasts of Spain, Portugal, and France.

German Democratic Republic Nation founded from the Soviet zone of occupation of Germany after World War II; also known as East Germany.

German Social Democratic Party Founded in 1875, the most powerful Socialist party in Europe before 1917.

Ghana The most celebrated medieval political kingdom in West Africa.

Ghost Dance American Indian ritual performed in the nineteenth century in the hope of restoring the world to precolonial conditions.

Gilgamesh Heroic narrative written in the Babylonian dialect of Semitic Akkadian. This story and others like it were meant to circulate and unify the kingdom.

Girondins Liberal revolutionary group that supported the creation of a constitutional monarchy during the early stages of the French Revolution.

global warming Release into the air of human-made carbons that contribute to rising temperatures worldwide.

globalization Development of integrated worldwide cultural and economic structures.

Gold Coast Name that European mariners and merchants gave to that part of West Africa from which gold was exported. This area was conquered by the British in the nineteenth century and became a British colony; upon independence, it became Ghana.

Goths One of the groups of "barbarian" migrants into Roman territory in the fourth century.

government schools Schools founded by the Han dynasty to provide an adequate number of officials to fill positions in the administrative bureaucracy. The Imperial University had 30,000 members by the second century BCE.

Gracchus brothers Two tribunes, the brothers Tiberius and Gaius Gracchus, who in 133 and 123–21 BCE attempted to institute land reforms that would guarantee all of Rome's poor citizens a basic amount of land that would qualify them for army service. Both men were assassinated.

Grand Canal Created in 486 BCE, a thousand-mile-long connector between the Yellow and Yangzi rivers, linking the north and south, respectively.

grand unity Guiding political idea embraced by Qin rulers and ministers, with an eye toward joining the states of the Central Plain into one empire and centralizing administration.

"Greased cartridge" controversy Controversy spawned by the rumor that cow and pig fat had been used to grease the shotguns of the sepoys in the British army in India. Believing that this was a British attempt to defile their religion and speed their conversion to Christianity, the sepoys mutinied against British officers.

Great Depression Worldwide depression following the U.S. stock market crash on October 29, 1929.

great divide The division between economically developed nations and less developed nations.

Great East Asia Co-Prosperity Sphere Term used by the Japanese during the 1930s and 1940s to refer to Hong Kong, Singapore, Malaya, Burma, and other states that they seized during their run for expansion.

Great Flood One of many traditional Mesopotamian stories that were transmitted orally from one generation to another before being recorded. The Sumerian King List refers to this crucial event in Sumerian memory and identity. The Great Flood was assigned responsibility for Uruk's demise to the gods.

Great Game Competition over areas such as Turkistan, Persia (present-day Iran), and Afghanistan. The British (in India) and the Russians believed that controlling these areas was crucial to preventing their enemies' expansion.

Great League of Peace and Power Iroquois Indian alliance that united previously warring communities.

Great Leap Forward (1958–1961) Plan devised by Mao Zedong to achieve rapid agricultural and industrial growth in China. The plan failed miserably and more than 20 million people died.

Great Proletarian Cultural Revolution (1966–1976) Mass mobilization of urban Chinese youth inaugurated by Mao Zedong in an attempt to reinvigorate the Chinese revolution and to prevent the development of a bureaucratized Soviet style of communism; with this movement, Mao turned against his longtime associates in the communist party.

Great Trek Afrikaner migration to the interiors of Africa after the British abolished slavery in the empire in 1833.

Great War (August 1914–November 1918) A total war involving the armies of Britain, France, and Russia (the Allies) against those of Germany, Austria-Hungary, and the Ottoman Empire (the Central Powers). Italy joined the Allies in 1915, and the United States joined them in 1917, helping tip the balance in favor of the Allies, who also drew upon the populations and material of their colonial possessions. Also known as World War I.

Greek Orthodoxy Enduring form of Christianity that used the framework of the "Roman" state inherited from Constantine and Justinian to protect itself from Roman Catholicism and Muslim forces. The Greek Orthodox capital was Constantinople and its spiritual empire included the Russian peoples, Baltic Slavs, and peoples living in southwest Asia.

Greenbacks Members of the American political party of the late nineteenth century that worked to advance the interest of farmers by promoting cheap money.

griots Counselors and other officials to the royal family in African kingships. They were also responsible for the preservation and transmission of oral histories and repositories of knowledge.

Group Areas Act (1950) Act that divided South Africa into separate racial and tribal areas and required Africans to live in their own separate communities, including the "homelands."

guerrillas Portuguese and Spanish peasant bands who resisted the revolutionary and expansionist efforts of Napoleon; after the French word *guerre*.

guest workers Migrants looking for temporary employment abroad.

Gulag Administrative name for the vast system of forced labor camps under the Soviet regime; it originated in a small monastery near the Arctic Circle and spread throughout the Soviet Union and to other Soviet-style socialist countries. Penal labor was required of both ordinary criminals (rapists, murderers, thieves) and those accused of political crimes (counterrevolution, anti-Soviet agitation).

Gulf War (1991) Armed conflict between Iraq and a coalition of thirty-two nations, including the United States, Britain, Egypt, France, and Saudi Arabia. It was started by Iraq's invasion of Kuwait, which it had long claimed, on August 2, 1990.

gunpowder Explosive powder. By 1040, the first gunpowder recipes were being written down. Over the next 200 years, Song entrepreneurs invented several incendiary devices and techniques for controlling explosions.

gunpowder empires Muslim empires of the Ottomans, Safavids, and Mughals that used cannonry and gunpowder to advance their military causes.

Guomindang Nationalist party of China, founded just before World War I by Sun Yat-sen and later led by Chiang Kai-shek.

Habsburg Empire Ruling house of Austria, which once ruled both Spain and central Europe but came to settle in lands along the Danube River; it played a prominent role in European affairs for many centuries. In 1867, the Habsburg Empire was reorganized into the Austro-Hungarian Dual Monarchy, and in 1918 it collapsed.

Hadith Sayings attributed to the Prophet Muhammad and his early converts. Used to guide the behavior of Muslim peoples.

Hagia Sophia Enormous and impressive church sponsored by Justinian and built starting in 532 CE. At the time, it was the largest church in the world.

Hajj Pilgrimage to Mecca; an obligation for Muslims.

Hammurapi's Code Legal code created by Hammurapi, the most famous of the Mesopotamian rulers, who reigned from 1792 to 1750 BCE. Hammurapi sought to create social order by centralizing state authority and creating a grand legal structure that embodied paternal justice. The code was quite stratified, dividing society into three classes: free men, dependent men, and slaves, each with distinct rights and responsibilities.

Han agrarian ideal Guiding principle for the free peasantry that made up the base of Han society. In this system, peasants were honored for their labors, while merchants were subjected to a range of controls, including regulations on luxury consumption, and were belittled for not engaging in physical labor.

Han Chinese Inhabitants of China proper who considered others to be outsiders. They felt that they were the only authentic Chinese.

Han Fei Chinese state minister who lived from 280 to 223 BCE; he was a proponent and follower of Xunzi.

Han military Like its Roman counterpart, a ruthless military machine that expanded the empire and created stable conditions that permitted the safe transit of goods by caravans. Emperor Wu heavily influenced the transformation of the military forces and reinstituted a policy that made military service compulsory.

Hangzhou City and former provincial seaport that became the political center of the Chinese people in their ongoing struggles with northern steppe nomads. It was also one of China's gateways to the rest of the world by way of the South China Sea.

Hannibal Great Roman general from Carthage whose campaigns in the third century BCE swept from Spain toward the Italian peninsula. He crossed the Pyrenees and the Alps mountain ranges with war elephants. He was unable, however, to defeat the Romans in 217 BCE.

Harappa One of two cities that, by 2500 BCE, began to take the place of villages throughout the Indus River valley (the other was Mohenjo Daro). Each covered an area of about 250 acres and probably housed 35,000 residents.

harem Secluded women's quarters in Muslim households.

Harlem Renaissance Cultural movement in the 1920s that was based in Harlem, a part of New York City with a large African American population. The movement gave voice to black novelists, poets, painters, and musicians, many of whom used their art to protest racism; also referred to as the "New Negro movement."

harnesses Tools made from wood, bone, bronze, and iron for steering and controlling chariot horses. Harnesses discovered by archaeologists reveal the evolution of headgear from simple mouth bits to full bridles with headpiece, mouthpiece, and reins.

Hatshepsut Leader known as ancient Egypt's most powerful woman ruler. Hatshepsut served as regent for her young son, Thutmosis III, whose reign began in 1479 BCE. She remained co-regent until her death.

Haussmannization Redevelopment and beautification of urban centers; named after the city planner who "modernized" mid-nineteenth-century Paris.

Hegira "Emigration" of Muhammad and his followers out of a hostile Mecca to Yathrib, a city that was later called Medina. The year in which this journey took place, 622 CE, is also year 1 of the Islamic calendar.

Heian period Period from 794 to 1185, during which began the pattern of regents ruling Japan in the name of the sacred emperor.

Hellenism Process by which the individuality of the cultures of the earlier Greek city-states gave way to a uniform culture that stressed the common identity of all who embraced Greek ways. This culture emphasized the common denominators of language, style, and politics to which anyone, anywhere in the Afro-Eurasian world, could have access.

hieroglyphs One of two basic forms of Egyptian writing that were used in conjunction throughout antiquity. Hieroglyphs are pictorial symbols; the term derives from a Greek word meaning "sacred carving"—they were employed exclusively in temple, royal, and divine contexts. *See also* Demotic writing.

Hijra Tradition of Islam, whereby one withdraws from one's community to create another, more holy, one. The practice is based on the Prophet Muhammad's withdrawal from the city of Mecca to Medina in 622 CE.

Hinayana (Lesser Vehicle) Buddhism Form of Buddhism that accepted the divinity of Buddha himself but not of demigods, or bodhisattvas.

Hinduism A refashioning of the ancient Brahmanic Vedic religion, bringing it in accord with rural life and agrarian values. It emerged as the dominant faith in Indian society in the third century CE. Believers became vegetarians and adopted rituals of self-sacrifice. Three major deities—Brahma, Vishnu, and Siva—formed a trinity representing the three phases of the universe (birth, existence, and destruction, respectively) and the three expressions of the eternal self, or *atma*.

Hindu revivalism Movement to reconfigure traditional Hinduism to be less diverse and more amenable to producing a narrowed version of Indian tradition.

Hiroshima Japanese port devastated by an atomic bomb on August 6, 1945.

Hitler, Adolf (1889–1945) German dictator and leader of the Nazi Party who seized power in Germany after its economic collapse in the Great Depression. Hitler and his Nazi regime started World War II in Europe and systematically murdered Jews and other non-Aryan groups in the name of racial purity.

Hittites One of the five great territorial states. The Hittites campaigned throughout Anatolia, then went east to northern Syria, though they eventually faced weaknesses in their own homeland. Their heyday was marked by the reign of the king Supiliulimua (1380 to 1345 BCE), who preserved the Hittites' influence on the balance of power in the region between Mesopotamia and the Nile.

Holocaust Deliberate racial extermination of the Jews by the Nazis that claimed around 6 million European Jews.

Holy Roman Empire Enormous realm that encompassed much of Europe and aspired to be the Christian successor state to the Roman Empire. In the time of the Habsburg dynasts, the empire was a loose confederation of principalities that obeyed an emperor elected by elite lower-level sovereigns. Despite its size, the empire never effectively centralized power; it was split into Austrian and Spanish factions when Charles V abdicated to his sons in 1556.

Holy Russia Name applied to Muscovy and then to the Russian Empire by Slavic Eastern Orthodox clerics who were appalled by the Muslim conquest in 1453 of Constantinople (the capital of Byzantium and of Eastern Christianity) and who were hopeful that Russia would become the new protector of the faith.

home charges Fees India was forced to pay to Britain as its colonial master; these fees included interest on railroad loans, salaries to colonial officers, and the maintenance of imperial troops outside India.

hominids Humanlike beings who walked erect and preceded modern humans.

Homo A word used by scientists to differentiate between pre-human and "true human" species.

Homo caudatus "Tailed man," believed by some European Enlightenment thinkers to be an early species of humankind.

Homo erectus Species that emerged about 1.5 million years ago and had a large brain and walked truly upright. *Homo erectus* means "Standing man."

Homo habilis Scientific term for "Skillful man." Toolmaking ability truly made *Homo habilis* the forerunners, though very distant, of modern humans.

Homo sapiens The first humans; they emerged in a small region of Africa about 200,000 years ago and migrated out of Africa about 100,000 years ago. They had bigger brains and greater dexterity than previous hominid species, whom they eventually eclipsed.

homogeneity Uniformity of the languages, customs, and religion of a particular people or place. It can also be demonstrated by a consistent calendar, set of laws, administrative practices, and rituals.

horses Animals used by full-scale nomadic communities to dominate the steppe lands in western Afro-Eurasia by the second millennium BCE. Horse-riding nomads moved their large herds across immense tracts of land within zones defined by rivers, mountains, and other natural geographical features. In the arid zones of central Eurasia, the nomadic economies made horses a crucial component of survival.

Huguenots French Protestants who endured severe persecution in the sixteenth and seventeenth centuries.

humanism The Renaissance aspiration to know more about the human experience beyond what the Christian scriptures offered by reaching back into ancient Greek and Roman texts.

Hundred Days' Reform (1898) Abortive modernizing reform program of the Qing government of China.

hunting and gathering Lifestyle in which food is acquired through hunting animals, fishing, and foraging for wild berries, nuts, fruit, and grains, rather than planting crops, vines, or trees. As late as 1500, as much as 15 percent of the world's population still lived by this method.

Hyksos A western Semitic-speaking people whose name means "Rulers of Foreign Lands"; they overthrew the unstable Thirteenth Dynasty in Egypt around 1640 BCE. The Hyksos had mastered the art of horse chariots, and with those chariots and their superior bronze axes and composite bows (made of wood, horn, and sinew), they were able to defeat the pharaoh's foot soldiers.

Ibn Sina Philosopher and physician who lived from 980 to 1037 CE. He was also schooled in the Quran, geometry, literature, and Indian and Euclidian mathematics.

ideology Dominant set of ideas of a widespread culture or movement.

Il Duce Term designating the fascist Italian leader Benito Mussolini.

Iliad Epic Greek poem about the Trojan War, composed several centuries after the events it describes. It was based on oral tales passed down for generations.

Il-khanate Mongol-founded dynasty in thirteenth-century Persia.

Imam Muslim religious leader and politico-religious descendant of Ali; believed by some to have a special relationship with Allah.

imperialism Acquisition of new territories by a state and the incorporation of these territories into a political system as subordinate colonies.

Imperium Latin word used to express Romans' power and command over their subjects. It is the basis of the English words *empire* and *imperialism*.

Inca Empire Empire of Quecha-speaking rulers in the Andean valley of Cuzco that encompassed a population of 4 to 6 million. The Incas lacked a clear inheritance system, causing an internal split that Pizarro's forces exploited in 1533.

Indian Institutes of Technology (IIT) Institutions originally designed as engineering schools to expand knowledge and to modernize India, which produced a whole generation of pioneering computer engineers, many of whom moved to the United States.

Indian National Congress Formed in 1885, a political party deeply committed to constitutional methods, industrialization, and cultural nationalism.

Indian National Muslim League Founded in 1906, an organization dedicated to advancing the political interests of Muslims in India.

Indo-Greek Fusion of Indian and Greek culture in the area under the control of the Bactrians, in the northwestern region of India, around 200 BCE.

Indu What we would today call India. Called "Indu" by Xuanzang, a Chinese Buddhist pilgrim who visited the area in the 630s and 640s CE.

indulgences Church-sponsored fund-raising mechanism that gave certification that one's sins had been forgiven in return for money.

industrial revolution Gradual accumulation and diffusion of old and new technical knowledge that led to major economic changes in Britain, northwestern Europe, and North America, catapulting these countries ahead of the rest of the world in manufacturing and agricultural output and standards of living.

industrious revolution Dramatic economic change in which households that had traditionally produced for themselves decided to work harder and longer hours in order to produce more for the market, which enabled them to increase their income and standard of living. Areas that underwent the industrious revolution shifted from peasant farming to specialized production for the market.

innovation Creation of a new method that allowed humans to make better adaptations to their environment such as the making of new tools.

Inquisition Tribunal of the Roman Catholic Church that enforced religious orthodoxy during the Protestant Reformation.

internal and external alchemy In Daoist ritual, use of trance and meditation or chemicals and drugs, respectively, to cause transformations in the self.

International Monetary Fund (IMF) Agency founded in 1944 to help restore financial order in Europe and the rest of the world, to revive international trade, and to support the financial concerns of Third World governments.

invisible hand As described in Adam Smith's *The Wealth of Nations,* the idea that the operations of a free market produce economic efficiency and economic benefits for all.

iron Malleable metal found in combined forms almost everywhere in the world; it became the most important and widely used metal in world history after the Bronze Age.

Iron Curtain Term popularized by Winston Churchill after World War II to refer to a rift, or an iron curtain, that divided western Europe, under American influence, from eastern Europe, under the domination of the Soviet Union.

irrigation Technological advance whereby water delivery systems and water sluices in floodplains or riverine areas were channeled or redirected and used to nourish soil.

Islam A religion that dates to 610 CE, when Muhammad believed God came to him in a vision. Islam ("submission"—in this case, to the will of God) requires its followers to act righteously, to submit themselves to the one and only true God, and to care for the less fortunate. Muhammad's most insistent message was the oneness of God, a belief that has remained central to the Islamic faith ever since.

Jacobins Radical French political group that came into existence during the French Revolution and executed the French king and sought to remake French culture.

Jacquerie (1358) French peasant revolt in defiance of feudal restrictions.

jade The most important precious substance in East Asia. Jade was associated with goodness, purity, luck, and virtue, and was carved into such items as ceremonial knives, blade handles, religious objects, and elaborate jewelry.

Jagat Seths Enormous trading and banking empire in eastern India.

Jainism Along with Buddhism, one of the two systems of thought developed in the seventh century BCE that set themselves up against Brahmanism. Its founder, Vardhamana Mahavira, taught that the universe obeys its own everlasting rules that no god or other supernatural being could affect. The purpose of life was to purify one's soul in order to attain a state of permanent bliss, which could be accomplished through self-denial and the avoidance of harming other creatures.

Janissaries Corps of infantry soldiers recruited as children from the Christian provinces of the Ottoman Empire and brought up with intense loyalty to the Ottoman state and its sultan. The Ottoman sultan used these forces to clip local autonomy and to serve as his personal bodyguards.

Jati Social groups as defined by Hinduism's caste system.

Jesuits Religious order founded by Ignatius Loyola to counter the inroads of the Protestant Reformation; the Jesuits, or the Society of Jesus, were active in politics, education, and missionary work.

Jihad Literally, "striving" or "struggle." This word also connotes military efforts or "striving in the way of God." It also came to mean spiritual struggles against temptation or inner demons, especially in Sufi, or mystical, usage.

Jih-pen Chinese for "Japan."

Jim Crow laws Laws that codified racial segregation and inequality in the southern part of the United States after the Civil War.

Jizya Special tax that non-Muslims were forced to pay to their Islamic rulers in return for which they were given security and property and granted cultural autonomy.

jong Large ocean-going vessels, built by Southeast Asians, which plied the regional trade routes from the fifteenth century to the early sixteenth century.

Judah The southern kingdom of David, which had been an Assyrian vassal until 612 BCE, when it became a vassal of Assyria's successor, Babylon, against whom the people of Judah rebelled, resulting in the destruction of Jerusalem in the sixth century BCE.

Julius Caesar Formidable Roman general who lived from 100 to 44 BCE. He was also a man of letters, a great orator, and a ruthless military man who boasted that his campaigns had led to the deaths of over a million people.

junks Trusty seafaring vessels used in the South China Seas after 1000 CE. These helped make shipping by sea less dangerous.

Justinian Roman or Byzantine emperor who ascended to the throne in 527 CE. In addition to his many building projects and military expeditions, he issued a new law code.

Kabuki Theater performance that combined song, dance, and skillful staging to dramatize conflicts between duty and passion in Tokogawa, Japan.

Kamikaze Japanese for "divine winds" or typhoons; such a storm saved Japan from a Mongol attack.

Kanun Highly detailed system of Ottoman administrative law that jurists developed to deal with matters not treated in the religious law of Islam.

Karim Loose confederation of shippers banding together to protect convoys.

karma Literally "fate" or "action," in Confucian thought; this is a universal principle of cause and effect.

Kassites Nomads who entered Mesopotamia from the eastern Zagros Mountains and the Iranian plateau as early as 2000 BCE. They gradually integrated into Babylonian society by officiating at temples. By 1745 BCE, they had asserted order over the region, and they controlled southern Mesopotamia for the next 350 years, creating one of the territorial states.

Keynesian Revolution Post-Depression economic ideas developed by the British economist John Maynard Keynes, wherein the state took a greater role in managing the economy, stimulating it by increasing the money supply and creating jobs.

KGB Soviet political police and spy agency, formed as the Cheka not long after the Bolshevik coup in October 1917. Grew to more than 750,000 operatives with military rank by the 1980s.

Khan Ruler who was acclaimed at an assembly of elites and supposedly descended from Chinngis Khan on the male line; those not descended from Chinggis continually faced challenges to their legitimacy.

Khanate Major political unit of the vast Mongol empire. There were four Khanates, including the Yuan Empire in China, forged by Chinggis Khan's grandson Kubilai.

Kharijites Radical sect from the early days of Islam. The Kharijites seceded from the "party of Ali" (who themselves came to be known as the Shiites) because of disagreements over succession to the role of the caliph. They were known for their strict militant piety.

Khmers A people who created the most powerful empire in Southwest Asia between the tenth and thirteenth centuries in what is modern-day Cambodia.

Khomeini, Ayatollah Ruhollah (1902–1989) Iranian religious leader who used his traditional Islamic education and his training in Muslim ethics to accuse the shah's government of gross violations of Islamic norms. He also identified the shah's ally, America, as the great Satan. The shah fled the country in 1979; in his wake, Khomeini established a theocratic state ruled by a council of Islamic clerics.

Khufu A pyramid, among those put up in the Fourth Dynasty in ancient Egypt (2575–2465 BCE), which is the largest stone structure in the world. It is in an area called Giza, just outside modern-day Cairo.

Khusro I Anoshirwan Sasanian emperor who reigned from 530 to 579 CE. He was a model ruler and was seen as the personification of justice.

Kiev City that became one of the greatest cities of Europe after the eleventh century. It was built to be a small-scale Constantinople on the Dnieper.

Kikuyu Kenya's largest ethnic group; organizers of a revolt against the British in the 1950s.

King, Martin Luther, Jr. (1929–1968) Civil rights leader who borrowed his most effective weapon—the commitment to nonviolent protest and the appeal to conscience—from Gandhi.

Kingdom of Awadh One of the most prized lands for annexation and the fertile, opulent, and traditional vestige of Mughal rule in India.

Kingdom of Jerusalem What Crusaders set out to liberate when they launched their attack.

Kizilbash Mystical, Turkish-speaking tribesmen who facilitated the Safavid rise to power.

Knossos Area in Crete where, during the second millennium BCE, a primary palace town existed.

Koine Greek Common form of Greek that became the international spoken and written language in the Hellenistic world. This was a simpler everyday form of the ancient Greek language.

Koprulu reforms Reforms named after two grand viziers who revitalized the Ottoman Empire in the seventeenth century through administrative and budget trimming as well as by rebuilding the military.

Korean War (1950–1953) Cold war conflict between Soviet-backed North Korea and U.S.- and UN-backed South Korea. The two sides seesawed back and forth over the same boundaries until 1953, when an armistice divided the country at roughly the same spot as at the start of the war. Nothing had been gained. Losses, however, included 33,000 Americans, at least 250,000 Chinese, and up to 3 million Koreans.

Koryo dynasty Leading dynasty of the northern-based Koryo kingdom in Korea. It is from this dynasty that the name "Korea" derives.

Kremlin Once synonymous with the Soviet government; refers to Moscow's walled city center.

Kshatriyas Originally the warrior caste in Vedic society, the dominant clan members and ruling caste who controlled the land.

Ku Klux Klan Racist organization that first emerged in the U.S. South after the Civil War and then gained national strength as a radically traditionalist movement during the 1920s.

Kubilai Khan (1215–1294) Mongol leader who seized southern China after 1260 and founded the Yuan dynasty.

kulak Originally a pejorative word used to designate better-off peasants, the term used in the late 1920s and early 1930s to refer to any peasant, rich or poor, perceived as an opponent of the Soviet regime. Russian for "fist."

Kumarajiva Renowned Buddhist scholar and missionary who lived from 344 to 413 CE. He was brought to China by Chinese regional forces from Kucha, modern-day Xinjiang.

Kushans Northern nomadic group that migrated into South Asia in 50 CE. They unified the tribes of the region and set up the Kushan dynasty. The Kushans' empire embraced a large and diverse territory and played a critical role in the formation of the Silk Road.

Labour Party Founded in Britain in 1900, the party that represented workers and was based on socialist principles.

laissez-faire The concept that the economy works best when it is left alone—that is, when the state does not regulate or interfere with the workings of the market.

"Land under the Yoke of Ashur" Lands not in Assyria proper, but under its authority; they had to pay the Assyrian Empire exorbitant amounts of tribute.

language System of communication reflecting cognitive abilities. Natural language is generally defined as words arranged in particular sequences to convey meaning and is unique to modern humans.

language families Related tongues with a common ancestral origin; language families contain languages that diverged from one another but share grammatical features and root vocabularies. More than a hundred language families exist.

Laozi Also known as Master Lao; perhaps a contemporary of Confucius and the person after whom Daoism is named. His thought was elaborated upon by generations of thinkers.

Latifundia Broad estates that produced goods for big urban markets, including wheat, grapes, olives, cattle, and sheep.

Laws of Manu Part of the handiwork of Brahman priests; a representative code of law that incorporated social sanctions and practices and provided guidance for living within the caste system.

League of Nations Organization founded after World War I to solve international disputes through arbitration; it was dissolved in 1946 and its assets were transferred to the United Nations.

Legalism Also called Statism, a system of thought about how to live an ordered life. It was developed by Master Xun, or Xunzi (310–237 BCE). It is based on the principle that people, being inherently inclined toward evil, require authoritarian control to regulate their behavior.

Lenin, Nikolai (1870–1924) Leader of the Bolshevik Revolution in Russia and the first leader of the Soviet Union.

Liangzhu Culture spanning centuries from the fourth to the third millennium BCE that represented the last new Stone Age culture in the Yangzi River delta. One of the Ten Thousand States, it was highly stratified and is known for its jade objects.

liberalism Political and social theory that advocates representative government, free trade, and freedom of speech and religion.

limited-liability joint-stock company Company that mobilized capital from a large number of investors, called shareholders, who were not to be held personally liable for financial losses incurred by the company.

Linear A and B Two linear scripts first discovered on Crete in 1900. On the island of Crete and on the mainland areas of Greece, documents of the palace-centered societies were written on clay tablets in these two scripts. Linear A script, apparently written in Minoan, has not yet been deciphered. Linear B was first deciphered in the early 1950s.

"Little Europes" Urban landscapes between 1100 and 1200 CE composed of castles, churches, and towns in what are today Poland, the Czech Republic, Hungary, and the Baltic States.

Liu Bang Chinese emperor from 206 to 195 BCE; after declaring himself the prince of his home area of Han, in 202 BCE, Liu declared himself the first Han emperor.

llamas Animals similar in utility and function to camels in Afro-Eurasia. Llamas could carry heavy loads for long distances.

Long March (1934–1935) Trek of over 10,000 kilometers by Mao Zedong and his communist followers to establish a new base of operations in northwestern China.

Longshan peoples Peoples who lived in small agricultural and riverine villages in East Asia at the end of the third millennium BCE. They set the stage for the Shang in terms of a centralized state, urban life, and a cohesive culture.

lord Privileged landowner who exercised authority over the people who lived on his land.

lost generation The 17 million former members of the Red Guard and other Chinese youth who were denied education from the late 1960s to the mid-1970s as part of the Chinese government's attempt to prevent political disruptions.

Louisiana Purchase (1803) American purchase of French territory from Napoleon, including much of the present-day United States between the Mississippi River and the Rocky Mountains.

Lucy Relatively intact skeleton of a young adult female australopithecine unearthed in the valley of the Awash River in 1974 by an archaeological team working at a site in present-day Hadar, Ethiopia. The researchers nicknamed the skeleton Lucy. She stood just over three feet tall and walked upright at least some of the time. Her skull contained a brain within the ape size range. Also, her jaw and teeth were humanlike. Lucy's skeleton was relatively complete and was the oldest hominid skeleton ever discovered.

Luftwaffe German air force.

Maastricht Treaty (1991) Treaty that formed the European Union, a fully integrated trading and financial bloc with its own bureaucracy and elected representatives.

Ma'at Term used in ancient Egypt to refer to stability or order, the achievement of which was the primary task of Egypt's ruling kings, the pharaohs.

Maccabees Leaders of a riot in Jerusalem in 166 BCE; the riot was a response to a Roman edict outlawing the practice of Judaism.

Madhyamika (Middle Way) Buddhism Chinese branch of Mahayana Buddhism established by Kumarajiva (344–413 CE) that used irony and paradox to show that reason was limited.

madrassas Higher schools of Muslim education that taught law, the Quran, religious sciences, and the regular sciences.

Mahayana (Greater Vehicle) Buddhism School of Buddhist theology that believed that the Buddha was a deity, unlike previous groups that had considered him a wise human being.

Mahdi The "chosen one" in Islam whose appearance was supposed to foretell the end of the world and the final day of reckoning for all people.

maize Grains, the crops that the settled agrarian communities across the Americas cultivated, along with legumes (beans) and tubers (potatoes).

Maji-Maji Revolt (early 1900s) Swahili insurrection against German colonialists; inspired by the belief that those who were anointed with specially blessed water (*maji*) would be immune to bullets. It resulted in 200,000–300,000 African deaths.

Mamluks (Arabic for "owned" or "possessed") Military men who ruled Egypt as an independent regime from 1250 until the Ottoman conquest in 1517.

Manaus Opera House Opera house built in the interior of Brazil in a lucrative rubber-growing area at the turn of the twentieth century.

Manchukuo Japanese puppet state in Manchuria in the 1930s.

Manchus Descendants of the Jurchens who helped the Ming army recapture Beijing in 1644 after its seizure by the outlaw Li Zicheng. The Manchus numbered around 1 million but controlled a domain that included perhaps 250 million people. Their rule lasted more than 250 years and became known as the Qing dynasty.

mandate of heaven Ideology established by Zhou dynasts to communicate the moral transfer of power. Originally a pact between the Zhou people and their supreme god, it evolved in the first century BCE into Chinese political doctrine.

Mande A people who lived in the area between the bend in the Senegal River and the bend in the Niger River east to west and from the Senegal River and Bandama River north to south. Also known as the Mandinka. Their civilization emerged around 1100.

Mandela, Nelson (1918–) Leader of the African National Congress (ANC) who was imprisoned for more than two decades by the apartheid regime in South Africa for his political beliefs; worldwide protests led to his release in 1990. In 1994 Mandela won the presidency in South Africa's first free mass elections.

Manifest Destiny Belief that it was God's will for the American people to expand their territory and political processes across the North American continent.

Mao Zedong (1893–1976) Chinese communist leader who rose to power during the Long March (1934). In 1949, he defeated the Nationalists and established a communist regime in China. Although many of Mao's efforts to transform China, such as the industrialization program of 1958 (known as the Great Leap Forward) and the Cultural Revolution of 1966, failed and brought great suffering to the people, he did instill a new spirit of independence in China and a sense of purpose after many decades of political and economic failure.

maroon community Sanctuary for runaway slaves in the Americas.

Marshall Plan Economic aid package given by the United States to Europe after World War II in hopes of a rapid period of reconstruction and economic gain, thereby securing the countries that received the aid from a communist takeover.

martyrs People executed by the Roman authorities for persisting in their Christian beliefs and refusing to submit to pagan ritual or belief.

Marx, Karl (1818–1883) German philosopher and economist who created Marxism and believed that a revolution of the working classes would overthrow the capitalist order and create a classless society.

Marxism Form of scientific socialism created by Karl Marx and Friedrich Engels that was rooted in a materialist theory of history: what mattered in history were the production of material goods and the ways in which society was organized into classes of producers and exploiters.

mass consumption Increased purchasing power in the early-twentieth-century prosperous and mainly middle-class societies, stemming from mass production.

mass culture Distinctive form of popular culture that arose in the wake of World War I. It reflected the tastes of the working and the middle classes, who now had more time and money to spend on entertainment, and relied on new technologies, especially film and radio, which could reach an entire nation's population and consolidate their sense of being a single state.

mass production System in which factories were set up to produce huge quantities of identical products, reflecting the early-twentieth-century world's demands for greater volume, faster speed, reduced cost, and standardized output.

Mastaba Word meaning "bench" in Arabic; it refers to a huge flat structure identical to earlier royal tombs of ancient Egypt.

Mau-Mau Revolt (1952–1957) Uprising orchestrated by a Kenyan guerrilla movement; this conflict forced the British to grant independence to the black majority in Kenya.

Mauryan Empire Dynasty extended by the Mauryans from 321 to 184 BCE, from the Indus Valley to the northwest areas of South Asia, in a region previously controlled by Persia. It was the first large-scale empire in South Asia and was to become the model for future Indian empires.

Mawali Non-Arab "clients" to Arab tribes in the early Islamic Empire. Because tribal patronage was so much a part of the Arabian cultural system, non-Arabs who converted to Islam affiliated themselves with a tribe and became clients of that tribe.

Maxim gun European weaponry that was capable of firing many bullets per second; it was used against Africans in the conquest of the continent.

Mayans Civilization that ruled over large stretches of Mesoamerica; it was composed of a series of kingdoms, each built around ritual centers rather than cities. The Mayans engaged neighboring peoples in warfare and trade and expanded borders through tributary relationships. They were not defined by a great ruler or one capital city, but by their shared religious beliefs.

McCarthyism Campaign by Republican senator Joseph McCarthy in the late 1940s and early 1950s to uncover closet communists, particularly in the State Department and in Hollywood.

Meat Inspection Act (1906) Legislation that provided for government supervision of meat-packing operations; it was part of a broader "Progressive" reform movement dedicated to correcting the negative consequences of urbanization and industrialization in the United States.

Mecca Arabian city in which Muhammad was born. Mecca was a trading center and pilgrimage destination in the pre-Islamic and Islamic periods. Exiled in 622 CE because of resistance to his message, Muhammad returned to Mecca in 630 CE and claimed the city for Islam.

Medes Rivals of the Assyrians and the Persians. The Medes inhabited the area from the Zagros Mountains to the modern city of Tehran; known as expert horsemen and archers, they were eventually defeated by the Persians.

megaliths Literally, "great stone"; the word *megalith* is used when describing structures such as Stonehenge. These massive structures are the result of cooperative planning and work.

Megarons Large buildings found in Troy (level II) that are the predecessors of the classic Greek temple.

Meiji Empire Empire created under the leadership of Mutsuhito, emperor of Japan from 1868 until 1912. During the Meiji period Japan became a world industrial and naval power.

Meiji Restoration Reign of the Meiji emperor, which was characterized by a new nationalist identity, economic advances, and political transformation.

Mencius Disciple of Confucius who lived from 372 to 289 BCE.

mercantilism Economic theory that drove European empire builders. In this economic system, the world had a fixed amount of wealth, which meant one country's wealth came at the expense of another's. Mercantilism assumed that colonies existed for the sole purpose of enriching the country that controlled the colony.

Mercosur Free-trade pact between the governments of Argentina, Brazil, Paraguay, and Uruguay.

meritocracy Rule by persons of talent.

Meroe Ancient kingdom in what is today Sudan. It flourished for nearly a thousand years, from the fifth century BCE to the fifth century CE.

mestizos Mixed-blood offspring of Spanish settlers and native Indians.

métis Mixed-blood offspring of French settlers and native Indians.

Mexican Revolution (1910) Conflict fueled by the unequal distribution of land and by disgruntled workers; it erupted when political elites split over the succession of General Porfirio Díaz after decades of his rule. The fight lasted over ten years and cost one million lives, but it resulted in a widespread reform and a new constitution.

Mfecane movement African political revolts in the first half of the nineteenth century that were caused by the expansionist methods of King Shaka of the Zulu people.

microsocieties Small-scale communities that had little interaction with others. These communities were the norm for peoples living in the Americas and islanders in the Pacific and Aegean from 2000 to 1200 BCE.

migration Long-distance travel for the purpose of resettlement. In the case of early man, the need to move was usually a response to an environmental shift, such as climate change during the Ice Age.

millenarian Convinced of the imminent coming of a just and ideal society.

millenarian movement Broad, popular upheaval calling for the restoration of a bygone moral age, often led by charismatic spiritual prophets.

Millets Minority religious communities of the Ottoman Empire.

minaret Slender tower within a mosque from which Muslims are called to prayer.

Minbar Pulpit inside a mosque from which Muslim religious speakers broadcast their message to the faithful.

Minoans A people who built a large number of elaborate, independent palace centers on Crete, at Knossos, and elsewhere around 2000 BCE. Named after the legendary King Minos, said to have ruled Crete at the time, they sailed throughout the Mediterranean and by 1600 BCE had planted colonies on many Aegean islands, which in turn became trading and mining centers.

mission civilisatrice Term French colonizers used to refer to France's form of "rationalized" colonial rule, which attempted to bring "civilization" to the "uncivilized."

mitochondrial DNA Form of DNA found outside the nucleus of cells, where it serves as cells' microscopic power packs. Examining mitochondrial DNA enables researchers to measure the genetic variation among living objects, including human beings.

Moche A people who extended their power and increased their wealth at the height of the Chimu Empire over several valleys in what is now modern-day Peru.

Model T First automobile, manufactured by the Ford Motor Company of Henry Ford, to be priced reasonably enough to be sold to the masses.

Modernists A generation of exuberant young artists, writers, and scientists in the late nineteenth century who broke with older conventions and sought new ways of seeing and describing the world.

Mohism School of thought in ancient China, named after Mo Di, or Mozi, who lived from 479 to 438 BCE. It emphasized one's obligation to society as a whole, not just to one's immediate family or social circle.

monarchy Political system in which one individual holds supreme power and passes that power on to his or her next of kin.

monasticism Christian way of life that originated in Egypt and was practiced as early as 300 CE in the Mediterranean. The word itself contains the meaning of a person "living alone" without marriage or family.

monetization An economic shift from a barter-based economy to one dependent on coin.

Mongols Combination of nomadic forest and prairie peoples who lived by hunting and livestock herding and were expert horsemen. Beginning in 1206, the Mongols launched a series of conquests that brought far-flung parts of the world together under their rule. By incorporating conquered peoples and adapting some of their customs, the Mongols created a unified empire that stretched from the Pacific Ocean to the shores of the eastern Mediterranean and the southern steppes of Eurasia.

Moors Term employed by Europeans in the medieval period to refer to Muslim occupants of North Africa, the western Sahara, and the Iberian Peninsula.

mosque Place of worship for the people of Islam.

"Mound people" Name for the people of Cahokia, since its landscape was dominated by earthen monuments in the shapes of mounds. The mounds were carefully maintained and were the loci from which Cahokians paid respect to spiritual forces. *See also* Cahokia.

Mu Chinese ruler (956–918 BCE) who put forth a formal bureaucratic system of governance, appointing officials, supervisors and military captains to whom he was not related. He also instituted a formal legal code.

muckrakers Journalists who aimed to expose political and commercial corruption in late-nineteenth- and early-twentieth-century America.

Muftis Experts on Muslim religious law.

Mughal Empire One of Islam's greatest regimes. Established in 1526, it was a vigorous, centralized state whose political authority encompassed most of modern-day India. During the sixteenth century, it had a population of between 100 and 150 million.

Muhammad (570–632 CE) Prophet and founder of the Islamic faith. Born in Mecca in Saudi Arabia and orphaned when young, Muhammad lived under the protection of his uncle. His career as a prophet began around

610 CE, with his first experience of spiritual revelation.

Muhammad Ali Ruler of Egypt between 1805 and 1848. He initiated a set of modernizing reforms that sought to make Egypt competitive with the great powers.

mullahs Religious leaders in Iran who in the 1970s led a movement opposing Shah Reza Pahlavi and denounced American materialism and secularism.

multinational corporations Corporations based in many different countries that have global investment, trading, and distribution goals.

Muscovy The principality of Moscow. Originally a mixture of Slavs, Finnish tribes, Turkic speakers, and many others, Muscovy used territorial expansion and commercial networks to consolidate a powerful state and expanded to become the Russian Empire, a huge realm that spanned parts of Europe, much of northern Asia, numerous North Pacific islands, and even—for a time—a corner of North America (Alaska).

Muslim Brotherhood Egyptian organization founded in 1938 by Hassan al-Banna. It attacked liberal democracy as a cover for middle-class, business, and landowning interests and fought for a return to a purified Islam.

Muslim League National Muslim party of India.

Mussolini, Benito (1883–1945) Italian dictator and founder of the fascist movement in Italy. During World War II, he allied Italy with Germany and Japan.

Muwahhidin Term meaning "unitarians"; these were followers of the Wahhabi movement that emerged in the Arabian Peninsula in the eighteenth century.

Mycenaeans Mainland competitors of the Minoans; they took over Crete around 1400 BCE. Migrating to Greece from central Europe, they brought their Indo-European language, horse chariots, and metalworking skills, which they used to dominate until 1200 BCE.

Nagasaki Second Japanese city to be hit by an atomic bomb near the end of World War II.

Napoleon Bonaparte (1769–1821) General who rose to power in a post-Revolutionary coup d'état, eventually proclaiming himself emperor of France. He placed security and order ahead of social reform and created a civil legal code. Napoleon expanded his empire through military action, but after his disastrous Russian campaign, the united European powers defeated Napoleon and forced him into exile. He escaped and reassumed command of his army but was later defeated at the Battle of Waterloo.

Napoleonic Code Legal code drafted by Napoleon in 1804; it distilled different legal traditions to create one uniform law. The code confirmed the abolition of feudal privileges of all kinds and set the conditions for exercising property rights.

National Assembly of France Governing body of France that succeeded the Estates-General in 1789 during the French Revolution. It was composed of, and defined by, the delegates of the Third Estate.

National Association for the Advancement of Colored People (NAACP) Founded in 1910, the U.S. civil rights organization dedicated to ending inequality and segregation for black Americans.

National Recovery Administration (NRA) New Deal agency created in 1933 to prepare codes of fair administration and to plan for public works. It was later declared unconstitutional.

nationalism The idea that members of a shared community called a "nation" should have sovereignty within the borders of their state.

nation-state Form of political organization that derived legitimacy from its inhabitants, often referred to as citizens, who in theory, if not always in practice, shared a common language, common culture, and common history.

native learning Japanese movement to promote nativist intellectual traditions and the celebration of Japanese texts.

native paramountcy British form of "rationalized" colonial rule, which attempted to bring "civilization" to the "uncivilized" by proclaiming that when the interests of European settlers in Africa clashed with those of the African population, the latter should take precedence.

natural rights Belief that emerged in eighteenth-century western Europe and North America that rights fundamental to human nature were discernible to reason and should be affirmed in human-made law.

natural selection Charles Darwin's theory that populations grew faster than the food supply, creating a "struggle for existence" among species. In later work he showed how the passing on of individual traits was also determined by what he called sexual selection—according to which the "best" mates are chosen for their strength, beauty, or talents. The outcome: the "fittest" survived to reproduce, while the less adaptable did not.

Nazis (National Socialist German Workers Party) German organization dedicated to winning workers over from socialism to nationalism; the first Nazi Party platform combined nationalism with anticapitalism and anti-Semitism.

Neanderthals Members of an early wave of hominids from Africa who settled in western Afro-Eurasia, in an area reaching from present-day Uzbekistan and Iraq to Spain, approximately 150,000 years ago.

needle compass Crucial instrument made available to navigators after 1000 CE that helped guide sailors on the high seas. It was a Chinese invention.

negritos Hunter-gatherer inhabitants of the East Asian coastal islands who migrated there around 28,000 BCE but by 2000 BCE had been replaced by new migrants.

Negritude Statement of the virtues of the black identity and the validation of African culture and the African past, even in a westernizing world. This idea was shaped by African and African American intellectuals like Senegal's first president, Léopold Sédar Senghor.

Nehemiah Jewish eunuch of the Persian court who was given permission to rebuild the fortification walls around the city of Jerusalem from 440 to 437 BCE.

Neo-Assyrian Empire Afro-Eurasian empire that dominated around 950 BCE. The Neo-Assyrians extended their control over resources and people beyond their own borders, and their empire lasted for three centuries.

Nestorian Christians Denomination of Christians whose beliefs about Christ differed from those of the official Byzantine church. Named after Nestorius, former bishop of Constantinople, they emphasized the human aspects of Jesus.

New Deal President Franklin Delano Roosevelt's package of government reforms that were enacted during the 1930s to provide jobs for the unemployed, social welfare programs for the poor, and security to the financial markets.

New Economic Policy Enacted decrees of the Bolsheviks between 1921 and 1927 that grudgingly sanctioned private trade and private property.

New Negro movement *See* Harlem Renaissance.

New World Term applied to the Americas that reflected the Europeans' view that anything previously unknown to them was "new," even if it had existed and supported societies long before European explorers arrived on its shores.

Nirvana Literally, nonexistence; nirvana is the state of complete liberation from the concerns of worldly life, as in Buddhist thought.

Nō drama Masked theater favored by Japanese bureaucrats and regional lords during the Tokugawa period.

Noble Eightfold Path Buddhist concept of a way of life by which people may rid themselves of individual desire to achieve nirvana. The path consists of wisdom, ethical behavior, and mental discipline.

Nok culture Spectacular culture that arose in what is today Nigeria, in the sixth century BCE. Iron smelting occurred there around 600 BCE. Thus the Nok people made the transition from stone to iron materials.

nomads People who move across vast distances without settling permanently in a particular place. Often pastoralists, nomads and transhumant herders introduced new forms of chariot-based warfare that transformed the Afro-Eurasian world.

non-governmental organizations (NGOs) Term used to refer to private organizations like the Red Cross that play a large role in international affairs.

nonviolent resistance (*Satyagraha*) Moral and political philosophy of resistance developed by Indian National Congress leader Mohandas Gandhi. Gandhi believed that if Indians pursued self-reliance and self-control in a nonviolent way, the British would eventually have to leave.

North American Free Trade Agreement (NAFTA) Treaty negotiated in the early 1990s to promote free trade between Canada, the United States, and Mexico.

North Atlantic Treaty Organization (NATO) International organization set up in 1949 to provide for the defense of western European countries and the United States from the perceived Soviet threat.

Northern Wei dynasty Regime founded in 386 CE by the Tuoba, a people originally from Inner Mongolia, that lasted one and a half centuries. The rulers of this dynasty adopted many practices of the earlier Chinese Han regime. At the same time, they struggled to consolidate authority over their own nomadic people. Ultimately, several decades of intense internal conflict led to the dynasty's downfall.

northwest passage Long-sought marine passageway between the Atlantic and Pacific oceans.

Oceania Collective name for the lands of Australia and New Zealand and the islands of the southwest Pacific Ocean.

**Odyssey* Composed in the eighth century BCE, an epic tale of the journey of Odysseus, who traveled the Mediterranean back to his home in Ithaca after the siege of Troy.

**Oikos* The word for "small family unit" in ancient Greece, similar to the *familia* in Rome. Its structure, with men as heads of household over women and children, embodied the fundamental power structure in Greek city-states.

oligarchy Clique of privileged rulers.

Olmecs A people who emerged around 1500 BCE and lived in Mesoamerica. The name means those who "lived in the land of the rubber." Olmec society was composed of decentralized villages. Its members spoke the same language and worshipped the same gods.

Open Door Policy Policy proposed by American Secretary of State John Hay that would give all foreign nations equal access to trade with China. As European imperial powers carved out spheres of trade in late-nineteenth-century China, American leaders worried that the United States would be excluded from trade with China. To prevent this, Hay proposed the Open Door Policy.

Opium War (1839–1842) War fought between the British and Qing China over British trade in opium; resulted in the granting to the British the right to trade in five different ports and the ceding of Hong Kong to the British.

oracle bones Animal bones used by Shang diviners. Diviners applied intense heat to the shoulder bones of cattle or to turtle shells,

which caused them to crack. The diviners would then interpret the cracks as signs from the ancestors regarding royal plans and actions.

Organization of Petroleum Exporting Countries (OPEC) International association established in 1960 to coordinate price and supply policies of oil-producing states.

orientalism Genre of literature and painting that portrayed the nonwestern peoples of North Africa and Asia as exotic, sensuous, and economically backward with respect to Europeans.

orientalists Western scholars who specialized in the study of the East.

**Orrorin tugenensis* Predecessor to hominids that first appeared 6 million years ago.

Ottoman Empire Rulers of Anatolia, the Arab world, and much of southern and eastern Europe in the early sixteenth century. They transformed themselves from nomadic warrior bands who roamed the borderlands between Islamic and Christian worlds in Anatolia into sovereigns of a vast, bureaucratic empire. The Ottomans embraced a Sunni view of Islam. They adapted traditional Byzantine governmental practices but tried new ways of integrating the diverse peoples of their empire.

Pacific War (1879–1883) War between Chile and the alliance of Bolivia and Peru.

**Pagani* Pejorative word used by Christians to designate pagans.

palace Official residence of the ruler, his family, and his entourage. The palace was both a social institution and a set of buildings. It first appeared around 2500 BCE, about a millennium later than the Mesopotamian temple, and quickly joined the temple as a defining landmark of city life. Eventually, it became a source of power rivaling the temple, and palace and temple life often blurred, as did the boundary between the sacred and the secular.

Palmyra Roman trading depot in modern-day Syria; part of a network of trading cities that connected various regions of Afro-Eurasia.

pan movements Groups that sought to link people across state boundaries in new communities based on ethnicity or, in some cases, religion (e.g., pan-Germanism, pan-Islamism, pan-Slavism).

Pansophia Ideal republic of inquisitive Christians united in the search for knowledge of nature as a means of loving God.

papacy The institution of the pope; the Catholic spiritual leader in Rome.

papal Of, relating to, or issued by a pope.

Parthians Horse-riding people who pushed southward around the middle of the second century BCE and wiped out the Greek kingdoms in Iran. They then extended their power all the way to the Mediterranean, where they ran up against the Roman Empire in Anatolia and Mesopotamia.

pastoral nomadic communities Groups of people that moved their domesticated animals from place to place to meet the animals' demanding grazing requirements. Around 3500 BCE, western Afro-Eurasia witnessed the growth and spread of pastoral nomadic communities.

pastoralism Herding and breeding of sheep and goats or other animals as a primary means of subsistence.

**Paterfamilias* Latin for "Father of the family," which itself was the foundation of the Roman social order.

**Patria* Latin, meaning "fatherland."

patrons In the Roman system of patronage, men and women of wealth and high social status who protected dependents or "clients" of a lower class.

**Pax Mongolica* Term that refers to the political and especially the commercial stability that the vast Mongol Empire provided for the travelers and merchants of Eurasia during the thirteenth and fourteenth centuries.

**Pax Romana* Latin for "Roman Peace"; refers to the period between 25 BCE and 235 CE during which conditions in the Roman Empire were settled and peaceful.

**Pax Sinica* Period of peace (149–87 BCE) during which agriculture, commerce, and industry flourished in East Asia under the rule of the Han.

Peace Preservation Act (1925) Act instituted in Japan that specified up to ten years' hard labor for any member of an organization advocating a basic change in the political system or the abolition of private property.

Pearl Harbor American naval base in Hawaii on which the Japanese launched a surprise attack on December 7, 1941, bringing the United States into World War II.

Peloponnesian War War fought between 431 and 404 BCE between two of Greece's most powerful city-states, Athens and Sparta.

Peninsular War (1808–1814) Conflict in which the Portuguese and Spanish populations, supported by the British, resisted the French invasion under Napoleon of the Iberian Peninsula.

Peninsulars Spaniards who, although born in Spain, resided in the Spanish colonial territories. They regarded themselves as superior to Spaniards born in the colonies (Creoles).

Peoples' Charter Document calling for universal suffrage for adult males, the secret ballot, electoral districts, and annual parliamentary elections. It was signed by over 3 million British between 1839 and 1842.

**periplus* Book that reflected sailing knowledge; in such books captains would record landing spots and ports. The word *periplus* literally means "sailing around."

Persepolis Darius I's capital city in the highlands of Fars; a ceremonial center and expression of imperial identity as well as an important administrative hub.

Peterloo Massacre (1819) The killing of 11 and wounding of 460 following a peaceful demonstration for political reform by workers in Manchester, England.

Petra City in modern-day Jordan that was the Nabataean capital. It profited greatly by supplying provisions and water to travelers and traders. Many of its houses and shrines were cut into the rocky mountains. *Petra* means "rock."

phalanx Military formation used by Philip II of Macedonia, whereby heavily armored infantry were closely arrayed in battle formation.

Philip II of Macedonia Father of Alexander the Great, under whose rule Macedonia developed into a large ethnic and territorial state. After unifying Macedonia, Philip went on to conquer neighboring states.

philosophia Literally "love of wisdom"; this system of thought originally included speculation on the nature of the cosmos, the environment, and human existence. It eventually came to include thought about the nature of humans and life in society.

Phoenicians Known as the Canaanites in the Bible, an ethnic group in the Levant under Assyrian rule in the seventh century BCE; they provided ships and sailors for battles in the Mediterranean. The word *Phoenician* refers to the purple dye they manufactured and widely traded, along with other commercial goods and services, throughout the Mediterranean. While part of wider Mesopotamian culture, their major contribution was the alphabet, first introduced in the second millennium BCE, which made far-reaching communication possible.

phonemes Primary and distinctive sounds that are characteristic of human language.

piety Strong sense of religious duty and devoutness, often inspiring extraordinary actions.

plant domestication Process of growing plants, harvesting their seeds, and saving some of the seeds for planting in subsequent growing cycles, resulting in a steady food supply. This process occurred as far back as 5000 BCE, when plants began to naturally retain their seeds. Plant domestication was practiced first in the southern Levant and spread from there into the rest of Southwest Asia.

Plato (427–347 BCE) Disciple of the great philosopher Socrates; his works are the only record we have of Socrates' teaching. He was also the author of formative philosophical works on ethics and politics.

plebs In Rome, term that referred to the "common people." Their interests were protected by officials called tribunes.

Pochteca Archaic term for merchants of the Mexicos.

polities Politically organized communities or states.

polyglot communities Societies composed of diverse linguistic and ethnic groups.

popular culture Affordable and accessible forms of art and entertainment available to people at all levels of society.

popular sovereignty The idea that the power of the state resides in the people.

populists Members of a political movement that supported U.S. farmers in late-nineteenth-century America. The term is often used generically to refer to political groups who appeal to the majority of the population.

potassium-argon dating Major dating technique based on the changing chemical structure of objects over time, since over time potassium decays into argon. This method makes possible the dating of objects up to a million years old.

potato famine (1840s) Severe famine in Ireland that led to the rise of radical political movements and the migration of large numbers of Irish to the United States.

potter's wheel Fast wheel that enabled people to mass-produce vessels in many different shapes. This advance, invented at the city of Uruk, enabled potters to make significant technical breakthroughs.

pottery Vessels made of mud and later clay that were used for storing and transporting food. The development of pottery was a major breakthrough.

Prague Spring (1968) Program of liberalization under a new communist party in Czechoslovakia that strove to create a democratic and pluralist socialism.

predestinarian Belief of many sixteenth- and seventeenth-century Protestant groups that God had foreordained the lives of individuals, including their bad and good deeds.

primitivism Western art movement of the late-nineteenth and early-twentieth centuries that drew upon the so-called primitive art forms of Africa, Oceania, and pre-Columbian America.

progressive reformers Members of the U.S. reform movement in the early twentieth century that aimed to eliminate political corruption, improve working conditions, and regulate the power of large industrial and financial enterprises.

proletarians Industrial wage workers.

prophets Charismatic freelance religious men of power who found themselves in opposition to the formal power of the kings, bureaucrats, and priests.

Prophet's Town Indian village that was burned down by American forces in the early nineteenth century.

Protestant Reformation Religious movement initiated by sixteenth-century monk Martin Luther, who openly criticized the corruption in the Catholic Church and voiced his belief that Christians could speak directly to God. His doctrines gained wide support, and those who followed this new view of the Christianity rejected the authority of the papacy and the Catholic clergy, broke away from the Catholic Church, and called themselves "Protestants."

Protestantism Division of Christianity that emerged in western Europe from the Protestant Reformation.

Proto-Indo-European The parent of all the languages in the Indo-European family, which includes, among many others, English, German, Norwegian, Portuguese, French, Russian, Persian, Hindi, and Bengali.

Pullman Strike (1894) American Railway Union strike in response to wage cuts and firings.

puppet states Governments with little power in the international arena that follow the dictates of their more powerful neighbors or patrons.

Puritans Seventeenth-century reform group of the Church of England; also known as dissenters or nonconformists.

Qadiriyya Sufi order that facilitated the spread of Islam into West Africa.

Qadis Judges in the Ottoman Empire.

qanats Underground water channels, vital for irrigation, which were used in Persia. Little evaporation occurred when water was being moved through qanats.

Qing dynasty (1644–1911) Minority Manchu rule over China that incorporated new territories, experienced substantial population growth, and sustained significant economic growth.

Questions of King Milanda (Milindapunha) Name of a second-century BCE text espousing the teachings of Buddhism as set forth by Menander, a Yavana king. It featured a discussion between the king and a sophisticated Buddhist sage named Nagasena.

Quetzalcoatl Ancient deity and legendary ruler of Native American peoples living in Mexico.

Quran The scripture of the Islamic faith. Originally a verbal recitation, the Quran was eventually compiled into a book in the order in which we have it today. According to traditional Islamic interpretation, the Quran was revealed to Muhammad by the angel Gabriel over a period of twenty-three years.

radicals Widely used term in nineteenth-century Europe that referred to those individuals and political organizations that favored the total reconfiguration of Europe's old state system.

radiocarbon isotope C[14] Isotope contained by all living things, which plants acquire directly from the atmosphere and animals acquire indirectly when they consume plants or other animals. When living things die, the C^{14} isotope they contain begins to decay into a stable nonradioactive element, C^{12}. The rate of decay is regular and measurable, making it possible to ascertain the date of fossils that leave organic remains for ages of up to 40,000 years.

raj British crown's administration of India following the end of the East India Company's rule after the Rebellion of 1857.

raja "King" in the Kshatriya period in South Asia; could also refer to the head of a family, but indicated the person who had control of land and resources in South Asian city-states.

Ramadan Ninth month of the Muslim year, during which all Muslims must fast during daylight hours.

Rape of Nanjing Attack against the Chinese in which the Japanese slaughtered at least 100,000 civilians and raped thousands of women between December 1937 and February 1938.

Rashtriya Swayamsevak Sangh (**RSS**) (1925) Campaign to organize Hindus as a militant, modern community in India; translated in English as "National Volunteer Organization."

Rebellion of 1857 Indian uprising against the East India Company to bring religious purification, an egalitarian society, and local and communal solidarity without the interference of British rule.

rebus Probably originating in Uruk, a representation that transfers meaning from the name of a thing to the sound of that name. For example, a picture of a bee can represent the sound "b." Such pictures opened the door to writing: a technology of symbols that uses marks to represent specific discrete sounds.

Reconquista Spanish reconquest of territories lost to the Islamic Empire, beginning with Toledo in 1061.

Red Guards Chinese students who were the shock troopers in the early phases of Mao's Cultural Revolution in 1966–1968.

Red Lanterns Female supporters of the Chinese Boxers who rebelled against foreign intrusions in China at the turn of the twentieth century. Most were teenage girls and unmarried women and dressed in red garments.

Red Turban movement Diverse religious movement in China during the fourteenth century that spread the belief that the world was drawing to an end as Mongol rule was collapsing.

Reds Bolsheviks.

Reich German empire composed of Denmark, Austria, and parts of western France.

Reichstag The German parliament.

Reign of Terror Campaign at the height of the French Revolution in the early 1790s that used violence, including systematic execution of opponents of the revolution, to purge France of its enemies and to extend the revolution beyond its borders; radicals executed as many as 40,000 persons who were judged enemies of the state.

Renaissance Term meaning "rebirth" that historians use to characterize the expanded cultural production of European nations between 1430 and 1550. Emphasized a break from the church-centered medieval world and a new concept of humankind as the center of the world.

republican government Government in which power and rulership rest with representatives of the people—not a king.

Res publica Literally "public thing"; this referred to the Roman republic, in which policy and rules of behavior were determined by the Senate and by popular assemblies of the citizens.

Restoration period (1815–1848) European movement after the defeat of Napoleon to restore Europe to its pre-French revolutionary status and to quash radical movements.

Rift Valley Area of northeastern Africa where some of the most important early human archaeological discoveries of fossils were found, especially one of an intact skull that is 1.8 million years old.

river basin Area drained by a river, including all its tributaries. River basins were rich in fertile soil, water for irrigation, and plant and animal life, which made them attractive for human habitation. Cultivators were able to produce surplus agriculture to support the first cities.

riverine Term denoting an area whose inhabitants depended on irrigation for their well-being and whose populations are settled near great rivers. Egypt was, in a sense, the most riverine of all these cultures, in that it had no hinterland of plains as did Mesopotamia and the Indus valley. Away from the banks of the Nile, there is only largely uninhabitable desert.

Roman army Military force of the Roman Empire. The Romans devised a military draft that could draw from a huge population. In their encounter with Hannibal, they lost up to 80,000 men in three separate encounters and still won the war.

Roman Catholicism Branch of Christianity established by 1000 CE in western Europe and led by the Roman papacy. In contrast to ancient Greek Orthodoxy, Western Catholics believed that their church was destined to expand everywhere, and they set about converting the pagan tribes of northern Europe. Western Catholics contemptuously called the East Romans "Greeks" and condemned them for their "Byzantine" cunning.

Roman law Roman legal system, under which disputes were brought to the public courts and decisions were made by judges and sometimes by large juries. Rome's legal system featured written law and institutions for settling legal disputes.

roving bandits Large bands of dispossessed and marginalized peasants who vented their anger at tax collectors in the waning years of the Ming dynasty.

Royal Road A 1,600-mile road from Sardis in Anatolia to Susa in Iran; used by messengers, traders, the army, and those taking tribute to the king.

Russification Programs to assimilate people of over 146 dialects into the Russian Empire.

S.S. (*Schutzstaffel*) Hitler's security police force.

Sack of Constantinople Rampage in 1204 by the Frankish armies on the capital city of Constantinople.

sacred kingships Institutions that marked the centralized politics of West Africa. The inhabitants of these kingships believed that their kings were descendants of the gods.

Sahel region Area of sub-Saharan Africa with wetter and more temperate locations, especially in the upland massifs and their foothills, villages, and towns.

St. Bartholomew's Day Massacre (1572) Roman Catholic massacre of French Protestants in Paris.

St. Patrick Former slave brought to Ireland from Briton who later became a missionary, or the "Apostle of Ireland." He died in 470 CE.

Salt March (1930) A 240-mile trek to the sea in India, led by Mohandas Gandhi, to gather salt for free, thus breaking the British colonial monopoly on salt.

Samurai Japanese warriors who made up the private armies of Japanese daimyos.

Sandinista coalition Left-leaning Nicaraguan coalition of the 1970s and 1980s.

Santería African-based religion, blended with Christian influences, that was first practiced by slaves in Cuba.

Sargon the Great King of Akkad, a city-state near modern Baghdad. Reigning from 2334 to 2279 BCE, Sargon helped bring the competitive era of city-states to an end and sponsored monumental works of architecture, art, and literature.

Sasanian Empire Empire that succeeded the Parthians in the mid-220s CE in Inner Eurasia. The Sasanian Empire controlled the trade crossroads of Afro-Eurasia and possessed a strong armored cavalry, which made them a powerful rival to Rome. The Sasanians were also tolerant of Judaism and Christianity, which allowed Christians to flourish.

Sati Hindu practice whereby a woman was burned to death on the pyre of her dead husband.

satrap Governor of a province in the Persian Empire. Each satrap was a relative or intimate associate of the king.

Satyagraha *See* nonviolent resistance.

scientific method Method of inquiry based on experimentation in nature. Many of its principles were first laid out by the philosopher Sir Francis Bacon (1561–1626), who claimed that real science entailed the formulation of hypotheses that could be tested in carefully controlled experiments.

Scramble for Africa European rush to colonize parts of Africa at the end of the nineteenth century.

scribes Those who wield writing tools; from the very beginning they were at the top of the social ladder, under the major power brokers.

Scythian ethos Warrior ethos that embodied the extremes of aggressive mounted-horse culture, c. 1000 BCE. In part the Scythian ethos was the result of the constant struggle between settlers, hunter-gatherers, and nomads on the northern frontier of Europe.

Sea Peoples Migrants from north of the Mediterranean who invaded the cities of Egypt and the Levant in the second millennium BCE. Once settled along the coast of the Levant, they became known as the Philistines and considerably disrupted the settlements of the Canaanites.

SEATO (Southeast Asia Treaty Organization) Military alliance of pro-American, anticommunist states in Southeast Asia in 1954.

Second World Term invented during the cold war to refer to the communist countries, as opposed to the West (or First World) and the former colonies (or Third World).

second-generation societies Societies that expanded old ideas and methods by incorporating new aspects of culture and grafting them onto, or using them in combination with, established norms.

Seleucus Nikator Successor of Alexander the Great who lived from 358 to 281 BCE. He controlled Mesopotamia, Syria, Persia, and parts of the Punjab.

Self-Strengthening movement In the latter half of the nineteenth century, a movement of reformist Chinese bureaucrats that attempted to adopt western elements of learning and technological skill while retaining their core Chinese culture.

Semu Term meaning "outsiders" or non-Chinese people—Mongols, Tanguts, Khitan, Jurchen, Muslims, Tibetans, Persians, Turks, Nestorians, Jews, and Armenians—who became a new ruling elite over a Han majority population in the late thirteenth century.

sepoys Hindu and Muslim recruits of the East India Company's military force.

serfs Peasants who farmed the land and paid fees to be protected and governed by lords under a system of rule called feudalism.

settled agriculture Application of human labor and tools to a fixed plot of land for more than one growing cycle. It entails the changeover from a hunting and gathering lifestyle to one based on agriculture, which requires staying in one place until the soil has been exhausted.

Seven Years' War (1756–1763) Worldwide war that ended when Prussia defeated Austria, establishing itself as a European power, and when Britain gained control of India and many of France's colonies through the Treaty of Paris.

sexual revolution Increased freedom in sexual behavior, resulting in part from the advances in contraception, notably the introduction of oral contraception in 1960, which allowed men and women to limit childbearing and to have sex with less fear of pregnancy.

shah Traditional title of Persian rulers.

shamans Certain humans whose powers supposedly enabled them to commune with the supernatural and to transform themselves wholly or partly into beasts.

Shamisen Three-stringed instrument, often played by Japanese geisha.

Shandingdong Man A *Homo sapiens* whose fossil remains and relics can be dated to about 18,000 years ago. His physical characteristics were closer to those of modern humans, and he had a similar brain size.

Shang state Dynasty in northeastern China that ruled from 1600 to 1045 BCE. Though not as well defined by borders as the territorial states in the southwest of Asia, it did have a ruling lineage. Four fundamental elements of the Shang state were a metal industry based on copper, pottery making, standardized architectural forms and walled towns, and divination using animal bones.

Shanghai School Late-nineteenth-century style of painting characterized by an emphasis on spontaneous brushwork, feeling, and the incorporation of western influences into classical Chinese pieces.

sharecropping System of farming in which tenant farmers rented land and gave over a share of their crops to the land's owners. Sometimes seen as a cheap way for the state to conduct agricultural affairs, sharecropping often resulted in the impoverishment and marginalization of the underclass.

Sharia Literally, "the way"; now used to indicate the philosophy and rulings of Islamic law.

Sharpeville Massacre (1960) Massacre of sixty-nine black Africans when police fired upon a rally against the recently passed laws requiring nonwhite South Africans to carry identity papers.

Shawnees Native American tribe that inhabited the Ohio valley during the eighteenth century.

Shays's Rebellion (1786) Uprising of armed farmers that broke out when the Massachusetts state government refused to offer them economic relief.

Shiism One of the two main branches of Islam, practiced in the Safavid Empire. Although always a minority sect in the Islamic world, Shiism contains several subsects, each of which has slightly different interpretations of theology and politics.

Shiites Group of supporters of Ali, Muhammad's cousin and son-in-law, who wanted him to be the first caliph and believed that members of the Prophet's family deserved to rule. The leaders of the Shiite community are known as "Imam," which means "leaders."

Shinto Japan's official religion; it promoted the state and the emperor's divinity. The term means "the way of the gods."

shoguns Japanese military commanders. From 1192 to 1333, the Kamakura shoguns served as military "protectors" of the ruler in the city of Heian.

Shotoku Prince in the early Japanese Yamoto state (574–622 CE) who is credited with having introduced Buddhism to Japan.

shudras Literally "small ones"; workers and slaves from outside the Vedic lineage.

Siddhartha Gautama Another name for the Buddha; the most prominent opponent of the Brahman way of life; he lived from 563 to 483 BCE.

Sikhism Islamic-inspired religion that calls on its followers to renounce the caste system and to treat all believers as equal before God.

Silicon Valley Valley between the California cities of San Francisco and San Jose, known for its innovative computer and high-technology industries.

silk Luxury textile that became a vastly popular export from China (via the Silk Road) to the cities of the Roman world.

Silk Road Trade route linking China with central Asia and the Mediterranean; it extended over 5,000 miles, land and sea included, and was so named because of the quantities of silk that were traded along it. The Silk Road was a major factor in the development of civilizations in China, Egypt, Persia, India, and even Europe.

Silla One of three independent Korean states that may have emerged as early as the third century BCE. These states lasted until 668 CE, when Silla took control over the entire peninsula.

Silver Islands Term used by European merchants in the sixteenth century to refer to Japan, because of its substantial trade in silver with China.

Sino-Japanese War (1894–1895) Conflict over the control of Korea in which China was forced to cede the province of Taiwan to Japan.

Sipahi Urdu for "soldier."

Siva The third of three Vedic deities, signifying destruction. *See also* Brahma *and* Vishnu.

slave plantations System whereby labor was used for the cultivation of crops wholly for the sake of producing surplus that was then used for profit; slave plantations were a crucial part of the growth of the Mediterranean economy.

small seal script Unified script that was used to the exclusion of other scripts under the Qin, with the aim of centralizing administration; its use led to a less complicated style of clerical writing than had been in use under the Han.

social contract The idea, drawn from the writings of British philosopher John Locke, that the law should bind both ruler and people.

Social Darwinism Belief that Charles Darwin's theory of evolution was applicable to humans and justified the right of the ruling classes or countries to dominate the weak.

social hierarchies Distinctions between the privileged and the less privileged.

Social Security Act (1935) New Deal act that instituted old-age pensions and insurance for the unemployed.

socialism Political ideology that calls for a classless society with collective ownership of all property.

Socrates (469–399 BCE) Philosopher in Athens who encouraged people to reflect on ethics and morality. He stressed the importance of honor and integrity as opposed to wealth and power. Plato was his student.

Sogdians A people who lived in central Asia's commercial centers and maintained the stability and accessibility of the Silk Road. They were crucial to the interconnectedness of the Afro-Eurasian landmass.

Solidarity The communist bloc's first independent trade union, it was established in Poland at the Gdansk shipyard.

Song dynasty Chinese dynasty that took over the mandate of heaven for three centuries starting in 976 CE. It ruled an era of many economic and political successes, but it eventually lost northern China to nomadic tribes.

Song porcelain Type of porcelain perfected during the Song period that was light, durable, and quite beautiful.

South African War (1899–1902) Conflict between the British and Dutch colonists of South Africa which resulted in bringing two Afrikaner republics under the control of the British. Often called the Boer War.

Soviet bloc International alliance that included the east European countries of the Warsaw Pact as well as the Soviet Union but also came to include Cuba.

Spanish-American War (1898) War between the United States and Spain in Cuba, Puerto Rico, and the Philippines. It ended with a treaty in which the United States took over the Philippines, Guam, and Puerto Rico; Cuba won partial independence.

speciation The formation of different species.

specie Money in coin.

species Group of animals or plants possessing one or more distinctive characteristics.

spiritual ferment Process that occurred after 300 CE in which religion touched more areas of society and culture than before and touched them in different, more demanding ways.

Spring and Autumn period Period between the eighth and fifth centuries BCE, during which China was ruled by the feudal system. Considered an anarchic and turbulent time, there were 148 different tributary states in this period.

Stalin, Joseph (1879–1953) Leader of the communist party and the Soviet Union; sought to create "socialism in one country."

steel A metal more malleable and stronger than iron that became essential for industries like shipbuilding and railways.

stoicism Widespread philosophical movement initiated by Zeno (334–262 BCE). Zeno and his followers sought to understand the role of people in relation to the cosmos. For the Stoics, everything was grounded in nature. Being in love with nature and living a good life required being in control of one's passions and thus indifferent to pleasure or pain.

Strait of Malacca Seagoing gateway to Southeast and East Asia.

Strategic Defense Initiative ("Star Wars") Master plan, championed by U.S. president Ronald Reagan in the 1980s, that envisions the deployment of satellites and space missiles to protect the United States from incoming nuclear bombs.

stupa Dome monument marking the burial site of relics of the Buddha.

Suez Canal Channel built in 1869 across the Isthmus of Suez to connect the Mediterranean Sea with the Red Sea and to lower the costs of international trade.

Sufi brotherhoods Mystics within Islam who were responsible for the expansion of Islam into many regions of the world.

Sufism Emotional and mystical form of Islam that appealed to the common people.

sultan Islamic political leader. In the Ottoman Empire, the sultan combined a warrior ethos with an unwavering devotion to Islam.

Sumerian King List Text that recounts the making of political dynasties. Recorded around 2000 BCE, it organizes the reigns of kings by dynasty, one city at a time.

Sumerian pantheon The Sumerian gods, each of whom had a home in a particular floodplain city. In the Sumerian belief system, both gods and the natural forces they controlled had to be revered.

Sumerian temples Homes of the gods and symbols of Sumerian imperial identity. Sumerian temples also represented the gods' ability to hoard wealth at sites where people exchanged goods and services. In addition, temples distinguished the urban from the rural world.

Sun Yat-sen (1866–1925) Chinese revolutionary and founder of the Nationalist Party in China.

Sunnis Orthodox Muslims. The majority sect of Islam, Sunnis originally supported the succession of Abu Bakr over Ali and supported the rule of consensus rather than family lineage for the succession to the Islamic caliphate. *See also* Shiism.

superior man In the Confucian view, a person of perfected moral character, fit to be a leader.

superpowers Label applied to the United States and the Soviet Union after World War II because of their size, their possession of the atomic bomb, and the fact that each embodied a model of civilization (capitalism or communism) applicable to the whole world.

supranational organizations International organizations such as NGOs, the World Bank, and the IMF.

survival of the fittest Charles Darwin's belief that as animal populations grew and resources became scarce, a struggle for existence arose, the outcome of which was that only the "fittest" survived.

Suryavamsha The second lineage of two (the solar) in Vedic society. *See* Chandravamsha.

Swadeshi movement Voluntary organizations in India that championed the creation of indigenous manufacturing enterprises and schools of nationalist thought, in order to gain autonomy from Britain.

Syndicalism Organization of workplace associations that included unskilled labor.

tabula rasa Term used by John Locke to describe the human mind before it begins to acquire ideas from experience; French for "clean slate."

Taiping Heavenly Kingdom (Heavenly Kingdom of Great Peace) Religious sect established by the Chinese prophet Hong Xiuquan in the mid-nineteenth century. Hong Xiuquan believed that he was Jesus's younger brother. The group struggled to rid the world of evil and "restore" the heavenly kingdom, imagined as a just and egalitarian order.

Taiping Rebellion Rebellion by followers of Hong Xiuquan and the Taiping Heavenly Kingdom against the Qing government over the economic and social turmoil caused by the Opium War. Despite raising an army of 100,000 rebels, the rebellion was crushed.

Taj Mahal Royal palace of the Mughal Empire, built by Shah Jahan in the seventeenth century in homage to his wife, Mumtaz.

Tale of Genji Japanese work written by Lady Murasaki that gives vivid accounts of Heian court life; Japan's first novel (early eleventh century).

talking cures Psychological practice developed by Sigmund Freud whereby the symptoms of neurotic and traumatized patients would decrease after regular periods of thoughtful discussion.

Talmud Huge volumes of oral commentary on Jewish law eventually compiled in two versions, the Palestinian and the Babylonian, in the fifth and sixth centuries BCE.

Talmud of Jerusalem Codified written volumes of the traditions of Judaism; produced by the rabbis of Galilee around 400 CE.

Tang dynasty (608–907 CE) Regime that promoted a cosmopolitan culture, turning China into the hub of East Asia cultural integration, while expanding the borders of their empire. In order to govern such a diverse empire, the Tang established a political culture and civil service based on Confucian teachings. Candidates for the civil service were required to take examinations, the first of their kind in the world.

Tanzimat Reorganization period of the Ottoman Empire in the mid-nineteenth century; modernizing reforms affected the military, trade, foreign relations, and civilian life.

tappers Rubber workers in Brazil, mostly either Indian or mixed-blood people.

Tarascans Mesoamerican society of the 1400s; rivals to and sometimes subjects of the Aztecs.

Tatish Ruler of Chan Santa Cruz during the Mexican Caste War. The term means "father."

Tecumseh (1768–1813) Shawnee who circulated Tenskwatawa's message of Indian renaissance among Indian villages from the Great Lakes to the Gulf Coast. He preached the need for Indian unity, insisting that Indians resist any American attempts to get them to sell more land. In response, thousands of followers renounced their ties to colonial ways and prepared to combat the expansion of the United States.

Tekkes Schools that taught devotional strategies and the religious knowledge for students to enter Sufi orders and become masters of the brotherhood.

temple Building where believers worshipped their gods and goddesses and where some peoples believed the deities had earthly residence.

Tenskwatawa (1768–1834) Shawnee prophet who urged disciples to abstain from alcohol and return to traditional customs, reducing dependence on European trade goods and severing connections to Christian missionaries. His message spread to other tribes, raising the specter of a pan-Indian confederacy.

Teotihuacán City-state in a large, mountainous valley in present-day Mexico; the first major community to emerge after the Olmecs.

territorial state Political form that emerged in the riverine cities of Mesopotamia, which was overwhelmed by the displacement of nomadic peoples. These states were kingdoms organized around charismatic rulers who headed large households; each had a defined physical border.

Third Estate The French people minus the clergy and the aristocracy; this term was popularized in the late eighteenth century and used to exalt the power of the bourgeoisie during the French Revolution.

Third Reich The German state from 1933 to 1945 under Adolf Hitler.

Third World Nations of the world, mostly in Asia, Latin America, and Africa, that were not highly industrialized like First World nations or tied to the Soviet Bloc (the Second World).

Thirty Years' War (1618–1648) Conflict begun between Protestants and Catholics in Germany that escalated into a general European war fought against the unity and power of the Holy Roman Empire.

Tiananmen Square Largest public square in the world and site of the pro-democracy movement in 1989 that resulted in the killing of as many as a thousand protesters by the Chinese army.

Tiers monde Term meaning "Third World," coined by French intellectuals to describe countries seeking a "third way" between Soviet communism and western capitalism.

Tiglath Pileser III Assyrian ruler from 745 to 728 BCE. This leader instituted reforms that changed the administrative and social structure of the empire to make it more efficient and introduced a standing army.

Tiwanaku Another name for Tihuanaco, the first great Andean polity, on the shores of Lake Titicaca.

Tlaxcalans Mesoamerican society of the 1400s; these people were enemies of the powerful Aztec Empire.

Tokugawa shogunate Hereditary military administration founded in 1603 that ruled Japan while keeping the emperor as a figurehead; it was toppled in 1868 by reformers who felt that Japan should adopt, not reject, Western influences.

Toltecs A Mesoamerican people who, by 1000 CE, had filled the political vacuum created by the decline of the city of Teotihuacán.

tomb culture Warlike group from northeast Asia who arrived by sea in the middle of the third century CE and imposed their military and social power on southern Japan. These conquerors are known today as the "Tomb culture" because of their elevated necropolises near present-day Osaka.

Topkapi Palace Political headquarters of the Ottoman Empire, located in Istanbul.

total war All-out war involving civilian populations as well as military forces, often used in reference to World War II.

transhumant migrants Nomads who entered settled territories in the second millennium BCE and moved their herds seasonally when resources became scarce.

Trans-Siberian Railroad Railroad built over very difficult terrain between 1891 and 1903 and subsequently expanded; it created an overland bridge for troops, peasant settlers, and commodities to move between Europe and the Pacific.

Treaty of Brest-Litovsk (1918) Separate peace between imperial Germany and the new Bolshevik regime in Russia. The treaty acknowledged the German victory on the Eastern Front and withdrew Russia from the war.

Treaty of Nanjing (1842) Treaty between China and Britain following the Opium War; it called for indemnities, the opening of new ports, and the cession of Hong Kong to the British.

Treaty of Tordesillas (1494) Treaty in which the pope decreed that the non-European world would be divided into spheres of trade and missionary responsibility between Spain and Portugal.

trickle trade Method by which a good is passed from one village to another, as in the case of obsidian among farming villages; the practice began around 7000 BCE. Also called "down the line trade."

Tripartite Pact (1940) Pact that stated that Germany, Italy, and Japan would act together in all future military ventures.

Triple Entente Alliance developed before World War I that eventually included Britain, France, and Russia.

Troy Important site founded around 3000 BCE in Anatolia, to the far west. Troy is legendary as the site of the war that was launched by the Greeks (the Achaeans) and that was recounted by Homer in the *Iliad*.

Truman Doctrine (1947) Declaration promising U.S. economic and military intervention, whenever and wherever needed, for the sake of preventing communist expansion.

Truth and Reconciliation Commission Quasi-judicial body established after the overthrow of the apartheid system in South Africa and the election of Nelson Mandela as the country's first black president in 1994. The commission was to gather evidence about crimes committed during the apartheid years. Those who showed remorse for their actions could appeal for clemency. The South African leaders believed that an airing of the grievances from this period would promote racial harmony and reconciliation.

truth commissions Elected officials' inquiries into human rights abuses by previous regimes. In Argentina, El Salvador, Guatemala, and South Africa, these commissions were vital for creating a new aura of legitimacy for democracies and for promising to uphold the rights of individuals.

tsar/czar Russian word derived from the Latin *Caesar* to refer to the Russian ruler of Kiev, and eventually to all rulers in Russia.

Tula Toltec capital city; a commercial hub and political and ceremonial center.

Uitlanders British populations living in Afrikaner republics; they were denied voting rights and subject to other forms of discrimination in the late nineteenth century. The term means "outsiders."

Ulama Arabic word that means "learned ones" or "scholars"; used for those who devoted themselves to knowledge of Islamic sciences.

Umayyads Family who founded the first dynasty in Islam. They established family rule and dynastic succession to the role of caliph. The first Umayyad caliph established Damascus as his capital and was named Mu'awiya ibn Abi Sufyan.

Umma Arabic word for "community"; used to refer to the "Islamic politu" or "Islamic community."

Universal Declaration of Human Rights (1948) U.N. declaration that laid out the rights to which all human beings are entitled.

universitas Term used from the end of the twelfth century to denote scholars who came together, first in Paris. The term is borrowed from the merchant communities, where it denoted the equivalent of the modern "union."

Untouchables Caste in the Indian system whose jobs, usually in the more unsanitary aspects of urban life, rendered them "ritually and spiritually" impure.

Upanishads Vedic wisdom literature collected in the first half of the first millennium BCE. It took the form of dialogues between disciples and a sage.

urban-rural divide Division between those living in cities and those living in rural areas. One of history's most durable worldwide distinctions, the urban-rural divide eventually encompassed the globe. Where cities arose, communities adopted lifestyles based on the mass production of goods and on specialized labor. Those living in the countryside remained close to nature, cultivating the land or tending livestock. They diversified their labor and exchanged their grains and animal products for necessities available in urban centers.

utopian socialism The most visionary of all Restoration-era movements. Utopian socialists like Charles Fourier dreamed of transforming states, workplaces, and human relations and proposed plans to do so.

Vaishyas Householders or lesser clan members in Vedic society who worked the land and tended livestock.

Vardhamana Mahavira Advocate of Jainism who lived from 540 to 468 BCE; he emphasized interpretation of the Upanishads to govern and guide daily life.

Varna Caste system established by the Vedas in 600 BCE.

vassal states Subordinate states that had to pay tribute in luxury goods, raw materials, and manpower as part of a broad confederation of polities under the kings' protection.

Vedas Rhymes, hymns, and explanatory texts composed by Aryan priests; the Vedas became their most holy scripture and part of their religious rituals. They were initially passed down orally, in Sanskrit. Brahmans, priests of Vedic culture, incorporated the texts into ritual and society. The Vedas are considered the final authority of Hinduism.

Vedic people People who came from the steppes of Inner Asia around 1500 BCE and entered the fertile lowlands of the Indus River basin, gradually moving as far south as the Deccan plateau. They called themselves Aryan, which means "respected ones," and spoke Sanskrit, an Indo-European language.

veiling Practice of modest dress required of respectable women in the Assyrian Empire, introduced by Assyrian authorities in the thirteenth century BCE.

Venus figures Representations of the goddess of fertility drawn on the Chauvet Cave in southeastern France. Discovered in 1994, they are probably about 35,000 years old.

Versailles Conference (1919) Peace conference between the victors of World War I; resulted in the Treaty of Versailles, which forced Germany to pay reparations and to give up its colonies to the victors.

Viet Cong Vietnamese communist group committed to overthrowing the government of South Vietnam and reunifying North and South Vietnam.

Viet Minh Group founded in 1941 by Ho Chi Minh to oppose the Japanese occupation of Indochina; it later fought the French colonial forces for independence. Also known as the Vietnamese Independent League.

Vietnam War (1965–1975) Conflict that resulted from concern over the spread of communism in Southeast Asia. The United States intervened on the side of South Vietnam in its struggle against peasant-supported Viet Cong guerrilla forces, who wanted to reunite Vietnam under a communist regime. Faced with antiwar opposition at home and ferocious resistance from the Vietnamese, American troops withdrew in 1973; the puppet South Vietnamese government collapsed two years later.

Vikings A people from Scandinavia who replaced the Franks as the dominant warrior class in northern Europe in the ninth century. They used their superior ships to loot other seagoing peoples and sailed up the rivers of central Russia to establish a trade route that connected Scandinavia and the Baltic with Constantinople and Baghdad. The Vikings established settlements in Iceland and Greenland and, briefly, North America.

Vishnu The second of three Vedic deities, signifying existence. *See also* Brahma *and* Siva.

viziers Bureaucrats of the Ottoman Empire.

Vodun Mixed religion of African and Christian customs practiced by slaves and free blacks in the colony of Saint Domingue.

Voting Rights Act (1965) Law that granted universal suffrage in the United States.

Wafd Nationalist party that came into existence during a rebellion in Egypt in 1919 and held power sporadically after Egypt was granted limited independence from Britain in 1922.

Wahhabism Early-eighteenth-century reform movement organized by Muhammad Ibn abd al-Wahhab, who preached the absolute oneness of Allah and a return to the pure Islam of Muhammad.

Wang Mang Han minister who usurped the throne in 9 CE because he believed that the Han had lost the mandate of heaven. He ruled until 23 CE.

war ethos Strong social commitment to a continuous state of war. The Roman army constantly drafted men and engaged in annual spring military campaigns. Soldiers were taught to embrace a sense of honor that did not allow them to accept defeat and commended those who repeatedly threw themselves into battle.

War of 1812 Conflict between Britain and the United States arising from U.S. grievances over oppressive British maritime practices in the Napoleonic Wars.

War on Poverty President Lyndon Johnson's push for an increased range of social programs and increased spending on social security, health, education, and assistance for the disabled.

Warring States period Period extending from the fifth century BCE to 221 BCE, when the regional warring states were unified by the Qin dynasty.

Warsaw Pact (1955–1991) Military alliance between the Soviet Union and other communist states that was established in response to the creation of the NATO alliance.

Weimar Republic (1919–1933) Constitutional Republic of Germany that was subverted by Hitler soon after he became chancellor.

Western Front Military front that stretched from the English Channel through Belgium and France to the Alps during World War I.

White and Blue Niles The two main branches of the Nile, rising out of central Africa and Ethiopia. They come together at the present-day capital city of Sudan, Khartoum.

White Lotus Rebellion Series of uprisings in northern China (1790–1800s) inspired by mystical beliefs in folk Buddhism and, at times, the idea of restoring the Ming dynasty.

White Wolf Mysterious militia leader, depicted in popular myth as a Chinese Robin Hood whose mission was to rid the country of the injustices of Yuan Shikai's government in the early years of the Chinese Republic (1910s).

Whites "Counterrevolutionaries" of the Bolshevik Revolution (1918–1921) who fought the Bolsheviks (the "Reds"); included former supporters of the tsar, Social Democrats, and large independent peasant armies.

witnessing Dying for one's faith, or becoming a martyr.

Wokou Supposedly Japanese pirates, many of whom were actually Chinese subjects of the Ming dynasty.

Works Progress Administration (WPA) New Deal program instituted in 1935 that put nearly 3 million people to work building roads, bridges, airports, and post offices.

World Bank International agency established in 1944 to provide economic assistance to war-torn and poor countries. Its formal title is the International Bank for Reconstruction and Development.

World War II (1939–1945) Worldwide war that began in September 1939 in Europe, and even earlier in Asia, and pitted Britain, the United States, and the Soviet Union (the Allies) against Nazi Germany, Japan, and Italy (the Axis).

Wu or Wudi Chinese leader known as the "Martial Emperor" because of his many military campaigns during the Han dynasty. He reigned from 141 to 87 BCE.

Wu Zhao Chinese empress who lived from 626 to 706 CE. She began as a concubine in the court of Li Shimin and became the mother of his son's child. She eventually gained power equal to that of the emperor, and named herself regent when she finagled a place for one of her own sons after their father's death.

Xiongnu The most powerful and intrusive of the nomadic peoples; originally pastoralists from the eastern part of the Asian steppe in what is modern-day Mongolia. They appeared along the frontier with China in the late Zhou dynasty and by the third century BCE had become the most powerful of all the pastoral communities in that area.

Xunzi Confucian moralist whose ideas were influential to Qin rulers. He lived from 310 to 237 BCE and believed that rational statecraft was more reliable than fickle human nature and that strict laws and severe punishments could create stability in society.

Yalta Accords Results of the meeting between President Roosevelt, Prime Minister Churchill, and Premier Stalin that occurred in the Crimea in 1945 to plan for the postwar order.

Yavana kings Sanskrit name for Greek rulers, derived from the Greek name for the area of western Asia Minor called Ionia, a term that then extended to anyone who spoke Greek or came from the Mediterranean.

yellow press Newspapers that sought a mass circulation by featuring sensationalist reporting.

Yellow Turbans One of several local Chinese religious movements that emerged across the empire, especially under Wang Mang's officials, who considered him a usurper. The Yellow Turbans, so called because of the yellow scarves they wore around their heads, were Daoist millenarians.

Yin City that became the capital of the Shang in 1350 BCE, ushering in a golden age.

Young Egypt Antiliberal, fascist group that gained a large following in Egypt during the 1930s.

Young Italy Nationalist organization made up of young students and intellectuals, devoted to the unification and renewal of the Italian state.

Yuan dynasty Dynasty established by the Mongols after the defeat of the Song. The Yuan dynasty was strong from 1280 to 1368; its capital was at Dadu, or modern-day Beijing.

Yuan Mongols Mongol rulers of China who were overthrown by the Ming dynasty in 1368.

Yuezhi A Turkic nomadic people who roamed on pastoral lands to the west of the Xiongnu territory of central Mongolia. They had friendly relationships with the farming societies in China, but the Yuezhi detested the Xiongnu and had frequent armed clashes with them.

Zaibatsu Large-scale, family-owned corporations in Japan consisting of factories, import-export businesses, and banks that dominated the Japanese economy until 1945.

Zamindars Archaic tax system of the Mughal Empire where decentralized lords collected tribute for the emperor.

Zapatistas Group of indigenous rebels that rose up against the Mexican government in 1994 and drew inspiration from an earlier Mexican rebel, Emiliano Zapata.

Zheng King during the Qin era who defeated what was left of the Warring States between 230 and 221 BCE. He assumed the mandate of heaven from the Zhou and declared himself First August Emperor, to distinguish himself from other kings.

Zheng He (1371–1433) Ming naval leader who established tributary relations with Southeast Asia, Indian Ocean ports, the Persian Gulf, and the east coast of Africa.

Zhong Shang Administrative central complex of the Shang.

Zhongguo Term originating in the ancient period and subsequently used to emphasize the central cultural and geographical location of China in the world; means "Middle Kingdom."

ziggurat By the end of the third millennium BCE, the elevated platform base of a Sumerian temple had transformed into a stepped platform called a *ziggurat*.

Zionism Political movement advocating the reestablishment of a Jewish homeland in Palestine.

Zoroaster Sometimes known as Zarathustra, thought to have been a teacher around 1000 BCE in eastern Iran and credited with having solidified the region's religious beliefs into a unified system that moved away from animistic nomadic beliefs. The main source for his teachings is a compilation called the Avesta.

Zoroastrianism Religion based on the teachings of Zoroaster that became the dominant religion of the Persian Empire.

Zulus African tribe that, under Shaka, created a ruthless warrior state in southern Africa in the early 1800s.

CHAPTER 15

Pages 560–61: Stefano Bianchetti/Corbis; p. 566: Library of Congress; p. 568: Granger Collection; p. 569: Hulton Archive/Getty Images; p. 570: Musee de la Ville de Paris, Musee Carnavalet/Giraudon/Art Resource, NY; p. 572: Lauros-Giraudon/The Bridgeman Art Library; p. 575: North Wind Picture Archives; p. 576: Granger Collection; p. 577: The Art Archive/ Museo Nacional de Historia, Castillo de Chapultepec, Mexico City/Dagli Orti; p. 578: Granger Collection; p. 580: Private Collection/The Bridgeman Art Library; p. 581–82: Granger Collection; p. 584: Granger Collection; p. 586: Novotsi/The Bridgeman Art Library; p. 588: Corbis; p. 589: Courtesy of the director, National Army Museum, London; p. 591: Granger Collection; p. 592: The Art Archive; p. 594 (left): The British Library, London/ The Bridgeman Art Library; (right): North Wind Picture Archives; p. 596: Roy Miles Fine Paintings/ The Bridgeman Art Library.

CHAPTER 16

Pages 598–99: Harvard-Yenching Library, Harvard University; p. 608 (left): The British Library, London; (right): National Archives, Zimbabwe; p. 610: Granger Collection; p. 612: Corbis; p. 615: Granger Collection; p. 616: Alamy; p. 620 (both): Granger Collection; p. 627 (top): Corbis; (bottom): Victoria & Albert Museum/Art Resource, NY.

CHAPTER 17

Pages 630–31: Granger; p. 637: (both): Granger Collection; p. 638: Granger Collection; p. 639: Time & Life Pictures/Getty Images; p. 640: Hulton/Getty Images; p. 646 (top): Dougal Waters/Getty Images; (bottom): Topham/The Image Works; p. 647: Hulton-Deutsch/Getty Images; p. 648: Bettmann/ Corbis; p. 650 (top): Illustrated London News/ Mary Evans Picture Library; (bottom): Private Collection (uncredited photo), from Judith Gutman's *Through Indian Eyes*, Oxford University Press; p. 653 (left): Hulton-Deutsch/ Getty Images; (right): The Warder Collection; p. 655: The Art Archive; p. 656: Illustrated London News/Mary Evans Picture Library; p. 657 (top): North Wind Picture Archives; (right): Erich Lessing/Art Resource, NY; p. 658: North Wind Picture Archives; p. 659 (top): The Art Archive; (bottom): Granger Collection; p. 664: Sovfoto/Eastfoto.

CHAPTER 18

Pages 668–69: Granger Collection; p. 674 (left): Hulton-Deutsch /Getty Images; (right): LL/Roger Viollet/Getty Images; p. 677 (top): Corbis; (bottom): Art Media/Heritage/The Image Works; p. 678: Empress Dowager Cixi and the imperial eunuchs, 1903–05. Photographer: Hsun-ling Tz-u-hi, Empress Dowager of China, 1835–1908, Photographs, negative 261. Freer Gallery of Art and the Arthur M. Sackler Gallery Archives, Smithsonian Institution, Washington, DC; p. 680: SuperStock; p. 682 (left): Underwood & Underwood/ Corbis; (right): Hulton-Deutsch Collection/Corbis; p. 684: Bettmann/ Corbis; p. 687: North Wind Picture Archives; p. 689 (left): Culver Pictures/Art Archive; (right): Sean Sprague/Mexicolore/The Bridgeman Art Library; p. 691: Library of Congress; p. 692: Snark/Art Resource, NY; p. 693 (clockwise from top left): © National Gallery, London/Art Resource, NY; Erich Lessing/Art Resource, NY; © Estate of Pablo Picasso/Artists Rights Society (ARS), New York. Digital Image © The Museum of Modern Art/Licensed by Scala/Art Resource, NY; Digital Image © The Museum of Modern Art/ Licensed by SCALA / Art Resource, NY. © 2010 Estate of Pablo Picasso/ Artists Rights Society (ARS), New York; p. 694 (top): Sigmund Freud Copyrights/Mary Evans Picture Library; (bottom): The Palace Museum, Beijing; p. 696–97: Corbis; p. 698: Schalkwijk/Art Resource, NY; p. 699 (left): The Warder Collection; (right): The Warder Collection; p. 702: E. O. Hoppe/ Corbis; p. 703: Domenica del Corriere/Dagli Orti/The Art Archive.

CHAPTER 19

Pages 706–07: The Illustrated London News Picture Library, London/The Bridgeman Art Library; p. 710: The Imperial War Museum; p. 714: Hulton-Deutsch Collection/Corbis; p. 715 (left): Sovfoto/Eastfoto; (right): Super-Stock; p. 718: Corbis; p. 719 (top): Culver Pictures/The Art Archive; (bottom): Hulton-Deutsch/Getty Images; p. 721: SF Palm/Stageimage/The Image Works; p. 722: Library Of Congress; p. 724: Hulton-Deutsch/Getty Images; p. 726: The Illustrated London News Picture Library; p. 727: Mary Evans Picture Library; p. 730: Bettmann/Corbis; p. 731: Heinrich Hoffmann/Time & Life Pictures/Getty Images; p. 732: The Art Archive; 733: Genevieve Naylor/ Corbis; p. 734: Granger Collection; p. 736 (left): The Illustrated London News Picture Library; (right): Private Collection/The Bridgeman Art Library; p. 738: Dinodia Picture Agency, Bombay; p. 739: Modern China Rare Photography Library, Sun Yat-Sen and the Guomindang Party, The Commercial Press, Ltd. 1994; p. 740: Getty Images.